ANTHROPOLOGY FOR THE NINETIES

ANTHROPOLOGY FOR THE NINETIES

Introductory Readings

Revised Edition of
ANTHROPOLOGY FOR THE EIGHTIES

Edited with Introductions by

Johnnetta B. Cole

THE FREE PRESS
A Division of Macmillan, Inc.
NEW YORK

Collier Macmillan Publishers
LONDON

The Free Press
A Division of Macmillan, Inc.
866 Third Avenue, New York, N.Y. 10022

Collier Macmillan Canada, Inc.

Printed in the United States of America

printing number

1 2 3 4 5 6 7 8 9 10

Library of Congress Cataloging-in-Publication Data

Anthropology for the nineties: introductory readings /
    edited with introductions by Johnnetta B. Cole.
        p.   cm.
        "Revised edition of Anthropology for the eighties."
        ISBN 0-02-906441-4
        1. Ethnology. 2. Anthropology. I. Cole, Johnnetta B.
    II. Anthropology for the eighties.
    GN316.A574   1988   87-28963
    306—dc19   CIP

Copyright Acknowledgments

**In memory of my colleague and friend,
Eleanor Burke Leacock**

For my sons, David, Aaron, and Che

To my sisters, the students of Spelman College

Not to know is bad
Not to wish to know is worse
Not to hope is unthinkable
Not to care is unforgivable
    —Ibo proverb (Nigeria)

Contents

Ritual and Belief Systems

III. Toward a New Anthropology: On Systems of Inequality

Preface and Acknowledgments

The inspiration for this anthology comes from the students I teach and learn from. Their gnawing questions about the very nature of being human and their insistence on relating knowledge of other cultures to their own set the theme for this book. I have drawn on a basic tenet in cultural anthropology in assuming that despite differences among the people who are studying in colleges and universities throughout the United States, there is a baseline of shared values, experiences, behaviors, and expectations common to students who will use this book.

A number of considerations guided the selection of the articles and the preparation of the introductions to each of the sections of the book:

1. Most of the students who take an introductory course in cultural anthropology do not go on to major in the field. They do so as part of a general education designed to help them become critical thinkers and creative and productive individuals in their particular era of world history. Anthropology has a contribution to make in the formation of an educated person as it instructs us in the accomplishments and problems of the past, informs us of the organization of societies today, and teaches respect for diversity in the human condition as a prerequisite for a better world. The emphasis in general education on integrative knowledge, an interdisciplinary approach, and a broadened or cross-cultural perspective is well served by an exposure to cultural anthropology. The readings in this anthology

were selected because they pose and discuss big questions about humankind and illustrate how anthropology can assist us in moving toward understandings of those questions. Accomplishing this objective has necessarily meant that not all of the issues, theories, and personalities of modern anthropology have been included.

2. The distinctiveness of cultural anthropology is its breadth. By definition it is concerned with *all* societies, from those small bands of fifty to one hundred people using rudimentary tools to highly technological societies composed of millions of people. This volume emphasizes this distinctiveness of anthropology and dispels the notion that anthropology only deals with "them," leaving "us" to sociology. Each section of the book contains articles on American culture, along with those on the cultures of various other peoples of the world; the articles illustrate the range of cultures and subcultures that are studied by anthropologists.

3. A book of readings that introduces anthropology to students living in today's world must give a sense of where the discipline has come from and the current state of the art, and must suggest the direction in which it is headed. For that reason, the anthology contains a mix of articles. Included are classic works that have had a profound impact on the discipline, even though the theoretical framework may currently be questioned. The bulk of the articles represent the most current and diversified thinking in the field; and a sample of articles are included that suggest new trends in the ever-evolving subject of anthropology.

4. In the selection of articles, consideration was given to the continuing call for relevant studies voiced by many students, practitioners, and subjects of anthropology. Today, as during the 1960s, the term "relevant" is defined and used in different ways. In terms of guiding the choice of articles for this volume, "relevant" very simply means that which is real and important in the lives of people whom anthropologists study and, therefore, that which aids us in understanding the world. Thus the volume contains articles on a feminist health clinic, witchcraft among Hispanic urban families, and a garbage workers' strike—not simply because they exist, but because they are a part of the current reality of the United States, and an understanding of these particular phenomena advances our overall understanding of the nature of American culture. The same consideration influenced the selection of articles on "other cultures."

5. A great deal of important material is dull, but material does not have to be dull to be important. In selecting articles for this anthology, thought was given to the writing style used to communicate the lessons of anthropology. Although no article was included simply because it is written in clear and stimulating terms, all of the works selected for the volume are clearly and interestingly written.

Organization and Features of the Anthology

The volume is designed to serve as the principal book for an introductory cultural anthropology course on the university level. It includes the topics traditionally covered in such courses (fieldwork in anthropology, language and culture, and the four major aspects of culture) and others that are often addressed only in supplementary readings (ethics in anthropology, the impact of Western technology and economics on the Third World, and issues of racism and sexism).

Each of the sections and subsections of the book is introduced by an essay, which points out the major issues in that particular area of anthropology and the relationship of the articles to those issues.

Viewed in totality, the various articles cover all areas of the world and are written by individuals who represent the growing diversity among anthropologists: individuals from European and American societies, individuals from Third World countries and communities, women and men, the "elders" of the field and the younger generation of anthropologists, anthropologists studying their own societies and the societies of other peoples.

Improvements in the Second Edition

Since *Anthropology for the Eighties* was published in 1982, cultural anthropology has not changed in radical ways; but the discipline has, of course, continued to develop. Among the areas in which this development is most noticeable are three which were identified as important in the 1982 text:

1. There is an increased focus on industrialized societies of the east and the west. The majority of the articles that are new in this edition are about such societies.

2. Today there is greater attention in anthropology to issues of race, ethnicity, gender, and class. In this volume, these issues are addressed in the chapters by Gilliam, Hansen, Morgen, Mullings, Price, A. Wilson, and L. Wilson.

3. In response to criticism of so-called value-free, objective social science, increasing numbers of anthropologists are engaged in "reflective anthropology." This involves conscious attention to the role of the anthropologist in the very process of fieldwork and theorizing. In this volume, the chapters by L. Wilson and Mitchell are examples of this approach.

This edition continues the distinctive features of the first edition and adds new ones.

1. More than any other introductory text, *Anthropology for the Nine-*

ties has a large percentage of works written by women anthropologists, anthropologists in the Third World, and "minority" anthropologists of the U.S. This means that taken as a whole, the volume presents a diverse set of field experiences, methodological approaches, and theoretical perspectives.

2. Because of the need to limit the total number of pages in an introductory anthology of readings, the first edition did not include articles on the arts. But expressive culture (music, art, dance, folklore, and drama) is an important part of the human condition; hence the inclusion of the article by Price in this edition.

3. In each section of this volume there is at least one article which did not appear in the first edition. Of the ten new inclusions, five are published here for the first time (A. Wilson, L. Wilson, Mitchell, Morgen, and Spears); one has been revised explicitly for this volume (Gilliam); and four have appeared in other places.

4. Minor changes have been made in the editor's introductions in response to criticisms and suggestions by faculty and students.

5. The new Instructor's Manual is updated in keeping with revisions in the text. It also reflects a number of current trends in the pedagogy of anthropology.

Acknowledgments

Although anthropologists keep asking the question, people cannot always explain *why* a particular tradition continues, other than to say "that is the way we have always done it." This is not the case with the tradition of acknowledgments in a book, for the people who have written and edited volumes can very quickly say why they wish to express their gratitude to those who have contributed to an effort that by its very nature reflects input from many sources and requires the cooperation of others.

I remain indebted to the three scholars who were my major professors. George E. Simpson first introduced me to the very word and reality of anthropology. Melville J. Herskovits helped me to understand my own culture as an expression of Africa in the New World. And Paul Bohannan's own work continues to exemplify what the best of teachers give to their students.

In addition, I am grateful to colleagues and friends in the interdisciplinary fields of Black Studies and Women's Studies; for it is often their critiques and insights that fuel creative improvements in the discipline of anthropology.

It is students—those I have taught and learned from, and those I look forward to working with—to whom I owe the greatest debt. The hundreds and hundreds of former students raised many questions to which parts of this book are not answers but possible responses; and at least some of what is written here is in anticipation of the kinds of points that my students of the future will want to discuss.

Laura Wolff was my editor for this volume, as she was for the first, with this difference: my respect for her work has soared higher, and our friendship has deepened.

During the last stages of preparing this volume, Marea Wexler, Kate Wilson, and Louise te Boekhorst each took care of a few straws that would have indeed broken the back of the production schedule. I am grateful to each of them. And I deeply appreciate the interest Karen Wanza and Wuletahemma-Frehiwot showed in the volume and their willingness to work on it during the final stage.

Ara Wilson's contribution to the book calls into serious question the distinction between serving as a research assistant and full scholarly partnership. From proposing articles to setting up the mechanics of revising a book, she brought to this work an exceptional mind and a very warm spirit. For her command of the discipline of anthropology, and appropriate compulsiveness, I as well as those who use this book owe a great deal to Ara Wilson.

To my immediate family, my extended family, friends, and colleagues whose understanding and patience make my work easier, I also wish to express my gratitude.

Contributors

John Beattie received his D.Phil in social anthropology from Oxford University where he has taught since 1953. Earlier in his career he served as a district officer in Tanzania (then called Tanganyika) for eight years. He has written extensively on the Nyoro.

Gerald D. Berreman, professor of anthropology at the University of California, Berkeley, has researched and written on the questions of research methods and ethics in anthropology, stratification, and social inequality. Among his books is *Caste in the Modern World* (1973). He has contributed a chapter to a book compilation entitled *Social Inequality: Comparative and Developmental Approaches* (1981).

Laura Bohannan received the D.Phil from Oxford University in 1951. Since that time, she has continued to conduct research in social anthropology, with particular interests in Africa, kinship, language, and culture, and theory of social structure. She is currently a professor at the University of Illinois, Chicago Circle.

Paul J. Bohannan, professor of anthropology and dean of the Social Sciences and Communications Department at the University of California, Los Angeles, has researched and published in the areas of law, social organization, economic anthropology, and psychoanalysis. His geographic areas of specialization are Africa and the United States.

Ernest Burch received his Ph.D. from the University of Chicago in 1966 and continues to conduct research in sociocultural anthropology, with a major interest in Eskimo culture. He is the author of *Eskimo Kinsman: Changing Family Relationships in Northwest Alaska* (1975).

Johnnetta B. Cole is president of Spelman College and formerly a professor of anthropology and director of the Latin American and Caribbean Studies Program at Hunter College of the City University of New York. She has conducted fieldwork in Liberia, West Africa, Cuba, and among Afro-Americans in the United States, with particular focus on the issues of race and gender.

Thomas W. Collins, professor and chair of the Department of Anthropology at Memphis State University, has done extensive research and writing on urban school desegregation and labor segmentation.

Patricia Fernandez-Kelly is currently teaching in the Sociology Department at Johns Hopkins University and is on the Editorial Board of *Signs*. With June Nash, she co-authored the book *Women, Men and the International Division of Labor* (1983).

James L. Gibbs, professor of anthropology at Stanford University, specializes in legal anthropology, psychological anthropology, and the cultures of Africa.

Angela Gilliam teaches at the State University of New York College at Old Westbury. She has investigated the relationship between language and power in Brazil, Mexico, and Papua, New Guinea.

Nelson H. H. Graburn, professor of anthropology at the University of Califorina, Berkeley, received his Ph.D. from the University of Chicago in 1963. His areas of interests are social structure and kinship, ethnic arts, tourism, and circumpolar peoples.

Edward C. Hansen, professor of anthropology at Queens College of the City University of New York and the City University of New York Graduate School, has conducted research in Spain, Brazil, and the United States. He is concerned with issues of elites, class, status groups, political orders, and their interrelationships. A consistent thread of his research has been an effort to bridge the gap between these concepts and the ways in which lives are actually led.

Delmos J. Jones, professor of anthropology at the City University of New York Graduate School, has conducted research among Native Americans in southern

Arizona, hill tribes of northern Thailand, Afro-Americans in the United States, and aborigines in Australia. His research focuses on the link between local communities and institutions of power and emphasizes neighborhood organizations as an example that provides this link.

Joseph Jorgensen, professor in the Social Science Department at the University of California, Irvine, was a member of the Committee on Ethics of the American Anthropological Association in 1969. His books include *The Sun Dance Religion* (1972) and *Western Indians* (1979).

Madeleine Leininger, professor of nursing and adjunct professor of anthropology, holds degrees in registered nursing and a Ph.D. in anthropology. She is founder of the field of transcultural nursing and director of the Transcultural Nursing Program at Wayne State University.

Kenneth L. Little, professor emeritus at the University of Edinburgh, has researched and taught in the areas of African and urban studies. Among his works in these areas is the book *African Women in Towns* (1973).

Bronislaw Malinowski was born in Poland in 1884 and died in 1942. His works on the Trobriand Islands are considered classics in anthropology.

John Middleton is professor of anthropology at Yale University. His publications on religion, political organization, change, and urbanization are based on his fieldwork in several African countries.

William E. Mitchell, professor of anthropology at the University of Vermont, is the author of *Mishpokeh* (1978), about Jews in New York City, and co-author (with Hope Jensen Leichter) of *Kinship and Casework* (1967). He has also conducted extensive fieldwork in Papua, New Guinea. His research interests center on problems of family and kinship, economic exchange, and the relationship between indigenous and introduced systems of therapeutic intervention.

Sandra Morgen, professor of women's studies at the University of Massachusetts, is currently editing a book entitled *Women and the Politics of Empowerment: Workplace and Community Activism*.

Leith Mullings is professor of anthropology in the biomedical program at City College and at the City University of New York Graduate School. Her research interests include Africa and the urban population of the United States.

Laura Nader, professor of anthropology at the University of California, Berkeley, is well known in anthropology for her work in the comparative ethnography of law. She also researches the anthropology of professional mind sets. Her geographical areas of interest include the Middle East, Mexico, Latin America, and the United States.

Bernard Nietschmann, professor of geography at the University of Michigan, has conducted research among the Miskito Indians of Nicaragua. His current focus is on conflicts among groups within states and between states, such as the conflict between Ethiopia and Eritrea.

Sally Price, author of *Co-Wives and Calabashes* (1984), has collaborated with Sidney Mintz on *Caribbean Contours* (1985) and with R. Price on *Afro-American Arts of the Suriname Rain Forest* (1980). Her future publications include *Primitive Art in Civilized Places* (1989). She currently divides her time among Paris, Minneapolis, and Martinique.

Roy A. Rappaport has conducted both archaeological and cultural fieldwork. He is particularly interested in cultural ecology. Among his books is *Ecology, Meaning and Religion* (1979).

Marshall Sahlins, professor of anthropology at the University of Chicago, has written extensively in the areas of anthropological theory, economic anthropology, and the ethnology of Oceania.

Surajit Sinha is an anthropologist from India who has conducted research on his own culture and that of the United States. One of his areas of specialization is religion. He is author of the *Junior Encyclopedia of Sikhism* (1985).

Arthur K. Spears, professor of anthropology and linguistics at City College of the City University of New York and the City University of New York Graduate School, is currently conducting research on language, symbolism, and ideology; language and education; and the sociolinguistics and grammatical analysis of Black English, Haitian Creole, and Caribbean Spanish.

Niara Sudarkasa, currently president of Lincoln University, is a former professor of anthropology and associate director of the Center for Afro-American and American Studies at the University of Michigan. She has conducted extensive research in Africa.

Ara Wilson, a doctoral student in anthropology at the City University of New York Graduate School, is studying the interconnections between gender, race, and sexuality, specifically in Southeast Asia and the United States.

Lynn Wilson, a graduate student in anthropology at the University of Massachusetts, centered her masters-level work on feminist resistance to nuclear militarism and spent five months in 1984 at the women's peace camp at Greenham Common in England. Her dissertation research will focus on social processes of nuclear militarism and, in particular, on the transformation of women's participation in political activity in Belau, Western Micronesia.

Introduction

ANTHROPOLOGY STANDS OUT as the broadest in scope of all of the humanities and social sciences. Defining their concern as no less than the study of humankind, anthropologists impose no restrictions in terms of time, space, or the aspect of humankind that is analyzed. Thus anthropology explores human biology, culture, and language from our origins through the long, slow, and continuing evolutionary process. The range of human societies, from the most technologically simple to the most technologically complex, are studied in terms of economic, social, political, religious, and aesthetic institutions.

At the same time that anthropology remains a unified and broadly comprehensive discipline, there are four distinct but related subfields: archaeology, which studies prehistoric and historic human societies; physical anthropology, which explores the biological base of humankind as it influences and interacts with culture; linguistics, which analyzes languages cross-culturally; and cultural or social anthropology, which studies similarities and differences in the organization of the societies of the world.

This reader introduces you to social or cultural anthropology (for convenience, referred to throughout the book as anthropology). Although the comprehensive view associated with the discipline as a whole contributes important insights, we have chosen to focus on one branch in order to provide more in-depth analysis.

Sociocultural Anthropology

The task of sociocultural anthropology is to study the range of human societies that are found throughout the world. Yet throughout most of the history of the discipline, this branch of anthropology was in fact the study of only a portion of humanity, the study of societies distant in miles from Europe and the United States, explorations of those societies which we too easily labeled as primitive.

The image of the anthropologist, an accurate image until recently, is of a Londoner, Parisian, or New Yorker setting out for some remote land—a coral lagoon in the South Pacific, a rain forest area in Africa, the vast plains of the North American West, the hills of Tibet. Arriving in one of these remote areas of the world, the anthropologist then set out to understand the lifeways of another people.

Cultural anthropology is still about such distant journeys, but it is also about travels closer to the lands of Londoners, Parisians, and New Yorkers. In this sense, the anthropology of today more closely approaches the objective of studying and understanding all of humankind, the study of others *and* ourselves. And thus the modern anthropologist is interested in dispute settlements in tribal societies and in an East European country; a coal miners' strike in England and a cooperative work group in Benin, West Africa; multinational corporations as well as tribal lineages; Melanesian witchcraft and San Francisco witches' covens; sexual division of labor in small-scale societies and sexism in technologically complex nation-states.

This anthology of readings reflects the expansive range of human culture, illustrating that our own way of life is in fact as exotic, interesting, and worthy of study as any other. The culture of the United States is a particular variant in the range of world cultures, and cultural anthropology is the point of view, the set of concepts for understanding *all* cultures. We might describe cultural anthropology as a particular set of lenses for viewing the diversity and similarities in the culture of human beings. If we continue with this metaphor, we can note that the lenses are bifocals, designed to permit the anthropologist to see near and afar. Since the discipline began in the eighteenth century and came of age in the 1900s, anthropologists have primarily used the upper part of the bifocals, looking outward to peoples distant from the cultures of Europe and the United States. Some of the pioneers of the discipline, such as Tylor and Morgan, did peer through the lower part of the lenses and examine ways of life in their own societies. This type of study was continued by anthropologists such as Kroeber, Benedict, Linton, Powdermaker, and Margaret Mead, and it continues today, as illustrated by several of the articles reprinted in this volume.

However, in the majority of cases, the bifocals of anthropologists have been used to focus on those particular societies variously referred to, as we continue to search for an appropriate term, as "primitive," "nonliterate," and "non-Western." This is an important task, and until recently it was uniquely the responsibility of anthropologists, as other social scientists concentrated on behavior in their own and similarly organized societies. Although sociologists tended to use a different methodology from that employed by anthropologists, they studied fundamentally the same phenomena in the U.S. and European societies as anthropologists were studying in the rest of the world. Europe and the United States were similarly the loci of study for economists, political scientists, and psychologists, but with concentration in each of these disciplines on singular aspects of those societies. Thus studies by anthropologists filled a void left by all the other social scientists.

Beginning in the 1960s, a number of forces exerted pressures on anthropologists to study "us" as well as "them," to genuinely study the range of human behavior. Political changes in the developing countries of Africa, Asia, and Latin America culminated in independence for many nations, and national liberation struggles heightened in a host of others. As the people of these Third World countries asserted their rights in the political and economic spheres, many also claimed the right to scrutinize more carefully studies of their history and culture by foreigners. In some cases, emerging independent nations charged that anthropologists had willingly and, more often, unknowingly aided the CIA. However, the principal charge was that studies by anthropologists did not assist in the development needs of the new nations.

During this same period of the 1960s groups within the United States called on anthropologists to turn their attention to studies that would contribute to solving social problems at home. In that period of protest and activism, when the issues of civil rights and the Vietnam War concerned many Americans, young people called for relevance in academia. Anthropology, along with the other university disciplines, came under sharp attack.

There were also criticisms from within the discipline itself. Sharp and difficult questions were posed by anthropologists: Why were the few studies of U.S. society of a particular type, concentrating on poor and relatively powerless Third World communities and never on the circles of power? Why had anthropologists studied hundreds of colonized African tribal groups and never conducted fieldwork among the European "tribes" who had colonized Africa? Why had anthropologists so little to say about the burning issues of the day: war, racial discrimination, poverty? What are the ethics of doing fieldwork, at home or abroad? Would the cry for Black studies and other ethnic studies have arisen if anthropologists and other social scientists had done their jobs? What specific contributions could anthropology make to women's studies? Shouldn't anthropology be an applied as well as a "pure" social science, addressing and helping to eliminate social problems as well as analyzing them?

The American Anthropological Association's resolution on ethics, passed in 1969 after much heated debate and soul-searching among anthropologists, expressed a serious attempt to address these questions. In addition to stipulating a code of ethics, the resolution recognized the importance and legitimacy for anthropologists of studying their own societies.

Today there is an additional reality that may well push anthropologists into more studies closer to home. The hallmark of anthropologists, based on intensive fieldwork usually conducted in a society very distant from the United States or Europe, is a costly process, made possible by substantial grants from government and foundation sources. But during periods of financial austerity in the United States and Western Europe many anthropologists, both the graduate students who are receiving their academic credentials and the professionals whose work depends on periodic trips to the field, may well have to identify studies in their own countries.

Finally, in terms of the forces that are motivating anthropologists to stay home and study "themselves," convincing arguments are made within the discipline for "native anthropology," that is, the study of a culture by a participant in a given way of life (see Jones's article in this volume). This too has a history in anthropology. For example, Franz Boas encouraged Zora Neale Hurston, an Afro-American woman, to return to her native town in Florida to collect folklore and describe the way of life of members of her original community. And in the literature of anthropology there are important works by individuals who have systematically studied their own societies (see, for example, Jomo Kenyatta's classic ethnography on the Gikuyu of Kenya).

Toward Understanding Others and Ourselves

A growing emphasis on studying others *and* ourselves encourages anthropologists to reexamine existing theories and methodologies, to question anew the most fundamental notions about the purpose and indeed the responsibilities involved in studying all the folk of the world. Ralph Linton, an anthropologist who did study American culture in the 1940s, quipped: "The last thing a fish would ever notice would be water!" Today, increasing numbers of anthropologists *are* noticing the "water," that is, the importance and relevancy of studying that which surrounds them.

As anthropologists explore the totality of human attitudes, values, and behavior, a number of issues come into sharper focus. We turn now to a discussion of these issues. The principal mode of anthropological inquiry is fieldwork, where the anthropologist lives among a people, observing their modes of behavior and participating in most aspects of their way of life. Basically, anthropologists are people-watchers and "snoopers"—social scientists who ask a million questions and look for invitations to join in a great deal of what is the private life of a people. By studying our own society, especially when it involves studying in our very own communities, we increase our sensitivity to how other people react to research practiced upon them.

Because our studies have disproportionately focused on a single village or a small "tribal" society, a number of exaggerations about a culture are perpetuated: that cultures are marked by coherence, and rarely by conflict; that stability grossly overshadows change; and that tribal societies were limited to localized organization, in contrast to regional and world routes of trade and exchange. Thus, studying our own and other complex societies not only serves as a mirror of ourselves, it helps us correct stereotypes and misconceptions about the very tribal societies that we assumed we understood.

Studying and understanding our own culture is also a means of countering ethnocentrism, the assumption that one's own way of life is superior to all others. And just as studying other cultures can increase an understanding of our own, studying phenomena in our own way of life can help us to understand certain attitudes and behaviors among other peoples.

Anthropological inquiries into racial and ethnic relations in England can open up a more meaningful interpretation of the caste system in India; investigations of attitudes about and involvements of the U.S. government and people in war can be the source of insight into why and how the Dani of New Guinea engage in war; and research into the phenomenon of "born again Christianity" in the United States today might well increase our understanding of the political elements associated with revivalist cults in Jamaica. Looking at ourselves puts brakes on the tendency to view attitudes and behavior patterns of others as inherently "inferior," "weird," and "exotic."

Studying "us" as well as "them" encourages anthropologists to explore the major social issues of our times. Anthropologists could more easily put up blinders to a number of vital world problems when studying small-scale societies in faraway lands than they can when the societies under scrutiny are their own technologically advanced states. The issues that anthropologists will inevitably confront in seeking to explain European and American societies—uneven distribution of resources among classes, racial and gender discrimination, pollution, depletion of natural resources, violence and war—these are in fact issues of the contemporary world. While the debate continues as to the responsibility of anthropologists to act as agents of change in terms of such problems, anthropologists, like all social scientists, at the very least have the obligation to study these social realities.

Analyzing these social issues at home encourages anthropologists to explore them abroad—both as they are a part of the history and culture of Third World countries and as they are exported from the "developed" to the "underdeveloped" world. A potent discovery results from anthropological attention to world problems: The very discipline of cultural anthropology has over the years amassed data that speak directly to these issues. Phrased in terms of two basic anthropological concepts, there is enormous relevance for international affairs that (1) war is not genetic but is a part of culture, and as such is a learned behavior which can be changed or abandoned, and that (2) there are no inferior and superior races.

The insights and rewards of studying the cultural universe are accompanied by certain difficulties and problems for anthropologists. For example, the mode of anthropological research appropriate for a small-scale, relatively self-contained society will be inadequate for doing research in our own society. And thus anthropologists must continue to develop a diversified set of techniques ranging from traditional participant observation to quantitative methods. Studies of our own society can challenge ethnocentrism, but they can also tempt us to explain the behavior of other peoples in our own codes and symbols rather than struggling to understand those of the people being studied.

The problems are greatly outbalanced by the insights that come from doing what anthropologists have purported to do: to explore and explain the rich array yet fundamentally similar expressions of human cultures—*all* human cultures. In this sense anthropology will help us learn about ourselves as we more sensitively and purposefully learn about others.

References

HURSTON, ZORA NEALE. 1935. *Mules and Men.* Philadelphia: J. B. Lippincott Company.

KENYATTA, JOMO. 1965. *Facing Mt. Kenya: The Tribal Life of the Gikuyu.* New York: Vintage Books.

The Practice and Ethics of Fieldwork

Fieldwork is at the very core of cultural anthropology. Although other social scientists are increasingly doing studies that involve participant observation, fieldwork remains the methodology most associated with anthropology. Participating in much of the daily life of a people over an extended period of time, the anthropologist seeks to understand their rules and patterns of behavior in the greatest possible depth, and thus to contribute to our ultimate understanding of the human condition. The articles in Part I explore the process of practicing anthropology: the techniques used in carrying out a field project; the pleasures and difficulties associated with fieldwork; and the ethical issues and problems that flow from close interaction in the life-ways of a people.

Anthropologists did not always "go to the field." When the discipline first emerged in the late nineteenth century, anthropologists collected data from books and reports written by explorers, missionaries, and colonial officials. The values, attitudes, and behaviors of non-Western peoples were gleaned from various Westerners' descriptions of them. It was not until the turn of the twentieth century that British and American anthropologists independently invented fieldwork as a specific method for studying and understanding societies different from their own.

It was well into the twentieth century before anthropologists in any numbers applied this particular methodology to their own societies. What distinguishes fieldwork in the anthropologist's own culture from that done among other peoples is not so much the techniques used nor the ease or difficulty of carrying out the research. In both field situations the anthropologist leads a dual existence: as a participant in and an analyst of a way of life. The crucial difference is in what the anthropologist brings to the field—not in terms of possessions and tools, but far more importantly in terms of ideas, values, knowledge, and experience. In studying others the anthropologist is seeing, feeling, knowing *for the first time* what it is to be a part of a particular culture. In studying ourselves we learn to see, feel, and know *anew* as we systematically examine and analyze those institutions, processes, and emotions of which we too are a part.

It is important to appreciate contrasts between conducting fieldwork in one's own and in another culture. Perhaps most difficult of all those situations is where the anthropologist shares citizenship with the people being studied, but comes from a different culture or subculture. The article by Mitchell illustrates some of these difficulties.

However, we must not overemphasize the differences in doing fieldwork at home and abroad. It is dangerous for the anthropologist to assume that because someone has grown up in a particular society, he or she necessarily has an analytic understanding of that society, indeed that the "native anthropologist" is *inherently* better equipped to study "the folks at home." As Delmos Jones points out in his chapter, the anthropologist who wanders no farther than down the street or over to the next town needs to be as critical and as well prepared to do fieldwork as the one who wanders thousands of miles away from home.

What is it like to do fieldwork? What is it really like to study a people's way of life by participating, as fully as possible, in the range of conversations, celebrations, activities, and conflicts that constitute culture? We are presented with a number of insights into fieldwork in John Middleton's article. In a candid tone, he assesses the various techniques he has used in conducting fieldwork among the Lugbara of Uganda, and he describes his feelings and emotions as well as changes in his role and views over time. Although there is considerable variety among fieldwork settings, anthropologists agree that fieldwork is among the most rewarding and difficult encounters of their lives.

Anthropologists' accounts of their months and years among the native peoples in the highlands of New Guinea or snow-filled lands of the Eskimo of Greenland document the physical hardships of fieldwork. Working in highly industrialized countries such as our own can also be a taxing physical experience. And in certain situations, such as the women's "peace camp" in England, where Lynn Wilson did fieldwork, an anthropologist can face daily harassment and violence.

But those physical obstacles are the easy ones to deal with; the truly difficult ones are problems of translation and of objectivity as against ethnocentrism. In discussing these issues briefly here, we shall see that preconceptions are often the underlying problem.

The Problem of Translation

The anthropologist doing fieldwork confronts translation problems in several forms. In the field, the anthropologist is surrounded by the everyday expressions and concepts of a culture, which are often stated in a foreign language. Once the anthropologist has learned the language of the people he or she is studying—and that alone can be a monumental problem—the very accomplishment of bilingualism sets up a trap. Is the people's term "X" best translated by the term "Y" in the anthropologist's language? Or is it in fact not translatable? Bohannan (1963:9) makes the point:

> There is no more complete way to misunderstand a foreign civilization than to see it in terms of one's own civilization. It was a common fault of colonial governments that they looked for "the indigenous authorities" instead of realizing that authority is a Western concept and that it may even be peculiar to the West. With half a dozen notable exceptions, it has been only within the last generation or two that missionaries have stopped calling all the indigenous spirits whose names and rites they encounter "devils."

Unfortunately, anthropologists make similar mistakes when they give in to the temptation to use their own concepts to explain the culture of others.

An interesting twist to this problem of translation is captured in Laura Bohannan's "Shakespeare in the Bush," included in the section on language and culture in this volume. The tables are turned as the Tiv of Nigeria translate her description of Shakespeare into their own language and reality.

What is the solution to this particular problem of translation? We take the first step toward a solution by recognizing the problem and exercising extreme care in our efforts to communicate the realities of a culture through a language foreign to that culture. Another step is taken when the anthropologist, informed by the concepts and realities of another culture, develops a sensitivity to the previously familiar terms and concepts of Western culture.

When the anthropologist studies "at home," using a language that is in fact the language of the anthropologist's native culture, problems of translation are not avoided, although they are somewhat different. There is, as in all social science research, the issue of how to translate correctly "what the folks say" into analytical terms that permit the construction of theories and laws. Yet another problem stems from the fact that the anthropologist studying among "us" can be overconfident with language, assuming that those who share a common language inevitably communicate well. One potential check on this assumption is of course that the natives of the anthropologist's own culture have the opportunity to read what is written about them, a possibility that raises other questions, such as, Who has the final say on whether or not material is included in the ethnography or ethnology? In his article in this section, William Mitchell raises in a direct way some of the problems of "miscommunication" in a fieldwork setting. It is cultural styles, not more narrowly defined language differences, that are at the base of the mistrust and miscommunication between the anthropologist and the people studied.

The Problem of Preconceptions

Focusing on these problems of translation emphasizes that the comparative method is fundamental to cultural anthropology as it is forged out of fieldwork. Each anthropologist's attempt to understand a particular way of life contributes to our understanding of the human condition through comparisons and contrasts. This is a strength of anthropology, for before we are confident that we know what "kinship" or "religion" or "conflict" is, the anthropologist warns us that we need to examine how those concepts and realities are defined and experienced cross-culturally.

In making comparisons, anthropologists must beware of distortions caused by preconceptions and biases. Conscious of this problem, anthropologists, like other social scientists, strive for that disengaged quality known as "objectivity": the ability to engage in scientific study free of judgments, values, and biases. Were anthropologists to give free rein to their own biases and judgments, their writings would be ethnocentric; that is, they would view other people's ways of life in terms of their own cultural assumptions and values and imply that their own is always the superior way of life.

The history of anthropology as a discipline has been marked by changing approaches to ethnocentrism. Following the early days when many anthropologists made value judgments, the pendulum swung to the other extreme, as some argued that it is not only desirable but possible for anthropologists to suspend all of their own values, and only evaluate a given cultural pattern within the context of a particular culture itself. Today this idea of cultural relativism is discussed and debated among anthropologists. Some defend the necessity and possibility of achieving cultural relativism. Others hold the view that fieldwork cannot be totally unaffected by preconceptions: those that come from one's life experiences, those that come from anthropologists' academic training, and, indeed, those that come from ideological and political commitments.

In her chapter in this section Lynn Wilson analyzes some of the ways in which being an insider can present difficulties in the field. But from these vantage points the anthropologist can also gain insights which the traditional methods of fieldwork do not offer. As with the problem of translation in fieldwork, it is far easier to identify the difficulty than to prescribe a guaranteed solution. But again, solutions lie first and foremost in the recognition of a problem. In short, we can better deal with our biases and preconceptions not by ignoring them and pretending that they do not exist, but by openly confronting the fact that we, like all human beings, have them. The more anthropologists study their own culture, the easier it becomes to look less judgmentally at others. This is true because studying ourselves will expose the assumptions and concepts of Western cultural traditions, which form a part of the anthropologist's way of seeing things. Secondly, the more we study our own culture, the more we are forced to see that our ways of doing certain things are best described as "habitual," not "natural"; that ours is a way of life, not *the* way of life to be imposed on the world.

If we are accurately to describe the importance of fieldwork to anthropology and anthropologists, we cannot simply focus on the problems and difficulties; we must also communicate a sense of the joys and rewards of fieldwork. On both a personal and an intellectual level, deep immersion in a way of life can be a profound and very special experience. On a personal level, anthropologists often develop deep friendships among the people they are studying. Much of the richness of these interpersonal relations is recorded in anthropologist's diaries and journals, and not in the ethnographies they write. And yet in some ethnographies we gain a glimpse of what it means to be an uninvited guest (and after all, that is what anthropologists are) who is at some point incorporated into the daily motion of a given way of life, sharing in the celebrations of birth and the sadness of deaths; hoping, like all others in the community that the rains will come and the crops will be plentiful, or that the hunt will be successful.

There are also intellectual and psychological rewards that accrue from the experiences of fieldwork. Whether an anthropologist studies at home or abroad, there comes the point when understanding distinct human conditions brings sharp insight into the very nature of humanness, and the world is more understandable because one has seen and experienced more than one small corner of it.

There are very serious ethical issues, moral questions and choices, that anthropologists must face throughout their fieldwork and, indeed, as long as they are practitioners of the discipline. Some anthropological readers and texts avoid discussions of ethics on the grounds that such issues are too complex and controversial for students. Those that do speak of the ethics of anthropology tend to do so in the concluding chapter. In this volume, we place these issues in Part I, for although the complexities involved may be more understandable after the range of anthropological inquiry is presented, the primacy of ethical issues requires that they be placed before the student of human behavior as a vital context within which the very stuff of anthropology is cast.

It is hoped that students using the volume will be conscious of the ethical questions inherent in each of the articles in this book.

There is enormous variety in the ethical issues anthropologists face, because they work among "human subjects." In order to communicate even a sense of that variety, we turn to a series of questions the "answers" to which are sometimes found in the professional code of ethics of the American Anthropological Society, but others ultimately rest in the conscience (and consciousness) of each anthropologist. Should anthropologists participate in clandestine research for their own government or that of the people being studied? When an anthropologist is aware of activities deemed illegal or immoral in the society being studied, is it the role of the anthropologist to expose that activity? Should an anthropologist always use pseudonyms in describing the people and places where work is being carried out? If members of a community under study request that an anthropologist serve as an advocate for them, should the anthropologist accept the role? Do anthropologists have the same responsibilities in reporting the behavior of the elite and powerful as of the poor among whom they have traditionally studied? Is an anthropologist's primary responsibility to the people being studied, to the agency that has supported the research, or to the more abstract traditions and ethics of anthropological science? Do anthropologists have the right to collect and publish information on any aspect of people's lives? If an anthropologist knows that publishing the truth about some aspect of a community will bring harm to that community, does he or she nevertheless have the responsibility to publish that information? Is the primary responsibility of all anthropologists to engage in social change? The articles in this section provide some answers to these questions. In some cases they are offered as a particular anthropologist's solution to a particular ethical problem encountered in his or her work; in others they are presented more definitively as the ethically correct stance for all anthropologists.

In reviewing these articles, it becomes clear that regardless of their individual politics, research topic, or research setting, anthropologists in the field are always working in terms of three "levels" or spheres of activities and responsibility: the personal (including interpersonal relationships), the political (that is, the politics of the particular community being studied), and the academic (that is, the concrete research project being carried out). Life is simple for those anthropologists who have an absolute commitment to one of these spheres as always primary over the other two. But most anthropologists value and respect all three. While willing in some cases to grant more importance to one, they are not willing to disregard the others.

For example, the anthropologist who feels that his or her research is ultimately more important than local politics and interpersonal relations may nevertheless decide not to ask certain questions because they are insulting or because they will expose politically sensitive issues. There are contradictions within a given fieldwork situation, which further complicate the life of the anthropologist. For example, respecting the friendship and confidentiality that define an anthropologist's relationship with one person may be the very thing that jeopardizes his or her relationship with another individual in the community.

As we have argued previously, the first step in solving a difficult problem rests in the very recognition of it, and thus, the more anthropologists are aware of these three "levels" of activity, the better the chance that difficult ethical choices will be faced with a consciousness of potential consequences.

Reference

BOHANNAN, PAUL. 1963. *Social Anthropology.* New York: Holt, Rinehart & Winston.

1

The End of Fieldwork

JOHN MIDDLETON

The Study of Cultural Variation

DURING THE TIME I was there I worked in four parts of Lugbaraland, as well as visiting other areas of the country. . . . After about nine months [in south central Lugbaraland] I decided that I should work elsewhere and moved to northern Lugbaraland for a few weeks, then to western Lugbara on the Congo border, then briefly to the eastern part of the country, and then back to the same part of northern Lugbara that I had already visited. I spent most of the second year there, with a couple of weeks in southern Uganda, in Lugbara settlement of cotton farmers in Buganda and Bunyoro.

The three other areas in Lugbaraland itself were basically very similar to that in which I had already spent many months. But, partly because I had taken care to spend those months in one area, so that I knew it very well (as well, I suppose, as I know any place on earth), the differences in detail were immediately obvious to me. The area of western Lugbara, on the Congo border, was A'dumi. I was very unhappy there. The main reason was that I was again in the position of a newly arrived stranger, without friends or "kin"; but in addition this was an area of much intermingling of small groups of different clan affiliations, which had taken refuge there after having moved from the harsher colonial regime over the border in the Congo. There was considerable competition for land and power, and it was an area notorious for its sorcery. For a time I thought that my discovery of the importance of sorcery and of the persistent malice and hostility that lay behind it were due to my own sense of frustration and longing for the relatively ordered life I had left behind me in my earlier place of work. But at least I was soon aware of this possibility and realized that it did not explain what I found, although it certainly was the cause for my sour remarks about the people there in my diary of the period.

After a short stay of four weeks, I spent some weeks among the eastern Lugbara of Omugo. This was an area much affected by Islam and the scene of some of the early hostility to the colonial administration that culminated in the Rembe-inspired revolt of 1919 at Udupi. . . . Here my dissatisfaction that had been so obvious during my stay at A'dumi died down, as I was able again to see the importance of the marked differences in cultural detail from the area I knew so well from my first year. Unfortunately I found that I could understand very little of the local dialect, so that my progress was very slow and the results as far as filling pages of notes very disappointing. The differences from the first area were also marked enough for me to realize that I could not build on what I had learnt there. But whereas A'dumi had struck me as an area of some disintegration from what I assumed to be a more "traditional" system, it was very clear that Omugo, Udupi, Aringa, and the other parts of eastern and northeastern Lugbaraland could in no way be regarded in that light. They were simply very different from what I had experienced during the previous year. This made me reconsider my view of A'dumi, and I returned there for a week to see whether I had merely been misled in what I had learnt there. That week, although short, enabled me to view A'dumi more dispassionately and to put my experience there in proper perspective. These weeks also taught me something that I was not fully to appreciate until much later, when I spent a short time in Metu, among the western Madi: that the cultural variations within Lugbara were as great as between them and the Madi, their related neighbors to the east.

I spent the remainder of my fieldwork period in one place in northcentral Lugbara, called Maraca. . . . I chose this for several reasons. It was the center of a densely populated region, near the heartland of the country close to Mounts Eti and Liru; it was said to be very "traditional" in many ways, yet had been the scene of the first colonial administrative center established by the Belgians in 1900. Also I had very friendly relations with the county chief who lived a few miles from where I did, at a place he called Ovujo, "the house of idleness"; with the local sub-county chief, he who introduced me to the men who told me about the prophet Rembe; and with my cook's father, who lived a little way from where I established myself. I had stayed there for short periods during the previous year. I knew, therefore, that here I had kin ready-made, as it were, and was able to gain a great amount of valuable data which provided me with the bulk of the worthwhile information I collected during the total research period. Much of the work described in previous chapters was done in Maraca, although I have not explicitly mentioned the changes in locale in them. I was able to come to this area with both a considerable knowledge of Lugbara culture in general, with a knowledge of what I was looking for, and with a fresh eye. I saw everything as though for the first time, but with some knowledge of its likely significance and its relevance to my own work. Here I also took on another helper, Oraa, a local man of some age but a younger full-brother of an Elder: he was therefore near the sources of local power and knowledge but was not himself concerned to exercise it. He was ideal as introducer and also as informant.

There is no need to relate what I did in Maraca in detail. . . . But there is one point that should be made. By this time I was aware of the general pattern of Lugbara culture and social organization, so that I no longer regarded items of behavior as isolated but could expect, and grasp when I saw them, the relations between them. In other words, I was able by this time to comprehend the totality of everyday social behavior much as did the Lugbara themselves. If I observed farming, for example, I was aware of the general cosmological background to it; if I heard a discussion about witchcraft I could place it within the wider system of notions of sin, sacrifice, lineage segmentation, conflict for authority, and so on. In brief, I was aware not only of the interrelationships between one item of behavior and another but also of the bounds of Lugbara culture. Before this I had always been aware that there could be a vast range of behavior of which I knew nothing; but now, although of course I continued to collect new details of culture until the last day of my stay, I knew what was the totality of cultural detail and variation that I was likely to find. This was not, however, a time when all I had left to do was to fill in a few gaps of detail; I had rather to continue to seek out those relations between items of behavior and belief that I had not realized existed, and—perhaps more important since after all everything is ultimately related in one way or another to everything else—to weigh the significance of each relationship in the totality of Lugbara culture.

Interviews and Other Mundane Matters

Although I do not wish to discuss field "techniques" as such, I should say something about how I carried out interviews with informants. I have read in accounts of fieldwork methodology about the various ways of structuring interviews, with the implication that this is necessary for any successful gathering of data. I do not believe that this is true. It is clear from my own experience among the Lugbara that I found myself in four kinds of interview situations. The first was that in which I would be sitting among a mass of people who were engaged in drinking beer or performing a ceremony or ritual where my presence was to them merely peripheral and of little importance. On these occasions I would participate as far as I could in whatever was going on, which usually meant drinking, eating, and making as much sense as I could out of the hubbub of conversation around me. I suppose this merits the term "interview-situation." I know that on many occasions I very much wanted to interrupt what was going on with questions, but I never did. The main point of my being there was to observe the whole process and flow of activity in a given situation and I tried to be as inconspicuous as I could and to observe as much as I could for later questioning. If you like, these were preparatory interviews in which I would mark in my notebook and in my own mind points that I could discuss more privately later. They were also important in that my mere presence as an observer and participant was witness to my role of merely being an observer. On these occasions I showed myself to be above board, to be interested in the everyday life around me, and as far as I was able to behave as an ordinary person. It was rare on these occasions that there was not some stranger present whom I would notice asking puzzled but discreet questions about me. He would be told that I was the man who was learning Lugbara culture and history so that I could tell people in Europe about it. The questioner would accept this information with a nod (as my reputation spread quickly) and often with a smile and a handshake for me. . . . From the point of view of filling out my notes these occasions yielded little, but from that of understanding the life around me they were invaluable.

The second type of interview situation was that in which I would sit with two or three people, perhaps a man, his wife, and children, or a couple of men working in a field, and would discuss matters of interest with some care and with myself asking fairly carefully thought out questions. By that I do not mean that I thought out the phrases that I would use, but that I would try to ask my questions in a particular sequence in order to fill in points on which I wanted particular information. On many occasions these discussions became inconsequential as the people themselves would grow interested and excited, either because I was talking about something that was important to be told to me or important to be hidden from me. I would always try not to guide the conversation too much since I found after the first few months that if I did so either the people would grow bored or it would not occur to them to fill in the gaps in my own knowledge that would have been of interest to me had I known about them. These interviews were important for two reasons: from them I could fill in gaps of information and could ask for more detailed accounts than would be possible to obtain in general discussions with large numbers of people present; and because again they enabled me to make friends and to see the main lines of Lugbara culture open out before me. At these times I always wrote in a notebook and would transcribe my notes the same evening if I could possibly do so, with the date and identity of the informants. I could also take photographs much more easily at these times than when in a large mass of people, when there was always likely to be someone who did not like the idea.

The third type of interview was probably the most profitable as far as filling up my notebooks was concerned. These were long discussions with one person. I found that at any one time I would have one or two cronies who would play for a period of a week or two the role of inseparable confidant. Their motives were many and mixed. At times they were people who would gain prestige by being with me. Sometimes they would get a great deal of beer from me; sometimes they thought they could pay off old grudges by gossiping about their enemies. I think that this kind of interview situation is universal in anthropological fieldwork, and although it is very valuable it is not always easy to deal with. The Lugbara, although they lack marked differences of wealth or status, are extremely competitive and jealous people. So that bosom friendships of this kind can be somewhat harmful unless very carefully handled. At the same time the Lugbara are friendly people and I was not willing to snub a man who was merely trying to be helpful because of the risk of being involved in personal quarrels. My childhood had been spent largely near a small town near London, but with regular and extended holidays among farm people of a small and remote hamlet. In that village I, as a kinsman of a locally important farmer, had been in a situation not unlike that in which I found myself among the Lugbara. I was a stranger, and though a fairly wealthy one was yet a young man who did not show obvious signs of snobbishness and wished to be friendly with everybody. In other words I am saying that I tended in Lugbaraland to play by ear and to let things come as they might. Looking back I think now that I should perhaps have taken greater care not to have let myself be involved in various obscure interpersonal quarrels and jealousies. On the other hand the mere fact that I was told about these quarrels and jealousies was extremely valuable and indeed essential, especially when I began to analyze the cycle of lineage segmentation and the concomitant rites of sacrifice. All that I can really say here is that I behaved in exactly the same way as would anyone involved in the everyday life of any small village or neighborhood. I respected confidences and tried not to give offense, and tried to preserve an Olympian detachment from local quarrels and a sense of understanding and compassion. I come here to what is probably the single most difficult problem that faces an anthropologist: living among people who are themselves living out their everyday lives as does everyone in any society anywhere, but at the same time trying hard to remain outside these local relationships and to be an impartial observer of them. I admit that living with people such as the Lugbara, whose culture is in many ways so different from my own, many events that caused them to feel anger, guilt, or shame, were not events that caused me to feel the same sentiments nor even to imagine myself feeling them in those situations. There were also many situations when by observation or from gossip I learned of various actions that I found objectionable, but I would later have to talk with their perpetrators as though I cared nothing about their doings and when I knew that by doing precisely nothing would cause those people who had told me about the actions to feel that I was two-faced or cowardly in not regarding the people concerned in the way that they did themselves. These are matters on which one can advise a would-be fieldworker only by suggesting to him that he observe common sense and good manners and maintain a sense of decency and of understanding the weaknesses of other people. If this sounds smug and pretentious then I can answer only that I know no other advice.

The last type of interview situation was the somewhat different one of interviewing a person while filling in a questionnaire. I used questionnaires on several occasions. The first comprised four surveys that I made in different parts of the country to obtain some basic demographic information, with emphasis on the patterns of marriage within the group and with its neighbors. In each case I took a major section as the relevant group (some five to eight hundred people), and obtained data from every household in the section's territory. I had the questionnaire duplicated, in Lugbara, a single form covering all the members of a single homestead. I found that it would take me almost a morning to complete one form, so that I obviously had to have help. I asked the local mission-run secondary schools for assistance, and found a few schoolboys from each of the actual groups I wished to survey who were willing to help me in their school vacations. These were the only people who I actually paid in cash, by the day, for helping me. After spending a few days showing them what was required, we would visit every compound covered by the survey to introduce ourselves, and my assistants returned later to fill in the forms. They were of much value to me, and I wish that I had been able to do more of this work. I should add here that this was done toward the end of my stay, when I knew exactly what I wanted and when I could use questionnaires not to elicit fresh cultural details but rather to provide quantitative demonstration of processes of which I already knew the outlines. The work took a couple of months in each area.

As I have said, this was a slow process and I left most of the donkeywork to my helpers. However, from the few questionnaires that I did myself I found that if I spent an hour in filling in the replies to the actual questions on the paper I would spend at least another hour and a half in discussing them. I found that it was usually impossible to answer the questions in the order set out on the paper but that I had instead to fill them in in the order in which they occurred spontaneously in the course of conversation. I found also, and this is perhaps important, that information gained by questionnaire could be of a very superficial and public nature and I always took great care to administer them in public with as many people standing around listening, giving advice, and volunteering information of their own, as cared to attend. On one occasion I remember clearly administering half a dozen questionnaires to half a dozen people at the same time, trying to go down the list of questions going from one informant to another before passing on to the next question. The noise of argument must have carried a good quarter of a mile, but at least it was obvious that I was not hiding anything; despite the grievous departure from strict canons of technique in administering a questionnaire, such a way of doing it was certainly better in the Lugbara situation than sitting carefully and cold-bloodedly with a single person at a time. One must remember that as far as Lugbara of that time were concerned, virtually no one in the audience could read the marks I wrote on the pieces of paper, so that the more publicity given to what I was doing the better it was.

In passing I must admit that I can still only wonder at the kindness and patience of the many people with whom I spoke, often about matters of considerable intimacy, and that the degree of trust shown in me was really astonishing. I think that it is important and indeed wish to stress the fact that all depends upon one's own approach to one's informants. I have heard of anthropologists who have had chiefs and others in power punish people who refused to give information, and I have heard of others who will pay people or even get them drunk to get them to divulge secret information on matters that they would normally prefer not to discuss with strangers. I have also known anthropologists who have acquired confidential information and then use it in later interviews to elicit still further confidential information from other informants. It seems to me that such behavior is intolerable. I am not saying that I made no mistakes with informants but at least I did not break confidences or publish confidential information. The Lugbara accepted me as a guest and a friend and I tried to behave properly in these roles.

The Role of Fieldworker

By the end of two years in the field I had acquired a status in Lugbara eyes that appeared to be a reasonably stable one. I have mentioned early in this book something of the rather ill-defined roles that I had been given at the beginning of my stay. I had essentially been given, first, the status of a human being; then the incipient or uncertain semi-status of an immature social being, a stranger; then a more clearly definable and acceptable full status of a social or socialized being. I had, as I have mentioned, begun the development into a fully mature social being that is gone through, much more gradually and carefully, by a growing child and by a stranger who enters a Lugbara community from outside.

In the beginning the role I played was associated—with one exception—with technical activities: I was concerned with farming, hut-building, making spears and drums, and the like. The symbolic content of what I did and learned was minimal, and whatever such content there was was at the time almost beyond my comprehension. The exception, of course, was that at first I was given the role of European and so a man of power and nontraditional authority: this role became increasingly anomalous as I was given a more socialized total status in Lugbara society, and eventually the contradiction had to be resolved.

The change in role in the first year was expressed mainly in being allotted a status defined in terms of quasi-kinship. I hope that I have explained the nature of this enough to make it meaningful. Its acquisition was preceded by the various events that marked a change in my status from "thing" to "person": eating, drinking, dancing, and so on, and with events that marked the gradual loss of my "European" status, such as the invitation to drink *waragi* at the site of an illicit still.

The status of European, insofar as it was possible for it to be dropped—after all, it was not possible for me to drop it completely, since I *was* a European and not a Lugbara in any final analysis—was removed from me after about eight months. I was not all that aware of this process at the time it took place, but I saw later what it represented. The first development was not a single event but a series of occasions at which I took part in various activities at which European administrators and missionaries as well as Lugbara—both "New People" and ordinary persons—participated. They included various government holidays, with parades at the district headquarters in Arua; religious festivals and school celebrations, held at the two missions, and odd meetings and conversations with European officials. I noticed more and more that on these occasions, some formal, others not, I was increasingly placed on the Lugbara side. Whatever the situation, it was not unexpectedly always regarded by the Lugbara as one for the expression of the then basic axis of conflict in the region—Lugbara versus the others, or less commonly, Africans versus the others. I was counted more and more as being on the Lugbara side, perhaps as a Fifth Column agent of the Lugbara pretending to be on the other side but in reality "our child," "the child of Nyio" and similar phrases. I need not enlarge on this point, and perhaps I am exaggerating the significance of these incidents, but I noticed that when later discussing them I was increasingly included among the "we" rather than among "those Europeans."

Another occasion was to me both important and frightening. I was called about midnight to go to the hut of a young married woman, whose family I by then knew quite well, who was in childbirth. It was a breech birth and she was very weak from pneumonia. After many hours' labor, her mother, an old lady with whom I had often joked using the obscenities of a Lugbara joking relationship (since by some roundabout way I was reckoned as her husband's sister's son), suggested that I be called in. By this time it was known that my closest friend among the local Europeans was the doctor, so that it was assumed that I had unlimited medical expertise. When I reached the hut the woman was very weak. Obviously I was medically unskilled and other than suggesting that fewer old women and less herbal smoke in the hut might help, there was not much that I could do. If she were to die, presumably I would be to blame, since men should not be present at a birth, yet I clearly had to do something. I remembered what little medical knowledge I did possess and tried to assist. The baby was finally born and lived, as did the mother. The following day her mother came to visit me, with her sisters and other members of both the wife's and the husband's lineages, and talked for some time. One statement made was "now we know you are not a European, but a good person, and we are glad you are here as sister's son." The mother added that although she had wanted to call me earlier than she had, she had been frightened lest I pollute the homestead and endanger the birth; but she had been overcome by the argument that as I was not a Lugbara this could not apply to the situation. She had been wrong in that regard and yet paradoxically here was I, not a European, but a proper, trustworthy, person; being a "sister's son" helped, since sisters' sons could perform certain actions for someone that were too intimate to be done by a person's patrilineal kin. She was puzzled, realizing that her argument was, in the terms of her own culture, paradoxical. Until the previous day I had been a European, or at least more a European than a Lugbara; the scale had now tilted slightly and I could be regarded as more a Lugbara than a European.

Somewhat cynically one might well ask what is the point of discussing all this about the fieldworkers' changing role. The anthropologist is not undergoing a course in psychoanalysis, although the experience of being a field anthropologist may almost certainly be as intensive as being under analysis—it is not guided but in many respects remarkably similar (I write as someone who has not experienced analysis, so any indignant analyst can contentedly shoot me down here). The anthropologist is engaged in an arduous task of trying to understand and interpret a culture other than his own, and must retain this as being his only task for a period of two years. His behavior in the role he is given by his hosts is determined—or should be determined—by this single aim. Ultimately I am here leading to the question of how and when does one know that one has a reasonable idea of the culture and organization that one is studying. With this problem goes another that is present throughout one's field research and that is implicit in all that I have written so far: this is how does one estimate the accuracy, relevance, and completeness of the information given by informants. Clearly there are times when one is deliberately misled but it is much more common for one to be given incomplete information through no bad intention or fault of informants. The criterion for knowing that one has understood a culture and the cultural behavior that one witnesses might be said to be that one can predict what is likely to be the answer given to questions about them. The word predict here raises many epistemological questions that cannot be discussed in a book of this size; but something should be said of them since it seems to me that they are important. One cannot predict human behavior in the way that an astronomer can predict the appearance of a comet. The Lugbara cannot do that for their own behavior nor we for ours. However, it is not so much a matter of prediction of the future as of understanding the completeness and complementarity of the set of roles played before one in a given social situation. For example, the sacrificial rites that I have mentioned earlier were dramas played out for a certain end, with the actors being those taking part, the dead ancestors, Divine Spirit, and myself. Perhaps it would be better to call them scenes in a long drawn out drama than individual dramas themselves: none could fully be understood in isolation from the others. Each of these scenes had an expected number of actors whose roles were in a certain pattern of relationships and were composed of certain expected items of behavior. If one of these were missing or were misplayed the Lugbara would realize this and would state that the ritual concerned would be ineffective and should therefore be performed on another occasion. My competence at analysis of the situation was made clear only when I could myself realize that a particular role was missing, miscast, misplayed, or in some other way out of its proper place in the whole constellation of roles whose correct performance made up the scene before me.

I come here to an important point when one is studying nontraditional or innovative social behavior. When the prophets and the Christian evangelists initiated their ritual performances in response to situations of radical conflict, ambiguity, and change, the response to them by ordinary Lugbara was precisely that of bewilderment, uncertainty, irritation, and even anger because they could not comprehend a total and expected pattern in the scene before them. It was only at the very end of my stay that I was able to interpret in this way the Lugbara reaction of such figures and to realize that I did in fact understand something of Lugbara ritual performances. The same applied of course to many other situations, such as the behavior of many administrators and missionaries to that of many "New People" and, of course, to my own behavior. I first noticed this when I heard some Lugbara telling other Lugbara of the events that had occurred when several of us had visited southern Uganda. Their description of what we had seen and done were couched in terms that were very different from my own and which I saw at first as a distortion of our experiences. During that visit we had been to one or two Lugbara settlements of labor migrants and the men with me could not place properly the behavior of those migrants because the scenes they were playing were as it were part of a different drama to that with which they were familiar in their homeland. It was after this that I began what I found to be extremely fruitful discussions in which I compared the accounts given to me by close informants of events and situations that we together had witnessed to my own description of the same events and situations that I had written down immediately on my return from them. The more I learned about Lugbara the closer were our various accounts of these same events, except on the few occasions when we had traveled into non-Lugbara situations, some of which I could interpret correctly by my own cultural traditions and others in which we were all ignorant of the expected dramatic structure of what we saw (such as a visit to the Kuku of the Sudan). In brief, what I am trying to say is that one cannot predict the events of a given situation but one can see the structure or pattern within the scene that is part of a total drama; and one then knows that one understands as much of another culture as one can hope to understand.

I had been warned by my teacher, Professor Evans-Pritchard, that there is a time when one thinks one is wasting one's time and is a failure. He was correct. In my case it was about nine months after I first entered Lugbaraland. I seemed to have no understanding of the language, I seemed to have no friends or confidants, I seemed to know nothing of the people or their culture. This sense of failure and of frustration would seem to affect us all sooner or later, I am told by colleagues. It was in my case compounded of several elements, most of them connected with my own somewhat romantic and optimistic expectations about my role among the Lugbara.

I had been trained to be a research anthropologist, and this stay among the Lugbara whom I wished to study was in a sense, as I saw it at that time, the culmination of a long period of apprenticeship: the apprentice, although hardly a master, was at least thrown on his own resources as a craftsman. I do not clearly remember exactly what I hoped to achieve even within a few months, but when very little seemed to have been achieved I felt lonely and despondent. I think that probably I had written too many initial field notes. My diary was another matter and when I look at it now I realize its value; but my first half-year's field notes are virtually useless except on a few matters such as technology, and these lack any sociological understanding.

I see also now how much of my sense of frustration, and much else of what I felt and did, were due to my own uncertainty as to my role among the Lugbara. It would be expected that one would have this sense of uncertainty during the period when one is being given a mature status by one's hosts: and indeed I experienced it at this precise time. It was clear to me, whether I liked always to admit it or not, that I was never completely accepted as one of themselves by the people among whom I worked—as I have mentioned before, a stranger can never be accepted, despite the self-deception of many sentimental travellers in Africa. I was always ultimately under the protection of the central government, whether they had wished to leave me alone or to deport me. The visitor longs to be accepted by his hosts, both emotionally and otherwise. I found for myself that there are likely to be three ways in which a fieldworker—or at least an anthropological fieldworker, whose position is very different from that of an economist, sociologist, teacher, historian, technician, or others—tries, consciously or not, to attain this affective link. I am assuming here, of course, that he is a fieldworker, that is, an objective observer; a full participant in the life of his hosts, even from his point of view if not from theirs, is no longer an observer in the anthropological sense. Perhaps this is both the easiest and emotionally the only satisfying course to take, but it makes research impossible and its findings unreliable. The three ways easily open to observer are to assist his hosts in such ways as providing them with medicine; to act as their spokesman vis-à-vis the central government or other external agency that his hosts find it diffcult to deal with; and to build up a series of mutual friendship obligations that in some way fall short of complete participant equality. It is clear that these three courses (with full participation as the fourth) differ in the degree to which the fieldworker regards his hosts as objects. As Lévi-Strauss has written, one can only observe people as objects, whether we or they like it or not. But we are also people, and find the objective role as an emotionally unsatisfying one. One problem is obvious: that if we play the roles I have mentioned above, since they are all to one degree or other asymmetrical, they become frustrating. Probably the first response of most people is to accuse the other party of being selfish, or greedy, or in some other way showing that they lack the purity of one's own motives. If one gives several hours a week to dressing dirty and unsightly wounds and sores, one becomes annoyed when one's patients do not follow medical routine; if one gives a patient drugs one gets angry if he gives or sells them to others. If one puts in a word to the agent of the central government on behalf of people who are badly represented there, one may grow resentful if one's advice in the matter to the people one is representing is not taken, or if they try to presume on one's powers and demand more help than one can give while still retaining the role of impartial observer. If one has a friend—and I acquired a handful of close friends about whose behavior I could not remain impartial or objective—one expects him not to abuse that friendship, even if the abuse is in our cultural terms and not in his.

I am not saying that one should not grow angry, resentful, or frustrated at these responses. I am saying merely that at times I did, and from conversations with anthropological colleagues I have found that they did the same. I am saying merely that the role of the anthropological fieldworker is one of paradox, ambiguity, and uncertainty, and these are increased with the greater degree of difference in cultural expectations between his hosts and himself. There is not much that one can do about his hosts' behavior, but there is quite a lot one can do about his own. In my view, the most important thing is to know exactly what is one's own role as an observer, however one's hosts may regard it or their own. As I have said at the beginning of this book, my teacher told me that the most important part of a fieldworker's abilities is to have good manners, since these imply a knowledge of one's own status and values in interpersonal relations. To have this knowledge is, of course, to avoid condescension and patronizing, faults that are found, I fear, most particularly among those fieldworkers who assume, for one reason or another, that they have some special innate sympathy for and intuitive understanding of the people among whom they are living. Most of these merely think that they have these desirable qualities and their behavior is usually, in my experience, one that generates ambiguity and misunderstanding. Let me give two trivial examples. Lugbara always insisted that I should behave as a "European," or rather as a European without power over them, although I behaved as a pleasant and powerless human being who happened to have been born "across Lake Albert." If I did not dress in a fairly formal and clean manner they did not approve, saying that I was behaving "like a Greek" (the nearest thing in their particular experience to a "poor white") and was regarding them as unworthy of respect and good manners. And whenever I invited acquaintances to my hut to drink or to eat they expected at least some of the beer to be "European" and served in glasses and at least some of the food to be served on a plate and eaten with fork or spoon. No one likes a slummer, whether in New York or in the Appalachians: why should people in an African city or village be expected to be any different? I am not saying, of course, that the observer should behave like a caricature of an Anglo-Indian colonel: that is as far on the other side; and one could argue that that kind of behavior is due also to uncertainty and often to fear, especially one expressed in collective and ethnic terms.

I am saying that the role of the anthropological fieldworker is not an easy one, and that the chief difficulty is usually one that arises from the paradox in his role, that he must be both objective and yet be a participant to the greatest degree that he can while still retaining objectivity. This is not advice for people who must cope with neighbors, or teach them, or administer them or have any other kind of role. Others with somewhat similar difficulties, of which the most obvious is probably the psychoanalyst, meet them differently. But there is here an essential difference that the analyst is an objective observer only with regard to individuals for ritually defined periods, whereas the anthropologist has the far harder task of being unable and unwilling to set aside ritually defined interview periods. There are, as we all know, many anthropologists who have done precisely this: they set certain times aside for clearly defined interviews, and live outside the fieldwork situation at other times. Except in the case engaged in ethnological reconstruction, as among certain American Indian groups, for example, I cannot see the value of doing this. It is a denial of the role of fieldworker.

Writing Up the Field Material

Finally I should say something about the writing-up of the data I had collected on my return to England from Uganda. After all, a man who has spent two years or twenty years on ethnographic field research but does not write up his findings for public use might just as well never have been to the field as far as the discipline of anthropology is concerned. As we all know there are some anthropologists who find it virtually impossible to set down their findings on paper. I assume that they find the paradox of being an anthropological fieldworker so difficult that they cannot readjust to their own culture.

I found on my return to England considerable difficulty in leaving one culture for another, even though the second had been my own. My first recollection is of noticing various minutiae of behavior in England of which I had previously been unaware. For example, I noticed how English women—but not English men—looked quickly at one another's clothing in passing in the streets. Coming as I had done from a virtually naked people I could perhaps hardly fail to see the social significance placed on wearing the clothes suitable to one's social position and aspirations. Again I soon noticed how English women would appear ashamed of being pregnant, whereas among the Lugbara to be pregnant is a source of pride and a cause for congratulation by patting the woman's stomach—something that I only just stopped myself doing on more than one occasion in England. I noticed what seemed to me to be the loudness and ill-manners of the children although what of course I was really seeing was the difference between Lugbara culture, in which children know their status as incipient adults, and English culture in which children have a subculture and an indeterminate status. I think that all anthropologists have similar experiences when returning from the field. This sense of strangeness and of awareness did not last for more than a few weeks, but it made clear to me my sense of uncertainty as to my proper role of a person who had lived in more than one culture and tried to observe more than one set of social values.

Looking back to my behavior after my return I see now that my uncertainty as to my role was expressed, as it is in most cases, by an excitement and a garrulousness concerning the Lugbara, whom I discussed avidly with anyone whom I met and was willing to listen to me. They were "my people," the object of an intense personal experience which I was willing to interpret to others although not totally willing to share with them. My own sense of uncertainty was lessened by the fact that I returned to a department in which all members had themselves done fieldwork or were planning to do it, and many of whom had only just returned from the field. This latter group was in the eyes of its own members set apart, and there can be no doubt that the excitement and fascination we felt for our common work was both helpful to us in a psychological sense and fruitful for us with regard to thinking about and interpreting our field experience and material.

I had one academic year in which to write a doctoral dissertation on my fieldwork, and I had chosen for the title of my thesis the very general one of "The social organization of the Lugbara of Uganda," which could of course cover virtually anything. I was fortunate at having no work other than to write the dissertation, although I did also have the immediate obligation of writing a report on labor migration. I was told that the dissertation would act as my formal report to those institutions that had sponsored my fieldwork. I spent those nine months mainly in writing the dissertation, which involved presenting some of the material I had collected so as to give an orderly picture of the society. This was not quite so easy as it may sound, since the various notions as to pattern and structure that I had held in my mind at the end of my actual field period soon proved not to be fully adequate when I attempted to put them down on paper. When I could no longer see the wood for the trees I was lucky in being able to turn to my labor migration report, in which the trees themselves were of major importance. By writing up the material for the thesis I was being made to objectivize my experiences and thus to resolve again the paradox of the anthropologist that I have mentioned above. I need not go into details of the thesis itself, which is from my viewpoint today a very inadequate presentation of Lugbara society. I think that there is often far too much pressure placed upon younger anthropologists to have a doctoral dissertation published immediately as a hardcover monograph. I would say that a thesis is one thing and a book is another; the former is something to be got rid of as soon as possible, whereas the latter is a much more important work which is the real *raison d'être* of one's being privileged to be an anthropologist at all. By the summer of 1953, therefore, I had written a report on labor migration for the Government of Uganda, and had submitted and had accepted the dissertation.

I was at this point extremely fortunate—more so than I realized at the time—to be able to return to Lugbaraland for a period of three months during the summer. I did this in the company of three other people, so I was able to finish my fieldwork among the Lugbara both while working with a team and also after I had had a long period of writing and thinking about the former material that I had collected. There is no need in discussing this work, since for my part I spent most of the time in filling in gaps of information that had become apparent to me during the time I was writing the dissertation. The people with me were three students, all of my own academic standing: one was a soil chemist, one a botanist, and the third a geographer. All were excellent at the work they did and between us we were able to collect a great deal of valuable data regarding Lugbara ecology and agriculture. I found that my style of work was hardly possible in the company of other people, since we were simply too many to be accepted easily by the Lugbara at any one time. We were able efficiently to measure fields and to discover details of ecology that I found extremely important and meaningful when added to my former information about such matters as patterns of settlement and processes of group segmentation. But it was not possible to set up the close personal ties that had been so important for me during my own previous work. One man may be accepted as a quasi-kinsman, but three more were too many. All I need say here is that if the four of us had gone to Lugbaraland in the way in which I had gone myself three years previously we could not have acquired any very close knowledge of the workings of Lugbara society. We might have been very efficient at collecting quantifiable data, but any close and intimate knowledge of Lugbara culture and its values would not have been possible for us to collect, due simply to the inhibiting factor of our being so many strangers that Lugbara could not easily have absorbed us as "kinsmen." I think that this would not hold true of a husband and wife team, for the simple reason that a husband and wife could easily be accepted into the kinship system. But this was not possible for four unrelated men and I do not think the Lugbara found it easy or possible to regard us as being in any sense brothers to one another, which might have resolved that particular problem. However, I shall not continue this particular discussion, because although we worked as a team our situation was unusual, in that one of us had already spent two years in the area. We were therefore not in the position of a newly arrived team and our particular experience is of little value to other people in a more usual situation.

What is worth saying about this final visit is that it was perhaps the most immediately productive of any three-month period I had spent there. First, because I knew at that time exactly what were the points that I was investigating, and that with my two-year former experience the very fact that I was forced by my company to behave somewhat distantly and objectively removed many of the personal difficulties as well as many of the personal delights of my main fieldwork tour. In later years I was able to do fieldwork in Zanzibar and in Nigeria, and much the same is true of those researches. I was in an objective sense a far more competent fieldworker, for the very reason that my tie with the people whom I was studying was much less emotionally laden than that I had had with the Lugbara. I was able on these later occasions not to put myself into the position of paradox that I had been in among the Lugbara. This was not merely because these were second and third field projects but also because they were shorter and directed to specific research projects: in Zanzibar the study of land tenure and in Lagos that of immigrant associations. I was able to control any sense of uncertainty and frustration to a far greater degree but my work was more superficial, more objective, and with much less understanding and less sympathy and affection. I was not involved in anything in the same sense as among the Lugbara. I do not mean to say that I could not have been if I had had longer and less clearly defined projects: I am merely reporting my own experience. But these several years later I do not remember the people of either Zanzibar or Lagos as I do the Lugbara.

2

Towards a Native Anthropology

DELMOS J. JONES

FIELD METHODOLOGY is currently a much-discussed subject in anthropology.[1] As usually conceived, research is a task carried out by an "outsider" or "stranger" who enters a society and attempts to learn about the way of life of its people. Thus, most discussions center on problems encountered by the outsider. But there is another vantage point from which research can be conducted—that of "insider," the person who conducts research on the cultural, racial, or ethnic group of which he himself is a member. The goal of this paper is to explore some of the problems of field work faced by such inside researchers.

The paper does not, however, focus entirely on the subject of field methodology; the epistemological dimension of field research will also be explored. I will attempt to show that the insider and the outsider do face different problems in the field situation. But as far as theory is concerned, there is as yet no set of theoretical conclusions generated from the point of view of native anthropologists. By a "native anthropology," I mean a set of

This paper is based on two research projects: one in Northern Thailand under a fellowship granted by the Foreign Area Fellowship Program of the Social Science Research Council and the American Council of Learned Societies, the second in Denver under a small grant from the National Institute of Health (MN-16242-01). The conclusions, opinions, and other statements in this paper are those of the author and not necessarily those of either of the above agencies.

theories based on non-Western precepts and assumptions in the same sense that modern anthropology is based on and has supported Western beliefs and values; for, as Maquet has pointed out:

> ... it seems clear that the existence of a particular discipline dedicated exclusively to the study of non-Western cultures reflected the Victorian sense of superiority of the 19th century Europe and was perfectly consistent with, and useful to, the colonial expansion of that period. Is it not striking that this situation persisted in Africa as long as did the Colonial system and had to wait the decolonization process to be questioned?[2]

So long as the use of native anthropologists does not lead to the development of a native anthropology, I disagree with the statement that "the science of anthropology has been greatly enriched by those informants who were influenced by anthropologists to become anthropologists."[3] This is a process not yet achieved; its occurrence will benefit anthropology as a whole and may well prevent the "death" of anthropology predicted by some current writers.[4]

Field research is of course a process of finding answers to certain questions, or solutions to certain theoretical or practical problems. As such, it involves a series of steps from a definition of the problem to be studied through the collection of data to the analysis of data and the writing up of the results. The general philosophy in anthropology is that a graduate student should do field research for his Ph.D. dissertation. Furthermore, it is thought that his research should take place in a culture other than his own. Students are generally taught that a person working among his own people cannot maintain the degree of objectivity desirable, hence research experiences must be gained initially in another culture. Thus, a philosophical element enters into the research process. Interestingly enough, however, the rule that the student should not work in his own culture seems to be reversed when it comes to the foreign student, the "native" who is studying for a Ph.D. in the United States. It is an undeniable fact that most African students in American universities are Africanists who have conducted field work in their own society and are specialists in their own people. The philosophy concerning the field training of foreign students, therefore, is opposite to that which pertains to training American students. This discrepancy can only be explained in terms of the way in which the native anthropologist is seen by the field as a whole—not as a professional who will conduct research and develop theories and generalizations, but as a person who is in a position to collect information in his own culture to which an outsider does not have access. There is, then, the expectation that the insider will know things in a different, more complete way than will the outsider.

A basic aim of anthropological field research is to describe the total culture of a group of people. This description, as much as possible, should be made from the point of view of the people—i.e., the inside view. For the anthropologist to obtain such a description, he must become actively involved in the life of the people, communicate with them, and spend a considerable period of time among them. With these general goals as the primary emphasis, it seems obvious that the trained native anthropologist can produce the best and most reliable data, since he knows the language, has grown up in the culture, and has little difficulty in becoming involved with the people.

According to Lowie, Boas encouraged the training of native anthropologists on the assumption that in describing the total way of life of a people from the point of view of the people themselves, it was the trained native who could best interpret native life from within. Materials collected by the trained native had "the immeasurable advantage of trustworthiness, authentically revealing precisely the elusive intimate thoughts and sentiments of the native, who spontaneously reveals himself in these outpourings."[5] In the same spirit that Boas encouraged natives to become anthropologists, he also encouraged women because they could collect information on female behavior more easily than a male anthropologist. This attitude strongly implies that native and female anthropologists are seen as potential "tools" to be used to provide important information to the "real," white male anthropologists.

It is undoubtedly true that an insider may have easier access to certain types of information as compared to an outsider. But it is consistent to assume, also, that the outsider may have certain advantages in certain situations. For example, in 1969-70, I conducted a research practicum for Health students at Denver General Hospital. The students, mostly white, were sent into the black community to inquire about health practices. One student returned with the information that some women had a craving for a particular type of dirt during pregnancy. On checking further, I found this to be quite a general practice, especially in the rural South. Although I was born and grew up in the rural South, I was unaware of the practice. None of the informants volunteered this information to me, probably because it did not occur to them that I did not already know about it, since I could be readily identified as both black and Southern. The crucial point is that insiders and outsiders may be able to collect different data; they also have different points of view which may lead to different interpretations of the same set of data.

The Problem of Point of View

As an outsider, I have done research among the Papago Indians of Southern Arizona and among the Lahu, a hill tribe of Northern Thailand. As an insider, I have done research in a black community in Denver, Colorado. In this paper I wish particularly to compare my experiences in Denver and Thailand. In both places, as a researcher (whether insider or outsider), I began with the formulation of the problem to be investigated. In Thailand the problem was to study intracultural variation among six villages of a hill tribe. In Denver the problem was to study the relationship between social structure and black self-concept. The logical processes of formulating a research problem were similar; however, the factor of point of view entered very strongly into the formulation of the Denver study, whereas it was virtually absent in the Thailand study. In Thailand, the questions relating to cultural variation were derived from the literature on the concept of culture and from the tendency of anthropologists to speak of a total population in terms of a study of one segment of that population.[6] The goal was to determine and to measure the range of variation in cultural behavior among villages of the same tribal (cultural) group.

The problem formulation for the Denver study, on the other hand, involved much more than logic. It involved intuition, experience, and self-interest (or more properly speaking, group interest). Current literature is filled with discussions concerning black self-image, and the conclusions are that in general blacks have a more negative self-image than whites.[7] First of all, there is some resentment over having one's own group described in this manner, although as a scientist, one must allow for the possibility that the findings are indeed correct. But as a skeptic, one can also consider the possibility that there may be something in the situation that other people are missing. For example, when I looked at my own experience of relating to other blacks within a black social context, I could not see the general conclusion of a negative self-image as being consistent with these experiences.

Before one can begin collecting data, it is necessary to gain access to the community. In this, the insider is faced with a much different set of problems than the outsider. But unless the insider returns to the same community in which he grew up, he still has the problem of developing contacts. Since I was new to the Denver area, I had to begin there (as I began in Thailand) with someone who knew someone, who in turn knew someone else in "a chain of introduction which leads at least to the threshold of his group."[8]

In the Thailand and Denver experiences, one of the biggest differences in gaining access to the community and establishing a continuing role for myself was the nature of the two social situations. In Thailand I was dealing with a small, close-knit village; but in Denver I was dealing with an urban neighborhood with little or no neighborhood-wide social organization. Once an anthropologist is accepted into a nonurban community, he takes a role for himself within the context of the community. In the urban situation, however, the researcher may have to establish a role for himself with each individual that he meets. . . .

The Lahu had seen only three types of outsiders: traders, missionaries, and government agencies of various sorts. When I first arrived in the village, there was immediate suspicion that I was a missionary since most of the Americans they had seen were missionaries. This suspicion was easily overcome by pointing out that many of the things that I did with them, such as dancing in their "pagan" rituals, would be considered sinful by a missionary. The ghetto dweller, on the other hand, is faced with many different types of outsiders, many of whom are greeted with a great deal of hostility. Among the types of people who may knock on their door are social workers (perhaps checking up on the behavior of welfare recipients), bill collectors, salesmen, researchers, and representatives from various agencies such as the Office of Economic Opportunity, Department of Health, local hospital, and the like. Most of these are white. Because I am black and did not wear a white shirt and tie, I was not viewed immediately as an undesirable stranger. I could just be someone looking for a friend. Thus the reaction to me was perhaps much less hostile than it would have been to a white anthropologist. Although I have no comparison of people's reaction to a white researcher, not a single person refused to be interviewed by me.[9]

This is not to say that conducting research in the black community of Denver was without problems. Sometimes people were a bit suspicious. On occasions I was suspected of being a Black Panther; alternatively, I was sometimes suspected of being connected with some of the agencies of the Establishment. Thus, the problems of establishing rapport involved similar elements in both Thailand and Denver. But convincing the few people in Denver who objected to the Panthers and thought that I might be one was much easier than convincing the Lahu that I was not a missionary. In the Denver case the problem arose when I said something about political and economic oppression. People would ask, "Are you one of those Panthers?" They always accepted my reply of "No," and got on with the interview. In Thailand, when the Lahu thought that I was a missionary, I had to demonstrate that I was not a missionary by pointing out that I participated in village activities which no missionary would ever do.

In order to collect data one has to communicate; but communication involves more than verbal exchanges. There are also facial expressions, hand movements, body movements, and tone of voice, to name just a few of the subtleties of communication. In my research experience among the Lahu of Northern Thailand there were certain mannerisms which I was able to understand only after a considerable amount of time. After about three months with the Lahu I discovered that I could tell when they were not telling me the whole truth by the way they answered questions. When I tried to collect information on a topic which people did not want to tell me about, such as religion, they would answer the question very softly; and on further checking, I would find their answers to be untrue. In most situations the good researcher reaches a point at which he is able to read meaning into the way a person says something as well as to record what is said. But where this was a level of understanding that I had to achieve as an "outsider" anthropologist, it was something that I began with as an "inside" anthropologist. That is, I have a core of common understanding with most black people: I grew up in a poor black community; I have experienced discrimination; and I can speak and understand the "dialect."

One task which most researchers face is how to explain what they are doing. A stranger coming to a remote village in Thailand has to have a reason for being there. How does he explain his research? Since the Lahu had not seen many outsiders and knew nothing about research, the problem was solved by simply stating that I wanted to learn all that I could about their way of life. Although they could not understand why anyone wanted to know about their life, they accepted the explanation. In contrast, most people in the urban black community *do* know what research is and are familiar with some of the implications and results of research. As stated previously, various types of research have taken place in Denver. Some of the people that I interviewed had been interviewed by other researchers as well, and some researchers have appeared on local television to discuss what they have discovered about the Denver community. In addition, many people have read descriptions of black behavior and do not like what they have read. More importantly, many persons see research as a process which takes the place of political action.[10] It is understandable, therefore, that explaining research in a context such as this takes on a different complexion than explaining the purpose of research to hill people in Thailand.

Negative feelings toward research are becoming more and more common among minority groups in the United States. Still, I found no single attitude towards research in the black community of Denver. Rather, I encountered three general reactions: The majority of the people I interviewed had no opinion or commitment toward research. The problem of explaining the purpose of research to this group was minor. The only real problem with them was that some felt that answering my questions would somehow harm them. There was no specific bit of information which seemed threatening—merely the task of giving answers. This was solved by not requiring names. The second general reaction was a feeling that research among black people by a black social scientist was a very good thing. This attitude was common among people who had read sociological discussions of blacks. They felt, for example, that the information contained in works such as the Moynihan report is distorted because reports written by whites cannot reflect an understanding of black people. Since people of this type felt that the record should be set straight and could only be done so by a black person, they were the most cooperative. The third reaction was the feeling that enough research has already been done, period. People with this attitude think that action is what is needed now; consequently, they were the least cooperative. However, because I am black, they did submit to an interview; but by and large, they made poor informants since they did not take the interview seriously.

One dimension of the Denver research experience which was completely absent in the Lahu experience was the very personal way in which many people reacted to me and the research itself. I have already explained that many people with whom I talked felt that information in the currently available literature about black people is untrue, and it is untrue because it was written by whites who were unable to understand black behavior. The desire to set the record straight, therefore, was very strong, as evidenced in one of my first encounters with a woman living in the housing project. After explaining the nature of my research project, she replied, "Finally!" And there were other ways in which people reacted to me in a very personal manner; I was, to many of them, not a social scientist but a black man who had overcome the barriers of American society and made good.

Data Analysis and Publication

A common problem confronting anthropologists when compiling their data is whether or not to withhold certain information from publication. Many who have done research in the Third World countries have withheld from their reports information which they thought would displease or embarrass the host country and jeopardize their chances of returning. As an inside researcher, I felt this emotion even more keenly than I did as an outsider. As an outsider, you work with people who, because of cultural, racial, or language differences, are always aware that you are an outsider. As an insider, people often do not look upon you as a researcher. You may be a friend, someone who is trusted.[11] In this capacity, people have revealed deeply personal things to me; and in this context also, I am in a position to learn many specific things about the people. Such revelations may be related to the research, but I would be both dishonest and disloyal to reveal such information.

Because of my emotional involvement, I am also inclined to question certain conclusions which have been reached concerning the behavior of black people, such as the conclusion that blacks have a negative self-image or that Africans were easily enslaved compared to the New World Indians whose nobility led them to prefer death to slavery. It might not occur to an outsider to question this theory about slavery because these conclusions do not involve his own identity. For example, in a conversation at one time with a white historian, it was apparent that he had never considered the high rate of suicide or the high death rate in general among the early African population as an indication of resistance to slavery.

The face that I may question many existing ideas about black people with which the white anthropologist might not be concerned is not in itself an argument for the advantages of either the inside or outside view.

To observe a way of life best, it seems, involves living that way of life. This assumption invites two criticisms, each of which has both a theoretical and a practical aspect. First, is "the inside" a privileged observation point? There is nothing especially privileged about the observations of a parade made by those in it. Spectators may be in a better position, television viewers in a still better one. Which vantage point you choose must surely be a matter of what you want to observe and why.[12]

One vantage point cannot be said to be better than the other. There are logical dangers inherent in both approaches. The outsider may enter the social situation armed with a battery of assumptions which he does not question and which guide him to certain types of conclusions; and the insider may depend too much on his own background, his own sentiments, his desires for what is good for his people. The insider, therefore, may distort the "truth" as much as the outsider. Since both positions involve the possibility of "distortion," which is better? . . .

Many anthropologists feel that the native's view of his own culture reflects the most accurate view. The aim of anthropological research, we are often told, is to see things from the point of view of the native. Although the inside view is loudly proclaimed by anthropologists, few go so far as to consider the belief in magic and witchcraft as an element of absolute truth. There is no escape from the idea that outsiders and insiders view social reality from different points of view and that no matter how hard each tries, neither can completely discard his preconceptions of what that social reality is or should be. From this point of view, neither is any more or less trustworthy than the other. Both have room for distortions, inaccuracies, half-truths. A social anthropologist who claims to have acquired a complete understanding of another culture stands self-condemned.[13] A lesson that most anthropologists have failed to learn is that a subsequent researcher will always find errors in one's data, no matter how many years one remains in the field, no matter how well one speaks the language, and no matter how far one thinks he has got under the skin of the native.

Since both the inside researcher and the outside researcher face the same empirical problems, is there any advantage to the native anthropologist at all? My answer is yes, potentially. The problem at this point is that there are native anthropologists, but there is no native anthropology. By this I mean there is little theory in anthropology which has been formulated from the point of view of tribal, peasant, or minority peoples. Thus, the whole value of the inside researcher is not that his data or insights into the social situation are better—but that they are *different*. Most of the few black anthropologists operating in this country are looking for something new, questioning old assumptions about social processes, developing new ones, exploding old myths, and in the process developing new ones. The work of the white anthropologist among non-Western people is not bad because he is white, but because the field of anthropology as a whole was dull and uncreative in the 1960's. Our concepts and theories, our way of looking at people have lost their relevance.[14]

Lehman, in an article on the problem of minority relations in Burma, concludes that social science theory has played a major role in generating the problem of majority/minority relations in Burma or "at least [has played a part] in obscuring the conditions required for their solution."[15] This is no less true of the situation in the United States. The theory to which Lehman refers is the consensus model of society which is the basis of much anthropological thinking about social problems.

In anthropology the conception of a primitive society has been one in which there is structure, function, and equilibrium. Consensus on values is the basic element which holds a society together. This means that the society operates without conflict, competition, or resentment. Everyone agrees upon the values, internalizes those values, and voluntarily follows the proper forms of behavior. Force is seldom needed to get this conformity. Everyone in the society does exactly as he is supposed to do at all times. This basic assumption about society leads to a description of the caste system of India as

> . . . an organic system with each particular caste and subcaste filling a distinctive functional role. It is a system of labor division from which the element of competition among workers has been largely excluded.[16]

Thus, the elements of oppression, frustration, resentment, aspirations, and hostility are not seen in most anthropological descriptions of social organization. The lower castes never rebel against the higher, nor do they resent their position in the system.

There is an alternative to the notion of primitive societies being held together by value consensus. Dahrendorf has written:

> From the point of view of coercion theory, . . . it is not voluntary cooperation or general consensus but enforced constraint that makes social organizations cohere. In institutional terms, this means that in every social organization some positions are entrusted with a right to exercise control over other positions in order to ensure effective coercion: it means, in other words, that there is a differential distribution of authority. . . . this differential distribution of authority invariably becomes the determining factor of systematic social conflict of a type that is germane to class conflict in the traditional (Marxian) sense of the term.[17]

Another important dimension to this problem involves the extremely high regard with which anthropologists tend to hold the traditions of other people. Sometimes anthropologists seem more attached to traditional behavioral patterns of a group than the people themselves, though as Maquet notes:

> I do not mean that anthropological writings, by enhancing African traditional values, have had a significant bearing on the upholding of the colonial system. . . . What matters is that anthropology was oriented as though it wanted to preserve the existing situation.[18]

Robert Redfield also recognized this in his *Peasant Society and Culture*.[19] He wondered whether differences reported about peasant values might be due to choices made by observers and writers as to which aspects of the social situation they chose to stress. He asserted that the observer of a people's values must answer such questions as "What do these people desire for themselves and for their children? To what kind of life do they attach highest esteem?" Many anthropologists never ask these questions. They assume that peasants find rural life to be just as romantic as they do. Lopreato, who did deal with this subject, found that the Italian peasant had an intense dislike of his life-situation and a strong desire to leave the inferno of his peasant community. It is unlikely, he writes, that the Italian peasant represents a special case.[20] Indeed, the concept of a culture of poverty deemphasizes the fact that poverty groups are concerned with their marginal economic position and have a strong desire for something better. This is one of the strongest elements which has come through in the interviews I have had with poor people.

It should be clear from the above that the native anthropologist should be one who looks at social phenomena from a point of view different from that of the traditional anthropologist. I feel that this point of view should be admittedly biased, in favor of the insider's own social group. Thus, when I seek to "set the record straight" about some of the things which have been written about black people, this is not only justified but necessary. It is unfortunate that Third World students who are trained in American universities have, in the past, been *unable* to do this. This came about because the process of training itself eroded what could have been a distinctive native point of view. But this is rapidly changing. The students that are now being trained are becoming aware of the biases in social science and are not bound by the old values of objectivity and neutrality. This change in mood may disturb many people. But if anthropology is to survive it must respond to the changing social and technological realities of the present. It is well known that part of the process of colonization involves the distortion of social, cultural, and historical facts about a colonized people. The emergence of a native anthropology is part of an essential decolonization of anthropological knowledge and requires drastic changes in the recruitment and training of anthropologists.

Notes and References

1. See, for example, Thomas Rhys Williams, *Field Methods in the Study of Culture*, Holt, Rinehart and Winston, New York, 1967; Ake Hulkrantz, "The Aims of Anthropology: A Scandinavian Point of View," *Current Anthropology*, Vol. 9, No. 4, 1968, pp. 289–296.

2. Jacques J. Maquet, "Objectivity in Anthropology," *Current Anthropology*, Vol. 5, No. 1, 1964, p. 51.

3. Allan R. Holmberg, "The Research and Development Approach to the Study of Change," *Human Organization*, Vol. 17, No. 1, 1958, p. 12.

4. Gerald D. Berreman, "Is Anthropology Alive? Social Responsibility in Social Anthropology," *Current Anthropology*, Vol. 9, No. 5, 1968, p. 391–396.

5. Robert Lowie, *The History of Ethnological Theory*, Holt, Rinehart and Winston, New York, 1937, p. 133.

6. E. R. Leach, *Political Systems of Highland Burma*, Beacon Press, Boston, 1954, p. 3.

7. See, for example, D. L. Noel, "Group Identification among Negroes: An Empirical Analysis," *Social Issues*, Vol. 20, No. 2, 1954, pp. 71–84; Ralph M. Dreger and Kent S. Miller, "Comparative Psychological Studies of Negroes and Whites in the United States: 1959–1965," *Psychological Bulletin Monograph Supplement*, Vol. 70, No. 3, Part 2, 1968, pp. 32–33.

8. B. D. Paul, "Interview Techniques and Field Relationships," in A. L. Kroeber (ed.), *Anthropology Today*, University of Chicago Press, Chicago, 1953, p. 430.

9. There does not seem to be complete agreement on whether the race of the interviewer is an important element of bias in the interview situation. Williams concludes that the race of the interviewer "is an important variable related to bias but . . . this is only under certain conditions with certain types of interview questions." Weller and Luchterhand, on the other hand, write: ". . . our findings indicate that . . . Negro respondents gave higher quality responses to white interviewers than to Negro interviewers in a personally sensitive research area." J. Allen Williams, Jr., "Interviewer-Respondent Interaction: A Study of Bias in the Information Interview," *Sociometry*, Vol. 27, No. 3, 1964, pp. 338–352; Leonard Weller and Elmer Luchterhand, "Interviewer-Respondent Interaction in Negro and White Family Life Research," *Human Organization*, Vol. 27, No. 1, 1968, pp. 50–55.

10. See, for example, Robert K. Merton and Daniel Lerner, "Social Scientists and Research Policy," in Daniel Lerner and Harold D. Lasswell (eds.), *The Policy Sciences*, Stanford University Press, Stanford, California, 1951, p. 299.

11. *Cf.* I. C. Jarvie, "The Problem of Ethical Integrity in Participant Observation," *Current Anthropology*, Vol. 10, No. 5, 1969, p. 505, who observes that the complete participant observer conceals his character as observer. There is the problem of striking a balance between being a "good friend" and a "snooping stranger." On the one hand is the aim of participating fully, or identifying entirely with the alien way of life; on the other is the danger of betraying "trust."

12. Jarvie, *op. cit.*, p. 506.

13. John Beattie, *Other Cultures*, The Free Press, New York, 1964, p. 90.

14. Gutorm Gjessing, "The Social Responsibility of the Social Scientist," *Current Anthropology*, Vol. 9, No. 5, 1968, p. 400.

15. F. K. Lehman, "Ethnic Categories in Burma and the Theory of Social Systems," in Peter Kunstadter (ed.), *Southeast Asian Tribes, Minorities, and Nations*, Vol. I, Princeton University Press, Princeton, New Jersey, 1967, p. 103.

16. E. R. Leach, *Aspects of Caste in South India, Ceylon and Northwest Pakistan*, Cambridge University Press, Cambridge, Massachusetts, 1960, p. 5.

17. Ralf Dahrendorf, *Class and Class Conflict in an Industrial Society*, Routledge and Kegan Paul, London, 1959, p. 165.

18. Maquet, *op. cit.*, p. 50.

19. Robert Redfield, *Peasant Society and Culture*, The University of Chicago Press, Chicago, 1956, p. 140.

20. Joseph Lopreato, "How Would You Like to Be a Peasant?" in Jack M. Potter, May N. Diaz, George M. Foster (eds.), *Peasant Society: A Reader*, Little, Brown and Company, 1967, p. 436.

3

Epistemology and Power: Rethinking Ethnography at Greenham

LYNN WILSON

SOON AFTER I BEGAN graduate studies in anthropology, I took advantage of a small departmental grant for fieldwork in Europe. My initial broader interests in studying feminist resistance to nuclear militarism narrowed to proposed research at the women's peace camp outside the air force base at Greenham Common in England, one of the intended sites for U.S. cruise missiles in Europe.[1] The primary field method I planned to use was that of participant observation, often referred to in both my department and the anthropological literature as the "hallmark" of anthropology. As an inexperienced anthropologist, I did not have the critical perspective at the outset of my research to question this concept. During the five months I lived at Greenham and since my return, it has become increasingly clear that the commonly accepted ethnographic posture of an independent, objective "participant observer" is an impossible one.

In the field, I was not a "marginal native" or a "professional stranger;"[2] I was not an outsider at all. The peace camp at Greenham is an international community where I could join in protest with other women from Australia, New Zealand, Japan, the United States, Britain, and from throughout Western Europe. My research agenda did not particularly distinguish me from other women at Greenham because, although I had been quite open about my being an anthropologist, that fact was not evident most of the time. And, certainly, I was not the only woman who intended to write about Greenham or to make the experience of living at Greenham relevant to my professional life.

Living as a member of this community of women actively resisting state military policy and nuclear weapons was demanding but also very satisfying in a number of ways. Some of my personal needs were met as I became vocal in opposing both the weapons and the authorities; at a time of intense political and social global tragedy, there are few vehicles available to most people for taking part in the process of decision making. Participating in an all-women's activity allowed me to distance myself from many of the multidimensions of gender hierarchy present in almost every institution of Western society. I was an equal participant in decision making and in community action rather than an invisible or partial one. I encountered women who, for the first time in their lives, could step out of their dominant roles as primary caretakers for others (i.e., the family) with its implicit sex-role stereotyping and devaluation. With many women there, I shared some sense of a common goal, and yet our ideas of how to reach that goal varied tremendously. Our diverse experiences brought us together in a way that made critical questioning of ourselves, of each other, and of other groups working toward similar goals an intimate part of the community experience.

Living at Greenham offered me the chance to integrate my concerns for contemporary social problems with my academic work within anthropology, but the experience also raised significant and disturbing questions. How could I combine my anthropologist "Self" with myself as simultaneously among the studied "Other"? How could I have stepped out of my full participation to "observing" from a distance, maintaining independence from those around me, when police, soldiers, and vigilantes threatened my friends and me with daily harassment, violence, and the potential of greater violence?[3] In a community such as Greenham, in constant and intense confrontation with state authority and in which I figured as a full member, is it possible to "do" anthropology, and, if so, how? What kinds of problems or dilemmas emerge for an insider anthropologist in a community of direct action? Had I conducted formal interviews or taken the time and space to write voluminous field notes while in camp, I would have alienated myself from the women there. Had I refrained from taking part in or initiating active resistance, I never would have been accepted as a member of the community. As it was, when I made it explicit to women at Greenham that I was a graduate student in anthropology planning to use this experience in my academic work, I was at times heavily questioned as to my reasons and intentions.[4]

Returning from the field, I encountered other dilemmas. My shock upon returning paralleled more that of a return from the "front" than from the "field." My body and my psyche were still tense from the daily threats of violence that I had left behind. Although my experience at Greenham strengthened my belief that "action" can effect political and social change, when I returned to the academic context, I began to feel inactive, worthless, and cutoff. I wondered how I could bring my experience at Greenham to bear upon anthropology while at the same time respecting the community of women of which I had been a part. Most theory seemed irrelevant. I felt more activist than academic, and yet I was becoming unsure about what being an activist means. I felt an intense pessimism about the state of the world—of the world as community—and as I considered what I needed to create in my personal and professional life to respond to that threat and pessimism, I had to confront another problem: namely, that research on topics such as feminist communities, social processes of nuclear militarism, and multinational militarism constitute areas that funding institutions and universities advertising for teaching positions might not support.

Instead of proceeding from the question, Why did I choose such an impossible research situation? I find it important to examine what it is in the discipline of anthropology that defines such a situation as "impossible." Why was I confronted by these dilemmas and contradictions? How can I now make sense of my experiences at Greenham? This chapter explores answers to these questions by reconsidering the history of ethnography in anthropology, by clarifying the positivist assumptions that have dominated ethnographic activity, and by examining contemporary challenges to positivist anthropology that arise both in the process of doing fieldwork and in the way anthropologists represent field experiences in ethnographic writing.

Fieldwork in Historical Perspective

> The research which had been done on native races by men of academic training has proved beyond doubt and cavil that scientific, methodic inquiry can give us results far more abundant and of better quality than those of even the best amateur's work. (Malinowski 1953:xv)

Until the end of the nineteenth century, ethnography and anthropology were, for the most part, separate enterprises. Missionaries, government officials, traders, and travelers, with no specific theoretical or methodological training, made records of various aspects of the cultures with which they came in contact. They then sent these records to trained anthropologists who would analyze the data and begin to apply them in cross-cultural comparisons. After the turn of the century, anthropologists became more aware of the need for greater control of the ethnographic process in order to standardize data for cross-cultural comparisons. In line with this objective, there was a move to professionalize the discipline by using theoretically trained, full-time ethnographers, who would not have to contend with possibly conflicting political, economic, or religious interests.

Concurrent with the shift from armchair to field, anthropologists fought for legitimation in order to become integrated into academic institutions. At the same time, ethnographers were placing greater emphasis upon the "scientific," maintaining that the methodology employed in studying the "human sciences" should parallel scientific investigations in the "natural sciences." Subjectivity was identified as an obstacle that a well-trained scientist should overcome.

Conventional Ethnographic Postures

The equating of "science" with "objective" and "neutral" investigation has dominated anthropological research for the greater part of this century. In this positivist approach, ethnographic "facts" become something like the specimens one can examine in a laboratory. The anthropologist takes on the role of a contemplative, passive observer and assumes that facts are disconnected from social processes, that anthropologists are uninvolved in the process of forming the perceived context of the informants.

What are the implications of these contemplative assumptions for ethnographic activity?[5] First, the anthropologist (and the anthropologist's culture) becomes "invisible" in the records of interactions. If the ethnographer discusses the fieldwork presence at all, it is usually relegated to prefaces and footnotes instead of being integrated into the body of the ethnographic report. The direct impact of the ethnographer's participation upon the research results and upon the studied community is largely ignored. The impact of anthropology's historical ties to colonialism, to neocolonialism, and to the inherent hierarchical power relationships between the societies and cultures involved rarely emerges as the focus or even as the explicit context of ethnographic activity. Another aspect of ethnographers' invisibility surfaces in their attempts to write about the experience of the informant as if it comprised the informant's perceptions, words, ideas, and feelings rather than an account mediated by the ethnographer's choices.

A second implication of contemplative approaches involves the ethnographer's heavy reliance upon generalization. Here, in attempting to present a "complete" description of the informants' society and culture, ethnographers tend to write about a "typical" informant, derived by collapsing the life experiences of several informants into one. The people in contemplative ethnographic writing then become "generic" or "composite" informants rather than specific individuals. This preference for generalization also means that who said what and the moment in time and space it was said becomes concealed. Therefore, readers must accept the ethnographer's generalizations and has no way of arriving at other interpretations.

The final implication of contemplative assumptions I will discuss concerns "authority" in ethnographic texts. Here, usually after some sort of acknowledged apprenticeship period, the ethnographer becomes omniscient and assumes that there is one "correct" interpretation of this particular ethnographic experience. The omniscience is based upon a belief that the ethnographer/Self can independently interpret the world of the informant/ Other. The ethnographer, however, rarely reveals to the reader the research process that brought about this expansive, unchallengeable knowledge. Ethnographers claim all-knowing objectivity in their ethnographic activity and attempt to validate the resulting texts by using, for example, "I was there" statements or by employing other forms of legitimation that attempt to demonstrate expert status.

Contemporary Challenges to Conventional Ethnographic Postures

Over the past twenty years, widespread criticism has emerged directed against the positivist assumptions in ethnographic activity that I have broadly outlined above. It would be a mistake to represent these challenges to the existence of independent "facts" and to the ethnographic posture of the "observer" as unilineal or monolithic; instead, they are complex, varied, and at times contradictory. In the following discussion, I will introduce critiques of contemplative ethnography that center on two different sets of concerns: power and epistemology.

Challenges to Power

Indigenous and activist anthropology, two clearly related ethnographic approaches concerned with issues of power, present substantive challenges to the contemplative stance and the assumed separation of ethnographer and informant as well as to the ethnographer's objectivity in research and writing. In both approaches, ethnographers are acutely aware of the power relationship that exists between researcher and informant. Both take into consideration the impact of the researcher upon the group studied, but because there are important differences in what these two approaches bring to the critique of contemplative anthropology, I will consider them separately.

Indigenous Anthropology: Until relatively recently, anthropology was carried out almost exclusively by white Western ethnographers, mostly men, who could afford an advanced education. Those engaged in ethnographic activity directly reflected the groups holding international economic and political privilege. Ethnographers ventured out from a "developed core" (countries such as the United States, England, and France) in order to study the "periphery" (that is, peoples of the non-Western world). They designed research in the context of less "technologically advanced" cultures where people knew little about the ethnographer's own society and culture. Consistently, the outsider's "objective" ethnography tended to overrule and ignore the insiders' perspectives.[6]

Indigenous anthropology, also referred to as "native" or "local" anthropology, calls into question the Western outsider's privileged position of power as the only viable means to ethnography. This approach gained strength and visibility in the 1960s when widespread critiques of colonial and neocolonial relations of power gained force; anthropology was one of the targets.[7] The number of ethnographic texts by indigenous anthropologists, who study their own cultures and who generally come from the periphery of economic and political privilege, whether inside or outside the core countries, is increasing rapidly.[8] This democratization of anthropology and the recognition of the value of insider perspectives challenge the authority inherent to contemplative approaches.

Who is right? Which is the correct view, the insider's or the outsider's? Indigenous anthropologists are not interested in answering these questions; instead, they recognize that the perspectives are simply different. Both have advantages and disadvantages, constraints and freedoms, clarities and confusions. The indigenous anthropologist contributes a different perspective to our disciplinary collection of ethnographic knowledge while also creating alternative ethnographic methods that are directly related to a particular cultural experience other than that of the core. How we *do* anthropology is therefore changed.[9]

Identifying the factors that constitute an insider's stance is a complex issue. Outside the core, state boundaries most often define an insider's position—for example, Indian anthropologists who are working in India. Inside the core, an insider's position is usually defined by racial or cultural group. A Black anthropologist in the U.S. studies Black U.S. communities (see Jones this volume), and a Moroccan in France examines problems of North African workers there (see ben Jelloun 1977). But, like so many aspects of culture and society we study, there is not a clear separation of "who's in" and "who's out." A variety of factors become significant in considering who is an indigenous or local anthropologist. How "local" is the Black ethnographer from the rural South who goes to study an inner-city Black community in Denver? How "indigenous" is an Indian ethnographer who travels 700 miles to study a group that lives in the same country but in a different linguistic or religious region? With these questions in mind, it is clear that other factors become important in defining an insider's position: factors such as sex, class or caste, age, ideological commitments, sexual preference, family status, etc., as well as the constitution of the community involved. Considering these diverse and interconnecting factors, it is clear that no position is solely one of an insider or an outsider.

Activist Anthropology: Although an important aspect of much indigenous anthropology is the goal of improving the living situations of communities studied, social change is generally not so central a concern as it is for activist anthropology, also referred to as "commitment" and "liberation" anthropology.[10] One could argue that anthropologists have always been activists, given their historical connections to governments and participation in sociocultural change; this "activism" however, has taken place primarily within a given power structure. Activist, or liberation, anthropologies operate outside of those structures. Activist ethnographers focus explicitly on aspects of systemic power relationships and participate in attempts to stimulate change in the related social inequalities. These ethnographic efforts are not simply altruistic acts made by kind-hearted anthropologists. Activist anthropologists, recognizing that they live in a world community where social inequalities impair *all* participants, are working for their own liberation as well.

The history of power relations within the discipline between researcher and informant demands that the activist anthropologist becomes self-conscious and critical in decision making during the ethnographic process. Activist anthropologists attempt to initiate and carry out research in ways that interrupt the patterns of those unequal ethnographic relationships. As a result, difficult ethical and political questions surface.

Working within groups attempting to effect change, activist anthropologists make conscious decisions about how the information they collect will be used.[11] Informant consent for the ethnographer's use of interviews and confidentiality become major concerns. Because anthropological data are not given privileged status through law, many ethnographers use number codes instead of informants' names and destroy original field notes after the research is written up. There is no one set of rules that will ensure protection of informants. Instead, activist ethnographers develop a wide range of tools to help them guard against contributing to the vulnerability of the communities they study.

Other ethical issues center around questions of what ethnographers write about and how they choose to represent the communities they have studied.

If the anthropologists are not insiders, and even for those who are, how closely does the research reflect the direction of change that is sought by those in the group being studied? Understanding that every community is diverse, how will the anthropologist determine whom to listen to in identifying how to contribute to change? Will the ethnographer popularize the research results, both in an attempt at broader education for the international community regarding the particular research situation and for the benefit of and responsibility to the studied community? The complexity of these questions leads many activist anthropologists to choose research within their own society and culture in order that their actions and representations be grounded within a position that is equivalent to others in the group.

Both indigenous and activist anthropologists recognize the impossibility of the ethnographic posture that calls for an independent, objective observer. The dissolution of ethnographer/Self and informant/Other occurs for the indigenous anthropologist because of his or her member or insider status; it occurs for the activist anthropologist because of commitment. These anthropologists take the contemplative charge of bias and turn it around, identifying it as a problem for the whole discipline and not only for anthropologists who work in their own group or for those ethnographers who have political interests different than those reflected in mainstream research.[12]

Challenges to Epistemology

These relatively recent challenges to contemplative ethnography discussed above developed at approximately the same time as challenges from other directions. Whereas indigenous and activist anthropology direct critique at power relationships within the research process, interpretive and reflexive anthropology question theoretical assumptions concerned with the construction of knowledge. The dialogue and thus the intersection between these two directions appears to be highly limited.

Interpretive Anthropology: Interpretive anthropology developed in the 1960s and subsequently. It challenges contemplative assumptions by creating a theoretical alternative to "objective" research that employs methods developed in the natural sciences. Clifford Geertz (1973), one of the leading exponents of the interpretive approach, defines anthropology as "not an experimental science in search of law, but an interpretive one in search of meaning" (1973: 5). Geertz is not interested in ethnography that is limited only to identifying the causes and effects of social events; he rejects a social science of postulations to be proved and measurements to be recorded. Instead, he identifies the object of ethnography as "a multiplicity of complex conceptual structures, which are at once strange, irregular, and inexplicit" (1973: 10). The anthropologist therefore directs ethnographic efforts toward "guessing at meanings, assessing the guesses, and drawing explanatory conclusions from the better guesses" (1973: 19, 20).

The interpretive approach challenges positivist assumptions by maintaining that theoretical activity is a constructive effort by culturally bound anthropologists whose choices express particular interests. Ethnography then strives to reject the contemplative separation of researcher and informant, to reject the false dichotomy between objectivity and subjectivity, and attempts to reveal the "inside" view by emphasizing how the informants define the world.[13]

Reflexive Anthropology: Building upon interpretive approaches, anthropologists have developed what has become known as reflexive anthropology.[14] Reflexive approaches, conscious of the ethnographer's position in ethnographic activity, recognize the theoretical challenge and textual alternatives that interpretive anthropology offers to the critique of contemplative ethnography but identifies this challenge as partial. Kevin Dwyer (1982), an anthropologist who uses a reflexive approach, criticizes Geertz for failing to recognize that the ethnographer does not merely record what is going on during the research process. The ethnographer, Dwyer holds, is an active participant in the context that forms the informants' explanations; these explanations are created in an environment where the anthropologist poses the questions and encourages certain kinds of responses. Thus, ethnographers become acknowledged "actors" in an historic, disciplinary encounter; informants become full participants; and ethnography becomes a written text that represents specific relationships between specific individuals and cultures.

This reflexive approach encourages a greater degree of self-consciousness in ethnographic activity, a self-consciousness that recognizes ethnography as a dynamic relationship encompassing both construction *and* truth. James Clifford (1986) refers to this as a "partial truth" that no ethnographer is able to transcend. Integrating self-consciousness into written texts, reflexive ethnographers create alternatives to conventional ethnography by attempting to disperse the "authority" that our discipline has so commonly considered a strength (Clifford 1983), by employing transcribed dialogues between ethnographer and informant to make these specific field encounters explicit (e.g., Crapanzano 1980, Dwyer 1982), and by representing the experience of field research in a way that challenges the conventional assumptions defining ethnography as a linear, unified whole (Clifford 1981). This self-consciousness assumes an importance for reflexive anthropology at a very basic level—the definition of the goal of anthropology offered by advocates of this approach emphasizes "the comprehension of self by detour of the comprehension of the other" (Ricoeur 1971; see also Rabinow 1977: ix).

Making Greenham Make Sense

What do these two major anthropological directions, one concerned with power and the other with epistemology, contribute toward an understanding of my field experience? At Greenham, my ethnographic posture was that of an insider and an activist. Some may be skeptical of my claiming an "insider" position. Although I was an American woman in Britain, a position that ordinarily would have defined me as an outsider, Greenham was an international community in which many women from the U.S. participated. This was an intentional community where women could choose to live for relatively short periods; therefore, my living at Greenham for five months did not differentiate me from others in the community, as so often happens in more "traditional" ethnographic research. In fact, after I had lived in the camp for one month, I was surprised to find that someone had pointed me out as a "regular." As my proposed departure date arrived, I postponed leaving Greenham because of my personal commitment to my friends and to the community of resistance that was continuously developing around me.

My position at Greenham as an insider is reinforced by two other factors. As a feminist, I shared with many women there the goals of wanting to better understand systemic power relationships and of challenging the institutions, individuals, and processes that contribute to the continuance of inequalities. As a lesbian in a community where a large number of women identified themselves as lesbians, I also shared the goals of challenging heterosexism both in public policy and in the personal assumptions of individuals.[15]

Even if I had been interested in remaining an independent Self observing an Other at Greenham, it would have been difficult. I became identified by police, soldiers, and people from the town nearby as one of "them" in what had become a largely bipolar, "us and them" situation. It was easy to discern from the way I dressed (e.g., three layers of sweaters smelling of woodsmoke, leg warmers, and muddy hiking boots) that I lived at Greenham, and although local citizens gave significant support both to the camp and to individual women living in it, women from Greenham also met considerable hostility in the town. I was asked to leave several business establishments, was spat upon and yelled at while walking through town, and was forced off the sidewalk into traffic by others on the sidewalk and by the driver of a car. Regardless of the nature of local responses towards me, the result was the same: I was identified as a "Greenham woman."

Many soldiers who stood inside the base guarding the perimeter fence also tended to identify me as one of "them." On a February morning shortly after I had arrived at Greenham, I was exhausted because the soldiers had kept up a persistent noise over loudspeakers to prevent us from sleeping. I went to the perimeter fence and asked them gently if they could be a little more considerate and stop making noise so that we could get some sleep. The only response to my request was that one soldier pulled a large burning stick from the nightwatch fire and threw it at my head. These soldiers did not distinguish among the women at the camp; whether I had come to Greenham as a participant observer or not, my role as one of "them" was reinforced on a deep level by these daily interactions.

The use of my camera, an instrument of "observation," exemplifies another aspect of the situation that dissolved any intentions I might have had of being a participant observer. At first, I carried my camera for the purpose of employing the method of "photo-documentation." For Greenham women, experiences with insensitive journalists and "tourists" had nurtured a kind of community reticence and disdain for cameras. For some, my camera was a reminder that I was attempting research at Greenham. As time went on and trust in my approach to photography increased, however, my camera became an effective tool for recording events in order to increase media coverage of the camp and of resistance to cruise missiles. It was also effective in contributing to the protection of the other women as well as myself when we were being harassed or abused by policemen and soldiers. In these instances, I would make my photography very obvious to the authorities. Even if there was no film in the camera, I would tell them as calmly as possible that I was recording their faces, their numbers, and their actions on film for later use in court, if necessary. During my last two months at Greenham, the camp collectively gave me money to buy film, and the police on two occasions tried to confiscate my camera. What had at first been a research tool developed into a vehicle for some of my most active, personal resistance.

Since my return from Greenham, I have had to "make sense" of my experience there. At first, I was primarily concerned with issues related to my insider and activist position in a discipline where most ethnography is done from an outsider, contemplative position. My interests were largely defined by ethical issues concerning my relationship to the women at Greenham and by the political effectiveness, or relevance, of what I chose to write about. The initial goal of my research was to better understand Greenham as a diverse social and political movement; I examined the debate among feminists in Britain as to whether Greenham is consistent with or in opposition to feminist values. More recently, in the process of reading interpretive and reflexive ethnography and theory, I have realized that my concerns for challenging systemic power relationships cannot remain limited to the definition of a "problem" involved in my work (e.g., social processes of nuclear militarism; inequality based upon race, class, gender, sexual preference, etc.). I found it imperative to my activist concerns to challenge the false boundaries of what has been identified as "political" by addressing the theoretical questions raised by the interpretive and reflexive literature.

What does combining these two approaches—challenges to power and challenges to epistemology—look like? What kind of ethnography emerges from this cross-fertilization? For the remainder of the chapter, I will discuss some aspects of what I think this could mean with regard to exploring alternatives in ethnography, both in terms of my fieldwork at Greenham and in moving toward future experimental ethnography.

Historically, anthropologists have chosen so-called powerless communities, those that represent a societal position of subordination. Many of these communities actively engage in resistance strategies or even in active confrontation in order to protest domination by other groups. Conventionally, ethnographers refrain from participating in this resistance, maintaining a distance in order to be able to make "observations." If we are to increase our understanding of social processes that are relevant to local and global problems, it is imperative to include in our research studies from "within" communities that engage in direct action against state authorities. Implicit in this approach is the ethnographer's commitment to be a full participant and to share the vulnerability that other participants experience.

Women at Greenham experienced this vulnerability in diverse ways. I have already mentioned the incident when one soldier threw a burning stick at me. This, or incidents like this, were daily occurrences and generally were not damaging except in contributing to create an environment where fear and hostility ran high. But there existed a vulnerability at Greenham that led to deeper consequences than the incidents of eggs, sticks, and rocks thrown by soldiers or the tires slit and property stolen by vigilantes who came into the camps at night. Many women there believed that getting arrested was an imperative means of nonviolent direct action. By this act, women "enter the mouth of the tiger" and submit themselves, albeit with protest, to the police, court, and prison systems. Arrests mean records— the military police compile names, addresses, and photographs that then become available to other national and international computer-communication networks. After arrest, many women experienced a lack of what would be considered humanitarian care and were even subjected to physical assault at the hands of the police—this included violence such as beatings, threats of sexual violence while being physically restrained, and, in one case, boiling tea poured on a woman's head while being interrogated. It was virtually impossible to remain for any length of time in these politically intense situations without taking on the same risks that everyone in the community faced.

Confrontation

By using "confrontation," I refer directly to the relationship between informant and researcher (cf., Dwyer 1982). Confrontation implies the ethnographic encounter, a moment of meeting between two distinct individuals and between their respective societies and cultures; it does not necessarily imply that the relationship is one of opposition, antithesis, or polarization.

By envisioning ethnographic activity as confrontation, we shatter the illusion of the ethnographer as removed and objective. Equally shattered is the illusion of the ethnographic endeavor in which the Other is described or inscribed; here, the confrontation, not the Other, becomes the object of ethnography. Ethnographic research becomes a series of specific encounters in which the relationship between ethnographer and informant, as well as its meaning, is continually reconstituted. Instead of perceiving ethnographic relationships as static and fixed, this new approach makes the negotiated and socially constructed process itself visible.

It is not enough to simply recognize the implications of this conceptual shift toward confrontation while in the field. The challenge is to embody the shift within written texts, to explore alternatives for making the confrontation explicit. What could this mean in the way we write ethnographic accounts? First, the written ethnography makes the historical context of the confrontation explicit; for example, the ethnographer integrates discussion of the process of identifying the research "problem" and of choosing the community involved into the ethnographic document thereby exposing the social and cultural interests that both the researcher and the informant bring to the confrontation. In the context of my research at Greenham, I would include a description of how I came to choose this specific project as an essential component of the ethnography.

Second, the written text reveals the actual process of field research by including the specific sequence of events and the interruptions, accommodations, and oppositions that occur within negotiated field encounters. Ethnographies many times imply that every aspect of the research process was carried out according to a plan, that nothing significant occurred spontaneously or unexpectedly. New approaches to ethnographic writing recognize the importance of unexpected events in forming the ethnographer's understanding. Writing about the specific sequence of fieldwork encounters becomes important in another way. How I interpreted events during my first month at Greenham would be very different from my interpretations during my last month there. Making these different understandings explicit can be essential to exposing the process of confrontation between ethnographer and informant.

Third, because ethnographers cannot present their complete field research experiences in ethnographic writing (one could write a whole volume on solely one interview), the written text is self-consciously partial. An experimental ethnography would therefore expose the ethnographer's decision making in the actual editing process by addressing questions concerning the manner in which the words of informants were chosen from conversations and concerning the extent to which the informants were involved in creating the final written texts.

With regard to my research at Greenham, it is impossible to go back in time in order to experience those dialogues and events again with my newly acquired awarenesses of "ethnography as confrontation." Although this limits my full experimentation in the areas I discuss above, it does not totally preclude my bringing these new awarenesses to already existing field notes or to my future ethnographic activity at Greenham. The point here is that there is no *one* path to follow in writing ethnographic texts describing a confrontation; it is important to realize that our work can only (and fully) be a process of creative experimentation in the context of our "partial truths."

Conclusion

This confluence of dilemma, critique, experimentation, and discovery following my fieldwork has convinced me that challenges to contemplative ethnographic activity based on power and on epistemology can no longer remain mutually exclusive efforts if we are to make our discipline more relevant to contemporary social problems and our research more relevant to problems within our discipline. "Making sense" of the women's peace camp has become a larger project for me than translating my field experiences into conventional ethnography where "political" or activist concerns remain separate from and supercede interpretive and reflexive concerns. Eliminating these false boundaries, we can bring anthropology to activism by focusing upon communities engaged in direct action and by participating in the concomitant vulnerability. We can also bring our activism to anthropology by exploring ethnography as confrontation and by anticipating risk in our research.

Notes

Acknowledgments

Many thanks to Brinkley Messick, whose help has been indispensible in my ethnographic exploration. Thanks also to Sylvia Forman, John Cole, Dena Dincauze, Oriol Pi-Sunyer, Ann Kingsolver, Paulla Ebron, Peg Connors, Sky Arndt, and Michele Melchionda for their support and constructive criticism. Field research at Greenham was funded through a grant from The European Field Research Training Program, Department of Anthropology, University of Massachusetts, Amherst. And of course, thanks to the women at Greenham.

1. For more details about the women's peace camp at Greenham, see Wilson 1986, where I discuss criticisms some British feminists have made of Greenham; see also Harford and Hopkins 1984.
2. In this paper, recognizing the possible derogatory aspects of the word in refer-

ring to indigenous people, I will not use the term "native" except when quoting directly from other sources. "Marginal native" is a term used by Freilich (1970); Agar uses "professional stranger" (1980).

3. Soldiers and police harassed us daily in surveilling the camp and attempting to procure lists of women's names and addresses. Women were abused by police while being held for interrogation as well as for sentences. Women were arrested when they had done nothing to warrant arrest. Some women were even harassed by the police in London and elsewhere. Vigilantes stole personal belongings and threw blood, urine, feces, stones, and burning sticks at women. Several women associated with the camp were raped either near or traveling to or from Greenham. One woman was murdered while traveling to Greenham.

4. One woman accused me of being a U.S. governmental agent. This may seem to some an overreaction on the part of women associated with Greenham. Actually, while I lived at Greenham, a CIA agent was exposed at a peace camp in the Netherlands, which was also opposing the deployment of cruise missiles to Europe. Additionally, some women at Greenham just could not understand why I would want to apply my activist interests to the academic context.

5. To answer this question, I will draw heavily from the Marcus and Cushman (1982) discussion of ethnographic realism, which is not exactly comparable with contemplative ethnography but which shares the assumption of an independence between researcher and informant. I will also use Clifford's excellent and engaging discussion of ethnographic authority (1983).

6. For a more extensive discussion of this, see Jones, this volume.

7. Examples of this literature include scholars such as Fahim (1982), Hare (1973), Jones (this volume), Khare (1983), Maruyama (1978), and Nakhleh (1979).

8. I realize that there are problems in referring to those in the "periphery" as homogenous without recognizing the diversity of experience depending upon factors such as race, class, gender, governmental affiliations, etc. For the purpose of this chapter, I acknowledge these differences but will not investigate them in further detail.

9. Jones, this volume, offers an extensive discussion of these issues.

10. Here, I include scholars such as Asad (1979, 1982), Caulfield (1969, 1979), Dubell et al. (1981), Huizer and Mannheim (1979), and Roberts (1981). I do not include other anthropologists whose work is important in studying relations in political-economic systems or in questioning our disciplinary ethics yet who are not actively involved in changing them. Making this distinction remains an ambiguous effort, because it is not possible to clearly identify which actions lead to sociocultural change and which do not.

11. Anthropology seems particularly susceptible to these concerns of informants' vulnerability and anonymity. Research in such disciplines as sociology and political science tends to use large samples and to focus more upon quantitative, statistical data rather than qualitative data.

12. It is important to recognize here that although many indigenous and activist ethnographers do challenge various aspects of contemplative anthropology, there are also many who have not made the theoretical shift related to challenging the belief in the "scientific" goal of objectivity.

13. It is interesting to note here that Geertz rejects aspects of insider's and outsider's views basing his criticism upon the distance of the researcher to the group studied rather than upon the researcher's abilities to combine this distance of nearness with an anthropological approach.

14. For example, Clifford (1981, 1983, 1986), Clifford and Marcus (1986), Dwyer (1982), Marcus and Cushman (1982), Ruby (1982), and Stocking (1983) are among the anthropologists who have contributed significantly to this approach.

15. Here again the one-word labels, such as "feminist" and "lesbian," imply well-defined categories; this implication masks the debates and the diversity of experience within these social groups. I use these terms in a nonspecific way, acknowledging their drawbacks and yet also recognizing their value in making general distinctions.

References Cited

AGAR, MICHAEL H. 1980. "Hermeneutics in Anthropology: A Review Essay." *Ethos* 8 (3):253–272.

ASAD, TALAL. 1979. "Anthropology and the Colonial Encounter," in *The Politics of Anthropology: From Colonialism and Sexism Toward a View from Below,* G. Huizer and B. Mannheim, eds. The Hague: Mouton Publishers.

———. 1982. "A Comment on the Idea of Non-Western Anthropology," in *Indigenous Anthropology in Non-Western Countries,* Proceedings of a Burg Wartenstein Symposium, H. Fahim, ed. Durham, N.C.: Carolina Academic Press.

BEN JELLOUN, TAHAR. 1977. *La Plus Haute des Solitudes.* Paris: Editions du Seuil.

CAULFIELD, MINA DAVIS. 1969. "Culture and Imperialism: Proposing a New Dialectic," in *Reinventing Anthropology,* D. Hymes, ed. New York: Random House.

———. 1979. "Participant Observation or Partisan Participation?" in *The Politics of Anthropology: From Colonialism and Sexism Toward a View from Below.* The Hague: Mouton Publishers.

CLIFFORD, JAMES. 1981. "On Ethnographic Surrealism." *Society for Comparative History of Society and History.*

———. 1983. "On Ethnographic Authority." *Representations* 2:118–146.

———. 1986. "On Ethnographic Allegory," in *Writing & Culture,* James Clifford and George Marcus, eds. Berkeley: University of California Press.

CLIFFORD, JAMES and GEORGE MARCUS, eds. 1986. *Writing Culture: The Poetics and Politics of Ethnography.* Berkeley: University of California Press.

DUBELL, FOLKE, THORD ERASMIE, and JAN DE VRIES, eds. 1981. *Research for the People Research by the People.* Selected Papers from the International Forum in Ljubljana, Yugoslavia. Linkoping, Sweden: Department of Education, Linkoping University.

DWYER, KEVIN. 1982. *Moroccan Dialogues: Anthropology in Question.* Baltimore: Johns Hopkins University.

FAHIM, HUSSEIN, ed. 1982. *Indigenous Anthropology in Non-Western Countries.* Proceedings of a Burg Wartenstein Symposium. Durham, N.C.: Carolina Academic Press.

FREILICH, MORRIS. 1970. *Marginal Natives: Anthropologists at Work.* New York: Harper and Row.

GEERTZ, CLIFFORD. 1973. *The Interpretation of Cultures.* New York: Basic Books.

HARE, NATHAN. 1973. "The Challenge of a Black Scholar," in *The Death of White Sociology,* Joyce Ladner, ed. New York: Random House.

HARFORD, BARBARA and SARAH HOPKINS. 1984. *Greenham Common: Women at the Wire.* London: The Women's Press.

HUIZER, GERRIT, and BRUCE MANNHEIM, eds. 1979. *The Politics of Anthropology: From Colonialism and Sexism Toward a View From Below.* The Hague: Mouton Publishers.

KHARE, R. 1983. "Between Being Near and Distant: Reflections on Initial Approaches and Experiences of an Indian Anthropologist," in *Fieldwork: The Human Experience,* Robert Lawless, Vincent H. Sutlive, Jr., and Mario D. Zamora, eds. New York: Gordon and Breach.

MALINOWSKI, BRANISLOW. 1953. *Argonauts of the Western Pacific.* New York: E. P. Dutton.

MARCUS, GEORGE and DICK CUSHMAN. 1982. "Ethnographies as Texts," in *Annual Review of Anthropology,* vol. 11. Palo Alto, Calif.: Annual Reviews.

MARUYAMA, MAGORAH. 1978. "Endogenous Research and Polyocular Anthropology," in *Perspectives on Ethnicity.* Regina E. Holloman and Serghei A. Arutiunov, eds. The Hague: Mouton Publishers.

NAKHLEH, KHALIL. 1979. "On Being a Native Anthropologist," in *The Politics of Anthropology: From Colonialism and Sexism Toward a View from Below,* G. Huizer and B. Mannheim, eds. The Hague: Mouton Publishers.

RABINOW, PAUL. 1977. *Reflections on Field Work in Morocco.* Berkeley: University of California Press.

RICOEUR, PAUL. 1971. "Model of the Text: Meaningful Action Considered as a Text." *Social Research* 38:529–562.

ROBERTS, HELEN. 1981. *Doing Feminist Research.* London: Routledge and Kegan Paul.

RUBY, JAY, ed. 1982. *A Crack in the Mirror: Reflexive Perspectives in Anthropology.* Philadelphia: University of Pennsylvania Press.

STOCKING, GEORGE W. JR., ed. 1983. *Observers Observed: Essays On Ethnographic Fieldwork.* Madison: University of Wisconsin Press.

4

A Goy in the Ghetto: Gentile–Jewish Communication in Fieldwork Research

WILLIAM E. MITCHELL

EARLY IN MY CAREER as an anthropologist I joined a small team of social scientists planning a study of New York City Jewish families. An important part of my work was to interview family members in their homes. As a Gentile from Kansas I knew that my cultural background was very different from theirs, so I asked two Jewish male social scientist friends born and raised in New York City for advice. With devastating frankness I was told that my "cool Wasp manner" would "scare the wits" out of my interviewees. As Kansas men are generally open and friendly—we smile a lot— I was discomforted by their view of me. But that was only the beginning.

My body language, they said, was too detached, too placid. They were concerned that I rarely gestured and, when I did, the gesture was so small and anemic that it was barely discernible. Besides, my gestures were all wrong; they were woodenly symmetrical rather than creatively baroque. My friends insisted that if I were to work successfully with New York City Jewish families of Eastern European background, I must look more "bright-eyed" and act "more lively." And, while they assured me that my speech pattern was not as slow and heavily accented as some midwesterners', it was obvious that I must "speed it up."

If I could not make these important behavioral accommodations, the research, according to my friends, would be a disaster. The families would find me "strange" and feel "uncomfortable" and "anxious" as long as I was around. In other words, if I wanted good rapport I would have to change. "Sure you're a Gentile," they seemed to be saying. "But you don't have to act like one!"

The personal experiences on which this chapter is based took place in two separate but related studies (Leichter and Mitchell 1978; Mitchell 1980) of New York City Jewish families of Eastern European background. The parent research project, "Studies in Social Interaction," was carried out with a large group of families who were clients of the Jewish Family Service of New York. Our primary research interest was in the extent and nature of the relationships these households of parents and children had with their other relatives and in the ways social workers assigned to the families intervened to support or change the relationships.

During this research we "discovered" an unusual kind of urban descent group organized as clubs called "family circles" or "cousins' clubs," and I did a separate study (Mitchell 1980) of the history, organization, and functioning of these groups that included individuals and families completely unrelated to the parent project. In both studies, I made interview visits to my informants' homes or places of business and also attended some of the family clubs' meetings and parties.[1]

How one "acts" in the research role, as my two friends knew, is a significant factor affecting rapport in behavioral research that may directly influence the outcome of the research itself. Behavioral scientists often consider "good rapport" as the *sine qua non* for "good research." It is an especially crucial dimension for anthropologists who are studying cultural groups that in some ways are very unlike their own. In these instances, anthropologists must be overtly sensitive to the customs and behavioral nuances of their own culture as well as that of their hosts.

I was aware, as were my two friends, that they were informing me about my own subculture as well as telling me about theirs, for anthropological rapport is a culturally symbiotic relationship. There must be a behavioral "fit" between the anthropologist and her or his informants for trust and understanding—essential ingredients in all anthropological research—to grow. If the anthropologist's behavior signifies a culturally antithetical persona, the wary informant will withdraw, and the research most certainly will flounder. So it is anthropologists as "cultural guests" who must make the accommodating moves if they want the approval and cooperation of informants.

Depending upon the society studied, these behavioral accommodations may take a variety of forms. For example, on my first research project I worked with college-educated Chinese from mainland China living in New York City (Hinkle et al. 1957). To gain their respect and establish rapport, I learned to sit much more quietly than was my usual wont and to ask personally sensitive questions indirectly. Fortunately, I already knew how to maintain a smile, as that too was important.

An even greater challenge to establishing behavioral rapport came on a field trip (Mitchell 1987) to Papua, New Guinea. Although American men generally avoid touching one another except for a ritual handshake or an occasional brusque slap on the back, men of the Wape tribe with whom I lived have a close physical relationship. Gathered together in the men's house, they visit amiably with legs intertwined and arms draped across each other's bodies, as if these were their own. And among the Iatmul, another New Guinea group I lived with, young men who are good friends sometimes stroll through the village holding hands by intertwining their little fingers. To the men of these societies such actions are commonplace, but for me they were emotionally charged. I was not aware of the affective strength behind the touching taboo of American males until I was in New Guinea and felt my personal space and body being "violated" by my new friends. My response was an almost overwhelming desire to pull away and draw myself in. Although I did not withdraw from their friendly touching and holding, it was only gradually that I learned to relax and enjoy their intimate camaraderie.

This account of fieldwork experiences may strike some as essentially trivial or inconsequential and not the critical factors in building rapport that I see them to be. Or some may view the anthropologist's behavioral adaptations to the host culture as contrived and manipulative. That would be unfortunate, because the motivation for "fitting in" goes far beyond the constraints of research methodology, important as this is. It also is intrinsically related to the strong humanist concern of anthropologists who spend years in the field augmenting their understanding of human nature, culture, and themselves. These behaviorally transforming fieldwork experiences serve the anthropologist as powerful entrees into the host culture. By adapting one's behavior to that of one's informants, a sense of empathy may be generated, and the work of learning the culture gets underway. This does not mean, however, that the anthropologist goes "native," nor am I espousing a "sentimental view of rapport as depending on the enfolding of anthropologist and informant into a single moral, emotional, and intellectual universe" that Clifford Geertz (1967:12) justly criticizes.

These personal fieldwork experiences are important because they help give the anthropologist a sense of the host culture and of its behavioral parameters. The field-worker begins to get the "feel" of the culture almost unwittingly as he or she succeeds in occasionally "fitting in" or receives a polite rebuke. Once, as a large group of New Guinea village children rushed onto our temporary and dangerously rickety porch, I called out loudly for them to get off. The children fled in terror. A nearby villager turned toward me and, his hushed voice filled with embarrassed anguish, said, "Speak gently!" My face burned with shame. But it was a lesson in Wape manners I never forgot.

This problem of how to communicate with one's informants and establish rapport in the field is an important methodological issue in modern anthropology.[2] "Communication"—or more properly in this context, "interpersonal communication"—specifically refers to face-to-face or two-way communication. It concerns the transmission of behavioral messages and how these messages are interpreted by others. In other words, the interpretation or "meaning" is separate from the act or "message." In this sense, communication is the process of creating a meaning from a message (Tubbs and Moss 1974:6). As my two Jewish friends had wisely advised me, the meaning my Jewish informants undoubtedly would give to my behavioral messages was, This man is a *goy*, beware!

When I joined the Jewish family research project I had little personal experience with Jewish–Gentile relations in American society. I did know that anti-Semitism was a chilling reality in American life and, as an anthropologist, I was certainly aware of the importance of cultural differences. But in my personal life I tended to play down ethnic differences among my friends and was impressed by the common humanity of New Yorkers amid such polyglot cultural diversity. So it came to me as a surprise when my two Jewish friends found my behavior and style of interaction so disturbingly different.

The social division between Gentiles and Jews is an ancient one, although what is meant by "gentile" depends upon the context. The term is from Latin and means "of the same clan or race." It formerly was used by Christians to refer to "heathens," is presently used by Mormons to refer to non-Mormons, and, of course, by Jews to refer to non-Jews, especially Christians. But here I will use the Yiddish term *goy* (*goyim,* pl.) to refer to the non-Jew, because it is a more culturally salient concept for the problem at hand.

While "gentile" is a somewhat neutral term, *goy* is loaded with cultural meaning stemming from the Jewish experience as a persecuted minority in the Diaspora. As used by Jews, it is a pejorative term, referring to someone who is "dull, insensitive, heartless." As Leo Rosten (1970:142) further points out in his discussion of the term, centuries of Jewish persecution have left a legacy of bitter sayings about *goyim*. For example, *"Dos ken nor a goy,"* translated from the Yiddish, means "That, only a *goy* would do." Or the exclamation of exasperation "A *goy!*" is used "when endurance is exhausted, kindliness depleted, the effort to understand useless" (Rosten 1970:142).

It was during the research discussed here that I first became aware of the Jewish view of a distinct Jewish–Gentile cultural dichotomy characterized by the *goy* as a symbol of callousness and danger; the kind of person one tries to avoid if possible. As my informants led me into their perceptual world, I too, albeit reluctantly, began to see individuals in terms of this dichotomy. I was so deeply imprinted with this ethnic duality during the research experience that it has been one of the most enduring personal effects of the study. Learning firsthand about the inexorableness of ethnic divisions was an emotionally powerful experience because it challenged and in some ways shattered my youthful "one world" idealism. An early response is recorded in my notebook:

> This family circle meeting was the first time I was accosted with a Jewish-Gentile dichotomy. It was presented to me in several quite personal ways. Some pleasant and some joking; others that were to me of a negative tinge. Aunt Edith, who is 50, kept coming up to me and telling me how fine the Jews were, that the Jews and Gentiles should learn to get together, that the Jews want to get along with the Gentiles, that most Jews are fine people like here at the family circle, all Jews want is to be friends with the Gentiles, isn't it a shame the way the Jews are sometimes treated, etc. I was quite amazed by all of this talk and even more at a loss as to how to handle the indomitable interaction entrances. It all seemed quite irrelevant, and it annoyed me that I was being accepted—provisionally—as a "good" Gentile rather than as a fellow human being.

In my research with other cultural groups—college-educated Chinese and Papua New Guineans, for example—it was obvious that I was an outsider because of my light skin color, but with my Jewish informants the situation was not as clear. Racially we were Caucasians, but culturally there were significant differences.[3] While I doubt that any of my informants seriously believed I was Jewish, it still was very important to them that they be absolutely sure. They knew that the research was sponsored in part by a Jewish social work agency and that we were studying Jewish family–kin relationships. Their underlying question seemed to be, What's he here for if he's not Jewish?

During the interviews at the beginning of the research, an informant would usually pause at some point and, eyebrows raised, diffidently ask, "You Jewish?" During one interview, an informant's elderly mother came into the room and, after listening to our conversation for a while, asked the inevitable question. When I said "No," she shook her head sagely and replied with a strong Yiddish accent, "You don't look Jewish!" The point is that unambiguous ethnic identification of me was of great importance to my informants. They needed to know if I was an "insider" or an "outsider"—did I "belong" or didn't I.

So I learned to volunteer during the first meeting that I was not Jewish and to offer other personal information about myself. While the New Guinea Wape were singularly disinterested in my cultural background, my Jewish informants seemed pleased when I gave them information placing me in a specific social context. Instead of waiting to be pumped for personal data, I could always count on an amused expression, for example, when I volunteered that I was born and raised in Wichita, Kansas.

In some of the Jewish homes that I visited, I was something of an "event" because I was the first *goy* guest. Many of my informants lived in an almost entirely Jewish world—socially if not physically ghettoized—in terms of significant relationships with their neighbors, fellow workers, friends, and, of course, relatives. This is possible in a city with several million Jews where large sections of the city and even certain industries have become predominantly Jewish in composition. For persons who have spent most of their lives in an almost totally Jewish milieu, social relations with *goyim* are unusual and, when they do occur, are touched with apprehension. After a pleasant visit with a Jewish family accompanied by an informant, I learned that I was the first "Wasp" to have entered the home. My informant's comment about our hostess was, "I bet she gave a sigh of relief when you went out the door!"

This sort of apprehensiveness was reflected in most of my initial interviews with informant families. There was always some hesitation on my first visit, a kind of cautious stiffness that I interpreted as misgivings, perhaps even overt suspiciousness. But that mood was never sustained. I found that the best way to break it was to begin collecting a genealogy as soon as possible. As we set to work on the family's genealogy with brown wrapping paper spread out on the kitchen table and usually a soft drink and cookies on the side, the tension would subside. Most of my informants became intensely engrossed in watching the social and cultural dimensions of their family network unfold before their eyes. "My," one woman exclaimed with enthusiasm, "isn't this interesting!"

However, there was always a certain amount of bemusement that I, a *goy*, was studying Jews. There was something wrong—intrusive maybe— about this *goy*, this outsider, trying to get "inside" Jewish family life. This "wonderment" regarding my involvement in the research project was expressed to me primarily via joking comments. Not only did my informants seem a bit muddled and amused about my research role, but so did my New York Jewish friends and colleagues. At the time, I did not know how to interpret this levity; I know I failed to see the humor to the extent they did. For me it was a serious and fascinating research project and my involvement did not strike me as odd or "funny." I could not help but feel that the smiles and laughter were tinged with disapproval, that the joking response was covering up at least some resentment towards this presumptuous *goy* who was trying to penetrate Jewish family life.

But once I was accepted, family members went out of their way to make me feel as though I were not the comparative stranger that I obviously was. Still, there were often problems if my informant had to go beyond the immediate family to get information or to grant me permission to attend a specific family function. There was then a need for the inevitable explanation of who I was and why did I want what I wanted. Sometimes the explanations didn't make much sense to older family members whose suspicions about the *goyim* had been documented, not just by social discrimination and negative insinuations, but by horrifying personal experiences in Eastern Europe and the genocidal murder of close relatives.

Because of my own idealism regarding intergroup interactions and because I was an "integrated" member of a Jewish social agency, I at first was unaware of any emotional connection between the holocaust and my research role. I could remember as an impressionable teenager photos and newsreels of the German concentration camps and the terrifying impact they had upon me, so it never occurred to me that such heinous events could be associated, even remotely, with my research. I can recall the sickening feeling I had when a male informant during the last week of interviewing wisecracked that I was collecting Jewish genealogies for "a giant Manhattan concentration camp." I laughed, but I was so struck by the monstrousness of the comment that I wrote it down. I was puzzled how a man of my own age and American-born could bring such a macabre association to my research. Then three days later while interviewing another informant, the "concentration camp" image appeared again. I wrote in my notebook:

> [My informant] said that he had asked his uncle, who is president of their Family Circle, for the documents and explained what I was doing. The uncle was skeptical and joked about my collecting all of the family names for a concentration camp. [My informant] said it was doubtful if he could get the documents for me.

The *goyim* issue was a pervasive problem that influenced all of my informant relationships. Establishing rapport undoubtedly would have been easier if I were a Jew but, as an outsider, I was able to see some things more clearly and with less distorting personal involvement than could a member of the group.[4] However, there were other problems less specifically ethnic in origin that in some instances also affected my relationships with informants.

Informant disapproval is not a unique response to anthropological research, especially in literate societies. To be "studied" is seen by some as demeaning; that one is being treated as an object rather than as a person. I occasionally ran into this type of resistance, especially when I tried to gain access to family social events and was turned away because some family members didn't want to be "studied." Family affairs, including meetings of family clubs, were generally considered private activities where relatives could relax and have fun. The presence of a researcher, I was once told, would put "a damper" on the festivities.[5]

There was also the problem of the popular view that anthropologists are primarily interested in "primitive peoples," hardly a flattering notion to a "civilized" person whose group has attracted anthropological interest. "A sociologist," said one informant, "I can understand, but why an anthropologist?"[6] Morton Fried (1959:351) faced a similar problem when, on beginning his anthropological fieldwork in east-central China, he was summoned to appear at the office of the county magistrate. "The magistrate was polite but cold: an anthropological study of his country was an affront; anthropologists, said the magistrate, studied only savages and barbarians."

There are, however, communication problems other than those directly related to informant rapport that have an impact upon the research process and the anthropologist's understanding of what is happening. Among these is how the anthropologist interprets an informant's "interaction style"; that is, the culturally patterned actions that characterize how a person initiates and/or responds to others. The anthropologist, like all other human beings, is culturally trained from infancy to interpret and respond to the behavioral patterns of her or his own culture in a specific and often unconscious way. When working in another culture, therefore, the anthropologist is always at risk of projecting a behavioral interpretation from his or her own culture onto the one being studied.

Anthropologists call this phenomenon "ethnocentrism" and recognize it as a common cause of distortion and misunderstanding among individuals of diverse ethnic backgrounds. Although a behavioral act in two different cultures may appear to be the same, the social meanings of the act can vary; what looks like one thing in one's own culture may have a very different meaning in the host culture. During the first months of the research as I was learning about the culture and its characteristic interaction style, I frequently misinterpreted an informant's behavior.

Initially, I was somewhat abashed by my informants' familiarity and verbal frankness. As a group they were quick to express their personal views, even very negative ones, about their relatives and family affairs. Their extreme candor about "family skeletons," as well as their boasting about family accomplishments, occasionally embarrassed me. I was unaccustomed to such bold forthrightness—it was almost the reverse of my own subculture and the Chinese I had studied. And, while I might marvel at their unreserved and seemingly uncensored presentation of themselves and their families, I wondered how family members could endure such brashness without alienating one another.

Although they treated me kindly as a guest in their home, these informants felt no constraint to defer to me politely as my Chinese informants had done. If I made some passing, and to me, innocuous comment, I might be challenged directly with an opposing view. If they thought I had misunderstood or not comprehended a point in the interview, they would abruptly correct me or ruefully continue their explanation. They were excellent informants, willing to instruct me in details but ever ready to chide me if they thought I didn't understand completely. Most of them quickly grasped the nature of my study, even anticipating my next question and volunteering information before I had the presence of mind to ask for it. It was exciting research, fast paced and fully developed, but it wasn't what I would call "easy." It demanded a great deal of mental discipline because the data and its nuances appeared so rapidly. It was very different from later work with the New Guinea Lujere (Mitchell 1977) when some of my informant interviews moved so slowly that I could occasionally daydream about home and still keep track of what was being said in a foreign language.

But there was no time to daydream with my Jewish informants. I was too busy keeping abreast of the interview action. At first, I tended to misinterpret their avid outspokenness and abrupt corrections and comments as "put-downs" of myself. It seemed as if I could do nothing right and that nothing was sacred; if they had a view it existed to be expressed. Even my own cultural background did not escape critical commentary. Once, in an interview on Jewish weddings, I commented that the giving of money as a wedding gift was different from my family's custom:

MRS. X: Well, you are not Jewish, or no?
WM: No.
MRS. X: No, then that's the difference. The style is entirely different! I know in your case they usually bring gifts in their display.
WM: That's right.
MRS. X: And everyone brings a piece of junk, and by the time you get through, half that stuff is thrown out. You don't even use it. Am I right?

This kind of critical forthrightness, to my chagrin, sometimes would throw me off balance. However, as I learned not to withdraw—for that only made the interviewee more impatient and anxious—my interviews became both more interesting and valuable. My informants seemed more comfortable because they had someone to "push" against or disagree with. I also learned that it wasn't really important for us to agree; no one had to "win." It was the disputation or "status jockeying" that was important; it made the interaction sequence exciting and, I can't help but thinking now, not blandly *goyish*.

Learning this disputatious interaction style was a challenge because it was different from my own more circumspect cultural style in which one should protect the feelings of the other person, and open disagreements, especially with relative strangers, are avoided. There is, however, a special exhilaration in the disputatious style. It is bold and assertive and intellectually stimulating. One must think quickly to marshall evidence for a convincing riposte. What once would have seemed like an inappropriate argument came to feel like a stimulating discussion about a disagreement. Later, when I asked an informant about conflicts or arguments with respect to her family circle organization, I knew exactly what she meant when she smilingly replied, "Oh, we don't have arguments! We have disagreements!" Nevertheless, because a disputatious interaction style is concerned with interpersonal conflict, it flirts with danger. A lively discussion may easily move into genuine quarreling if a participant "pushes" too hard, is too intractable, or is insulting.[7]

Related to this assertive interaction style is the phenomenon of "overtalking"—two or more individuals speaking simultaneously. Again, this was different from my own subculture where it is considered either "rude" or "aggressive" to speak when another person is talking. To keep from losing control of an interview when my informant interrupted me, I learned how to "overtalk" by raising my voice as I persisted in asking a question or making a comment; however, I never succeeded in feeling at ease with this tactic. The problem was even more difficult when I did a family interview with parents and children. Verbatim transcriptions of these interviews presented a complex methodological problem when, for example, the wife, husband, teen-age daughter, and I were each competing verbally for attention.

In an important way, this chapter is about language—language in its widest application to include the symbolic display of both the voice and the body. I have emphasized the differences between Gentiles and Jews in these communicative displays as exemplified by my experience as an anthropologist studying New York City Jewish families of Eastern European ethnic background. It is an anthropological truism that one's culture helps to shape how we perceive ourselves and others. It is also true that intimate experience with another culture can affect one's perceptions and understanding. In the Jewish research, I learned that I was a *goy,* a pejorative term signifying that I was a callous outsider and potential enemy. My physical appearance and style of interaction further corroborated the cultural differences between my informants and me. These were facts embedded in deep and compelling cultural histories. Nothing I might do could completely change or transcend them.

There is an old Yiddish saying, "A *goy bleibt a goy!*" that translates loosely as, "Once a *goy,* always a *goy!*" I was a *goy,* but in my role as an anthropologist, I made a concerted attempt to modify my *goyisher kop,* my "Gentile ways." By consciously working to accommodate my behavior and interaction style to that of my Jewish informants, I was able to feel my way into this host culture and gradually develop a sense of empathy and "connectedness" that facilitated the communication process. Although I never completely attained the easy verbal and gestural expressiveness of my Jewish informants (or, for that matter, the easy physical intimacy of my Wape male informants), I did achieve an approximation that made me feel and look less behaviorally foreign. And once I understood that my informants' disputatious interaction style was not a personal attack but an elaborated form of provocative play, I could enter into the exchange without fear of hurting someone's feelings or suffering a damaged ego myself.

At the end of the project I moved to northern Vermont to work with rural and village families and encountered yet another problem in cultural adaption. Compared to the placid mien of many rural Vermont Yankee males, my indigenous Kansas style of interaction was rather lively and when augmented by the expressive behaviors learned during the Jewish project, it became explosively dynamic. My wife, a native Vermonter, admonished me to modify my interaction style. There it was the "village idiot," not the successful man, who cultivated verbal and behavioral expressiveness.

Communication problems are a "given" of anthropological fieldwork. The nature of the problems and how they are revealed depends partly upon the culture of the anthropologist and the culture of the informant. To what extent the anthropologist is successful in adapting his or her behavior patterns to those of the host culture will vary greatly. It is a problem area that has had little, if any, formal discussion among anthropologists, although it is a crucial dimension of fieldwork that may have an enduring effect on the anthropologist's life. Each group with whom an anthropologist works, if one is sensitive to the kinds of communication problems explored here, helps to change and/or augment one's behavioral repertoire. In this sense, fieldwork research is a transforming experience.

My research with New York City Jewish families was no exception. Like most anthropological fieldwork, it has had a lasting influence upon me. Encountering the profound rigidity of ethnic divisions was, in spite of my Kansas optimism, a disillusioning experience. Nevertheless, my personal life has been enriched by learning a lively cultural style of interaction quite different from my own. Perhaps of even more significance, I learned something known by members of this culture for many centuries: how it feels to be a dangerous outsider.

Notes

For comments on a draft of this paper, I am grateful to Jack Kugelmass, Annette B. Weiner, and Jonathan B. Weiner.

1. The parent project was cosponsored by the Jewish Family Service of New York and the Russell Sage Foundation. The project was directed by Hope Jensen Leichter, and the regular research staff included Fred Davis, Judith Lieb, Alice Liu Szema, Dianne Tendler, Candace Rogers, and myself. A detailed account of the samples, methodology, and findings of this study are reported in Leichter and Mitchell (1978). For similar information on the study of Jewish family clubs, see Mitchell (1980). The majority of the data for both studies was collected between 1958 and 1962.

2. See, e.g., Freilich (1970); Hammersley and Atkinson (1983); Lawless, Sutlive, Jr., and Zamora (1983); Mead (1970); and Pelto and Pelto (1973). More recently, some anthropologists, e.g., Marcus and Fischer (1986), Ruby (1982) and Stocking (1983) have developed a critical interest in the anthropologist's fieldwork experience in a particular society and how this is reflected in resulting publications.

3. Although Jews are sometimes collectively called, "the Jewish race," this is scientifically incorrect. Race is a biological concept. There is great variation among Jews in terms of physical characteristics, and this disqualifies them from being a race per se. On this subject, see Newman (1965:21–30) and Shapiro (1960).

4. For example, even Jewish social scientists who were members of a "family circle" or "cousins' club" did not recognize the uniqueness of these urban descent groups in the ethnographic record or their importance for kinship theory but tended to react to them as annoyances that demanded an occasional appearance at a meeting or special event.

5. This negative response to anthropological research has become a frequent response in the Third World, where anthropologists are sometimes viewed as having been handmaidens to an exploitative colonialism and are now barred from doing fieldwork in some countries. See, e.g., Strathern (1983).

6. It is true that it is very unusual for a Gentile to study and publish on Jewish life. As Mayer (1973:152) has noted, "the sociology of Jews has been written almost exclusively by Jews."

7. For substantive data on conflict among Jews of Eastern European descent and its cultural background see Leichter and Mitchell (1978:166–184); Mitchell (1978:155–168); and Zborowski and Herzog (1952).

References Cited

FRIED, MORTON H. 1959. *Readings in Anthropology,* Vol. 2. New York: Thomas Y. Crowell.

FREILICH, MORRIS, ed. 1970. *Marginal Natives: Anthropologists at Work.* New York: Harper & Row.

GEERTZ, CLIFFORD. 1967. "Under the Mosquito Net." *New York Review of Books* 9:12–13.

HAMMERSLEY, MARTYN and PAUL ATKINSON. 1983. *Ethnography: Principles in Practice.* London: Tavistock.

HINKEL, LAWRENCE *et al.* 1957. "Factors Relevant to the Occurrence of Bodily Illness and Disturbances in Mood, Thought and Behavior in Three Homogeneous Population Groups." *American Journal of Psychiatry* 114:212–220.

LAWLESS, ROBERT, VINCENT H. SUTLIVE, JR., and MARIO D. ZAMORA, eds. 1983. *Fieldwork: The Human Experience.* New York: Gordon and Breach.

LEICHTER, HOPE JENSEN and WILLIAM E. MITCHELL. 1978. *Kinship and Casework: Family Networks and Social Intervention.* New York: Teachers College Press.

MARCUS, GEORGE E. and MICHAEL M. J. FISCHER. 1986. *Anthropology as Cultural Critique: An Experimental Moment in the Human Sciences.* Chicago: University of Chicago Press.

MAYER, EGON. 1973. "Jewish Orthodoxy in America: Towards the Sociology of a Residual Category." *Jewish Journal of Sociology* 15:151–165.

MEAD, MARGARET. 1970. "The Art and Technique of Fieldwork," in *Handbook of Method in Cultural Anthropology,* Raoul Naroll and Ronald Cohen, eds. New York: Columbia University Press.

MITCHELL, WILLIAM E. 1977. "Sorcellerie chamanique: Sanguma chez lez Lujere de cours supérieur de Sépik." *Journal de la Société des Océanistes* 33:178–189.

———. 1980. *Mishpokhe: A Study of New York City Jewish Family Clubs*, 2nd ed. Hawthorne, N.Y.: Aldine. Reprinted in *Anthropology for the Eighties*, Johnnetta B. Cole, ed. New York: Free Press, 1982.

———. 1987. *The Bamboo Fire: Field Work with the New Guinea Wape*, 2nd ed. Prospects Heights, Ill.: Waveland Press.

NEWMAN, LOUIS I. 1965. *The Jewish People, Faith and Life.* New York: Bloch.

PELTO, PERTTI J. and GRETEL H. PELTO. 1973. "Ethnography: The Fieldwork Enterprise," in *Handbook of Social and Cultural Anthropology*, John J. Honigmann, ed. Chicago: Rand McNally.

ROSTEN, LEO. 1970. *The Joys of Yiddish.* New York: Simon and Schuster.

RUBY, JAY, ed. 1982. *A Crack in the Mirror: Reflexive Perspectives in Anthropology.* Philadelphia: University of Pennsylvania Press.

SHAPIRO, HARRY I. 1960. *The Jewish People: A Biological History.* Paris: UNESCO.

STOCKING, GEORGE W. JR., ed. 1983. *Observers Observed: Essays on Ethnographic Fieldwork.* Madison, Wis.: University of Wisconsin Press.

STRATHERN, ANDREW. 1983. "Research in Papua New Guinea: Cross-Currents of Conflict." *Royal Anthropological Institute News*, No. 58.

TUBBS, STEWART L. and SYLVIA MOSS. 1974. *Human Communication: An Interpersonal Perspective.* New York: Random House.

ZBOROWSKI, MARK and ELIZABETH HERZOG. 1952. *Life Is With People: The Culture of the Shtetl.* New York: Schocken.

PART II

Aspects of Culture

Culture is the most discussed concept in anthropology, and yet a great deal of disagreement surrounds those discussions. Anthropologists are quite certain about what they *do not* mean by the term; the problem centers on determining what it *is*. Culture, in the anthropological sense, does not refer to the cultivation of the soil, nor a growth, like bacteria, nor some intellectual or artistic activity. As anthropologists debate what in fact they do mean by culture, they often go back, at least as a starting point, to the definition articulated by the father of anthropology, E. B. Tylor, in 1871. Culture is, Tylor wrote, "that complex whole which includes knowledge, belief, art, morals, law, custom and any other capabilities and habits acquired by man as a member of society."

Since Tylor's time, when "culture" was earmarked as the primary conceptual tool of anthropologists, there has been a profusion of definitions.

Referring to culture as the way of life of human groups brings us closer to a consensus on what is meant by culture—until we discover that the debate is reopened by a set of probing questions. Is culture the patterns *of* behavior or the patterns *for* behavior of human groups? Ward Goodenough, in an article written in 1957, prodded anthropologists to make up their minds which of these meanings they refer to when they speak of culture. If we accept the first meaning, culture can be studied directly because it refers to observable acts; but according to the second meaning culture cannot be studied directly, because it is the ideas, concepts, and knowledge that are expressed in and underlie observable behavior.

The distinction becomes clearer when we examine an example from our own way of life. Imagine that you and a friend go to a baseball game. An anthropologist could observe you sitting on bleachers, talking, eating hotdogs, cheering, booing, perhaps arguing over which team is better. A definition of culture as patterns of behavior would thus lead the anthropologist to describe you and your friend (the people), the hotdogs (objects), and the stadium (the place). Another anthropologist might, however, describe yet another order of what went on: what you and your friend know and believe about baseball games and the appropriate way to act when attending them; in short, the knowledge and concepts that you and your friend use to structure your behavior at the game.

In the articles in Part II, culture is used in each of these two senses. Clearly, as anthropologists engage in technical discussions, it is most important that they distinguish the sense in which they are using this primary conceptual tool of the discipline. However, at this stage of the development of anthropological theory, and also for students of anthropology, there is value in continuing to look at culture in two ways: as shared, learned patterns of *and* for behavior.

Culture Is Learned

It would be difficult to overestimate the importance of the anthropologists' statement that culture is learned. But how *much* of human behavior is learned is the hotly debated question. The recently developed interdisciplinary field of sociobiology is at the center of this debate.

Drawing on the principles of natural selection, sociobiologists seek to explain the evolution of animal—including human—social behavior. Among sociobiological explanations of human behavior there is a range, from those based in the genetic heritage of all *Homo sapiens* to theories which see much of human behavior (culture) as genetically determined. Taken as a group, anthropologists tend to differ from sociobiologists by identifying very little of human behavior, including warfare or racism, as expressions of the genetic heritage of *Homo sapiens*. And anthropologists stress the enormous variation in human behavior at any given moment in history in support of the conclusion that behavior is learned and shaped by culture.

The statement that culture is learned is on the surface obvious; the implications of its negation are enormous. Behind notions of the inevitability of war or the inherent superiority of one group of people over another is a denial of the fact that men and women are biological creatures whose ideas and behavior are, with few exceptions, learned. Why do Haitians conceive of and worship gods (orishas) in organized voodoo cults? Why do Toda women of southern India marry a group of brothers? Why did the various tribal groups in Liberia traditionally isolate young men in a secret society known as the Poro, and young women in a similar organization known as the Sande? Why did young men from the United States go thousands of miles away from their homes to engage in warfare in Vietnam? Why do the Dani of New Guinea cut off the tips of the fingers of women when their male relatives die? The assumption underlying any anthropological discussion of each of these specific ethnographic examples is of course that these are ideas and behaviors that were learned, not genetically transmitted.

It is so easy to forget how very much we *learn* to eat certain things and not others, to marry certain "categories" of people and not others, to define certain forces as supernatural and not others, to perform certain tasks and call them work while we engage in other activities and call them play. For once we have learned these patterns of and for behavior, and learned them at an early age, they seem to us to be natural, not simply in the sense that they are the ways in which we are comfortable thinking and behaving, but "natural" in the sense of genetically—some would say "racially"—determined.

How people map out their world and move within it is not only learned but acquired in large measure from observation and imitation, rather than from specific instruction. Stop and think about when and how you learned to eat an ice cream cone, to run for shelter when a sudden rain storm breaks while you are taking a stroll, to sing a song. It will also be instructive to try to remember if any one individual or "teacher" instructed you on the "proper" roles and statuses of men and women; on "race relations," "democracy," "freedom," and a host of similarly complex ideas.

In sum, the tenacity of culture and the ease with which we come to think, value, and behave in certain ways must not deceive us into thinking that it is somehow instinctual. We grasp the most important contribution anthropology has made to understanding human behavior when we understand that culture is learned. For if human beings have learned to think and do in a certain way, then they can also learn to think and do differently.

Culture Is Shared

Culture, the particular way in which a people generates behavior, is not simply the sum total of every individual's ideas and actions. Culture is shared in the sense that it is a social process. This attribute of culture is easier to comprehend in small tribal societies because of the *relative* absence of different and conflicting interest groups. But care must be taken not to assume, as too many anthropologists have, that tribal societies are homogeneous collections of individuals. In large and technologically complex societies such as our own, societies with different ethnic, racial, and class formations, there is a distribution of "partial versions" of a cultural tradition among the various individuals who constitute a society. In our own society, the version of the North American cultural tradition that is conceptualized and acted out by members of the New York Stock Exchange differs sharply from that which is held by a group of men on skid row. The perspective of Afro-Americans will differ in certain ways from that of Euro-Americans; that of women will differ from that of men; that of farmers from that of industrial workers; that of Southerners from the perspective of Westerners. North American culture, then, is that complex pool of knowledge and patterns of and for behavior to which various gender, racial, economic, and other interest groups contribute.

Society

A second key conceptual term in anthropology, also of central importance in sociology, is "society." If anthropologists limited themselves to studying the imagined or real Robinson Crusoes of the world, solitary individuals washed ashore on some desert island, there would be no meaning to the concept of society, for there would be only one, not the necessary two individuals who, when they interact in a social relationship, form the basis of a society. Put differently, society is the complex of social relationships, each of which involves individuals (in their various roles and statuses), bound together by a common language and cultural tradition.

American anthropologists have placed more weight on the concept of culture, while British anthropologists have tended to use the notion of society. Recently French anthropologists, especially the structuralists such as Levi-Strauss, have sought to understand the relationship between these two as complementary abstractions.

Just as we have suggested that students who are being introduced to anthropology might well explore the notion of culture as patterns both of and for behavior, we suggest here that students should not concentrate on viewing human behavior in terms of either society or culture, but rather in "sociocultural" terms.

Sociocultural Universals

When anthropologists examine the organization and integration of human societies, they explore the means by which individuals communicate with each other—particularly that form of human communication which is language. They also note how the sociocultural systems (economic, political, social, and religious) interlock. It is to an exploration of these universals in human societies that we now turn.

References

GOODENOUGH, W. H. 1957. "Cultural Anthropology and Linguistics," in *Report of the Seventh Annual Round Table Meeting on Linguistics and Language Study,* P. Garvin, ed. Monograph Series on Language and Linguistics, 9. Georgetown University, Washington, D.C.

TYLOR, E. B. 1871. *Primitive Culture.* London: Murray.

Language and Culture

We have all observed groups of animals communicating in some way: parents nurturing their offspring, pairs of animals mating, animals involved in aggressive acts. No one has observed a group of animals engaged in a philosophical discussion about the nature of language. We human beings are distinguished from all other animals by language. Recent experiments among primates, especially chimpanzees, do not invalidate this statement, but these data do prompt anthropologists to be quite specific about what language is and how it is used.

In the 1940s, in one of the earlier experiments in primate communication, researchers taught a chimpanzee named Viki to speak, but her vocabulary never advanced beyond three words: mama, papa, and cup. Twenty years after that experiment, Beatrice and Allen Gardner lived in close contact with Washoe, a female chimpanzee. The Gardners taught Washoe to use more than two hundred words in American sign language and to use this vocabulary in a grammatically correct way. The Gardners claim that Washoe can generalize (for example, using the sign for "dog," which she learned from a picture, in connection with the bark of a dog she could not see) and express abstract ideas (Washoe used the sign for "dirty" in reference to a monkey that she did not like). Another chimpanzee, Sarah, has learned to manipulate plastic signs (which she has learned to use as symbols) to build what we might call sentences and to answer questions posed by researchers.

No matter how impressive these feats, they are pale when compared with the complex set of verbal symbols for communication that constitute human language. The distinctiveness of language can be illustrated by the following exchange between two young children:

"Let's pretend we're dinosaurs!"

"I don't want to. We always play that old stuff. Let's pretend we live on another planet in the year 3000."

Language allows one human being to communicate with another about things that are of the past or future, as well as the present; to discuss facts or engage in fantasies; to refer to abstract notions that are not connected to the speaker's or hearer's immediate sensory experiences.

Language comprises a set of symbols and a set of rules (a grammar) used in a meaningful way that permits communication. The symbols are expressed orally by sounds, or they can be communicated in a written form. There is no resemblance between the sound we English-speaking humans write as "dinosaur" and the class of animals we label with that sound. The sound could just as well refer to what we all know as a cucumber, a computer, or a washing machine. In short, the labels languages assign to classes of things are consistently applied, but they are arbitrary. Language, a distinctively human means of communication, involves a patterning whereby smaller units (sounds) are combined into meaningful larger units (words) that are then constructed into sentences. Human language is also highly productive. Drawing on some of the several thousand words an individual knows and combining them according to grammatical rules, any human being can create new messages.

Not all scholars endorse the position that human language differs qualitatively from other forms of communication. The psychologist B. F. Skinner and the linguist Charles Hockett are among those who hold that language is the end result of a long and gradual evolutionary process of increased intelligence and the ability to communicate. Thus, they argue, human language is only quantitatively different from some other communication systems used by animals. For example, Hockett suggests that productivity is not peculiar to human languages since it is also a feature of bee communication, as when a worker performs a dance that signals the location of nectar in an area not previously visited by the colony. Hockett compares what he calls "design features" (productivity, arbitrariness, duality of patterning, and so on) among humans and other animals and concludes that many of these features of communication are widespread among various animal species, although they are most developed in human language.

The alternative language theory, associated with the linguist Noam Chomsky, advances the position that human languages are qualitatively different from all other forms of communication. In addition, Chomsky holds the view that human beings are born with specific brain patterns for language. Chomsky suggests that there is a universal general grammar coded in the brains of all normal human beings (there is no similar universal grammar among nonhumans), and thus children articulate sentences they have never heard. As to the suggestion that chimpanzees almost speak, Chomsky retorts that such a view is analogous to saying that the difference between jumping and flying is only one of degree, and thus people can really fly, just like birds, only not as well!

Language is not only distinctive to our species, it is central to our lives. It is one of the first forms of behavior that children learn, and much of the later learning of every human being requires language. Try for a moment to divorce what you think and believe and do from language, and its centrality in your life becomes obvious. But language is not the only communicative code used by human beings. We also relate to and communicate with each other through body language, gestures, smells, and indeed by silence and the use of space. A person tapping his or her fingers on a table is probably impatient. An individual who keeps watching the clock may well be bored. One who pushes another and occupies that individual's space is signaling hostility. Waving the hand means "goodby," and a clenched fist is a sign of protest. You are no doubt in agreement with these interpretations of body language, but of course that is because you and I share a particular culture. Outside of our culture, these same nonverbal clues can connote quite different meanings.

There are, as you know, many different languages throughout the world. We do not increase our understanding of the variety in human languages by simplistic categorizations into value-laden pigeonholes such as "primitive" and "advanced." Every language has a complete and ordered set of rules for phonology, syntax, and grammar, and all languages are flexible and constantly changing. Because the people of New Guinea do not speak about computers does not mean that their language is incapable of addressing that concept. After all, it is only recently that we have spoken of and understood each other when sounds have been uttered such as "I bought an apple II," "the computer is down," and "do you know fortran?"

Linguists use the fact that all languages are constantly changing to date the length of time two peoples speaking related languages have been separated. Developed by the linguist Morris Swadesh, the technique is called glottochronology or lexicon statistics. Using a basic word list of one hundred words that are assumed to change at a known rate, the differences between two related languages are recorded. The degree of difference in the basic word list indicates the date at which the two peoples separated.

Such technical and rather complex analyses as glottochronology are carried out by linguists, those scholars who study language for its own sake. In the early stages of the development of their field, linguists saw language in isolation from the range of human behavior, and thus they could focus on the internal organization of aspects of a linguistic system. Following the rapid development of linguistics—and perhaps because of its more narrow focus—linguists turned to the relationship between language and its social and cultural setting. The difference between linguists (some of whom are anthropologists and are distinguished by their expertise in non-European languages) and those social scientists (mainly anthropologists) who are interested in the relationship between language and culture is somewhat like the difference between a meteorologist and a barber/beautician. Each can tell you a great deal about the weather: The meteorologist can speak in very specific and technical terms; the barber/beautician can tell you what people of different genders, races, classes, occupations, and ages say and feel about the weather in nontechnical but descriptive and meaningful terms. Each set of information, from the meteorologist and the barber/beautician, like the linguist and the student of language and culture, is important and useful, and both are necessary if one wishes fully to understand "weather" or "language." In this anthology, we are focusing on language and culture but encourage students to explore the wealth of insight contributed by linguistic studies. Today few cultural anthropologists ignore the findings of linguistics, for they often have a bearing on anthropological theory. A major influence in current cultural anthropology, structuralism as associated with Levi-Strauss, draws heavily on language as a source of theory. Levi-Strauss posits that we can take the sound systems of languages as conceptual models for unraveling the human mind, perception, and culture. As people think and perceive, they use a logical order similar to the organization of sound systems.

In the articles that follow, two fundamental issues in the study of the relationship between language and culture are explored: the Whorfian position on language as a determinant of perception and thought; and language as a reflection of roles and status, of the various bases of stratification in a society.

Edward Sapir, an anthropologist writing in the 1920s, opened a crucial debate in the study of language and culture when he wrote that "the worlds in which different societies live are distinct worlds, not merely the same world with different labels attached." One of Sapir's students, Benjamin Whorf, developed this idea that language is central in structuring these distinct worlds. Whorf's observations as an insurance investigator (an occupation he pursued when he was not engaged in linguistic studies) suggested that the impact of language on thought was the explanation for some rather foolish behavior by obviously intelligent workers. For example, he noticed that workers smoked around empty gas drums, but not around full ones. Whorf concluded that it was because the workers associated the word "empty" with ideas like "void," "inert," and "unhazardous" while they associated the word "full" with the concept of "dangerous substance present." A series of such observations led Whorf to study systematically the way we code reality in language and the way we think. He made a series of comparisons between what he called Standard Average European language (like American English) and the languages of tribal people such as the Hopi and Eskimo. From contrasts such as those in the following example Whorf concluded that the way we categorize events linguistically determines the way we think about them.

> We have the same word for falling snow, snow on the ground, snow packed hard like ice, slushy snow, wind-driven flying snow—whatever the situation may be. To an Eskimo, this all-inclusive word would be almost unthinkable; he would say that falling snow, slushy snow, and so on, are sensuously and operationally different things to contend with; he uses different words for them and for other kinds of snow. [Whorf 1956:216]

Today, most anthropologists reject the deterministic position of Whorf; but the insights from Sapir and Whorf remain a part of the way that language, thought, and world view are analyzed. For example, Whorf liked to use Hopi verb tenses and vocabulary about "time" to prove that the Hopi notion of time is a kind of cylinder that turns over slowly—contrasted to the Euro-American concept of time (dictated by our language), which has a beginning and runs forward in one direction at a uniform pace. The many statements and expressions about time in American English certainly reflect the importance of this concept in our way of life, but it does not prove that it is our language that forces us to be preoccupied with time. The linguistic features Whorf used to show the contrasts between what he called Standard American English (SAE) and Hopi certainly do reflect differences in ways of *expressing* the same thoughts—but that is a far cry from saying that they reflect differences in thought.

The main criticism of Whorf is that he saw linguistic categories as the very units of thinking itself. Modern evidence suggests that thinking and manipulating linguistic categories are not ultimately the same thing. But we remain indebted to Benjamin Whorf for initiating the debate among anthropologists and linguists. Perhaps the point of common agreement among these scholars today is that linguistic categories do in fact set up a kind of screen between an individual and the world that he or she perceives. But to most scholars, the screen seems less all-powerful than it did to Benjamin Whorf.

In Laura Bohannan's article, "Shakespeare in the Bush," we see the importance of concepts of time, kinship, religious and magical power notions of cause and effect, and so forth in a people's world view—and the difficulty of describing events of one cultural and linguistic tradition so that they are "understood" by people of another tradition. As Laura Bohannan told a group of Tiv the story of Hamlet, based on her culture's notion of what was the proper behavior for each of Shakespeare's characters, the Tiv had quite different views and interpretations, based, of course, on their cultural values and practices. The result is a graphic statement on cross-cultural understanding and misunderstanding.

Language is fundamentally a social act, and thus the particular content used in specific social settings is an important indicator of the various roles and statuses in a society. Price's chapter considers how the different material of Suriname women's and men's folk songs relates to their differences in social status. In those societies marked by class, racial, and similar sharp divisions, speech patterns (dialects) mirror stratification. We tend to associate dialects and particular accents with geographical regions. However, throughout the world there are also dialects (varieties of a language) that are characteristic of a particular social class, caste, racial or ethnic group, and gender and accents associated with a given occupation or group. For example, in a few tribal societies men and women speak different dialects; in our own and other technologically complex societies, class is often associated with an accent, such as the working-class "New York accent" as opposed to the Beacon Hill upper-class Boston accent. In our society there is also the use of special or exotic terms by professionals or enthusiasts of one sort or another.

Many Afro-Americans in the United States speak a dialect known as Black English, which differs from "standard English" in its grammar, vocabulary, and pronunciation. In Arthur Spears's article in this section, the point is made that when Afro-Americans speak Black English, they are not speaking standard English badly, they are speaking Black English correctly. For example, in standard English the use of double negatives is incorrect (I ain't got none); but in Black English, double negatives are consistently and unambiguously used so that the phrase, "I ain't got none" is a correct way of saying in Black English what standard English speakers mean when they no less correctly say "I haven't got any."

A dialect can also serve as a basis of social solidarity, as Black English does among many Afro-Americans. Individuals who speak both Black English and standard English will, as we all must, use the standard dialect in the many day-to-day interactions of U.S. society. However, among members of the black community, or as an act of solidarity, when speaking with other Afro-Americans in the presence of Euro-Americans, Black English will be used.

The experiences of many speakers of Black English are intensified in the daily lives of the group that will soon be the largest "minority" in the United States, Spanish-speaking peoples. Even where there are laws requiring bilingual education in public schools, what often happens is that native Spanish-speaking youngsters never fully develop their capacities as Spanish speakers and never fully acquire proficiency in English. One also must ask what is lost culturally and psychologically in the process. Oriol Pi-Sunyer, writing of a broadly similar phenomenon in another part of the world, explains the importance of language as a symbol of identity among the Catalans of Spain:

But at the very core of Catalan nationalism, as something that all could share, as something that would differentiate them from other peoples, was the language. This raises what I believe is the key question, the most important cultural and political consideration with which this generation of Catalans must struggle: is it possible to be Catalan without speaking the language? If the answer is in the affirmative, what does it mean to be Catalan once language takes a secondary position as a symbol of identity? [1980:114]

Pi-Sunyer's challenging questions have relevance for the ethnic and racial minorities *and* majorities of every part of the world.

Beyond spoken language, the identities of groups within a society emerge in other forms of communication. The material culture of a people—the arts, crafts, clothing, utensils—quite generally, their things— also symbolically expresses the thoughts of those who produce and use them. This form of communication might be more difficult to "hear," but it can be no less important and revealing.

In examining Suriname women's arts, Price finds that both their folk songs and their carvings and textiles convey their lower social status. A. Wilson also considers how language, in writing, and visual representation, in photographs, construct women's identity, but in her example American entrepreneurs create identities of Asian women.

As a group, these articles on language and representation demonstrate the ways in which the production and evaluation of linguistic and artistic expressions reflect social relations of the culture that creates these expressions.

References

CHOMSKY, NOAM. 1975. *Reflections on Language.* New York: Pantheon.

HOCKETT, C. F. 1958. *A Course in Modern Linguistics.* New York: Macmillan.

LEVI-STRAUSS, CLAUDE. 1963. *Structural Anthropology.* New York: Basic Books.

PI-SUNYER, ORIOL. 1980. "Dimensions of Catalan Nationalism," in Charles R. Foster, ed., *Nations Without a State: Ethnic Minorities in Western Europe.* New York: Praeger.

WHORF, B. L. 1956. *Language, Thought, and Reality: Selected Writings of Benjamin Lee Whorf.* Edited by J. B. Carroll. Cambridge: MIT Press.

5

Shakespeare in the Bush

LAURA BOHANNAN

JUST BEFORE I LEFT OXFORD for the Tiv in West Africa, conversation turned to the season at Stratford. "You Americans," said a friend, "often have difficulty with Shakespeare. He was, after all, a very English poet, and one can easily misinterpret the universal by misunderstanding the particular."

I protested that human nature is pretty much the same the whole world over; at least the general plot and motivation of the greater tragedies would always be clear—everywhere—although some details of custom might have to be explained and difficulties of translation might produce other slight changes. To end an argument we could not conclude, my friend gave me a copy of Hamlet to study in the African bush: it would, he hoped, lift my mind above its primitive surroundings, and possibly I might, by prolonged meditation, achieve the grace of correct interpretation.

It was my second field trip to that African tribe, and I thought myself ready to live in one of its remote sections—an area difficult to cross even on foot. I eventually settled on the hillock of a very knowledgeable old man, the head of a homestead of some hundred and forty people, all of whom were either his close relatives or their wives and children. Like the other elders of the vicinity, the old man spent most of his time performing ceremonies seldom seen these days in the more accessible parts of the tribe. I was delighted. Soon there would be three months of enforced isolation and leisure, between the harvest that takes place just before the rising of the swamps and the clearing of new farms when the water goes down. Then, I thought, they would have even more time to perform ceremonies and explain them to me.

I was quite mistaken. Most of the ceremonies demanded the presence of elders from several homesteads. As the swamps rose, the old man found it too difficult to walk from one homestead to the next, and the ceremonies gradually ceased. As the swamps rose even higher, all activities but one came to an end. The women brewed beer from maize and millet. Men, women, and children sat on their hillocks and drank it.

People began to drink at dawn. By midmorning the whole homestead was singing, dancing, and drumming. When it rained, people had to sit inside their huts: there they drank and sang or they drank and told stories. In any case, by noon or before, I either had to join the party or retire to my own hut and my books. "One does not discuss serious matters when there is beer. Come, drink with us." Since I lacked their capacity for the thick native beer, I spent more and more time with *Hamlet*. Before the end of the second month, grace descended on me. I was quite sure that *Hamlet* had only one possible interpretation, and that one universally obvious.

Early every morning, in the hope of having some serious talk before the beer party, I used to call on the old man at his reception hut—a circle of posts supporting a thatched roof above a low mud wall to keep out wind and rain. One day I crawled through the low doorway and found most of the men of the homestead sitting huddled in their ragged cloths on stools, low plank beds, and reclining chairs, warming themselves against the chill of the rain around a smoky fire. In the center were three pots of beer. The party had started.

The old man greeted me cordially. "Sit down and drink." I accepted a large calabash full of beer, poured some into a small drinking gourd, and tossed it down. Then I poured some more into the same gourd for the man second in seniority to my host before I handed my calabash over to a young man for further distribution. Important people shouldn't ladle beer themselves.

"It is better like this," the old man said, looking at me approvingly and plucking at the thatch that had caught in my hair. "You should sit and drink with us more often. Your servants tell me that when you are not with us, you sit inside your hut looking at a paper."

The old man was acquainted with four kinds of "papers": tax receipts, bride price receipts, court fee receipts, and letters. The messenger who brought him letters from the chief used them mainly as a badge of office, for he always knew what was in them and told the old man. Personal letters for the few who had relatives in the government or mission stations were kept until someone went to a large market where there was a letter writer and reader. Since my arrival, letters were brought to me to be read. A few men also brought me bride price receipts, privately, with requests to change the figures to a higher sum. I found moral arguments were of no avail, since in-laws are fair game, and the technical hazards of forgery difficult to explain to an illiterate people. I did not wish them to think me silly enough to look at any such papers for days on end, and I hastily explained that my "paper" was one of the "things of long ago" of my country.

"Ah," said the old man. "Tell us."

I protested that I was not a storyteller. Storytelling is a skilled art among them; their standards are high, and the audiences critical—and vocal in their criticism. I protested in vain. This morning they wanted to hear a story while they drank. They threatened to tell me no more stories until I told them one of mine. Finally, the old man promised that no one would criticize my style "for we know you are struggling with our language." "But," put in one of the elders, "you must explain what we do not understand, as we do when we tell you our stories." Realizing that here was my chance to prove *Hamlet* universally intelligible, I agreed.

The old man handed me some more beer to help me on with my storytelling. Men filled their long wooden pipes and knocked coals from the fire to place in the pipe bowls; then, puffing contentedly, they sat back to listen. I began in the proper style, "Not yesterday, not yesterday, but long ago, a thing occurred. One night three men were keeping watch outside the homestead of the great chief, when suddenly they saw the former chief approach them."

"Why was he no longer their chief?"

"He was dead," I explained. "That is why they were troubled and afraid when they saw him."

"Impossible," began one of the elders, handing his pipe on to his neighbor, who interrupted, "Of course it wasn't the dead chief. It was an omen sent by a witch. Go on."

Slightly shaken, I continued. "One of these three was a man who knew things"—the closest translation for scholar, but unfortunately it also meant witch. The second elder looked triumphantly at the first. "So he spoke to the dead chief saying, 'Tell us what we must do so you may rest in your grave,' but the dead chief did not answer. He vanished, and they could see him no more. Then the man who knew things—his name was Horatio—said this event was the affair of the dead chief's son, Hamlet."

There was a general shaking of heads round the circle. "Had the dead chief no living brothers? Or was this son the chief?"

"No," I replied. "That is, he had one living brother who became the chief when the elder brother died."

The old men muttered: such omens were matters for chiefs and elders, not for youngsters; no good could come of going behind a chief's back; clearly Horatio was not a man who knew things.

"Yes, he was," I insisted, shooing a chicken away from my beer. "In our country the son is next to the father. The dead chief's younger brother had become the great chief. He had also married his elder brother's widow only about a month after the funeral."

"He did well," the old man beamed and announced to the others, "I told you that if we knew more about Europeans, we would find they really were very like us. In our country also," he added to me, "the younger brother marries the elder brother's widow and becomes the father of his children. Now, if your uncle, who married your widowed mother, is your father's full brother, then he will be a real father to you. Did Hamlet's father and uncle have one mother?"

His question barely penetrated my mind; I was too upset and thrown too far off balance by having one of the most important elements of *Hamlet* knocked straight out of the picture. Rather uncertainly I said that I thought they had the same mother, but I wasn't sure—the story didn't say. The old man told me severely that these genealogical details made all the difference and that when I got home I must ask the elders about it. He shouted out the door to one of his younger wives to bring his goatskin bag.

Determined to save what I could of the mother motif, I took a deep breath and began again. "The son Hamlet was very sad because his mother had married again so quickly. There was no need for her to do so, and it is our custom for a widow not to go to her next husband until she has mourned for two years."

"Two years is too long," objected the wife, who had appeared with the old man's battered goatskin bag. "Who will hoe your farms for you while you have no husband?"

"Hamlet," I retorted without thinking, "was old enough to hoe his mother's farms himself. There was no need for her to remarry." No one looked convinced. I gave up. "His mother and the great chief told Hamlet not to be sad, for the great chief himself would be a father to Hamlet. Further-more, Hamlet would be the next chief: therefore he must stay to learn the things of a chief. Hamlet agreed to remain, and all the rest went off to drink beer."

While I paused, perplexed at how to render Hamlet's disgusted soliloquy to an audience convinced that Claudius and Gertrude had behaved in the best possible manner, one of the younger men asked me who had married the other wives of the dead chief.

"He had no other wives," I told him.

"But a chief must have many wives! How else can he brew beer and prepare food for all his guests?"

I said firmly that in our country even chiefs had only one wife, that they had servants to do their work, and that they paid them from tax money.

It was better, they returned, for a chief to have many wives and sons who would help him hoe his farms and feed his people; then everyone loved the chief who gave much and took nothing—taxes were a bad thing.

I agreed with the last comment, but for the rest fell back on their favorite way of fobbing off my questions: "That is the way it is done, so that is how we do it."

I decided to skip the soliloquy. Even if Claudius was here thought quite right to marry his brother's widow, there remained the poison motif, and I knew they would disapprove of fratricide. More hopefully I resumed, "That night Hamlet kept watch with the three who had seen his dead father. The dead chief again appeared, and although the others were afraid, Hamlet followed his dead father off to one side. When they were alone, Hamlet's dead father spoke."

"Omens can't talk!" the old man was emphatic.

"Hamlet's dead father wasn't an omen. Seeing him might have been an omen, but he was not." My audience looked as confused as I sounded. "It *was* Hamlet's dead father. It was a thing we call a 'ghost.' " I had to use the English word, for unlike many of the neighboring tribes, these people didn't believe in the survival after death of any individuating part of the personality.

"What is a 'ghost?' An omen?"

"No, a 'ghost' is someone who is dead but who walks around and can talk, and people can hear him and see him but not touch him."

They objected. "One can touch zombis."

"No, no! It was not a dead body the witches had animated to sacrifice and eat. No one else made Hamlet's dead father walk. He did it himself."

"Dead men can't walk," protested my audience as one man.

I was quite willing to compromise. "A 'ghost' is the dead man's shadow."

But again they objected. "Dead men cast no shadows."

"They do in my country," I snapped.

The old man quelled the babble of disbelief that arose immediately and told me with that insincere, but courteous, agreement one extends to the fancies of the young, ignorant, and superstitious, "No doubt in your country the dead can also walk without being zombis." From the depths of his bag he produced a withered fragment of kola nut, bit off one end to show it wasn't poisoned, and handed me the rest as a peace offering.

"Anyhow," I resumed, "Hamlet's dead father said that his own brother, the one who became chief, had poisoned him. He wanted Hamlet to avenge him. Hamlet believed this in his heart, for he did not like his father's brother." I took another swallow of beer. "In the country of the great chief, living in the same homestead, for it was a very large one, was an important elder who was often with the chief to advise and help him. His name was Polonius. Hamlet was courting his daughter, but her father and her brother . . . [I cast hastily about for some tribal analogy] warned her not to let Hamlet visit her when she was alone on her farm, for he would be a great chief and so could not marry her."

"Why not?" asked the wife, who had settled down on the edge of the old man's chair. He frowned at her for asking stupid questions and growled, "They lived in the same homestead."

"That was not the reason," I informed them. "Polonius was a stranger who lived in the homestead because he helped the chief, not because he was a relative."

"Then why couldn't Hamlet marry her?"

"He could have," I explained, "but Polonius didn't think he would. After all, Hamlet was a man of great importance who ought to marry a chief's daughter, for in his country a man could have only one wife. Polonius was afraid that if Hamlet made love to his daughter, then no one else would give a high price for her."

"That might be true," remarked one of the shrewder elders, "but a chief's son would give his mistress's father enough presents and patronage to more than make up the difference. Polonius sounds like a fool to me."

"Many people think he was," I agreed. "Meanwhile Polonius sent his son Laertes off to Paris to learn the things of that country, for it was the homestead of a very great chief indeed. Because he was afraid that Laertes might waste a lot of money on beer and women and gambling, or get into trouble by fighting, he sent one of his servants to Paris secretly, to spy out what Laertes was doing. One day Hamlet came upon Polonius's daughter Ophelia. He behaved so oddly he frightened her. Indeed"—I was fumbling for words to express the dubious quality of Hamlet's madness—"the chief and many others had also noticed that when Hamlet talked one could understand the words but not what they meant. Many people thought that he had become mad." My audience suddenly became much more attentive. "The great chief wanted to know what was wrong with Hamlet, so he sent for two of Hamlet's age mates [school friends would have taken long explanation] to talk to Hamlet and find out what troubled his heart. Hamlet, seeing that they had been bribed by the chief to betray him, told them nothing. Polonius, however, insisted that Hamlet was mad because he had been forbidden to see Ophelia, whom he loved."

"Why," inquired a bewildered voice, "should anyone bewitch Hamlet on that account?"

"Bewitch him?"

"Yes, only witchcraft can make anyone mad, unless, of course, one sees the beings that lurk in the forest."

I stopped being a storyteller, took out my notebook and demanded to be told more about these two causes of madness. Even while they spoke and I jotted notes, I tried to calculate the effect of this new factor on the plot. Hamlet had not been exposed to the beings that lurk in the forests. Only his relatives in the male line could bewitch him. Barring relatives not mentioned by Shakespeare, it had to be Claudius who was attempting to harm him. And, of course, it was.

For the moment I staved off questions by saying that the great chief also refused to believe that Hamlet was mad for the love of Ophelia and nothing else. "He was sure that something much more important was troubling Hamlet's heart."

"Now Hamlet's age mates," I continued, "had brought with them a famous storyteller. Hamlet decided to have this man tell the chief and all his homestead a story about a man who had poisoned his brother because he desired his brother's wife and wished to be chief himself. Hamlet was sure the great chief could not hear the story without making a sign if he was indeed guilty, and then he would discover whether his dead father had told him the truth."

The old man interrupted, with deep cunning, "Why should a father lie to his son?" he asked.

I hedged: "Hamlet wasn't sure that it really was his dead father." It was impossible to say anything, in that language, about devil-inspired visions.

"You mean," he said, "it actually was an omen, and he knew witches sometimes send false ones. Hamlet was a fool not to go to one skilled in reading omens and divining the truth in the first place. A man-who-sees-the-truth could have told him how his father died, if he really had been poisoned, and if there was witchcraft in it; then Hamlet could have called the elders to settle the matter."

The shrewd elder ventured to disagree. "Because his father's brother was a great chief, one-who-sees-the-truth might therefore have been afraid to tell it. I think it was for that reason that a friend of Hamlet's father—a witch and an elder—sent an omen so his friend's son would know. Was the omen true?"

"Yes," I said, abandoning ghosts and the devil; a witch-sent omen it would have to be. "It was true, for when the storyteller was telling his tale before all the homestead, the great chief rose in fear. Afraid that Hamlet knew his secret he planned to have him killed."

The stage set of the next bit presented some difficulties of translation. I began cautiously. "The great chief told Hamlet's mother to find out from her son what he knew. But because a woman's children are always first in her heart, he had the important elder Polonius hide behind a cloth that hung against the wall of Hamlet's mother's sleeping hut. Hamlet started to scold his mother for what she had done."

There was a shocked murmur from everyone. A man should never scold his mother.

"She called out in fear, and Polonius moved behind the cloth. Shouting, 'A rat!' Hamlet took his machete and slashed through the cloth." I paused for dramatic effect. "He had killed Polonius!"

The old men looked at each other in supreme disgust. "That Polonius truly was a fool and a man who knew nothing! What child would not know enough to shout, 'It's me!'" With a pang, I remembered that these people are ardent hunters, always armed with bow, arrow, and machete; at the first rustle in the grass an arrow is aimed and ready, and the hunter shouts "Game!" If no human voice answers immediately, the arrow speeds on its way. Like a good hunter Hamlet had shouted, "A rat!"

I rushed in to save Polonius's reputation. "Polonius did speak. Hamlet heard him. But he thought it was the chief and wished to kill him to avenge his father. He had meant to kill him earlier that evening...." I broke down, unable to describe to these pagans, who had no belief in individual afterlife, the difference between dying at one's prayers and dying "unhousell'd, disappointed, unaneled."

This time I had shocked my audience seriously. "For a man to raise his hand against his father's brother and the one who has become his father, that is a terrible thing. The elders ought to let such a man be bewitched."

I nibbled at my kola nut in some perplexity, then pointed out that after all the man had killed Hamlet's father.

"No," pronounced the old man, speaking less to me than to the young men sitting behind the elders. "If your father's brother has killed your father, you must appeal to your father's age mates; they may avenge him. No man may use violence against his senior relatives." Another thought struck him. "But if his father's brother had indeed been wicked enough to bewitch Hamlet and make him mad that would be a good story indeed, for it would be his fault that Hamlet, being mad, no longer had any sense and thus was ready to kill his father's brother."

There was a murmur of applause. *Hamlet* was again a good story to them, but it no longer seemed quite the same story to me. As I thought over the coming complications of plot and motive, I lost courage and decided to skim over dangerous ground quickly.

"The great chief," I went on, "was not sorry that Hamlet had killed Polonius. It gave him a reason to send Hamlet away, with his two treacherous age mates, with letters to a chief of a far country, saying that Hamlet should be killed. But Hamlet changed the writing on their papers, so that the chief killed his age mates instead." I encountered a reproachful glare from one of the men whom I had told undetectable forgery was not merely immoral but beyond human skill. I looked the other way.

"Before Hamlet could return, Laertes came back for his father's funeral. The great chief told him Hamlet had killed Polonius. Laertes swore to kill Hamlet because of this, and because his sister, Ophelia, hearing her father had been killed by the man she loved, went mad and drowned in the river."

"Have you already forgotten what we told you?" The old man was reproachful. "One cannot take vengeance on a madman; Hamlet killed Polonius in his madness. As for the girl, she not only went mad, she was drowned. Only witches can make people drown. Water itself can't hurt anything. It is merely something one drinks and bathes in."

I began to get cross. "If you don't like the story, I'll stop."

The old man made soothing noises and himself poured me some more beer. "You tell the story well, and we are listening. But it is clear that the elders of your country have never told you what the story really means. No, don't interrupt! We believe you when you say your marriage customs are different, or your clothes and weapons. But people are the same everywhere; therefore, there are always witches and it is we, the elders, who know how witches work. We told you it was the great chief who wished to kill Hamlet, and now your own words have proved us right. Who were Ophelia's male relatives?"

"There were only her father and her brother." Hamlet was clearly out of my hands.

"There must have been many more; this also you must ask of your elders when you get back to your country. From what you tell us, since Polonius was dead, it must have been Laertes who killed Ophelia, although I do not see the reason for it."

We had emptied one pot of beer, and the old men argued the point with slightly tipsy interest. Finally one of them demanded of me, "What did the servant of Polonius say on his return?"

With difficulty I recollected Reynaldo and his mission. "I don't think he did return before Polonius was killed."

"Listen," said the elder, "and I will tell you how it was and how your story will go, then you may tell me if I am right. Polonius knew his son would get into trouble, and so he did. He had many fines to pay for fighting, and debts from gambling. But he had only two ways of getting money quickly. One was to marry off his sister at once, but it is difficult to find a man who will marry a woman desired by the son of a chief. For if the chief's heir commits adultery with your wife, what can you do? Only a fool calls a case against a man who will someday be his judge. Therefore Laertes had to take the second way: he killed his sister by witchcraft, drowning her so he could secretly sell her body to the witches."

I raised an objection. "They found her body and buried it. Indeed Laertes jumped into the grave to see his sister once more—so, you see, the body was truly there. Hamlet, who had just come back, jumped in after him."

"What did I tell you?" The elder appealed to the others. "Laertes was up to no good with his sister's body. Hamlet prevented him, because the chief's heir, like a chief, does not wish any other man to grow rich and powerful. Laertes would be angry, because he would have killed his sister without benefit to himself. In our country he would try to kill Hamlet for that reason. Is this not what happened?"

"More or less," I admitted. "When the great chief found Hamlet was still alive, he encouraged Laertes to try to kill Hamlet and arranged a fight with machetes between them. In the fight both the young men were wounded to death. Hamlet's mother drank the poisoned beer that the chief meant for

Hamlet in case he won the fight. When he saw his mother die of poison, Hamlet, dying, managed to kill his father's brother with his machete."

"You see, I was right!" exclaimed the elder.

"That was a very good story," added the old man, "and you told it with very few mistakes. There was just one more error, at the very end. The poison Hamlet's mother drank was obviously meant for the survivor of the fight, whichever it was. If Laertes had won, the great chief would have poisoned him, for no one would know that he arranged Hamlet's death. Then, too, he need not fear Laertes' witchcraft; it takes a strong heart to kill one's only sister by witchcraft.

"Sometime," concluded the old man, gathering his ragged toga about him, "you must tell us some more stories of your country. We, who are elders, will instruct you in their true meaning, so that when you return to your own land your elders will see that you have not been sitting in the bush, but among those who know things and who have taught you wisdom."

6

Black American English

ARTHUR K. SPEARS

Introduction

WHEN I WAS VERY YOUNG, probably before I entered elementary school, I remember becoming aware of a difference. It was a difference I encountered repeatedly in my social environment and finally felt compelled to ask about. "What's the difference between a thing and a thang?" My parents laughed when I posed the question. An older brother, with all the seriousness he could muster at such a young age—surely no more than eight or nine years old—proposed an answer, which went roughly as follows: a thing is a specific thing; a thang is any old thang.

I have never known precisely why this has stuck in my mind. Perhaps it has something to do with my becoming a linguist. In any case, this vignette is an instructive one. My brother's answer points out two facts about language. First, our statements about language reflect our norms, values, and attitudes. Second, language variation, or language differences, are not only present but ineradicable, reflecting as they do differences in individual personalities and group identities. In the Black neighborhood where I was growing up, people generally said *thang*; but sometimes, some of them said *thing*. This was what gave rise to the question in the first place.

Students of language variation—that is, how language varies with social groups and individual members of such groups—know that *thing* and *thang* are prime examples of variation. When speaking some varieties, or dialects, of English, we use *thing*. When using other varieties, we use *thang*. The difference has nothing to do with specificity or precision, as my brother erroneously believed. These are simply two instances of the same word. Each variety of English gives the word its own pronunciation.

But why did my brother, as do many people, assume that *thing* was more specific, while *thang* was relatively vague—somehow involved in a loose way of speaking. The answer has to do with issues of norms and attitudes. *Thing* is the standard English pronunciation of the word. *Thang* is the pronunciation we find in several nonstandard varieties of English. One of these nonstandard varieties is what linguists refer to as Black Vernacular English.

Since standard English is the version of the language used in the schools, government, most literature, the mass media, and other controlling and officially promoted institutions of society, most people think it must be somehow better; for example, more precise. Nonstandard dialects are associated with ordinary people, not those who run the nation. Also, they are often associated with groups that are poor and disadvantaged. So, many people mistakenly believe nonstandard dialects are somehow inferior; for example, less precise or less elegant. These kinds of erroneous assumptions were reflected in my brother's comments.

What Black English Is

Grammar, Dialect, and Language

It is best to think of the term *Black English* as comparable to terms such as *British English, New Zealand English,* and *Australian English.* Each of these terms embraces an array of dialects. Some of the dialects are standard varieties, used in government, education, law, and other arenas where the controlling decisions of a society are made. Some are nonstandard. Accordingly, we have the British standard called *Received Pronunciation.* (This term focuses on pronunciation rather than aspects of grammar.) Received Pronunciation is exemplified by the speech of Queen Elizabeth and other British notables, very often those born to privilege. In the U.S., *Cockney* is probably the best known nonstandard variety of British English, having been immortalized by the eminently malleable Eliza Doolittle and a number of characters in Charles Dickens's novels. Each of the cover terms for varieties of English spoken throughout the world refers to a cluster of dialects that are considered to share in common something that sets them off from other clusters. This is in theory. In fact, there may be some overlap between dialect clusters of distinct geographical areas such as Britain and Australia, especially if we consider the historical patterns of population exchanges.

When we use the term *Black English*, we are referring to a cluster of

American English dialects, both standard and nonstandard, which have properties setting them off from other dialect clusters. We use *Black* in the name of these dialects because their distinctive features are found almost exclusively in the speech of Blacks. Non-Blacks speaking these dialects have had close contact with Black people.

One point that should be emphasized is that Black English does not refer to the speech of anyone and everyone who is Black. There are, of course, Black people who have grown up isolated from any Black community and others who, for different reasons, speak varieties of the language devoid of specifically Black traits. Their English would typically be that of the group with which they have had most contact. One also encounters people such as the Black television journalists Max Robinson and Ed Bradley, who speak what we call the *network standard*. Of course, just because they use the network standard when delivering news over the air does not necessarily mean that they also use it at home playing with their children, or when reminiscing with buddies from the old neighborhood. Like many Black people, they undoubtedly use the neutral type of standard English in formal, professional situations, while reserving more informal varieties for home and leisure. (Note that the formality of speech varieties is not inherent; the level of formality associated with them depends on the kinds of social situation in which people actually tend to use them.)

The reader will have noticed that I have been using the terms *language* and *dialect*, but so far I have not distinguished between them. However, it is important to do so because in popular usage *dialect* is usually derogatory. In linguistics, *dialect* is used in a neutral, nonjudgmental sense, just as the term *language* is in popular usage.

When I worked as an interpreter (someone who provides spoken translations), I traveled to many American cities with foreign groups. The people that my groups and I met casually on buses, trains, and airplanes were often curious about what language we were speaking. I began to notice that whenever I was with an African group, people asked what dialect they were speaking. (They were speaking French or Spanish.) When I was with a White group from Europe or Latin America, people asked what language they were speaking. (They were also speaking French or Spanish—and sometimes Portuguese.) The inquisitive reader is now probably wondering what happened when there were mixed groups of Black and Whites—or even mulattoes. It just so happens that in these cases, the question asked was what language we were speaking. Apparently, the presence of some whiteness among members of a group linguistically "purifies" the whole group.

Now it is obvious that certain assumptions underlay these questions. One assumption, apparently, is that dark-skinned people—Africans—speak dialects while light-skinned ones and Whites speak languages. Why the difference? Usually, when I answered that a group of Africans was speaking

French or Spanish, the question generally asked next was did they also speak some native dialect. (Here we go again.) Sometimes I was asked if I spoke a native dialect, too. Many people would go on to comment how difficult it must be to learn a "native dialect, what with it not having a grammar and all."

The correlation of skin color with *language* or *dialect* was only a derivative one. The more basic assumption was that languages have grammars, are written, and are spoken in the more "advanced" parts of the world by more "advanced" people, and one can guess who they are supposed to be.

The terms *language* and *dialect* are used in several ways by linguists, but rest assured that none of them correlate with factors such as skin color or writing. *Language* is the more inclusive term, and a language is seen as including a number of dialects, all of which have a grammar. Dialects, as languages, may or may not be written.

In the sense that *grammar* is used by linguists, there is no such thing as a dialect or language without one. The term *grammar* is intentionally ambiguous and can refer either to written grammars or the system of rules that is internalized in the mind of a speaker. (Note that no complete grammar or codification has been prepared for any language spoken anywhere. Some cover more than others, but none is complete.) A grammar consists of the rules for the combination of the units of a language. What are those units? Sounds, words (which are made by combining sounds), phrases (made by combining words), and so on. To be sure, the complete set of rules describing these combinations is complex, but, again, all grammars are basically about possibilities of combination.

English, Swahili, Hausa, French, and Arabic, for example, are languages each of which comes in several dialects. English includes American English, Canadian English, New Zealand English, and so forth. Note also that the term *dialect* can be applied at several levels. So we can talk about dialects of the American dialect of English: Black English dialects, Midland dialects, Appalachian English, and Brooklynese, to give a few examples.

In linguistic usage, everybody speaks a dialect—and a language, too, depending on what level of generalization one wishes to use. Queen Elizabeth II speaks a British dialect of English. Muhammad Ali, the well-known boxer, speaks a Black (American) dialect of the English language. Television talk show hosts, such as Dick Cavett or Johnny Carson, speak another American dialect.

Much of the confusion about the term *Black English* stems from its equivalence, in the usage of too many who have written about Black language, to what is nowadays labeled with clarifying care as *Black Vernacular English*. It is Black Vernacular English that has been the sole concern of practically every published treatment of Black language. This is the non-standard variety of Black English, usually spoken by members of lower income groups with limited formal education, that embraces sentences without a copula (*She pretty*); those with the celebrated invariant *be* (*Joe always be runnin' his mouth*); and those with double negatives (*It ain't nobody in there*).

Various epithets have been hurled at Black Vernacular English: it is charged with being "the language of slavery" and "the dialect of oppression." The invective heaped on it is due primarily to its status as a nonstandard form of English and its association with the most underprivileged segment of the Black community. Few of those who have directed such vituperation at Black Vernacular English have paused long enough to realize that nonstandard and standard dialects of any language are the products of historical, economic, and political realities. Today's standard dialects, typically, are not only the languages of those who wield power in a society but are also the contemporary form of a dialect that became standard because it was spoken by those wielding power. It is not by chance, for example, that a Parisian dialect became the French standard only after the emergence of Paris as a political and commercial center. If Paris had remained an inconsequential village on the Seine, what we today call (standard) French might be mocked and ridiculed as a badge of sloth and ignorance.

As I pointed out, Black Vernacular English, like Appalachian English and Cockney, is neither grammarless nor grammatically defective. It has its own grammar, which is systematic and rule-governed and also fully adequate for the communicative needs of its speakers. Its status is that of its speakers, and the abuse heaped on it echoes the abuse heaped on its speakers.

Linguistic and Social Definitions of Black English

The question of what Black English is is further complicated by the fact that there are several definitions of it. These definitions are of two types: social and linguistic. The social one is quite straightforward but is not precise. According to the social definition, Black English is the form of English that Black speakers label as such. The lay person, in labeling someone's speech as Black, would typically be unable to come up with the specific criteria on which the classification is based. Black English is what people say it is, just as a good Baptist sermon is what good Baptists say it is. The labeling is quite consistent, but the basis for it can be difficult to articulate.

Consider the case of Carla, a thirteen-year-old White girl growing up in a nearly all-Black neighborhood in Camden, New Jersey. Carla's speech was studied by Ellen Hatala while a graduate student at the University of Pennsylvania. Carla was classified by Blacks—solely on the basis of listening to her recorded speech—as being Black.

Let us look at a sample of Carla's speech:

They were, they were—oh Lord, they were slaughterin' that child! . . . So uh—
so I had to git Koko, right, because like he is one of the big guys. . . . an' he's
BI-IG. . . . ain't nobody gonna touch them. . . . [Hatala 1976, cited in Labov
1980]

Carla gave the impression to Black listeners that she was speaking Black
Vernacular English. When they were asked, "Could this girl pass for White,
speaking as she does?" the answer was a unanimous "No." When asked,
"Could this girl pass for Black?" the response was confusion, as if they
had been asked, "Could Richard Pryor pass for Black?"

Linguists, however, would fail to find Carla's speech sample an example
of Black Vernacular English, defined on the basis of certain grammatical
features. For example, the copula (some form of the verb *to be*) was consistently present, as it is in ". . . he is one of the big guys. . . . an' he's
BI-IG." What is certain is that Carla effectively used linguistic features of
Black Vernacular English, such as tempo, stress, and intonation, and certain vocabulary items typical in Black usage, such as *child* in "slaughterin'
that child."

Black English as socially defined is largely a function of word use and
pronunciation features, for example, the particular vowel quality used in
pronouncing a word that is typical of Black speakers, or suprasegmental
features of pronunciation such as intonation (nonlinguists sometimes talk
in terms of the inflections in the voice of the speaker), tempo or speed,
volume, and rhythm. (The term *suprasegmental* is used for these features of
pronunciation because in phonetic transcription—which seeks to represent
sounds in a scientific, accurate way—they are written above, i.e., *supra*,
segmental symbols. Segmental symbols in phonetic transcription are written
on the line and represent vowels, semi-vowels, and consonants.)

Now we can focus on linguistic terms for Black language. As I noted,
practically all linguists have directed their attention to Black Vernacular
English exclusively. To a large extent, this has been because the vernacular
is the form that differs most from the standard and is believed to interfere
with the acquisition of reading and writing skills. The impetus for research
on Black language in the 1960s was the hypothesis that a better understanding of Black Vernacular English might reveal the source of the problems in
skills acquisition by Black children. Although linguists realized that not all
Black school children speak the vernacular, they also realized that those
with the most severe academic problems do.

The kind of English that the term *Black Vernacular English* refers to
has previously been called Nonstandard Black English, Nonstandard Negro
English, colored lingo—it gets worse from here on. One thing we notice is
that the further we go back in time, the more derogatory the terms become.
Even during the 1960s, one came across studies purporting to be scientific
investigations of Black speech that offered up litanies of what I call

"mises"—mispronunciations, misarticulations, misconjugations, and, in the words of one misguided speech pathologist, "Mississippi-isms." There is now, thankfully, more enlightenment in the discussion of nonstandard Black language, with more people realizing that what we have are dialect differences, not deficits—differences similar to those existing, for example, between British English and American English. The differences are just that; they do not make either dialect "bad." It is more than a good guess that if the boards of directors of the Fortune 500 corporations, major network newsrooms, the White House, and Congress were monopolized by Black Vernacular English speakers, attitudes toward this kind of speech would be more benign. These points about the evaluation of Black Vernacular English cannot be overemphasized. The term *Black Vernacular English* is the current favorite because it does not call forth invidious comparisons, nor does it cast aspersions on its speakers.

There is another variety of Black English, singled out and discussed almost exclusively by the few linguists who are Black, that is labeled *Standard Black English*. This version of Black English is on a par with other standard varieties of English. The question is, how is it different from Black Vernacular English and other nonstandard varieties? The answer: It differs from them in the same way that all standard and nonstandard dialects differ from one another. In other words, it has none of the grammatical features that are considered nonstandard, but yet it does have distinctive features. Many of these are quite subtle; it is possible that most—but not all—of them are suprasegmental. Frequently, these distinctive features would identify a speaker as Black, just as comparable features in Received Pronunciation or Standard Australian English would identify speakers of these dialects as British and Australian respectively. The crucial point is that Standard Black English has none of the features that are commonly considered nonstandard, even though it does have features that distinguish it from other standard dialects. How can this be so? The reason is that only some aspects of standard English—any standard English—have been codified.

In addition to the grammatical properties of Black Vernacular English, there are other properties commonly associated with nonstandard forms of English. The list is long, but a few can be singled out:

(1) *Done* as a marker of perfect tense (*she done took it and gone*). *Done* can be heard in the speech of a good number of Whites in the South. Blacks use it in the South and in Northern urban areas.

(2) Double or multiple negatives. This phenomenon goes beyond double negatives, as in *he ain't got none*. One also finds *he ain't never got none* and even *he ain't never got none you cain't see*, meaning "he never has any that you can see." These sentences contain more than two negatives.

The following passage, taken from the transcript of a recording of a Black Vernacular English speaker, appears in William Laboy's (1972) cele-

brated article in which he demonstrates the use of Black Vernacular English
to express logical thought in elegantly structured discourse:

> Why? I'll tell you why. "CAUSE, you see, doesn' nobody really know that IT's
> a God, y'know, 'cause I mean I have seen black gods, pink gods, white gods,
> all color gods, and DON'T NOBODY know it's really a God. An' when they
> BE sayin' if you good, you goin' t'heaven, tha's bullshit, 'cause you AIN'T
> GOIN' TO NO HEAVEN, 'cause it ain't no heaven for you to go to. [Labov
> 1972:214–215, emphasis added]

Several grammatical features of this passage deserve mentioning. First, note
the absence of the prefix on *because* (the first item in Capital letters). Prefix
absence is, of course, not unique to Black Vernacular English, but it occurs
frequently enough to merit pointing it out. The second capitalized item is
what linguists call "existential *it*." This is the Black Vernacular English
equivalent of existential *there*, used in standard English dialects. The third
item in capitals, *don't nobody*, is what linguists refer to as "negative inversion." This clause in standard English would be *and nobody knows there's
really a God*. The next capitalized item is "invariant *be*," which refers to
actions or situations that occur repeatedly. Invariant *be* is one of the most
discussed grammatical features of Black Vernacular English. The last item
is an example of double negation, discussed above.

There are several features of grammar that distinguish Standard Black
English from its sister standard dialects: (1) words, their frequency of use,
and sometimes certain shades of meaning; (2) grammatical constructions;
and (3) perhaps most important of all, suprasegmental features. But again,
none of these grammatical features are associated with nonstandard speech.
Indeed, this is most likely a major reason for their persistence in Standard
Black English, which is spoken most often by middle-class Blacks.

So far, I have discussed two varieties of Black English: the standard one
and the nonstandard one, Black Vernacular English. Both have features
unique to Black dialects. In dealing with these two dialects, it should be
remembered that a hard and fast distinction cannot be drawn; the two varieties represent points on a continuum. Think of the situation as a line drawn
in linguistic space. At one end is Black Vernacular English, at the other,
Standard Black English, and between them, speech varieties that are more
or less like each. Black people do not all speak one or the other. They often
shift along the line, back and forth, in order to produce the speech they
feel most appropriate for whatever social situation they find themselves in.
This phenomenon is called code-shifting. In moving back and forth along
the continuum, speakers add or subtract particular traits of grammar to
make their speech either more or less like the standard dialect.

Accordingly, a churchwoman, for example, in reporting before her
church on the activities planned for Women's Day, might well employ a

more standard variety of English (but not necessarily one that could be accurately called Standard Black English) than she uses when sitting in the kitchen chatting with her dearest friend. In a way, that is parallel to what people do all around the world; when the churchwoman changes occasions, clothes, roles, and motives, she changes her speech to match them. A proper Baptist churchwoman wouldn't think of saying, "Ain't nothing we ain't gone do to have the best Women's Day we ever had." Then, too, there is even a time to say something like that when addressing the congregation, but one has to be intimately familiar with the culture's rules of behavior in order not to cause a serious breach of decorum. One has to know not only the rules, but also the rules for breaking the rules.

Black Vernacular English and Standard Black English are two varieties of Black English that can be characterized with reasonable accuracy, but they are the only ones at this stage in linguistic research. It should be kept in mind that these are language varieties with characteristics that are exclusive to Blacks—and, of course, scattered non-Black individuals and groups who have had intimate contact with Black people; examples are Whites and Asian-Americans raised in largely Black neighborhoods and Puerto Ricans raised in the eastern sector of the Black community of Harlem in New York City. These two varieties of Black English do not, however, account for all the distinctively Black dialects spoken in the U.S., nor do they account for all varieties—Black or non-Black—used by Blacks. Remember that some Blacks speak types of English that show no Black features, and some speak varieties of other languages—Cajun French, Louisiana French Creole, Spanish, Arabic, Portuguese, Cape Verdean Portuguese Creole, and various Native American languages. The linguistic heterogeneity not only of the Black population but also of the U.S. as a whole is often sorely underestimated.

Gullah

Another language variety spoken almost exclusively by Blacks is Gullah, first described by Lorenzo Dow Turner, the father of Black language study in the United States. Turner's detailed and scholarly study of Gullah, *Africanisms in the Gullah Dialect*, appeared in 1949. Gullah is spoken by several thousand people in the Sea Islands off South Carolina, Georgia, and Florida, in adjacent mainland areas, and in certain inland areas in Texas and Georgia. Other names for Gullah are *Guichee* and *Sea Island Creole*; Linguists usually use the term *Gullah* because it is not pejorative, unlike *Guichee*, and is more established than *Sea Island Creole*.

Any discussion of Black English calls for a discussion of Gullah because many scholars believe that Gullah is very much like—or essentially the same as—the creole English spoken during slavery, which today's Black English is probably descended from (Dillard 1972, Rickford 1977). According to the most widely supported theory on the origins of Black English, the earlier creole language gradually lost most of its creole grammatical traits as Black people gained more educational opportunities and were exposed to more standard forms of English. Today's Black English does not have enough unarguably creole grammatical features to be classified as a creole language.

Before discussing creole languages, I should point out a general preference for limiting *Black English* to Black Vernacular English, Standard Black English, and varieties in between. This delimitation of the term recognizes the basic, important difference between these dialects and Gullah: Gullah is a creole language, while they are not.

Creole languages can be defined from both historical and contemporary perspectives, but the historical is the more important for us because it emphasizes the defining property of creole languages: they descend from earlier contact languages. The contact languages in this case are those that formed from the interaction of West Africans and Europeans during the period of European commercial and, subsequently, colonial expansion. All languages undergo change, and those changes sometimes reflect influences from other languages. With contact languages, created often for purposes of commerce, the changes are so drastic that a new language is created. This new contact language—no one's native language—takes elements of grammar from the two or more languages that come into contact. (A native language is one learned from childhood as one grows up in a community.) In many cases, the vocabulary comes mainly from one language. Other aspects of grammar may come from another language or, possibly, may not be traceable directly to any previously existing language.

The new contact language has no native speakers—no one begins speaking it in childhood. The term for this type of language is *pidgin*. If a pidgin language becomes fixed in a community, used for the many types of social interactions communities engage in—not only for commerce—it may become the first language of more and more people; in other words, it may become nativized. Once nativized, it is referred to as a creole language.

Many of the creole languages that exist around the world have an African component in their history. This is notably true of creole languages of the Caribbean such as Haitian French Creole, Jamaican Creole English, and Guyanese Creole English. (The European language names included in the full names of these creoles indicate the language from which most of the vocabulary comes.) The ancestors of many of the native speakers of these creole languages came from West Africa. Not surprisingly, West African languages are represented in some areas of the grammars of modern-day creole languages (their vocabularies, for example). Gullah is in a sense kin to the other creoles of the Western Hemisphere in that it also carries an historical West African influence, as does Black English, although to a considerably lesser extent.

These creole languages also share other grammatical features. For example, they use the same basic pattern to express tense (past, present, and future) and aspect (the difference between *I ate it* and *I was eating it*). Because of this, we can also identify present-day creoles largely on the basis of their grammar.

The following passage in Gullah is part of a recollection about slavery:

> When dee Yankee come troo [through], I bin up dee country. An' I git dee fire 'n set dee house fire—set dee big house afire. An' I took out ewyting [everything] out dee house. I done it; dee Yankee done it . . . an ca' [carry] 'im owuh [over] dee udduh [other] side on dee street an' gi' [give] 'im somebody deh [there]. [Turner 1973 (1949):280; explanations in brackets added by editor]

There is not enough space to explain how the verb system in Gullah works, but several observations can be made. First, simply note how the verb forms in this passage differ from those that would be used in standard English. Notice also that certain sounds in standard English are consistently realized as other sounds in Gullah, for example, "th" as in *the* is "d" in Gullah, as in the Gullah word *dee*. Also, Gullah often has "w" where standard English has "v."

As noted, linguists believe that contemporary Gullah is much like the language that the majority of Blacks must have spoken during slavery. Assuming this to be true, why was Gullah retained in the areas where it is still spoken, while in other parts of the country, Blacks moved away from creole speech? The answer primarily has to do with isolation—geographical and social. The main areas where Gullah is spoken have always been heavily, if not mostly, Black. Formal education has been scant and poor, contact with mainstream culture limited. Note also that Black people were arriving directly from Africa as late as the 1850s, speaking, of course, their native West African languages. (This traffic in slaves was illegal at the time but continued, nevertheless.) Thus, the kind of intergroup contact involved in the creation of creole languages as well as the kind that aids in maintaining them, existed in the Gullah-speaking areas.

So Gullah was able to survive, especially in the Sea Islands, relatively unchanged. However, since World War II, Blacks in these areas have had increasingly more contact with the outside and better educational opportunities. With the development of a resort area, Hilton Head, on one of the Sea Islands, there has been a mild but constantly growing influx of Whites into the area.

These and other factors have combined to create a situation in which classic Gullah, described by Turner, is now found principally among older residents. Some of the younger residents with college experience cannot be recognized by their speech alone when they are talking to outsiders. So, in the Gullah area, as in other Black communities, there is a speech continuum. The Gullah area continuum ranges from classical Gullah all the way to Standard Black English. Gullah, then, has taken very rapid steps along the road of decreolization, the process whereby a language variety moves from creole status toward the standard dialect. This is the same process that was seen earlier in other Black communities and, to a certain extent, can still be witnessed now.

The integration of Gullah speakers into the main currents of American life has clear advantages for them, but it may turn out to be a tragic loss of the study of Black culture. The Sea Islands are perhaps the richest reservoir of African influences in Black America. If island culture disappears rapidly, scholars may never have the chance to gain a full understanding of it and its implications for clarifying Black identity. As a result of their continued poverty and limited formal education, Gullah speakers have in a sense helped to keep the African past alive so that the rest of the Black community might one day gain a deeper self-knowledge.

Who Speaks Black English

There remains the question of who speaks Black English. Can anything more than "some Black people" be said? I have already stated that not only do everyday Blacks speak Black English, but also, as my great-uncle used to say, "the bigshots and bigwigs," those high up on the socioeconomic scale. Even Black teachers of English in the public and private schools speak it (but not at school, in the normal situation). Given the many kinds of Black people who do indeed speak Black English, we have to take the foregoing discussion into consideration and ask, what kind of Black English do they speak and on what occasions do they speak it?

Because there are no large-scale empirical studies of the varieties of English spoken by different groups of Black people and the occasions on which they are spoken, it is difficult to talk about the distribution of language varieties in the Black community as a whole. At this point we can only say that certain kinds of people have been observed to speak such and such a variety, and then go on to draw whatever conclusions we can from these observations.

One point that empirical studies do make clear over and over again is that, as one would expect, the higher one's socioeconomic status, the more standard one's language. Socioeconomic status is based on income, education, residence type, and other objective factors, in addition to subjective factors, such as the status a person is assigned by others in the community.

In the absence of useful empirical data, I will make some observations based on what I observed in the Midwestern community in which I was raised during the 1950s and 1960s.

The Blacks there who were at the very top of the income pile—but not the educational achievement pile or the social status pile—were among those who spoke a Black Vernacular English. It lacked all the grammatical features associated with Black Vernacular English but had too many of them to be labeled Standard Black English. These were people who had acquired much real estate, had some businesses, but had no college background and in many cases little or no high school training. There were only a few people like this. They were prime examples of the pull-yourself-up-by-your-bootstraps philosophy, who had evidently not seen education as the means to pull themselves up.

They were followed by doctors and then dentists, speaking Standard Black English, but in no case that I was aware of, an ethnically unmarked, neutral standard English such as the network standard. It was Standard Black English all the way down through the middle class—including, among others, lawyers, school teachers, and postal employees (who had relatively high status, because post office jobs offered some of the most secure and highest paying positions available to Blacks; many were college-educated but preferred post office work to teaching). This group probably had expunged all Black Vernacular English traits from their speech at a relatively young age—if indeed their speech ever included them at all. When my parents' middle-class friends gathered (*Black* would have been redundant during those days; if they were friends, they had to be Black), one heard an occasional *ain't*, perhaps a double negative or two, but nothing that could reasonably be called Black Vernacular English. These nonstandard features of grammar were usually employed for stylistic effect. Among these same people, solidarity and intimacy typically correlated with more typically Black speech patterns, but more Black along the lines of suprasegmentals—intonation, rhythm, and tempo.

Members of this group normally did not use any non-Black speech variety, but there was a phenomenon referred to as "sounding White" or "talking White." One would sometimes hear a husband say of his wife, "Of course, she sounds just like she's White on the phone." This would often be followed by an anecdote involving some negative remarks about Blacks or an invitation or bit of information that was offered and would not have been had her racial identity been known. (Notice that it was typically women who sometimes talked White, which was more socially acceptable for women. In talking White, these women used a markedly standard form of English with pronunciation typical of Whites.)

Talking White was for the telephone only, however; there was no point in talking White in person. With Blacks, it would be interpreted negatively. This was probably because distinctively White behavior of any kind—dancing, dressing, singing—was generally held in low esteem. This was, no doubt, partly a reaction to racism, partly a product of cultural chauvinism created by the very insularity of the culture, but also, significantly, a product of a strong pride that survived adversity. Talking White face-to-face with Whites would not have helped to gain any advantage, of course, because one's Black identity would be apparent.

In some instances, there were middle-class Blacks who showed features in their speech that clearly marked it as Black Vernacular English—but only a few such features. I can think of two older Black teachers, both in their seventies, who today use invariant *be* (*She always be talking so loud*), which is part of the Black vernacular. Vernacular features are used only in small-group, intimate situations, however.

J. L. Dillard, in his book *Black English*, estimates that 80 percent of Afro-Americans speak Black Vernacular English, but he gives no basis for this figure. If Black Vernacular English is understood to include all of the grammatical features discussed in the literature on it, the figure is probably significantly lower, perhaps as low as 10 or 20 percent. The major problem in trying to pinpoint who speaks Black Vernacular English is that, in reality, people speak it to varying degrees. Many use some of the features included in the linguistic definition, but never all of them.

As to how many Blacks speak some form of Black English, whether standard or vernacular, my estimate would be 85 percent. Clearly, this is only an estimate. In my travels around the country in the last ten years, I have been surprised by how many Blacks—especially young people, thirty-five and under—speak an ethnically unmarked English even in informal, intimate, all-Black situations. This points to the major difference between what I find now in Northern urban areas and the situation that existed where I grew up: now there are significantly more Blacks who do not speak Black English. (Presumably, if they had some Black variety, they would use it in informal, all-black, small-group contexts.)

Current Issues

My remarks on who speaks Black English indicate that, generally, the English of Blacks is moving toward that of Whites. Certainly among younger Blacks there is more of a tendency than among older Blacks to speak in a way that is not distinctively Black. These remarks are in line with what Black English scholars have said about Black English since a significant number of them began studying it in the early 1960s. In an ongoing process of decreolization (discussed above), Black English has increasingly lost its creole grammatical features. In addition, in a process of convergence, Black English has increasingly lost those grammatical features that make it distinctively Black.

In the spring of 1985, William Labov, an eminent linguist at the University of Pennsylvania who was responsible for the resurgence of interest in Black English studies in the 1960s, announced that, contrary to what most scholars believed, his research group had discovered evidence of divergence. The implication of his statement was that Black English was not becoming more like White dialects (or standard English, for that matter), that is, converging. Instead, it was diverging: it was in the process of developing even more distinctively Black grammatical features as it went through the process of grammatical change that all languages undergo over time. (Note that no one today speaks the English of Shakespeare and his contemporaries.)

Labov claimed that this linguistic divergence was due to the increasing isolation of low-income Blacks in inner city ghettos such as those of Philadelphia, where his research group discovered the evidence for their claim of divergence. Sociological studies had already indicated a pattern of increasing residential segregation in major American urban areas. The language of the Philadelphia Black community, as that of all isolated groups, was changing independently of the language spoken in communities socially separated from it. (Generally, the more communication there is between groups, the more their language is likely to be homogeneous and undergo the same linguistic changes in grammar over time.) After Labov's announcement of the findings of his research group, several linguists challenged his evidence. However, even if the evidence is invalidated, there are general sociolinguistic principles that predict the probability of just the kind of divergence Labov claimed.

Labov saw this divergence as reason for great concern. There was already general concern among linguists and educators over the widespread educational failure of many Black pupils in inner-city schools and the fact that this failure seemed to be worsening over time. Labov also felt that the language division was caused by decreasing personal contact between Blacks and Whites, and that the most effective way for Black children to learn other dialects of English in addition to their own dialects was through more interaction with Whites. He noted that contrary to widespread opinion, the mass media had had little influence on the speech patterns of Blacks—or any other group for that matter.

First of all, it should be pointed out that understanding the role of language in the widespread failure of Black students in the inner-city schools presents several problems. Joshua Fishman, a well-known linguist, has noted that differences between standard and nonstandard dialects in several countries—Switzerland, Finland, Japan, to name some—are much more radical than those existing between Black English Vernacular and the Standard American English of American schools. Yet, one finds significantly less educational failure in those countries. Thus, while language differences can have some effect on the ease with which a child acquires literacy skills, there is no reason to believe they will actually hinder the child from acquiring them. The conclusion that comes from a number of studies is that the real problems are attitudinal and social and are related to the general problem of institutional racism in America, that is, racism that permeates the very structure and daily workings of all societal institutions—so much so that individuals do not have to be racist for racism to effect the lives of minorities. Frantz Fanon, the widely read Black psychiatrist from Martinique, was the first to articulate the theory of institutional racism (in *The Wretched of the Earth*), and it has been elaborated by others. Institutional racism is the culprit involved in many problems, among them low teacher expectations and disrespect for the home language and culture of inner-city students.

Now let us consider the acquisition by Blacks of dialects other than Black Vernacular English. (Remember that Standard Black English has never been implicated in the educational failure of Black students.) First, the acquisition of standard English would appear to be more important than simply acquiring White dialects. This is true because many of the White dialects in question are nonstandard ones also, and there is no reason to believe that acquiring them would have any positive effect on educational achievement. Furthermore, it is quite unwarranted to assume that the most effective way for Black children to learn standard English is through increased interaction with Whites. This view ignores an important factor, if not the most important one, in the acquisition of standard English by Black Vernacular English speakers: contact with middle-class Blacks who speak some form of standard English.

Consequently, we must separate the issue of Blacks acquiring White dialects from that of Blacks acquiring standard dialects. In order to explain any divergence between Black Vernacular English and standard English specifically, we must consider not only Black–White segregation but also the increasing separation between middle- and lower-income Blacks as a result of the widespread move by middle-class Blacks to better neighborhoods outside of the inner cities, an especially strong trend over the last thirty years. Historically, Blacks not speaking some form of standard English, have in most cases learned the standard through contact with standard-speaking Blacks, not Whites. One can begin to appreciate the truth of this statement in considering that, overwhelmingly, Blacks have had more overall contact with Blacks than with Whites.

We must also carefully scrutinize the underlying assumption in Labov's statements, which is shared by many scholars and social commentators. This assumption is that the lot of Black people in the U.S. would improve, educationally and otherwise, if more Blacks acquired standard English.

Obviously, standard English is an important tool in our society. There is a consensus that it is the schools' job to teach it, and it is incumbent upon teachers in the nation's schools to do it well. Some people, however, go on to claim that standard English is essential for overcoming the economic handicaps facing Blacks. This is not true.

Standard English is indeed important for some types of jobs, not all. There are many well-paying jobs for which the ability to speak it is irrelevant, for example, the overwhelming majority of skilled labor jobs. While it is true that the service sector in the U.S. accounts for a steadily increasing percentage of all jobs and that service jobs typically require standard English, there remain many jobs for which standard English is not required.

Also, we must ask, if Black Vernacular English has economically handicapped Blacks, why have the nonstandard varieties of English spoken by Whites not economically handicapped the American Whites who speak them? After all, the great majority of Whites, and of the entire population, speak nonstandard English. Many people are not aware of this fact. Why are the economic woes of Whites, where they exist, not blamed on their nonstandard English? This discussion of economic handicaps, as other discussions, has a tendency to sidestep the fundamental issue of institutional racism.

This is not to deny that more stigma is often attached to nonstandard Black dialects than to nonstandard White ones. The real question is, why is nonstandard Black speech more stigmatized? As students of language attitudes know, it is because its speakers are more stigmatized. After all, what would happen if all Black people in the U.S. suddenly woke up tomorrow morning speaking like the president and vice-president or the British monarch? Even with such a scenario, Blacks would still be faced with problems of structured inequality. Ultimately, we must face the fact that language for the most part reflects social realities; it does not create them.

Bibliography

ABRAHAMS, ROGER D. 1976. *Talking Black*. Rowley, Mass.: Newbury House.

"Are Black and White Vernaculars Diverging? Papers from the NWAVE XIV Panel Discussion." *American Speech* (Spring 1987) 62(1).

BAUGH, JOHN. 1983. *Black Street Speech: Its History, Structure, and Survival*. Austin: University of Texas Press.

BURLING, ROBBINS. 1973. *English in Black and White*. New York: Holt, Rinehart and Winston.

CHAMBERS, JOHN, JR., ed. 1983. *Black English: Educational Equity and the Law*. Ann Arbor: Karoma.

DILLARD, J. L. 1972. *Black English: Its History and Usage in the United States*. New York: Random House.

FISHMAN, JOSHUA. 1972. "What Has the Sociology of Language to Say to the Teacher?" in *Language in Sociocultural Change*, Anwar S. Dil, ed. Stanford: Stanford University Press.

HATALA, EILEEN. 1976. "Environmental Effects on White Students in Black Schools." (Unpublished Master's essay, University of Pennsylvania.)

KOCHMAN, THOMAS. 1981. *Black and White Styles in Conflict*. Chicago: University of Chicago Press.

LABOV, WILLIAM. 1972. "The Logic of Nonstandard English," in *Language in the Inner City: Studies in the Black English Vernacular*, William Labov, ed., 201–240. Philadelphia: University of Pennsylvania Press.

———. 1980. "Is There a Creole Speech Community?" in *Theoretical Orientations in Creole Studies*. Albert Valdman and Arnold Highfield, eds., 369–388. New York: Academic Press.

RICKFORD, JOHN R. 1977. "The Question of Prior Creolization in Black English." In *Pidgin and Creole Linguistics*, Albert Valdman, ed., 190–221. Bloomington: Indiana University Press.

SMITHERMAN, GENEVA. 1977. *Talkin' and Testifyin'*. Boston: Houghton Mifflin.

SPEARS, ARTHUR. 1984. "Towards a New View of Black English." *The Journal* 1(1):94–103.

TURNER, LORENZO DOW. 1973 (1949). *Africanisms in the Gullah Dialect*. Ann Arbor: University of Michigan Press.

7

American Catalogues of Asian Brides

ARA WILSON

THE WEST PRODUCES AND CONSUMES vast quantities of information concerning "exotic" peoples and cultures: those to the north, south, and east of it. Professional anthropologists supply scholarly knowledge about "other" cultures based on their fieldwork in far-off lands. But the discipline of anthropology has never held a monopoly on representing foreign peoples and places, and the academic media of ethnographic books, films, articles, and lectures are not the only source of cross-cultural information available to the general population. Representations of the rest of the world occur in abundance and in a myriad of forms. The written descriptions in literature, in the mass media, and in vacation travel guides are supplemented by the visual depictions provided by postcards, pornography, and movies. The anthropological, the artistic, and the commercial renditions present the exotic "others" of Africa, Asia, and Oceania to European and American audiences.

These texts, these words and images representing distant cultures, are themselves elements of American culture, produced by and for people of the West. In the hands of the anthropologist they are equivalent to the masks and myths of faraway cultures and can be analyzed towards the same end: to reveal the cultural themes and patterns that shape their form, meaning, and use. In this case the ethnographic gaze turns homeward. By understanding how "we" represent "them," the "other," the anthropologist illuminates not only what "we" see in "them," but also what we see in ourselves.[1]

This chapter examines the representation of Southeast Asian women in the "mail-order marriage" trade.[2] "Introductory" or "pen-pal" services sell photographs, descriptions, and addresses of "Oriental" women, usually Southeast Asian, to American, European, and Australian men for large profits.

> *Sometimes you have to look to another culture to find that special girl. Faithful Oriental girls make the best wives—by far. . . . Many feel it's just about the only way left to find someone who is sweet and unspoiled.*
>
> *(Advertisement)*

These matchmaking enterprises construct and sell images of the Oriental woman as an "other." They do not literally sell women from catalogues, and these women are not the "picture brides" familiar from the time of early Asian immigration to North America, when men selected spouses from an album of photographs (Kobayashi 1978). Rather, Rainbow Ridge, Paradise Connections, and a hundred or so other North American companies offer "introductions" to "Oriental ladies" in the form of catalogues. Clients who subscribe (for fees of one hundred to five hundred dollars per year) can write to and possibly marry the women described. In addition to the monthly or bimonthly catalogues, more costly services are offered as well: for example, information booklets, such as the Asian Perspective Company's "From 'Dear Lady' to 'I do.'"

Basically what these agencies provide is access to women, rather than the women themselves. How do the pen-pal companies obtain this access? They place ads in Southeast Asian newspapers, particularly in the Philippines, which solicit women interested in corresponding with Western men. The women submit their photograph, address, and a description; some agencies require the completion of a detailed questionnaire asking for intimate information, especially sexual history and physical appearance. Thus, these women supply the raw materials of faces, names, and addresses (Belkin 1986, Krich 1986).

Mail-order marriage firms then sell the addresses and descriptions of Southeast Asian women in the form of subscription catalogues. Their product is text: brochures, catalogues, and letters, which present information on specific women. However, the way these businesses market access to a particular Oriental woman is by selling the representation of Asian women in general; the literature distributed circulates a construction of the "other." In the language of Levi-Strauss (1969), Asian women have become complete "signs" in the mail-order marriage trade: pictures and words exchanged and shared.

"Oriental" clearly means something in this market for brides: it has significance. How the catalogues represent Asians and Asian qualities reveals what the Oriental woman signifies to the packagers and their clientele. Examining the mail-order catalogues as cultural texts means reading them closely, but rather than focusing on the content of individual elements (such as the photograph and description of one specific woman), each portion is treated as a part of a larger whole. Such an examination attends to themes or patterns in the features that are stressed, repeated, and omitted in the presentations of Asian women.

This view of the mail-order catalogues separates the text from the people behind their production: the Southeast Asian women and the matchmaker entrepreneurs. As texts, women's self-representations can travel from Filipina women to companies in the United States, whose agents select, edit, cut and paste to assemble their new text, the catalogue. This text, too, travels; as language and pictures, it will be interpreted by those who look at it.[3]

To the anthropologist, and to other readers, these catalogues do not describe "real" Southeast Asian women neutrally or objectively. The creators of these documents construct imagined Oriental ladies that draw upon traditional representations of Asian women. The Orient has kindled the fantasies of the Occident for hundreds of years, with Asian women consistently entering into Western imagery as exotic, enigmatic, submissive, and erotic (Alloula 1986).

The mail-order marriage companies rely on this collective representation of Asian women in selling their services. In order to peddle their catalogues, the companies must represent Asian women in media, and these representations form part of the overall depiction that this chapter analyzes. Classified advertisements for agencies like Interpacific and Asian Worldwide Services appear in the back pages of magazines ranging from pornographic publications to *Rolling Stone,* and, until recently, the politically progressive *Mother Jones* magazine. Here are two typical ads:

> *Attractive Orientals Overseas. Singles Seeking Friendship, Correspondence.*
>
> *Filipinas! Young! Beautiful! Love to meet Americans. Brochure $2.*

These lines are short and telegraphic, relying on the reader's prior understanding of what "Oriental" means to catch his interest. The men who answer these classified ads (paying up to ten dollars to receive more information) share a cultural imagery of the Oriental woman and know what they want in her. These classifieds aim at reaching as wide an audience as possible with vague yet inviting phrases, so they stress friendship and "singles" over marriage.

The companies send brochures and sample catalogues to respondents in order to strengthen the sales pitch. This literature offers concrete and persuasive testimony from satisfied customers of the respective firms. They mention the great number of pen pals they have brought together and successful matches they have initiated. One of the operations, Asian Perspectives, consists of a husband and wife team who are themselves the product of the matchmaking trade. The husband, George Elkington, writes:

> My adorable little Asian princess and I are so deliriously happy with one another that we wish to share our experience with others like yourself.

Physically, the catalogues, the mainstay of the pen-pal services, consist of photographs and descriptions printed in black and white on cheap paper. Asian Perspectives' booklet is bordered in red; like the others, its basic format resembles catalogues of machine parts, hardware, or seeds.

The photographs attract the eyes' attention immediately. A single photograph, an image of a person, seems to offer an objective truth: this is the real Asian woman. However, the rows of two-dimensional images repetitiously lining the pages appear standardized and mass-produced. These flat, black or white-and-gray multiple images of Asian women are almost all the same size and mostly show faces. All the women look posed: self-conscious set-ups for the photographer, and for another's gaze. In some sense, these are passport photos for foreign eyes and a ticket out of Southeast Asia.

Some of the photographs actually are passport photos, but most strongly resemble American high school yearbook pictures. The unmistakable frontal or three-quarter head shot with hazy lighting, the traces of airbrush, a soft focus, and the youthful appearance of the subjects strongly suggest this genre. In fact, a woman in one of the catalogues appears in cap and gown. The association with school simultaneously suggests youth and marriageability, while demonstrating education and modernization. Other images are awkward snapshots, with instant-camera displays of the women's figures and surroundings.

Asian faces, and occasional Asian bodies, offer themselves up in columns and rows for choice and selection. Their framed faces, their self-conscious posture, the lack of artistry in the composition and lighting, and the naivete and familiarity of the format of the catalogue all suggest an innocence and vulnerability that the facial expressions of the young women confirm. In fact, they are vulnerable, having submitted their images to be sold, gazed at, and perhaps selected; their very appearance in the catalogue testifies to their need. These photographs offer the Oriental women to the viewer.

The images offer no ethnographic illustrations of the Orient: there are no exotic customs depicted, and markers of Asian culture are minimal. The Orient is not made into a fetish as it is in the artistic traditions of Orientalism, which painted the Orient through the symbols of Asia: opium pipes, kimonos, or harems (Alloula 1986). In fact, the West appears in frequent guises: the cap and gown, denim jackets, a cheerleader's outfit, and a checkered table cloth. These American elements, like the yearbook photo style, render Oriental women familiar and make them more American. This shortens the distance between the two regions—American and Asian—and makes any potential marriage less exogamous. In the pictures, the only sign of Asian background remains the phenotypic display of the women's faces.

Beneath these images of faces and bodies, and sometimes over them, are printed identifying numbers. This labeling offers the starkest demonstration of the market character of these pen-pal services: numbers cataloguing women to facilitate access to them. The digits also hint at large quantities of women who must be organized, labeled, and arranged for convenient selection and service. In addition, the cataloguing system of numbers and letters suggests the ability to organize an expanding supply of available women. It indicates that this company hosts a large supply of women who are available to the reader: greater availability of and greater accessibility to a vast supply of women means better service and a better company.

The identifying numbers link the numerous adjacent photographs to the specific descriptions beneath them. The images are satisfying as visual stimulation that seems human and real, but they are not complete. They provoke fascination and curiosity; who these specific women are is unclear. Words provide what the pictures cannot: identity and knowledge. By selecting the relevant details for description—name, age, and a few key words—the words offer a way of interpreting the photograph and the identity of the woman. The written word has authority while the picture has reality; it adds knowledge to the evocative image. The descriptions make the woman more specific and more familiar, thus making selection feasible and even necessary. This selection requires the numbers, because the relation between the photographs and the captions assigned to them seems arbitrary. Consider this caption:

> Flora (25) Philippines. 5'1'', 104. Protestant. Dental Assistant. Prefers corresponding with men 30 to 40 years of age.

Flora could be any one of the faces on this page, but her number, 4F, links the description with the photograph of the woman with the wide smile wearing the simple V-neck shirt.

While the pictures present Western or Westernized images, the written words reveal what the agencies think are desirable traits in the marriage market. Captions beneath the photographs include first names and descriptions of the numbered women, including their ages (usually young), nationality (usually the Philippines), height, weight, hobbies, jobs, and wishes. Sometimes these captions are in a woman's "own" words:

> *14F Imelda (17) Philippines. 5'1. 108. "Interest—*
> *must be Catholic, all ages. I'm pure Filipina citi-*
> *zen have good looking, good personality and*
> *body slim."*

Sometimes they are in the third person:

> *Norma (23) Philippines. A saleslady who enjoys*
> *volleyball and decorating the home in her spare*
> *time.*

The women's names, hobbies, and occupations are not Asian markers. The names are frequently Western. The hobbies, such as lawn tennis and tandem bicycle, are also Western, if somewhat eccentric: this makes the women familiar yet different. These recreational activities generally signify good, clean fun.

Religion is rarely mentioned, but when cited, it is almost always Christian. The occupations listed for the women sound familiar, and fall within the proper sphere of our own sexual division of labor: secretary, teacher, nurse, and student. These jobs are appropriate for women in the labor market and in the marriage market; they prepare a woman for wifely duties and complement men's work, while demonstrating a fair degree of competence and responsibility.

The captions reinforce the impression of innocence and vulnerability conveyed by the photographs through the quirky and unrealistic hobbies mentioned and through the women's expressed desire to serve. Much of the content concerns emotions and wishes: "sincerity" and "honesty" and "friendship." Significantly absent from these lines is any mention of economics or politics in their lives, in Southeast Asia, or in the world.

Many of the descriptions are in broken English. Their errors in our language make them seem awkward with speech in general, naive, and ignorant, which heightens the impression of vulnerability. The native English speaker has an expertise that they lack; since the pen-pal relationship involves an exchange of letters, of language, and the introduction occurs through printed media, this relationship between the American and the Asian is asymmetrical. The women are at a disadvantage in any communication, and they are the ones who speak first, through the catalogues. What kind of conversation can they start with their fractured language?

In fact, the visual and rhetorical vulnerability of these women is a selling point: it makes them attractive and desirable. In addition to the representations of specific women, the brochures offer more direct explanations of why Asian women make good wives. The agencies' scripts offer a kind of ethnographic report on Asia, providing facts that demonstrate what Asian women are like, and how it is that they are available. It is explained that the economic situation and the Oriental tradition of Asia produce women who desire to please a man, which, according to this literature, is the quality American men want. The poverty of Southeast Asia means that these women find shelter and solid meals luxuries. The low standard of living in these regions makes Asian women unmaterialistic but longing to escape to a better life. Thus, they will be grateful.

One way that this literature demonstrates the value of Asian women is to compare them, either explicitly or implicitly, with American women. The pen-pal material knowingly presents American men's criticisms of American women: that they are rude and sloppy or demanding, power-hungry feminists. Disillusionment, disgust, and dissatisfaction with the disorder of North American women pervades the prose. For example:

> Naturally the idea of wooing and winning the exotic beauty by mail is not for every male, so this whole idea might be a turn-off for the guy who wants to convert the local hash-slinger into the world's most perfect wife.

According to this literature, Asian women are, for some American men, the only acceptable marriage option. For these men who find women in the United States too loud, too unfeminine, or too close, matchmaker services offer subscriptions to their catalogues.

This background material explains how tradition, or culture, make these women so different from American women and, therefore, such good wives. The following example is unusual in its mention of Western influence, but the general message is typical:

> Although indoctrinated in Western culture and religion, the women of the Philippines still cling to some of their own customs. For them the man is lord. They treat their men with respect. The old women still teach the young girls how to please their future husbands and lovers.

The ethnography of the mail-order agencies presents Southeast Asian women as desperate to correspond with and possibly marry North American men. They are unspoiled, unliberated, devoted, obedient, and faithful because of their cultural ways and their economic positions.

Race, though essential in marking these women as the "other," does not appear in these discussions. What does stand out are elements that are part of the overall meaning of "Oriental": the faces, the broken English, the vulnerability, and the devotion. Phenotype, culture, and economics substitute for the all-encompassing, but unspoken, factor of "race." The almost complete lack of reference to children or reproduction magnifies the silence on race; the specter of miscegenation is absent, and the interracial nature of the potential matches is not discussed. The thrust of the mail-order marriage literature is to bring these women closer, to render them familiar and Western and make them marriageable.

The ethnographic situation of Southeast Asia is considered only for its instrumental value in providing the commodities of subservient wives. The aims of knowing about the Orient in these brochures are not conquest or exploration or pure knowledge of the unknown and exotic, as they were in Orientalist work during colonial and postcolonial periods (Said 1978, Alloula 1986). Rather, the aims are to make use of the images, services, and personages of Asian women, who are conquered and complacent and almost Westernized but with just enough Oriental flavor left to be different. They are not so American that they are noisy hash-slingers, and they are not too Oriental, which would make them unmarriageable. What "Oriental"—the race and culture conflated under one term—signifies is a bargain for the First World consumer in desired services and security. The information presented in these catalogues conveys this idea in a streamlined and efficient manner, without excess or lyrical exoticism.

Where, then, is the mystery of the Orient and the eroticism of the exotic? The representations in the catalogues are not sensuously alluring or romantically enigmatic. When references to the erotic aspects of Asian women appear, they seem almost an afterthought. For example, one brochure says of Oriental brides:

> They are giving and caring—while at the same time romantic and sexy.

In general, the catalogues exhibit a dearth of sensuality or sexuality in the photographs and in the descriptions.

The absence of explicit erotica presupposes the collective cultural fantasies of the Orient. With their generalizing shorthand, the classified advertisements for mail-order marriage agencies exploit the sexual implications of "Oriental," but they need not and do not elaborate those themes. Excluding explicit references to Oriental sexuality allows the mail-order catalogues to present the women as innocent and naive and, therefore, attractive. The catalogues suggest a latent eroticism in these women, who inherit cultural skills and values that make them gifted lovers. Preceded by the Orientalist legacy, by the depictions of geishas and harems and Oriental ladies, the pen-pal services need merely allude to these representations in order to conjure up the image of alluring Oriental women.

The absence of an explicit erotic dimension in these texts serves another purpose. It allows for private fantasy. Each viewer can construct his own picture of the Oriental women, drawing on the cultural Orientalist conventions of the enigmatic Oriental lover; he merely pays for the representations of specific women in the catalogues. In this way the customer's construction of an Asian woman is his alone; it is not mass-produced by the agencies to be shared by all. The viewer's fantasizing is promoted by the form of the catalogues. In the repetition of pictures and descriptions, each separate face and caption is embedded within a whole field of representations of Asian women. This whole evokes Oriental women generally, rather than providing concrete and complete information on one woman. There is room for wondering: "Who are these women?" "Who is number 298F?" "Which one is Venus, and which is Dinah?" The structure of the catalogues offers an overwhelming selection of Oriental ladies, and sparks curiosity about individual ones. This interest pushes the viewer to identify a particular woman, to put together the picture, number and words, to make her more whole and distinct.

The matchmaking sequence begins with the public, shared representation of the general exotic "other" but, with the catalogues, becomes more private, allowing private fantasy and private ownership. For additional fees, a customer can purchase from the company the original letter of one woman, thereby making her communication his private property and limiting the access of other men to her. The progression of intimacy, as individual women take on specific and recognizable identities for the reader, corresponds to an increased need for privacy. The purported goal of this courtship is marriage, which, after all, procures complete private access to (and, in some senses, ownership of) one woman, removing her from the supply of available women in the marriage market.

The shift from public to private representations means a shift from the collective erotic fantasy to a specific romantic one. But the implications of "Oriental" still exist, and they shape the attraction to a particular Southeast Asian woman. And though these catalogues are not pornographic—they are not sexually explicit, nor do they contain degrading depictions of Asian women—the display of the women involves relations that parallel pornographic relations. The creation of the catalogues, their sale, and their use is for American men, not for Southeast Asian women. This power imbalance is furthered by the content of the catalogues, which present their subjects, the Southeast Asian women, as vulnerable and needy. Women offer themselves to men for selection and for fantasy in a representational form familiar to pornography: images of women coupled with identifying captions. The form, the content, and the purpose of the catalogues render the Southeast Asian woman powerless and encourage a voyeuristic objectification of Oriental women as the "other."

The attraction of American men for Asian women is not a timeless, spontaneous, biological phenomenon. Desire expresses itself in specific cultural forms and emerges within a culture at a particular period in time. Sexuality and attraction do not form a "natural" realm separate from the "cultural" realms of kinship, politics, and economics; rather, they take their place within the overall system of social relations. Where inequality and domination exist among the members of a society or community, sexuality and "eros" will embody this pattern of relationships (Hartsock 1983).

The phenomenon of mail-order marriage occurs in America (and Europe and Australia) in the late twentieth century, when interracial marriage is (relatively) acceptable and where mass-media technology is available.

Though it is interracial, the desire for the Oriental other is not an instance of racial egalitarianism. Frantz Fanon, writing about racial relations in the Caribbean, argues that the attraction of one race for another, in fact, manifests racial inequality and hostility or domination. This especially describes colonial and postcolonial situations, such as those of Southeast Asia, where relations with the "other" society have been politically and economically exploitative (Fanon 1967). The allure of Asian women stems from their Oriental heredity, which signifies eroticism, enigma, and weakness.

Mail-order marriage companies design their products with a specific population in mind, anticipating the desires of their clients. These catalogues are tailored texts, which can reveal something about their readers. Who is it that wishes to court through pen-pal agencies? And what people desire the vulnerability and powerlessness of the depicted Asian women? The mail-order marriage trade serves American men who are neither colonizers, explorers, nor conquerors. Their clients do not yearn to invade foreign terrain or to violently pillage and plunder the Orient. As pen pals, these men stay at home and receive letters through the safe and slow mediation of the mail. American women are too loud, too pushy, too strong, and too forceful for them, and Southeast Asian women, who need and want them, offer an available alternative.

The catalogues do draw on an ideology of chivalry and offer an opportunity to rescue an Oriental damsel in distress. The matchmaking publications in this way resemble "Sponsor a Child" advertisements, presenting vulnerable and innocent Asian women trapped in Third World poverty. Southeast Asian women are suitable heroines in a rescue fantasy, because, according to these representations, they need and want to be rescued and protected by American men.

The intended audience for these catalogues seeks to reproduce or return to a perceived older order, where men had unambiguous power over women. In some sense, these men want to rescue and marry the girl next door, only the girl next door is now the hash-slinger. Southeast Asian women, less urban, less modern, less spoiled, offer the men old-fashioned power and service. The following excerpt makes the point:

> Joe P., Chicago, says: Every evening there's a hot bath waiting for me. She bathes me, dries me off, and even helps me into my robe. Later she gives me a refreshing massage as only an Oriental can. She's a fantastic cook, has a great sense of humor, enjoys staying home, and is always there when I

*need her. Now honestly—what more could a man
ask for?*

(Advertisement)

Representations of "others" are not windows onto foreign lands: they do
not transparently convey "reality." Rather than being a window onto
Southeast Asian women, the mail-order catalogues more closely resemble a
painting: the catalogues obtain their value not because they "realistically"
present Southeast Asian women but because they evoke meanings and engender fantasies in the viewers.

"Texts"—masks or myths, paintings or catalogues—exist only through
the people who create them, buy them, and use them. The anthropological
gaze must look up from the pages of the mail-order marriage catalogue
to encounter the American men and Southeast Asian women beyond the
representations.

Notes

This paper derives from shorter versions presented at the American Anthropological
Association Annual Meeting in Philadelphia, December 1986, and the Northeastern
Anthropological Association Meeting at the University of Massachusetts, March
1987.

For their references, advice, and encouragement I thank Vincent Crapanzano,
Elizabeth Brusco, Katherine Wilson, and especially my editor, Johnnetta B. Cole.
For his compassionate labors I offer William Wilson my gratitude.

1. Anthropologists and students of anthropology have already analyzed specific
ethnographic texts as cultural documents, demonstrating how anthropological
writers construct the "other." See, for example, Clifford and Marcus (1986) and
Said (1978).
2. There are "introductory" services specifically to Latin American and to European women as well, although the "Oriental mail-order marriage" trade receives
the most publicity (Belkin 1986, Krich 1986). The term "Oriental" lumps together women from many different Asian countries whose identity derives from
its geographical relationship to the Occident, the West.
3. The analysis of these works draws on Barthes (1983), Ricoeur (1971), and Alloula
(1986) for their methods of studying text. Barthes's analysis of the written descriptions accompanying fashion photography and Alloula's interpretation of
colonial French postcards depicting Moroccan women were especially useful.

References

ALLOULA, MALEK. 1986. *The Colonial Harem.* Myrna Godzich and Wlad Godzich,
trans. Minneapolis: University of Minnesota Press.

ASAD, TALAL. 1973. "The European Images of Non-European Rule" in *Anthropology and the Colonial Encounter*, T. Asad, ed., 103–118. New York: Humanities Press.

BARTHES, ROLAND. 1983. *The Fashion System*. Matthew Ward and Richard Howard, trans. New York: Farrar, Straus and Giroux.

BELKIN, LISA. 1986. "The Mail-Order Marriage Business." *The New York Times Magazine*, Sunday, May 11: 28pp.

CLIFFORD, JAMES and GEORGE MARCUS, eds. 1986. *Writing Culture: The Poetics and Politics of Ethnography*. Berkeley: University of California Press.

FANON, FRANTZ. 1967. *Black Skin, White Masks*. C. L. Markmann, trans. New York: Grove Press.

HARTSOCK, NANCY. 1983. *Money, Sex and Power: Towards a Feminist Historical Materialism*. Boston: Northeastern University Press.

KOBAYASHI, CASSANDRA. 1978. "Sexual Slavery in Canada: Our Herstory." *The Asianadian* Fall/Winter: 4–7.

KRICH, JOHN. 1986. "Here Come the Brides." *Mother Jones* 40 (11) February/March: 34–46.

LEVI-STRAUSS, CLAUDE. 1969. *The Elementary Structures of Kinship*. James Harle Bell, John Richard Von Sturmer, and Rodney Needham, trans. Boston: Beacon Press.

RICOEUR, PAUL. 1971. "Model of the Text: Meaningful Action Considered as a Text." *Social Research* 38: 529–562.

SAID, EDWARD. 1978. *Orientalism*. New York: Vintage Books, Random House.

8

Sexism and the Construction of Reality: An Afro-American Example

SALLY PRICE

The literature on the art of the Suriname Maroons depicts men as active artists producing decorative woodcarvings as gifts of love for their women, who are passive connoisseurs. This paper explores the ways by which Maroon women use their own arts to affirm their social relationships and to reflect on them. It also traces misconceptions about Maroon women and their arts to notions of gender that are held by ethnographers and by the Maroons themselves.

THROUGHOUT THEIR HISTORY, the Suriname Maroons (often called "Bush Negroes") have excited the romantic imaginations of outsiders—from the 18th-century soldiers who fought against them in their original wars of liberation to the 20th-century anthropologists who live among them, and from the coastal Surinamers who see them walking barefoot in the streets of the capital city to the foreign tourists who sign up for one-day jungle excursions to the interior. All of these observers have been captivated by the story of the Maroons' heroic struggle for freedom from slavery, by their striking independence in the South American rain forest, and by the visible debt their way of life owes to the many African societies from which their early ancestors came.

Two aspects of Maroon society—the place of women and the role of art in social life—have attracted considerable attention and have contributed importantly to the image of Maroon life as it is constructed by non-Maroons. This paper, based on long-term fieldwork with the Saramaka Maroons, suggests that the social and artistic life of women has generally been misunderstood by outsiders at least in part because of ideas about gender that are held by both outsiders and by Maroons themselves.

The fascination of Westerners with the place of women in Maroon societies can be traced to two central features of Maroon life: a strongly matrilineal kinship system and the evident independence of women in many contexts. Because residence, political succession, ritual involvements, marriage prohibitions, land tenure, and countless other aspects of their life are regulated by a kinship system centered on relations traced through women, outsiders are often inspired to speculate as to the political/ritual/social influence that they imagine Maroon women must exercise within their communities. Because they often see Maroon women conducting themselves quite independently—maintaining a household separate from their husband's, growing their own food in an individually owned garden, rearing children largely as single parents, and, in the most literal sense, paddling their own canoes—many outsiders assume that Maroon women's freedom from the domination of men extends over the whole of their domestic life. In other words, the pivotal position of women in defining the basic structure of social relations has often been misread as a central role for women in directing social life itself; matriliny has been read as matriarchy.

The evident independence of Maroon women in housing, subsistence activities, child rearing, and intervillage transportation is occasionally misinterpreted as a kind of 1970s-style liberation; women's independence is viewed as their own conscious choice. As a result of this kind of speculation, the literature on Maroons is sprinkled with characterizations of the following sort:

> The women essentially rule the entire people because they are the main ones who deal with the gods (Kersten 1770:137).

> It is chiefly the women who see that the ancestral and village customs are enforced. They are the guardians of the ancient traditions and customs of the race (Kahn 1931:98).

> . . . the [Maroon] woman, . . . jealous of her independence from the man, places her pride in being able to get along on her own (Hurault 1961:158).

> The women . . . participate fully in the . . . major decisions about village life. Women sit on the high councils, equal to the men (Counter and Evans 1981:92).

This image, frequently reinforced by an ideologically motivated glorification of Maroon society, sometimes leads to ironic distortions. For example, the explicit purpose of the custom of menstrual seclusion is to protect men's ritual powers from pollution. This period of seclusion is viewed by Maroon women as one of the more distasteful, inconvenient, and burdensome necessities of their life. However, two recent male visitors whose only verbal contact with the Maroons was through an interpreter misrepresent the periodic banishment of women from social life by presenting the menstrual hut as the location of a kind of feminist escape from the burdens of daily life, asserting that

> rules governing the practice [of menstrual seclusion] are made by the women themselves . . . the women seem to enjoy this opportunity to get away from the village chores and family and join their friends in the woman's *oso* [house] for several days of gossip and laughter (Counter and Evans 1981:133).

Outsiders give even more attention to Maroon art than to Maroon women, resulting in a large body of literature, both popular and scholarly, published in English, Dutch, French, German, Spanish, and other languages. Books and articles on "Bush Negro art" have always been devoted to decorative woodcarving—the stunning and elaborately developed medium that every Maroon man is expected to master (see, e.g., Dark 1954; Herskovits 1969 [1930]; Kahn 1931; Hurault 1970; Muntslag 1966). The received wisdom about Maroon art (i.e., woodcarving) is that it functions importantly in the context of male-female relations, especially in courtship and marriage. Such gift giving is traditionally viewed as a one-way street, with men actively producing and proffering artistic objects and women passively receiving and admiring them. Herskovits (1969:159), whose first foreign fieldwork was among the Saramaka in the late 1920s, offered a quotation in pseudo-Saramaccan to support this picture of Maroon art: "'*Tembe no muje sundi*,' . . . 'Woodcarving is not a woman's affair.'" Another writer, working with secondary sources, generalized confidently that "the role of the men is primarily concerned with creation, that of the women with appreciation" (Dark 1951:57).

My own experience with Maroons does not contradict the image of Maroon women as enthusiastic and admiring connoisseurs of men's woodcarving, nor does it lead to doubts as to how meaningful these decorated objects are to them as symbols of sexual love. At the same time, however, my experience makes it very clear that artistic creativity and productivity are not confined to men; Maroon women have developed forms of artistic expression that are every bit as richly elaborated. If we look at what is actually happening in Maroon villages, we see women as active artists, producing beautifully carved calabashes and a wide range of textile arts that rival their more well known counterparts in other areas of the world. We also see that the use of art in courtship and marriage is very much a two-way street, with Maroon women expressing their love through artistic gifts just as men do.[1]

Over the past 16 years, in the course of general ethnographic research with Saramaka Maroons, I have attempted to understand women's social and artistic life from their own perspective.[2] Particularly in informal settings—while cutting rice in their gardens, sewing clothes and carving calabashes on their doorsteps, preparing meals in their cooking sheds, doing laundry at rocks in the river, and gossiping together in the menstrual hut—Saramaka women have provided interesting clues as to how their place in the society is reflected in their arts, as well as how their arts are used in social life. They have spoken eloquently and perceptively about their place in the society, about their view of men's arts and women's arts, and about the potential of decorative and verbal arts for expressing their joys and sorrows.

The image that Maroon women present of themselves is quite different from that of defiantly independent matriarchs who run council meetings, preside over social and religious life, and delight in the conviviality of the menstrual hut. Rather, when women speak of their participation in public life it is with recognition of the dominant role of men as social and religious leaders. When women speak of menstrual seclusion it is with resignation rather than joy. The bulk of their conversations center on their involvements in a polygynous marriage system that strongly favors men. Moreover, their daily life during the years I spent in the field offered strong support for these views, in the form of countless specific incidents.

Art in Social Life

Several features of Saramaka social life are particularly relevant to a full understanding of their arts. First, husbands are scarcer than wives. Second, women are more dependent on their husbands, in terms of material well-being, than men are on their wives. Third, women attach more affective value than men do to both the giving and the receiving of conjugal gifts.

The Relative Scarcity of Husbands Compared to Wives

Even though many Saramaka men have two, three, or even four wives, there are at any one time many more women without husbands than men without wives. Furthermore, while being unmarried is for men virtually always a temporary state to be altered more or less when they choose, women's opportunities for remarriage decline sharply with age, so that women who are widowed or divorced in their 40s face a very real prospect of remaining permanently without a husband, and women past menopause virtually never remarry. Several different features of Saramaka life are responsible for this surplus of older, marriageable women, but the two most important contributing factors are (1) that women enter into their first marriage in their mid-teens, while men do so in their mid-20s and (2) that Saramaka men spend long periods of their life earning money on the coast, effectively removing themselves from the marriage pool. With teenage girls and non-Saramaka women acquiring a significant portion of the potential husbands, the scarcity of marriageable men for older Saramaka women is not only a perceived problem but a statistical reality.[3]

The Greater Material Dependence of a Woman on Her Husband Than of a Man on His Wife

A Saramaka woman is dependent for a wide range of goods and services on *one* man, her husband, who should provide her house, her canoe, her household furnishings, the bulk of the fish and game in her diet, and the male labor needed for clearing gardens in the forest. When she has no husband, or when her husband is absent for long periods of time, her standard of living is significantly lowered. During these times she is put in the position of "begging" a kinsman—a brother or an uncle, for example—to help out. When a woman's house is built by a kinsman, however, it is not expected to be as beautifully decorated as the one her husband would have provided; fish and game are supplied by her kinsmen only when there is some left over from what they give their own wives; and unmarried women must often make do with reworking old gardens rather than planting newly cleared ones, because their male kinsmen are too busy to spend time felling trees and cutting underbrush for them.

By contrast, there is very little variation among Saramaka men in how adequately they are supplied with the goods and services for which women are responsible. The most important material contributions that women make to men are meals and clothing, and it is rarely difficult for a man to obtain either of these. Not only are men generally married for most of their lives but because of widespread polygyny a man is frequently in the position of being provided for by two or three women at a time, all of whom are consciously competing for his favor. As a result, men often have valises and trunks filled with beautifully decorated clothing, much of which they have never worn. In terms of food, the practice of communal meals for the men of a neighborhood, as well as for any men visiting in the neighborhood, means that meals are always available to men whether or not their wives are around to cook for them.

Sexual opportunities are similarly tilted in favor of men. Ideals for women's behavior require sexual fidelity to one husband at a time, sexual abstinence during that husband's years away from Saramaka, and resignation to a sharply reduced sex life during old age. By contrast, men are expected to have several wives at a time, to engage in frequent extramarital affairs, to take lovers and wives during their years away from Saramaka, and to continue to be sexually active well into old age.

In short, women sometimes have access to the goods and services that are supplied by men and sometimes not. But men are almost never deprived to any significant extent of the goods and services that are provided by women.

Women Value Conjugal Exchanges More Than Men Do

There is no doubt that Saramaka women are more insecure than Saramaka men when it comes to pleasing their spouses in terms of both the proper fulfillment of their own obligations and the adequate reciprocation of their spouses' offerings. It is perhaps significant that a special phrase, *nyá papái*, which refers to the shame of not being able to reciprocate a gift properly, is used frequently by and about women but is not generally applied to men. Even the etiquette of conjugal exchange is different for men and women. Saramaka women, upon receiving a gift from a husband, are expected to offer more effusive expressions of gratitude, to display it to a wide range of other people, and to indulge in dramatic, excited behavior similar to that of American women on television game shows who win fur coats or washing machines or trips to Hawaii. Saramaka men who receive a conjugal gift are also expected to express thanks, but in a much more subdued style. The main contribution women make to men's life—prepared food—is treated not as a gift that must be acknowledged but rather as the simple fulfillment of a woman's duties.

Male and Female Artists

Just as husbands are scarcer than wives in Saramaka, so too are male-made woodcarvings scarcer than female-made decorative textiles. This alone confers on woodcarvings a special value. Inventories of a number of women's possessions indicate that although women may have two or three carved combs and up to five or six carved stools, they tend to own only one or two examples of most kinds of decoratively carved objects—paddles, food stirrers, peanut-grinding boards, and so forth. These objects are displayed in the woman's house, and women are always able to supply a detailed account of which man made each one and when it was presented. Woodcarvings, then, represent to women tangible and very visible symbols of specific personal relationships.

Textiles are a very different matter. Because most men have two or three wives at a time, as well as a large number of lovers who also offer decorated textiles as gifts of affection, their storage trunks tend to be filled with literally hundreds of capes, breechcloths, dance aprons, calfbands, and neckerchiefs. When I discussed these collections with their owners, it became clear that only a very few of the individual textiles retained specific romantic meanings. Men often did not know which wife or lover had sewn a particular textile, and they tended to see their clothing as a largely undifferentiated accumulation of gifts from the women in their life.[4]

Women's carved calabashes are also intended for use in the context of marriage, but unlike woodcarvings and textiles, they are never conjugal gifts. Decorated calabashes are understood primarily to reflect the care and aesthetic taste of the woman who sets them out when serving her husband's meals; as such, they form an important part of the Saramaka conception of a woman's role in marriage. The display of calabashes is also an important aspect of the ceremonial presentation that occurs when a woman pays her first formal visit to a new husband's village. Women often decorate the interior of their house with extensive arrays of carefully selected calabashes that they have carved (see S. Price and R. Price 1980: Figures 23-24).[5]

Woodcarving, decorative sewing, and calabash carving—the three main artistic media in Saramaka villages—thus play complementary roles in social life. Woodcarvings are highly valued by women, and each carved object is understood as a specific symbol of the relationship between the man who created it and the woman to whom he gave it. Textiles offer an idiom for women to express their love for a man, but they do not generally retain individualized romantic associations by the men who own them. And carved calabashes communicate the care with which a woman fulfills her conjugal duties, without ever serving as a conjugal gift.

Saramakas not only have firm opinions about the relative value of artistic media, such as woodcarvings and textiles, they also have definite ideas on a more general level about the "natural" artistic aptitudes of men versus women. Even when considering the arts that women have developed and personalized, such as embroidery or interior-carved calabashes, there is still a general belief among both men and women that men could do them better. Women like to ask men for help in laying out an embroidery design, sometimes even seeking instructions as to which lines to execute in which colors.[6] Men often say they are too busy to help, but when a man does sit down to draw out the lines of a design with pencil, the woman embroiders it extremely conscientiously, treating it as a valuable asset. As one woman commented, "Embroidered neckerchiefs that men design are more handsome than women's because they design them like a woodcarving." What she was referring to was the achievement of geometric precision and exact symmetry in men's designs, for these are the features of men's carving that women consider themselves incapable of producing. Men have always used imported tools, such as compasses, in their art, and they produce designs with rigorous geometric regularity, a quality that is strongly valued by all Saramakas, both men and women.

Women's more flowing free-form designs are also admired, but to Saramakas they reflect a lesser artistic accomplishment. Women see themselves as striving in their arts toward the kind of symmetry and geometric precision that characterize men's woodcarving, but generally failing to achieve it. Their narrow-strip textile compositions are consciously planned in terms of symmetry around a vertical center strip, but they exhibit a tendency—viewed by Saramakas as typically feminine "mistakes"—to stray from the perfect regularity of a pattern (e.g., by the insertion of an extra bit of embroidery or the reversal of one of two "matching" strips of cloth). Capes embroidered by women are similarly designed around a center, but the sides rarely come out perfectly even. Figuring out how to balance the elements of a calabash design in order to produce a proper mirror image between the two sides is seen by women as one of the most difficult parts of getting the design the way they want it. Those few women who teach themselves how to mark out geometric embroidery designs, rather than asking a man to help or embroidering a more typical woman's design, show pride in their accomplishment, but their behavior is considered by most people to be rather unfeminine. Young girls who show an artistic inclination in this direction (like girls in a traditional community in the United States who aspire to an expertise in physics or construction work rather than in literature or nursing) are made to understand that the precision involved in such designs represents a somewhat "unnatural" skill for their sex[7] (see Figures 1–4, which illustrate the contrast between men's and women's artistic styles).

Men's Art, Women's Doodling

In the hands of Western observers (brought up with their own definite notions about men and women), the Maroons' cultural bias toward male artistic styles has been accepted not as an aesthetic preference but rather as a statement of ethnographic reality. The consequences of this interpretive error have ranged from the academic to the economic: men's woodcarving is the only Maroon art treated seriously in the literature and it is the only Maroon art that has any commercial value in the tourist shops of coastal Suriname.

Even when outsiders *do* acknowledge the existence of women's arts, their perceptions still tend to reflect Western preconceptions about men and women. For example, in one of the very rare attempts to deal seriously with Maroon women as artists, Philip Dark (1951) projected some traditional Euro-American notions about women onto Maroon calabash arts and reached some rather questionable conclusions about what he called the "personality configurations" of Maroon men and women.[8] In an analysis of the differences between men's calabash carving (executed on the exterior surfaces of two-piece containers, with compasses, chisels, and knives) and women's calabash carving (executed on the interior surfaces of bowls and ladles, with pieces of broken glass), Dark evaluated their distinctive features in the following terms. The men's designs were described as "always clearly marked," "always well considered and apt," and "always conceived as

FIGURE 1.   A Male-Carved Calabash Container and Three Female-Carved Cala-bash bowls. (a) Surinaams Museum, Paramaribo H685; (b, c, d) Private collection. Photos by Antonio Graeber.

having to fill a definite surface,'' and they were said to exhibit ''apt consid-eration of the relationship of design to design space'' (Dark 1951:58–59). By contrast, the women's carvings were described as ''alien'' (to the men's), and it was said that they ''may or may not'' overflow the design space, ''may or may not'' be conceived as having to fill a definite surface, and ''may or may not'' be ''apt'' in terms of the relationship of design to design space (Dark 1951:59).

To understand the differences that he perceived between men's and women's styles of carving, Dark looked to published ethnographic reports

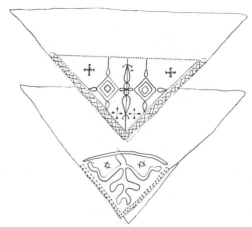

FIGURE 2.   Male- and Female-Designed Embroidery. The Neckerchief on the Top Was Designed in Pencil by a Man Before Being Sewn by a Woman; The One on the Bottom Was Designed and Sewn by a Woman. Sketches by Sally Price (Dangogo 1968).

FIGURE 3.   A Wooden Tray, Carved Ca. 1969 by Tebini of Kampu, Who Inscribed on It the First Letter of His Own Name and That of the Wife for Whom It Was a Gift. Private collection. Photo by David Porter.

FIGURE 4.   A Cape, Sewn 1900–10 by a Woman for a Man. Saramakas View This
Kind of "Imperfect" Symmetry in Design as Typically Feminine. Field photo by
Richard Price (Asindoopo, 1978).

on Maroon life. There he found comments that allowed him to characterize
Maroon marriage as a "tenuous" relationship in which "women appear to
have the whip hand" (1951:59) and "divorce is quite an informal matter,
a woman being able to break a union on some slight pretext" (1951:57).
Combining his own museum analysis of calabash carvings with these
impressionistic ideas of Maroon social life (provided by Morton Kahn, a
physician who visited Suriname in the 1920s), Dark (1951:59) arrived at the
remarkable speculation that both indicate

> a distinct difference in temperament between the men and women of this cul-
> ture. The men would appear to be definite in their actions and probably more
> conservative than the women. The women may perhaps be thought more fickle
> and more easily susceptible to novelty. Perhaps the decoration of calabashes by
> the women is their form of doodling.[9]

Although based purely on secondary sources, Dark's reading of the contrast between the "personality configurations" of Maroon men and women as artists presented ironic similarities to the ideas of Maroons themselves. His comparative assessment of male and female styles of carving led to the notion that one is art, the other doodling. Maroon "sexism," while not reaching such an extreme position, also encourages the view that women's art is inferior to men's art. We are told by Dark that women's designs are less consistently "well considered and apt" than those of the men; we are told by Maroons that women's designs exhibit less technical skill than those of the men. We thus have two independent assessments of these decorative styles that strongly reinforce one another—one from a museum researcher and another from the artists themselves. In both cases, however, it might be useful to attempt to disaggregate the visual properties of women's art (such as features of design and technical control) from the cultural and social settings in which it is being evaluated, after which we should be able to reintegrate them in a more perceptive understanding of the ways in which they interrelate. For the fact that Dark's evaluation of male versus female arts in a sense corresponds to that of Maroons does not make either one of them any less a culturally conditioned aesthetic response.

Having observed the production, evaluation, and uses of Saramaka arts over an extended period of field experiences, I have come to the firm conclusion that the differential status of men's and women's arts stems more from social dynamics and gender constructs in that society than from the Saramakas' abstract aesthetic preferences.[10] If we do not simply assume that Maroon women are fickle doodlers, it becomes possible to appreciate the arts they produce and the ways in which they use art in their daily lives. Women's calabash carvings and textile designs, viewed from a more purely aesthetic perspective, represent richly elaborated artistic traditions.[11] Regardless of the status of women's arts relative to men's, the appreciation of women's artistic expression among both men and women is still a strong, positive aspect of Saramaka life. The importance of these arts in social life is equally undeniable. We can no longer accept the idea that Maroon men are active artists and Maroon women are passive connoisseurs, that Maroon men give art and Maroon women receive it. On the contrary, women spend a great deal of time engaged in artistic activities and most of what they produce is used to express and reaffirm the love that they feel for a man. By embroidering a handsome cape for her husband, a woman communicates her affection; by carving beautiful calabashes to set out at his meals, she reasserts her commitment to their marriage. Their arts, like men's woodcarving, are used to express love and solidarity.

Popular Songs

When love turns sour, when jealousy over a rival builds, when anger dominates, and when divorce threatens, however, the decorative arts are not viewed by Saramakas as a proper expressive outlet, and people turn instead to the performing arts. In the remainder of this paper I present Saramaka women's songs as a reflection of their self-image and an example of the gap between the way these women view their social position and the way it is traditionally portrayed in the literature. I suggest that their social position, as they themselves view it, has exerted a fundamental influence on the Saramaka construction of the relative merits of men's and women's arts.

Popular songs (sêkêti kandá) are the preferred artistic medium for the expression of love and hate, joy and despair, desire and rejection. Two representative examples give an idea of the range of emotions that these songs cover. In one a man expands the standard Saramaka "good morning" (I wéki nô?, "Did you awake?" or Fá i wéki?, "How did you awake?") into a song of admiration for his tall wife:

Gadja mazó, a póbiki bùka,	Statuesque nun, with the mouth of a doll,
Un fá i wéki-o, mama?	How did you awake, momma?
Mi wéki-o, mi wéki-é.	I awoke, I awoke [the reciprocal greeting].
Mama, i wéki hànse sèmbè.	Momma, you awoke [as] a beautiful person.

In another, a woman calls out for help after a dramatic verbal and physical fight with her husband, mother-in-law, and co-wife; this song employs the standard term for a co-wife adversary and addresses a plea for help to Gaan Gadu, the "supreme deity" of Saramaka whose "voice" is heard in the form of thunder.

Kabitên, baáa-o. Kéé!	Headman, oh brother. *Kéé!* [expression of alarm]
Dí soní miti mi,	The thing that's happened to me,
Un tá yéi-ó?	Do you hear?
Dí gaamá-dê,	The tribal chief there,
Dí soní míti mi,	The thing that's happened to me,
Un tá yéi, nô?	Do you hear?
Téé u mi yéi dí Gaán Gádu bái	When I hear the thunder roll
Mi kái Gaán Gádu-éé,	I call out to Gaan Gadu,
Mi bái goòn líba-o.	I shout out to the world.
U dí yayó u mi édi	It's because of that slut-of-mine [co-wife]
Mi kái ên-éé.	That I'm calling him.

Sêkêti songs are created spontaneously by both men and women, usually about specific incidents in their own lives. In some songs people deal with problems that they share with others. For example, there were many songs in the 1960s about the hydroelectric dam that flooded about half of Saramaka territory and forced some 6000 people to evacuate to government-built towns near the coast. There were also many songs composed after a man tried to assassinate the Saramaka tribal chief that commented on the event and offered condolences to the chief. Most songs, however, are more personal and refer to the ups and downs of individual relationships. A Saramaka woman once suggested to me that all *sêkêti* songs are either songs of love, songs of cursing, or songs of hardship; that is, they either express the passions of a particular relationship, attack a specific enemy, or voice despair over personal hardships such as loneliness or poverty.

People most often compose new *sêkêti* songs in solitary and relaxed settings—for example, while paddling a canoe, cutting rice in a garden, or daydreaming at home. A person sitting idly on a doorstep may break into a spontaneous song as a way of commenting on the passing scene. An appropriate way to react to a gift is through a sung expression of delight. Even very young children are actively encouraged to invent *sêkêti* songs. One girl set the name of a kinsman to a little melody when she was three or four years old, singing "*Peléki-éé, Peléki-oo,*" and was warmly embraced by everyone around, who interpreted this simple song as the beginning of a promising *sêkêti* career. Children just a few years older enjoy performing their own songs in groups, with a soloist, a choral response, and an accompaniment of rhythmic handclapping.

If a person's new *sêkêti* song catches the fancy of others, it is sung and talked about and eventually performed for the community at large, usually at one of several types of all-night funeral ceremonies. In the presence of perhaps a hundred or more people, a carefully groomed and attired performer sings the solo while executing a special dance (see Figure 5). A line of women and girls, bent forward at the hips, provide a steady beat of handclapping and punctuate the soloist's phrases with a simple choral response. At the end, the performer is embraced and congratulated by others and another *sêkêti* song begins, either by the same person or by someone else.

Because of the frequency and spontaneity of *sêkêti* song composition, many are almost immediately forgotten and even those that become popular have a relatively brief active life. There were several hundred *sêkêti* songs being sung in Saramaka during 1967–68, but a year or two later these had all gone out of style and had been replaced by new ones that reflected incidents of more current interest—from love affairs and divorces to gift presentations and petty crime. When asked to do so, Saramakas can still sing the songs of the past decade, and the older women I worked with derived great pleasure from providing me with nostalgic renditions of songs that were popular in the early 20th century. But in the absence of an anthropologist's urging, the performance of outdated songs is limited to an occasional brief session at the very end of a wake, when most of the participants have already gone home to sleep.

Unlike some genres of Saramaka singing, *sêkêti* songs are composed in the everyday language of Saramaccan, but their verbal style is subtly different. Occasionally a person introduces a new word or phrase that becomes part of *sêkêti* vocabulary, more for the way it sounds than for what it

FIGURE 5. Performers at Large Community Events Execute the *Tiêke* Dance While Singing Currently Popular *Sêkêti* Songs. Left: photo by Richard Price (Dangogo 1968); right: photo by Terry Agerkop (Saramaka 1970s).

means. *Sêkêti* lyrics also include more metaphorical words and expressions than does ordinary speech. For example, various kinds of Western-style communication that Saramakas view partly as foreign novelties are used to symbolize irresponsible gossiping: when a nonliterate woman sings that her name is "written down in a book," or when a man who has never used a telephone sings to someone, "Your mother just phoned," they are very explicitly accusing another person of spreading malicious rumors. Similarly, a faithful wife is often referred to metaphorically as a nun (*mazó*); a beautiful woman may be called Queen Wilhelmina (*Kónu Wemina*) because of the romantic attitude that Saramakas have toward Dutch royalty.

Women's Songs

The spontaneity of *sêkêti* composition allows these songs to express emotions directly and forcefully through phrases that are also used in gossip sessions and other conversational settings. The commentary in songs closely parallels the attitudes that people voice in other contexts. The emotions that women's songs express are extremely varied, from tender love to bitter jealousy, but there is a statistical tendency for them to be more negative than those composed by men.[12] The image of life that women project in their songs, like that expressed in other settings, contradicts quite strongly the notion that they hold the "whip hand" in marriage. Rather, they tend to present themselves as individuals deeply involved in love relationships that constantly run into snags and inspire intense rivalries. They also make clear that they are rarely in a position to control their personal lives as much as they would like to. Women's love songs are generally simple lyrical expressions of affection; they require no social science analysis. However, some commentary about women's other songs, which make up the statistical majority, may offer partial support for my argument that the position of Maroon women in their own society is not as privileged as some outsiders have imagined.

Women most frequently focus their songs on relationships with their husbands, their husbands' kin, and their husbands' other wives (their arch enemies in this polygynous society). While relations with their own kinswomen (especially mother, sisters, and mother's sisters) tend to be friendly, solidary, and relaxed, those relationships acquired through marriage are more often distinctly strained, and women view themselves as relatively impotent in dealing with the conflicts thereby produced. A woman's husband may fail to provide well for her, or he may show preference for another of his wives, but she is acutely aware that if she leaves him she not only will suffer in terms of material goods but she may well never have a chance to remarry. A woman's in-laws may spread malicious gossip about her, but if she leaves their village to establish full-time residence in her own village, she loses status in her husband's eyes and weakens her marriage. A woman's co-wives may make life extremely trying for her, but there is nothing she can do about the fact that her husband enjoys spending time with them. Many women's *sêkêti* songs address these dilemmas, not as general social problems but in terms of particular situations and individual relationships.

Several songs that one Saramaka woman made up in despair and anger over a particular rival are illustrative. In the first one, composed while she was cutting rice in her in-laws' horticultural camp, the woman attempted (at least rhetorically) to elicit sympathy from her husband through exaggerated self-deprecation:

Kiólo-éé,	Young dandy,
Wómi án dê a kamía kê mi môò-nô.	There's no other man around who wants me anymore.
I wánwán sí mi kê.	Only you have ever wanted me.
Wè dí fési Gaán Gádu dá mi,	Well, the face that God gave me,
Dí u hònyò-hônyò,	That of a wasp,
I wánwán sí mi kê.	Only you have ever wanted me.
Wè, dí fési Gaán Gádu dá mi,	Well, the face that God gave me,
Dí u mbéti u mátu,	That of a forest beast,

I wánwán sí mi kê.	Only you have ever wanted me.
Wè, dí fési Gaán Gádu dá mi,	Well, the face that God gave me,
Dí u zandibô, wè,	That of a cartoon character, well,
I wánwán sí mi kê.	Only you have ever wanted me.
Wè, dí fési Gaán Gádu dá mi,	Well, the face that God gave me,
Dí u basikáanu,	That of a funeral mask,
I wánwán sí mi kê.	Only you have ever wanted me.

A second song was inspired when people told her husband that she had taken a lover; she called out to the gods in despair at being the victim of ugly rumors:

Dí gádu a dí lío,	Oh god that presides over this river,
Mi bái helú dá i,	I call out in despair to you
Dí sondí míti mi a mùndu	[About] the thing that's happened to me in the world
Sôndò mi sábi.	Without my even knowing.

In a third song she accused her husband's kin of making life in their village unbearable for her.

M'án ó téi ên,	I won't take it,
Bigá ná mi á dí lío.	Because this isn't my river [home village].
Sèmbè sitááfu u tjái. . .	Accepting punishment from others. . .
M'án ó tjái dí f'ên môò.	I'm not going to take *his* anymore.

And finally, when her efforts to save her marriage failed, she sang a bitter concession of defeat to her co-wife:

Kambósa-éé,	Co-wife,
Ná wái dá mi môò.	Don't celebrate to me anymore.
Muyêè,	Woman,
I ku i mánu toóu.	You and your husband have a church marriage.

(Or, more freely, "Co-wife, you don't need to strut around so smugly for my benefit anymore. Woman, it's clear that you and your husband have as monogamous a pact as city people who get married in a church.")

Many women's songs about marital problems have a distinctly bitter, sarcastic tone. In one a woman effectively characterized her co-wife as the kind of person who could have committed the worst atrocities of World War II, referring to her as a "German" (*Alumá*). In another song a woman inquired solicitously whether her husband was in menstrual seclusion, since that would explain why he never came to her house to sleep anymore. One woman sarcastically addressed her husband's sister by the term for a co-wife, feigning understanding for the sister's hostility toward her by pretending that they were both married to the same man. Another woman ridiculed her husband's obsession for assuring her sexual fidelity by singing a song of mock gratitude for his assistance in keeping her virtuous:

A púu mi a yayó-yéé.	He saved me from promiscuity.
Dísi púu mi a môntjo-éé.	This one saved me from becoming a whore.

A á mánu f'i téi,	When you marry certain kinds of men,
Nòò, i án tá yayó môò.	You don't fool around anymore.

Women frequently compose sarcastic songs extolling the passionate love of their husband and their co-wife:

Fá a namá ku i dê,	The way she's pressed up against you,
Fá a namá ku i dê,	The way she's pressed up against you,
Sébitaa ku yái, Sébitaa ku yái,	From May to January, from May to January,
Un án ó lúsu môò.	You two will never break apart.
A dóu a búnu;	He's arrived at [something] good;
Dí wómi téi sindò muyêè.	The man's taken a "sit-still" [faithful] wife.
Dí wómi táa mi yayó,	The man said I was fooling around,
Téé án tá yéi m'wootu seéi.	So he wasn't even hearing my words [of protest]
A dóu a búnu.	[But now] he's arrived at [something] good.
Dí wómi téi sindò muyêè.	The man's taken a "sit-still" wife.

Saramaka women commemorate both their victories and their defeats in song. One woman, for example, sensing that her co-wife's marriage was on rocky ground, suggested to her that she should admit defeat quickly and gracefully:

Adjóísi u gó dá dí wómi	Saying goodbye to the man
An taánga môò-éé.	Isn't so hard.
Adjóísi u gó dá dí wómi	Saying goodbye to the man
An taánga môò-éé.	Isn't so hard.
Dí a dá i pási f'i sa gó,	Since he's given you an opportunity to leave,
Nôò, i gó dé ên,	Just go and say it,
Nôò, i tooná-éé.	And then be on your way.

Another woman, recognizing that her own marriage was falling apart, composed a song of concession:

Mi pii lái-éé.	I've packed my things.
Mi pii lái-éé.	I've packed my things.
A di wán wósu nôò	It's just at that one house [the co-wife's]
I tá kê duumi.	That you keep wanting to sleep.

Art, Gender, and Social Consciousness

One of the most important contrasts between Saramaka men and women is their differential involvement in the world beyond their tribal territory. This involvement has left its mark on their respective material lives, sexual histories, linguistic patterns, personal styles, and philosophical orientations. It has also been a crucial influence on their respective artistic styles and on the ways that art fits into their social lives.

Saramaka masculinity, in addition to specific expectations regarding sexual virility, hunting skills, verbal eloquence, and ritual competence, has long required an ability to function in "foreign" settings, as well as an active enthusiasm for dabbling in non-Saramaka culture. Whether in the streets of Paramaribo, the construction sites at Afobaka, the Djuka villages in eastern Suriname, the towns of French Guiana, or the diamond-mining camps of Brazil, Saramaka men must know how to converse in foreign languages, deal with people from other ethnic backgrounds, hold down a job, and make wise purchases for the return home. Men enjoy displaying symbols of this aspect of their lives, mixing into their speech words they have picked up from different languages, decorating their houses with non-functional items of Western culture (e.g., light bulbs in villages with no electricity), working the antics of coastal personalities into their songs, and reminiscing about the novelties of life outside Saramaka, from elevators and supermarkets to prostitutes and motorbikes. Men sometimes ostentatiously consume foods they have imported from the coast; one man, for example, occasionally opened a can of evaporated milk and poured it into a cup of coffee, enjoying it especially because of the reaction of his great-grandmother, who considered imbibing the bodily fluids of a cow to be the ultimate sign of the decadence of city life.

By contrast, women's lives have always been envisioned by Saramakas more purely in the context of their home environment. While men often talk about their own alternation between Saramaka and coastal societies, women tend to see their life experiences as an alternation between villages and horticultural camps. Women's subsistence activities require a higher proportion of native materials and locally made tools than do men's, and their houses have fewer manufactured furnishings. Their speech is less sprinkled with foreign terms, and their dress includes fewer store-bought items. Their view of city streets, buses, stores, and other features of life outside Saramaka exhibits a stronger ratio of apprehension to fascination. While men take pride in mastering appropriate etiquettes and styles of interaction for their dealings with outsiders, women tend, in the presence of non-Saramakas, either to become very withdrawn or to adopt a crude brashness, both of which reflect their lack of confidence and their discomfort in such situations.

The different orientations of Saramaka men's and women's lives vis-à-vis the outside world are reflected quite directly in their arts. In terms of tools, men's use of store-bought compasses, chisels, and knives for both calabash decoration and woodcarving contrasts with women's use of broken glass for calabashes and threads pulled from scraps of cloth for embroidery. In terms of design styles, men's compositions tend to be rigorously geometric, with straight lines, perfect arcs and circles, and exacting symmetry—the very features that they are familiar with from printed signs, machinery, and Western architecture; by contrast, women's design styles more often center on free-form "organic" shapes, with stubby appendages and irregular symmetries. In terms of the place of the various arts in social life, the long-term absences of men from tribal territory, which are a fundamental influence on the nature of male-female relationships in this society, are also crucial in delineating the social meaning of the artistic gifts that flow within these relationships.

In Saramaka, the value of men's artistry is closely linked with the value of men. The explicit association that women make between particular woodcarvings and particular relationships contrasts with the less attentive attitude of men toward the social origins of their decorative textiles, in a way that corresponds directly to the respective concerns of women and men about marriage itself. The insecurities that women express in their songs are the same insecurities that inspire their unbounded joy at receiving a carved comb or food stirrer. The security that men enjoy in terms of ongoing marriage prospects is similarly related to their more subdued reaction to the artistic gifts they receive from women.

From an anthropological perspective, it should not be surprising that women in Saramaka villages express fundamental dissatisfactions in their personal lives without generally going on to assess critically the cultural attitudes and institutions that lie behind their difficulties. In most cases, a Saramaka woman suffering material deprivations because she has no husband does not wish that her culture provided equal money-earning opportunities for men and women; she wishes only that she could find a husband. Because of their relative isolation from other ways of life, the cultural setting in which these women grow up has provided the framework for their social consciousness; alternatives have traditionally carried connotations of deviance and impropriety for women as much as they have carried a sense of excitement and adventure for men. During my residence in Saramaka, women reacted with strong moral indignation to stories of women from villages closer to the city who "hid their periods" in order to avoid the inconveniences of menstrual seclusion; they expressed resentment about their husbands' sexual freedom in the same culturally prescribed rhetoric that their grandmothers had used; they never failed to distinguish their husbands' meals from their own through rigorous attention to special details of service, such as smooth mounds of rice and specially chosen calabash bowls; and they were rearing their daughters to expect the same satisfactions and frustrations in life that they were experiencing.

As Michelle Rosaldo (1980:417) has argued, the relevance of sexual asymmetries for social scientists is not that they exist but that they are closely linked, like other phenomena such as racism and social class, to the particulars of women's (and men's) lives, activities, and goals. The strong sexual asymmetries of Maroon life—material, social, and conceptual—are as deeply embedded in the arts as they are in subsistence practices, in marriage patterns, or in religious beliefs. Each Maroon woman's life experience represents, in part, a response to the attitudes and institutions that define her as a woman. The creative arts, whether calabash carving, decorative sewing, song composition, body cicatrization, or any other medium, form a dynamic and richly expressive part of that response.

Notes

Acknowledgments

This paper has benefited from constructive criticisms by Richard Price, Roberta Johnson (commentator on an earlier version presented at the 1982 Caribbean Studies Association Conference in Kingston, Jamaica), and participants in the Johns Hopkins Seminar in Atlantic History, Culture, and Society.

1. Perhaps because of the strong association of each medium with maleness or femaleness, the decorative arts are not considered appropriate as gifts within same-sex dyads. That is, a man would not make a woodcarving for another man, and a woman would not embroider a textile for another woman.

2. My fieldwork, conducted jointly with Richard Price, has been largely in Saramaka villages on the Pikilio, an upriver tributary of the Suriname River (see S. Price and R. Price 1980:Figures 3–4); the demographic and ethnographic details in this paper refer primarily to that region. My comments on gender and the arts reflect observations on the life of Suriname Maroons more generally. In this paper, Saramaccan words are written with a modified version of the orthography developed by Jan Voorhoeve: vowels have "Italian" values except that *è* represents the vowel in English "met" and *ò* represents the vowel in English "all"; vowel extension is indicated by double vowels; and high tones are indicated by acute accents, while low tones are left unmarked.

3. For a more detailed discussion of the effects of labor emigration on Saramaka marriage, see R. Price (1970, 1975).

4. The only portion of a man's personal textile collection that is certain to evoke memories of specific women is a small, distinctly private and rarely contemplated set of memorabilia. Somewhere in each man's trunks is a tied kerchief containing all the adolescent girls' aprons that he has been given during his life, either on wedding nights with never-married girls or as gifts from adolescent lovers. For example, one 92-year-old man, who kindly spent three days opening his trunks of clothing for my inspection, came upon such a kerchief in the course of the project. Excusing himself with obvious delight and commenting that he had not seen this bundle in over 25 years, he turned his back to me (and to one of his wives, who was also present) and unfolded each cloth in turn, reminiscing silently and announcing proudly at the end, in the language that he associated with his youth as a wage laborer in French Guiana, "*Quinze!*"

5. For a comparative discussion of Maroon and West African calabashes, see S. Price (1982).

6. The reliance of women on men for help in planning designs dates to the very beginning of Maroon decorative sewing (see van Panhuys 1899:81). Until several decades ago, men also lent their artistic skills to the designing stage of women's body cicatrizations, but this practice was discontinued as men allegedly proved increasingly unable to resist the sexual temptations it presented.

7. The style of Saramaka women's arts has changed visibly over the past century, with symmetry becoming more precisely executed by each succeeding generation of artists. At every point, however, women's designs have been less geometric and less perfectly symmetrical than those of men. See S. Price (1983) for a detailed discussion of these developments and the aesthetic attitudes and perceptions that have changed along with them.

8. My commentary on this analysis of Maroon "personality configurations" is in no way intended as an attack on Dark. Rather, it is a caution about the power of any observer's social and cultural environment to color his or her perceptions of other societies, especially in the absence of first-hand fieldwork. It seems unlikely that Dark's paper, published in 1951, would have reflected the same perspective if he had written it in 1981. Similarly, the idyllic feminism that Counter and Evans (1981:92, 96, 133) imagine to exist among the Maroons— with men and women sharing political responsibilities and domestic chores and women fashioning the rules of menstrual seclusion as a way of liberating themselves periodically to relax in the company of other women—is clearly a product of its time.

9. Dark's (1951) characterization of Maroon marriage inspired a cryptic but vehement rebuttal by Melville Herskovits (1951), whose book on Maroon life (Herskovits and Herskovits 1934) would have provided a somewhat more sophisticated first-hand description of Maroon marriages than Kahn's (1931). See also Dark's (1952) reply.

10. This is clearly a judgmental assertion, proof for which would require discussion of many facets of Saramaka social and artistic life and their development through time, a task undertaken at some length in S. Price (1983).

11. For several hundred examples, see the illustrations in S. Price and R. Price (1980).

12. A sample of songs from the Pikilio region reveals that about half of those composed by men expressed positive emotions such as admiration or love and only about one-fourth expressed negative feelings such as anger. By contrast, those composed by women were about one-fifth "positive" and about three-fourths "negative." In general, about two-thirds of sêkêti songs are composed by women. The corpus on which this discussion is based includes 178 songs, a minority of which cannot be classified as either "negative" or "positive." A more detailed discussion of sêkêti songs, including several dozen transcriptions/ translations, is contained in S. Price (1983). See also S. Price and R. Price (1980:174–178) and, for ten recorded examples, R. Price and S. Price (1977).

References Cited

COUNTER, S. ALLEN and DAVID I. EVANS. 1981. I Sought My Brother: An Afro-American Reunion. Cambridge: MIT Press.

DARK, PHILIP J. C. 1951. Some Notes on the Carvings of Calabashes by the Bush Negroes of Surinam. *Man* 51:57–60.

———. 1952. Bush Negro Calabash-Carving. *Man* 52:126.

———. 1954. Bush Negro Art: An African Art in the Americas. London: Tiranti.

HERSKOVITS, MELVILLE J. 1951. Bush Negro Calabash Carving. Man 51:163–164.

———. 1969[1930]. Bush Negro Art. *In* The New World Negro: Selected Papers in Afroamerican Studies. Frances S. Herskovits, ed. pp. 157–167. New York: Minerva Press.

HERSKOVITS, MELVILLE J., and FRANCES S. HERSKOVITS. 1934. Rebel Destiny: Among the Bush Negroes of Dutch Guiana. New York: McGraw-Hill.

HURAULT, JEAN. 1961. Les Noirs Réfugiés Boni de la Guyane Français. Mémoires de l'Institut Français d'Afrique Noire (Dakar) 63.

———. 1970. Africains de Guyane: La Vie Matérielle et l'Art des Noirs Réfugiés de Guyane. The Hague: Mouton.

KAHN, MORTON C. 1931. Djuka: The Bush Negroes of Dutch Guiana. New York: Viking Press.

KERSTEN, CHRISTOPH. 1770. Letter of 12 February. *In* Die Mission der Brüdergemeine in Suriname and Berbice im achtzehnten Jahrhundert (1913–19), F. Staehelin, ed. 3(1):137–139. Herrnhut: Vereins für Brüdergeschichte in Kommission de Unitätsbuchhandlung in Gnadau.

MUNTSLAG, F. H. J. 1966. Tembe: Surinaamse Houtsnijkunst. Amsterdam: Prins Bernhard Fonds.

PANHUYS, L. C. VAN. 1899. Toelichting Betreffende de Voorwerpen Verzameld bij de Aucaner Boschnegers. *In* Catalogus der Nederlandsche West-Indische Tentoonstelling te Haarlem, pp. 74–82. Haarlem.

PRICE, RICHARD. 1970. Saramaka Emigration and Marriage: A Case Study of Social Change. Southwestern Journal of Anthropology 26:157–189.

———. 1975. Saramaka Social Structure: Analysis of a Maroon Society in Surinam. Caribbean Monograph Series 12. Rio Piedras: Institute of Caribbean Studies of the University of Puerto Rico.

PRICE, RICHARD, and SALLY PRICE. 1977. Music from Saramaka: A Dynamic Afro-American Tradition. Phonograph record with ethnographic notes. New York: Folkways Records FE 4225.

PRICE, SALLY. 1982. When Is a Calabash Not a Calabash? Nieuwe West-Indische Gids 56:69–82.

———. 1983. Co-wives and Calabashes. Ann Arbor: University of Michigan Press.

PRICE, SALLY, and RICHARD PRICE. 1980. Afro-American Arts of the Suriname Rain Forest. Berkeley: University of California Press.

ROSALDO, M. Z. 1980. The Use and Abuse of Anthropology: Reflections on Feminism and Cross-cultural Understanding. Signs 5:389–417.

Social Systems

We humans are social creatures, involved in constant interactions with others, which range from "one-to-one" relationships to complex group interactions. In the processes of these interactions, each of us assumes a number of roles: that of kin, friend, worker, boss or headman, parishioner or priest, teacher or student, and a host of others. Here we introduce the rules for and the behaviors characteristic of the kinship and nonkinship relationships that social systems comprise.

In their studies of marriage and kinship, anthropologists describe the specifics of a particular society, but always with the objective of making the kinds of cross-cultural comparisons on which we can ultimately construct laws of human behavior. In the article by Burch, for example, the focus of the study is on traditional and current patterns of marriage and divorce among the Eskimos of North Alaska. He follows that description and analysis with comparisons between Eskimo and what he calls "middle-class American" marriage and divorce.

Kinship Groups

The literature of anthropology is filled with descriptions of marriage and kinship among tribal peoples, and a complex method for analyzing kinship terminologies has been a part of the discipline since the pioneering work of the early anthropologist Lewis H. Morgan.

There is much about kinship in the tribal world that is intriguing. Among the Nuer of Africa there is "ghost marriage," a pattern by which a woman whose husband has died remains married to his "ghost" in the sense that the rights to the children she bears belong to her husband's lineage. Thus her subsequent children will be sired by her deceased husband's brother, but the children are socially defined as the offspring of her deceased husband. Among the Trobriand Islanders of Melanesia, descent is traced matrilineally, that is, through the mother and her kin. In that society, and others with matrilineal descent, a paramount role vis-à-vis children is played by the uncle who is the mother's brother. It is he who is the major disciplinarian and provider of their material needs. In the traditional culture of Dahomey, in what is now the nation of Benin in West Africa, there is woman-to-woman marriage. A woman who becomes wealthy through trading may desire dependents and secure them by marrying another woman in the sense of acquiring social rights as "father" to children and serving as the "householder" to a woman who plays the role of "house-wife." The sexual rights to the wife are held by the "woman father's" son or a trusted employee. Whereas the marriage of one man to several wives (polygyny) is the preferred form of marriage in many societies—an ideal reached by only a certain percentage of men—the Toda of Tibet and India practice polyandry, the "legal" marriage of a woman to two or more men. In many societies the same term meaning father is used with reference to one's biological father and all other male ascendants: father's father, father's father's father, mother's father, mother's mother's father, and so on. In other words, there is one kinship term for "male ancestor."

Each of these ethnographic examples highlights how much kinship is a social category, as opposed to a biological one. A kin is as much an individual who acts like a kin—that is, who treats one in a certain way and expects to be treated in certain ways—as it is a relationship based on a biological reference. This is illustrated in our own society by the use of the term uncle or aunt for individuals who are close to our biological mothers and fathers but are not biologically related to them. We call them Aunt Bess or Uncle George because we behave toward them, and they toward us, as if they were our biological aunts and uncles.

In the context of my initial fieldwork in Liberia, West Africa, Faya, the individual who served as my translator and principal informant, quickly taught me this fundamental rule about kinship. A man twenty years my senior but of no biological relationship, on some occasions Faya would refer to me as "my child," especially when I had made a stupid mistake or once again butchered a word in the Kissi language. When he wished me to do him a favor, he referred to me by the Kissi term for "mother." And when he was vexed with me or wished to anger me, he called me "missy," a term reserved for white women from Europe and America.

In studying kinship, anthropologists have gained increasing sensitivity to the differences between "ideal" and "real" standards of behavior between relatives. When an anthropologist sits in a tribal village and asks an individual to describe how "brothers" relate to each other, the question is usually interpreted to mean how are brothers *expected* to behave toward each other. The response may well be that they look out for each other's welfare, they do not argue and fight, and in general it is a very warm and close relationship. That same day, the anthropologist may witness a heated argument between two brothers as accusations are traded back and forth.

Kinship has been of paramount focus in anthropology precisely because in those societies that anthropologists traditionally studied, groups, decisions, and interactions are so importantly centered on kinship. Put differently, in tribal societies most of an individual's relationships are with relatives. The contrast with our own society is clear when we realize how few of our relatives are our neighbors, co-workers, and best friends. In industrialized societies such as our own, common interest has replaced kinship as a primary organizing principle.

However, among Afro-Americans and other ethnic and racial groups, families and extended kin groups continue to provide important services. Niara Sudarkasa argues, in the article reprinted here, that in terms of both structure and functions, the Afro-American family and kinship system represent a retention of African patterns, recreated by the first black people brought to the United States as slaves.

Nonkinship Groups

In concentrating on kinship because of its preeminence in tribal societies, anthropologists have given far less attention to nonkinship groupings as aspects of a people's social organization. Once again, turning to the anthropology of our own and other industrialized societies "forces" a broader view of the range of human organization, for in such societies, as we noted above, nonkinship social relations have taken on increased importance.

There are three major principles on which individuals are recruited into membership in nonkin groupings: gender, age, and agreement. While there is no society without some interaction organized around these principles, societies differ in terms of the degree to which these principles form the basis of structured groups. For example, in all societies there is a concept of groupings by rough chronological age. In the vernacular of our society, the terms used are children, teenagers, middle-aged adults, and old folks. But in some societies, such as those in East Africa, age is the primary criterion for membership in a group. Among the Karimojong cattle herdsmen of Uganda, an age set consists of all of the adult males who were initiated into manhood within a five- to six-year time period. A single named generation is composed of all of the men who were initiated during a twenty-five to thirty-year time span.

These age sets of East African peoples such as the Karimojong perform a range of functions: They determine an individual's social status; they mirror and reinforce economic, social, and political relationships; and perhaps their primary function is to maintain internal order and mobilize manpower for defense against outsiders.

Demographic, social, and economic conditions in our own society have led to organized groups based on age. Senior citizen organizations and groups are now involved in a range of activities: recreational, political lobbying, and others associated with shared residential units.

Gender as the only basis of recruitment into a social group is rare but when combined with other criteria it is a common basis for organized activity. Looking at our own society illustrates the difference between an unorganized group of individuals categorized by gender (all men, all women) and the combination of gender with other factors—e.g., religious or political beliefs, economic activity—as the basis of recruitment into an organized social group. All women form a category based on their biological sex, but in the United States today the "new" women's movement, which grew up in the 1970s, has spun off a multitude of organizations based on gender *and* notions of shared economic, political, and social oppression. All men are likewise of one category, but when combined with other criteria, they can form business*men*'s clubs, social organizations like fraternities, and hate groups such as the Ku Klux Klan.

The third kind of social group based on mutual agreement is by far the most elusive to analysis because of their tremendous variety in form and functions. Basically, their common distinctions are that their members have voluntarily "agreed" to participate in such a formation and that association with each other brings benefits to each of the individuals. These groups differ from the other types because they are not primarily based on kinship, age, gender, ethnicity, or nationality.

Included in the readings in this section are a description and analysis of voluntary associations in West Africa. Little argues that these tribal unions, occupational associations, and entertainment and recreational associations may well reflect the needs of a basically immigrant and heterogeneous urban population and the adaptation of traditional institutions to urban conditions. Edward Hansen's chapter illustrates a similar phenomenon in Spain. Here men establish and maintain networks in bars which are crucial to business success in the modernization period he describes.

Changing Definitions of Kinship and Nonkinship Groups

When anthropologists describe the kin and nonkinship groupings found throughout the world, we are initially struck by what appears to be an infinite variety: residence based on living with or near various relatives (patrilocal, matrilocal, avunculocal, matri-patrilocal) or, as is often the case in our society, not living necessarily near any of one's relatives (neolocal). Preferred marriage arrangements include monogamy, polyandry, and polygyny. Descent systems include patrilineal, matrilineal, bilateral and double unilineal descent systems. And nonkinship associations appear even more varied.

On second examination, however, we realize that one of the striking things about kinship is that there are in fact a limited number of patterns. In all societies the majority of people live in residential kinship groups of some kind, only one form of which is the nuclear family. Another "universal" pattern is that in all societies a particular kind or kinds of relationships are defined as marriage. And in every human society some individuals are set apart from others as kinsmen. As is the case with all aspects of a society, new variations on the old patterns are often in process.

Marriage in our own society is a case in point. How the ideal marriage is defined as well as the actual patterns of behavior practiced in marriage (or "marriage-like" situations) have changed markedly since the early nineteenth century in the United States. Some of these variations reflect changes in attitudes that lead to more open expressions of old patterns, for example, the "marriage" of two individuals of the same sex. Others reflect adaptations to change in other aspects of our society, such as the increased desire and necessity for women to work outside of the home. One result of this change is that many American couples now find it necessary to live in different cities in order to pursue their individual occupations. While they may not share a common household, an integral part of our "old" definition of marriage, they may maintain other rights associated with the institution of marriage.

Summary

Kinship is a universal construct employed in the organization of human behavior, and marriage and family—defined differently in different societies—are at the very core of kinship. Although kinship rests on a biological base, notions of expected behavior are far more important in determining definitions of relatedness. This is the sense in which kinship is most fundamentally a social phenomenon. Other bases on which human behavior is organized include age, gender, and agreement. These nonkinship groupings exist universally, although in any given society they take specific forms.

Because both kinship and nonkinship groupings are interconnected with the economic, political, and ideological spheres of a society, they change over time in response to changes in these spheres of activity.

Reference

MORGAN, LEWIS H. 1871. *Systems of Consanguinity and Affinity of the Human Family.* Smithsonian Contribution to Knowledge, Vol. 17. Washington, D.C.

9

Marriage and Divorce Among the North Alaskan Eskimos

ERNEST S. BURCH, JR.

Introduction

"Do THE ESKIMOS *really* trade wives?" This is a question that seems invariably to greet travelers returning from the Far North. Obviously, the American public is generally aware of the custom and is fascinated by it. Unfortunately, the practice has been exploited by the movies and the popular press more for its dramatic effect than for its educational value. More seriously, even the professional anthropological literature contains more fiction than fact when dealing with Eskimo "wife-trading." Consequently, social scientists as well as laymen tend to be grossly misinformed on the subject.

Recent research, however, has provided new information on numerous aspects of Eskimo* social life. Specialists have also been re-evaluating the earlier material, and are now in a position to correct some of the errors present in the literature. Far from being the casual and promiscuous affair that it is generally pictured to have been, "wife-trading" was a very serious matter to the Eskimos. We now know that it was an integral part of their system of marriage, which also included polygamous as well as monogamous

---

*Eskimos resident in Alaska are American citizens. However, when the word American is used in this essay, it should be understood to mean "middle-class American of whatever race, color, or national origin." The point is to separate the Eskimo traditional and present-day usages from those that the readers of this book are accustomed to, and any other way of saying it eventually becomes stilted as the reader proceeds.

forms of union. Both "wife-trading" and polygamy, once thought to be manifestations of "anarchy," turn out to have been components of a complex but well-ordered system. In addition, it has been learned that the marriage system meshed with the other aspects of Eskimo kinship in an entirely consistent pattern. Many questions about Eskimo kinship (including marriage) remain unanswered, but the outlines of the system are now fairly clear.

The purpose of this paper is to present a general description of Eskimo marriage and divorce as we have now come to understand it, but it has been necessary to impose certain restrictions on the scope of the discussion. The first of these is with regard to the geographic area covered. The Eskimos formerly occupied a vast portion of northern North America, extending from the eastern tip of Siberia clear across the top of the continent to the east coast of Greenland. The people inhabiting this huge area were by no means as homogeneous as they are generally assumed to have been, and there were many regional variations in all aspects of social life. That such differences occurred in the realm of kinship specifically has been made quite clear by the best of the recent (and relevant) studies.[1] There do seem to be some common threads running through at least the marital customs of many Eskimo groups, but it will be difficult to know what they are with any precision until more of the research now in progress has been published. Tenable generalizations on the subject may be forthcoming in the near future, but it would be premature to attempt them at this time. Consequently, in an effort to keep the presentation on as firm ground as possible, the discussion will be limited to the group that has been more thoroughly studied[2] than any of the others. This group, the "North Alaskan Eskimos," inhabit the northern portion of Alaska between (roughly) Bering Strait and the Canadian border.

A second limitation on the scope of the essay is based on the difference between the "traditional," and the "modern" or contemporary periods in North Alaska. While the North Alaskan Eskimos were by no means isolated from other peoples prior to the arrival of Europeans, they did operate in terms of what is properly regarded as an indigenous system of behavior. Around the middle of the nineteenth century, however, whaling ships began to arrive in the area in substantial numbers. The whalers were followed by traders, missionaries, government representatives, and various others, and the native ways of doing things began to undergo numerous changes as a result of this contact. The process was greatly accelerated when the United States Government established schools and government-directed reindeer herds in the area around the turn of the century. Since the agents of change have been largely American, the changes which have occurred have generally been toward the American way of doing things, and away from the traditional Eskimo one. Since the purpose of this paper is to describe a system that is quite different from our own, my concern will be solely with the former Eskimo ways of doing things rather than with the current ones, which approximate ours in many respects.

Eskimo Marriage

For purposes of scientific analysis, a "marital" relationship can be defined usefully as any relationship in which sexual intercourse is an integral component. In our society, sexual intercourse is institutionalized *only* between husband and wife. Sexual relations between other categories of individuals do in fact occur, however, even though generally considered morally wrong. In other words, from a scientific point of view, only one of the several forms of marriage which *actually* occur in our society is of the single type *ideally* permitted. This monogamous approach of "one man-one woman" is by no means universal in human affairs, however, and numerous peoples around the world permit or even highly value marital ties of various other kinds. Eskimo societies were of the latter type, with the result that the Eskimo marriage system was more complicated than our own.

The basic building block of the North Alaskan Eskimo marriage system, the *ui-nuliaq* relationship, is illustrated in Figure 1.[3] This relationship obtained between a man and a woman who lived together and who had socially approved sexual relations. Superficially, this relationship appears identical to our own husband-wife relationship. As will become apparent later on, however, the two relationships differ in quite significant respects. In addition, where the American husband-wife relationship comprises virtually all there is to marriage in our society, at least ideally, the *ui-nuliaq* relationship was merely the keystone of a more extensive system. (In order to keep the two clearly distinguished from one another, I will use the Eskimo words when referring to their system, and the English terms when referring to ours. Other Eskimo relationships that ideally have no counterparts in our system will be referred to alternately by English and Eskimo terms.)

The establishment of the *ui-nuliaq* relationship depended on two factors, those of coresidence and socially approved sexual intercourse. In other words, all that was required for this kind of marriage was for a man and woman to live together in the same house (which was usually shared with other relatives) and have sexual intercourse. Once these two conditions had been met even for a brief period, the relationship was considered established. The Eskimos did not have any marriage ceremony and in fact, there seems to have been no ritual whatsoever associated with the founding of the *ui-nuliaq* relationship. Not only is this total lack of ceremonial embellishment unusual from a cross-cultural perspective, it was in distinct contrast to other aspects of

ui   *nuliaq*

FIGURE 1.   Simple Residential Marriage

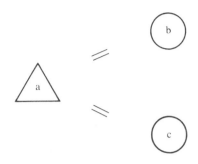

(ab) *ui-nuliaqpak;* (ac) *ui-nukarak;* (bc) *aipaq-aipaq*

FIGURE 2.   Polygynous Residential Marriage

Eskimo life. Taboos, rituals, and ceremonies of various kinds were associated with almost every daily activity and, to me, their absence here is indicative of the rather unimportant place that the *ui-nuliaq* relationship had in the ideal[4] Eskimo scheme of things.

The primary elaboration on the *ui-nuliaq* theme is illustrated in Figure 2, which represents the polygynous[5] residential marriage situation. Here we have a single man living together with two women, and having socially approved sexual relations with both of them. The *nuliaqpak* is the *nuliaq* the man acquired first, and the *nukarak* is the one he married second (regardless of the relative ages of the two women). His relationship with each followed the basic *ui-nuliaq* pattern almost completely, at least ideally. Having the two women living together, however, resulted in the existence of still another relationship within the general marital context, namely that of "co-wives," or the *aipaq-aipaq* relationship (an analysis of which is outside the scope of this paper).

We have no exact figures on the frequency of polygynous unions in the traditional society, but there were, of course, strict demographic limitations on the possibilities. If men and women were roughly equal in number in the society,[6] either the number of polygynous unions was very low, or many men had to go unmarried. Since we know that virtually every man in the society did get married, and spent most of his adult life that way, we must conclude that polygynous marriages were fairly uncommon. They were highly acceptable, however, and numerous cases have been attested. Rather than being commonplace, they seem to have been more on the order of a luxury: something to be achieved when a man was rich enough to support more than one wife. Generally, polygynous unions involved only two women, but there are cases on record of especially wealthy men in the larger villages having three wives. One man at Point Hope was said to have had five at the time of his death.

The other primary elaboration on the *ui-nuliaq* theme, namely, the polyandrous union, is illustrated in Figure 3. In this case, there were two men

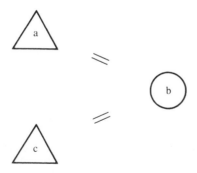

(ab) *uikpak-nuliaq;* (cb) *nukarak-nuliaq;* (ac) *nuliaqan-nuliaqan*

FIGURE 3. Polyandrous Residential Marriage

involved, both of whom had approved sexual relations with one woman within the coresidential context. The woman was the *nuliaq* of both men. The man whom she married first was her *uikpak*, and the one she married second was her *nukarak*. The relationship between the two men was that of *nuliaqan-nuliaqan*, or "cohusbands."

The frequency of polyandrous unions in the traditional society cannot be determined with precision, but it is certain that they were extremely rare, much more so than their polygynous counterparts. Actual cases have been documented, however, and it is clear that the system had a place for such marriages if people wished to get involved in them. It seems that the scarcity of polyandrous marriages was a function of the strains that were inherent in them. On the one hand, problems resulted from the competition of the two men for the sexual relations with the one woman. On the other hand, they stemmed from the tremendous economic burden placed on one woman having to do all the butchering, sewing, and other work that being married to two hunters would entail. These tasks would of course be in addition to the duties of childbearing and child rearing that would devolve upon her. When people did align themselves in a polyandrous marriage, it usually did not last long as a result of these factors. The Eskimos themselves were aware of the problems involved, and most of them simply avoided getting into such situations.

The final form of institutionalized marriage among the North Alaskan Eskimos was the celebrated "wife-exchange" situation.[7] This arrangement, illustrated in Figure 4, involved *two ui-nuliaq* pairs becoming associated with each other, the participants engaging in sexual relations with each other's spouse. This is different from any of the other forms of marriage in that here the individuals involved did not reside together on a permanent basis, but merely exchanged sexual partners for brief periods. The relationships established through the sexual exchange were binding outside of the scope of the exchange itself however. Because of its intimate connection with the other forms of marriage, and its general importance in Eskimo life, I shall refer to

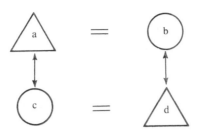

(ab) *ui-nuliaq;* (dc) *ui-nuliaq;* (ac) *uiNuzaq-nulizaq;*
(db) *uiNuzaq-nulizaq;* (ad) *nuliaqan-nuliaqan;* (bc) *aipaq-aipaq*

FIGURE 4.   Comarriage

this custom as "comarriage." The older labels of "wife-trading" and "wife-exchange" have connotations which are misleading in a number of respects.

It is important to remember that while sexual relations were repeated often in most (but not all) comarriages, intercourse was really nothing more than the validating act of the union. Significantly, it had to take place only on one occasion for the relationships to be established for the lifetimes of the participants. Thus, if two couples agreed to unite in comarriage, all that was required was that each man spend a single night with the other man's wife. After that, even if the exchange was never repeated, the participants were considered to be cospouses.

In a comarriage, the relationships that were considered to be the most important were those between the two men, on the one hand, and the two women, on the other. For the co-wives (*aipaq*) and cohusbands (*nuliaqan*), comarriage meant strong bonds of friendship, mutual aid, and protection. The tie between each man and the other's *nuliaq* was institutionalized as a superficial one, and sex was of secondary importance once the union had been established. If the ties between cospouses (*uiNuzaq-nulizaq*) did in fact become stronger than the two *ui-nuliaq* relationships, the participants had the option of exchanging on a permanent basis rather than a temporary one. In any case, the cospouse relationship was the weakest of the four. Both popular and scientific writers have consistently failed to appreciate this fact.

One of the obvious implications of the terms "wife-exchange" and "wife-trading" is that it was the *nuliaq* alone who was traded.[8] This implication is incorrect, for the *ui* was exchanged just as surely as was the *nuliaq*, if not more so. Just how the exchange was effected depended on the circumstances, but, whenever possible, the wives stayed home and the husbands traded places for the night, returning home during the day. Most often, however, comarriages were established between couples who normally resided in different villages. Under such conditions, the principals might exchange sex partners whenever they happened to come together in the same place. This might occur fairly frequently if the home villages were not too far apart, but otherwise might take place only once a year or so, or perhaps even less. In some cases, they only took place once, even though the bonds thus established were permanent.

The term "wife-exchange" implies that the decision about establishing an exchange was taken solely at the discretion of the husband, but here again the popular conception is incorrect. As Heinrich has so clearly demonstrated, and as my own research has confirmed, the *ui* had absolutely no right to order his *nuliaq* around in such matters. On the contrary, the women had just as much to say about whether or not an exchange union would be established as did the men. Moreover, the women as well as the men could take the initiative in getting one started. In any case, the matter of "trading" never entered the situation.

There is little doubt that comarriage was institutionalized to a high degree among the traditional North Alaskan Eskimos. Statistics are lacking, but there is reason to believe that it was very widespread. Indeed, the majority of the adult population of the society may well have been involved in comarriage situations. Unfortunately, the extreme disfavor with which the practice was viewed by the American teachers and missionaries in the region was quickly and thoroughly impressed upon the Eskimos, with the result that nowadays it is extremely difficult to get information about it. Nonetheless, the following considerations have been established with sufficient thoroughness as to be considered facts: (1) comarriage was an integral part of the more general marriage system; (2) it involved behavioral patterns that were highly institutionalized; and (3) promiscuity had virtually nothing to do with it.

It has sometimes been alleged that part of Eskimo hospitality involved loaning a wife to a visiting male guest, and much has been made of this in the popular literature on the Eskimos. Since the distinction between "wife-trading" and "wife-lending" is a rather fine one, I would like to clarify the matter at this point. To put it briefly, the available information suggests that "wife-lending," in the sense of letting a stranger have sexual relations with one's wife, was totally non-existent among the North Alaskan Eskimos. It is well known, for example, that in the traditional society, complete strangers were invariably killed on sight[9] unless one of the following conditions was met: (1) the strangers were numerous enough to be able to protect themselves; (2) the strangers had relatives in the area to serve as their guarantors and protectors; or (3) the strangers were encountered on certain special occasions, such as a Messenger Feast (cf. Spencer, 1959:210 ff.) or a summer trading festival when hostility of this sort was temporarily put aside. Strangers were despised and feared, and it is rather difficult to reconcile this thoroughly documented fact with the alleged practice of sexual hospitality. If a visitor had any sexual relations with a host's wife, one may be sure that the individuals were well known to each other, and that they were merely continuing a previously established relationship.

It seems that it was the American whalers and traders who in fact instituted something that might be called "wife-lending" in North Alaska. These strangers to the region took advantage of the peculiarities of the Eskimo marriage system on the one hand, and of their own wealth and power relative to that of the Eskimos on the other. In the former case, the white men pretended that they were getting into some sort of institutionalized marriage arrangement with the Eskimos, then refused to abide by the appropriate Eskimo rules of behavior. In the latter situation, the white men sometimes took Eskimo women by force, knowing that the Eskimos would not dare retaliate. In other cases (probably most frequently), the Eskimos themselves agreed on such sexual liaisons in the hope of getting some trade goods or whisky, more or less on the order of prostitution. In any case, such affairs were not native to the Eskimo way of life, but a consequence of the social breakdown which followed the arrival of rich and powerful outsiders.

Returning now to the institutionalized Eskimo marriage system, one can see that the several forms of marriage fit together rather neatly. A comparison of Figures 1 through 4 will reveal that the keystone of the system, the *ui-nuliaq* relationship, was common to all the marital arrangements. The other forms of marriage can be most easily understood simply as elaborations of this basic theme. Sexual intercourse was the common feature running through all the marriage forms, and residence was the variable. In the case of the *ui-nuliaq* type of marriage, there were two people involved, and they lived together and apart from any other spouses. In the plural forms of residential marriage, there were simply two or more members of the one sex or the other living with a single member of the opposite sex. Finally, in comarriage, the cospouses simply did not live together on a regular basis. The two additional relationships, those of cohusbands and co-wives, served to relate any members of the same sex who happened to be involved in *any* of the plural forms of marriage.

It is interesting to note that the various forms of marriage do not seem to have been mutually exclusive. An *ui-nuliaq* marriage, of course, was not only compatible with but was a prerequisite for each of the other alternatives. It is not certain, however, just how either of the plural forms of residential marriage co-ordinated with comarriage. Thus, if a man had two *nuliaqs*, just how would an exchange have been effected with another marital unit having only one man and one woman? Or how did two polygynous (or polyandrous) units establish an exchange union with each other, if they could do so at all? One can readily see that if all the logical combinations of the various basic forms of marriage could have been participated in at the same time by the same people, the real-life situations must have been quite complex. Unfortunately, the answers to the above and related questions are as yet unanswerable, although educated guesses could perhaps be made. Since all the forms of plural marriage are now either carried on in secret or are no longer practiced in North Alaska, they may remain unanswered forever. About the only thing that appears definite at this point is that a single couple could be associated through comarriage with more than one other couple at the same time.

It is instructive to consider the implications of the various forms of Eskimo marriage on subsequent generations. In the gross sense, all the offspring of *any* kind of marital arrangement were considered to be siblings to one another. Finer distinctions[10] were made as to "full," "half," "step-" and "co-" siblings, but the children were nonetheless considered to be brothers or sisters of one sort or another. This fact is significant, for in the Eskimo scheme of things, sibling relationships were extremely important, much more so than they are in the contemporary United States. Eskimo siblings were morally bound to co-operate in almost all the major activities of life, an obligation that held regardless of the form of marriage that produced or connected them.

The marital ties made at one generation level, which resulted in sibling connections at the second-generation level, produced cousin relationships at the third, and so on. The ties of kinship, once established, continued down-ward through the generations regardless of the form of marriage that was involved initially.[11] The same obligations and activities that were appropriate to the descendants of a simple residential marriage also held for the descen-dants of all the plural-marriage forms. The descendants of *any* sort of marital connection were ideally forbidden to marry one another as a result of the incest restrictions placed on relatives. This fact lends considerable support to the conclusion that each of the several forms of Eskimo marriage was really a form of marriage and not something else, for they all resulted in what was regarded as true kinship for the descendants.

Eskimo Divorce

The most fruitful application of the concept of "divorce" to the Eskimo situation is clearly in connection with the *ui-nuliaq* relationship since it was the keystone of the entire system. In this case what is said applied equally to the polygynous and polyandrous situations except that only one man and one woman were normally involved in each instance of divorce. (There was no rule preventing a person from divorcing two spouses simultaneously; how-ever, it just does not seem to have happened very often.) There is also a practical reason for excluding the cospouse relationship from this discussion, namely, a lack of relevant data. Whether or not anything which might be usefully labeled "divorce" ever occurred in connection with comarriage has not yet been determined as far as I know.

For all practical purposes, Eskimo divorce consisted in the breaking of the residence tie, and the termination of sexual relations invariably followed. Like marriage, divorce was accomplished without ceremony. All that was involved was one or the other spouse leaving the other, or else making the other one go, depending on the circumstances.[12]

If they were living with the *ui's* relatives and the *nuliaq* wished to leave, she could simply walk out on him. Ideally, at least, he could do nothing to stop her. Likewise if they were living with his relatives and the *ui* wished his *nuliaq* to leave, he had only to wait until she was out of the house, then scatter all her belongings outside the door. When she returned, the hint would be obvious. If they were living with the *nuliaq's* relatives, similar procedures in reverse would be followed. Ideally, either spouse could take the initiative in breaking off the residence tie, although in fact husbands had a bit more control over such situations than did wives simply by virtue of their superior physical strength. If a wife was really determined, however, the husband could not stop her from leaving him, regardless of how he felt about the situation.[13] If both the *ui* and *nuliaq* were agreed on a separation, an immediate result was assured.

One significant feature of Eskimo divorce was that the breaking of the residence tie did not terminate the marital relationship. Once such a relationship had been established, it held for the lifetimes of its members, regardless of whether or not either sexual relations or coresidence were continued. What divorce did was to *deactivate* the relationship. In other words, when the residence tie was broken, the relationship was generally ignored in the course of daily life even though it was still there in theory. In the United States we sometimes have inactive relationships with relatives outside our immediate family, such as cousins, especially second cousins. We may know who our cousins are and perhaps where they live, but we may never have any contact with them directly, even though the relationship is still there. If the members of such a relationship ever have occasion to activate it, it is a simple matter for them to do so.

In Eskimo divorce, the individuals either avoided each other altogether, or they acted as *ui* and *nuliaq*. There was nothing on the order of the "exspouse" relationship that so frequently occurs in our society, and even divorced Eskimo spouses thought of and referred to each other as *ui* and *nuliaq*. Indeed, it not infrequently happened that divorced spouses got back together again. Since the relationship had never been dissolved in the first place, re-establishment of the residence tie simply meant the reactivation of an already existing relationship. In America, if a husband and wife get divorced and then decide to get back together again, they would ideally have to go through the entire marriage procedure again, although actually they sometimes do not.

On the basis of the above considerations, it may be argued that the Eskimos did not have an institution which can appropriately be called "divorce." Indeed, Eskimo "divorce" was more like our separation than our "divorce." Properly speaking, of course, the American institution is a legal proceeding, nothing more and nothing less. In that sense it is correct to say that the Eskimos did not have "divorce." But, when you disregard the technicalities and look at situations, the two systems are not so different. The basic point is whether or not two spouses stay together or separate. It has been shown by Goode (1956:186, 187), for example, that the greatest emotional disturbance in the American situation comes at the time of physical separation, not at the time of a legal action. Hunt (1966:5) echoes Goode's conclusion, saying that "an emotionally genuine separation constitutes the death of a marriage, and divorce is merely its burial." On the other hand, the legal proceeding by no means necessarily terminates interaction between spouses. Indeed, Hunt[14] goes so far as to say that "divorce, though it cancels the partnership of man and wife, *never* severs their relationship entirely" [italics mine]. In short, in America, the legal matter of divorce has relatively little effect on the *de facto* aspects of the overall situation. It seems to be more of a symbol than anything else. Consequently, while the Eskimos did not have divorce in the technical sense of that term, I feel justified in maintaining that situations occur(red) in both societies, which are usefully compared under the rubric of "divorce."

It is of course impossible to know with certainty the extent of divorce among the traditional North Alaskan Eskimos, but there is reason to believe that the divorce rate (in the Eskimo sense) approached 100 per cent. That is, virtually everyone broke the residence tie with their spouse at least once, and many did so several times. What is not clear is the extent to which the initial tie was later reactivated as opposed to the frequency with which totally new spouses were acquired. Even here, however, the rate seems to have been fairly high, especially in the first years of married life.

The conditions which resulted in divorce among the Eskimos varied, of course, but some factors were clearly more significant than others. The most frequently cited source of strain in the *ui-nuliaq* relationship was infidelity on the part of one or both spouses. "Infidelity," in this case, means sexual relations outside the scope of the marriage system. Those involved in plural marriage were institutionalized, and hence did not constitute infidelity. Infidelity alone, however, did not necessarily result in divorce (although it might), but it certainly placed a strain on the *ui-nuliaq* relationships involved.

Another serious source of strain was the failure on the part of one or the other spouse to meet his or her economic obligations. In the traditional society, the family was economically self-sufficient to a high degree. It was the major locus of production, and both spouses were involved to an equal extent. The division of labor along sex lines was so complete, however, that there was virtually no overlap in the activities of the two. Consequently, when either shirked his or her responsibilities, the whole family suffered. In a society where life hovered around the subsistence level a good bit of the time, there were rather strict limits on the extent to which laziness and/or incompetence in economic pursuits could be tolerated. If a person was working hard, and his (or her) spouse was either unwilling or unable to carry her (or his) proper share of the load, it was only a matter of time before the strains in the relationship would become intolerable.

Disputes over child rearing also seem to have been a significant source of strain, although for different reasons than are usually involved in our society. When an American husband and wife argue about how to raise children, they are generally disagreeing on one of the two following points: (1) how to handle a specific incident; or (2) a general aspect of the upbringing of *all* their children. For the Eskimos on the other hand, the methods involved were pretty much agreed on, and followed traditional lines. The problems resulted from the apparently widespread tendency for a parent to strongly favor one child, who was usually *not* favored by the other parent. The favored child was exempt from normal rules of behavior as far as the favoring parent was concerned, but not from the viewpoint of the non-favoring parent. Consequently, when one parent scolded his or her spouse's favorite child, regardless of the reason, the other parent would become extremely incensed, and a quarrel would result. The depth of the emotions which could be generated in such situations was considerable.

The above seem to have been the major sources of strain in the *ui-nuliaq* relationship, but they were by no means the only ones. Other sources included personality clashes, with all that they entailed, in-law trouble, jealousy, barrenness, and minor irritations of all kinds. Significantly, the *ui-nuliaq* relationship was not expected to contain any serious strains. Indeed, some things we would scarcely regard as justification for an argument were sufficient grounds for an Eskimo divorce. If friction developed between spouses, separation was an acceptable alternative at all times. Divorces also resulted from factors other than strains within a marital union, however. For example, a person might leave a spouse to go live with someone else who seemed more desirable even though the first one was generally quite acceptable. Divorce could be instituted on purely individual initiative, and justification for such action did not have to be made to anyone. Irresponsibility in such matters was not encouraged, however, and a person who evidenced extreme instability in marital associations would eventually have a difficult time obtaining a spouse.

One of the more interesting things about Eskimo divorce is the consequences that remarriage had for the various individuals involved. A hypothetical remarriage situation is illustrated in Figure 5, in which two

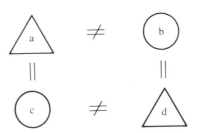

(ab) *ui-nuliaq;* (dc) *ui-nuliaq;* (ac) *ui-nuliaq;* (db) *ui-nuliaq;*
(ad) *nuliaqan-nuliaqan;* (bc) *aipaq-aipaq*

FIGURE 5.   Divorce and Remarriage

couples who were divorced then married each other's spouses. It should be noted that remarriage rarely followed this particular pattern because two divorced couples were not likely to remarry on a parallel basis such as this one. More often, an *ui* would marry someone that had no or only distant connections with the person that his *nuliaq* married. The resulting types of relationships would be the same regardless of the number of individuals involved, however, hence the utility of the diagram.

Since the *ui-nuliaq* relationship, once established, held for the lifetimes of its members, the original link between the two marital couples in Figure 5 is not broken by divorce; it is merely deactivated. Since everyone in the diagram got remarried, however, two new *ui-nuliaq* pairs were created in addition to, not in replacement of, the original pair. The interesting thing is the relationships that resulted for the two men and the two women involved. As Figure 4 indicates, the women stood in the relationship of co-wives (*aipaq-aipaq*) and the two men were cohusbands (*nuliaqan-nuliaqan*). A comparison to Figures 8 and 9 will indicate that divorce and remarriage was almost identical in its formal aspects with the highly institutionalized comarriage situation. The only difference is that the relationship between cospouses (*uiNuzaq-nulizaq*) was not established in the case of divorce and remarriage, being replaced there by the residential marital relationship of *ui-nuliaq*. The similarity that Eskimo divorce and remarriage had with the basic forms of plural marriage has prompted Heinrich (1963) to label it "marriage in lesser degree," rather than as divorce.

Divorce, with the virtually universal remarriage, was for all practical purposes an integral part of the Eskimo marriage system because it resulted in the establishment of the same set of relationships as did marriage itself. Consequently, the four relationships in the system can be defined as follows: (1) the *ui-nuliaq* relationship existed between any man and woman who had *ever* had socially approved sexual relations while living together; (2) the cospouse relationship (*uiNuzaq-nulizaq*) relationship obtained between any man and woman who had had socially approved sexual relations with each other while *not* living together; (3) the cohusband (*nuliaqan-nuliaqan*) relationship held between two men who had had socially approved sexual intercourse with the same woman; (4) the co-wife (*aipaq-aipaq*) relationship obtained between two women who had had socially approved intercourse with the same man. The "had had" feature is an essential component of the above definitions because in no case did the defining criteria have to be maintained for a very long time. Likewise, a considerable length of time could elapse between the establishment of one relationship and the setting up of another. Thus, a man could enter into an *ui-nuliaq* relationship with a woman, divorce her, and marry another woman twenty years later, and the two women would still be in the co-wife relationship.

The above consequences of divorce and remarriage were of considerable importance in the traditional society. If a man and the new husband of his divorced wife had anything to do with each other at all, they were expected to behave in terms of the same highly structured relationship that obtained between the two men in an exchange-marriage arrangement. This meant that they were under obligations of mutual friendship and support. A similar situation held for the women. In short, they had the choice of avoiding each other altogether, or of getting along on very good terms indeed. The jealousy and mutual antagonism which might be expected in such situations were considered inappropriate. They did in fact occur sometimes, of course, but were considered wrong by the other members of the society. In any case, the ideal alternatives were clearly defined, as were the resulting behavior patterns once a choice had been made.

The effect that Eskimo divorce had on the children is not clear at our present state of knowledge, but was probably minimal in its negative aspects. The results varied considerably depending on the situation. If a single, very young child was involved, it was generally adopted by another family, usually relatives of one of the parents. Since the Eskimos had a well-established, highly institutionalized, and generally very satisfactory system of adoption (which cannot be gone into here), such a procedure was not upsetting to anyone. The child would not lose his ties with his real parents when taken in by someone else, it would merely gain some additional ones. When more and/or older children were involved, they usually stayed with the mother. Even while fairly young, however, Eskimo children were permitted to exercise a fair amount of individual discretion as to the person with whom they wished to live. Adolescents could pretty much make up their own minds on the subject. As was the case for marriage proper, divorce and remarriage resulted in the establishment of sibling ties for all the children of all the participants; hence there were no problems in this area either.

Property rarely caused any difficulties in Eskimo divorce because, on the whole, goods were individually owned, with fairly little overlap between the sexes. Consequently, when a divorce was effected, each person simply kept his or her own belongings. If there was any trouble at all, it usually occurred in situations where a man had been living with his wife's relatives and had helped them in some major construction effort, such as building the house in which they were living, which would entitle him to part ownership in it. Here, of course, the problem was not between the *ui* and *nuliaq*, but between the man and his *nuliaq's* relatives.[15] Its resolution depended on a number of situational factors that need not be considered here.

Discussion

It is revealing, in the analysis of divorce, to consider what the marital relationship would be like if it were functioning normally. It is also instructive in the attempt to understand any institution in one society to contrast it with the appropriate one in another. The traditional North Alaskan Eskimo *ui-nuliaq* relationship and its contemporary American counterpart, for example, differed in a number of ways. For the remainder of the paper, therefore, I am going to compare the two systems and outline their similarities and differences as I see them with respect to both marital relationships and the divorce situation. Although my primary concern here is with the Eskimos, it will sometimes be necessary to discuss our own system in some detail to bring out the contrast between the two.

One distinctive feature of the *ui-nuliaq* relationship is its similarity to what we call a "contract" relationship. Such a relationship is known in professional jargon as a "functionally specific" one. As defined by Levy,[16] this means that the various "activities or rights and obligations or performances that [were] covered by the relationship [were] precisely defined and delimited." If someone had asked a traditional Eskimo couple to list what was supposed to be involved in their relationship, they probably could have answered quickly and precisely, and then stop, having listed everything they thought relevant. If the same question were put to a contemporary American couple, however, they would probably have some difficulty in answering. They could perhaps name a few especially important things in relatively short order, but beyond that they would likely be overwhelmed by the number and variety of considerations involved.

It should be recognized, however, that the *ui-nuliaq* relationship was not functionally specific to the extent that is the case with a true contract relationship, in which both definition *and* delimitation are quite precise. In the *ui-nuliaq* case most of the considerations were relatively precisely defined, but the relationship was not precisely *delimited* to the extent that an Eskimo could state exactly where his duties vis-à-vis his spouse ended and where they began. The data suggest, however, that in both respects the Eskimos went far beyond our own husband-wife relationship, and I strongly suspect that they were relatively extreme from the viewpoint of marital relationships in any society in the world.

Of the various orientations involved in the *ui-nuliaq* relationship, sexual relations were obviously important, but the relationship was economically oriented to a degree that must be unusual for relationships in the marital category.[17] That is to say, the production of goods and services occupied an especially important place among all the activities involved in *ui-nuliaq* interaction from the Eskimos' own point of view. The *ui* was primarily a hunter, and most of his activities revolved around the chase, and the manufacture and maintenance of hunting and household implements. He was also primarily responsible for the education of his sons. The *nuliaq*, on the other hand, was responsible for the skinning and butchering of the game that her husband killed. She also had to make and maintain the family clothing, store and prepare the food, look after the small children, and educate her daughters. The duties of the spouses overlapped very little. Beyond these predominantly economically oriented activities and sexual intercourse, there was little involved in the relationship, at least ideally.

With respect to the contemporary American situation, however, the same assertions could not be made, at least with reference to the ideals of married life. While it is clear that economic considerations are very important in the relationship between husband and wife, I think it fair to say that a marriage in which they are emphasized to the same extent as was ideally the case among the Eskimos would be regarded by most Americans as one which is headed for disaster. Indeed, I would not be surprised if the American husband-wife relationship was found to be one of the most diffusely oriented marital relationships of any in the world, certainly at the opposite end of the continuum from its Eskimo counterpart.

So far, of course, I have been talking about the ideal situation with respect to the substantive definition of the relationships. Actually, however, many Eskimo marriages were relatively functionally diffuse, while many American marriages are relatively functionally specific. The interesting thing about the North Alaskan situation is that to the extent that the individuals involved in a particular *ui-nuliaq* relationship were living under favorable economic circumstances, the greater the extent to which their relationship was likely to approach the ideal of functional specificity. Couples who were living in isolated camps of perhaps one or two families were generally involved in very diffuse relationships, but the larger the settlement in which the same couples might live, the less that *ui* and *nuliaq* would have to do with each other outside of sexually and economically oriented activities. In some of the larger maritime villages, *ui* and *nuliaq* might only see one another at sporadic intervals.

There was very little communication between an *ui* and his *nuliaq*, and little was expected. Furthermore, as one might suppose in a functionally specific relationship of this sort, the communication that did take place dealt largely with the practical problems of the day, and little else. Indeed, as was mentioned above, Eskimo husbands and wives were not often in one another's company.[18] The men spent their time hunting or visiting with other men, while women were either working in the house, or visiting with other women. In the larger villages and elsewhere whenever conditions permitted, the men generally spent most of their waking hours in a special building known as a *kazgi*,[19] and even ate their meals there, completely separated from their wives and young children.

In the contemporary United States, however, the situation is quite the opposite, at least ideally. Husbands and wives are expected to share experiences, ideas, secrets, and so forth, and to spend a major portion of their free time in one another's company. Not only is communication between husband and wife supposed to be frequent and informative, it is expected to be of an emotionally satisfying kind that theoretically cannot be found outside of marriage. Actually, of course, many husbands and wives interact more along the lines of their Eskimo counterparts than according to the American ideal, but, when they do, it is a sign of breakdown in the relationship. To the Eskimos, lack of communication between spouses was not only the normal state of affairs, it was regarded as the "right" one. An interesting point made by Dr. Jessie Bernard . . . is that the requirements of the American custom greatly increase the opportunities for communication at *cross-purposes*. The result is that one of the most highly institutionalized aspects of the husband-wife relationship is also one of the primary loci of strain in that relationship. The Eskimos, by minimizing communication of any kind, were able to avoid this particular problem.

Another important difference between the Eskimo and American systems is in the intensity of the emotional involvement in the marital situation. It is well known, of course, that love is considered the keystone of American marriage, and a vast folklore and literature has grown up to tell us why this must be so. Not only are American couples expected to be in love with each other, they are expected to demonstrate that affection in a variety of ways, both publicly and privately. The *ui-nuliaq* relationship, however, was much less intense than its American counterpart. Cases of romantic unions did in fact occur, but they do not seem to have been overly common. In any case, love certainly was not institutionalized as a component of the relationship. One was expected to feel affection for a spouse, but not necessarily a great deal of it. And, regardless of one's actual feelings, the demonstration of affection for one's spouse in public was regarded as being improper. It was probably minimal (although present) even in private.

Perhaps the most significant contrast of all between the two systems is in the relative strength of the appropriate relationships. In the Eskimo case, the *ui-nuliaq* relationship was ideally a very weak one (although strong ones did sometimes occur in fact). In other words, if one had to choose between the obligations to one's spouse and those to almost any kind of "blood" relative, one was expected to choose in favor of the latter in virtually every case. In America, however, there are rather few obligations and commitments that take precedence over those between husband and wife. The general obligations to "God and country" are perhaps the only ones that unequivocally come before those to one's spouse, at least ideally. Even here, provision is made for the spouse wherever possible (such as when married men are deferred from the draft). Actually, of course, it often happens that individuals choose in favor of their job, their golf partners, their parents, their bridge club, or whatever, over their spouse. Doing so constitutes a breakdown of the marriage, however. Continued deferment of one's obligations to one's spouse in favor of those to virtually anything *but* "God and country" will frequently lead to severe strains in the relations between husband and wife, and perhaps to separation and divorce.

It is sometimes argued that the rising divorce rate in the United States is a sign that the husband-wife relationship is rapidly losing its former strength. One implication of such a conclusion for the present discussion would be that the American marital relationship is becoming more like the traditional Eskimo one, at least in this particular respect. I think that such a conclusion is unwarranted, however. I suspect that a thorough examination of the *actual* reasons behind the divorces in the United States, without any regard for what is said in court, would reveal that, on the contrary, the husband-wife relationship is even stronger than it was in former decades. What is happening, I suggest, is that since divorces are becoming progressively easier to come by, people are beginning to demand that their spouses live up to the ideals of the relationship to a higher degree *in fact* than was formerly the case, or forfeit the relationship altogether. Easy divorce in both the Eskimo and American systems provides a means by which a person can hold a spouse effectively responsible for his or her behavior. The difference lies in the kinds of behavior which are expected in the first place.

It is clear that the *ui-nuliaq* and husband-wife relationships, however similar they might appear in a diagram, occupied vastly different niches in quite different systems. It is not surprising, therefore, that divorce should have different causes and consequences in each. If it were possible to measure such things with any precision, I am sure that we would find that the *ui-nuliaq* relationship was generally subjected to fewer, and usually weaker, strains than is the case for its American counterpart. This, despite the fact that divorce was probably much more frequent among the Eskimos than in the contemporary United States. The major difference, however, lies in the fact that in America there is an overwhelming obligation to contain any and all strains which might be generated in such a relationship, whereas the Eskimos felt very little responsibility of this sort. No wonder, then, that in America[20] the divorce of mature, stable individuals is preceded by varying amounts of anguish, soul searching, sleepless nights, and so forth. It is an unhappy event for the people involved, and usually for their relatives and close friends as well. Indeed, the more one has accepted the values of our society, the more extreme the emotional strain of a divorce is likely to be. This does not mean that even the most stable person will not get divorced under the right conditions, but when he does, it is usually an extremely painful experience.

To the Eskimos, however, divorce was hardly a catastrophe. As far as economic considerations were concerned, the separated spouses could turn to relatives for temporary support. Since they usually remarried within a relatively short time,[21] divorce generally caused few difficulties in the economic sphere. Furthermore, in the case of famine or any other crisis, the full obligations of mutual support were incumbent on the individuals involved regardless of how antagonistic they might be at the time. Unfortunately, we do not know with any certainty what the psychological consequences of divorce were in the traditional period. We do know, however, that the individuals involved in a divorce situation were often extremely aroused, usually in the form of anger. The psychological impact was probably very superficial in nature, however, certainly much less than what it seems to be in the contemporary United States. For the Eskimos, a rift with one's parents or siblings was an infinitely more traumatic experience than was a break with one's spouse.[22]

There is also a distinct difference between the two societies with regard to the extent to which the postdivorce situation is structured. That is, they differ with respect to the extent to which behavioral guidelines for divorcees are institutionalized. When an American couple gets divorced, for example, their obligations to one another, usually with reference to the children (if any), property, and economic support, are generally fairly carefully defined in the courts. Outside of these few, albeit important considerations, however, the divorce situation seems to be almost totally unstructured. The individuals involved have to improvise their own rules of behavior. Indeed, it is just this lack of definition which Goode[23] cites as the major cause of the high remarriage rate among divorced Americans. The situation is so poorly defined, he argues, that most people find it very uncomfortable to stay in it, and they seek the only acceptable way out, namely, remarriage.[24]

Divorced Eskimos, however, were in no such position. On the whole, they were expected to avoid each other, but even when confronting each other face to face they knew how they were supposed to act. They could follow socially approved alternatives which they knew in advance, and they did not have to make things up as they went along. There was considerable pressure on Eskimos to remarry, but in their case the pressure stemmed from the need to have an economic partner of the opposite sex. Lack of social definition of their status in life was never a factor.

Another difference between Eskimos and Americans is the position of the children in a divorce situation. For the Eskimos divorce was not only clearly defined with respect to any children involved, it was fully integrated with the kinship system in general. Eskimos generally had several sets of siblings, a full biological set, possibly a set or two of half-siblings, and probably one or more sets of exchange siblings. Likewise, an Eskimo was liable to have more than one set of parents, a full biological pair, perhaps an adoptive pair, and possibly one or more stepparents. Since the notion of multiple sets of siblings and parents was a feature of Eskimo kinship at its *best*, it is unlikely that the new relationships created through divorce and remarriage caused any serious problems.

In America, however, it is generally agreed that divorce produces trauma of varying degrees of severity for children involved. Even if the degree of psychological and emotional impact of divorce on the children is not known with precision, it is clearly negative. The picture of estranged parents staying together "for the children's sake," long after their own relationship has failed, is a familiar one to all of us. The argument that the strains resulting from two such people living together might be even harder on the children than a divorce would be is beside the point, regardless of what truth it might contain in a given case.

Interestingly enough, when an American couple gets divorced, especially if there are children, the resulting situation is in some respects not unlike the one described for the Eskimos. Goode[25] and Hunt[26] have both found that divorce by no means necessarily breaks the bond between husband and wife in our society, and that often the behavior of a divorced person continues to be shaped by the attitudes of the former spouse for some time. As a minimum, certain economic obligations tie the two ex-spouses together, and if there are children involved, it is very difficult for them to avoid seeing each other on occasion. In America, the illusion is that divorce terminates interaction between spouses altogether, while in fact it is rarely the complete break we tend to think it is. In the Eskimo case, the illusion was that the divorce situation meant a continued active relationship, while in fact interaction between spouses was either greatly reduced or ceased completely.

A similar situation obtains for the other relationships involved. Say, for example, that American children of a first marriage go with the mother, as is normally the case. When she remarries, which she is likely to do, these children suddenly find themselves with two fathers, a "real" one and a "step" one. Now, if the mother has children by her second husband, they become half-siblings to the children she had by her first. If the second husband had children of his own by a previous marriage, the situation is even more complex, but rather similar to the *standard* Eskimo situation.

Likewise, if the first husband remarries and has children by his second wife, then those children are half-siblings to those he had by his first wife, and so on. To the American mind this is an extremely complicated situation, and probably a highly ambiguous one.[27] What are the relationships of the several sets of half- and step- and full-siblings to be like? How are the two husbands supposed to behave toward each other when they meet (which may be unavoidable at times)? How are the two women supposed to act toward each other? The Eskimos would have had a set of ready answers for questions like these because such situations were not only commonplace in their society even without divorce, they were highly institutionalized. Many Americans are now in situations similar to the hypothetical ones outlined above, yet they have no standards of behavior to guide them.

Superficially, at least, the traditional North Alaskan Eskimos and the contemporary Americans are rather similar with respect to the *de facto* consequences of divorce, no matter how different the two systems might be ideally. The most obvious difference is that for the Eskimos the postdivorce situation was clearly defined and institutionalized for *all* parties, whereas in the United States it is not. It is clear, however, that due to radically different conceptions of what marriage is supposed to be like in the first place, divorce has quite a different type of impact on the individuals involved. Goode (1956:216) argues that life goes on, and that the wounds of an American divorce heal in time, as do those of a loved one's death and other life crises. There, however, lies the rub, for a wound always leaves a scar. For the

Eskimos there was no wound, hence no scar. For them it was not a matter of "life going forward" in spite of it all, for there was no crisis to be overcome; life merely went on pretty much as usual, with perhaps a few temporary complications.

In conclusion, it seems apparent that divorce can never be understood except in relation to the whole of which it is a part. More specifically, divorce is non-existent apart from marriage, and neither can be understood without a consideration of their positions in the society as a whole. Eskimo society was set up in such a way that divorce was neither greatly upsetting to the principals involved nor disruptive of the community at large. Emotional and social stability depended on the operation of other relationships which, to them, were more important. This does not mean, as has sometimes been claimed, that the Eskimos were totally lacking in moral standards. On the contrary, they had very definite values—values which were strongly held. They were simply different than ours. In the final analysis, the problem seems to be largely one of emphasis. The degree to which a particular marital relationship is emphasized in a society is of crucial importance in this respect and must be taken into consideration in any analysis of divorce.

Notes

1. (Befu, 1964; Ben-Dor, 1966; Damas, 1963, 1964: Gradburn, 1964; Guemple, 1965, 1966; Heinrich, 1960, 1963; Hughes, 1958, 1960; and Lantis, 1946, 1960.)

2. The studies most relevant to this paper are the following, only a portion of the total literature on North Alaska: Burch, 1966; Gubser, 1965; Heinrich, 1955a, 1955b, 1960, 1963; Pospisil, 1964; Pospisil and Laughlin, 1963; and Spencer, 1959. For a general description of the life of the people living in the northern portion of this region, see Chance, 1966.

3. In this and subsequent diagrams, a triangle indicates a male and a circle a female. An equal sign indicates a marital tie. These symbols are in common use among anthropologists.

4. *Actually*, of course, the relationship was a crucial one for the society from a number of points of view.

5. In everyday American speech, we are accustomed to using the term "polygamy" to refer to the situation of a man having two or more wives. Technically, however, such a situation is known as "polygyny." Its counterpart, where one woman has two husbands, is called "polyandry." Both polygyny and polyandry are included under the rubric "polygamy," which means simply "plural marriage" of any kind.

6. It has sometimes been claimed that baby girls were frequently put to death at birth in the traditional society. This situation would have resulted in more men than women, a further limitation on the possibilities for polygyny. The *actual frequency* of infanticide of any kind has been questioned (Burch, 1966), however, at least insofar as the North Alaskan Eskimos are concerned. On the other hand,

it has been suggested that the hazards of hunting would have resulted in a higher death rate for men than for women. This would have increased the opportunities for polygyny. While this seems a reasonable proposition, it is one that has yet to be examined with sufficient thoroughness to permit definite statements on the subject one way or the other. Consequently, we must assume that males and females were roughly equal in number in the society until it is demonstrated to have been otherwise.

7. The field research which formed the basis for the "breakthrough" in our understanding of this custom was conducted by Albert Heinrich (1955a, 1955b, 1960, 1963). Heinrich's work was followed by a study in which Guemple (1961) reviewed the entire literature, both published and unpublished, dealing with exchange practices. Subsequent field research of my own has confirmed the general conclusions reached by Heinrich and Guemple, and has started to fill in the details.

8. Heinrich, 1955a: 134 ff.

9. The North Alaskans were apparently more extreme in their treatment of strangers than were other Eskimo groups.

10. As is true of most aspects of kinship, the Eskimos divided siblings along different lines than we do, a matter which cannot be more fully explored here.

11. After a time, almost everyone in an Eskimo village could become related through this process if carried on over even a few generations. There were, however, various social mechanisms for getting around this problem when necessary. In addition, certain factors operated to counteract this unifying tendency, so that actual situations were generally less complicated in this respect than one might be led to suspect.

12. Heinrich, 1955a: 170.

13. This greatly minimized the possibility of a wife being "exchanged" or "loaned" by her *ui* to another man. If she did not approve, she could divorce her husband on the spot.

14. Hunt, 1966: 203.

15. This raises the question of where the *relatives* of the spouses fit into the divorce situation. This question, which is not often dealt with, would probably be a most interesting one to consider, especially in any sort of cross-cultural analysis of marriage, divorce, and their implications.

16. Levy, 1952: 256.

17. I do not mean to imply by this remark that economic functions alone were served by this relationship. On the contrary, numerous others, many of them crucial for the operation of the society, were also fulfilled through the operation of the *ui-nuliaq* relationship, but on the whole they seem either to have been unrecognized or were simply considered relatively unimportant by the Eskimos themselves.

18. The North Alaskan Eskimos seem to have been more extreme in this respect than their relatives to the east in Canada and Greenland. This is possibly a consequence of the fact that subsistence conditions were generally more favorable in Alaska than they were to the east, hence this particular ideal would have been more easily attained there.

19. Spencer, 1959: 182 ff.

20. My remarks on the postdivorce situation in the United States are based largely on Goode's study *After Divorce* (Free Press, 1956), and Hunt's *The World of the Formerly Married* (McGraw, 1967). The discussion is most applicable to the middle and upper levels of United States society, and less so at the lower levels.

21. Precise data are lacking but the "between-marriage" period for the traditional North Alaskan Eskimos was probably measured in terms of days, weeks, or months, but rarely, if ever, in years. This is in sharp contrast with our own system.

22. This brings up an important point which should not be overlooked, namely, that the Eskimos did have other, non-marital relationships which were very strong indeed. Among the Eskimos, parent-child, sibling, and cousin relationships *at least* were all much stronger than are the comparable relationships in our own society.

23. Goode, 1956: 207, 216.

24. Hunt's (1966) more recent account of the postmarital situation indicates that the patterns which are now beginning to develop to guide behavior during this period are overwhelmingly oriented to getting people over the trauma of their divorce, and to the location and recruitment of new spouses. In other words, the "formerly married" state remains highly unsatisfactory to most people involved in it even though some sort of structure is beginning to evolve. This suggests that it is not lack of definition that is the key to remarriage. On the contrary, I see it as another affirmation of the great strength which marriage has in our society.

25. Goode, 1956:306.

26. Hunt, 1966: Chapter 7.

27. Even though the postmarriage situation is becoming increasingly structured in the United States with respect to husband-wife interaction, I have yet to hear of any satisfactory developments along these lines as far as children are concerned.

References

ABERLE, DAVID F.; BRONFENBRENNER, URIE; HESS, ECKHARD H.; MILLER, DANIEL R.; SCHNEIDER, DAVID M.; and SPUHLER, JAMES N. 1963. "The Incest Taboo and the Mating Pattern of Animals." *American Anthropologist* 65:253-65.

ALEXANDER, FRANZ. 1930. "The Neurotic Character." *International Journal of Psychoanalysis* 11:292-311.

ARDENER, E. 1962. *Divorce and Fertility: An African Study*. Nigerian Social and Economic Studies, No. 3. (Nigerian Institute of Social and Economic Research.) London: Oxford University Press.

BEFU, HARUMI. 1964. "Eskimo Systems of Kinship Terms—Their Diversity and Uniformity," *Arctic Anthropology* 2:(1):84-98.

BEN-DOR, SHMUEL. 1966. *Makkovik: Eskimos and Settlers in a Labrador Community. A Contrastive Study in Adaptation.* St. John's, Newfoundland: Memorial University of Newfoundland, Institute of Social and Economic Research. Newfoundland Social and Economic Studies No. 4.

BERGLER, EDMUND. 1948. *Divorce Won't Help.* New York: Harper & Row.

BERNARD, JESSIE. 1942. *American Family Behavior.* New York: Harper & Row.

BERNARD, JESSIE. 1956. *Remarriage, A Study of Marriage.* New York: Dryden Press.

BERNARD, JESSIE. 1964. "Adjustments of Marital Partners," in HAROLD T. CHRISTENSEN, *Handbook of Marriage and the Family.* Chicago: Rand McNally.

BERNARD, JESSIE. 1969. "Infidelity, A Moral or Social Issue?" *Science and Psychoanalysis,* vol. 16.

BLOS, PETER. 1962. *On Adolescence: A Psychoanalytic Interpretation.* New York: The Free Press of Glencoe.

BOHANNAN, PAUL and KARAN HUCKLEBERRY. 1967. "Institutions of Divorce, Family and the Law." *Law and Society Review,* vol. I, no. 2, pp. 81-102.

BURCH, ERNEST S., JR. 1966. "Authority, Aid and Affection: The Structure of Eskimo Kin Relationships." (Unpublished Ph.D. dissertation, Department of Anthropology, University of Chicago.)

CHANCE, NORMAN A. 1966. *The Eskimo of Northern Alaska.* New York: Holt, Rinehart & Winston.

CHRISTENSON, CORNELIA and GAGNON, JOHN. 1955. "Sexual Behavior in a Group of Older Women." *Journal of Gerontology,* vol. 20, No. 3, pp. 351-55.

CHRISTENSEN, HAROLD and BARBER, KENNETH E. 1967. "Interfaith versus Intrafaith Marriage in Indiana," *Journal of Marriage and the Family.* 29, August, pp. 461-549.

COHEN, RONALD. 1966. "The Bornu King Lists," in *Boston University Publications in African History,* vol. II, J. Butler, ed. (pp. 41-83). Boston: Boston University Press.

COHEN, RONALD. 1967a. *The Kanuri of Bornu.* New York: Holt, Rinehart & Winston.

COHEN, RONALD. 1967b. "Social Stratification in Bornu," in *Class and Status in Sub-Saharan Africa.* A. Tuden and L. Plotnicov, eds. New York: The Free Press of Glencoe.

COHEN, RONALD. In press. "From Empire to Colony: Bornu in the Nineteenth and Twentieth Centuries," in *The Impact of Colonialism.* Victor W. Turner, ed. Stanford: The Hoover Institute.

COHEN, YEHUDI A. 1964. *The Transition from Childhood to Adolescence.* Chicago: Aldine Press.

CUBER, JOHN F. and HARROFF, PEGGY. 1966. *Sex and the Significant Americans.* Baltimore: Penguin Books.

DAMAS, DAVID. 1963. *Igluligmiut Kinship and Local Groupings: A Structural Approach.* Ottawa: National Museum of Canada Bulletin No. 196.

DAMAS, DAVID. 1964. "The Patterning of the Igluligmiut Kinship System." *Ethnology* 3:(4):377-88.

DESPERT, J. LOUISE. 1962. *Children of Divorce.* New York: Doubleday & Co. (Dolphin Books).

ERICKSON, ERIK H. 1956. "The Problem of Ego Identity." *Journal of the American Psychoanalytic Assoc.* 4:56-121.

FENICHEL, OTTO. 1945. *The Psychoanalytic Theory of Neurosis.* New York: W. W. Norton & Co.

FORTUNE, R. F. 1932. *Sorcerers of Dobu; The Social Anthropology of the Dobu Islanders of the Western Pacific.* New York: E. P. Dutton & Co.

FREUD, ANNA (1936). 1946. *The Ego and the Mechanisms of Defense.* New York: International Universities Press.

FREUD, SIGMUND (1910). 1948. "Contribution to the Psychology of Love. A Special Type of Choice of Object made by Men." *Collected Papers* 4:192-202. London: Hogarth Press.

FREUD, SIGMUND (1921). 1949. *Group Psychology and the Analysis of the Ego.* New York: Liveright Publishing Corp.

GEBHARD, PAUL. 1966. "Factors in Marital Orgasm." *The Journal of Social Issues,* Vol. 22, No. 2, pp. 88-95.

GITELSON, MAXWELL. 1963. "On the Problem of Character Neurosis." *Journal of the Hillside Hospital* 12:3-17.

GOODE, W. J. 1956. *After Divorce.* Chicago: Free Press.

GOODE, W. J. 1963. *World Revolution and Family Patterns.* New York: Free Press.

GRADBURN, NELSON H. H. 1964. "Taqagmiut Eskimo Kinship Terminology." Ottawa: Northern Co-ordination and Research Centre, Department of Northern Affairs and National Resources.

GREENBERG, JOSEPH H. 1954. "Studies in African Linguistic Classification, VIII." *Southwestern Journal of Anthropology* 10:405-15.

GUBSER, NICHOLAS J. 1965. *The Nunamiut Eskimos: Hunters of Caribou.* New Haven: Yale University Press.

GUEMPLE, D. L. 1961. *Innuit Spouse-Exchange.* Chicago: Department of Anthropology, University of Chicago.

GUEMPLE, D. L. 1965. "Saunik: Name-Sharing as a Factor Governing Eskimo Kinship Terms." *Ethnology* 4:(3):323-35.

GUEMPLE, D. L. 1966. "Kinship-Reckoning among the Belcher Island Eskimo." (Unpublished Ph.D. dissertation, Department of Anthropology, University of Chicago.)

HEINRICH, ALBERT C. 1955a. "An Outline of the Kinship System of the Bering Straits Eskimos." (Unpublished M.A. thesis, Department of Education, University of Alaska.)

HEINRICH, ALBERT C. 1955b. "A Survey of Kinship Forms and Terminologies Found among the Inupiaq-Speaking Peoples of Alaska." (College, Alaska: Unpublished manuscript in the University of Alaska library.)

HEINRICH, ALBERT C. 1960. "Structural Features of Northwestern Alaskan Eskimo Kinship." *Southwestern Journal of Anthropology* 16:(1):110-26.

HEINRICH, ALBERT C. 1963. "Eskimo-Type Kinship and Eskimo Kinship: An Evaluation and a Provisional Model for Presenting the Evidence Pertaining to Inupiaq Kinship Systems." (Unpublished Ph.D. dissertation, Department of Anthropology, University of Washington).

HENRY, JULES. 1941. *Jungle People.* New York: Augustin. [Reprinted 1964, Vintage V521, Random House]

HUGHES, CHARLES C. 1958. "An Eskimo Deviant from the 'Eskimo Type' of Social Organization." *American Anthropologist* 60:(6):1140-47.

HUGHES, CHARLES C. 1960. *An Eskimo Village in the Modern World.* Ithaca: Cornell University Press.

HUNT, MORTON M. 1966. *The World of the Formerly Married.* New York: McGraw-Hill Book Co.

JACOBSON, PAUL H. 1959. *American Marriage and Divorce.* New York: Rinehart & Co.

KINSEY, ALFRED C.; POMEROY, WARDELL B.; and MARTIN, CLYDE E. 1948. *Sexual Behavior in the Human Male.* Philadelphia: W. B. Saunders Company.

KINSEY, ALFRED C., POMEROY, WARDELL B., MARTIN, CLYDE E., and GEBHARD, PAUL. 1953. *Sexual Behavior in the Human Female.* Philadelphia: W. B. Saunders Company.

KOMAROVSKY, MIRRA. 1966. *Blue-Collar Marriage.* New York: Random House, Inc.

LANDES, RUTH and ZBOROWSKI, MARK. 1950. "Hypotheses Concerning the Eastern European Jewish Family." *Psychiatry* 13:447-64.

LANTIS, MARGARET. 1946. *The Social Structure of the Nunivak Eskimo.* Transactions of the American Philosophical Society, ns., Vol. 35, Part 3.

LEVY, M. J., JR. 1952. *The Structure of Society.* Princeton: Princeton University Press.

LEVY, R. 1957. *The Social Structure of Islam* (2nd ed.). Cambridge: The University Press.

LEVY, ROBERT. No date. *Uniform Marriage and Divorce Legislation: A Preliminary Analysis.* Prepared for the Special Committee on Divorce of the National Conference of Commissioners on Uniform State Laws (mimeographed).

LIEBOW, ELLIOTT. 1967. *Fathers Without Children.* Boston: Little, Brown & Co., Inc.

MEAD, MARGARET. 1935. *Sex and Temperament in Three Primitive Societies.* New York: William Morrow & Co. [Reprinted 1963, Apollo A-67, Morrow]

MEAD, MARGARET. 1949. *Male and Female.* New York: William Morrow & Co. [Reprinted 1955, Mentor MD150, New American Library]

MEAD, MARGARET. 1955. "Implications of Insight—II" in *Childhood in Contemporary Cultures.* Margaret Mead and Martha Wolfenstein, eds. (pp. 449-61). Chicago: University of Chicago Press. [Reprinted 1963, Phoenix P124, University of Chicago Press]

MEAD, MARGARET. 1965. "Outdoor Recreation in the Context of Emerging American Cultural Values." In *Trends in American Living and Outdoor Recreation.* Reports to the Outdoor Recreation Resources Review Commission No. 22 (pp. 2-25). Washington: Government Printing Office.

MEAD, MARGARET. 1968. "Incest" for the *International Encyclopedia of the Social Sciences.* New York: Macmillan and Free Press.

NIMKOFF, M. F. 1952. "Contributions to a Therapeutic Solution to the Divorce Problem: Sociology," paper in Conference on Divorce: The Law School, University of Chicago, 9, pp. 55-62.

NYE, F. IVAN and HOFFMAN, LOIS W. 1963. *The Employed Mother in America.* Chicago: Rand McNally & Co.

PARSONS, TALCOTT. 1954. "The incest taboo in relation to social structure and the socialization of the child." *British Journal of Sociology* 5:101-17.

PESHKIN, A. and COHEN, R. 1967. "The Values of Modernization." *Journal of the Developing Areas,* vol. 2, pp. 7-22.

POSPISIL, LEOPOLD. 1964. "Law and Societal Structure among the Nunamiut Eskimo," in *Explorations in Cultural Anthropology: Essays in Honor of George Peter Murdock*, Ward H. Goodenough, ed. (pp. 395-431). New York: McGraw-Hill.

POSPISIL, LEOPOLD and LAUGHLIN, WILLIAM S. 1963. "Kinship Terminology among the Nunamiut Eskimos." *Ethnology* 2:(2):180-89.

RAINWATER, LEE. 1966. "Some Aspects of Lower-Class Sexual Behavior." *Journal of Social Issues*, vol. 22, April.

RANGELL, LEO. 1963. "On Friendship." *Journal of the American Psychoanalytic Assoc.* 11:3-54.

RUBEL, ARTHUR J. 1961. "Partnership and Wife-Exchange Among the Eskimo and Aleut of Northern North America." *Anthropological Papers of the University of Alaska* 10:(1):59-72.

SPENCER, ROBERT F. 1959. *The North Alaskan Eskimo: A Study in Ecology and Society*. BAE Bulletin No. 171. Washington: Government Printing Office.

SUMNER, WILLIAM GRANT. 1906. *Folkways*. Boston: Ginn & Co.

SUSSMAN, MARVIN. 1955, 1963. *Sourcebook in Marriage and the Family*. Boston: Houghton Mifflin Co.

TERMAN, L. M. and WALLIN, PAUL. 1949. "The Validity of Marriage Prediction and Marital Adjustment Tests." *American Sociological Review* 14 (August).

TERMAN, L. M. 1938. *Psychological Factors in Marital Happiness*. New York: McGraw-Hill Book Company.

TUMIN, MELVIN. 1965. "The Functionalist Approach to Social Problems." *Social Problems*, Spring, p. 383.

UNITED STATES GOVERNMENT National Center for Health Statistics. 1969. *Monthly Vital Statistics* Report, March 12.

UNITED STATES GOVERNMENT U. S. Census of Population. 1960. *Employment Status and Work Experience*. Washington: Government Printing Office.

UNITED STATES GOVERNMENT U. S. Census of Population 1960. *Marital Status*. Washington: Government Printing Office.

UNITED STATES GOVERNMENT U. S. Census of Population. 1960. *Persons by Family Characteristics*. Washington: Government Printing Office.

UNITED STATES GOVERNMENT U. S. Department of Health, Education, and Welfare, Public Health Service. 1963. *Divorce Statistics Analysis*. Washington: Government Printing Office.

UNITED STATES GOVERNMENT U. S. Department of Health, Education, and Welfare, Public Health Service. 1969. *Divorce Statistics*, 1966. Washington: Government Printing Office.

VERNIER, CHESTER G. and FRANK, R. A. 1938. *American Family Laws*. Stanford: Stanford University Press.

WEINBERG, S. KIRSON. 1955. *Incest Behavior*. New York: Citadel Press.

WOLFENSTEIN, MARTHA. 1946. *The Impact of a Children's Story on Mothers and Children*. Monographs of the Society for Research in Child Development, vol. 11, Ser. 42. Washington: National Research Council.

10

African and Afro-American Family Structure

NIARA SUDARKASA

Introduction

NOT SINCE THE PUBLICATION of Herskovits's *Myth of the Negro Past* in 1941 has there been such an interest as there is today in the relationship between Black American family structure and indigenous African family structure. The writings of a number of scholars, including Ladner (1971), Nobles (1974a, 1974b, 1978), and Shimkin and Uchendu (1978), essentially reaffirm the position articulated by DuBois in his pioneering study *The Negro American Family*, first published in 1908. Noting that he had made an attempt "to connect present conditions with the African past," DuBois stated:

> This is not because Negro-Americans are Africans, or can trace an unbroken social history from Africa, but because there is a distinct nexus between Africa and America, which, though broken and perverted, is nevertheless not to be neglected by the careful student. [DuBois 1908, p. 9]

It should not be necessary at this juncture in the study of the Black family to argue anew for the significance of the linkage between African and Black American families. The early historical and sociological writings of DuBois

The author, known also as Gloria A. Marshall, expresses her thanks to her former student Bamidele Agbasegbe for bringing to her attention a number of sources used in this paper, for his helpful comments on it, and for the final rendering of the kinship diagrams contained in it.

(1908), Woodson (1936), and Herskovits (1941), and the recent historical studies of Blassingame (1972), Genovese (1974), Owens (1976), Haley (1976), Gutman (1976), and others knowingly or unknowingly reveal many of the continuities as well as the changes in African family structure that resulted from the descent into slavery. Nevertheless, in view of some of the generalizations that have been put forth concerning African family patterns and the principles that are said to link Afro-American family structure to its African antecedents (Nobles 1974a, 1974b, 1978), it seems appropriate for a student of continental African societies to help shed light on some of the issues that have been raised.

The purpose of the present paper is twofold: (1) to analyze and interpret the structure of African families, with the aim of clarifying the operation of the principles of consanguinity and conjugality in the formation and maintenance of these groups,[1] and (2) to show how the data on African family structure point to a need for studying the process by which, in the changing socio-economic and political contexts of the United States, Afro-American family organization evolved from the African patterns re-created by the first Blacks brought here as slaves.

It is important to note, by way of a preface, that when the concept of "African family structure" is used, it implies generalization along two dimensions. First, there is an attempt to delineate those features of African family organization that underly and unify the variety of specific familial patterns and kinship ideologies that exist among the indigenous peoples of the African continent. Secondly, there is an attempt to describe those features of African family organization that have had relative permanence or persistence over time, so that they represent aspects of kinship that are legitimately termed a part of *the African heritage*. This is not to say that such structural features are unchanging, but rather that if one studies African families of the sixteenth century or the twentieth century, one would find remarkable similarities in the institutional features described.

African Kin Groups Defined

Basic to an understanding of African kinship is an understanding of (1) the composition of the *lineage* and the *extended family*; (2) the differences between these two kin groupings and their relationship to one another; and (3) the relationship of the lineage and the extended family to the typical African residential grouping known as the *compound*.

The *lineage* is a kin group in which the members, living and deceased, are related to each other and to a common ancestor through a line of descent traced through mothers *or* through fathers, but not through both. In the case of a *matrilineage*, the males and females who belong to it trace their kinship to each other and to their common female ancestor through their mothers, their mothers' mothers, their mothers' mothers' mothers, and so on. In the case of a *patrilineage*, the males and females who belong to it trace their kinship to each other and to their common male ancestor through their fathers, their fathers' fathers, their fathers' fathers' fathers, and so on.

Stated another way, this means that in a matrilineal society, a woman's children, male and female, belong to the lineage to which she herself belongs. That lineage would also include her brothers and sisters born of the same mother; her mother and her mother's brothers and sisters born of the same mother; her mother's mother, and so on. By the same principle, it follows that children of uterine sisters also belong to the same matrilineage. (See Figure 1.)

In a patrilineal society, a woman's children, male and female, belong to the lineage to which their respective fathers belong. They *do not* belong to the lineage to which their mother belongs. A woman's children would belong to a lineage comprising their father and his sisters and brothers sired by the same father; their father's father and his sisters and brothers of the same father, and so on. By extension of this principle, it follows that all children of a set of paternally-linked brothers belong to the same patrilineage. (See Figure 2.)

Two points are immediately apparent regarding the concept of "brothers and sisters" in societies where people are born into lineages. First, in a matrilineal society, children of the same mother belong to the same ma-

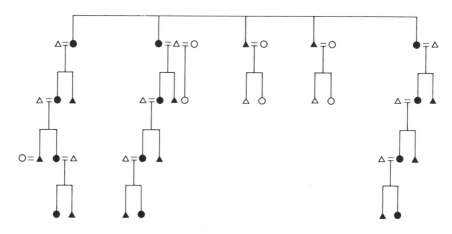

▲ Male member of the matrilineage
● Female member of the matrilineage
△ Male from another matrilineage
○ Female from another matrilineage
⊓ Sibling bond
| Parent-child link
= Marriage

FIGURE 1.   Schematic View of a Matrilineage

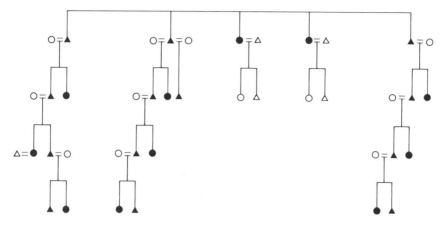

▲	Male member of the patrilineage
●	Female member of the patrilineage
△	Male from another patrilineage
○	Female from another patrilineage
⊓	Sibling bond
│	Parent-child link
=	Marriage

FIGURE 2.   Schematic View of a Patrilineage

trilineage, regardless of differences in paternity. Correspondingly, in a patrilineal society, children of the same father are members of the same patrilineage, without regard to differences in maternity.

Although it is beyond the scope of this paper to discuss all the functions of lineages in African societies, suffice it to say that where they existed in precolonial times, they were landholding corporate entities charged with the allocation of land, titles, and other properties among their members. In virtually all cases, lineages were identified with particular ancestral homelands; in some instances, they had special deities as well. Although there have been some changes in the function of lineages in contemporary Africa, where they exist they are still a vital part of the social structure. Ultimately, because of the actual and fictive links that connect the living members to the founding ancestor, lineages were and are the kin groups that signify and symbolize social continuity in African societies.

Through rules of lineage exogamy, i.e., rules that mandate marriages *outside* the lineage,[2] African lineages become linked with one another in networks of alliance and cooperation (see Marshall 1968). Traditionally, through ties of marriage, members of different lineages are drawn together into extended families. Even though marriage is not necessarily expected of all members of contemporary African communities, in traditional African societies it was customary for all adults except holders of certain offices and persons with severe mental or physical disabilities to get married and have children (see, e.g., Kenyatta 1938; Mbiti 1969 and 1973; Radcliffe-Brown and Forde 1950). It is important to note that when Africans got married, *they did not "start families," they joined existing families*. Upon marriage, a couple joined a cluster of related families who resided together in a single compound. This *extended family* comprised resident members of a lineage, their spouses (from other lineages), and children (who, of course, were also members of the resident lineage).

Depending upon the prevailing rules governing residence after marriage, the newly married couple joined either an extended family, where the groom's relatives formed the core of the group, or one where the bride's relatives formed the core of the group. In actuality, only one of the spouses normally *changed* residence at marriage, because the other was usually already living in the compound of the extended family which they would join.

It is important to understand the differences between the lineage and the extended family in African kinship, for although the two groupings are closely related, they are not the same. From what I have said so far, it should be apparent first of all that extended families are based on marriage and descent, whereas lineages are based solely on descent. It is important to realize also that the living adult members of a lineage form the core of consanguineal ("blood") relatives around whom the extended family is built.[3] Furthermore, as Uchendu notes, even in those African societies where corporate lineages are absent or exist only in rudimentary form, the extended families are still based around consanguineal cores, that is, persons linked by parent–child and/or sibling ties (Shimkin and Uchendu 1978).

A second difference between the lineage and the extended family concerns the manner in which descent is reckoned in the two groupings. In the lineage descent is traced through one line only, whereas in the extended family descent (or more technically, filiation) is traced bilaterally, through both parents. Thus, in a patrilineal or matrilineal society, from the point of view of any given person, the lineage comprises relatives linked through the father-line or the mother-line, as the case may be. In both types of society, however, *the extended family* comprises relatives on *both* the mother and the father side.

A third point of contrast between the lineage and the extended family is that lineage membership is discrete and nonoverlapping whereas extended family membership is always overlapping. Ideally, a society can be divided into a finite number of lineages, and each person in the society would be a member of only one of those lineages.[4] The situation is different with extended families. Given the different marital connections of the various members of the lineage, it is obvious that even brothers and sisters do not have precisely the same constellation of relatives in their extended families. African extended families were and are transresidential groupings, even though in day-to-day affairs the particular extended family constellation that actually resides together in the same compound is the group that carries out most of the mutual aid and socialization functions normally ascribed to African extended families.

A fourth distinction between the lineage and the extended family concerns the relative permanence and the generational depth of the two types of groups. Lineages are conceptualized as existing in perpetuity, involving the living and the dead, going back to the founding ancestor. Extended families are essentially constellations of living relatives. Their precise composition will vary depending upon the person who is taken as the "central ego" from whom the extended family is being reckoned. When deceased persons are remembered, they are always identified by their lineage (or compound) affiliation, not simply by their extended family connections to some living person. For example, one's deceased maternal grandfather would be remembered as a son of a particular lineage and compound rather than recalled simply as one's "mother's father."

Although African extended families tend to be large, labyrinthine groupings, for illustrative purposes an extended family occupying a single compound in a patrilineal society (such as that of the Yoruba of Nigeria) might be diagrammed as a group of brothers, their wives, their adult sons and grandsons and their wives, and any unmarried children in the group. (See Figure 3.) The married daughters and sisters of the adult males would be resident in the compounds of their husbands. Thus, the consanguineal core of the domiciled extended family consists of the adult males and their unmarried children. The core might also include a divorced or widowed sister or daughter who has returned to live in her father's compound until such time as she remarries.

From one perspective, members of the patrilineage view the wives collectively as the "in-law" (affinal) component of the resident extended family. That is, the wives represent the component of the domiciled extended family that is created "by law" rather than "by blood" (see Sudarkasa 1973, Ch. V). And whereas only in the most extraordinary circumstances do African societies provide for the legal severance of *consanguineal* kinship bonds, they all provide for the "severance 'by law' of those bonds that are based 'in law' " (Marshall 1968, p. 9).

From another very important perspective, however, *as mothers* the women married into the compound are the very persons through whom the patrilineage achieves continuity. Hence, as the "mothers of the lineage" they have a significance that transcends their relationship to the particular men who happen to be their husbands. Moreover, women as wives and mothers of a lineage are the connecting links with other lineages and as such are very important to their husbands and their husbands' kin. Understanding these points helps one to understand why divorce was not common in most in-

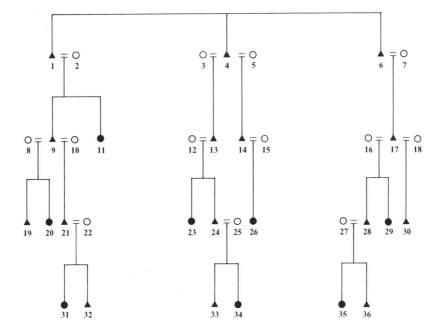

▲ Male member of the patrilineal core of the extended family

● Female member of the patrilineal core of the extended family

O "Wives of the compound"

⊓ Sibling bond

| Parent-child link

= Marriage

FIGURE 3.   Schematic View of an Extended Family Occupying a Single Compound

digenous African societies. It also helps to explain why in many African societies widows normally married men from their deceased husbands' lineages.

In this paper I cannot go into the differences in structure and functioning between lineages and extended families in patrilineal societies and those in matrilineal societies. A moment's reflection should reveal that males in matrilineal societies cannot occupy roles that are strictly analogous to those of females in patrilineal societies. In both instances, it is the *women* who bear the children, and that in itself has important implications.

I have already noted that in day-to-day affairs it is the *co-residential* extended family that carries out most of the functions normally associated with African extended families. These compound-based groupings vary considerably in size within the same society and across different societies. In the small town of Awe, Nigeria, I studied Yoruba compounds that had as few as fifteen and as many as sixty adults in them (Sudarkasa 1973). In large Yoruba cities, many compounds, especially those headed by indigenous rulers, had hundreds of adults living in them. The number of dependent children in the compounds was difficult to obtain, but in most compounds they outnumbered the adults.

Subdivisions of the African Extended Family

Having described the structure of the lineage and its relationship to the compound and the extended family, we turn now to an examination of the families based on marriage that exist within the traditional extended family. The first point to be made is that these conjugal families are not "nuclear families" in the common usage of the term. They are actually or potentially polygamous families (usually involving polygyny, i.e., a plurality of wives, but in some societies polyandry, i.e., a plurality of husbands, was permitted). Seemingly, in traditional African societies most men were involved in a polygynous marriage for at least some part of their married life. In fact, traditionally the normal developmental cycle of a conjugal family would involve a monogamous and then a polygamous phase. But even when a couple had a monogamous union throughout their married life, in the context of the extended family, where many people were involved in polygamous unions and where everyone had obligations to their own lineages as well as to their conjugal families, this monogamous family was not the insular type of institution implied in the Western concept of the nuclear family.

A second and equally important point concerning conjugal families within the extended family is that from the perspective of the larger family group the monogamous and polygamous families within it were structurally equivalent to each other. In other words, whether a man had one wife and children, two wives and children, or many wives and children, his was only one family. This very important point concerning the structural equivalence of monogamous and polygamous families within the extended family has been overlooked in many discussions of African families. The Western preoccupation with "reducing" polygamous families to their "minimal constituents" has led various writers, including W. H. R. Rivers (1924, p. 12) and Murdock (1949, p. 2), to propose that these families be viewed as "multiple families" with a husband-father in common. Elizabeth Colson even went so far as to maintain that a mother and her children constituted *the nuclear family* in traditional Africa, and that this nuclear family could best be viewed as having been incorporated into various types of larger units.[5] If one logically pursued these arguments, the monogamous family would be one family, and the polygamous family many families within the extended family.

Although Africans recognize the mother–child dyad as a primary social and affective unit (as do most of the world's peoples), it is erroneous to characterize this unit as a separate "nuclear family" within the African extended family. Such a formulation has no explanatory value since none of the normal functions of a family were traditionally performed by this unit in isolation. It was not a unit of socialization in and of itself; it was not a unit of economic production or consumption in and of itself; it was not an isolated unit of emotional support or mutual aid; it obviously was not a procreative unit. Why then term it a "nuclear family"?

The obsession of anthropologists with nucleation within the extended family stems from the *a priori* assumption of Westerners that anything larger than the nuclear family must be reducible to it or to something smaller. It is undeniable that in all societies, including those of Africa, the procreative unit is normally a male and a female, and that this unit, together with its offspring, can be profitably isolated for study or analysis. It does not follow, however, that this unit should be conceptualized as *the building block* for families in every society where it is found. Labeling the father-mother-child unit as the "nuclear family" does not make it invariably so. Other role configurations are sometimes more appropriately designated as the *nuclear* family in a given society. It is clear that in many African societies what is most appropriately designated as the *nuclear* unit within the extended family is not the "nuclear family" of the West; nor is it the *minimal* unit into which, for analytical purposes, the extended family can be divided. Depending on the purpose of the division, there can be said to be two nuclear groups within the African extended family. The consanguineal core (excluding spouses) forms the *nucleus* of the African extended family. The nuclear *families* (including spouses) within the traditional African extended family are normally built around polygamous, not monogamous, marriages.

If there is one thing that anthropologists should have learned from the study of African societies, it is that large and complex family groupings do not present to Africans the "problems" that they present to Europeans. In fact, what P. A. Tetteh observed concerning Ghana is true of indigenous Africa in general: "when the word 'family' is used, it does not usually refer to the nuclear or elementary family based on the husband–wife relationship but to the extended family based on descent" (Tetteh 1967, p. 201). Given the "naturalness" of the extended family to Africans, one would have thought that anthropologists would have sought to explore the implications of this reality rather than obscure it by conceptual analyses that seek to reduce it to Western-derived paradigms.

The polygamous families that form one of the basic subdivisions of the extended family can indeed be further subdivided *for certain purposes*, but the rationales for these divisions constitute one of the variable aspects of African kinship that have to be understood by looking closely at each society in question. From my own researches among the Yoruba, I can illustrate one manner in which the polygamous family is subdivided and give a brief introduction to its functioning within the extended family that resides in a single compound. I will caution the reader that the practice of polygyny *as described below* is disappearing in Nigeria and elsewhere under the impact of Christianity, Western education, internal demographic and economic changes, and so on.

In a typical traditional Yoruba compound, each man had a section of the dwelling, or a separate dwelling, for himself and his family. Whether he was married monogamously or polygynously, he had a separate room apart from his wife or wives. Each wife also had her own room, her own household furnishings, cooking utensils, and so forth. Nevertheless, each polygynous family was *one* family. Any other interpretation misrepresents the structure and functioning of the unit. To speak of separate families with a husband/father in common would overlook, for example, the important integrative role of the senior wife. Traditionally, the Yoruba expected the senior wife to be a companion and confidante to her co-wives, as well as to her husband (Mabogunje 1958). She was often called upon to intercede with her husband on behalf of a co-wife, and wives of the same husband often cooperated in domestic activities and sometimes in economic activities as well (Sudarkasa 1973, Chs. V and VI).

Moreover, on many occasions, including naming ceremonies for newborn babies, weddings, and funerals, the wives of each man, together with other wives of the compound, collectively carried out specific roles that were traditionally assigned to them. On these occasions, the wives were collectively responsible for some of the preparation and distribution of food that took place. They might also have specific social or ceremonial roles to play. For example, during a traditional wedding, as the bride and her procession moves through the town, the wives of her father's compound (excluding her own mother and some of the older women) bring up the rear of the group, singing traditional songs of sorrow at the loss of a daughter from their husbands' lineage. In positioning and in demeanor, the wives provide the counterpoint to the brides' attendants who dance and rejoice with her at the head of the procession.[6]

Generally, it might be said that among the Yoruba the wives of a compound traditionally constituted a quasi-kin group within the extended family. They were and are referred to as "wives" by both the females and the males of their husbands' lineage. They also refer to each other by terms that mean senior or junior wife. (They are usually addressed as "mother of So-and-So even though they are referred to and refer to each other as "wives.") During my research, I found that even though there was some rivalry and competition among wives of the same husband, the relationships among wives of the entire compound were characterized by a considerable degree of camaraderie and cooperation (Sudarkasa 1973, pp. 104–109, 146–152).

The cohesion of the polygynous Yoruba family derived in large measure from the existence of explicit rules or codes defining appropriate behavior for all persons in the group. Within the polygynous family, the children are referred to as *Omo Baba* or *Obakan*, i.e., "children of one father." According to the indigenous protocol governing kin behavior in day-to-day affairs as well as in matters of succession to office, differential and deferential behavior among and toward siblings is based on seniority as determined by age, irrespective of differences in maternity. However, the Yoruba also have the concept of *Omo Iya*, meaning "children of the same mother [by the same father]."[7] The concept of *Omo Iya* comes into prominence mainly in matters of inheritance. Certain of a deceased man's properties are divided into as many parts as there are wives with children. Thus, for certain purposes, a mother and her children do constitute a *subunit* within the family, but they do not constitute a *separate unit* within that family.

The Yoruba recognize that the emotional bond between the children of the same mother and father (*Omo Iya*) is not necessarily found among all the children of the same father by different mothers (*Omo Baba*). However, in day-to-day affairs all children of the same father are expected to behave toward each other as if there were no differences in maternity. As far as the behavior of the husband/father is concerned, it is considered very re-prehensible for him to show favoritism toward any wife other than a new bride during the "honeymoon" period, or to treat the children of one wife differently from the children of the other wives (Sudarkasa 1973, Chs. V and VI).

No institution has been more maligned by observers of African societies than the institution of polygyny (popularly termed polygamy). The an-thropological and popular literature abounds with discussions of rivalry and jealousy among co-wives but contains almost no reports of affection, mutual respect, and cooperation among co-wives. Even when anthropologists de-scribe the bond between co-wives, they tend to refer back to an underlying conflict between the women (see, e.g., Fortes 1949, pp. 126 ff.). When men-tion is made of the fact that women themselves often encouraged their husbands to take additional wives, it is usually explained solely in terms of the economic or material benefits of polygyny. For example, it is often noted, as I myself did, that the addition of a junior co-wife frees the senior wife from certain domestic chores (Sudarkasa 1973).

It does not seem to occur to most Western students of African societies that before the bombardment of Africa with propaganda against polygamy, African women valued the companionship of co-wives. In fact, in a recent study of Nigerian women it was reported that the majority of women still said they would be "pleased" to have a second wife in the home (Ware 1979). The negative attitudes of some Western-educated African women toward polygyny cannot be taken as representative of the traditional attitudes toward the institution.

After years of studying African social organization I have come to the view that the premium Africans placed on having children led women as well as men to place a high value on a system (namely polygyny) that afforded all women the possibility of motherhood within the context of a family. According to African values, having a system of co-wives was preferable to having a system where women bore children outside of marriage or where women could live out their lives as childless spinsters. In fact, in traditional Africa these occurrences would have been perceived as outside the normal and appropriate mode of behavior.

Conjugality and Consanguinity in the African Extended Family

Paradoxically, although "the concept of the extended family itself developed from studies of African peoples" (Aldous 1965, p. 109), the "classical" model of the extended family described by Murdock (*Social Structure* 1949), missed one of the most distinctive features of these families. Murdock, who appears to have coined the phrase "nuclear family", also put forth the polar concept of the "extended family" as *two or more nuclear families* linked by the parent–child tie or the sibling tie (Murdock 1949, pp. 2, 23).

Anxious to confirm his hypothesis concerning the universality of the nuclear family and its centrality in all other types of family groupings, Murdock imposed upon the empirical reality of the extended family an analytical paradigm that emphasized the primacy of the nuclear family. Of course, in some parts of the world there are extended families built upon nuclear families, as Murdock's model suggests. However, this model does not fit the reality of African extended families, and, as I shall attempt to show, it has obscured some of the important realities of Afro-American families.

The Murdock model of the extended family did not take into account the important contribution to comparative family studies made by Ralph Linton in *The Study of Man* (1936). Linton had proposed a generic division of all families into two types: "conjugal" (built around the marital pair) and "consanguineal" (built around "blood relatives"). Linton and Murdock were seeking concepts to describe the same empirical realities. Linton defined his types by reference to principles of family formation, whereas Murdock defined his types by reference to presumed basic structural characteristics. It appears, unfortunately, that Murdock's preoccupation with the nuclear family led him to misrepresent the structural characteristics he encountered. Nevertheless, Murdock's *terminology* seems to be with us to stay, hence we must stress the *consanguinity within African extended families* rather than speak of consanguineal families as Linton had done.

The primacy of the consanguineal core over the conjugal family as the "building block" of the African extended family is attested to in a number of ways. First of all, the stability of the family is not dependent upon the

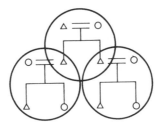

Δ Male
O Female
⊓ Sibling bond
| Parent-child link
⹀ Marriage

FIGURE 4.   The Murdock Model of the Extended Family

stability of conjugal unions. Although for reasons alluded to earlier in this paper divorce was relatively rare in most precolonial African societies, nonetheless, when divorces did occur, they did not cause the "dissolution of the family." Spouses could come and go, as it were, but the extended family remained intact. In the patrilineal societies, when a divorce occurred, the wife would return to her natal compound or move to that of her new husband. Her older children would remain behind to be cared for by their paternal grandmother (who resided in the same compound as her husband and sons), by one of their father's other wives, or by one of the other women resident in their compound. Conceivably also, one of the children could go to live with the father's sister in the compound of her husband. In a matrilineal situation women often did not change residences at marriage, and when a divorce occurred, they simply remained in their natal compounds with their children and members of their lineage.

A second indicator of the primacy of the consanguineal group over the conjugal group in the African extended family is the contrast in the consequences of the departure of a spouse versus the departure of a member of the lineage core. As I indicated, when a spouse leaves the compound, the stability of the family is not seriously jeopardized. On the other hand, when a member of the lineage core of the extended family decides to make a permanent break away from the compound, this starts a process of fission that could have serious disruptive consequences. For example, in the case of patrilineal groups one brother's departure could trigger the exodus of several other males and their wives and children. Eventually the process could culminate in the formation of a new lineage segment and a new branch of the extended family. Interestingly, in virtually all African societies stories recalling this process of lineage and family segmentation describe it as resulting from a quarrel between brothers (see, e.g., Radcliffe-Brown and Forde 1950).

A third clue to the preeminence of consanguinity in the African extended family is the fact that in various societies, when a member of the core dies or is barren or impotent, his or her procreative functions would be assumed by a brother or sister. Thus, a man might marry his deceased brother's widow or sire a child on behalf of an impotent brother or "cousin" within the lineage. A woman might replace her deceased sister in a marital union or bear a child in her barren sister's stead. These practices are usually discussed in terms of their importance to the maintenance of marriage alliances between lineages or in terms of their contribution to the continuity of the lineage (Radcliffe-Brown 1950, pp. 64–65; Marshall 1968). Looked at from another perspective, however, they demonstrate that within the extended family the priorities of the consanguineal core group can determine the manner in which the conjugal family's procreative functions will be carried out.

A fourth consideration that negates the primacy of the conjugal family within the African extended family is the fact that two of the important functions that are attributed to families cross-culturally, namely socialization and economic cooperation, are not carried on by separate conjugal families within the extended family but are shared, albeit in varying degrees, by all members of the larger group. For example, all adult members of a Yoruba compound share in the upbringing of children in that compound. Extended family members in other compounds are also called upon to assist in the socialization process (Sudarkasa 1973). Similarly, among the Yoruba and in virtually all other African societies, people are linked into extensive networks of financial obligation and economic cooperation. These networks embrace not only family members who are co-resident in a given compound or a given locality but extend to distant communities and foreign lands (Sudarkasa 1974, 1975b, 1977; Eades 1979; Shimkin and Uchendu 1978).

Having shown that the consanguineal core is the building block of African extended families, it is important to reiterate that marriage was a stable institution in traditional African communities. Most marriages were lifelong unions. It was through marriage that families as well as individuals were conjoined and the linkages formed were valued for their political and economic entailments as well as for the social and psychological solidarity they fostered.

The point I am making here, then, is not that conjugality was unimportant in African extended families; it was very important. After all, it was only through procreation that the consanguineal kin groups could continue to exist, and most African societies had strong negative sanctions against having children outside of marriage. The point that I am making is that important though it was, marriage did not have the primacy of place in kinship that it has in the nuclear family of the West.

The Extended Family in African Communities

The extended family was a unit wherein the basic production and distribution of material goods and services took place.[8] Because of its relatively large size and composition (including both sexes and members of all generations in the society), it was an efficient economic mechanism. The skills that had been accumulated over centuries were harnessed and utilized within the extended family, with the elders providing the know-how based on experience and the younger members providing the labor to get various tasks accomplished. Innovation and change also resulted from the interaction between young and old.

The size of the extended family and the division of labor by sex and age made it possible for all persons within it to make concrete contributions to the economic activities that took place outside the domestic unit as well as within it. Thus, for example, young married women could engage in productive work outside the home because older women assisted with childrearing and young unmarried women helped with other domestic chores (Sudarkasa 1976). Moreover, both males and females could accomplish a variety of complex productive and distributive tasks because the work was done in cooperative groups rather than in isolation.

The responsibilities for socialization and social control that were carried out by the family also involved the cooperation of the entire unit, although some of the tasks were allocated at different times to different segments or persons within the larger unit. Because of the structure of the extended family, it could serve as the society's basic educational facility, imparting both skills and values to the youth. It could also function as an effective agent of social control, because it was the source of much of the satisfaction and many of the "rewards" its members received. By having the power to withdraw sources of emotional support, which might be done, for example, by ostracizing recalcitrant members of the family, the leadership of the extended family was able to serve as a basic law enforcement agency. The strength of the extended family explains in part the absence of elaborate policing mechanisms and penal institutions in precolonial Africa. Moreover, through the use of arbitration and diplomacy, the male and female elders in the extended family were able to settle many disputes without recourse to the courts that did exist.

The extended family provided social security in the form of companionship, counseling, and emotional reinforcement for the society's youth, adults, and aged. Africans did not subscribe to the view that "true" emotional gratification, satisfaction, and support come mainly through groups based on sexuality. In fact, husbands and wives looked to their wider extended family relations as well as to each other (sometimes more than to each other) for companionate, gratifying, and satisfying relationships. The extended family also provided care for the infirm as well as the emotionally or mentally disabled, with the burden of these responsibilities being shared among various members of the units.

Principles Governing African Family Relations

Interpersonal relations within the extended family were guided by a number of ethical principles as well as by the various sanctions that could be brought to bear on members whose behavior was considered too deviant to be tolerated. In this paper I can not attempt to summarize the vast amount of data that exist on patterns of authority, decision-making, and other aspects of interpersonal behavior in African kin groups. I have elsewhere suggested that four principles—namely, *respect, restraint, responsibility,* and *reciprocity*—underlie and undergird interpersonal behavior in the family and the wider community in most indigenous African societies (Marshall 1970b).

Two of these principles, namely respect and responsibility, are often mentioned in discussions of African kinship. Reciprocity is usually held to be a principle governing economic relations, but as Mauss (1954), Sahlins (1972, Ch. 5), and others have shown, it is equally applicable to the broad spectrum of behavior within the family. It is only the principle of restraint that might seem unfamiliar to students of African societies. Any questions about this concept should be dispelled when it is realized that I use it to refer to the quality that causes individual desires or proclivities to be weighed against, and possibly subordinated to, the sentiment of the group.

Respect is the cardinal guiding principle for behavior within the family and in the society at large. It not only governs the behavior of family members toward the head of the compound and the other male and female elders, it is expected of siblings and is the key to harmonious relations within the polygamous family. Displayed primarily through patterns of deference and forms of address, children learn to show respect even before they learn to speak. It manifests itself in greetings, bows, curtsies, and other gestures signaling recognition of seniority; it manifests itself in knowing when to be seen and not heard; it requires acknowledgment of and submission to persons in authority.

Restraint is the principle that makes possible communalism within the family and in the wider society. Restraint means that a person cannot "do his or her own thing." The rights of any person must always be balanced against the requirements of the group. In the family restraint is manifest in many ways: It is evident in patterns of consumption, it governs verbal communication, it is necessary in the management of polygamous connubial relations. Restraint is related to the notion of "sacrifice." Parents exercise restraint over their own desires in order to provide for their children, who, in turn, repay the "sacrifice" by putting their parents' needs before their own in many instances.

Responsibility is manifest in every area of family life and is the principle that needs the least elaboration. It is obviously closely related to the foregoing principle of restraint. What needs to be emphasized, perhaps, is that given the size of African families, the lines or chains of responsibility extend much farther than they do in most Western family situations. For Africans, kinship offers a network of security, but it also imposes the burden of obligations.

Reciprocity "ties it all together." Without the principle of reciprocity, the other principles would not stand. Traditionally, it is expected that generousity will prevail, especially among relatives, but it is also expected that good deeds will be reciprocated either in the short run or in the distant future. Sometimes obligations are carried over from one generation to the next, but they are eventually reciprocated.

African and Afro-American Family Structure: Clarifying the Issues

The earliest forms of African family organization re-created in America by enslaved Blacks represented both an amalgamation of specific features from different ethnic groups and an adaptation of these features to the realities and demands of the slave regime. The foregoing description and interpretation of African family organization provide some of the "baseline" data needed to study the transformation of the African family patterns re-created in America into Afro-American family patterns reflecting changes developed over time in the context of different social, economic, and political conditions. Research into the continuities and changes in African-derived family patterns among Black Americans must be undertaken in a historical context and must begin with models of African kinship that accurately depict past realities on that continent.

In this regard, the oft-cited writings of Wade Nobles deserve comment. The "principles" he describes as underlying African family organization ("oneness of being" and "survival of the tribe") are of such a level of generality as to be of little use in explaining recurrent patterns or variations in the behavioral and structural aspects of African family life. Moreover, some of Nobles's formulations are inaccurate and misleading. He states, for example, that "the Black African definition of the family, prior to the intrusion of the European presence on the continent, included every member of the tribe" (Nobles 1974b, p. 15; see also Nobles 1974a, 1978, and King 1976). Only in a strictly metaphorical sense can it be said that all members of a given community, or a given "tribe," belonged to one family. When it is realized that many of the so-called tribes to which Nobles refers were nations embracing millions of people, it becomes apparent that this part of his description of African kinship cannot be taken literally.

Moreover, while it is true that the idea of a founding ancestor for an entire people was widespread in precolonial Africa, and the ideology of common descent was used to mobilize some of the so-called segmentary societies,[9] neither of these facts should be construed to mean that Africans considered everyone in their ethnic group or their nation to be members of *one family*. In precolonial Africa as in other parts of the world, the very notion of kin implied its opposite, namely, nonkin. Thus, some people were defined as relatives and some were not. Those who were nonkin constituted the pool from which spouses were taken.

Turning to the areas that require clarification in the study of the relationship between African and Afro-American family structure, I want to discuss briefly three: (1) the issue of documenting continuities as well as discontinuities between African and Afro-American family patterns; (2) the necessity of studying the operation of the principles of consanguinity and conjugality in Afro-American families without the acknowledged or implicit assumption that the conjugally based nuclear family is superior to any other form of the family (Sudarkasa 1975a); and (3) the need to study the temporal and spatial aspects of the adaptation of African-derived family patterns to different American environs, defined in geographic, sociopolitical, and economic terms.

The issues involved in documenting continuities and changes in African family patterns transplanted in America have been the subject of decades of debate (Frazier 1939; Herskovits 1941; Bracey et al. 1970; Shimkin and Uchendu 1978). Without attempting to cite all the parties and positions in this debate, let me outline the situation as I see it, recognizing that not all of my formulations are original or unique.

It is necessary, first of all, to establish that we are seeking to understand the processes by which *Africans* and *African institutions* were transplanted and transformed in America. This might seem a simple or obvious point to make, but it is not one which undergirds most of the historical scholarship on Blacks in America. Enslaved Africans are *generically* referred to as "slaves" and their institutions as "slave" institutions, as if their identity were totally determined by the condition of their oppression. (Note that Israelites enslaved in Egypt for centuries are always referred to as Israelites in a state of bondage or in slavery.)

Yet, despite mainstream academia's attempt to deny the cultural heritage of early America's enslaved population, their own researches belie their efforts. Even in the hands of writers such as Herbert Gutman who are skeptical of "African survivals" (his quotation marks), the data show that most of the patterns of family and kinship (and patterns in other areas outside the purview of this paper) found among enslaved Africans were basically "retentions and reinterpretations" of patterns found on the continent of Africa (Woodson 1936; Herskovits 1941).

As a student of continental African societies, it is not surprising to me that contemporary writings on Afro-American history, most notably those of Blassingame (1972), Genovese (1974), and Gutman (1976), reveal the presence of African patterns in Afro-American consanguineal kin groupings ("kin networks"), husband–wife relations, sibling bonds, socialization practices, patterns of exogamy, marriage rules and rituals, naming practices, relationships between alternate generations (i.e., grandparents and grandchildren), patterns of respect and deference, and the extension of kinship terminology to elders throughout the community. As I pointed out in the first section of this paper, in the realm of kinship more than in any other aspect of social organization, there was variation only in details, not in essentials, from one indigenous African society to the next. Furthermore, as has been repeatedly shown, most of the Africans enslaved in America came from contiguous areas in the western part of the continent, where there had been a long history of culture contact and a high degree of institutional similarity (see, e.g., Herskovits 1941, pp. 1–85).

Lineages, extended families, polygynous conjugal families, large residential units, and other structural features and behavioral patterns described in the preceding sections of this paper were found throughout the area from which the African captives were taken to America. Eyewitness descriptions of late seventeenth, eighteenth, and nineteenth century Africa and ethnographic reconstructions of precolonial social organization provide evidence of the prevalence of the kinship patterns noted.[10] These patterns were found in precolonial states as well as in the so-called stateless or segmentary societies. They were found in the savanna (or Sahel) as well as along the coast. They cut across almost every type of grouping into which African societies have been divided.

Thus, regardless of the "diverse" backgrounds of the Africans enslaved in America (a diversity that is usually greatly exaggerated), there was a commonality in the familial patterns known to them. It was this shared social organizational "baseline" that enabled the Africans enslaved in America to create recognizably *African* patterns where they lived. Obviously, these captive people had to adapt to the realities of the savage system of slavery in which they existed, but that did not obliterate the fact of their origin. If Israelites enslaved in Egypt for centuries could remain Israelites, if diverse European peoples in the twentieth century can still acknowledge cultural survivals from ancient Greece and Rome, I wonder why it is considered so preposterous that Africans only a few generations removed from their homelands would show evidence of their cultural roots. Unfortunately, in this area of scholarship as in many others we are confronted with persistent and pervasive pseudo-scientific "postulates" about the nature of African people. These so-called theories and the so-called facts adduced to support them do nothing but pervert and prevent the progress of reasonable scholarship.

As an Africanist reading historical writings on the Black family in America, I have to marvel at the refusal of many scholars to make the most obvious interpretations of their data when these data point to the fundamental Africanity of Blacks enslaved in America. One has only to note Gutman's reluctance to attribute the most obvious African patterns to their cultural source. In his speculation over the origin of the marriage ritual of "jumping over the broomstick," he includes the possibility that it was "learned from whites" (1976, p. 277)! In a discussion of naming practices described as African in origin by a former enslaved woman, Gutman seemed to think it unusual that the practice survived among people who "had been separated from direct contact with West Africa at least a half century and probably much longer" (1976, p. 193). European peoples are considered to have what might be termed cultural memories that span millennia; apparently those of Africans, on the other hand, cannot be expected to last the lifetime of a single person!

Gutman also illustrates another tendency among certain scholars of early Afro-American life, namely the tendency to discount a practice as being African when it becomes fused with some Euro-American elements. Herskovits long ago appropriately referred to such manifestations as "syncretisms" (in the case of certain religious practices) and "reinterpretations" (in more general instances). It is very interesting in this connection that when Gutman labels an institution or custom *Afro-American*, he seems to assume that the Americanness, as it were, is more significant than the Africanity. This is revealed, for example, in his discussion of the practice of naming babies after siblings who died in infancy. Gutman almost triumphantly labels the practice Afro-American (rather than African) because the names used were Euro-American names (1976, p. 193). It is as if he thought Africans were free to give or use African names whenever they wanted to. One has only to recall the renaming of Kunta Kinte as Toby (Haley 1976).

It appears that to most Euro-American and to some Afro-American scholars the social science axiom about the tenacity of culture is inapplicable when describing the experience of Africans transplanted in America. All too often we are confronted with variations of Elkins's view of "the slave":

> Much of his past had been annihilated; nearly every prior connection had been severed. Not that he had really "forgotten" all these things—his family and kinship arrangements, his language, the tribal religion, the taboos, the name he had once borne, and so on—but *none of it any longer carried much meaning*. The old values, the sanctions, the standards, already unreal, could no longer furnish him guides for conduct, for adjusting to the expectations of a complete new life. Where then was he to look for new standards, new cues—who would furnish them now? He could now look to none but his master, the one man upon whose will depended his food, his shelter, his sexual connections, whatever moral instruction he might be offered, whatever "success" was possible within the system, his very security—in short, everything. [Elkins 1959, pp. 101–2. Emphasis added]

This statement was born of Elkins's own imagination, not from the evidence that existed at the time he wrote and that is coming to light more and more with each new publication.

The writings of Blassingame, Owens, Genovese, Gutman, and others suggest that Blacks on the plantations *behaved as slaves* toward whites and in relation to matters concerning the "Masters" or their surrogates. Most of the older literature on slavery would have us believe that the slave role was all-consuming. The more recent historical writings point to the fact that in some areas of their lives, enslaved Blacks *behaved toward each other as Africans*, albeit Africans whose customs had to be adapted to the context of slavery.

The interpreter of early Afro-American life cannot be misled by the fact that Blacks on the plantations almost literally ran away from the label "African" or hid from the "Master" anything that could be labeled "voodoo." They denied their Africanity because in so doing they sought to enhance their chances of survival in a situation where to be African was to invite the whip or worse. But the point is, *they lived out much of their lives as Africans.* Their Africanity was manifest in their family and community relations; in their music and their recreation; in their spirituality; and in their rituals and rites of passage (most especially in the way they mourned their dead). The point is that certain manifestations of Africanity could be tolerated or overlooked ("that's jes' the way the Niggers is"). It was those aspects of Africanity that were perceived as dangerous to the survival of the slave regime that were outlawed or forbidden. Thus, African religions, Islam, secret societies, "voodoo," night funerals, any evidences of the recreation of political structures, such as "chieftaincies," were among the practices that were banned. Ironically, neither the "Masters" nor the "slaves" seemed to realize that the most powerful "Africanism" of all was the extended family, which did survive, and thereby enabled a people to survive.

One of the most important areas for research is the reassessment of the extent to which and the ways in which the slave status was prevented from intruding upon the daily round of life in the "slave quarters." Many of the recent descriptions of these quarters suggest African-derived communities where the internal behavioral norms were almost as foreign to the whites as would have been customs on the African continent. Gutman's book provides a wealth of data on early Afro-American families, but we have yet to see an ethnohistorical study of enslaved African families and communities. This is a piece of research that is urgently needed.

The second issue that requires clarification in studies of African and Afro-American family structure concerns the principles upon which these families are organized. The implications of the operation of the principle of consanguinity in relation to that of conjugality must be fully explored before the dynamics of Afro-American families can be appreciated and their similarities to African families and differences from Euro-American families fully understood. This point was the main theme of a lecture I presented to the National Medical Association in 1972. At that time, I stated:

> Black families are not necessarily centered around conjugal unions, which are the *sine qua non* of the nuclear family. Among blacks, households centered around

consanguineal relatives have as much legitimacy (and for most people, as much respectability) *as family units* as do households centered around conjugal unions. When this fact is understood, it becomes clear that the instability of conjugal relations cannot be taken as the sole measure of instability of the family. That black families exhibit considerable stability over time and space is evidenced by the enduring linkages and bonds of mutual obligation found among networks of consanguineal kin. [Sudarkasa 1975a, p. 238]

A number of studies that have appeared since 1972, including those by Stack (1974), Ashenbrenner (1975), Agbasegbe (1976), McAdoo (1978), Shimkin et al. (1978), Martin and Martin (1978), and Kennedy (1980) have provided documentation and amplification of those observations.

The question of the relationship between consanguinity and conjugality in Black families is not to be broached in terms of the prevalence of one *or* the other. We need to study the circumstances and conditions under which one or the other predominates in matters of family and/or household formation, delegation of authority, maintenance of solidarity and support, and so on. This implies, of course, that we must study the operation of these principles in transresidential family groupings as well as in individual households.

When the study of Black families is approached from this perspective, it becomes apparent that the old debate (enjoined most recently by Gutman) as to whether historically blacks lived mostly in one-parent or two-parent families requires reformulation. Virtually all of Gutman's extraordinary data should be evaluated from another perspective. He was concerned with proving the antiquity of "the nuclear family" among Blacks; this he considered to have been accomplished by his abundant documentation of the stability of conjugal unions over time. From the data I presented on African families, it should be clear that stable conjugal unions are not to be taken as necessary indicators of the prevalence of nuclear families of the Western type. What is critical to investigate are the ways in which and the extent to which the conjugally based groupings described by Gutman were embedded in or articulated with the wider kin networks also described by him.

By now it should be apparent that the old (and unfortunately continuing) debate about the presence or absence of the nuclear family among Blacks rests on the assumption that the nuclear family represents a form of family organization that is superior to all others. As I noted previously:

A survey of the literature on comparative family organization shows that the emphasis on the nuclear family . . . does not derive from its universality or its structural primacy, but rather from the *value* placed upon it in Western societies. What European . . . scholars did was to take the type of family . . . that existed in their own societies and rationalize its existence elsewhere. Where other types of family existed, they construed these to be "built upon" nuclear families. Moreover, where nuclear families did not exist as the normal or preferable form of family organization, they were promoted through the various propaganda agencies and techniques utilized by European missionaries, political officials, and scholars. . . .

[S]tudies of black families in the U.S. must be viewed in the general context of the development of comparative family studies. The value premise undergirding these comparative studies asserted (and still asserts) that the conjugally based nuclear family is the "healthy," "normal," "organized," and "stable" form of family whereas families that depart from the nuclear family ideal are "unhealthy," "abnormal," "disorganized," and "unstable." [Sudarkasa 1975a, p. 237]

One would hypothesize that the farther we go back in time in the study of Afro-American families, the more likely we are to find that, barring direct interference from "Masters," both two-parent households and one-parent households would be conceptualized by the enslaved Africans as parts of interlocking family networks in which consanguinity played a significant organizing role. This is not to imply that conjugality and the stable conjugal unions documented by Gutman were unimportant. Indeed, given that the constraints of slavery did not permit the replication of African consanguineal kin groups, one would expect that the bond between husband and wife as elders in the family would assume an even greater importance than they did in the context of full-fledged lineages and extended families with *various elders* domiciled in one large compound.

What I am suggesting is that the conjugally based groupings described by Gutman probably should not be conceptualized as nuclear families, as he is inclined to do, but rather as groups linked to others through ties of consanguinity and affinity which involved the types of obligations and mutual assistance associated with African family organization. A corollary of this interpretation is that *it was after slavery*, when Black American extended family organization was not encumbered by the restraints of the slave regime, that we find the reemergence of kinship groupings that exhibited many of the features of their African antecedents. The data on families in rural and urban Black communities tend to support this interpretation (Agbasegbe 1976; Shimkin et al. 1978; Aschenbrenner 1975; Martin and Martin 1978).

Of course, as many writers have pointed out, these multifunctional mutual assistance kin groupings that are Black extended families were vital to the survival and, as Billingsley and McAdoo have shown, to the upward mobility of Blacks in America (Billingsley 1968; Hill 1971; McAdoo 1978). However, it is important to reiterate that *these groups did not originate in America in response to the adverse socioeconomic and political circumstances in which Blacks found themselves.* The groups originated in Africa, where they had served many of the same purposes they came to serve in America. The various adaptations of these groups to American conditions, the changes that occurred in the process thereof, remain to be systematically explored (see Green 1978).

Such a study would involve the third issue I wish to touch upon, namely, the need to identify those factors that account for the evolution or development of different family patterns in different circumstances and different time periods in America. Certain patterns were obviously due to regulations and conditions imposed by the regime of slavery as manifested in different areas. For example, the size and configuration of the living quarters as well as the small size of many of the plantations and farms on which enslaved Blacks lived prevented the replication of African compounds and African extended families. Nevertheless, consanguineal kin networks and stable conjugal unions did persist (Gutman 1976). Other patterns may have been due to other factors—for example, to the proximity of free Black families to native American communities. In a manner similar to Jacquelyne Jackson's researches on contemporary Black families (1971), we need to know more about the impact of varying economic conditions and demographic factors, such as sex ratios, on black family and household configurations over time. Studies such as those of Furstenberg et al. (1975) on female-headed households in nineteenth century Philadelphia are useful in this connection.

Gutman's intriguing data on patterns of kin and community exogamy point to another area that should be studied for evidence on factors underlying changes in African patterns. Moreover, the whole question of the disappearance of the lineage principle or its absorption into the concept of extended family requires research. Gutman's data on the practice of naming children after their fathers suggests an attempt to keep the lineage principle alive for some time.

As we move farther and farther away from Africa in time and as the Afro-American population increases in size, socioeconomic complexity, and geographical diversity, we must become increasingly involved in studying the process by which patterns of Afro-American family life diverged significantly from those found in Africa. And, of course, in many respects *contemporary* Afro-American families, extended as well as all other types, differ considerably from those of precolonial and present-day Africa.[11] Interestingly, however, the operation of various factors associated with Westernization and modernization in contemporary Africa are leading to the emergence of family patterns similar to those found among Blacks in the United States. Clearly, a comparative study of changes in the African family, both on the continent and in the American diaspora, would contribute enormously to our understanding of what happens to the structure and functioning of extended families in different socioeconomic environments.

Conclusion

In this paper I have outlined the main features of African family organization and indicated some of the issues to be taken into account in relating the African patterns to those that developed among the Africans who were captured and enslaved in America. The task of actually specifying the continuities and discontinuities in African and Afro-American family structure and of analyzing the bases for these is obviously too vast for the present paper. It does seem, however, that such an undertaking would make an important contribution to the ongoing reinterpretation of much of the data on Black families (English 1974; Staples 1978; Allen 1978). Such a study would also provide a synthesis of the various approaches to Black family studies which Staples (1978) describes as "conceptual models" under the headings "Pan-Africanism," "Historical Materialism," and "Domestic Colonialism."

From my perspective the approach to Black family studies that starts from the premise that African familial patterns were re-created in a modified form in America is not properly termed a "conceptual model," if by that is meant that some other "conception" has equal validity. It is a *fact*, supported by evidence that accumulates with each new historical and sociological study of Black families, that African patterns of family organization survived among enslaved Blacks and continue to be manifest to the present day. This fact is not inconsistent with a view that takes into account economic forces and racist ideologies in studying the changes that have occurred in African-derived family patterns over time and in different geographical and political environments.

As regards the studies that would specifically focus on illuminating the African family patterns that were transplanted and transformed in America, I would reiterate that we should begin to look comparatively at *specific* behavioral patterns, *specific* structural features, and *specific* values rather than continue to generalize about African cosmological views that are said to undergird Black American life (Nobles 1978). Not only is it extremely difficult to substantiate this claim (one has only to study an African society to appreciate how complex a matter this is), but so long as we continue our discussions at such highly abstract levels, we make it possible for those who are doing the concrete historical and sociological studies from Eurocentric perspectives to continue to misinterpret or misrepresent the data they uncover.

Notes

1. This essay is not intended as an exhaustive treatment of African kinship. The analyses and interpretations presented should enable scholars from various disciplines to delve into the anthropological and historical literature for further information specific to their research needs. It should be noted also that the paper does not deal with the important subject of African kinship terminology.

2. Among the Yoruba of Nigeria, the rule of exogamy prohibits marriage within one's own patrilineage, one's mother's patrilineage, one's father's mother's patrilineage and one's mother's mother's patrilineage.

3. The reader is reminded that kinship is fundamentally a *social* phenomenon, not merely a biological one. In some societies, certain genetically related persons are defined as marriageable nonkin. For example, one's mother's brother's son or daughter might be so defined. In other societies the same relative might be defined as too close for marriage. Moreover, in all societies there are provisions for making nonkin into kin (adoption is one such process). When we use the term "consanguineal" or "blood" relatives, we are referring to persons so defined by the rules of their society or ethnic group.

4. Here we are excluding the so-called double descent systems in which a person belongs to a matrilineage traced through the mother and a patrilineage traced through the father.

5. Colson begins her analysis by terming this the "nuclear group"; later she terms it the "family nucleus" to which "the husband and father is attached." Subsequently, she refers to the mother–child grouping as the "nuclear family" (1962).

6. I observed such weddings during my fieldwork in the Yoruba town of Awe in 1961 and 1962 (Marshall 1970a).

7. Children of the same mother by different fathers are termed *Iyekan*, but inasmuch as they belong to different lineages and normally reside in the compounds of their respective fathers, they do not come under discussion here.

8. This section of the paper is revised from Sudarkasa 1975c. For other discussions of the functioning of African extended families, see Tetteh (1967), Okediji (1975a), Shimkin and Uchendu (1978), and Kerri (1979).

9. Sahlins (1961) refers to these as "tribal" societies based upon segmentary lineage systems.

10. The bibliography in Herskovits's *Myth of the Negro Past* cites many of the early accounts of precolonial West Africa. An introduction to the vast ethnographic literature can also be gleaned from that source or from others cited in this paper.

11. In a pilot study measuring extended family interaction among Nigerians, Black Americans, and white Americans, Okediji (1975b) shows that Nigerians scored highest on his scale of intensity and frequency of such interaction, followed by Black Americans and then white Americans. There was a significant difference between Black and white Americans, but there was an even greater difference between Nigerians and Black Americans.

Bibliography

AGBASEGBE, BAMIDELE, "The Role of Wife in the Black Extended Family: Perspectives from a Rural Community in Southern United States" in *New Research on Women and Sex Roles*, Dorothy McGuigan, ed., Center for Continuing Education of Women, The University of Michigan, Ann Arbor, 1976.

ALDOUS, JOAN, "Urbanization, the Extended Family and Kinship Ties in West Africa" in *Africa: Social Problems of Change and Conflict*, Pierre van den Berghe, ed., Chandler Publishing Co., San Francisco, 1965.

ALLEN, WALTER R., "The Search for Applicable Theories of Black Family Life," *Journal of Marriage and the Family*, Vol. 40:1:117-129, 1978.

ASCHENBRENNER, JOYCE, *Lifelines: Black Families in Chicago*, Holt, Rinehart, & Winston, New York, 1975.

BILLINGSLEY, ANDREW, *Black Families in White America*, Prentice Hall, Englewood Cliffs, N.J., 1968.

BLASSINGAME, JOHN W., *The Slave Community: Plantation Life in the Antebellum South*, Oxford University Press, New York, 1972.

BRACEY, JOHN H., AUGUST MEIER, and ELLIOTT RUDWICK, eds., *Black Matriarchy: Myth or Reality*, Wadsworth Publishing Co., Belmont, California. 1970.

COLSON, ELIZABETH, "Family Change in Contemporary Africa," *Annals of the New York Academy of Sciences,f* Vol. 92:2:641-52, 1962. Cited from *Black Africa*, John Middleton, ed., The Macmillan Co., New York, 1970.

DuBois, W.E.B., *The Negro American Family*, Atlanta University Press, 1908. Cited from the New American Library edition, New York, 1969.

EADES, JEREMY, "Kinship and Entrepreneurship among Yoruba in Northern Ghana" in *Strangers in African Societies*, William A. Shack and Elliott P. Skinner, eds., University of California Press, Berkeley, 1979.

ELKINS, STANLEY, *Slavery: A Problem in American Intellectual Life*, University of Chicago Press, 1959. Cited in the Universal Library edition, Grosset & Dunlap, 1963.

ENGLISH, RICHARD, "Beyond Pathology: Research and Theoretical Perspectives on Black Families" in *Social Research and the Black Community: Selected Issues and Priorities*, Lawrence E. Gary, ed., Institute for Urban Affairs and Research, Howard University, Washington, D.C., 1974.

FORTES, MEYER, *The Web of Kinship among the Tallensi*, Oxford University Press, Oxford, 1949.

FRAZIER, E. FRANKLIN, *The Negro Family in the United States*, University of Chicago Press, 1939.

FURSTENBERG, FRANK, T. HERSHBERT, and J. MODELL, "The Origins of the Female-Headed Black Family: the Impact of the Urban Experience," *Journal of Interdisciplinary History*, Vol. 6:211-33, 1975.

GENOVESE, EUGENE D., *Roll Jordan Roll: The World the Slaves Made*, Random House, New York, 1974.

GREEN, VERA, "The Black Extended Family in the U.S.: Some Research Suggestions" in *The Extended Family in Black Societies*, D. Shimkin, et al., eds., Mouton, The Hague, 1978.

GUTMAN, HERBERT, *The Black Family in Slavery and Freedom: 1750-1925*, Random House, New York, 1976. Cited Vantage edition, 1977.

HALEY, Alex, *Roots: The Saga of an American Family*, Doubleday & Co., Garden City, New York, 1976.

HILL, ROBERT, *The Strengths of Black Families*, Emerson Hall Publishers, New York, 1971.

HERSKOVITS, MELVILLE J. *The Myth of the Negro Past*, Harper & Brothers, New York, 1941. Cited Beacon Press edition, Boston, 1958.

JACKSON, JACQUELYNE J., "But Where are the Men?" *The Black Scholar*, December 1971, pp. 30-41, 1971.

KENNEDY, THEODORE R., *You Gotta Deal With It: Black Family Relations in a Southern Community*, Oxford University Press, New York, 1980.

KENYATTA, JOMO, *Facing Mt. Kenya: The Tribal Life of the Gikuyu*, 1938. Vintage edition, 1965.

KERRI, JAMES N., "Understanding the African Family: Persistence, Continuity, and Change," *The Western Journal of Black Studies*, Vol. 3:1:14-17, 1979.

KING, JAMES R., "African Survivals in the Black American Family: Key Factors in Stability," *Journal of Afro-American Issues*, Vol. 4:2:153-67, 1976.

LADNER, JOYCE, *Tomorrow's Tomorrow: The Black Woman*, Doubleday & Co., Garden City, New York, 1971.

LINTON, RALPH, *The Study of Man*, Appleton-Century, New York, 1936.

MABOGUNJE, AKIN, "The Yoruba Home," *Odu: Journal of Yoruba and Related Studies*, No. 5, 1958.

MARSHALL, GLORIA A. [Niara Sudarkasa], "Marriage: Comparative Analysis," *International Encyclopedia of the Social Sciences*, Macmillan Co. and The Free Press, New York, 1968.; "In a World of Women: Field Work in a Yoruba Community; in *Women in the Field*, Peggy Golde, ed., Aldine Publishing Co., Chicago, 1970a; "Interpersonal and Institutional Relationships in African Society" and "Integrative Elements in African Social Life" in *Black Perspectives in the Social Sciences*, Video Lecture Series, Institute for African American Affairs, Kent State University, Kent, Ohio, 1970b.

MARTIN, ELMER P. and JOANNE M. MARTIN, *The Black Extended Family*, University of Chicago Press, Chicago, 1978.

McADOO, HARRIETTE P., "Factors Related to Stability of Upwardly mobile Black Families," *Journal of Marriage and the Family*, Vol. 40:4:761-76, 1978.

MAUSS, MARCELL, *The Gift*, translated by Ian Cunnison, Cohen and West, Ltd., London, 1954.

MBITI, JOHN, *African Religions and Philosophy*, Praeger, New York, 1969. *Love and Marriage in Africa*, Longman Group Ltd., London, 1973.

MURDOCK, GEORGE PETER, *Social Structure*, The Macmillan Co., New York, 1949.

NOBLES, WADE, "African root and American Fruit: The Black Family," *Journal of Social and Behavioral Sciences*, Vol. 20:2:52-63. "Africanity: Its Role in Black Families," *The Black Scholar*, June 1974b, pp. 10-17. "Toward an Empirical and Theoretical Framework for Defining Black Families," *Journal of Marriage and the Family*, Vol. 40:4:679-88, 1978.

OKEDIJI, PETER ADE, "A Psychosocial Analysis of the Extended Family: the African Case," *African Urban Notes*, Series B, I:3:93-99. (African Studies Center, Michigan State University), 1975a. "Developing a Measure of Extended Family and Kinship System," *Nigerian Journal of Sociology and Anthropology*, Vol. 2:1:75-79, 1975b.

OWENS, LESLIE H., *This Species of Property: Slave Life and Culture in the Old South*, Oxford University Press, New York, 1976.

RADCLIFFE-BROWN, A.R., "Introduction," *African Systems of Kinship and Marriage*, A.R. Radcliffe-Brown and D. Forde, eds., Oxford University Press, London, 1950.

RADCLIFFE-BROWN, A.R. and DARYLL FORDE, eds., *African Systems of Kinship and Marriage*, International African Institute, by the Oxford University Press, London, 1950.

RIVERS, W.H.R., *Social Organization*, Alfred A. Knopf, New York, 1924.

SAHLINS, MARSHALL, "The Segmentary Lineage: an Organization of Predatory Expansion," *American Anthropologist*, Vol. 63:322-43, 1961. *Stone Age Economics*, Aldine Publishing Co., Chicago, 1972.

SHIMKIN, DIMITRI, EDITH M. SHIMKIN, and DENNIS A. FRAKE, eds., *The Extended Family in Black Societies*, Mouton Publishers, The Hague, 1978.

SHIMKIN, DIMITRI and VICTOR UCHENDU, "Persistence, Borrowing, and Adaptive Changes in Black Kinship Systems: Some Issues and Their Significance" in *The Extended Family in Black Societies*, D. Shimkin, et al., eds., Mouton Publishing, The Hague, 1978.

STACK, CAROL, *All Our Kin*, Harper & Row, New York, 1974.

STAPLES, ROBERT, "The Black Family Revisited" in Robert Staples, ed., *The Black Family: Essays and Studies, Second Edition*, Wadsworth Publishing Co., Belmont, California, 1978.

SUDARKASA, NIARA, *Where Women Work: A Study of Yoruba Women in the Marketplace and in the Home.* Museum of Anthropology, University of Michigan, Ann Arbor, 1973. "Commercial Migration in West Africa, with Special Reference to the Yoruba in Ghana," *African Urban Notes*, Series B, 1:1:61:103 (African Studies Center, Michigan State University, East Lansing), 1974. "An Exposition on the Value Premises Underlying Black Family Studies," *Journal of the National Medical Association*, Vol. 67:3:235-39, 1975a. "The Economic Status of the Yoruba in Ghana Before 1970," *The Nigerian Journal of Economic and Social Studies*, Vol. 17:1:93-125, 1975b. "National Development Planning for the Promotion and Protection of the Family," *Proceedings of the Conference on Social Research and National Development*, The Nigerian Institute of Social and Economic Research, Ibadan, 1976c. "Female Employment and Family Organization in West Africa" in *New Research on Women and Sex Roles*, Dorothy McGuigan, ed., Center for Continuing Education of Women, the University of Michigan, Ann Arbor, 1976. "Women and Migration in Contemporary West Africa," *Signs*, Vol. 3:1:178-189 (Special Issue entitled *Women and Development*, University of Chicago Press, 1977).

TETTEH, P.A., "Marriage, Family and Household" in *A Study of Contemporary Ghana*, Vol. 2, W. Birmingham, et al., eds., Allen & Unwin, London, 1967.

WARE, HELEN, "Polygyny: Women's Views in a Transitional Society, Nigeria 1975," *Journal of Marriage and the Family*, Vol. 41:1:185-195, 1979.

WOODSON, CARTER G. *The African Background Outlined*, Association for the Study of Negro Life and History, Washington, D.C., 1936.

11

The Role of Voluntary Associations in West African Urbanization

KENNETH LITTLE

Introduction

TAKEN AS A WHOLE, the West African region was relatively unaffected by the modern world until the end of the 19th century. Modern development of the hinterland began with the British adoption of trusteeship as colonial policy and with the British and French realization that these territories constituted an expanding market for imported goods as well as important sources of mineral and raw materials needed by the metropolitan country. The French were also concerned with the question of military manpower. These factors were finally crystallized by World War II and the events following it. The British war effort demanded greatly increased supplies of palm kernels, cotton, cocoa, and other locally grown products as well as hides, tin, iron ore, etc., which the colonial governments concerned were required to stimulate (cf. Fortes 1945:205–219). Since the War there have been resettlement schemes, new industries and constructional projects have been instituted, and there has been a general improvement in communications by road, rail, and air. With the strategic implications of West Africa in the struggle against Communism also becoming manifest, political development has also gone on very rapidly, and there has been a corresponding expansion of education and the social services.

The consequence of all these technical and other changes is that there are now many more different models of life and ways of earning a living than existed in West Africa some fifty years ago. It also goes without saying that its inhabitants have acquired a taste for the material elements of Western civilization, including consumer goods of every possible kind. In addition to new economic incentives, Western interests ranging from Christianity and nationalism to football and ballroom dancing have also been generated on a wide scale. In short, there has been produced the kind of phenomenon which anthropologists have customarily studied under the heading of culture contact, or acculturation. This term, however, is not precise enough for purposes of present analysis. First, many of the principal agents of cultural change nowadays are Africans themselves, and second, many Western ideas, practices, and procedures have already been fully assimilated to African culture. Africans became important as "acculturative agents" about the middle of the 19th century when Western-educated Creoles from Sierra Leone went off evangelizing and trading down the Coast. All the way from the Gambia in the west to the Congo in the south they constituted, in many cases, little oases of westernized culture. Consequently, although much of the traditional life has disintegrated, new forms of social organization have arisen out of the older structure. There are, moreover, considerable differences in the extent to which given peoples and groups of Africans have undergone so-called detribalization, and it is rare to find whole communities which have completely severed all traditional loyalties and oblications. More often is it the case, as I propose to show, that the African individual moving out of the tribal area continues to be influenced by tribal culture. In other words, instead of viewing the contemporary West African situation in terms of the juxtaposition of two entirely different cultures, we shall do better to conceive it as a process of adaptation to new circumstances and conditions. Cultural contact still go on, but between westernized Africans and other Africans, as well as between Westeners and Africans; so that the changes occurring are no different in kind from those within a single society (cf. Little 1953:4).

The Urbanization of West Africa

What, in effect, this transformation of West Africa involves is a social process somewhat analogous to the social changes that resulted in the urbanization of Western Europe during the 19th century. Western contact with Africa, like the Industrial Revolution in Europe, has created new social and psychological needs which life in the countryside is rarely able to satisfy. The consequence is a tremendous migration of men and women to the towns, and to places where money can be earned to pay taxes, to provide bridewealth, and to buy manufactured goods and appliances.

Many of these people are in search of a higher standard of living in the shape of the more up-to-date amenities and better housing as well as the higher income that the town can offer. But this is not the only motivation. A large number of the younger men are looking for further educational opportunities, or are hoping to start a fresh career. Others move as a means of escaping from the restrictions of village life, and some of the younger girls, as well as the boys, out of love of adventure and desire for fresh experiences (cf. Balandier 1955a). As Fortes has written in reference to the Gold Coast: "Labour, enterprise, and skill are now marketable in their own right anywhere in the country. . . . People feel that there is little risk in moving about, especially if, as appears to be the case with most mobile elements, their earning capacity is low. A clerk getting £ 2.10 a month feels that he cannot go much lower if he moves" (Fortes 1947:149–179). The development of motor transport, in the shape of the ubiquitous lorry, is an important factor in these respects. Not only has it greatly increased local mobility between town and town, and between town and surrounding countryside, but it has created a new and influential social role—that of the lorry-driver, as a go-between between the urban labor market and the rural village.

Most of this migration is in the direction of towns already established as large centers of Western commerce and administration, of the rapidly growing ports, and of places where mining and other industries are being developed. Its effect has been to swell the population of such places far beyond their previous size, as well as to convert a good many villages into urban areas. For example, the principal towns of Senegal in French West Africa increased their populations by 100 percent between 1942 and 1952 and those of the French Ivory Coast by 109 percent during the same decade. In the Gold Coast there was an increase of 98 percent in the populations of the five largest towns between 1931 and 1948 (Balandier 1955b). Cotonou in Dahomey grew from 1,100 in 1905 to 35,000 in 1952 and Lunsar, in Sierra Leone, which was a village of 30 inhabitants in 1929, has a population today of nearly 17,000 (Lombard 1954:3, 4; Littlejohn n.d.).

Although urbanism in terms of "a relatively large, dense, and permanent settlement of socially heterogeneous individuals" (Wirth 1938) is not a general characteristic of traditional life, it is far from being a unique phenomenon in West Africa. In 1931, some 28 percent of the Yoruba population of Western Nigeria lived in 9 cities of over 45,000 inhabitants, while a further 34 percent lived in cities of over 20,000 inhabitants (Bascom 1955). However, what distinguishes the "new" African city—"new" in the sense, as Georges Balandier points out, that they were built by European colonists—from traditional urbanism is that a large part of its population is industrial, depending upon the labor market for a living. This is particularly evident in the case of towns of recent growth. In Cotonou, for example, some 10,000 persons out of a population of some 35,000 are in wage employment (Lombard 1954).

A further point is that the modern town is much more heterogeneous. It has groups of professionals, office workers, municipal employees, artisans, etc., and in addition to its indigenous political and social segmentation, it also accommodates a large proportion of "strangers." Not only do the latter frequently outnumber the native inhabitants of the town, but they include a wide diversity of tribes. For example, Kumasi, although the capital of Ashantiland, contains as many non-Ashantis as Ashantis; Takoradi-Sekondi contains representatives of more than 60 different tribes (Busia 1950); and less than 10 percent of the inhabitants of Poto-Poto, one of the three African towns of Brazzaville, were born in that city (Balandier 1955a). In the Gold Coast, as a whole, more than two-thirds of the inhabitants of the big towns have been there for less than five years. A further significant characteristic of these urban populations is the numerical preponderance of young people over old and, to a less appreciable extent, the preponderance of men over women. For example, only 2.4 percent of the population of Cotonou are over 60 years of age. In 1921, men considerably outnumbered women, but by 1952 the masculinity rate had dropped to 111. In an area of Poto-Poto, on the other hand, where the average age of the population is about 25, there are only 515 females to every 1,000 males (Balandier 1955a).

Voluntary Associations

Tribal Unions

From the point of view of social organization one of the most striking characteristics of these modern towns is the very large number and variety of voluntary associations.[1] These include a host of new political, religious, recreational, and occupational associations as well as the more traditional mutual aid groups and secret societies out of which some of these more recent organizations have developed. What generally distinguishes the latter kind of association is its more formal constitution and the fact that it has been formed to meet certain needs arising specifically out of the urban environment of its members. It is also more "modern" both in respect to its aims and the methods employed to attain them. One of the best illustrations of these points is provided by certain tribal associations of an extraterritorial kind, known in Nigeria and the Gold Coast as Tribal Unions.

These tribal unions range from little unions, consisting of a few members of the same extended family or clan (Aloba 1954), to much larger bodies like the Ibo State Union which is a collection of village and clan unions. In Nigeria, these associations were originally formed by Ibo and other migrants from Eastern Nigeria to protect themselves from the hostile way in which they were received when they took jobs as policemen, traders, and laborers in the towns of the West and the North. Their aim is to provide members with mutual aid, including support, while out of work, sympathy and financial assistance in the case of illness, and the responsibility for the funeral and the repatriation of the family of the deceased in the case of death. The main raison d'etre, however, is that of fostering and keeping alive an interest in tribal song, history, language, and moral beliefs, and thus maintaining a person's attachment to his native town or village and to his lineage there. In furtherance of this sentiment, money is collected for the purpose of improving amenities in the union's home town and to provide its younger people with education. Social activities include the organization of dances on festival days and of sports meetings and games for their young people. Some of these unions also produce an annual magazine, called an Almanac, in which their members' activities are recorded (Offodile 1947:937, 939, 941).

Associations based upon membership of the same ethnic group also exist in French and Belgian Africa where they perform somewhat similar functions. In Cotonou, for example, such groups welcome and look after persons newly arrived from the country. They provide a means whereby both the old people and the "evolué" can keep in touch with their rural relatives and friends. Each such association has an annual feast and celebration which brings together everyone from the same region. It is also a means of helping the needy and aged members of the group (Lombard 1954).

In Nigeria there have also been developed home branches of the tribal union abroad; and as a final step, State unions have been created, comprising every union of members of the same tribe. It is not surprising, therefore, that these Nigerian tribal unions have obtained a power and influence far beyond their original objectives. The larger unions have played an important part in the expansion of education. They offer scholarships for deserving boys and girls and run their own schools. In some places, the monthly contributions of members for education are invested in some form of commercial enterprise, and appeals for money to build schools seem to meet with a particularly ready response. One observer claims that he saw an up-country union raise in six hours and in a single meeting over £16,000 for such purposes. Some higher education overseas has also been provided, and several leading members of the Nigerian Eastern House of Assembly owe their training in British universities to State union money (Aloba 1954). Even more ambitious plans have included the building of a national bank where people can obtain loans for industrial and commercial purposes. In this connection, some unions have economic advisers who survey trade reports for the benefit of members (Offodile 1947). These tribal unions also serve a number of important political purposes and are recognized as units for purposes of tax collection. In addition to pressing local authorities for better roads, dispensaries and hospitals, and other public amenities, they have been a powerful force in the democratizing of traditional councils; in the multitribal centers they were for many years the recognized basis for representation on Township Advisory Boards or Native Authority Councils. They have also provided a forum for the expression of national politics and for the rise to positions of leadership of the younger educated element (Coleman 1952).

Friendly Societies

In addition to the tribal union, there are also a large number of tribal societies where objectives are limited to mutual aid and benefit. One of the most complicated of these organizations is run by the wives of Kru immigrants in Freetown. This kind of society is divided into three classes. A member pays an admission fee of one guinea and enters the class of least importance. He or she may subsequently be promoted to a higher class and in this event will be expected to make members of that class a present of several pounds. On his or her death, the relatives receive a sum of money commensurate with the deceased person's status. These societies endeavor to develop a high esprit de corps and have been known to impose fines of as much as £ 20 on members guilty of unfriendly conduct toward each other (Banton 1956).

Kru men go to sea for a living and so the members of their societies are divided into "ships," named after various recent additions to Messrs. Elder Dempster's fleet, instead of classes. The Kru also have so-called "family societies' comprising the migrant members of a particular class, or *dako* (a small local federation of patriclans). These groups also provide bereavement benefits. In Freetown there are also a number of traditional organizations, including so-called secret societies and dancing groups, which provide funeral expenses, presents, and entertainment for members when they marry. The congregations of mosques, too, usually have what is loosely called a *Jama Compin* (Compin = Krio, "Company") whose members help each other over funerals. Up country, another Moslem group, composed of women, endeavors to intervene in domestic quarrels and to reconcile man and wife. In this case, a sixpenny subscription is collected every Sunday, and persons joining as new members have to pay the equivalent of what a foundation member has already paid in subscriptions. Some of this money is disbursed as alms, but most of it is used to provide sickness and funeral benefits (Little 1955).

A different kind of mutual aid group is the *esusu*, which is of Yoruba origin. Members of the group pay in at regular intervals a fixed sum and the total is given each time to one of the members. This is an important method for buying trading stock, expensive clothing, etc. (Banton 1956; Bascom 1952). In southeastern Nigeria, a somewhat similar kind of "contribution club" is divided into seven sections, each under a headman. Each member pays one or more weekly subscriptions. The headmen are responsible for collecting the shares from their members, and when the shares have all been collected, the money is handed over to a member nominated by the headman in turn. The recipient has a number of obligations, including that of supplying a quantity of palm wine for the refreshment of club members (Ardener 1953:128-142).

A further organization serves all three functions—providing funeral benefits, charity, and helping its members to save. This is the *Nanamei Akpee*, or "mutual help" society. It has its headquarters in Accra and branches in several other Gold Coast towns, including Keta. The Keta branch has well over 400 members, the great majority of whom are educated or semiliterate women traders. There is a monthly subscription of one shilling and when a member dies, the surviving relatives are given at least £ 10 towards the cost of funeral expenses. Money for loans is raised at weekly collections which begin with community singing. All the women present give as much money as they feel they can afford, and their contributions are written down in a book which also contains a list of the society's members, in order of seniority. When the collection is finished, all the money is given to the member whose name takes first place; the following week it is given to the second, then to the third, and so on. Eventually, all members will in this way receive a contribution, though the process as a whole naturally takes a very long time. However, the man or woman receiving a collection is also given a list showing the amount of money contributed by other members. This determines, during later weeks, the amounts he must contribute himself. For example, if A has given B two shillings then B must raise the same amount when eventually A's turn arrives to receive a weekly collection. In effect, this arrangement means that senior members, i.e., those who have joined early, receive an interest-free loan, which they repay weekly by small contributions; those on the bottom of the list, on the other hand, are saving in a small way, for their own ultimate benefit. In a period of rising prices, those at the top of the list naturally have the advantage, but on the other hand those who wait longer may receive more because the society's membership will in the meantime have increased. There is an element of chance in all this which adds spice to the normally dull business of saving, and this partly explains the society's popularity. Finally, when a member falls ill he is visited in the hospital, given small gifts of money, and so on. At times the society also gives presents and small sums of money to old and sick people even if they are not members (Carey n.d.).

Occupational Associations

In addition to raising loans through such organizations as *Nanamei Akpee*, African market women also form associations in order to control the supply or price of commodities in which their members trade. Some of the larger markets have a woman in charge, and each of the various sections which women monopolize, such as the sale of yams, gari, cloth, etc. is also headed by a woman, who represents them in relation to customers and the market authorities. In Lagos market each such section has its own union, which discourages competition between women trading in that particular commodity (Comhaire-Sylvain 1951). Another women's association is the Fish Sellers Union at Takoradi-Sekondi. The members of this association may club together to raise money to buy fishing nets. The group then sells the nets to fishermen on agreed terms. A fisherman who receives a net sells his catches during the fishing season to the creditor group, and the value of the fish is reckoned against the net. In this way, the members are able to obtain the fish on which their livelihood depends (Busia 1950). Women also associate for industrial purposes. In southern Nigeria, for example, there are women's societies which run a bakery, a laundry, a calabash manufactory, and a gari mill. One of the most interesting of these associations, the Egba Women's Union in Abeokuta, claims a membership of 80,000 women, paying subscriptions of 13 shillings a year. It operates as a weaving co-operative, and runs a maternity and a child welfare clinic as well as conducting classes for illiterate women.

Other occupational and professional associations are concerned with the status and remuneration of their members as workers. Such groups include modern crafts such as goldsmiths, tinkers, gunsmiths, tailors, and barbers, as well as certain trade unions which, unlike Government sponsored trade unions, have come spontaneously into being. One example of these is the Motor Drivers Union at Keta which is now a branch of a nationwide union which negotiates freight rates, working conditions, and so on. Unlike European trade unions, this Motor Drivers Union is an association of small entrepreneurs owning their own vehicles rather than an association of employees. Its main purpose is to look after the interests of drivers generally and in particular to offer them legal assistance and insurance. When a driver is convicted, the Union tries as far as possible to pay his fine; and when a driver dies the Union provides part of the funeral expenses. There are also smaller sickness and accident benefits. The entrance fee is 14 shillings and there is a monthly subscription of one shilling. In addition, the Union organizes meetings and dances (Carey n.d.).

The organization of modern crafts, on the other hand, takes on the form of guilds resembling those of medieval Europe. The first rule of all these guilds in Yoruba towns, where many of them have developed, is that every craftsman, whether master, journeyman or apprentice, must be registered with the guild, must attend meetings, and must pay his dues. One of the guild's prime functions is to maintain a reasonable standard of work in the craft. It determines the rules of apprenticeship; fixes prices of workmanship; and settles disputes, whether between master and apprentice or between craftsman and customer. On the other hand, the guild does not undertake to care for its members in sickness or old age; neither does it function as a bank, lending money to members for tools. Most forms of social security are still organized by the lineage—in which the guild members still retain full membership—and not by the guild (Lloyd 1953).

Unions of a different kind which are also concerned with the status and remuneration of their members are associations of prostitutes. These have been reported from Takoradi and also from Brazzaville. In the latter city, the members of such organizations try to improve their own social and economic position by insisting on a high standard of dress and deportment, and by ostracizing other women who are too casual or too free with their sexual favors. Each group has its own name, such as *La Rose, Diamant,* etc. and is under a leader, an elderly woman, who can set a pattern of elegance and sophistication. Membership is limited and is regulated by a committee. There is also a common fund out of which members in financial straits are helped and their funeral expenses paid should they die. In the latter event, the association behaves as if it were the family of the deceased. Every girl goes into mourning, giving up her jewelry and finer clothes for six months, at the end of which there is a night-long celebration in some "bar-dancing" establishment hired for the occasion (Balandier 1955a:145-148).

Entertainment and Recreational Associations

A large number of associations are concerned with dancing and musical forms of entertainment. Many of these, such as the drumming companies found in Ewe villages in the Gold Coast, still retain much of their traditional character. A number of groups in Brazzaville also perform traditional music, but on a commercial basis. These societies consist of young men who have formed themselves into an orchestra under the presidency of an older man whose compound they use for the purpose of staging an evening's "social" on Saturdays and Sundays. The public is charged for admission on these occasions and the "band," which goes by such appropriate titles as *Etoile, Jeunesse, Record de la Gaieté,* etc. undertakes outside engagements. The receipts are divided among the members according to their position in the society and anything left over goes toward the purchase of new instruments and the provision of further conviviality (cf. Balandier 1955a:143-144). Other such associations, which began as simple dancing societies, have developed under urban conditions into a relatively complex organization and set of modern objectives. A striking example of this kind of phenomenon is the dancing *compin* of Sierra Leone. This is a group of young men and women concerned with the performance of "plays" of traditional music and dancing and with the raising of money for mutual benefit. The music is provided mainly by native drums, xylophones, and calabash rattles, and is accompanied by singing. The dancing which, like the drumming, shows signs of Western influence, is somewhat reminiscent of English country dancing. A "play" is generally given in connection with some important event, such as the close of Ramadan, or as part of the ceremonies celebrating a wedding or a funeral.

The general public as well as the persons honored by the performance are expected to donate money to the compin on these occasions. Money is also collected in the form of weekly subscriptions from the members (Banton 1956; Little 1955).

In one of these organizations, which are particularly numerous among Temne and Mandinka immigrants in Freetown, this amount goes into a general fund to cover corporate expenses of the society's activities—rent of yard, provision of lamps, replacement of drum skins, etc. Then, when any member is bereaved, a collection is held to which all must contribute. However, quite an elabroate procedure is necessary before the money can be paid. The bereaved person must first notify the Reporter with a reporting fee. This is passed on to the company's Doctor, who investigates the circumstances of death, for the company will fine any member who has not notified them of a relative's illness so that they can see that the sick person receives attention. The Doctor washes the body and sends the Prevoe (Provost) round to the other members, telling them to gather that evening when they must pay their contributions. When anyone avoids payment without good cause, the Bailiff may sieze and item of his property of equal value. The evening's meeting is organized by the Manager. He will bring the company's lamps, for members are under an obligation to take part in a wake which will last into the early hours. At the wake the bereaved person will provide cigarettes, kola nuts, bread, and coffee, and will employ a singer. Another duty of the Doctor is to examine members before admission, and to attend them if sick. The Commissioner or Inspector is the disciplinary officer and he can arrest or eject trouble makers, the Prevoe acting on his orders. The Clerk or Secretary keeps accounts and writes letters, and the Cashier receives from the Sultan for safe keeping any money accuring to the society. The Sultan is the chief executive; his female counterpart, who has charge of the women members, is the Mammy Queen. For the dancing there is a leader who directs it, and a Conductor who supervises the band. There is also a Sister in charge of the Nurses, young girls who bring round refreshments at dances, often in white dresses with a red cross on the breast and the appropriate headgear. If there is no woman Doctor, an older Nurse or Sister may assist the Doctor with the invalids, or the washing of the corpse. There may also be further officials, such as an Overseer, an M.C., a Solicitor, a Lawyer, Sick Visitor, etc. Many of these titles involve no work, but they can be given to honor even the least deserving member and to strengthen his identification with the group's company (Banton n.d.).

Other groups concerned with recreation range from Improvement Leagues and Women's Institutes to cricket and football clubs. Some of the latter are characterized by such colorful titles as Mighty Poisons, Hearts of Oak, Heroes, etc. (Hodgkin 1956). Football teams are also run by associations of the former pupils of certain schools, known as Old Boys Associations, which also organize receptions and "send-offs" and sometimes hold evening classes. Most organizations of the latter kind are modeled rather closely on European lines, particularly the so-called "social club." This is constituted for dining and drinking purposes as well as for tennis, whist, billiards, ballroom dancing, amateur dramatics, and other European recreational and cultural activities. For the latter reasons, "social clubs" are mainly confined to the most Westernized section of the population, including well-to-do professionals and businessmen as well as teachers, clerks, and other white collar workers. Such clubs are open to persons of any tribe, but members are expected to conform to European patterns of social etiquette. Europeans themselves are frequently admitted either as members or as guests. Examples of this kind of institution are the Rodgers Club in Accra, the Island Club in Lagos, and the Bo African Club in Sierra Leone. In the latter association, all official business and proceedings, including lectures, debates etc., are conducted in English. At the weekly dance, which is one of the club's principal activities, the general rule is for the women to wear print or silk dresses (without the head tie), and the men open-necked shirts with a blazer or sports jacket. On special occasions evening dress is worn by both sexes. In addition to its ordinary activities, this club undertakes a number of public functions, including special dances to honor visiting notables. It also entertains the teams of visiting football clubs, and its premises are used for such purposes as political meetings and adult education classes (Little 1955).

Women, too, have their social clubs which broadly complement those under the control of men. These are very often known as Ladies' Clubs and Women's Institutes. Many of the latter have been formed under the auspices of churches. A large number of literate husbands have nonliterate wives, and some of these women's clubs reflect the sociological situation in that they are divided into "literate" and "illiterate" sections which hold separate meetings. "Literate" activities consist mainly in sewing and crochet work, in practicing the cooking of European and native dishes, and in listening to talks about household economy. Individual literate women give instruction in these arts to the "illiterate" meeting, and in return nonliterate women sometimes teach the literate group native methods of dyeing, spinning, basketry, and traditional songs and dances (Little 1955).

Women's Institutes are primarily the result of the initiative of educated women. For example, the President and leading officers of the Keta Women's Institute in the Gold Coast are teachers, although the bulk of its membership consists of market women. It is principally a social club, but it has certain other more important interests. For example, it has acted as a "pressure group," intervening with the Urban Council in support of a plan for improving amenities at the local markets. Among other local changes, the women achieved the provision of ambulance services, and the employment of a larger number of female nurses at the Keta hospital (Carey n.d.).

The Organization of Voluntary Associations

Before we attempt to generalize about these voluntary associations, it necessary to distinguish between three rather different types. The first is sti basically concerned with traditional activities, although with some sligl modification; in the second type, traditional activities have been deliberatel modified or expanded to suit modern purposes; and the third type is wholl modern in organization and objectives. It will be convenient to term thes three types respectively "traditional," "traditional-modernized" an "modern."

The function of the "traditional" association is generally limited to th organization of some particular religious, occupational, or recreational intei est, such as a cult, a trade, or some form of dancing or drumming. Spac unfortunately prevents description of religious associations in general. Thes exist alongside Islam and the ancestral cult, and according to Hofstra (195! they may be divided into four categories: (1) Christian churches organized b missionaries, (2) so-called African churches, (3) looser, smaller groups of syncretistic character, (4) irregularly organized movements of a messianic o prophetic kind. In the traditional type of association some provision may b made for mutual benefit, but this is incidental to the main purpose of th society. Membership in the group is usually confined to persons belonging tc the same village or ward of a town and is often related to other traditiona institutions, such as an age set. For example, drumming companies amon⟨ the Ewe are organized on a ward basis, and usually there are three in ever⟩ ward. The first comprises children up to the age of about fifteen; the second consists of the so-called "young men," ranging in age from about fifteen tc thirty; and the third comprises "elders," i.e. the male population over thirty or so. The senior companies usually give themselves names such as "Patience" or "U.A.C." (abbreviation for United Africa Company), and some of these are, in effect, associations of semiprofessional entertainers who travel about the country in search of engagements (Cary, n.d.). Although the organization of such "traditional" associations is generally quite simple and informal, a number of them have adapted to modern conditions by incorporating literate persons as officials and by widening the scope of their function. In the traditional economy of the Gold Coast, for example, each trade or occupation normally had a chief-practitioner who settled disputes and represented his associates in relation to outsiders. This is largely true today, but in addition some of these groups have turned themselves into local branches of a nationwide union. In the case of the goldsmiths, this involved appointing its chief-practitioner as Life-Chairman of the association, while an educated man who could deal adequately with its business affairs was elected President. Similarly, the semiliterate president of the Carpenters Union now has a literate secretary and treasurer to help him (Carey n.d.).

It goes without saying that the great majority of people who belong to "traditional" associations are unlettered. The number of persons who can read and write or speak a European language is larger in the "traditional-modernized" association, but what mainly distinguishes the latter is its syncretistic character, its relatively formal organization, and the variety of its functions. A particularly striking example of the latter point is *La Goumbé*, a Moslem and predominantly Dioula youth organization for both sexes in the Ivory Coast. This combines the functions of emancipating young women from family influence; assisting the process of marital selection; providing, on a contributory basis, marriage and maternity benefits (including perfume and layettes for the newborn); preserving the Dioula tribal spirit; running an orchestra; and acting as the local propaganda agent for *Rassemblement Démocratique Africain*. It also maintains its own police force (cited by Hodgkin from Holas 1953:116-131). In addition to a written constitution which embodies the declared aims and rules of the society, this kind of association sometimes has its own name and a special uniform of its own, and generally follows such Western practices as the holding of regular meetings, keeping of minutes, accounts, etc. The wearing of a uniform type of dress is probably more characteristic of women's societies than those formed by men. The women members of *Nanemei Akpee*, for example, all dress in white for meetings, and the practice of appearing in the same kind of dress, including head-tie, necklace, and sandals, is followed by other women's groups on formal occasions. Finance plays an important part in its affairs, and there is a regular tariff of entrance fees; weekly or monthly dues are collected and fines are sometimes levied. These funds are administered by a Treasurer or Financial Secretary, sometimes supervised by a committee which also conducts the everyday business of the association, including the sifting of fresh applications for membership, settlement of disputes, etc. Related partly to the wide diversity of functions performed is the large number of persons holding official positions in some of these societies. Many of these office-bearers, as exemplified by the dancing compin, have European titles, or, as in the case of the Kru women's societies, are known by the native equivalents of such titles.[2] This enactment of European roles, as in the dancing compin, is a fairly common feature of associations of the "traditional-modernized" type. It has been termed "vicarious participation in the European social structure" by J. Clyde Mitchell, but as Michael Banton points out (1956), this possibly places too much emphasis on the process of westernization and too little on the independent process of change in the tribal group. An assistant official sometimes has the duty of conveying information about the society's activities to the general public as well as to members. *La Goumbé*, for example, has a number of town criers, members of the *griot* caste, to carry news through the town (Holas 1953).

The organization of the "traditional-modernized" association is also rendered more elaborate by a tendency toward affiliation. This ranges all the way from a fully centralized organization of individual branches to a loose fraternal arrangement between entirely autonomous branches of the same movement. Affiliation of individual branches sometimes seems to be the result of traditional conditions. Thus, the "village-group union" of the Afikpo Ibo of Nigeria is apparently modelled largely upon the indigenous age-set structure of the people concerned (cf. Ottenberg 1955:i-28). The *Goumbé* movement comprises a number of local "cells" co-ordinated by a central committee, which settles disputes between them and lays down general policy (Holas 1953). The dancing compin movement, on the other hand, consists of a large number of separate societies which occasionally exchange visits and information and extend hospitality to each other's members, but are otherwise entirely independent. Finally, although membership of these associations tends to be tribally or regionally circumscribed, this is not invariably so. Even tribal unions sometimes have persons from more than one tribe among their members. The Benin Nation Club (Nigeria), for example, provides facilities for all natives of the Benin Province (Comhaire-Sylvain 1950:246 ff.). Several occupational and other groups recruit their members on an intertribal basis, and this also applies to some of the societies run by women.

The "modern" association has already been briefly described in terms of the "social club," and so it will suffice merely to add that its organization is broadly the same as that of any European association of a comparable kind. Like its European counterpart, it is often a medium for social prestige.

Despite their wide variety, one objective common to all types of voluntary association is that of sociability and fraternity. Not only is the serving of refreshments, including such beverages as tea, palm wine, beer, or stronger drink, an integral part of any formal gathering of members, but the latter are expected and encouraged to visit each others' homes, especially in the event of illness or bereavement. Again, although some groups, including certain guilds and occupations, are confined to persons of the same sex, it seems to be a fairly common practice for women to be admitted into associations under the control of men, and for men to be members of certain associations in which women predominate. Some associations organized by men deliberately encourage the recruitment of female members but have them under a more or less separate administration, with the women's leader responsibile to the head of the society. A further fairly common feature of all kinds of voluntary associations is the fact that most of their personnel are young people. Indeed, some societies expect their members to retire at the age of thirty (Holas 1953), and it is rare for persons over middle age to play an active part in their affairs. This, however, is less typical of the "traditional" organizations that it is of the other types of association which, nevertheless, quite often like to have an elderly man or woman as an honorary president. The role of such a person is to uphold the association's reputation for respectability and to help its relations with the wider community. The fact that he is not infrequently a person of importance in tribal society is indicative of the desire of such associations to keep on good terms with the traditional authorities. The size of membership is a more variable factor. It ranges from a mere handful of individuals to several hundred or even thousands, in the case of the larger tribal associations. In the smaller societies, which are often very ephemeral, the amount of support given is probably bound up as much with the personality and personal influence of the leader as it is with the popularity of the institution.

Voluntary Associations as an Adaptive Mechanism

It was suggested earlier that the social changes resulting from culture contact may be seen as an historical process of adaptation to new conditions. Adaptation in the present context implies not only the modification of African institutions, but their development to meet the demands of an industrial economy and urban way of life. In effect, as Banton has shown in reference to Temne immigrants in Freetown, this sometimes amounts to a virtual resuscitation of the tribal system in the interests of the modernist ambitions and social prestige of the younger educated element concerned (Banton 1956:354-368). The unpublished findings of Jean Rouch seem to give even greater emphasis to this kind of phenomenon, which he has labelled "super-tribalization." Some of the immigrants into the Gold Coast, whom he has studied, have gained sufficient solidarity through their associations and cults to dominate over the local population, achieving monopolies in various trades (cf. Forde 1956:389). A further important effect of this kind of development, as both Busia (1950) and Banton (n.d.) have pointed out, is to inhibit the growth of civic loyalty or responsibility for the town concerned. Modern urbanism, in other words, is the conditioning factor in contemporary African society as well as the culmination of so-called acculturation. West African urbanism of course differs from comparable Western situations in being less advanced, although it is probably more dynamic. It involves a particularly rapid diffusion of entirely new ideas, habits, and technical procedures, and a considerable restructuring of social relationships as a consequence of the new technical roles and groups created.

Voluntary associations play their part in both these processes through the fresh criteria of social achievement that they set up and through the scope that they offer, in particular, to women and to the younger age groups. Women, and younger people in general, possess a new status in the urban economy, and this is reflected in the various functions which these associations perform as political pressure groups, in serving as a forum for political expression, and in providing both groups with training in modern methods of business. Equally significant is the fact that women's participation in societies with a mixed membership involves them in a new kind of social relationship with men, including companionship and the opportunity of selecting a spouse for oneself. In particular, voluntary associations provide an outlet for the energies and ambitions of the rising class of young men with a tribal background who have been to school. The individuals concerned are debarred by their "Western" occupations as clerks, school teachers, artisans, etc. and by their youth from playing a prominent part in traditional society proper; but they are the natural leaders of other young people less Western ized and sophisticated than themselves. This is largely because of their abilit to interpret the "progressive" ideas they have gained through their work and travel, and through reading newspapers and books, in terms that are mean- ingful to the illiterate rank and file of the movement.

It is, in fact, in relation to the latter group, particularly the urban immi- grant, that the significance of voluntary associations as an adaptive mech- anism is most apparent. The newly arrived immigrant from the rural areas has been used to living and working as a member of a compact group of kinsmen and neighbors on a highly personal basis of relationship and mu- tuality. He knows of no other way of community living than this, and his natural reaction is to make a similar adjustment to urban conditions.

This adjustment the association facilitates by substituting for the ex- tended group of kinsmen a grouping based upon common interest which is capable of serving many of the same needs as the traditional family or lineage. In other words, the migrant's participation in some organization such as a tribal union or a dancing compin not only replaces much of what he has lost in terms of moral assurance in removing from his native village, but offers him companionship and an opportunity of sharing joys as well as sorrows with others in the same position as himself. (Probably an important point in this regard is the large number of offices available in some associa- tions, enabling even the most humble member to feel that he "matters.") Such an association also substitutes for the extended family in providing counsel and protection, in terms of legal aid; and by placing him in the company of women members, it also helps to find him a wife. It also substi- tutes for some of the economic support available at home by supplying him with sickness and funeral benefits, thereby enabling him to continue his most important kinship obligations. Further, it introduces him to a number of economically useful habits and practices, such as punctuality and thrift, and it aids his social reorientation by inculcating new standards of dress, etiquett, and personal hygiene. Above all, by encouraging him to mix with persons outside his own lineage and sometimes tribe, the voluntary association helps him to adjust to the more cosmopolitan ethos of the city (Banton 1956; Offodile 1947:937, 939, 941). Equally significant, too, is the syncretistic char- acter of associations of the "traditional-modernized" type. Their combina- tion of modern and traditional traits constitutes a cultural bridge which conveys, metaphorically speaking, the tribal individual from one kind of sociological universe to another.

The latter point is also indicative of various ways in which these voluntary associations substitute for traditional agencies of social control. Not only are positive injunctions to friendly and fraternal conduct embodied in the constitution by which members agree to bind themselves,[3] but many associations have rules proscribing particular misdemeanors and what they regard as antisocial behavior. In this respect, the frequent inclusion of sexual offenses, such as the seduction of the wife or the daughter of a fellow member, is very significant. The association also sets new moral standards and attempts to control the personal conduct of its members in a number of ways. For example, the Lagos branch of *Awo Omama* Patriotic Union resolved not to marry any girl of their town so long as the prevailing amount of money asked for bride-wealth was not reduced (Comhaire-Sylvain 1950). The dancing compin will withhold its legal aid from a member unless the company's officials examining the case feel that he is in the right. Also, there are women's groups concerning themselves specifically with the settlement of domestic quarrels, which expel members who are constant troublemakers in the home and among other women. More frequently, punishment takes the form of a fine, but the strongest sanction probably lies in the fact that every reputable association is at pains to check fresh applications for membership (Offodile 1947:939, 941). In other words, a person who has earned a bad name for himself in one organization may find it difficult to get into another; and this form of ostracism may in some cases be as painful as exile from the tribe.

A final important point is the extent to which disputes of a private or domestic nature, which would formerly have been heard by some traditional authority such as the head of a lineage, are now frequently taken to the head of an association, even when the matter is quite unconcerned with the life of that particular body (Kurankyi-Taylor n.d.; Offodile 1947:28).

Conclusion

Theorists of Western urbanism have stressed the importance of voluntary associations as a distinctive feature of contemporary social organization. Wirth, in particular, has emphasized the impersonality of the modern city, arguing that its psychological effect is to cause the individual urbanite to exert himself by joining with others of similar interests into organized groups to obtain his ends. "This," wrote Wirth (1938) "results in an enormous multiplication of voluntary organizations directed towards as great a variety of objectives as are human needs and interests." However, this thesis has not been strongly supported by empirical enquiry. According to Komarovsky (1946:686–698), who studied voluntary associations in New York, the old neighborhood, the larger kin group, might have broken down, but they have not been replaced by the specialized voluntary groups to the extent usually assumed. Floyd Dotson, who conducted a similar investigation in Detroit, also failed to find a wholesale displacement of primary by secondary groups.

He concludes that the majority of urban working class people do not participate in formally organized voluntary associations (Dotson 1951:687-693). Perhaps more significant for the present context is the fact that the same writer found even less participation in voluntary organizations among the working class population of Guadalajara, the second largest city of Mexico (Dotson 1953:380-386).

The quantitative methods used in obtaining the latter results have not as yet been employed in African towns, so it is impossible to make exact comparisons. Also, the investigations concerned appear to have been made among relatively stable populations. Further study is therefore needed of the two factors which seem to be largely instrumental in the growth of these African voluntary associations. The first of these factors is the existence of an urban population which is largely immigrant, unstable, and socially heterogeneous. The second is the adaptability of traditional institutions to urban conditions. Possibly, it is the existence and interrelationship of these two factors rather than "anomie" which creates the essential conditions for the "fictional kinship groups," which, according to Wirth, substitute for actual kinship ties within the urban environment.[4]

Notes

1. Michael P. Banton (n.d.) estimates that some 130 registered societies were in existence in Freetown in 1952. The number of unregistered societies is unknown. Pierre Clément (1956:470-471) reports some 62 "authorized" and "unauthorized" societies from Stanleyville, Belgian Congo. There are very few data concerning individual participation, although J. Lombard (op. cit.) reports of Cotonou that out of 35 persons who belonged to one or more associations, 20 belonged to regional groups, 17 to professional associations, 13 to political groups, 3 to musical societies, 1 to an athletic club.

2. For example, *Chelenyoh*, Secretary; *Weititunyon*, Treasurer (Banton n.d.).

3. "Added . . . is the internal discipline which is often maintained among members of well organized tribal unions. Where there is perfect control of extraneous activities of the members, it is hard to see two litigants in court being members of the same tribal unions. I remember at Makurdi the Ibo Federal Union there had a strict regulation, which was observed to the letters . . . that no Ibo man shall send another to court under any pretext without first bringing the matter to the union for trial and advice. The result of this was that in that town the Ibo deserted the courts, except if drawn there by members of different tribes or by disloyal members of their own union, but this later case is rare" (Offodile 1947).

4. It has been noted in this connection that voluntary associations among Mexican immigrants in Chicago are participated in by only a small minority. Nevertheless, they play an important role which directly and indirectly affects the life of the entire colony (Taylor 1928:131-142).

References

ALOBA, ABIODUN 1954 Tribal unions in party politics. West Africa, July 10.

ARDENER, SHIRLEY G. 1953 The social and economic significance of the Contribution Club among a section of the Southern Ibo. Annual Conference, West African Institute of Social and Economic Research. Ibadan.

BALANDIER, GEORGES 1955a Sociologie des Brazzavilles Noires, Paris, Colin.
1955b Social changes and problems in Negro Africa. In Africa in the modern world, edited by Calvin W. Stillman. Chicago, University of Chicago Press.

BANTON, MICHAEL 1956 Adaptation and integration in the social system of Temne immigrants in Freetown. Africa, Vol. XXVI, No. 4
1957 West-African city: A study of tribal life in Freetown. O. U. P.

BASCOM, WILLIAM 1952 The Esusu: a credit institution of the Yoruba. Journal of the Royal Anthropological Institute, Vol. LXXXII.
1955 Urbanization among the Yoruba. American Journal of Sociology, Vol. LX, No. 5.

BUSIA, K. A. 1950 Social survey of Sekondi-Takoradi. Accra, Gold Coast Government Printer.

CAREY, A. T., N.D. Unpublished study of Keta, Gold Coast. Department of Social Anthropology, Edinburgh University.

CLÉMENT, PIERRE 1956 In Social implications of urbanization and industrialization in Africa south of the Sahara. Edited by Daryll Forde. (Prepared by the International African Institute, London.) Paris, UNESCO.

COLEMAN, J. S. 1952 The role of tribal associations in Nigeria. Annual Conference, West African Institute of Social and Economic Research, Ibadan.

COMHAIRE-SYLVAIN, SUZANNE 1950 Associations on the basis of origin in Lagos, Nigeria. American Catholic Sociological Review, Vol. 11.
1951 Le travail des femmes à Lagos. Zaire, Vol. 5, Nos. 2 and 5.

DOTSON, FLOYD 1951 Patterns of voluntary association among urban working-class families, American Sociological Review 16:687–693.
1953 Voluntary associations in a Mexican city. American Sociological Review 18:380–386.

FORDE, DARYLL 1956 Introduction. Social implications of urbanization and industrialization in Africa south of the Sahara. Daryll Forde, ed.

FORTES, M. 1945 The impact of the war on British West Africa. International Affairs, Vol. XXI, No. 2.
1947 Ashanti survey, 1945-46: an experiment in social research. Geographical Journal, Vol. CX.

HODGKIN, THOMAS 1956 Nationalism in Colonial Africa. London, Muller.

HOFSTRA, S. 1955 De Betekenis van Enkele Niewere Groepsverchijnselen voor de Sociale Integratie van Veranderend Afrika. Medelingen der Koninklijke Nederlandse Akademie van Wetenschappen, ofd. Letterkunde, Nieuwe Reeks, Deel 18, No. 14.

HOLAS, B. 1953 La Goumbé. Kongo-Overzee, Vol. 19

KOMAROVSKY, MIRRA 1946 The voluntary associations of urban dwellers. American Sociological Review, Vol. 11, No. 6.

KURANKYI-TAYLOR, E. E., N.D. Ashanti indigenous legal institutions and their present role. Ph.D. Dissertation, Cambridge University.

LITTLE, KENNETH 1950 The significance of the West African Creole for Africanist and Afro-American studies. African Affairs, Vol. XLIX.
1953 The study of "social change" in British West Africa. Africa, Vol. XXIII, No. 4.
1955 Structural change in the Sierra Leone Protectorate. Africa, Vol. XXV, No. 3.

LITTLEJOHN, JAMES, N.D. Unpublished pilot study of Lunsar, Sierra Leone Protectorate. Department of Social Anthropology, Edinburgh University.

LLOYD, PETER 1953 Craft organization in Yoruba towns. Africa, Vol. XXIII, No. 4.

LOMBARD, J. 1954 Cotonou: ville africaine. de l'Institut Français Afrique Noire (Dakar), Vol. XVI, Nos. 3 and 4.

OFFODILE, E. P. OYEAKA 1947 Growth and influence of tribal unions. West African Review, Vol. XVIII, No. 239.

OTTENBERG, S. 1955 Improvement associations among the Afikpo Iko. Africa, Vol. XXV, No. 1.

TAYLOR, PAUL S. 1928 Mexican labor in the United States. University of California Publications in Economics, Vol. VI, VII.

WIRTH, L. 1938 Urbanism as a way of life. American Journal of Sociology, Vol. XLIV, No. 8.

12

Drinking to Prosperity: Hedonism and Modernization in Vilafranca

EDWARD C. HANSEN

THE INFORMATION PRESENTED in this chapter is based on intensive participant observation carried out in three of the six major bars in Vilafranca where the coalitions are formed and maintained. All these bars came to exist in their present form between 1959 and 1967, and all occupy prominent spots on the two main thoroughfares of Vilafranca. Their newness stands in stark contrast to the timeworn stolidity of the buildings that surround them. They physically resemble the fancy tourist bars of the nearby Mediterranean coast.[1] Since 1960, these few bars have become the most dynamic forums of public intercourse in the Alto Panadés, and bar culture has spread at the expense of the major voluntary associations that used to monopolize public recreation and intercourse.

Even to the most casual observer, these bars have an obvious dynamism, marked by the volume of people that pass their portals from as early as six in the morning to as late as six on the following morning. On weekdays, there is a continuous trickle of people from early morning to late afternoon, and by seven in the evening there is a veritable avalanche of patrons, who stay until just before the evening meal at ten. On Saturdays and Sundays, the flow of humanity is so great at all hours of the day that there is barely

Editor's note: Research for this chapter was carried out in the Alto Panadés province of Barcelona over a period of 20 months during 1965 to 1969.

elbow room indoors and standing room only at the outdoor tables on the *ramblas*.

The bar's role as a center of communications is perhaps its most important. An essential part of this function entails keeping track of other people's whereabouts and doings. This sort of information is very useful in the Alto Panadés, since the economic pursuits of many people are diversified enough so that they do not remain in one place (e.g., an office) all day long. Even an efficient telephone system (which Vilafranca does not have) would not relieve the problem. The solution to finding people is to repair to the bar. If the person in question cannot be immediately located, the bartender takes a message for him. On an average day, a bartender takes well over 200 such messages, storing most of them in his head. The bar also serves as a gossip mill recording the activities of almost anyone in town. Discussing other people's activities and evaluating their characters is an essential of bar conversation. Far from being idle chatter, such conversations prove extremely useful in ferreting out news of coming economic possibilities and gaining insights about whom to ally with and whom to avoid. Such news and evaluations are absolutely essential in the drama of modernization in the Alto Panadés because people themselves are the resources in the process.[2]

The vital role of the bar in mediating human contacts has specialized importance for a certain type of small businessman. In Vilafranca, a number of men specialize in the sale of machinery, particularly agricultural machinery, but also automobiles and motor bikes. These men usually operate with precarious capitalization and a scarcity of goods. Rather than risk further capital by renting an office (which would isolate them from contacts anyhow), they simply circulate from bar to bar in search of customers. I recorded an interesting example. A young automobile salesman, Señor Llops, operated in this fashion to study the psychology of potential customers who were often unaware of their desire to purchase an automobile. Llops began his career as a garage mechanic; scraping together several weeks' earnings, he bought a second-hand motorcycle, reconditioned it, and sold it at a sufficient profit to buy two more motorcycles. In a few years, he had generated enough capital to move into the automobile business. As cars are costly in Spain, he must buy one and sell it before he can purchase another. Because his business is so small, he must actually guess who will be in the market for an auto and when. The logical marketplace is in the best bar in town, where he can measure psychologically the desires of affluent people for an auto. Through his understanding of the behavior appropriate to bar culture, he is able to meet and mix with all his potential clientele. Having ingratiated himself with a prospective buyer, Llops purchases a car he believes will interest his hoped-for client. He cleans and polishes the car and parks it in front of the potential customer's habitual bar. Almost always it is love at first sight between buyer and auto. Over a few hours of drinks, the deal is concluded, with a handsome profit for Llops. In the more than two years I observed him in action, he never failed to make a sale. Though few are so successful as Llops, such entrepreneurs abound in Vilafranca.

The principal social goals of participation in bar culture are to build new networks and maintain old ones. For the bourgeois with estates to modernize and for members of other social classes intent on social mobility, specific kinds of networks have to be cultivated that involve only specific people drawn from the various classes. From the perspective of the other classes and of government officials, the bourgeoisie has the lion's share of property, capital, and knowledge of economic opportunities in the *comarca* [province]. Members of the haute bourgeoisie own the best agricultural land, the wineries, much real estate, factories; several have seats on the Barcelona stock exchange, and one owns a local bank as well as the most important bar. What lands and businesses they do not own are not worth owning, foreign-owned,[3] or government-owned. The bourgeoisie is thus in an excellent position to do favors for people less well endowed. Such favors can consist of taking a talented partner into an enterprise or merely furnishing information and influence to enable a person to set up business on his own.

From the perspective of the bourgeois, the modernization of his estate requires him to assemble, on an informal basis, a team of loyal dependents. Minimally he must be able to acquire the talents of various technicians: skilled agricultural workers; mechanics (to service the new machinery); machinery salesman (machines are still in short supply); experts on fertilizer, hybridization, and scientific cultivation. Additionally, if he is to take advantage of state aid to agriculture, he must deal on good terms with a wide range of government officials: bank officials from the Agrarian Credit Bank, technical personnel from the Agrarian Extension Service, provincial officials related to the viniculture cooperative, officials of the government labor syndicates. All these personnel are in short supply. In addition, each is at once a potential ally and a potential enemy: a potential ally in the sense that he could become a happy (dependent) partner in a prosperous business venture; a potential enemy in that his refusal or disaffection could cause serious reverses for the modernizing landowner.

The high stakes involved on all sides, the history of social conflicts, and the vagaries of informal coalition formation explain why personal prestige plays such an important role in the success or failure of individuals trying to reap the benefits of modernization. To succeed, an individual must live up to a complex code of good-fellowship. The playing out of this drama constitutes a great part of the bar culture and in itself is worthy of anthropological inquiry. To evaluate the role of prestige in bar culture, I have followed Silverman's (1966) variant of the reputational method, which stresses eliciting the criteria of prestige from the subjects themselves. Eight informants were given a list of 100 names, 25 from each of the four major social classes of the *comarca* (haute bourgeoisie, petite bourgeoisie, workers, and *rabassaires* [or sharecroppers]), and asked to rank each name according to the level of prestige its owner enjoyed in local society. The informants were then asked to explain their classification. Then each individual listed was discussed to ascertain how he fit the criteria defined by the informant. Informants' classifications were cross-checked by a number of simple card sorts done by other people and by direct observations of prestige-deference behavior in the local bars.

The object of the study was not just to classify individuals according to the prestige they enjoyed in local society. Because personal prestige is essential to individual success in getting into coalitions, an effort was made to crack the code of personal prestige as a necessary step to an understanding of coalition formation in the Alto Panadés. The magnitude of this problem for a foreign anthropologist can be readily understood when one considers that no Catalan entirely understands the code himself. Apart from presenting some of the results of prestige classification and their relationship to informal social organization, I can provide only a rough idea of the ideological component of the code of bar culture.

In the bar culture of Vilafranca, a person's prestige is a direct function of how well he is able to live up to the complex code of good-fellowship that mediates relationships between individuals. According to informants' criteria, the ability to get along with others (*relacionarse con otros, relacionarse con los demás*) far outweighs any other criterion of gaining prestige. Any discussion of a person's ability to get along with others automatically includes an analysis of the individual's personality; the key formula for such an analysis is: "*(X) tiene un carácter (cerrado, alegre, abierto, adusto,* etc.)" ("So and so has a [closed, happy, open, brusque, etc.] personality"). In turn, the strength of an individual's personality is the key to his success (or lack of it) in attaining prestige and is a crucial factor in his ability to claim a spot in one of the coalitions.

Personality is viewed locally as a multifaceted entity, just as being able to get along with others is viewed as a complex process. Judgments about the nature of a man's personality are filtered through at least four major cultural constructs long familiar to students of Hispanic society: *cultura, gracia, simpatía,* and *honra.* The first refers to the upbringing of the individual, his breeding; the second is a quality of the essential personality and refers to charm and wit; the third refers to the quality of empathizing with others and evoking empathy in return; and the fourth refers to a person's ability to protect his familial and personal reputation from the depredations of immoral individuals and from abusive encroachments by diverse authority figures (e.g., bosses, the government). These four concepts hang together like a constellation, and failure to develop them successfully is reflected in diminished prestige, which in turn reduces the range of social action an individual enjoys.

The importance of these concepts is further highlighted by informants' evaluations of some of the more spectacular social failures in Vilafranca. Six individuals were ranked at the bottom of the prestige hierarchy for being given over to vice (*"entregado al vicio"*). Two were homosexuals, one a prostitute (the only one in the town), one too devoted to the pleasures of Barcelona whorehouses (*"demasiado putero"*), and two incorrigible drunks.[4] Failure of this sort is viewed as a serious deficiency in breeding (*"gran falta de cultura"*). Such deficiencies in breeding lead to the dimunition of honor as well, rendering such individuals outside the boundaries of normal social intercourse.

Far more serious personality deficiencies derive from abuse of power, which is viewed as stemming from wealth, political position, or both. Abuse of power is not viewed as an abstract matter, but as something that can occur in the context of dyadic relationships, man-to-man. The mere possession of public office in an area hostile to the central government is sufficient to engender a host of anecdotes relating to the abuse of power. Thus the mayor of the town, an able administrator cursed with a dour personality, was placed at or near the bottom of the hierarchy by all my informants and described by one as "the ideal chief of a Nazi concentration camp" (*"el jefe perfecto de un campo de concentración nazi"*). A working-class man who had risen to the post of councilman in the municipal government was even more rigorously downgraded than the mayor. He had arbitrarily instituted a system of alternate-side-of-the-street parking in Vilafranca, causing great inconvenience to the auto owners of the town. For this, he is shunned on the street and has received the nickname Don Disco (Mr. Parking Sign); it is reputed that "he even hangs those signs on his mother's balls" (*"hasta los cojones de su madre cuelga discos"*).

Abuses of power stemming from disparities in wealth are much more common than abuses deriving from the exercise of public office. The owner of a business can lose his prestige either by attempting to exact extraordinary services from his employees or by issuing commands to an employee that the latter considers degrading. Such commands or extraordinary services always have to be refused with great dramatic vigor, at least in the recounting of the incident to a foreign anthropologist. Minimally, negation of the demand involves an emphatic, "No, Señor," followed by the resignation of the employee on the spot. Various informants stressed that not only had they refused and resigned, but they had also had their revenge, including physical reprisals.[5] Such abuses are felt to constitute a direct affront to personal honor, which is precarious and must be maintained at all costs. As the abuse of power in this fashion could potentially occur in any situation where there is a disparity in wealth between partners, bar culture comes to stress a nearly exaggerated courtesy between such people.

In addition to the major social sins and personality defects discussed above, informants provided me with a catalog of less grievous, but still significant, social sins that have a direct bearing on bar culture. All these sins have ambiguous qualities, but ambiguity is part of any prestige-deference system. The first sin is to be pretentious or presumptuous (*presumido*), to pretend to be more than one actually is. The second is interfering in the affairs of others (*metirse*). The third is being overconcerned with one's economic affairs (*siempre al negocio*). The ambiguity stems from the fact that bar culture involves doing all three of these things as vigorously as possible. The people who fail to attain the upper reaches of the prestige hierarchy are those who do these necessary operations in bad style. Acquiring the proper style becomes a life-long preoccupation for participants in bar culture, and the statistical probabilities of personal success are stacked against them.

What kind of behavior is associated with the prestige code in the context of bar culture? The demonstration of good-fellowship involves spending a great deal of time, money, and effort buying drinks for one's cohorts at local bars and organizing impromptu suppers for them in a variety of regional restaurants. Success in the demonstration of good-fellowship is contingent on having a solid physical constitution, because eating and drinking are done in heroic proportions, repetitively and at irregular hours. Absenting oneself from the bar for several days brings complaints from companions of inattention to their primary needs. The stress on eating and drinking has evolved into an ideology in which hedonism is a reciprocal of ingestion. The organization of action invariably begins with statements such as: "We've go to go to bar *X* to drink Priorato wine." "Let's go to restaurant *Y* to get some of those octopuses." "A fine afternoon like today means we can drive over to Casa Marisco for those special prawns." Regardless of the hour, a gustatory excursion for eight to twenty persons is organized within five minutes. On two occasions within five years, this ideology led to the development of a quasiformal men's supper club, with membership of about fifty.

The proper atmosphere for these activities is one of enforced jollity; everyone must appear to be amusing himself to the utmost, without a care in the world (*sin preocupaciones*). Anyone appearing momentarily preoccupied is gently prodded by his companions, who inevitably ask: "Why are you so serious, man?" ("*¡Hombre! ¿Porqué tan serio?*") Anyone wishing to start a somewhat serious conversation is reminded: "But we are here to amuse ourselves, don't be such a bore" ("*Estamos aquí para divertirnos, no seas tan pesado*"). Should the immediate realities of food and drink not be sufficient to amuse those present, then either joking (each group inevitably seems to contain one joker) or singing will fill the void. Judged by its atmosphere, bar culture appears to involve a certain amount of just plain frivolity.

Nothing could be further from the truth in terms of social outcomes, however. Minimally, the emphasis on pleasures of the moment allows people who are suspicious of each other for any of the reasons outlined earlier in this chapter to suspend traditional judgments, as a prelude to becoming friends and allies or, if such relationships have already been achieved, to maintaining them. It allows them also to avoid considering the impact of the social changes their alliance will bring about in the *comarca*. As the directions of such changes have been hotly contested in recent history, the functional advantages of such a code are obvious. All are striving to enrich themselves as individuals, not as representatives of any identifiable social group. In the code of good-fellowship, society is blurred in a haze of alcohol and a whiff of garlic. Both were always important in local society, but they have not heretofore served to sublimate its realities.

A more mundane consideration also explains the premiums placed on *gracia, cultura, simpatía,* and general good-fellowship. The bars, as I have described above, serve as clearinghouses for all manner of small businesses in the Alto Panadés. Because the business situation is at once small-scale and fluid, men often have to wait for long periods at the bars to make contacts. There is a need to while away the waiting time, to alleviate the boredom of waiting and the tiring repetitiveness of cementing one's interpersonal relationships with hours of social drinking. In such circumstances, an entertainer is a godsend. A person can, with jokes, songs, and conviviality, make his hearers forget the repetitiveness of their life circumstances and the precariousness of their social and economic standing. By lightening the spirits of all present, the wit or the comic may also enhance his own business interests. A fine example is the car salesman, Señor Llops. Llops has a huge amount of animal vitality; he is proud that he is more of a glutton for food and drink than even the most prosperous men of the *comarca,* that he is always the first to form an impromptu party and to sponsor a quick foray to Sitges or Barcelona. When conversation lags at the bar, Llops uses his fine baritone voice to belt out old regional and new popular songs. Shortly, everyone joins in, and the singing usually continues until the small hours of the morning, improving as vocal cords are loosened with champagne. When everyone else is sagging from food, drink, and plain exhaustion, Llops is as bright-eyed as he was at midday and ready to continue the battle indefinitely. Apart from entertaining his friends, Llops has simultaneously laid the groundwork for new business transactions and shored up old friendships. As business transactions are completed only after friendships are established, Llops' virtuoso performance is rooted in sound business principles.

Whereas the code of the bar culture stresses individualism, it also stresses a kind of egalitarianism that suppresses overt differences of social class. Anyone can enter a bar and seek companionship; participation in bar culture is one of the few democratic aspects remaining in local life. The stress on succeeding by dint of individual personality reinforces this kind of democracy and levels social claims based on inequalities in wealth and power. There are subtleties to this facet of bar culture that were brought to my attention by both informants and casual discussants. For example, since the advent of bar culture and the possibilities of modernization, the more clever wealthy bourgeoisie have begun to dress more humbly; today they wear the pants and shirts of clerks and workers, whereas fifteen years ago all wore suits.[6] And in spite of their wealth, many purchase small autos, such as the Citroen Deux Cheveaux or SEAT coupé, instead of the Rolls Royce they would have bought only a short while ago. One working-class informant commented on this trend by stating in exasperation: "*Ni saben ser ricos*" ("They don't even know how to be rich").

Once the stylistic nuances of the code of good-fellowship have been mastered to some degree, the business of serious coalition formation can take place: Alliances can be successfully forged between previously unaffiliated individuals. Yet the development of substantive relationships depends upon the ability to continuously demonstrate one final aspect of the code. Although this is often left unstated, it is certainly implied in informants' statements that success in both achieving prestige and making alliances depends upon an individual's ability *to perform favors for others*. This can be attempted gracefully only *after* a person has established himself according to the criteria discussed above.

Doing favors in the Alto Panadés consists of having the knowledge and connections to intervene decisively and favorably in the life problems of others, great and small. The range of favors done in this context is far too great to be detailed here: Some examples are illustrative. "*Me hizo el gran favor de ——*" ("He did me the favor of ——") is the stock phrase used to describe everything from fixing a traffic ticket of Don Disco's to making a government official a consultant to a company. It includes things like providing transportation for those who need it, being able to intervene with officials over pending legal matters, providing introductions for people in need of contacts generally, getting the best deal for a friend at a shop, and providing useful information about pending business deals before they are known to the general public. None of these examples is idiosyncratic; such favors are recorded again and again in my notes and I have often observed them as a participant.[7] But doing favors in isolated incidents is not sufficient to guarantee high prestige; everyone does this to a greater or lesser extent. The most prestigious individual is able to do such favors consistently, and gracefully, so that the recipient can never be seen as a dependent of the donor.

The obstacles to success in the bar culture are legion. For persons whose economic activities are so diverse and far-flung as to necessitate much traveling, absence prevents the required good-fellowship. Local hostilities impede the success of many, and others are the victims of schemes that were improbable in the first place. There are in fact a number of highly successful individuals, but the life trajectories of most are at best erratic.[8]

We can now turn to the actual prestige classification of the 100 individuals in the sample and try to explain the results. The statistical results are displayed in the accompanying table. I have followed the informants' ranking system closely as to the number of categories and the classification of individuals,[9] but it is necessary to make explicit what is only implicit in many of their explanations of local prestige hierarchies. What is readily apparent but emphatically denied by the code is that only members of the haute bourgeoisie can become "*gente de primera categoría*" ("first-class people"). Though very few of the haute bourgeoisie were categorized as first class, nobody else was even considered for this category. It is significant that the six men at the apex of the prestige hierarchy were also those who stood at the apex of the coalitions in the bars. All these men were heavily committed to the modernization of their estates and were involved in many other business ventures as well, so that they were ideally placed to do favors for clients in search of a patron. All had considerable social skills and amazing energy, much of which was poured into the bar culture, building and maintaining ties of loyalty and dependence.

Most men in Vilafranca believe that members of the wealthy bourgeoisie are ideally "doers of favors." When they do them consistently, gracefully, and publicly, they rise in the local prestige hierarchy. The converse is also true, as illustrated by the three bourgeois classed as third rate. These three men were so wealthy and powerful that they needed no dependents locally. All had the deserved reputation of doing nothing for others. The rage against them for this neglect was apparent in the informants' tales about these men. For example, one was reputed to amuse himself by humiliating the workers at his factory by taking them to lunch in fancy restaurants,

Prestige Classification of 100 Men Sampled in Study of Bar Culture in Vilafranca

SOCIAL CLASS[a]	PRESTIGE CATEGORY				
	1	2	3	4	Total
Haute bourgeoisie	6	16	3	0	25
Petite bourgeoisie	0	14	11	0	25
Workers	0	10	11	4	25
Rabassaires	0	0	10	15	25
Total	6	40	35	19	100

[a] Social class is here defined in standard political economic terms. For a full account of local class structure, see Hansen (1969).

even though they were dressed in their working clothes. Another cared so little about local society that he was reputed to associate only with Americans and Germans at a ritzy Barcelona golf club. Such stories may be fanciful, but they underlie the popular expectations of generosity from the wealthy.

Second-class people, those described as *"normal y correcto"* ("normal and correct"), come from three different social classes. Included are minor patrons from the haute bourgeoisie and successful clients recruited from the petite bourgeoisie and the workers. These men are all well liked and respected, but lack the social vigor and generally the economic power of those ranked first class. They are commonly described as having the continued ability *"relacionarse con gente de primera categoría"* ("to have relations with first-class people"). It is noteworthy that no *rabassaire* was placed in this grouping; modernization of estates means the elimination of the *rabassaires* as a social class and, consequently, their ineligibility for clienthood in bar culture. It is rare to see a sharecropper in the bars, and few of them are known to the bar habitués.

Third-class people, those described as *"normal y corriente"* ("normal and ordinary"), seem generally to be failed clients in search of a patron, although there is a small number of antisocial haute bourgeoisie in this category as well. These third-rate people are hangers-on in the bars. Many have a history of defaulting on their obligations to others, and some are downgraded for character defects that lead them to violate the code. Several are newcomers to the area, who have not yet learned how to manipulate the code. In short, people in this category have at least one outstanding social defect, but are still in the running for client positions within the coalitions.

The fourth class is my own creation, based on implicit evidence supplied by informants about people who were known either not at all or not very well. Such men did not frequent the bars, out of choice or out of fear. Not to be known in Vilafranca is to be suspected of gross character defects, to become a "nonperson." Such people were consistently referred to by informants as lacking in either sufficient "category" or "balls" to get along with other people (*"no tiene la categoría [los huevos] sufficiente[s] para relacionarse con la gente"*). Apart from bestowing a profoundly negative rating in the prestige hierarchy, such statements underline the tensions involved in bar culture, which is seen as a contest where one's manhood is on the line. In a situation where people themselves are resources, withholding oneself is the most sublime but the most difficult of social skills. Subsequent interviews with people classified as fourth rate revealed that many find the social climbing in the bars repugnant. In their view, the bars are the places where the "rich and presumptuous" (*"los ricos y presumidos"*) make fools of themselves publicly.

One more implicit prestige category was suggested by several informants who were attempting to connect the prestige system of the Alto Panadés to one that was nationwide. The informants who were concerned about this stated that Vilafranca did not *really* have any first-class people because no one from the *comarca* was a national figure, such as a prominent politician or an economic titan. They stressed that this was a recent development, that before the civil war there had been seven or eight individuals who were nationally known and whose portraits still hang in the Gallery of Illustrious Vilafrancans in the town hall. Their concern underlines the fact that people in Vilafranca (and elsewhere in rural Catalonia) have no real power on a national level and little leverage in the process of modernization that is so dramatically changing the *comarca*.

This lack of power and control over the process of social change in the Alto Panadés goes a long way toward explaining the precarious nature of both individual prestige and the coalitions themselves. As no one in the *comarca* is involved in the decision-making process that formulates the major outlines of modernization, local strategies can only be reactive and speculative to whatever is decreed from above. As conditions are always in flux, the requirements for instrumental relationships on the part of the local bourgeoisie can change quickly, closing off avenues of mobility for some old allies and creating chances for new ones. This process probably lies behind the many stories of interpersonal treason that make up bar culture. It also may inhibit the size of coalitions that can be constructed, which generally include no more than twenty people.

Notes

1. Women, although not excluded from the bars, participate in very restricted ways in the coalitions and have no decision-making power in the establishment of alliances. A woman's role in the bar culture is to promote friendships among families, not to create instrumental relationships among men. The tourist bars are, of course, also products of modernization, but of a different kind. Such bars should in no way be confused with traditional *cantinas* found in most Spanish villages and towns. For the role of tourism in Mediterranean modernization, see Schneider et al. (1972:342–3).

2. A similar point is made in a different context for Sicily by J. Schneider (1969) and P. Schneider (1969).

3. Foreign industry has penetrated the *comarca* in the form of Cinzano vermouth, Krupp cement, and Purina Chow (Hansen 1970).

4. An individual is drunk by local standards, not when he is inebriated, which is a common occurrence, but when he falls down, which is a disgrace.

5. I believe most of the tales of reprisal were escapes into fantasy. I never heard of a verifiable physical confrontation between boss and employee, although I did witness a few angry resignations.

6. This observation was corroborated by photographs of these individuals taken before 1960.

7. Two of many cases I myself was involved in were the following. I was once victimized by Don Disco to the tune of 1,000 pesetas; connections were able to quash the ticket in half an hour, and I received a cheerful apology from the chief of police. Near the end of my stay in 1966, my stipend check was delayed and my funds were low. A friend, conveniently owner of a local bank, simply instructed the head of foreign exchange to issue any sum I requested. While I pride myself on having an honest face, my anthropological training suggests that an honest face without connections would have had to take up a beggar's bowl under similar circumstances.

8. Murphy's law states: "If anything can go wrong, it will."

9. I was surprised to find such high degrees of correspondence between informants in both respects. Particularly startling was the 85 percent correspondence in placing individuals in the prestige slots they had created. Their correspondence could be stretched even higher by using the results of back-up interviews concerning the fourteen to sixteen individuals who were initially controversial.

Bibliography

HANSEN, E. 1969. "The State and Land Tenure Conflict in Rural Catalonia, Spain." *Anthropological Quarterly* 42(3):214–43.

———. 1970. "Political Dimensions of Social Change in Rural Catalonia." Doctoral dissertation, University of Michigan.

SCHMITTER, P. 1971. *Interest, Conflict, and Political Change in Brazil,* Stanford University Press, Stanford, Calif.

SCHNEIDER, J. 1969. "Family Patrimonies and Economic Behaviour in Western Sicily." *Anthropological Quarterly* 42:109–29.

SCHNEIDER, P., SCHNEIDER, J., and HANSEN E. 1972. "Modernization and Development: The Role of Regional Elites and Noncorporate Groups in the European Mediterranean." *Comparative Studies in Society and History* 14:328–50.

SILVERMAN, S. 1966. "An Ethnographic Approach to Social Stratification: Prestige in a Central Italian Community." *American Anthropologist* 68:899–921.

Economic Systems, Changing Technology, and the Impact of the West

There is a great deal taking place in societies around the world that anthropologists agree constitutes economic organization: the assembly line in a Japanese automobile factory; the harvesting of crops on a state farm in Poland; the herding of reindeer by the Lapp—done today with snowmobiles, but in the past on sleds drawn by reindeer; and the activity at the stock exchange on Wall Street. There are many other activities about which anthropologists disagree as to whether or not they are conceptualized as economic by the participants and constitute "economic behavior." For example, is the potlatch of the Kwakiutl Indians, involving the giveaway and destruction of material goods an economic matter or one of social prestige? When a West African man works on the farm of his future in-laws, is that an issue of productive labor, and therefore economic behavior, or is it in fact best understood in terms of kinship and social organization?

Once again we can note that the variety in the specific ways that societies organize some aspect of their lives leads anthropologists to pose the most fundamental of questions. In this case the basic question is: What is economic behavior? Economists, rightly sensing that this is a discussion which involves their area of study, have joined in the debate.

There is agreement on two important points: (1) that universally, societies engage in processes that can be called "production" and "distribution" and (2) that production is organized, and products are distributed not by happenstance but on the basis of some principle or principles. It is with respect to the latter point that the debate reenters a discussion of cross-cultural economics.

Production

In every society, human labor transforms material items for use. These acts of production involve an allocation of resources, the tools and technology of work, and an organization of labor. Thus we can speak of the physical and social aspects of production: the resources and technology on the one hand, and the actions of individuals as laborers on the other.

In surveying the various technologies used by peoples throughout the world, anthropologists describe five major types: hunting and gathering, horticulture, pastoralism, agriculture, and industrialism. Hunting and gathering (also called foraging) is the chronologically oldest form of technology, and when compared to the others the least productive. Found among small bands of fifty to a hundred persons, hunting and gathering relies on human energy, with only the most basic of tools such as a digging stick, bows and arrows, spears, traps, and nets. It often is associated with a seminomadic way of life in relatively harsh environments. The !Kung San of southern Africa are among the best studied of hunting and gathering groups.

In the article reprinted here, Sahlins challenges the assumption that the life of hunters and gatherers is dominated by a never satisfied search for food. Drawing on the ethnographic cases of the !Kung and the Arnhem Landers of Australia, he concludes that these hunters and gatherers work neither particularly hard nor continuously, for the search for food is highly intermittent. Thus there is considerable free time. Anthropologists' long-held assumptions concerning hunters and gatherers now appear to be based on Western values and experiences: that people are driven to incessant labor by insatiable wants.

Certainly there are severe difficulties facing hunters and gatherers today, but those difficulties are due less to the society's indigenous form of technology, to which its members have adapted, than to the expansion of industrial "civilization," which is driving them out of their original areas.

Horticulture is a rudimentary form of farming dependent on human labor and hand tools, without the use of draft animals or plows, and with little or no use of fertilizers or irrigation. Except in those cases where the land is especially fertile, horticulturalists must abandon their land after a few seasons and allow it to lie fallow until it has naturally regenerated. Societies at this technological level, such as the majority of the peoples of Africa, are able to support larger populations and more permanent settlements than hunters and gatherers.

Pastoralism involves a primary dependence on herding and animal husbandry in areas where other forms of technology would be difficult or impossible. Thus pastoralists are found on desert fringes, open grasslands, and steppes. There are very few peoples who are "pure pastoralists." Most are part-time farmers or are involved in a symbiotic relationship with neighboring farmers. The animals must be herded through a sequence of ecological niches, and thus a degree of mobility is associated with this form of technology. Pastoralists secure numerous products from their herds: milk products, fuel, leather goods. Differences in individual access to grazing lands and to water lead to differences in individual wealth among pastoralists, and a centralized political system is often found among such groups as a response to the presence of neighbors at a state level of organization. Pastoralism is a primary technology in East Africa and in a dry belt from North Africa across the Middle East to Central Asia.

Agriculturalists replace the hoe and digging stick with the plow, which in turn necessitates the use of draft animals; fertilizers and irrigation techniques often increase productivity even more. Most agriculturalists are able to produce more than they consume, and the surpluses can therefore be stored, taken to markets, or used in exchanges or to pay taxes. The impact of a surplus is far-reaching, for when groups of individuals can pursue non-food-producing work, the possibility is created for stratified social classes and state organization. These far-reaching consequences of agriculture as a technology led anthropologists to refer to its development in ancient societies as a revolution.

Industrialism involves the use of energy beyond that of human beings and domesticated animals. The profound consequences of this form of technology are captured in the phrase used to describe its first appearance: the industrial revolution. We are familiar with the modern form of industrialism, as it predominates in our own society. But ours is not the only industrialized society in the world.

In Japan, for example, much of the economic organization and decision making are not very different from practices in the U.S. On the other hand, there are characteristics of the Japanese economic system that are the result of Japan's particular history and culture. One way of summarizing the economic and other societal characteristics of industrialism is to compare it with hunting and gathering societies.

Factory industrialism is, in one sense at least, the logical opposite of hunting and gathering societies. In hunting and gathering societies there is minimal separation of domestic and community economy. In factory industrialism, the domestic economy and the economy of the community are almost totally separated. The household remains the major consuming unit, but it is no longer a basic production unit. Production is carried out by new social groups, of which business firms are representative, that are based on the ethic of contract rather than on the principle and ethic of kinship. Linkage between the household, or consuming unit, and the firm, or producing unit, is by two means: secondary syndromes of roles link the families' husbands/fathers, as breadwinners, to the firm's technicians or executives; material items and overwhelmingly powerful ideas such as money provide the means for movement of goods both from producer to consumer and from one producer to the next. [Bohannan 1963:216–217]

The allocation of resources into production cannot be understood divorced from how a people conceptualize rights to the ownership or use of material resources. In our own society so much of what exists in terms of resources is owned by individuals or groups that we can mistakenly assume that such notions of "ownership" are inherent in economic systems. But in the tribal world it is more common for individuals to exercise rights to *use* resources, as opposed to exercising exclusive rights of ownership. This plot of land belongs to Mr. X or Corporation Y in our society, whereas in tribal societies land is either collectively held by a kinship or political unit or, in the absence of such a concept of collective ownership, individuals, through their kinship and political affiliations, are given access to land.

When Westerners interact with tribal peoples the radical differences between their two ways of conceptualizing resources come into sharp focus; for in one system the means of production, specifically the land, tools, and technical knowledge, are collectively held; in the other, they are "private property."

There are universal similarities in how labor is organized into production processes, as well as stark cross-cultural differences in other economic areas. Anthropologists speak of a division of labor on the basis of gender and age as universal. Exactly how this is played out can vary, however, as when we note that women engage in deep sea diving in certain Japanese and Korean communities, while the men have considerable responsibility for child care. The far more common division of labor gives women primary responsibility for child care, a pattern which many theorists suggest is at the root of the subjugation of women.

Explanations of this sexual division of labor vary. One theory sees biological differences between women and men as the determining factor. In her article in this section, Leith Mullings presents a clear statement against such biological reductionist explanations of the sexual division of labor. She argues that social organization (especially when geared towards economic profit) determines the meaning of sex roles and the division of labor.

We note differences in the way that work is organized as a function of such factors as climate and the types and availability of tools and techniques. But the organization of work is also affected by the prevailing concept of ownership and the political and ideological systems. In this sense, the organization of work in a technologically advanced capitalist society such as our own is radically different from that of a hunting and gathering people such as the !Kung of southern Africa. Maurice Godelier makes the point that in contrast with our own society, in tribal societies there is only limited accumulation of the products of human labor, there is little wealth, there are few tools, and there are no social classes. What there is then is living human labor, and thus the kinship institutions that actually reproduce the labor force are dominant in production.

Distribution

Every society must not only produce goods and services in order to address biological as well as social needs and wants, but must also distribute those "items" of production. There are three main explanations as to exactly how these products and services are dispersed within a society: the formalist, the substantivist, and the Marxist.

The Formalist Camp

According to the formalist view, the formal theories of neoclassical economics are applicable to *all* economies. The neoclassical economists argue that choices that *maximize* values are fundamental to economics. Thus the behavior of corporation heads is to be understood in terms of maximization of profit for the firm as well as personal gain and prestige. The behavior of the son-in-law in the West African village involves the maximization of kinship ties. Thus, according to this approach, the world is populated by rational, economic men and women who make choices in order to maximize something or other.

The Substantivists

The other "camp" of economic anthropology, referred to as "substantivist," holds that we must analyze the *substance* or content of people's behavior to determine if it is economically rational. The substantivist camp was pioneered by an economic historian, Karl Polanyi, and it has been defended by economists such as George Dalton and anthropologists such as Paul Bohannan. According to this view, we cannot explain all distributive processes according to such Western economic concepts as supply and demand, maximization and profit. The substantivists suggest that distribution of goods and services is carried out according to three basic forms of exchange: market exchange, reciprocity, and redistribution. Each of these exchange systems involves a set of rules. Market exchange involves a transfer of goods and services based on price, which is set by supply and demand— such as when you buy a television at a price determined by the relationship between the supply of sets and the demand for them. Reciprocity is the form of exchange whereby goods and services are distributed according to kinship and other social relationships—such as when the !Kung distribute meat after a hunt, or when some individuals in the United States exchange Christmas gifts. Redistribution is exchange based on the movement of these goods or services by the authorities at the center. Our tax structure is an example of redistribution. In societies where there are political and religious heads, such as chiefs and kings, a considerable amount of economic exchange takes this form.

Substantivists insist that in most economies more than one of these principles of allocation is at work. However, in societies such as our own one is dominant: the market principle.

The substantivists' notion of the "clash" of principles when traditional societies dominated by reciprocity and redistribution come up against the Western market-exchange system is discussed by Bohannan in his article on the Tiv.

The Marxist Camp

Anthropologists and economists in the Marxist camp agree with the formalist position that economic action is rational. Indeed, Marxists hold that we all—Kwakiutl and Americans alike—choose from among alternative options. But Marxists strongly protest the idea that maximization is a universal motivation for economic behavior. On the contrary, they argue that this notion of the universality of maximization is a rationalization of capitalist economic relationships. And in contrast to both formalists and substantivists, Marxists lay primary stress on class relations within a society.

It is not likely that this debate among formalists, substantivists, and Marxists will be settled in the near future. However, there is one reality on which the three camps are in agreement in terms of the most basic statement of the problem, namely, that few societies today are "untouched" by the Western economic system.

The Impact of the West's Economic System on Much of the Rest of the World

The societies traditionally studied by anthropologists—Third World societies of Africa, Asia, the Middle East, and the Americas—are characterized by their economic poverty and "underdevelopment." The conventional explanation of these conditions is that the obstacle to development is the traditional cultural modes of these societies, which must be left behind in favor of Western technology. In short, the problem, according to this view, is that the impact of the West on the Third World has not yet been profound enough. The alternative view is that Third World underdevelopment is not fundamentally a result of traditional cultural modes, but rather of Western colonialist exploitation. Thus, the problem is that the impact of the West has been too profound.

Keesing (1980:443) makes explicit three assumptions that underlie the conventional view of underdevelopment. The first assumption is that "traditional" culture is by its very nature conservative and thus is a deterrent to social change (traditional modes involve the antithesis of what is required for social change, namely individual initiative, freedom from kinship and other customary obligations, and so forth). A second assumption is that Third World countries and societies are plagued by "tribalism" and internal conflicts—problems that flow from their patchwork composition of culturally and linguistically disparate groupings. African situations are the most often cited as cases in point. The final assumption behind the conventional view of underdevelopment is that rural areas in Third World countries are trapped into poverty by large and growing populations that have a traditional outlook and fail to export products on a scale which would generate the capital required for economic growth.

These assumptions then are at the base of a theory that is frequently articulated in anthropological and other social science literature. Its basic tenets involve dual economies or sectors, with the subsistence or traditional economy viewed as a drain on development and the market or modernizing one as the basis for economic growth. Put in sharpest focus, this view argues the following:

> [T]hese "traditional" modes of life, structures of economy and society, were there when colonialism began, were only partly transformed in the colonial period and must now be left behind if modernization is to succeed. [Ibid.:443]

The alternative view of Third World underdevelopment rests on a theory of dependency as articulated by Andre Gunner Frank.[1] Frank (1969, 1973) advances the view that underdevelopment in Latin America (the area that he has studied—but by extension his theory applies to the Third World) is neither a historical accident nor the consequence of traditional culture. Rather, Frank argues, underdevelopment has been systematically *created* by Western colonialist exploitation. And therein lies the notion of the development of underdevelopment.[2]

Frank notes that the very regions of Latin America which are the most backward are the very areas where there was the most extreme exploitation of natural and human resources. And thus he suggests that the "degree and type of dependence on the metropolis of the world capitalist system is the key factor in the economic and class structures of Latin America" (Frank 1973:21–22). During the colonial and postcolonial periods Latin America's indigenous economic development was stymied and its wealth was exported. Noting that exploitation of indigenous wealth involved different products—sugar in some areas, coffee in others, mining in still others—

Frank argues that the determining factor was fluctuations of world capitalism. Those areas which because of sparse population and resources and poor climate did not attract foreign exploitation of mines and plantations are today, according to Frank, the most developed areas of the Americas.

Within the countries of Latin America, landed aristocracies developed, gaining their wealth from the ownership of land and the export of products at the expense of the rural peasantry. In this way were developed the class structure and internal colonialism of Latin America that persist today. Frank speaks of constellations of economic interest, each with a "metropolis" at its center and "satellite" economic regions. These satellites may consist on a smaller scale of a minor metropolis and its satellites. Thus a metropolis at one level is a satellite of a larger metropolis (Frank 1969:15–17).

There are criticisms of and modifications of this theory of dependency as the explanation for underdevelopment in the Third World. However, it remains a viable alternative to the conventional view. Joseph Jorgensen explicitly uses this theory in his analysis of the poverty and underdevelopment of Native Americans in the United States. He argues that the underdevelopment of American Indians, whereby they rank significantly below the white population and below all other ethnic groups in education, health, housing, and employment, is the result of the development of the white-controlled national economy in the United States.

In an article written before the Sandinistas came to power in 1979, Nietschmann describes the development of poverty and underdevelopment among the Miskito Indians off the eastern coast of Nicaragua. Until the 1960s, turtle meat was both the mainstay of subsistence and the item most often shared in a social network among Miskito kin and friends. There was sufficient turtle meat for the subsistence and social needs of the Miskito without overexploiting any one species of turtle or fishing site. Intensive exploitation of turtles, motivated by cash payments from foreign companies, eventually led to the depletion of this vital source of Miskito nutrition and had serious consequences for Miskito culture. Nietschmann said, "The turtles are going down and along with them, the Miskito."[3]

The case of the Miskito Indians is not an isolated one. For in those societies traditionally studied by anthropologists, the destruction of indigenous subsistence economies has left no choice for many people but to struggle in an economic system that

(a) is beyond their control, (b) keeps the raw materials they produce at artificially low prices, (c) makes them dependent on the purchase of imported manufactured goods for their subsistence, (d) keeps these manufactured goods at artificially high prices, and (e) keeps low the wages with which they must purchase these imported goods. [Henderson 1976:369–370]

In her study of the predominately female labor force in the border industries of Mexico—electronics and apparel—Patricia Fernandez-Kelly analyzes the commonly held view that employment in these transnational assembly plants has improved the condition of women in the sense of increased autonomy and decreased responsibility for domestic chores. She concludes that such employment has not allowed women to escape female subordination, break out of established norms, or develop a class- or gender-based solidarity. Kelly's conclusions are consistent with the pioneering work by Boserup (1970) and a number of other studies which demonstrate that "economic development" and "modernization" do not automatically improve the lot of women and, in fact, may worsen their condition.

It is, of course, far easier to identify problems associated with the impact of the West on the Third World than to offer workable solutions to those problems. There is a kind of arrogance in suggesting that Third World peoples should be blockaded from the technologies and goods of the West, and a naivete in assuming that such a blockage is possible in the highly interdependent modern world. However, students of anthropology must be aware of the irresponsibility of pretending that the intrusion of the West in traditional cultures does not have social consequences—at times, devastating ones. And while it is crucial to recognize the effects of Western colonialism, we must understand that today much of the Third World is formally independent. Phrased in the form of a question, we must ask: If underdevelopment is the product of colonialism, how is it being perpetuated? The answer is found in a term popularized by Third World scholars: neocolonialism. This is the new form of colonialism in which nominally independent countries remain tied in quasicolonial relationships with the metropolitan countries. Often the same multinational corporations that extracted natural resources from a colony continue to do so; and an indigenous class of elites are in charge of assuring the stability, often by internal repression, which is said to offer an attractive investment climate.

Our discussion of the impact of the West on most of the rest of the world has taken us into sensitive and indeed controversial areas where there are no easy solutions. But as anthropologists continue to conduct studies in the Third World, the more than one hundred nations in Africa, Asia, the Middle East, and Latin America, these are inescapable issues.

Notes

1. Modifications to that theory are introduced in Wallerstein's conceptualization of a center and peripheries in a world economic system.
2. See Walter Rodney's *How Europe Underdeveloped Africa* (1972) for an analysis

of the relationship between Europe's development and Africa's underdevelopment.

3. Since Nietschmann's article was written, the Miskito Indians have gained prominence in the public debate centering on questions of autonomy and place of ethnic communities in Nicaragua today.

References

BOHANNAN, PAUL. 1963. *Social Anthropology.* New York: Holt, Rinehart & Winston.

BOSERUP, E. 1965. *The Conditions of Agricultural Growth: The Economics of Agrarian Change Under Population Pressures.* Chicago: Aldine Publishing Co.

FRANK, A. G. 1969. *Latin America: Underdevelopment or Revolution.* New York: Monthly Review Press.

———. 1973. *Lumpenbourgeoisie: Lumpendevelopment; Dependence, Class, and Politics in Latin America.* New York: Monthly Review Press.

GODELIER, M. 1978. "Infrastructures, Society and History." *Current Anthropology* 19:4:763–768.

KEESING, ROGER. 1981. *Cultural Anthropology A Contemporary Perspective.* New York: Holt, Rinehart & Winston.

WALLERSTEIN, I. 1974. *The Modern World-System: Capitalist Agriculture and the Origins of the European World-Economy in the Sixteenth Century.* New York: Academic Press.

13

The Original Affluent Society

MARSHALL SAHLINS

IF ECONOMICS IS THE DISMAL SCIENCE, the study of hunting and gathering economies must be its most advanced branch. Almost universally committed to the proposition that life was hard in the paleolithic, our textbooks compete to convey a sense of impending doom, leaving one to wonder not only how hunters managed to live, but whether, after all, this was living? The specter of starvation stalks the stalker through these pages. His technical incompetence is said to enjoin continuous work just to survive, affording him neither respite nor surplus, hence not even the "leisure" to "build culture." Even so, for all his efforts, the hunter pulls the lowest grades in thermodynamics—less energy/capita/year than any other mode of production. And in treatises on economic development he is condemned to play the role of bad example: the so-called "subsistence economy."

The traditional wisdom is always refractory. One is forced to oppose it polemically, to phrase the necessary revisions dialectically: in fact, this was, when you come to examine it, the original affluent society. Paradoxical, that phrasing leads to another useful and unexpected conclusion. By the common understanding, an affluent society is one in which all the people's material wants are easily satisfied. To assert that the hunters are affluent is to deny then that the human condition is an ordained tragedy, with man the prisoner at hard labor of a perpetual disparity between his unlimited wants and his insufficient means.

253

For there are two possible courses to affluence. Wants may be "easily satisfied" either by producing much or desiring little. The familiar conception, the Galbraithean way, makes assumptions peculiarly appropriate to market economies: that man's wants are great, not to say infinite, whereas his means are limited, although improvable: thus, the gap between means and ends can be narrowed by industrial productivity, at least to the point that "urgent goods" become plentiful. But there is also a Zen road to affluence, departing from premises somewhat different from our own: that human material wants are finite and few, and technical means unchanging but on the whole adequate. Adopting the Zen strategy, a people can enjoy an unparalleled material plenty—with a low standard of living.

That, I think, describes the hunters. And it helps explain some of their more curious economic behavior: their "prodigality" for example—the inclination to consume at once all stocks on hand, as if they had it made. Free from market obsessions of scarcity, hunters' economic propensities may be more consistently predicated on abundance than our own. Destutt de Tracy, "fish-blooded bourgeois doctrinaire" though he might have been, at least compelled Marx's agreement on the observation that "in poor nations the people are comfortable," whereas in rich nations "they are generally poor."

This is not to deny that a preagricultural economy operates under serious constraints, but only to insist, on the evidence from modern hunters and gatherers, that a successful accommodation is usually made. After taking up the evidence, I shall return in the end to the real difficulties of hunting-gathering economy, none of which are correctly specified in current formulas of paleolithic poverty.

Sources of the Misconception

"Mere subsistence economy" "limited leisure save in exceptional circumstances," "incessant quest for food," "meagre and relatively unreliable" natural resources, "absence of an economic surplus," "maximum energy from a maximum number of people"—so runs the fair average anthropological opinion of hunting and gathering. . . . In reference to South American hunters:

> The nomadic hunters and gatherers barely met minimum subsistence needs and often fell far short of them. Their population of 1 person to 10 or 20 square miles reflects this. Constantly on the move in search of food, they clearly lacked the leisure hours for nonsubsistence activities of any significance, and they could transport little of what they might manufacture in spare moments. To them, adequacy of production meant physical survival, and they rarely had surplus of either products or time (Steward and Faron, 1959, p. 60; cf. Clark, 1953, p. 27 f; Haury, 1962, p. 113; Hoebel, 1958, p. 188; Redfield, 1953, p. 5; White, 1959).

But the traditional dismal view of the hunters' fix is also preanth-ropological and extra-anthropological, at once historical and referable to the larger economic context in which anthropology operates. It goes back to the time Adam Smith was writing, and probably to a time before anyone was writing.[1] . . .

Current low opinions of the hunting-gathering economy need not be laid to neolithic ethnocentrism, however. Bourgeois ethnocentrism will do as well. The existing business economy, at every turn an ideological trap from which anthropological economics must escape, will promote the same dim conclu-sions about the hunting life.

Is it so paradoxical to contend that hunters have affluent economies, their absolute poverty notwithstanding? Modern capitalist societies, however richly endowed, dedicate themselves to the proposition of scarcity. In-adequacy of economic means is the first principle of the world's wealthiest peoples. The apparent material status of the economy seems to be no clue to its accomplishments; something has to be said for the mode of economic organization (cf. Polanyi, 1947, 1957, 1959; Dalton, 1961).

The market-industrial system institutes scarcity, in a manner completely unparalleled and to a degree nowhere else approximated. Where production and distribution are arranged through the behavior of prices, and all livelihoods depend on getting and spending, insufficiency of material means becomes the explicit, calculable starting point of all economic activity.[2] The entrepreneur is confronted with alternative investments of a finite capital, the worker (hopefully) with alternative choices of remunerative employ, and the consumer. . . . Consumption is a double tragedy: what begins in inadequacy will end in deprivation. Bringing together an international division of labor, the market makes available a dazzling array of products: all these Good Things within a man's reach—but never all within his grasp. Worse, in this game of consumer free choice, every acquisition is simultaneously a de-privation, for every purchase of something is a foregoing of something else, in general only marginally less desirable, and in some particulars more desira-ble, that could have been had instead. (The point is that if you buy one automobile, say a Plymouth, you cannot also have the Ford—and I judge from current television commercials that the deprivations entailed would be more than just material.)[3]

That sentence of "life at hard labor" was passed uniquely upon us. Scarcity is the judgment decreed by our economy—so also the axiom of our Economics: the application of scarce means against alternative ends to derive the most satisfaction possible under the circumstances. And it is precisely from this anxious vantage that we look back upon hunters. But if modern man, with all his technological advantages, still hasn't got the wherewithal, what chance has this naked savage with his puny bow and arrow? Having equipped the hunter with bourgeois impulses and paleolithic tools, we judge his situation hopeless in advance.[4]

Yet scarcity is not an intrinsic property of technical means. It is a relation between means and ends. We should entertain the empirical possibility that hunters are in business for their health, a finite objective, and that bow and arrow are adequate to that end.

But still other ideas, these endemic in anthropological theory and ethnographic practice, have conspired to preclude any such understanding.

Considering the poverty in which hunters and gatherers live in theory, it comes as a surprise that Bushmen who live in the Kalahari enjoy "a kind of material plenty," at least in the realm of everyday useful things, apart from food and water:

> As the !Kung come into more contact with Europeans—and this is already happening—they will feel sharply the lack of our things and will need and want more. It makes them feel inferior to be without clothes when they stand among strangers who are clothed. But in their own life and with their own artifacts *they were comparatively free from material pressures*. Except for food and water (important exceptions!) of which the Nyae Nyae !Kung have a sufficiency—but barely so, judging from the fact that all are thin though not emaciated—they all had what they needed or could make what they needed, for every man can and does make the things that men make and every woman the things that women make. . . . *They lived in a kind of material plenty* because they adapted the tools of their living to materials which lay in abundance around them and which were free for anyone to take (wood, reeds, bone for weapons and implements, fibers for cordage, grass for shelters), or to materials which were at least sufficient for the needs of the population. . . . The !Kung could always use more ostrich egg shells for beads to wear or trade with, but, as it is, enough are found for every woman to have a dozen or more shells for water containers—all she can carry—and a goodly number of bead ornaments. In their nomadic hunting-gathering life, travelling from one source of food to another through the seasons, always going back and forth between food and water, they carry their young children and their belongings. With plenty of most materials at hand to replace artifacts as required, the !Kung have not developed means of permanent storage and have not needed or wanted to encumber themselves with surpluses or duplicates. They do not even want to carry one of everything. They borrow what they do not own. With this ease, they have not hoarded, and the accumulation of objects has not become associated with status (Marshall, 1961, pp. 243-44, emphasis mine).

Analysis of hunter-gatherer production is usefully divided into two spheres, as Mrs. Marshall has done. Food and water are certainly "important exceptions," best reserved for separate and extended treatment. For the rest, the nonsubsistence sector, what is here said of the Bushmen applies in general and in detail to hunters from the Kalahari to Labrador—or to Tierra del Fuego, where Gusinde reports of the Yahgan that their disinclination to own more than one copy of utensils frequently needed is "an indication of self-confidence." "Our fuegians," he writes, "procure and make their implements with little effort" (1961, p. 213).[5]

In the nonsubsistence sphere, the people's wants are generally easily satisfied. Such "material plenty" depends partly upon the ease of production, and that upon the simplicity of technology and democracy of property. Products are homespun: of stone, bone, wood, skin—materials such as "lay in abundance around them." As a rule, neither extraction of the raw material nor its working up take strenuous effort. Access to natural resources is typically direct—"free for anyone to take"—even as possession of the necessary tools is general and knowledge of the required skills common. The division of labor is likewise simple, predominantly a division of labor by sex. Add in the liberal customs of sharing, for which hunters are properly famous, and all the people can usually participate in the going prosperity, such as it is.

But, of course, "such as it is": this "prosperity" depends as well upon an objectively low standard of living. It is critical that the customary quota of consumables (as well as the number of consumers) be culturally set at a modest point. A few people are pleased to consider a few easily-made things their good fortune: some meagre pieces of clothing and rather fugitive housing in most climates;[6] plus a few ornaments, spare flints and sundry other items such as the "pieces of quartz, which native doctors have extracted from their patients" (Grey, 1841, vol. 2, p. 266); and, finally, the skin bags in which the faithful wife carries all this, "the wealth of the Australian savage" (p. 266).

For most hunters, such affluence without abundance in the nonsubsistence sphere need not be long debated. A more interesting question is why they are content with so few possessions—for it is with them a policy, a "matter of principle" as Gusinde says (1961, p. 2), and not a misfortune.

Want not, lack not. But are hunters so undemanding of material goods because they are themselves enslaved by a food quest "demanding maximum energy from a maximum number of people," so that no time or effort remains for the provision of other comforts? Some ethnographers testify to the contrary that the food quest is so successful that half the time the people seem not to know what to do with themselves. On the other hand, *movement* is a condition of this success, more movement in some cases than others, but always enough to rapidly depreciate the satisfactions of property. Of the hunter it is truly said that his wealth is a burden. In his condition of life, goods can become "grievously oppressive," as Gusinde observes, and the more so the longer they are carried around. Certain food collecters do have canoes and a few have dog sleds, but most must carry themselves all the comforts they possess, and so only possess what they can comfortably carry themselves. Or perhaps only what the women can carry: the men are often left free to react to the sudden opportunity of the chase or the sudden necessity of defense. As Owen Lattimore wrote in a not too different context, "the pure nomad is the poor nomad." Mobility and property are in contradiction.

That wealth quickly becomes more of an encumbrance than a good thing is apparent even to the outsider. Laurens van der Post was caught in the contradiction as he prepared to make farewells to his wild Bushmen friends:

> This matter of presents gave us many an anxious moment. We were humiliated by the realization of how little there was we could give to the Bushmen. Almost

everything seemed likely to make life more difficult for them by adding to the litter and weight of their daily round. They themselves had practically no possessions: a lion strap, a skin blanket and a leather satchel. There was nothing that they could not assemble in one minute, wrap up in their blankets and carry on their shoulders for a journey of a thousand miles. They had no sense of possession (1958, p. 276).

. . . Here then is another economic "peculiarity"—I will not say it is general, and perhaps it is explained as well by faulty toilet training as by a trained disinterest in material accumulation: some hunters, at least, display a notable tendency to be sloppy about their possessions. They have the kind of nonchalance that would be appropriate to a people who have mastered the problems of production, even as it is maddening to a European:

> They do not know how to take care of their belongings. No one dreams of putting them in order, folding them, drying or cleaning them, hanging them up, or putting them in a neat pile. If they are looking for some particular thing, they rummage carelessly through the hodgepodge of trifles in the little baskets. Larger objects that are piled up in a heap in the hut are dragged hither and yon with no regard for the damage that might be done them. The European observer has the impression that these [Yahgan] Indians place no value whatever on their utensils and that they have completely forgotten the effort it took to make them.⁷ Actually, no one clings to his few goods and chattels which, as it is, are often and easily lost, but just as easily replaced. . . . The Indian does not even exercise care when he could conveniently do so. A European is likely to shake his head at the boundless indifference of these people who drag brand-new objects, precious clothing, fresh provisions, and valuable items through thick mud, or abandon them to their swift destruction by children and dogs. . . . Expensive things that are given them are treasured for a few hours, out of curiousity; after that they thoughtlessly let everything deteriorate in the mud and wet. The less they own, the more comfortable they can travel, and what is ruined they occasionally replace. Hence, they are completely indifferent to any material possessions (Gusinde, 1961, pp. 86-87).

The hunter, one is tempted to say, is "uneconomic man." At least as concerns nonsubsistence goods, he is the reverse of that standard caricature immortalized in any *General Principles of Economics*, page one. His wants are scarce and his means (in relation) plentiful. Consequently he is "comparatively free of material pressures," has "no sense of possession," shows "an undeveloped sense of property," is "completely indifferent to any material pressures," manifests a "lack of interest" in developing his technological equipment.

In this relation of hunters to worldly goods there is a neat and important point. From the internal perspective of the economy, it seems wrong to say that wants are "restricted," desires "restrained," or even that the notion of wealth is "limited." Such phrasings imply in advance an Economic Man and a struggle of the hunter against his own worse nature, which is finally then subdued by a cultural vow of poverty. The words imply the renunciation of an acquisitiveness that in reality was never developed, a suppression of desires that were never broached. Economic Man is a bourgeois construction—as Marcel Mauss said, "not behind us, but before, like the moral man." It is not that hunters and gatherers have curbed their materialistic "impulses"; they simply never made an institution of them. "Moreover, if it is a great blessing to be free from a great evil, our [Montagnais] Savages are happy; for the two tyrants who provide hell and torture for many of our Europeans, do not reign in their great forests,—I mean ambition and avarice . . . as they are contented with a mere living, not one of them gives himself to the Devil to acquire wealth" (LeJeune, 1897, p. 231).

We are inclined to think of hunters and gatherers as *poor* because they don't have anything; perhaps better to think of them for that reason as *free*. "Their extremely limited material possessions relieve them of all cares with regard to daily necessities and permit them to enjoy life" (Gusinde, 1961, p. 1).

Subsistence

When Herskovits was writing his *Economic Anthropology* (1958), it was common anthropological practice to take the Bushmen or the native Australians as "a classic illustration of a people whose economic resources are of the scantiest," so precariously situated that "only the most intense application makes survival possible." Today the "classic" understanding can be fairly reversed—on evidence largely from these two groups. A good case can be made that hunters and gatherers work less than we do; and, rather than a continuous travail, the food quest is intermittent, leisure abundant, and there is a greater amount of sleep in the daytime per capita per year than in any other condition of society.

Some of the substantiating evidence for Australia appears in early sources, but we are fortunate especially to have now the quantitative materials collected by the 1948 American-Australian Scientific Expedition to Arnhem Land. Published in 1960, these startling data must provoke some review of the Australian reportage going back for over a century, and perhaps revision of an even longer period of anthropological thought. The key research was a temporal study of hunting and gathering by McCarthy and McArthur (1960), coupled to McArthur's analysis of the nutritional outcome.

Figures 1 and 2 summarize the principal production studies. These were short-run observations taken during nonceremonial periods. The record for Fish Creek (14 days) is longer as well as more detailed than that for Hemple Bay (seven days). Only adults' work has been reported, so far as I can tell. The diagrams incorporate information on hunting, plant collecting, preparing foods, and repairing weapons, as tabulated by the ethnographers. The

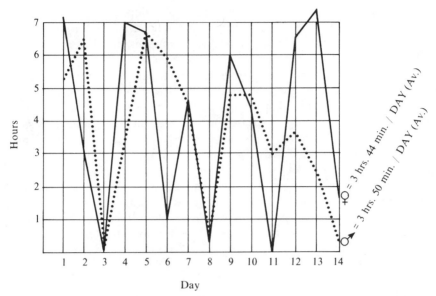

FIGURE 1.   Hours per Day in Food-connected Activities: Fish Creek Group (Mc-Carthy and McArthur, 1960)

people in both camps were free-ranging native Australians, living outside mission or other settlements during the period of study, although such was not necessarily their permanent or even their ordinary circumstance.[8]

One must have serious reservations about drawing general or historical inferences from the Arnhem Land data alone. Not only was the context less than pristine and the time of study too brief, but certain elements of the modern situation may have raised productivity above aboriginal levels: metal tools, for example, or the reduction of local pressure on food resources by depopulation. And our uncertainty seems rather doubled than neutralized by other current circumstances that, conversely, would lower economic efficiency: these semi-independent hunters, for instance, are probably not as skilled as their ancestors. For the moment, let us consider the Arnhem Land conclusions as experimental, potentially credible in the measure they are supported by other ethnographic or historic accounts.

The most obvious, immediate conclusion is that the people do not work hard. The average length of time per person per day put into the appropriation and preparation of food was four or five hours. Moreover, they do not work continuously. The subsistence quest was highly intermittent. It would stop for the time being when the people had procured enough for the time being, which left them plenty of time to spare. Clearly in subsistence as in other sectors of production, we have to do with an economy of specific, limited objectives. By hunting and gathering these objectives are apt to be

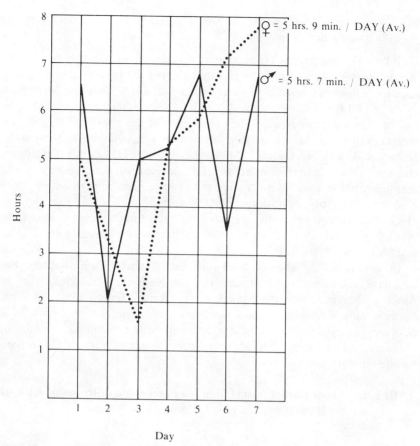

Day

FIGURE 2.   Hours per Day in Food-connected Activities: Hemple Bay Group (Mc-Carthy and McArthur, 1960)

irregularly accomplished, so the work pattern becomes correspondingly erratic.

In the event, a third characteristic of hunting and gathering unimagined by the received wisdom: rather than straining to the limits of available labor and disposable resources, these Australians seem to *underuse* their objective economic possibilities.

The quantity of food gathered in one day by any of these groups could in every instance have been increased. Although the search for food was, for the women, a job that went on day after day without relief [but see our Figures 1 and 2], they rested quite frequently, and did not spend all the hours of daylight searching for and preparing food. The nature of the men's food gathering was more sporadic, and if they had a good catch one day they frequently rested the next. . . . Perhaps unconsciously they weigh the benefit of greater supplies of food against the effort involved in collecting it, perhaps they judge what they consider to be enough, and when that is collected they stop (McArthur, 1960, p. 92).

It follows, fourthly, that the economy was not physically demanding. The investigators' daily journal indicates that the people pace themselves: only once is a hunter described as "utterly exhausted" (McCarthy and McArthur, 1960, pp. 150f). Neither did the Arnhem Landers themselves consider the task of subsistence onerous. "They certainly did not approach it as an unpleasant job to be got over as soon as possible, nor as a necessary evil to be postponed as long as possible" (McArthur, 1960, p. 92).[9] In this connection, and also in relation to their underuse of economic resources, it is noteworthy that the Arnhem Land hunters seem not to have been content with a "bare existence." Like other Australians (cf. Worsley, 1961, p. 173), they become dissatisfied with an unvarying diet; some of their time appears to have gone into the provision of diversity over and above mere sufficiency (McCarthy and McArthur, 1960, p. 192).

In any case, the dietary intake of the Arnhem Land hunters was adequate—according to the standards of the National Research Council of America. Mean daily consumption per capita at Hemple Bay was 2,160 calories (only a four-day period of observation), and at Fish Creek 2,130 calories (11 days). Table 1 indicates the main daily consumption of various nutrients, calculated by McArthur in percentages of the NRCA recommended dietary allowances.

TABLE 1. Mean Daily Consumption as Percentage of Recommended Allowances (from McArthur, 1960)

	CALORIES	PROTEIN	IRON	CALCIUM	ASCORBIC ACID
Hemple Bay	116	444	80	128	394
Fish Creek	104	544	33	355	47

Finally, what does the Arnhem Land study say about the famous question of leisure? It seems that hunting and gathering can afford extraordinary relief from economic cares. The Fish Creek group maintained a virtually full-time craftsman, a man 35 or 40 years old, whose true specialty however seems to have been loafing:

He did not go out hunting at all with the men, but one day he netted fish most vigorously. He occasionally went into the bush to get wild bees' nests. *Wilira* was an expert craftsman who repaired the spears and spear-throwers, made smoking-pipes and drone-tubes, and hafted a stone axe (on request) in a skillful manner; apart from these occupations he spent most of his time talking, eating and sleeping (McCarthy and McArthur, 1960, p. 148).

Wilira was not altogether exceptional. Much of the time spared by the Arnhem Land hunters was literally spare time, consumed in rest and sleep (see Tables 2 and 3). The main alternative to work, changing off with it in a complementary way, was sleep:

> Apart from the time (mostly between definitive activities and during cooking periods) spent in general social intercourse, chatting, gossiping and so on, some hours of the daylight were also spent resting and sleeping. On the average, if the men were in camp, they usually slept after lunch from an hour to an hour and a half, or sometimes even more. Also after returning from fishing or hunting they usually had a sleep, either immediately they arrived or whilst game was being cooked. At Hemple Bay the men slept if they returned early in the day but not if they reached camp after 4.00 p.m. When in camp all day they slept at odd times and always after lunch. The women, when out collecting in the forest, appeared to rest more frequently than the men. If in camp all day, they also slept at odd times, sometimes for long periods (McCarthy and McArthur, 1960, p. 193).

The failure of Arnhem Landers to "build culture" is not strictly from want of time. It is from idle hands.

So much for the plight of hunters and gatherers in Arnhem Land. As for the Bushmen, economically likened to Australian hunters by Herskovits, two excellent recent reports by Richard Lee show their condition to be indeed the same (Lee, 1968; 1969). Lee's research merits a special hearing not only because it concerns Bushmen, but specifically the Dobe section of !Kung

TABLE 2. Daytime Rest and Sleep, Fish Creek Group (data from McCarthy and McArthur, 1960)

Day	♂ Average	♀ Average
1	2'15"	2'45"
2	1'30"	1'0"
3	Most of the day	
4	Intermittent	
5	Intermittent and most of late afternoon	
6	Most of the day	
7	Several hours	
8	2'0"	2'0"
9	50"	50"
10	Afternoon	
11	Afternoon	
12	Intermittent, afternoon	
13	—	
14	3'15"	3'15"

TABLE 3.   Daytime Rest and Sleep, Hemple Bay Group (data from McCarthy and McArthur, 1960)

Day	♂ Average	♀ Average
1	—	45″
2	Most of the day	2′45″
3	1′0″	—
4	Intermittent	Intermittent
5	—	1′30″
6	Intermittent	Intermittent
7	Intermittent	Intermittent

Bushmen, adjacent to the Nyae Nyae about whose subsistence—in a context otherwise of "material plenty"—Mrs. Marshall expressed important reservations. The Dobe occupy an area of Botswana where !Kung Bushmen have been living for at least a hundred years, but have only just begun to suffer dislocation pressures. (Metal, however, has been available to the Dobe since 1880-90). An intensive study was made of the subsistence production of a dry season camp with a population (41 people) near the mean of such settlements. The observations extended over four weeks during July and August 1964, a period of transition from more to less favorable seasons of the year, hence fairly representative, it seems, of average subsistence difficulties.

Despite a low annual rainfall (6 to 10 inches), Lee found in the Dobe area a "surprising abundance of vegetation." Food resources were "both varied and abundant," particularly the energy-rich mangetti nut—"so abundant that millions of the nuts rotted on the ground each year for want of picking" (all references in Lee, 1969, p. 59).[10] His reports on time spent in food-getting are remarkably close to the Arnhem Land observations. Table 4 summarizes Lee's data.

The Bushman figures imply that one man's labor in hunting and gathering will support four or five people. Taken at face value, Bushman food collecting is more efficient than French farming in the period up to World War II, when more than 20 percent of the population were engaged in feeding the rest. Confessedly, the comparison is misleading, but not as misleading as it is astonishing. In the total population of free-ranging Bushmen contacted by Lee, 61.3 percent (152 of 248) were effective food producers; the remainder were too young or too old to contribute importantly. In the particular camp under scrutiny, 65 percent were "effectives." Thus the ratio of food producers to the general population is actually 3 : 5 or 2 : 3. *But*, these 65 percent of the people "worked 36 percent of the time, and 35 percent of the people did not work at all"! (Lee, 1969, p. 67).

For each adult worker, this comes to about two and one-half days labor per week. ("In other words, each productive individual supported herself or himself and dependents and still had 3-1/2 to 5-1/2 days available for other activities.") A "day's work" was about six hours; hence the Dobe work week is approximately 15 hours, or an average of 2 hours 9 minutes per day. Even lower than the Arnhem Land norms, this figure however excludes cooking and the preparation of implements. All things considered, Bushmen subsistence labors are probably very close to those of native Australians.

Also like the Australians, the time Bushmen do not work in subsistence they pass in leisure or leisurely activity. One detects again that characteristic paleolithic rhythm of a day or two on, a day or two off—the latter passed desultorily in camp. Although food collecting is the primary productive

TABLE 4.   Summary of Dobe Bushmen Work Diary (from Lee, 1969)

Week	Mean Group Size*	Man-Days of Consumption†	Man-Days of Work	Days of Work/ Week/Adult	Index of Subsistance Effort‡
1 (July 6-12)	25.6 (23-29)	179	37	2.3	21
2 (July 13-19)	28.3 (23-37)	198	22	1.2	11
3 (July 20-26)	14.3 (28-40)	240	42	1.9	18
4 (July 27-Aug. 2)	18.6 (32-40)	249	77	1.2	14
4-week totals	30.9	866	178	2.2	24
Adjusted totals§	31.8	668	156	2.5	23

*Group size shown in average and range. There is considerable short-term population fluctuation in Bushmen camps.

†Includes both children and adults, to give a combined total of days of provisioning required/week.

‡This index was constructed by Lee to illustrate the relation between consumption and the work required to produce it: $S = W/C$, where W = number of man-days of work, and C = man days of consumption. Inverted, the formula would tell how many people could be supported by a day's work in subsistence.

§Week 2 was excluded from the final calculations because the investigator contributed some food to the camp on two days.

activity, Lee writes, "the majority of the people's time (four to five days per week) is spent in other pursuits, such as resting in camp or visiting other camps" (1969, p. 74):

> A woman gathers on one day enough food to feed her family for three days, and spends the rest of her time resting in camp, doing embroidery, visiting other camps, or entertaining visitors from other camps. For each day at home, kitchen routines, such as cooking, nut cracking, collecting firewood, and fetching water, occupy one to three hours of her time. This rhythm of steady work and steady leisure is maintained throughout the year. The hunters tend to work more frequently than the women, but their schedule is uneven. It is not unusual for a man to hunt avidly for a week and then do no hunting at all for two or three weeks. Since hunting is an unpredictable business and subject to magical control, hunters sometimes experience a run of bad luck and stop hunting for a month or longer. During these periods, visiting, entertaining, and especially dancing are the primary activities of men (1968, p. 37).

The daily per-capita subsistence yield for the Dobe Bushmen was 2,140 calories. However, taking into account body weight, normal activities, and the age-sex composition of the Dobe population, Lee estimates the people require only 1,975 calories per capita. Some of the surplus food probably went to the dogs, who ate what the people left over. "The conclusion can be drawn that the Bushmen do not lead a substandard existence on the edge of starvation as has been commonly supposed" (1969, p. 73).

Taken in isolation, the Arnhem Land and Bushmen reports mount a disconcerting if not decisive attack on the entrenched theoretical position. Artificial in construction, the former study in particular is reasonably considered equivocal. But the testimony of the Arnhem Land expedition is echoed at many points by observations made elsewhere in Australia, as well as elsewhere in the hunting-gathering world. Much of the Australian evidence goes back to the nineteenth century, some of it to quite acute observers careful to make exception of the aboriginal come into relation with Europeans, for "his food supply is restricted, and . . . he is in many cases warned off from the waterholes which are the centers of his best hunting grounds" (Spencer and Gillen, 1899, p. 50).

> Constantly under pressure of want, and yet, by travelling, easily able to supply their wants, their lives lack neither excitement or pleasure (Smyth, 1878, vol. 1, p. 123).

Clearly, the hunting-gathering economy has to be revaluated, both as to its true accomplishments and its true limitations. The procedural fault of the received wisdom was to read from the material circumstances to the economic structure, deducing the absolute difficulty of such a life from its absolute poverty. But always the cultural design improvises dialectics on its relationship to nature. Without escaping the ecological constraints, culture would negate them, so that at once the system shows the impress of natural conditions and the originality of a social response—in their poverty, abundance.

What are the real handicaps of the hunting-gathering *praxis*? Not "low productivity of labor," if existing examples mean anything. But the economy is seriously afflicted by the *imminence of diminishing returns*. Beginning in subsistence and spreading from there to every sector, an initial success seems only to develop the probability that further efforts will yield smaller benefits. This describes the typical curve of food-getting within a particular locale. A modest number of people usually sooner than later reduce the food resources within convenient range of camp. Thereafter, they may stay on only by absorbing an increase in real costs or a decline in real returns: rise in costs if the people choose to search farther and farther afield, decline in returns if they are satisfied to live on the shorter supplies or inferior foods in easier reach. The solution, of course, is to go somewhere else. Thus the first and decisive contingency of hunting-gathering: it requires movement to maintain production on advantageous terms.

But this movement, more or less frequent in different circumstances, more or less distant, merely transposes to other spheres of production the same diminishing returns of which it is born. The manufacture of tools, clothing, utensils, or ornaments, however easily done, becomes senseless when these begin to be more of a burden than a comfort. Utility falls quickly at the margin of portability. The construction of substantial houses likewise becomes absurd if they must soon be abandoned. Hence the hunter's very ascetic conceptions of material welfare: an interest only in minimal equipment, if that; a valuation of smaller things over bigger; a disinterest in acquiring two or more of most goods; and the like. Ecological pressure assumes a rare form of concreteness when it has to be shouldered. If the gross product is trimmed down in comparison with other economies, it is not the hunter's productivity that is at fault, but his mobility.

Almost the same thing can be said of the demographic constraints of hunting-gathering. The same policy of *débarassment* is in play on the level of people, describably in similar terms and ascribable to similar causes. The terms are, cold-bloodedly: diminishing returns at the margin of portability, minimum necessary equipment, elimination of duplicates, and so forth—that is to say, infanticide, senilicide, sexual continence for the duration of the nursing period, etc., practices for which many food-collecting peoples are well known. The presumption that such devices are due to an inability to support more people is probably true—if "support" is understood in the sense of carrying them rather than feeding them. The people eliminated, as hunters sometimes sadly tell, are precisely those who cannot effectively transport themselves, who would hinder the movement of family and camp. Hunters may be obliged to handle people and goods in parallel ways, the draconic population policy an expression of the same ecology as the ascetic economy. More, these tactics of demographic restraint again form part of a larger policy for counteracting diminishing returns in subsistence. A local group becomes vulnerable to diminishing returns—so to a greater velocity of movement, or else to fission—in proportion to its size (other things equal). Insofar as the people would keep the advantage in local production, and maintain a certain physical and social stability, their Malthusian practices are just cruelly consistent. Modern hunters and gatherers, working their notably inferior environments, pass most of the year in very small groups widely spaced out. But rather than the sign of underproduction, the wages of poverty, this demographic pattern is better understood as the cost of living well.

Hunting and gathering has all the strengths of its weaknesses. Periodic movement and restraint in wealth and population are at once imperatives of the economic practice and creative adaptations, the kinds of necessities of which virtues are made. Precisely in such a framework, affluence becomes possible. Mobility and moderation put hunters' ends within range of their technical means. An undeveloped mode of production is thus rendered highly effective. The hunter's life is not as difficult as it looks from the outside. In some ways the economy reflects dire ecology, but it is also a complete inversion.

Reports on hunters and gatherers of the ethnological present—specifically on those in marginal environments—suggest a mean of three to five hours per adult worker per day in food production. Hunters keep banker's hours, notably less than modern industrial workers (unionized), who would surely settle for a 21–35 hour week. An interesting comparison is also posed by recent studies of labor costs among agriculturalists of neolithic type. For example, the average adult Hanunoo, man or woman, spends 1,200 hours per year in swidden cultivation (Conklin, 1957, p. 151); which is to say, a mean of three hours twenty minutes per day. Yet this figure does not include food gathering, animal raising, cooking and other direct subsistence efforts of these Philippine tribesmen. Comparable data are beginning to appear in reports on other primitive agriculturalists from many parts of the world. The conclusion is put conservatively when put negatively: hunters and gatherers need not work longer getting food than do primitive cultivators. Extrapolating from ethnography to prehistory, one may say as much for the neolithic as John Stuart Mill said of all labor-saving devices, that never was one invented that saved anyone a minute's labor. The neolithic saw no particular improvement over the paleolithic in the amount of time required per capita for the production of subsistence; probably, with the advent of agriculture, people had to work harder.

There is nothing either to the convention that hunters and gatherers can enjoy little leisure from tasks of sheer survival. By this, the evolutionary inadequacies of the paleolithic are customarily explained, while for the provision of leisure the neolithic is roundly congratulated. But the traditional formulas might be truer if reversed: the amount of work (per capita) increases with the evolution of culture, and the amount of leisure decreases. Hunters' subsistence labors are characteristically intermittent, a day on and a day off, and modern hunters at least tend to employ their time off in such activities as daytime sleep. In the tropical habitats occupied by many of these existing hunters, plant collecting is more reliable than hunting itself. Therefore, the women, who do the collecting, work rather more regularly than the men, and provide the greater part of the food supply. Man's work is often done. On the other hand, it is likely to be highly erratic, unpredictably required; if men lack leisure, it is then in the Enlightenment sense rather than the literal. When Condorcet attributed the hunter's unprogressive condition to want of "the leisure in which he can indulge in thought and enrich his understanding with new combinations of ideas," he also recognized that the economy was a "necessary cycle of extreme activity and total idleness." Apparently what the hunter needed was the *assured* leisure of an aristocratic *philosophe*.

Hunters and gatherers maintain a sanguine view of their economic state despite the hardships they sometimes know. It may be that they sometimes know hardships because of the sanguine views they maintain of their economic state. Perhaps their confidence only encourages prodigality to the extent the camp falls casualty to the first untoward circumstance. In alleging this is an affluent economy, therefore, I do not deny that certain hunters have moments of difficulty. Some do find it "almost inconceivable" for a man to die of hunger, or even to fail to satisfy his hunger for more than a day or two (Woodburn, 1968, p. 52). But others, especially certain very peripheral hunters spread out in small groups across an environment of extremes, are exposed periodically to the kind of inclemency that interdicts travel or access to game. They suffer—although perhaps only fractionally, the shortage affecting particular immobilized families rather than the society as a whole (cf. Gusinde, 1961, pp. 306-307).

Still, granting this vulnerability, and allowing the most poorly situated modern hunters into comparison, it would be difficult to prove that privation is distinctly characteristic of the hunter-gatherers. Food shortage is not the indicative property of this mode of production as opposed to others; it does not mark off hunters and gatherers as a class or a general evolutionary stage. Lowie asks:

> But what of the herders on a simple plane whose maintenance is periodically jeopardized by plagues—who, like some Lapp bands of the nineteenth century were obliged to fall back on fishing? What of the primitive peasants who clear and till without compensation of the soil, exhaust one plot and pass on to the next, and are threatened with famine at every drought? Are they any more in control of misfortune caused by natural conditions than the hunter-gatherer? (1938, p. 286)

Above all, what about the world today? One-third to one-half of humanity are said to go to bed hungry every night. In the Old Stone Age the fraction must have been much smaller. *This* is the era of hunger un-precedented. Now, in the time of the greatest technical power, is starvation an institution. Reverse another venerable formula: the amount of hunger increases relatively and absolutely with the evolution of culture.

This paradox is my whole point. Hunters and gatherers have by force of circumstances an objectively low standard of living. But taken as their *objective*, and given their adequate means of production, all the people's material wants usually can be easily satisfied. The evolution of economy has known, then, two contradictory movements: enriching but at the same time impoverishing, appropriating in relation to nature but expropriating in relation to man. The progressive aspect is, of course, technological. It has been celebrated in many ways: as an increase in the amount of need-serving goods and services, an increase in the amount of energy harnessed to the service of culture, an increase in productivity, an increase in division of labor, and increased freedom from environmental control. Taken in a certain sense, the last is especially useful for understanding the earliest stages of technical advance. Agriculture not only raised society above the distribution of natural food resources, it allowed neolithic communities to maintain high degrees of social order where the requirements of human existence were absent from the natural order. Enough food could be harvested in some seasons to sustain the people while no food would grow at all; the consequent stability of social life was critical for its material enlargement. Culture went on then from triumph to triumph, in a kind of progressive contravention of the biological law of the minimum, until it proved it could support human life in outer space—where even gravity and oxygen were naturally lacking.

Other men were dying of hunger in the market places of Asia. It has been an evolution of structures as well as technologies, and in that respect like the mythical road where for every step the traveller advances his destination recedes by two. The structures have been political as well as economic, of power as well as property. They developed first within societies, increasingly now between societies. No doubt these structures have been functional, necessary organizations of the technical development, but within the communities they have thus helped to enrich they would discriminate in the distribution of wealth and differentiate in the style of life. The world's most primitive people have few possessions, *but they are not poor*. Poverty is not a certain small amount of goods, nor is it just a relation between means and ends; above all it is a relation between people. Poverty is a social status. As such it is the invention of civilization. It has grown with civilization, at once as an invidious distinction between classes and more importantly as a tributary relation—that can render agrarian peasants more susceptible to natural catastrophes than any winter camp of Alaskan Eskimo.

All the preceding discussion takes the liberty of reading modern hunters historically, as an evolutionary base line. This liberty should not be lightly granted. Are marginal hunters such as the Bushmen of the Kalahari any more representative of the paleolithic condition than the Indians of California or the Northwest Coast? Perhaps not. Perhaps also Bushmen of the Kalahari are not even representative of marginal hunters. The great majority of surviving hunter-gatherers lead a life curiously decapitated and extremely lazy by comparison with the other few. The other few are very different. The Murngin, for example: "The first impression that any stranger must receive in a fully functioning group in Eastern Arnhem Land is of industry . . .

And he must be impressed with the fact that with the exception of very young children . . . there is no idleness" (Thomson, 1949a, pp. 33-34). There is nothing to indicate that the problems of livelihood are more difficult for these people than for other hunters (cf. Thomson, 1949b). The incentives of their unusual industry lie elsewhere: in "an elaborate and exacting ceremonial life," specifically in an elaborate ceremonial exchange cycle that bestows prestige on craftsmanship and trade (Thomson, 1949a, pp. 26, 28, 34 f, 87 passim). Most other hunters have no such concerns. Their existence is comparatively colorless, fixed singularly on eating with gusto and digesting at leisure. The cultural orientation is not Dionysian or Apollonian, but "gastric," as Julian Steward said of the Shoshoni. Then again it may be Dionysian, that is, Bacchanalian: "Eating among the Savages is like drinking among the drunkards of Europe. Those dry and ever-thirsty souls would willingly end their lives in a tub of malmsey, and the Savages in a pot full of meat; those over there talk only of drinking, and these here only of eating" (LeJeune, 1897, p. 249).

It is as if the superstructures of these societies had been eroded, leaving only the bare subsistence rock, and since production itself is readily accomplished, the people have plenty of time to perch there and talk about it. I must raise the possibility that the ethnography of hunters and gatherers is largely a record of incomplete cultures. Fragile cycles of ritual and exchange may have disappeared without trace, lost in the earliest stages of colonialism, when the intergroup relations they mediated were attacked and confounded. If so, the "original" affluent society will have to be rethought again for its originality, and the evolutionary schemes once more revised. Still this much history can always be rescued from existing hunters: the "economic problem" is easily solvable by paleolithic techniques. But then, it was not until culture neared the height of its material achievements that it erected a shrine to the Unattainable: *Infinite Needs*.

Notes

1. At least to the time Lucretius was writing (Harris, 1968, pp. 26-27).
2. On the historically particular requisites of such calculation, see Codere, 1968, [especially pp. 574-575.]
3. For the complementary institutionalization of "scarcity" in the condition of capitalist production, see Gorz, 1967, pp. 37-38.

4. It deserves mention that contemporary European-Marxist theory is often in accord with bourgeois economics on the poverty of the primitive. Cf. Boukharine, 1967; Mandel, 1962, vol. 1; and the economic history manual used at Lumumba University.

5. Turnbull similarly notes of Congo Pygmies: "The materials for the making of shelter, clothing, and all other necessary items of material culture are all at hand at a moment's notice." And he has no reservations either about subsistence: "Throughout the year, without fail, there is an abundant supply of game and vegetable foods" (1965, p. 18).

6. Certain food collectors not lately known for their architectural achievements seem to have built more substantial dwellings before being put on the run by Europeans. See Smythe, 1871, vol. 1, pp. 125-128.

7. But recall Gusinde's comment: "Our Fuegians procure and make their implements with little effort" (1961, p. 213).

8. Fish Creek was an inland camp in western Arnhem Land consisting of six adult males and three adult females. Hemple Bay was a coastal occupation on Groote Eylandt, there were four adult males, four adult females, and five juveniles and infants in the camp. Fish Creek was investigated at the end of the dry season, when the supply of vegetable foods was low; kangaroo hunting was rewarding, although the animals became increasingly wary under steady stalking. At Hemple Bay, vegetable foods were plentiful; the fishing was variable but on the whole good by comparison with other coastal camps visited by the expedition. The resource base at Hemple Bay was richer than at Fish Creek. The greater time put into food-getting at Hemple Bay may reflect, then, the support of five children. On the other hand, the Fish Creek group did maintain a virtually full-time specialist, and part of the difference in hours worked may represent a normal coastal-inland variation. In inland hunting, good things often come in large packages; hence, one day's work may yield two days' sustenance. A fishing-gathering regime perhaps produces smaller if steadier returns, enjoining somewhat longer and more regular efforts.

9. At least some Australians, the Yir-Yiront, make no linguistic differentiation between work and play (Sharp, 1958, p. 6).

10. This appreciation of local resources is all the more remarkable considering that Lee's ethnographic work was done in the second and third years of "one of the most severe droughts in South Africa's history" (1968, p. 39; 1969, p. 73 n.).

Bibliography

BOUKHARINE, N. 1967. *La Théorie du matérialism historique.* Paris: Editions Anthropos (First Russian edition, 1921).

CLARK, GRAHAM. 1953. *From Savagery to Civilization.* New York: Schuman.

CODERE, HELEN. 1968. "Money-Exchange Systems and a Theory of Money," *Man,* (n.s.) 3:557-77.

CONKLIN, HAROLD C. 1957. *Hanunóo Agriculture.* Rome: Food and Agriculture Organization of the United Nations.

DALTON, GEORGE. 1961. "Economic Theory and Primitive Society," *American Anthropologist* 63:1–25.

GORZ, ANDRE. 1967. *Le socialisme difficile*. Paris: Seuil.

GREY, SIR GEORGE. 1841. *Journals of Two Expeditions of Discovery in North-West and Western Australia, During the Years 1837, 38, and 39. . . .* 2 vols. London: Boone.

GUSINDE, MARTIN. 1961. *The Yamana*. 5 vols. New Haven, Conn.: Human Relations Area Files. (German edition 1931).

HARRIS, MARVIN. 1968. *The Rise of Anthropological Theory*. New York: Thomas Y. Crowell.

HAURY, EMIL W. 1962. "The Greater American Southwest," in J. Braidwood and G. R. Willey (eds.), *Courses toward Urban Life*. Chicago: Aldine.

HERSKOVITS, MELVILLE J. 1952. *Economic Anthropology*. New York: Knopf.

HOEBEL, E. ADAMSON. 1958. *Man in the Primitive World*. 2nd Ed. New York: McGraw-Hill.

LEE, RICHARD. 1968. "What Hunters Do for a Living, or, How to Make Out on Scarce Resources," in R. Lee and I. DeVore (eds.), *Man the Hunter*. Chicago: Aldine.
    1969. "!Kung Bushman Subsistance: An Input-Output Analysis," in A. Vayda (ed.), *Environment and Cultural Behavior*. Garden City, N.Y.: Natural History Press.

LEJEUNE, le PÈRE PAUL. 1897. "Relation of What Occurred in New France in the Year 1634," in R. G. Thwaites (ed.), *The Jesuit Relations and Allied Documents*, Vol. 6. Cleveland: Burrows. (First French edition, 1635.)

LOWIE, ROBERT H. 1938. "Subsistence," in F. Boas (ed.), *General Anthropology*. Boston: Heath.

MCARTHUR, MARGARET. 1960. "Food Consumption and Dietary Levels of Groups of Aborigines Living on Naturally Occurring Foods," in C. P. Mountford (ed.), *Records of the Australian-American Scientific Expedition to Arnhem Land, Vol. 2: Anthropology and Nutrition*. Melbourne: Melbourne University Press.

MCCARTHY, FREDERICK D., and MARGARET MCARTHUR. 1960. "The Food Quest and the Time Factor in Aboriginal Economic Life," in C. P. Mountford (ed.), *Records of the Australian-American Scientific Expedition to Arnhem Land, Vol. 2: Anthropology and Nutrition*. Melbourne: Melbourne University Press.

MANDEL, ERNEST. 1962. *Traite d'économie marxiste*. 2 Vols. Paris: Julliard.

MARSHALL, LORNA. 1961. "Sharing, Talking, and Giving: Relief of Social Tensions Among !Kung Bushmen," *Africa* 31:231–49.

Mauss, Marcel 1966. "Essai sur le don: Dorme et raison de l'échange dans les sociétés archaiques," in *Sociologie et anthropologie*. (First published 1923–24 in *L'Année Sociologique.*) Paris: Presses Universitaires de France.
    1967. *Manuel d'etnographie*. (First published 1947.) Paris: Payot.

POLANYI, KARL. 1947. "Our Obsolete Market Mentality," *Commentary* 3:109–17.
    1957. "The Economy as Instituted Process," in K. Polanyi, C. Arensberg and H. Pearson (eds.), *Trade and Market in the Early Empires*. Glencoe: The Free Press.
    1959. "Anthropology and Economic Theory," in M. Fried (ed.), *Readings in Anthropology*. Vol. 2. New York: Crowell.

QUIMBY, GEORGE I. 1962. "A Year with a Chippewa Family, 1763–1764," *Ethnohistory* 9:217–39.

REDFIELD, ROBERT. 1953. *The Primitive World and its Transformations.* Ithaca, N.Y.: Cornell University Press.

SHARP, LAURISTON. 1958. "People without Politics," in V. F. Ray (ed.), *Systems of Political Control and Bureaucracy in Human Societies.* American Ethnological Society. Seattle: University of Washington Press.

SMYTH, R. BROUGH. 1878. *The Aborigines of Victoria.* 2 vols. Melbourne: Government Printer.

SPENCER, BALDWIN, and F. J. GILLEN. 1899. *The Native Tribes of Central Australia.* London: Macmillan.
1927. *The Arunta.* 2 vols. London: Macmillan.

STEWARD, JULIAN H., and LOUIS C. FARON. 1959. *Native Peoples of South America.* New York: McGraw-Hill.

THOMSON, DONALD F. 1949a. *Economic Structure and the Ceremonial Exchange Cycle in Arnhem Land.* Melbourne: Macmillan.
1949b. "Arnhem Land: Explorations Among an Unknown People," *The Geographical Journal* 113:1–8, 114, 54–67.

TURNBULL, COLIN. 1965. *Wayward Servants.* Garden City, N.Y.: Natural History Press.

VAN DER POST, LAURENS. 1958. *The Lost World of the Kalahari.* New York: Morrow.

WHITE, LESLIE A. 1949. *The Science of Culture.* New York: Farrar, Strauss.
1959. *The Evolution of Culture.* New York: McGraw-Hill.

WOODBURN, JAMES. 1968. "An Introduction to Hadza Ecology," in R. Lee and I. DeVore (eds.), *Man the Hunter.* Chicago: Aldine.

WORSLEY, PETER M. 1961. "The Utilization of Food Resources by an Australian Aboriginal Tribe," *Acta Ethnographica* 10:153–90.

14

The Impact of Money on an African Subsistence Economy

PAUL BOHANNAN

IT HAS OFTEN BEEN CLAIMED that money was to be found in much of the African continent before the impact of the European world and the extension of trade made coinage general. When we examine these claims, however, they tend to evaporate or to emerge as tricks of definition. It is an astounding fact that economists have, for decades, been assigning three or four qualities to money when they discuss it with reference to our own society or to those of the medieval and modern world, yet the moment they have gone to ancient history or to the societies and economies studied by anthropologists they have sought the "real" nature of money by allowing only one of these defining characteristics to dominate their definitions.

All economists learned as students that money serves at least three purposes. It is a means of exchange, it is a mode of payment, it is a standard of value. Depending on the vintage and persuasion of the author of the book one consults, one may find another money use—storage of wealth. In newer books, money is defined as merely the means of unitizing purchasing power, yet behind that definition still lie the standard, the payment, and the exchange uses of money.

It is interesting that on the fairly rare occasions that economists discuss primitive money at all—or at least when they discuss it with any empirical referent—they have discarded one or more of the money uses in framing their definitions. Paul Einzig,[1] to take one example for many, first makes a plea for "elastic definitions," and goes on to point out that different economists have utilized different criteria in their definitions; he then falls into the trap he has been exposing: he excoriates Menger for utilizing only the "medium of exchange" criterion and then himself omits it, utilizing only the standard and payment criteria, thus taking sides in an argument in which there was no real issue.

The answer to these difficulties should be apparent. If we take no more than the three major money uses—payment, standard and means of exchange—we will find that in many primitive societies as well as in some of the ancient empires, one object may serve one money use while quite another object serves another money use. In order to deal with this situation, and to avoid the trap of choosing one of these uses to define "real" money, Karl Polanyi[2] and his associates have labeled as "general purpose money" any item which serves all three of these primary money uses, while an item which serves only one or two is "special purpose money." With this distinction in mind, we can see that special-purpose money was very common in pre-contact Africa, but that general purpose money was rare.

This paper is a brief analysis of the impact of general purpose money and increase in trade in an African economy which had known only local trade and had used only special purpose money.

The Tiv are a people, still largely pagan, who live in the Benue Valley in central Nigeria, among whom I had the good fortune to live and work for well over two years. They are prosperous subsistence farmers and have a highly developed indigenous market in which they exchanged their produce and handicrafts, and through which they carried on local trade. The most distinctive feature about the economy of the Tiv—and it is a feature they share with many, perhaps most, of the pre-monetary peoples—is what can be called a multi-centric economy. Briefly, a multicentric economy is an economy in which a society's exchangeable goods fall into two or more mutually exclusive spheres, each marked by different institutionalization and different moral values. In some multicentric economies these spheres remain distinct, though in most there are more or less institutionalized means of converting wealth from one into wealth in another.

Indigenously there were three spheres in the multi-centric economy of the Tiv. The first of these spheres is that associated with subsistence, which the Tiv call *yiagh*. The commodities in it include all locally produced foodstuffs: the staple yams and cereals, plus all the condiments, vegetable side-dishes and seasonings, as well as small livestock—chickens, goats and sheep. It also includes household utensils (mortars, grindstones, calabashes, baskets and pots), some tools (particularly those used in agriculture), and raw materials for producing any items in the category.

Within this sphere, goods are distributed either by gift giving or through marketing. Traditionally, there was no money of any sort in this sphere—all goods changed hands by barter. There was a highly developed market organization at which people exchanged their produce for their requirements, and in which today traders buy produce in cheap markets and transport it to sell in dearer markets. The morality of this sphere of the economy is the morality of the free and uncontrolled market.

The second sphere of the Tiv economy is one which is in no way associated with markets. The category of goods within this sphere is slaves, cattle, ritual "offices" purchased from the Jukun, that type of large white cloth known as *tugudu*, medicines and magic, and metal rods. One is still entitled to use the present tense in this case, for ideally the category still exists in spite of the fact that metal rods are today very rare, that slavery has been abolished, that European "offices" have replaced Jukun offices and cannot be bought, and that much European medicine has been accepted. Tiv still quote prices of slaves in cows and brass rods, and of cattle in brass rods and *tugudu* cloth. The price of magical rites, as it has been described in the literature, was in terms of *tugudu* cloth or brass rods (though payment might be made in other items); payment for Jukun titles was in cows and slaves, *tugudu* cloths and metal rods.[3]

None of these goods ever entered the market as it was institutionalized in Tivland, even though it might be possible for an economist to find the principle of supply and demand at work in the exchanges which characterized it. The actual shifts of goods took place at ceremonies, at more or less ritualized wealth displays, and on occasions when "doctors" performed rites and prescribed medicines. Tiv refer to the items and the activities within this sphere by the word *shagba*, which can be roughly translated as prestige.

Within the prestige sphere there was one item which took on all of the money uses and hence can be called a general-purpose currency, though it must be remembered that it was of only a *very limited range*. Brass rods were used as means of exchange *within the sphere*; they also served as a standard of value within it (though not the only one), and as a means of payment. However, this sphere of the economy was tightly sealed off from the subsistence goods and its market. After European contact, brass rods occasionally entered the market, but they did so only as means of payment, not as medium of exchange or as standard of valuation. Because of the complex institutionalization and morality, no one ever sold a slave for food; no one, save in the depths of extremity, ever paid brass rods for domestic goods.

The supreme and unique sphere of exchangeable values for the Tiv contains a single item: rights in human beings other than slaves, particularly rights in women. Even twenty-five years after official abolition of exchange marriage, it is the category of exchange in which Tiv are emotionally most entangled. All exchanges within this category are exchanges of rights in human beings, usually dependent women and children. Its values are expressed in terms of kinship and marriage.

Tiv marriage is an extremely complex subject.[4] Again, economists might find supply and demand principles at work, but Tiv adamantly separate marriage and market. Before the coming of the Europeans all "real" marriages were exchange marriages. In its simplest form, an exchange marriage involves two men exchanging sisters. Actually, this simple form seldom or never occurred. In order for every man to have a ward (*ingol*) to exchange for a wife, small localized agnatic lineages formed ward-sharing groups ("those who eat one Ingol"—*mbaye ingol i mom*). There was an initial "exchange"—or at least, distribution—of wards among the men of this group, so that each man became the guardian (*tien*) of one or more wards. The guardian, then, saw to the marriage of his ward, exchanging her with outsiders for another woman (her "partner" or *ikyar*) who becomes the bride of the guardian or one of his close agnatic kinsmen, or—in some situations—becomes a ward in the ward-sharing group and is exchanged for yet another woman who becomes a wife.

Tiv are, however, extremely practical and sensible people, and they know that successful marriages cannot be made if women are not consulted and if they are not happy. Elopements occurred, and sometimes a woman in exchange was not forthcoming. Therefore, a debt existed from the ward-sharing group of the husband to that of the guardian.

These debts sometimes lagged two or even three generations behind actual exchanges. The simplest way of paying them off was for the eldest daughter of the marriage to return to the ward-sharing group of her mother, as ward, thus cancelling the debt.

Because of its many impracticalities, the system had to be buttressed in several ways in order to work: one way was a provision for "earnest" during the time of the lag, another was to recognize other types of marriage as binding to limited extents. These two elements are somewhat confused with one another, because of the fact that right up until the abolition of exchange marriage in 1927, the inclination was always to treat all non-exchange marriages as if they were "lags" in the completion of exchange marriages.

When lags in exchange occurred, they were usually filled with "earnests" of brass rods or, occasionally, it would seem, of cattle. The brass rods or cattle in such situations were *never* exchange equivalents (*ishe*) for the woman. The only "price" of one woman is another woman.

Although Tiv decline to grant it antiquity, another type of marriage occurred at the time Europeans first met them—it was called "accumulating a woman/wife" (*kem kwase*). It is difficult to tell today just exactly what it consisted in, because the terminology of this union has been adapted to describe the bridewealth marriage that was declared by an administrative fiat of 1927 to be the only legal form.

Kem marriage consisted in acquisition of sexual, domestic and economic rights in a woman—but not the rights to filiate her children to the social group of the husband. Put in another way, in exchange marriage, both rights *in genetricem* (rights to filiate a woman's children) and rights *in uxorem* (sexual, domestic and economic rights in a woman) automatically were acquired by husbands and their lineages.[5] In *kem* marriage, only rights *in uxorem* were acquired. In order to affiliate the *kem* wife's children, additional payments had to be made to the woman's guardians. These payments were for the children, not for the rights *in genetricem* in their mother, which could be acquired only by exchange of equivalent rights in another woman. *Kem* payments were paid in brass rods. However, rights in women had no equivalent or "price" in brass rods or in any other item—save, of course, identical rights in another woman. *Kem* marriage was similar to but showed important differences from bridewealth marriage as it is known in South and East Africa. There rights in women and rights in cattle form a single economic sphere, and could be exchanged directly for one another. Among Tiv, however, conveyance of rights in women necessarily involved direct exchange of another woman. The Tiv custom that approached bridewealth was not an exchange of equivalents, but payment in a medium that was specifically not equivalent.

Thus, within the sphere of exchange marriage there was no item that fulfilled any of the uses of money; when second-best types of marriage were made, payment was in an item which was specifically not used as a standard of value.

That Tiv do conceptualize exchange articles as belonging to different categories, and that they rank the categories on a moral basis, and that most but not all exchanges are limited to one sphere, gives rise to the fact that two different kinds of exchanges may be recognized: exchange of items contained within a single category, and exchanges of items belonging to different categories. For Tiv, these two different types of exchange are marked by separate and distinct moral attitudes.

To maintain this distinction between the two types of exchanges which Tiv mark by different behavior and different values, I shall use separate words. I shall call those exchanges of items within a single category "conveyances" and those exchanges of items from one category to another "conversions."[6] Roughly, conveyances are morally neutral; conversions have a strong moral quality in their rationalization.

Exchanges within a category—particularly that of subsistence, the only one intact today—excite no moral judgments. Exchanges between categories, however, do excite a moral reaction: the man who exchanges lower category goods for higher category goods does not brag about his market luck but about his "strong heart" and his success in life. The man who exchanges high category goods for lower rationalizes his action in terms of high-valued motivation (most often the needs of his kinsmen).

The two institutions most intimately connected with conveyance are markets and marriage. Conveyance in the prestige sphere seems (to the latter-day investigator, at least) to have been less highly institutionalized. It centered on slave dealing, on curing and on the acquisition of status.

Conversion is a much more complex matter. Conversion depends on the fact that some items of every sphere could, on certain occasions, be used in exchanges in which the return was *not* considered equivalent (*ishe*). Obviously, given the moral ranking of the spheres, such a situation leaves one party to the exchange in a good position, and the other in a bad one. Tiv say that it is "good" to trade food for brass rods, but that it is "bad" to trade brass rods for food, that it is good to trade your cows or brass rods for a wife, but very bad to trade your marriage ward for cows or brass rods.

Seen from the individual's point of view, it is profitable and possible to invest one's wealth if one converts it into a morally superior category: to convert subsistence wealth into prestige wealth and both into women is the aim of the economic endeavor or individual Tiv. To put it into economists' terms: conversion is the ultimate type of maximization.

We have already examined the marriage system by which a man could convert his brass rods to a wife: he could get a *kem* wife and *kem* her children as they were born. Her daughters, then, could be used as wards in his exchange marriages. It is the desire of every Tiv to "acquire a woman" (*ngoho kwase*) either as wife or ward in some way other than sharing in the ward-sharing group. A wife whom one acquires in any other way is not the concern of one's marriage-ward sharing group because the woman or other property exchanged for her did not belong to the marriage-ward group. The daughters of such a wife are not divided among the members of a man's marriage-ward group, but only among his sons. Such a wife is not only indicative of a man's ability and success financially and personally, but rights in her are the only form of property which is not ethically subject to the demands of his kinsmen.

Conversion from the prestige sphere to the kinship sphere was, thus, fairly common; it consisted in all the forms of marriage save exchange marriage, usually in terms of brass rods.

Conversion from the subsistence sphere to the prestige sphere was also usually in terms of metal rods. They, on occasion, entered the market place as payment. If the owner of the brass rods required an unusually large amount of staples to give a feast, making too heavy a drain on his wives' food supplies, he might buy it with brass rods.

However, brass rods could not possibly have been a general currency. They were not divisible. One could not receive "change" from a brass rod. Moreover, a single rod was worth much more than the usual market purchases for any given day of most Tiv subsistence traders. Although it might be possible to buy chickens with brass rods, one would have to have bought a very large quantity of yams to equal one rod, and to buy an item like pepper with rods would be laughable.

Brass rods, thus, overlapped from the prestige to the subsistence sphere on some occasions, but only on special occasions and for large purchases.

Not only is conversion possible, but it is encouraged—it is, in fact, the behavior which proves a man's worth. Tiv are scornful of a man who is merely rich in subsistence goods (or, today, in money). If, having adequate subsistence, he does not seek prestige in accordance with the old counters, or if he does not strive for more wives, and hence more children, the fault must be personal inadequacy. They also note that they all try to keep a man from making conversions; jealous kinsmen of a rich man will bewitch him and his people by fetishes, in order to make him expend his wealth on sacrifices to repair the fetishes, thus maintaining economic equality. However, once a conversion has been made, demands of kinsmen are not effective—at least, they take a new form.

Therefore, the man who successfully converts his wealth into higher categories is successful—he has a "strong heart." He is both feared and respected.

In this entire process, metal rods hold a pivotal position, and it is not surprising that early administrators considered them money. Originally imported from Europe, they were used as "currency" in some part of southern Nigeria in the slave trade. They are dowels about a quarter of an inch in diameter and some three feet long; they can be made into jewelry, and were used as a source of metal for castings.

Whatever their use elsewhere, brass rods in Tivland had some but not all of the attributes of money. Within the prestige sphere, they were used as a standard of equivalence, and they were a medium of exchange; they were also a mode for storage of wealth, and were used as payment. In short, brass rods were a general purpose currency *within the prestige sphere*. However, outside of the prestige sphere—markets and marriage were the most active institutions of exchange outside it—brass rods fulfilled only one of these functions of money: payment. We have examined in detail the reasons why equivalency could not exist between brass rods and rights in women, between brass rods and food.

We have, thus, in Tivland, a multi-centric economy of three spheres, and we have a sort of money which was a general purpose money within the limited range of the prestige sphere, and a special purpose money in the special transactions in which the other spheres overlapped it.

The next question is: what happened to this multi-centric economy and to the morality accompanying it when it felt the impact of the expanding European economy in the 19th and early 20th centuries, and when an all-purpose money of very much greater range was introduced?

The Western impact is not, of course, limited to economic institutions. Administrative organizations, missions and others have been as effective instruments of change as any other.

One of the most startling innovations of the British administration was a general peace. Before the arrival of the British, one did not venture far beyond the area of one's kinsmen or special friends. To do so was to court death or enslavement.

With government police systems and safety, road building was also begun. Moving about the country has been made both safe and comparatively easy. Peace and the new road network led to both increased trade and a greater number of markets.

Not only has the internal marketing system been perturbed by the introduction of alien institutions, but the economic institutions of the Tiv have in fact been put into touch with world economy. Northern Nigeria, like much of the rest of the colonial world, was originally taken over by trading companies with governing powers. The close linkage of government and trade was evident when taxation was introduced into Tivland. Tax was originally paid in produce, which was transported and sold through Hausa traders, who were government contractors. A few years later, coinage was introduced; taxes were demanded in that medium. It became necessary for Tiv to go into trade or to make their own contract with foreign traders in order to get cash. The trading companies, which had had "canteens" on the Benue for some decades, were quick to cooperate with the government in introducing a "cash crop" which could be bought by the traders in return for cash to pay taxes, and incidentally to buy imported goods. The crop which proved best adapted for this purpose in Tivland was beniseed (*sesamum indicum*), a crop Tiv already grew in small quantities. Acreage need only be increased and facilities for sale established.

There is still another way in which Tiv economy is linked, through the trading companies, to the economy of the outside world. Not only do the companies buy their cash crops, they also "stake" African traders with imported goods. There is, on the part both of the companies and the government, a desire to build up "native entrepreneurial classes." Imported cloth, enamelware and ironmongery are generally sold through a network of dependent African traders. Thus, African traders are linked to the companies, and hence into international trade.

Probably no single factor has been so important, however, as the introduction of all-purpose money. Neither introduction of cash crops and taxes nor extended trading has affected the basic congruence between Tiv ideas and their institutionalization to the same extent as has money. With the introduction of money the indigenous ideas of maximization—that is, conversion of all forms of wealth into women and children—no longer leads to the result it once did.

General purpose money provides a common denominator among all the spheres, thus making the commodities within each expressible in terms of a single standard and hence immediately exchangeable. This new money is misunderstood by Tiv. They use it as a standard of value in the subsistence category, even when—as is often the case—the exchange is direct barter. They use it as a means of payment of bride-wealth under the new system, but still refuse to admit that a woman has a "price" or can be valued in the same terms as food. At the same time, it has become something formerly lacking in all save the prestige sphere of Tiv economy—a means of exchange. Tiv has tried to categorize money with the other new imported goods and place them all in a fourth economic sphere, to be ranked morally below subsistence. They have, of course, not been successful in so doing.

What in fact happened was that general purpose money was introduced to Tivland, where formerly only special purpose money had been known.

It is in the nature of a general purpose money that it standardizes the exchangeability value of every item to a common scale. It is precisely this function which brass rods, a "limited-purpose money" in the old system, did not perform. As we have seen, brass rods were used as a standard in some situations of conveyance in the intermediate or "prestige" category. They were also used as a means of payment (but specifically not as a standard) in some instances of conversion.

In this situation, the early Administrative offices interpreted brass rods as "money," by which they meant a general-purpose money. It became a fairly easy process, in their view, to establish by fiat an exchange rate between brass rods and a new coinage, "withdraw" the rods, and hence "replace" one currency with another. The actual effect, as we have seen, was to introduce a general purpose currency in place of a limited purpose money. Today all conversions and most conveyances are made in terms of coinage. Yet Tiv constantly express their distrust of money. This fact, and another—that a single means of exchange has entered all the economic spheres—has broken down the major distinctions among the spheres. Money has created in Tivland a unicentric economy. Not only is the money a general-purpose money, but it applies to the full range of exchangeable goods.

Thus, when semi-professional traders, using money, began trading in the foodstuffs marketed by women and formerly solely the province of women, the range of the market was very greatly increased and hence the price in Tiv markets is determined by supply and demand far distant from the local producer and consumer. Tiv react to this situation by saying that foreign traders "spoil" their markets. The overlap of marketing and men's long-distance trade in staples also results in truckload after truckload of foodstuffs exported from major Tiv markets every day they meet. Tiv say that food is less plentiful today than it was in the past, though more land is being farmed. Tiv elders deplore this situation and know what is happening, but they do not know just where to fix the blame. In attempts to do something about it, they sometimes announce that no women are to sell any food at all. But when their wives disobey them, men do not really feel that they were wrong to have done so. Tiv sometimes discriminate against non-Tiv traders in attempts to stop export of food. In their condemnation of the situation which is depriving them of their food faster than they are able to increase production, Tiv elders always curse money itself. It is money which, as the instrument for selling one's life subsistence, is responsible for the worsened situation—money and the Europeans who brought it.

Of even greater concern to Tiv is the influence money has had on marriage institutions. Today every woman's guardian, in accepting money as bridewealth, feels that he is converting down. Although attempts are made to spend money which is received in bridewealth to acquire brides for one's self and one's sons, it is in the nature of money, Tiv insist, that it is most difficult to accomplish. The good man still spends his bridewealth receipts for brides—but good men are not so numerous as would be desirable. Tiv deplore the fact that they are required to "sell" (*te*) their daughters and "buy" (*yam*) wives. There is no dignity in it since the possibility of making a bridewealth marriage into an exchange marriage has been removed.

With money, thus, the institutionalization of Tiv economy has become unicentric, even though Tiv still see it with multicentric values. The single sphere takes many of its characteristics from the market, so that the new situation can be considered a spread of the market. But throughout these changes in institutionalization, the basic Tiv value of maximization—converting one's wealth into the highest category, women and children—has remained. And in this discrepancy between values and institutions, Tiv have come upon what is to them a paradox, for all that Westerners understand it and are familiar with it. Today it is easy to sell subsistence goods for money to buy prestige articles and women, thereby aggrandizing oneself at a rapid rate. The food so sold is exported, decreasing the amount of subsistence goods available for consumption. On the other hand, the number of women is limited. The result is that bridewealth gets higher: rights in women have entered the market, and since the supply is fixed, the price of women has become inflated.

The frame of reference given me by the organizer of this symposium asked for comments on the effects of increased monetization on trade, on the distribution of wealth and indebtedness. To sum up the situation in these terms, trade has vastly increased with the introduction of general purpose money but also with the other factors brought by a colonial form of government. At the same time, the market has expanded its range of applicability in the society. The Tiv are, indigenously, a people who valued egalitarian distribution of wealth to the extent that they believed they bewitched one another to whittle down the wealth of one man to the size of that of another. With money, the degree and extent of differentiation by wealth has greatly increased and will probably continue to increase. Finally, money has brought a new form of indebtedness—one which we know, only too well. In the indigenous system, debt took either the form of owing marriage wards and was hence congruent with the kinship system, or else took the form of decreased prestige. There was no debt in the sphere of subsistence because there was no credit there save among kinsmen and neighbors whose activities were aspects of family status, not acts of money-lenders. The introduction of general purpose money and the concomitant spread of the market has divorced debt from kinship and status and has created the notion of debt in the subsistence sphere divorced from the activities of kinsmen and neighbors.

In short, because of the spread of the market and the introduction of general-purpose money, Tiv economy has become a part of the world economy. It has brought about profound changes in the institutionalization of Tiv society. Money is one of the shatteringly simplifying ideas of all time, and like any other new and compelling idea, it creates its own revolution. The monetary revolution, at least in this part of Africa, is the turn away from the multicentric economy. Its course may be painful, but there is very little doubt about its outcome.

Notes

1. Paul Einzig, *Primitive Money in its Ethnological, Historical and Economic Aspects* (London: Eyre and Spottisworde, 1949), pp. 319–26.

2. Karl Polanyi, "The Economy as Instituted Process," in Karl Polanyi, Conrad M. Arensberg and Harry W. Pearson, eds., *Trade and Market in the Early Empires* (Glencoe, Ill.: The Free Press and The Falcon's Wing Press, 1957), pp. 264–66.

3. B. Akiga Sai, *Akiga's Story* (London: International Institute of African Languages and Cultures, 1939), p. 382 and passim.

4. Akiga, *Akiga's Story*, pp. 120–27. Laura and Paul Bohannan, *The Tiv of Central Nigeria* (London: International African Institute), pp. 69–78 and Paul and Laura Bohannan, *Three Source Notebooks in Tiv Ethnography* (New Haven: Human Relations Area Files, 1958), pp. 384–444.

5. Laura Bohannan, "Dahomean Marriage: A Revaluation," *Africa*, XIX (1949), pp. 273–87.

6. Franz Steiner, "Notes on Comparative Economics," *British Journal of Sociology*, V (June 1954), 118–29.

15

Indians and the Metropolis

JOSEPH G. JORGENSEN

Introduction[1]

How MODERN AMERICAN INDIANS are integrated into the American political economy has received some anthropological analysis during the past thirty years. Anthropologists who have concerned themselves with *contemporary* Indian life have usually disregarded the political economic causes of Indian conditions and have employed an "acculturation" schema to explain why living Indian societies differ from their precontact forbears and from the dominant, contemporary, white or "Anglo" society as well. Stages, contexts, or levels of acculturation achieved by Indians are usually loosely defined and measured in relation to the hypothesized norms for white society. Though actual measurements of white society are seldom made and variation in white society is almost never accounted for, in general, the more similar an Indian society is said to be to white society, the more "acculturated" the Indian society is. In this view the dominated society accommodates itself to the dominant society in stages.

The underlying assumption in these studies is that the direction change takes is from a primitive, underdeveloped society—i.e., a society with low economic output and low standard of living—to a civilized, developed society that becomes fully integrated into the dominant white society. Integration is achieved when "acculturation" is complete. The actual steps involved vary from context to context. There is no single path.

The acculturation framework provides a rather euphoric way to think and talk about what has happened to American Indians since contact. It assumes that before white contact Indians were "underdeveloped" and avoids analysis of why Indians are as they are today. Because this framework assumes that Indians will eventually become fully integrated into the United States polity, economy, and society just like whites, it is also meaningless. No matter what the condition of Indian society is when analyzed by the anthropologist, it is always somewhere along the acculturation path, headed toward full acculturation. Because acculturation explains everything, it explains nothing.

Recently the clichés and erroneous concepts of acculturation research have been challenged by Vine Deloria, Jr. (1969), an Indian author. Although Deloria's criticisms are sound, he does not adequately explain why Indians are as they are. It is clear, however, that the political, economic, and social conditions of American Indians are not improving, and this is the nub of the issue.

Underdevelopment, in my view, has been caused by the *development* of the white-controlled national economy, and the political, economic, and social conditions of Indians are not improving because *the American Indian is, and has been for over one hundred years, fully integrated into the national political economy.* Underdevelopment, paradoxically then, has been caused by the development of the capitalist political economy of the United States. This postulate is in direct opposition to the postulate that seems to underlie acculturation, and also suggests a basic contradiction in the American political economy. Before exploring this postulate, let us survey Indian conditions in the past several decades since they have *become* underdeveloped, and in a very cursory way, let us develop some idea of what the basic features of modern Indian life have been for these "acculturating" or "developing" people.

The Problem: the Persistence of Indian Poverty

The History of Indian Deprivation

In 1926 Lewis Meriam was commissioned by Secretary of Interior Hubert Work to survey Indian administration and Indian life. His report demonstrated that federal legislation and the niggardly funds allocated for Indian programs had injured rather than helped American Indians (Meriam 1928). It also showed that the Bureau of Indian Affairs (BIA), the government agency responsible for implementing federal policies and managing Indian affairs, had a long tradition of dry rot—i.e., unimaginative and undereducated mismanagers caught up in red-tape procedures—that had made it incapable of helping Indians particularly with their economic, health, education, housing, and legal problems.

Since the passage of the General Allotment Act (Dawes Act) of 1887, which was intended to civilize Indians and "free" them from communal land ownership, Indian reservation land had been drastically reduced by allotting acreage to each Indian family head and in some instances, to other living Indians. The unallotted land became part of the public domain. By 1926, much Indian land was tied up in complicated heirship status, much had been sold or leased by Indians to whites, and Indian economic conditions, in general, were deplorable. Employment was almost nonexistent; family farming and ranching were not meeting subsistence needs. Thus, between 1887 and 1926 the underdeveloped Indians became more underdeveloped.

Meriam and his associates further showed that Indian health was particularly poor with a high incidence of disease—especially diseases that are correlated with poverty, like tuberculosis and trachoma—and a high infant mortality rate. Indian housing was so substandard—dirt floors, no doors, wretched sanitation, no running water—and Indian diet so poor that the two coalesced greatly to exacerbate Indian health problems.

Federal education policy since the 1880's took preadolescent children away from their homes and the so-called restrictive backward influences of tribal life, and educated them in all-Indian boarding schools. The intention of the policy was to force rapid acceptance of white ways, and the optimistic notion behind it was that if a man is given an education, he will, ipso facto, make his own way successfully as a wage earner or petty capitalist-farmer or shopkeeper in white society. The Meriam report was critical of this education policy as well as the General Allotment Act of 1887, which was intended to bring the education-economic program to fruition and in a short time, to achieve the desired effects.

The Meriam report criticized the current state of Indian affairs, especially land and education policies, and made suggestions to solve the problems: Indian health and housing were to be improved; preadolescents were to be educated on home reservations; loss of Indian land through sale or lease was to be stopped; and greater federal appropriations were to be made to increase salaries to entice better qualified people to join the BIA. Characteristically, the report did not cover such questions as the need for massive funds to develop industries—agricultural or otherwise—under the ownership and control of Indians. Rather, it directed itself to the symptoms of the Indians' problems and to cleaning up the bumbling, underfunded BIA, hoping that good advice administered through this special appendage of the federal welfare enterprise would improve the individual Indian's lot until he became self-sufficient.

During the Hoover administration, federal appropriations doubled from 1929 to 1932, but slackened by nearly 20 percent in 1933 during the depths of the Depression. Most of the money went for education expenses, salaries of better trained personnel, and health and medical expenses, including the salaries of doctors, nurses, nutrition experts, and others involved in Indian health programs. Thus, funds were provided for the education dream, for a larger and better trained welfare bureaucracy to administer Indian affairs, and for maintaining and hopefully improving Indian health. This welfare program served to expand the BIA, improve health slightly, and keep the Indian education system going.

In 1934 during Roosevelt's first administration, the Wheeler-Howard Act, known best as the Indian Reorganization Act (IRA), was passed. The IRA provided for sweeping changes in Indian policies. Following the recommendations of the Meriam report it allowed for consolidation of Indian land and purchase of more land; development of tribal governments with constitutions and charters; financial loans to the tribal governments for the development of tribal resources; and development of day schools for Indian children on home reservations. John Collier was appointed Commissioner of Indian Affairs to implement these policies which were considered "radical" at the time (see Haas 1957).

The IRA did *not* decrease the powers of the BIA over Indian lives, even though tribal governments with constitutions were created. In fact, the IRA actually *increased* the powers of the Secretary of Interior over Indians. Many Congressmen and many lobbyists became irritated at Collier's implementation of the IRA, but their irritations and fears were premature. Because the program allowed land to be purchased for Indians, thus removing the land from state tax rolls, and because it was thought that it would be more difficult for private corporations to exploit resources on those lands if they fell into Indian ownership, state governments as well as agribusiness and mineral lobbies were opposed to the IRA and to Collier. Actually, mineral, farm, and rangeland exploitation became cheaper on Indian-owned land than on company-owned or leased federal land because a special tax exemption was implemented for lessees of Indian lands.

Shortly after World War II, Commissioner Collier was replaced and the Indian Claims Commission Act was passed allowing Indian tribes to sue the United States for redress of grievances, particularly for the loss of lands and broken treaties. Many thought that legal redress for these things and for inhumanities perpetrated against the American Indians was only just.

The Indian Claims legislation also paved the way for a new federal policy whose goal was the dissolution of the BIA and the termination of all treaty obligations of the United States to American Indians. It was argued that once the old scores over land thefts and other inhumanities had been settled and Indians were taught how to spend money wisely, they could make their own way as responsible citizens (see Lurie 1957). . . .

The results of the commission's [Commission on the Rights, Liberties, and Responsibilities of the American Indian] investigation showed the economic position of the Indian about 1960 to be less favorable than that of any other American minority group. Indian income was scandalously low; employment was meager, unstable, and temporary; and the Indian land base was smaller than in the previous decade. Indian health was poor when contrasted with whites, as was Indian housing, education, and local government (see Brophy and Aberle 1966). Relatively nothing had changed for the American Indian since 1934, except that some land had been reacquired, schools had been developed near reservations—about *half* of all funds went to education—the BIA staff had grown, and Indian governments exercised a modicum of control over reservation societies which were poverty-ridden and often pervaded with factionalism. . . .

These statistics lay bare the discrepancy between the non-Indian and Indian norms. In the mid-1960's as in the mid-1920's, despite all programs, the American Indians were relatively as underdeveloped as in the past. Even in a statement of averages, as opposed contrasting the Indian minimum to the non-Indian maximum in education, skills, employment, income, and comforts, Indian conditions are extremely low on all measures and suggest extreme deprivation. The *acculturation* has been to rural poverty and, more recently, urban poverty as well. Surprisingly, the Indians of California on all these measures of the quality of life are *much* better off than their counterparts in other states and *much* closer to the standards of living considered adequate for the average United States citizen than their congeners (SACIA 1966).

The Endemic Poverty of Contemporary Indians

To consider the endemic poverty of United States' Indians generally, we shall contrast California Indians with other groups and assess how Indian family household organizations have adjusted to economic deprivation.

The relative "prosperity" of California Indians is partly due to the self-selected migrants to major urban areas, many of whom have some employment, and to generally high welfare standards observed in that state. For the nation as a whole, the average family income of Indians is $1500 per year, $1300 *less* than for California Indian families and about $2000 *under* the currently specified "poverty line." The unemployment rate is between 40 and 50 percent on almost all reservations; that rate is calculated on the BIA's narrow definition of employability. That pegs the employment rate at 50–60 percent; over half represents temporary or part-time employment, i.e., underemployment.

According to the President's Task Force on American Indians (Brophy and Aberle 1966), the present poverty on Indian reservations and among urban ghetto Indians is deplorable. Housing is grossly dilapidated; the incidence of disease, especially upper respiratory and gastrointestinal forms, is seven or eight times the national average; Indian life expectancy is only two-thirds the national expectancy; and one-third of all adult Indians are illiterate. As youthful populations grow on the reservations, many spill off into the ghettos of urban areas replacing rural poverty with urban poverty. Though adequate statistics on urban Indians are not available, particularly from the BIA—the agency responsible for sending many of them to the cities—it is estimated that 200,000 of the 600,000 American Indians currently live in urban areas.

In contrast to California Indians, 38 percent of whom use contaminated water, the national average of such usage by Indians is 74 percent. Forty-eight percent of California Indian families haul all domestic water, whereas 81 percent is the national average. Seventy-three percent of California Indians have unsatisfactory facilities for disposal of excreta; 83 percent is the national average. All Indian households, as well as the California Indian household, average more than five (5.4) occupants. The average size of Indian houses nationally is less than two rooms. The non-Indian household, however, averages only 2.9 occupants and occupies more than four rooms (SACIA 1966; Wagner and Rabeau 1964; SAUS 1966).

The composition of Indian households differs significantly from the nuclear-family, conjugal-pair, and single-person types that predominate in white America. In California 30 percent of all Indian households are composite, including such combinations of kin and non-kin as grandchildren, nieces and nephews, brothers or sisters of the husband or wife, a married child with spouse or children or both, and even more distantly related kin and affines (in-laws). Sixty-one percent of all California household heads are men and 39 percent are women—the latter being widowed, separated, or divorced. The composition of California Indian households is not an anomaly, but is a regular feature of Indian poverty and poverty in the Western Hemisphere generally.

Though there are no national statistics on the subject, the research of Munsell (1967) among the Salt River Pima-Papago of Arizona, Robbins (1968) among the Blackfeet of Montana, and Jorgensen (n.d.) among Shoshones and Utes on five reservations in Idaho, Wyoming, Colorado, and Utah confirms the California Indian household composition distribution. A difference is that these recent studies demonstrate that there are relatively *more* composite Indian households outside of California than in California, and that those outside of California are also larger. This is to be expected, given the greater average family income for California Indians.

The studies cited above clearly demonstrate that household size varies inversely with the amount and stability of income. The less stable and lower the amount of income among American Indian family households, the larger the households. The explanation for this phenomenon is that people with meager means join together to pool resources. It is better to crowd together under a single roof, or adjacent roofs, and share resources than it is to live apart in less crowded households where resources are less predictable. This grouping together characterizes poverty-stricken households among other ethnic and racial minorities within, as well as outside of, the United States (cf. footnote 2).

Through sharing funds from several diverse sources—welfare (e.g., Aid for Dependent Children, Old-Age Assistance, Federal Aid to the Blind), per capita payments from Indian Claims Commission judgments, lease income from land, wages from part time labor, cash from piece work, goods received as welfare commodities or procured in hunting and fishing—these composite family households have adjusted to their lack of resources. Where nuclear family households occur among American Indians, they usually have a *stable* source of income, males tend to be the household heads, and to a lesser extent, someone in the household is employed.

American Indian family household compositions tend to change in a rather predictable cyclic manner from composite to nuclear. If a son gains regular employment, he and his wife and children move out of his father's home and establish a separate household. In fifteen years or so, this man's nuclear family is likely to become a composite household as his own, or his wife's parents move in to share his resources, or as his own children marry and establish temporary residence in the household.

American Indian composite households and family household cycle are not retentions of aboriginal customs, but are products of their meager and unstable incomes, lack of skills, and lack of control over resources. They do not have money or resources to allow them to cope with life as do the gainfully employed and nonpaternalistically guided lower (working), middle, and upper classes of United States' society. Indian family households change from composite to nuclear to composite as their economic conditions change, making the Indian family similar to other families living in poverty in the Western world. Yet the peculiar niche occupied by the Indians in the American culture of poverty—that of superexploited and paternalistically guided wards of neocolonialism, the vast majority of whom reside on reservations—separates them, say, from the Mestizo in Mexico, the Callampa dwellers in Chile, the rural poor and the Black urban ghetto dwellers in the United States, and the Black Caribs of Latin America and the West Indies.

Although the major problems of American Indians are rooted in economy and polity as are the problems of the other groups mentioned, a difference is that Indians often have resources. But the *access* of American Indians to their resources is severely restricted, and the major exploitation of these resources is carried out by non-Indian local, national, and multi-national corporations.

The Political Economic Niche Occupied by American Indians

A brief survey of the niche of reservations in the national economy reveals that reservations generally have land bases that are arid or semi-arid, and because some segments of the land are tied up in heirship, they are not feasible for development of profitable agribusiness. Moreover, most reservations do not have sufficient land, even if all of it were consolidated, to provide decent livelihoods from agriculture for all inhabitants on those reservations (the rural economies surrounding most reservations are basically agricultural). Reservations are generally located long distances from major markets, big cities, and industrial plants, so there are no large job markets. Moreover, the greater distance to market, the less profitable, generally, the agribusiness on reservations. Reservations are also often located considerable distances from railroads and major highways, making transportation expensive and profitable development of heavy industry on reservations unlikely. Industrial development has been further inhibited because Indian populations are undereducated and underskilled (Brophy and Aberle 1966:62–116).

Rural economies adjacent to reservations in most of the western half of the United States have withered, as large farms in the midwest with access to capital and improvements in technology, including hybrid crops, fertilizers, and pesticides, have become more productive and have grown at the expense of small agricultural operations everywhere. Federal farm policies have worked with the large farm corporations to protect them through price supports and soil-bank payments, encouraging further expansion of large farm corporations to gobble up small farms (USPNACRP 1967). In general, the greater the productivity, the greater the government assistance. Since 1920 the farm population of the United States has decreased by two-thirds and its percentage of the total population has plummeted from 30 to 6. Although the average size of all farms has increased, the number of farms has decreased by more than half since 1920. Since 1940 alone the average size of farms in the United States has increased by well over 200 percent (SAUS 1966:613–624, 1967:608). As examples of federal benefits, in 1967, 43 percent of United States farmers with incomes of less than $2500 per year received 4.5 percent of the federal farm subsidies. On the other hand, 65 percent of federal subsidies went to the *top* 10 percent of earners in the farm production pyramid, most of them being large corporations or food processing trusts. (See USPNACRP 1967 for a complete analysis of the subsidy program, especially the programs designed to "encourage, promote, and strengthen the family farm.")

The livestock business has followed a similar course in the past decade as quasi-cartels are beginning to control all aspects of beef production from feeder lots, to packing houses, to supermarket distribution. Grass-fed (range-fed) mature beef is less and less marketable because of the time needed for fattening the animals for slaughter and the difficulty in controlling the size of range-fed beef. Weight can be controlled on feeder lots, yielding animals of standardized size, and greatly easing slaughtering and packing because the animals can also be fattened quicker. In addition, there is a dwindling demand for grass-fed beef by packing houses and distributors (both processes often carried out by the same corporation) because, they allege, the meat is not sufficiently marbled with fat, and the increased production costs, including transportation for range-fed beef, are pushing the producers of grass-fed beef off the market. This squeezes small operators out of business, especially those in the western United States who are long distances from the main markets.

Though the rural economies around Indian reservations are dwindling and farm consolidation is occurring at a rapid rate, there is some money to be made in agriculture on reservations. The BIA (1968) reports that 170 million dollars were grossed from agriculture on all reserves (50 million acres) in 1966. These figures are rather liberal as they include the *estimated* value of all fish and game taken by Indians on their reservations (perhaps 20 million dollars) and consumed by the procurers, but this modest amount of overes-timating is not the critical point. Of the 170 million dollars, the Indians realized only 58.6 million, 16 million of which was derived from rents and permits to non-Indians. This means that 127.4 million dollars, or 75 percent of the gross from agriculture, went to *non-Indians* who paid Indians 16 million dollars, or roughly 12 percent of their gross, for exploitation of Indian lands.

The BIA statistics clearly reveal what can happen to Indian resources when Indians have neither access to capital nor the skills or adequate counsel to exploit their own resources. Of the estimated 170 million dollars from agriculture in 1966, the Indian share approximates 58.6 million of which 16 million (27 percent) is from leasing to non-Indians, 23 million (39 percent) is from farming and ranching (this too is an estimate and includes all goods produced *and* consumed by Indians), and 19.6 million (34 percent) is from hunting and fishing for their own consumption. There is no way to know how inaccurate the latter two estimates are.

The BIA statistics on further exploitation of Indian resources are also revealing. In 1967 about 803 million board feet of lumber were cut. Only 100 million board feet, or about 12 percent, were processed in tribal sawmills. Indians were selling their natural resources yet maintaining practically no control over production. Timber sale brought 15 million dollars to Indian tribes in 1967. There are no figures pertaining to the non-Indian gross, non-Indian profits, or the costs to Indian tribes to maintain their resources (see BIA 1968).

As for oil and all other minerals, including uranium, sand, gravel, phos-phate, gilsonite, gypsum, coal, limestone, copper, lead, and zinc, the exploi-tation of these resources by national and multi-national corporations brought 31 million dollars to tribal coffers in 1967 through bids and lease royalties. Again, the tribes do not control production and few jobs are generated for Indian employees. Though there are no figures on corporate profits or gross income, the corporations are generating capital for themselves and offering

Indian tribes carrots in the form of lease and royalty incomes, and the Indians are losing their resources.

Finally, since the early 1950's the BIA (1955) has encouraged the location of industries on or near reservations to provide employment for Indians. The emphasis has not been on development of Indian-owned and controlled industries. Tribes have been urged to use their modest amounts of capital from land-claims judgments and mineral royalties to build plants and lease them to private corporations at low rates. The corporations, the Indians have been told, will then move onto the reservations, even though they are a great distance from markets, because they can operate at low costs and use cheap Indian labor.

Nothing much came of this program until 1962 when a few industries moved onto reserves to take advantage of provisions made for them. Between 1962 and 1968, 10,000 jobs were created through the development of industries on or near reserves. Characteristically, 6,000 (60 percent) of these jobs have gone to *non-Indians* (USDI 1968:7). Private corporations are using Indian capital to expand, yet using Indian labor only when it is adequate to the task. Indians do not maintain ownership or control.

"Industrial development" has been mostly talk; development has accrued to industry and not to Indians or Indian-owned and controlled industry. In 1967 private non-Indian development of Indian lands on a lease basis, including all industrial, commercial, and recreational uses, brought 4 million dollars to Indian tribes. Recreation brought 1.9 million dollars of that total (BIA 1968). The irony of this is that whites are paying low-lease fees to exploit Indian lands for white leisure use.

Why are things as they are, even after so much has been done to improve the Indians' lot? From 1955 to 1968 the BIA has grown from 9,500 employees to 16,000 (BIA 1955, 1968). From 1949 to 1969, federal government appropriations for American Indian affairs have increased from 49 million dollars to 241 million (BIA 1949, 1968). In fact, in the 1968–1969 fiscal year, about 430 million dollars were spent on federal programs intended to benefit Indians; yet the average annual income for all Indian families was about $1500.

Part of the failure of Indian policies is attributable to mismanagement by the BIA. For example, the BIA has encouraged the development of livestock operations at a time when quasi-cartels have been taking over the industry, and the bureau has advised tribes to allow non-Indian corporations to exploit Indian resources. But the causes of persistent Indian problems cannot be solely attributed to the BIA. Indeed, the growth of the BIA and the federal budget for Indian affairs are indicative of the more important causes of Indian poverty. Federal welfare institutions and funds have increased as exploitation has continued. The growth of the BIA is an effect of the way in which the national political economy has grown. Poverty is perpetually created and welfare measures are used to heal the most gaping wounds.

A Hypothesis About Indian Underdevelopment: The Metropolis- Satellite Political Economy

The Indians of the United States, in my opinion, have been integrated into the United States political economy since they were conquered. As shown above, Indians are currently deprived and have been deprived for the past several decades. This is not a coincidence or a fortuity; Indian poverty does not represent an evolutionary "stage of acculturation" somewhere between the underdeveloped tabula rasa and the developed non-Indian polity, economy, and society. In my hypothesis, Indian underdevelopment is the product of the full integration of United States Indians into the United States political economic society—albeit as super-exploited victims of that society. . . .

The conditions of the "backward" modern American Indians are not due to rural isolation nor a tenacious hold on aboriginal ways, but result from the way in which United States' urban centers of finance, political influence, and power have grown at the expense of rural areas. The rapid development of urban areas after the mid-nineteenth century brought the Indian social ruin, as measured in status and self-worth; poverty, as measured in access to strategic resources, the distribution of surpluses from one's own region, employment, housing, and general welfare; and political oppression and neocolonial subjugation, as measured by decimation of Indian populations through warfare, the dissolution of aboriginal polities, the loss of self-direction, the lack of access to the locus of political power, the general denial of citizenship (with a few exceptions) until 1924, and the increasing role of the BIA and the Secretary of Interior in approving the conduct of Indian affairs.

These results were brought about by expropriation of Indian land and resources by the railroads, mining corporations, farmers, and ranchers. Economic surpluses were taken from the rural areas, and used for the growth of the metropolis. For instance, from an estimated 16 million bison on the American plains in 1860, the bison population was reduced to about one thousand in 1885 through systematic killing by whites (Klose 1964:79–80) because there was a market for tongues and skins in the eastern United States, and more importantly because the plains could then be farmed and cattle raised without interference from the bison or the Indians who lived off them (Klose 1964:83–84). The railroads, which received vast amounts of right-of-way—i.e., Indian territory—free from the United States government, in turn sold this land to farmers and ranchers. The railroad profited from the sales and later began moving products from these farms and ranches to markets in the east.[3] Indians were the first rural inhabitants to suffer from this development and the first people to be forced into underdevelopment from their previous condition of self-support and self-governance. Mining industries expanded throughout the west from the 1850's to the turn of the century, and they too expropriated Indian land and resources.

With the growth of technology influenced and controlled by the metropolis, particularly as it affected agribusiness and the mineral industries, non-Indian ranchers, farmers, and miners in rural areas, too, became "underdeveloped." For instance, the beef production industry, once based on range-fed cattle, has been revolutionized by development of hybrid crops, feeder lots, mechanized packing techniques, and the growth of large supermarket quasi-cartels which are beginning to control all aspects of production. Since 1935 the man-hours (labor-time) to produce beef (measured in live weight) has been cut nearly in half, and it has been cut by one-fourth since 1959 alone (SAUS 1967:629). Only those producers who control the greatest amount of capital are able to survive. Technology has influenced the grain, vegetable, and cotton industries through mechanization and fertilizers. Again, only the largest producers are able to survive. The small producer is losing his land due to costs or taxes, or both. He cannot get loans because he is a bad risk and the large producer in turn, is consolidating the land made available through the former's liquidation. But this trend is not solely a product of technology and capital; political influence and power, too, are critical in maintaining this trend.

Underdevelopment of rural areas is a product of the development of urban centers of finance and the latter wield considerable influence in enacting legislation to maintain their growth. The mineral industries have long lived under special tax-privilege umbrellas; they have profited from the special-use tax (allowance) applicable to the exploitation of Indian lands, as well as the tax-depletion allowances offered to oil, gas, and mineral producers generally. The influence of the mining lobbies prior to the General Allotment Act and the multi-national oil and mineral corporations in maintaining the privileged tax-depletion and protective import laws that have sheltered them for decades is solid evidence of the relationship between polity and the growth of the metropolis. . . .

As the metropolis grows and the resources of the satellites nourish that growth, many people living in rural areas choose to better their conditions by moving to urban areas. Some are successful, especially if they are white, yet many trade rural poverty for urban poverty. For Indians who stand in a special neocolonial relationship to the rest of society, the latter is usually the case (Price 1968; Hodge 1969, and Graves in this volume). This is not to say that all Indians are doomed to poverty. Just as some native Africans once living in colonial Kenya can for example, be educated at Oxford and through help open businesses in London or Nairobi or even enter the British colonial service, so can some United States Indians move from reservations, gain university educations, and become popular authors or high ranking officials in the Indian Service. But the odds and the context in which both colonial Africans and neocolonial Indians live weigh heavily against such happenings. . . .

To summarize the hypothesis presented here, the growth of the metropolis caused the Indians of the United States to be underdeveloped; Indians did not begin that way. Non-Indians who originally settled in rural areas, expropriated Indian land and the resources thereon, and manned the satellite sector of the economy, met with some success. Yet the past four decades have brought economic reversals for their progeny. Only the largest producers have been able to cope, profitably, with the changes in their industries as the metropolis has grown. As a consequence, out-migration of rural non-Indians has been substantial since 1920, farm and ranch consolidation has been enormous, and rural labor needs have been greatly reduced.

As the satellite economies, especially in the western states, have withered and the threat of economic demise has become more pressing, the non-Indians who own the shops, manage the banks, and operate the ranches and farms in rural areas have hired non-Indians rather than Indians for the permanent and temporary jobs they control. They tend to provide jobs for kin, friends, and others of the same race as the owner or manager. The Indian is most generally a consumer, seldom a wage earner, almost never an owner or controller of the production of anything in the economic satellites. Just as in the initial westward expansion of the metropolis-satellite economy, the Indians have been the first to suffer in the subsequent growth of the economy.

As a corollary, the greater the contribution of a producer to the national farm, ranch, or mining economy, the greater the federal benefits accruing to the producer. Those that have, get. Though the rural areas exert little political influence, any influence that is felt, especially in state government, is that of the non-Indian. Another corollary is that as satellites have withered and small producers have gone bankrupt, those people who contribute least to the economy also exert the least political influence and receive the fewest benefits—usually only welfare assistance. The Indian, who has almost never produced anything, has the least influence and the least control over his own resources and the federal welfare he receives.

Finally, because Indians have few skills, little education, no capital, poor housing, poor health, and no influence or power, they are discriminated against by local non-Indians. The people who took their resources have denied status to Indians and have rebuked their morality because they have not been productive members of the society and because they have been special wards of the federal government. The cycle is vicious. . . .

The modern American Indians are the progeny of the super-exploited Indians of the nineteenth century who were forced to relinquish their territory, their self-governance, and their self-esteem so that the metropolis could grow. Some Indians have worked their way, through one means or another, to regular employment, even to positions of prestige. The average Indian has not. The reasons why he has not have been explicated here: simply enough, the modern exploited.

Notes

1. *Metropolis*, as used in the chapter title is not synonymous with *urban area, location, or city*. The hypothesis advanced in the third part of this chapter reveals its special meaning in this context.

2. See, for example, the following analyses of family household organization among people living in poverty who have little access to resources: Black Caribs of Guatemala and British Honduras (Gonzalez 1969); Mestizos of Latin America (Adams 1960); Blacks of the West Indies (Smith 1962; Otterbein 1965); Mestizos in Mexico and Mexican-Americans (Borah and Cook 1966); and Blacks in the United States (Moynihan 1965).

3. The transcontinental railroad, completed in 1869 with the extensive use of Chinese labor, was such an expensive project that the railroads could not foreseeably pay off their loans from the federal government. The government, in turn, cleared the loans without payment and left ownership in the hands of the railroad "financiers."

Bibliography

ABERLE, DAVID F. 1966. *The Peyote Religion among the Navaho.* Viking Fund Publications in Anthropology, no. 42.

ADAMS, RICHARD N. 1960. "An Inquiry into the Nature of the Family." In *Essays in the Science of Culture,* Gertrude E. Dole and Robert L. Carneiro (eds.). New York: Crowell, pp. 30–49.

BIA (BUREAU OF INDIAN AFFAIRS). 1949. *Answers to Your Questions about American Indians.* Washington, D.C.: U. S. Government Printing Office.
1955 *Answers to Your Questions about American Indians.* Washington, D.C.: U.S. Government Printing Office.
1968. *Answers to Your Questions about American Indians.* Washington, D.C.: U.S. Government Printing Office.

BORAH, WOODROW, and SHERBURN F. COOK. 1966. "Marriage and Legitimacy in Mexican Culture: Mexico and California." In *The Law of the Poor,* Jacobus tenBroek (ed.). San Francisco: Chandler Publishing Company, pp. 622–684.

BROPHY, WILLIAM, and SOPHIE D. ABERLE. 1966. *The Indian: America's Unfinished Business.* Norman: University of Oklahoma Press.

CFEPC (CALIFORNIA FAIR EMPLOYMENT PRACTICE COMMISSION). 1966. "Minority Groups in California." *Monthly Labor Review.* Bureau of Labor Statistics, U.S. Department of Labor.

CHCIIA (CHAIRMAN, HOUSE COMMITTEE ON INTERIOR AND INSULAR AFFAIRS). 1963. *Indian Unemployment Survey.* Committee Print no. 3, 88th Cong., 1st sess.

DELORIA, VINE, JR. 1969. *Custer Died for Your Sins: An Indian Manifesto.* New York: Macmillan.

FRANK, ANDRÉ GUNDAR. 1967. *Capitalism and Underdevelopment in Latin America: Historical Studies of Chile and Brazil.* New York and London: Monthly Review Press.

GONZALEZ, NANCIE L. SOLIEN. 1969. *Black Carib Household Structure*. Seattle: University of Washington Press.

HAAS, THEODORE H. 1957. "The Legal Aspects of Indian Affairs from 1887 to 1957." In *American Indians and American Life. The Annals of the American Academy of Political and Social Sciences*, vol. 311, George Simpson and Milton Yinger (eds.).

HCIIA (HOUSE COMMITTEE ON INTERIOR AND INSULAR AFFAIRS). 1953. *Investigation of the Bureau of Indian Affairs*. United States Congress House Report.
1954. *Investigation of the Bureau of Indian Affairs*. United States Congress House Report.

HODGE, WILLIAM H. 1969. "The Albuquerque Navahos." *Anthropological Papers of the University of Arizona*, no. 11.

INDIAN RECORD. 1968. "Special Issue: Economic Development." *Indian Record*. October, 1968. Department of Interior. Washington, D.C.: U.S. Government Printing Office.

JORGENSEN, JOSEPH G. 1964. "The Ethnohistory and Acculturation of the Northern Ute." Ph.D. dissertation, Indiana University, University Microfilms.
n.d. "Conquest, Neo-colonialism and the Modern Sun Dance Religion of the Shoshones and Utes." Mimeographed.

KLOSE, NELSON. 1964. *A Concise Study Guide to the American Frontier*. Lincoln: University of Nebraska Press.

LURIE, NANCY O. 1957. "The Indian Claims Commission Act." In *American Indians and American Life*, pp. 56-70. *The Annals of the American Academy of Political and Social Sciences*, vol. 311, George Simpson and Milton Yinger (eds.).

MERIAM, LEWIS. 1928. *The Problems of Indian Administration*. Baltimore: The Johns Hopkins University Press.

MOYNIHAN, DANIEL. 1965. *The Negro Family—the Case for National Action*. Office of Policy Planning and Research, United States Department of Labor.

MUNSELL, MARVIN. 1967. "Land and Labor at Salt River." Ph.D. dissertation, University of Oregon, University Microfilms.

OTTERBEIN, KEITH F. 1965. "Caribbean Family Organization: A Comparative Analysis." *American Anthropologist* 67:66-79.

PRICE, JOHN A. 1968. "The Migration and Adaptation of American Indians in Los Angeles." *Human Organization* 27:168-175.

ROBBINS, LYNN A. 1968. "Economics, Household Composition, and the Family Cycle: The Blackfeet Case." *Proceedings of the American Ethnological Society*, Spring, 1968.

SACIA (STATE ADVISORY COMMISSION ON INDIAN AFFAIRS). 1966. "Indians in Rural and Reservation Areas." Submitted to the Governor and Legislature of California. Sacramento.

SAUS (U.S. BUREAU OF THE CENSUS). 1966. *Statistical Abstract of the United States: 1966*. Washington, D.C.: U.S. Government Printing Office.
1967. *Statistical Abstract of the United States: 1967*. Washington, D.C.: U.S. Government Printing Office.

SHANNON, LYLE W. 1969. "The Economic Absorption and Cultural Integration of Immigrant Workers: Characteristics of the Individual vs. the Nature of the System." *American Behavioral Scientist* 13:36-56.

———, AND MAGDALINE SHANNON. 1967. "The Assimilation of Migrants to Cities: Anthropological and Sociological Contributions." In *Urban Affairs Annual Review*, Lyle W. Shannon and Magdaline Shannon (eds.). New York: Sage, pp. 49–75.

SIMPSON, GEORGE, AND MILTON YINGER (EDS.). 1957. *American Indians and American Life. The Annals of the American Academy of Political and Social Sciences*, vol. 311 (May, 1957).

SMITH, M.G. 1962. *West Indian Family Structure*. Seattle: University of Washington Press.

UINTAH AND OURAY AGENCY. 1968. "Report of Labor Force." Submitted to Bureau of Indian Affairs and Department of Labor.

USPNACRP (UNITED STATES PRESIDENT'S NATIONAL ADVISORY COMMISSION ON RURAL POVERTY). 1967. *The People Left Behind*. Washington, D.C.: U.S. Government Printing Office.

USPNACCD (UNITED STATES PRESIDENT'S NATIONAL ADVISORY COMMISSION ON CIVIL DISORDERS). 1968. *Report of the National Advisory Commission on Civil Disorders*. New York: Bantam Books.

UTE INDIAN TRIBE. 1956. "Ten-Year Development Program." Fort Duchesne. Mimeographed.

WAGNER, CARRUTH J., AND ERWIN S. RABEAU. 1964. "Indian Poverty and Indian Health." *Health, Education and Welfare Indicators*. March, 1964.

16

When the Turtle Collapses,
the World Ends

BERNARD NIETSCHMANN

After delivering a lecture on the solar system, philosopher-psychologist William James was approached by an elderly lady who claimed she had a theory superior to the one described by him.

"We don't live on a ball rotating around the sun," she said. "We live on a crust of earth on the back of a giant turtle."

Not wishing to demolish this absurd argument with the massive scientific evidence at his command, James decided to dissuade his opponent gently.

"If your theory is correct, madam, what does this turtle stand on?"

"You're a very clever man, Mr. James, and that's a good question, but I can answer that. The first turtle stands on the back of a second, far larger, turtle."

"But what does this second turtle stand on?" James asked patiently.

The old lady crowed triumphantly, "It's no use, Mr. James—it's turtles all the way down."

IN THE HALF-LIGHT OF DAWN, a sailing canoe approaches a shoal where nets have been set the day before. A Miskito turtleman stands in the bow and points to a distant splash that breaks the gray sheen of the Caribbean waters. Even from a hundred yards, he can tell that a green turtle has been caught in one of the nets. His two companions quickly bring the craft alongside the turtle, and as they pull it from the sea, its glistening shell reflects the first rays of the rising sun. As two men work to remove the heavy reptile from the net, the third keeps the canoe headed into the swells and beside the anchored net. After its fins have been pierced and lashed with bark fiber cord, the 250-pound turtle is placed on its back in the bottom of the canoe. The turtlemen are happy. Perhaps their luck will be good today and their other nets will also yield many turtles.

These green turtles, caught by Miskito Indian turtlemen off the eastern coast of Nicaragua, are destined for distant markets. Their butchered bodies will pass through many hands, local and foreign, eventually ending up in tins, bottles, and freezers far away. Their meat, leather, shell, oil, and calipee, a gelatinous substance that is the base for turtle soup, will be used to produce goods consumed in more affluent parts of the world.

The coastal Miskito Indians are very dependent on green turtles. Their culture has long been adapted to utilizing the once vast populations that inhabited the largest sea turtle feeding grounds in the Western Hemisphere. As the most important link between livelihood, social interaction, and environment, green turtles were the pivotal resource around which traditional Miskito Indian society revolved. These large reptiles also provided the major source of protein for Miskito subsistence. Now this priceless and limited resource has become a prized commodity that is being exploited almost entirely for economic reasons.

In the past, turtles fulfilled the nutritional needs as well as the social responsibilities of Miskito society. Today, however, the Miskito depend mainly on the sale of turtles to provide them with the money they need to purchase household goods and other necessities. But turtles are a declining resource; overdependence on them is leading the Miskito into an ecological blind alley. The cultural control mechanisms that once adapted the Miskito to their environment and faunal resources are now circumvented or inoperative, and they are caught up in a system of continued intensification of turtle fishing, which threatens to provide neither cash nor subsistence.

I have been studying this situation for several years, unraveling its historical context and piecing together its past and future effect on Miskito society, economy, and diet, and on the turtle population.

The coastal Miskito Indians are among the world's most adept small-craft seamen and turtlemen. Their traditional subsistence system provided dependable yields from the judicious scheduling of resource procurement activities. Agriculture, hunting, fishing, and gathering were organized in accordance with seasonal fluctuations in weather and resource availability and provided adequate amounts of food and materials without overexploiting any one species or site. Women cultivated the crops while men hunted and fished. Turtle fishing was the backbone of subsistence, providing meat throughout the year.

Miskito society and economy were interdependent. There was no economic activity without a social context and every social act had a reciprocal economic aspect. To the Miskito, meat, especially turtle meat, was the most esteemed and valuable resource, for it was not only a mainstay of subsistence, it was the item most commonly distributed to relatives and friends. Meat shared in this way satisfied mutual obligations and responsibilities and smoothed out daily and seasonal differences in the acquisition of animal protein. In this way, those too young, old, sick, or otherwise unable to secure meat received their share, and a certain balance in the village was achieved: minimal food requirements were met, meat surplus was disposed of to others, and social responsibilities were satisfied.

Today, the older Miskito recall that when meat was scarce in the village, a few turtlemen would put out to sea in their dugout canoes for a day's harpooning on the turtle feeding grounds. In the afternoon, the men would return, sailing before the northeast trade wind, bringing meat for all. Gathered on the beach, the villagers helped drag the canoes into thatched storage sheds. After the turtles were butchered and the meat distributed, everyone returned home to the cooking fires.

Historical circumstances and a series of boom—bust economic cycles disrupted the Miskito's society and environment. In the seventeenth and eighteenth centuries, intermittent trade with English and French buccaneers—based on the exchange of forest and marine resources for metal tools and utensils, rum, and firearms—prompted the Miskito to extend hunting, fishing, and gathering beyond subsistence needs to exploitative enterprises.

During the nineteenth and early twentieth centuries, foreign-owned companies operating in eastern Nicaragua exported rubber, lumber, and gold, and initiated commercial banana production. As alien economic and ecological influences were intensified, contract wage labor replaced seasonal, short-term economic relationships; company commissaries replaced limited trade goods; and large-scale exploitation of natural resources replaced sporadic, selective extraction. During economic boom periods the relationship between resources, subsistence, and environment was drastically altered for the Miskito. Resources became a commodity with a price tag, market exploitation a livelihood, and foreign wages and goods a necessity.

For more than 200 years, relations between the coastal Miskito and the English were based on sea turtles. It was from the Miskito that the English learned the art of turtling, which they then organized into intensive commercial exploitation of Caribbean turtle grounds and nesting beaches. Sea turtles were among the first resources involved in trade relations and foreign commerce in the Caribbean. Zoologist Archie Carr, an authority on sea turtles, has remarked that "more than any other dietary factor, the green turtle supported the opening up of the Caribbean." The once abundant turtle populations provided sustenance to ships' crews and to the new settlers and plantation laborers.

The Cayman Islands, settled by the English, became in the seventeenth and eighteenth centuries the center of commercial turtle fishing in the Caribbean. By the early nineteenth century, pressure on the Cayman turtle grounds and nesting beaches to supply meat to Caribbean and European markets became so great that the turtle population was decimated. The Cayman Islanders were forced to shift to other turtle areas off Cuba, the Gulf of Honduras, and the coast of eastern Nicaragua. They made annual expeditions, lasting four to seven weeks, to the Miskito turtle grounds to net green turtles, occasionally purchasing live ones, dried calipee, and the shells of hawksbill turtles (*Eretmochelys imbricata*) from the Miskito Indians. Reported catches of green turtles by the Cayman turtlers generally ranged between 2,000 and 3,000 a year up to the early 1960s, when the Nicaraguan government failed to renew the islanders' fishing privileges.

Intensive resource extraction by foreign companies led to seriously depleted and altered environments. By the 1940s, many of the economic booms had turned to busts. As the resources ran out and operating costs mounted, companies shut down production and moved to other areas in Central America. Thus, the economic mainstays that had helped provide the Miskito with jobs, currency, markets, and foreign goods were gone. The company supply ships and commissaries disappeared, money became scarce, and store-bought items expensive.

In the backwater of the passing golden boom period, the Miskito were left with an ethic of poverty, but they still had the subsistence skills that had maintained their culture for hundreds of years. Their land and water environment was still capable of providing reliable resources for local consumption. As it had been in the past, turtle fishing became a way of life, a provider of life itself. But traditional subsistence culture could no longer integrate Miskito society and environment in a state of equilibrium. Resources were now viewed as having a value and labor a price tag. All that was needed was a market.

Recently, two foreign turtle companies began operations along the east coast of Nicaragua. One was built in Puerto Cabezas in late 1968, and another was completed in Bluefields in 1969. Both companies were capable of processing and shipping large amounts of green turtle meat and by-products to markets in North America and Europe. Turtles were acquired by purchase from the Miskito. Each week company boats visited coastal Miskito communities and offshore island turtle camps to buy green turtles. The "company" was back, money was again available, and the Miskito were expert in securing the desired commodity. Another economic boom period was at hand. But the significant difference between this boom and previous ones was that the Miskito were now selling a subsistence resource.

As a result, the last large surviving green turtle population in the Caribbean was opened to intensive, almost year-round exploitation. Paradoxically, it would be the Miskito Indians, who once caught only what they needed for food, who would conduct the assault on the remaining turtle population.

Another contradictory element in the Miskito–turtle story is that only some 200 miles to the south at Tortuguero, Costa Rica, Archie Carr had devoted fifteen years to the study of sea turtles and to the conservation and protection of the Caribbean's last major sea turtle nesting beach. Carr estimates that more than half the green turtles that nest at Tortuguero are from Nicaraguan waters. The sad and exasperating paradox is that a conservation program insured the survival of an endangered species for commercial exploitation in nearby waters.

Green turtles, *Chelonia mydas*, are large, air-breathing, herbivorous marine reptiles. They congregate in large populations and graze on underwater beds of vegetation in relatively clear, shallow, tropical waters. A mature turtle can weigh 250 pounds or more and when caught, can live indefinitely in a saltwater enclosure or for a couple of weeks if kept in shade on land. Green turtles have at least six behavioral characteristics that are important in their exploitation: they occur in large numbers in localized areas; they are air breathing, so they have to surface; they are mass social nesters; they have an acute location-finding ability; when mature, they migrate seasonally on an overlapping two- or three-year cycle for mating and nesting; and they exhibit predictable local distributional patterns.

The extensive shallow shelf off eastern Nicaragua is dotted with numerous small coral islands, thousands of reefs, and vast underwater pastures of marine vegetation called "turtle banks." During the day, a large group of turtles may be found feeding at one of the many turtle banks, while adjacent marine pastures may have only a few turtles. They graze on the vegetation, rising periodically to the surface for air and to float for awhile before diving again. In the late afternoon, groups of turtles will leave the feeding areas and swim to shoals, some up to four or five miles away, to spend the night. By five the next morning, they gather to depart again for the banks. The turtles' precise, commuterlike behavior between sleeping and feeding areas is well known to the Miskito and helps insure good turtling.

Each coastal turtling village exploits an immense sea area, containing many turtle banks and shoals. For example, the Miskito of Tasbapauni utilize a marine area of approximately 600 square miles, with twenty major turtle banks and almost forty important shoals.

Having rather predictable patterns of movement and habitat preference, green turtles are commonly caught by the Miskito in three ways: on the turtle banks with harpoons; along the shoal-to-feeding area route with harpoons; and on the shoals using nets, which entangle the turtles when they surface for air.

The Miskito's traditional means of taking turtles was by harpoon—an eight- to ten-foot shaft fitted with a detachable short point tied to a strong line. The simple technology pitted two turtlemen in a small, seagoing canoe against the elusive turtles. Successful turtling with harpoons requires an extensive knowledge of turtle behavior and habits and tremendous skill and experience in handling a small canoe in what can be very rough seas. Turtlemen work in partnerships: a "strikerman" in the bow; the "captain" in the stern. Together, they make a single unit engaged in the delicate and almost silent pursuit of a wary prey, their movements coordinated by experience and rewarded by proficiency. Turtlemen have mental maps of all the banks and shoals in their area, each one named and located through a complex system of celestial navigation, distance reckoning, wind and current direction, and the individual surface-swell motion over each site. Traditionally, not all Miskito were sufficiently expert in seamanship and turtle lore to become respected "strikermen," capable of securing turtles even during hazardous sea conditions. Theirs was a very specialized calling. Harpooning restrained possible overexploitation since turtles were taken one at a time by two men directly involved in the chase, and there were only a limited number of really proficient "strikermen" in each village.

Those who still use harpoons must leave early to take advantage of the land breeze and to have enough time to reach the distant offshore turtle grounds by first light. Turtlemen who are going for the day, or for several days, will meet on the beach by 2:00 A.M. They drag the canoes on bamboo rollers from beachfront sheds to the water's edge. There, in the swash of spent breakers, food, water, paddles, lines, harpoons, and sails are loaded and secured. Using a long pole, the standing bowman propels the canoe through the foaming surf while the captain in the stern keeps the craft running straight with a six-foot mahogany paddle. Once past the inside break, the men count the dark rolling seas building outside until there is a momentary pause in the sets; then with paddles digging deep, they drive the narrow, twenty-foot canoe over the cresting swells, rising precipitously on each wave face and then plunging down the far side as the sea and sky seesaw into view. Once past the breakers, they rig the sail and, running with the land breeze, point the canoe toward a star in the eastern sky.

A course is set by star fix and by backsight on a prominent coconut palm on the mainland horizon. Course alterations are made to correct for the direction and intensity of winds and currents. After two or three hours of sailing the men reach a distant spot located between a turtle sleeping shoal and feeding bank. There they intercept and follow the turtles as they leave for specific banks.

On the banks the turtlemen paddle quietly, listening for the sound of a "blowing" turtle. When a turtle surfaces for air it emits a hissing sound audible for fifty yards or more on a calm day. Since a turtle will stay near the surface for only a minute or two before diving to feed, the men must approach quickly and silently, maneuvering the canoe directly in front of or behind the turtle. These are its blind spots. Once harpooned, a turtle explodes into a frenzy of action, pulling the canoe along at high speeds in its hopeless, underwater dash for escape until it tires and can be pulled alongside the canoe.

But turtle harpooning is a dying art. The dominant method of turtling today is the use of nets. Since their introduction, the widespread use of turtle nets has drastically altered turtling strategy and productivity. Originally brought to the Miskito by the Cayman Islanders, nets are now extensively distributed on credit by the turtle companies. This simple technological change, along with a market demand for turtles, has resulted in intensified pressure on green turtle populations.

Buoyed by wooden floats and anchored to the bottom by a single line, the fifty-foot-long by fourteen-foot-wide nets hang from the surface like underwater flags, shifting direction with the current. Nets are set in place during midday when the turtlemen can see the dark shoal areas. Two Miskito will set five to thirty nets from one canoe, often completely saturating a small shoal. In the late afternoon, green turtles return to their shoals to spend the night. There they will sleep beside or beneath a coral outcrop, periodically surfacing for air where a canopy of nets awaits them.

Catching turtles with nets requires little skill; anyone with a canoe can now be a turtleman. The Miskito set thousands of nets daily, providing continuous coverage in densely populated nocturnal habitats. Younger Miskito can become turtlemen almost overnight simply by following more experienced men to the shoal areas, thus circumventing the need for years of accumulated skill and knowledge that once were the domain of the "strikermen." All one has to do is learn where to set the nets, retire for the night, remove the entangled turtles the next morning, and reset the nets. The outcome is predictable: more turtlemen, using more effective methods, catch more turtles.

With an assured market for turtles, the Miskito devote more time to catching turtles, traveling farther and staying at sea longer. Increased dependence on turtles as a source of income and greater time inputs have meant disruption of subsistence agriculture and hunting and fishing. The Miskito no longer produce foodstuffs for themselves; they buy imported foods with money gained from the sale of turtles. Caught between contradictory priorities—their traditional subsistence system and the market economy—the Miskito are opting for cash.

The Miskito are now enveloped in a positive feedback system where change spawns change. Coastal villages rely on turtles for a livelihood. Decline of subsistence provisioning has led to the need to secure food from local shopkeepers on credit to feed the families in the villages and the men during their turtling expeditions. Initial high catches of turtles encouraged more Miskito to participate, and by 1972 the per person and per day catch began to decline noticeably.

In late 1972, several months after I had returned to Michigan, I received a letter from an old turtleman, who wrote: "Turtle is getting scarce, Mr. Barney. You said it would happen in five or ten years but it is happening now."

Burdened by an overdependence on an endangered species and with accumulating debts for food and nets, the Miskito are finding it increasingly difficult to break even, much less secure a profit. With few other economic alternatives, the inevitable step is to use more nets and stay out at sea longer.

The turtle companies encourage the Miskito to expand turtling activities by providing them with building materials so that they can construct houses on offshore cays, thereby eliminating the need to return to the mainland during rough weather. On their weekly runs up and down the coast, company boats bring food, turtle gear, and cash for turtles to fishing camps from the Miskito Cays to the Set Net Cays. Frequent visits keep the Miskito from becoming discouraged and returning to their villages with the turtles. On Saturdays, villagers look to sea, watching for returning canoes. A few men will bring turtle for their families; the majority will bring only money. Many return with neither.

Most Miskito prefer to be home on Sunday to visit with friends and for religious reasons. (There are Moravian, Anglican, and Catholic mission churches in many of the villages.) But more and more, turtlemen are staying out for two to four weeks. The church may promise salvation, but only the turtle companies can provide money.

Returning to their villages, turtlemen are confronted with a complex dilemma: how to satisfy both social and economic demands with a limited resource. Traditional Miskito social rules stipulate that turtle meat should be shared among kin, but the new economic system requires that turtles be sold for personal economic gain. Kin expect gifts of meat, and friends expect to be sold meat. Turtlemen are besieged with requests forcing them to decide between who will or will not receive meat. This is contrary to the traditional Miskito ethic, which is based on generosity and mutual concern for the well-being of others. The older Miskito ask why the turtlemen should have to allocate a food that was once abundant and available to all. Turtlemen sell and give to other turtlemen, thereby insuring reciprocal treatment for them-

Distribution of Turtle Meat by Gift and Purchase

PERCENT OF VILLAGERS*	POUNDS RECEIVED PER PERSON
18	10–14+
28	6–9
32	2–5
22	0–1.9

During the one-month period from April 15 to May 15, 1971, 125 green turtles were caught by the turtlemen of Tasbapauni, Nicaragua. Of these, 91 were sold to turtle companies; the remaining 34 were butchered and the meat sold or given to villagers. In all, 3,900 pounds of turtle meat were distributed, but 54 percent of the villagers received 5 pounds or less, an insufficient amount for adult dietary protein requirements.
* Population of 998 converted to 711 adult male equivalents.

selves, but there simply are not enough turtles to accommodate other economic and social requirements. In order to have enough turtles to sell, fewer are butchered in the villages. This means that less meat is being consumed than before the turtle companies began operations. The Miskito presently sell 70 to 90 percent of the turtles they catch; in the near future they will sell even more and eat less.

Social tension and friction are growing in the villages. Kinship relationships are being strained by what some villagers interpret as preferential and stingy meat distribution. Rather than endure the trauma caused by having to ration a limited item to fellow villagers, many turtlemen prefer to sell all their turtles to the company and return with money, which does not have to be shared. However, if a Miskito sells out to the company, he will probably be unable to acquire meat for himself in the village, regardless of kinship or purchasing power. I overheard an elderly turtleman muttering to himself as he butchered a turtle: "I no going to sell, neither give dem meat. Let dem eat de money."

The situation is bad and getting worse. Individuals too old or sick to provide for themselves often receive little meat or money from relatives. Families without turtlemen are families without money or access to meat. The trend is toward the individualization of nuclear families, operating for their own economic ends. Miskito villages are becoming neighborhoods rather than communities.

The Miskito diet has suffered in quality and quantity. Less protein and fewer diverse vegetables and fruits are consumed. Present dietary staples—rice, white flour, beans, sugar, and coffee—come from the store. In one Miskito village, 65 percent of all food eaten in a year was purchased.

Besides the nutritional significance of what is becoming a largely carbohydrate diet, dependence on purchased foods has also had major economic reverberations. Generated by national and international scarcities, inflationary fallout has hit the Miskito. Most of their purchased foods are imported, much coming from the United States. In the last five years prices for staples have increased 100 to 150 percent. This has had an overwhelming impact on the Miskito, who spend 50 to 75 percent of their income for food. Consequently, their entry into the market by selling a subsistence resource, diverting labor from agriculture, and intensifying exploitation of a vanishing species has resulted in their living off poorer-quality, higher-priced foods.

The Miskito now depend on outside systems to supply them with money and materials that are subject to world market fluctuations. They have lost their autonomy and their adaptive relationship with their environment. Life is no longer socially rewarding nor is their diet satisfying. The coastal Miskito have become a specialized and highly vulnerable sector of the global market economy.

Loss of the turtle market would be a serious economic blow to the Miskito, who have almost no other means of securing cash for what have now become necessities. Nevertheless, continued exploitation will surely reduce the turtle population to a critical level.

National and international legislation is urgently needed. At the very least, commercial turtle fishing must be curtailed for several years until the *Chelonia* population can rebound and exploitation quotas can be set. While turtle fishing for subsistence should be permitted, exportation of sea turtle products used in the gourmet, cosmetic, or jewelry trade should be banned.

Restrictive environmental legislation, however, is not a popular subject in Nicaragua, a country that has recently been torn by earthquakes, volcanic eruption, and hurricanes. A program for sea turtle conservation submitted to the Nicaraguan government for consideration ended up in a pile of rubble during the earthquake that devastated Managua in December, 1972, adding a sad footnote to the Miskito—sea turtle situation. With other problems to face, the government has not yet reviewed what is happening on the distant east coast, separated from the capital by more than 200 miles of rain forest—and years of neglect.

As it is now, the turtles are going down and along with them, the Miskito—seemingly, a small problem in terms of the scale of ongoing ecological and cultural change in the world. But each localized situation involves species and societies with long histories and, perhaps, short futures. They are weathervanes in the conflicting winds of economic and environmental priorities. As Bob Dylan sang: "You don't need a weatherman to tell which way the wind blows."

17

Notes on Women, Work, and Society

LEITH MULLINGS

ONE OF THE MOST PERNICIOUS THEORIES that has, for centuries, consistently promoted and rationalized the differential access of human beings to the resources of society is that of genetic determinism. In its various forms, this view serves to justify the ranking of people on the basis of class, race, ethnicity and sex. It suggests that such distinctions have biological implications, determining potential, ability and, ultimately, life chances. This concept serves to rationalize the sentiment that categories of people, defined by class, race and gender, are relegated to certain tasks and socioeconomic levels because their biological programming limits them to such statuses.

That there are anatomical differences between males and females is undisputed; what remains very much at issue is the meaning of this differentiation. In general, genetic determinists have argued that biological differences have "natural" consequences, that the division of labor—usually some variant of the home/work, private/public dichotomy—and, indeed, the inequalities between men and women have a genetic origin and therefore will persist in some form regardless of the structural arrangements of society. Much of the cross-cultural and historical data calls such a view into question. In this chapter, I will review some of the evidence which suggests that the sexual division of labor and the ideology of sex roles are not ultimately

I would like to thank Jean Carey Bond and Eleanor Leacock for reading and commenting on this paper.

determined by biological constraints, but by the structural arrangements of a given society.

Upon examination of the cross-cultural evidence, anthropologists of very different perspectives find that in general, the way in which labor is divided between the sexes is so diverse that it is difficult to correlate the division of tasks with the biological or physical attributes of either sex.[7, 11, 12] We find that assignments vary from one culture to another. Such tasks as agriculture, animal herding, marketing, or the transporting of heavy loads are performed by women in some cultures and by men in others. Whatever the nature of the division of labor, however, the rationale for it is usually biological. For example, the Arapesh say that women have stronger heads than men and it is the women rather than the men who transport heavy loads on their heads. The Kota of India claim that women have stronger heads, but weaker arms; women carry all loads on their heads while men carry the loads in their arms.[7] Even within the same geographical area, neighboring societies may make different assignments of sex-related roles: Navaho women in the southwest United States do the weaving, but among the neighboring Pueblos, weaving is undertaken by the men.[7]

It is not necessary to look to other societies to find that assignment of sex-segregated tasks are more related to the exigencies of historical development than to biological differences. Blau[3] notes that in the sex-segregated United States, the gender composition of occupations is subject to regional variation. For example, in the Midwest cornhuskers are traditionally women, while trimmers are always men; in the Far West, cornhuskers are men and trimmers are women. An occupation that is predominantly female in one industry may be predominantly male in another; thus, in electrical machinery equipment and supplies, the 1960 census reported that 67% of the assemblers were women, while in motor vehicles and motor vehicle equipment only 16% of the assemblers were women.

The correlation between anatomical differences and sex-related tasks, then, is far from clear. Historically, the major exception seems to be hunting, which was thought to be almost universally assigned to men, leading investigators to conclude that the biological fact of women's reproductive capacities constrained their ability to hunt, determining this initial division of labor. Sociobiologists have taken this further to suggest that because the early division of labor revolves around the anatomical difference between males and females, it is likely to persist in all types of societies:

> In hunter-gatherer societies men hunt and women stay home. This strong bias persists in most agricultural and industrial societies, and on that ground alone appears to have a genetic origin. . . . My own guess is that the genetic bias is intense enough to cause a substantial division of labor even in the most free and most egalitarian of future societies . . . even with identical education and equal access to all professions, men are likely to continue to play a disproportionate role in political life, business and science.[21]

Recent evidence calls many of these assumptions into question. In a provocative account of the evolution of the family and women's roles, Lila Liebowitz argues persuasively that the early division of labor was molded by socioeconomic considerations, not by biological imperatives in and of themselves.[12] Greatly simplified, her argument runs as follows: rather than the division of labor whereby men hunt and women gather and care for the children being a "natural" and perpetual outcome of anatomical differences, the sexual division of labor was the result of specific socioecological transformations. It is not the case, as is generally assumed, that women were excluded from all types of hunting.[1] The division of labor was associated with the development of hunting with projectile weapons—pursuing and killing large mobile animals—as opposed to earlier forms of hunting, such as drives, individual hunting of small game or "surround" hunting. It was in the specific conditions where meat became a regular part of the diet and resources were scarce, thus making dispersal into small groups a necessity, that projectile hunting was associated with a sexual division of labor. As the ability to remain inconspicuous and to surprise the animal was key in this type of hunting, small groups became more efficient, as opposed to surround or drive hunting where large groups were required to surround or drive the animal.

It was with the development of these socioecological circumstances, characterized by small groups and projectile hunting, that a woman with children found herself encumbered as a hunter. Nursing children must be fed and young children need constant care. In a small social unit having few nursing mothers and in which a nursing mother could not easily count on another nursing mother for care of her children, the assignment of men to hunt and women to gather and take care of the children becomes predictable, practical and adaptive. Moreover, since men cannot nurse children, the loss of a woman in the relatively dangerous occupation of hunting would have been more serious than the loss of a man. Since effective hunting requires a certain skill acquired through training, differential training and socialization of the sexes established, reinforced and perpetuated this division of labor.

If Liebowitz's assertions are valid, it seems that while anatomical differences determined which sex cared for the children, the necessity for a sexual division of labor arose not from biological or genetic imperatives, but became necessary only as a result of a particular configuration of ecological, economic and historical transformations. Thus, the sexual division of labor might not be "natural" and therefore enduring, but social and subject to change as social arrangements change. Numerous studies have pointed to the impact of such factors as private property, the evolution of the state, and warfare on the status of women, often transforming the division of labor into relationships of domination and subjugation. (For example, see[8, 9, 14, 17].)

Although the evidence is not yet all in and reconstruction of earlier epochs must be undertaken with caution, a glance at the history of women's roles in the United States suggests similar conclusions: that it is not biology, but society which ultimately determines the division of labor. The sexual division of labor has not been fixed, but has varied according to historical circumstances, and it has been very different for different classes. During the colonial period, although in England and Europe women were routinely employed as mowers, reapers and haymakers,[3] in the colonies among the non-slave population, agricultural tasks were primarily the domain of men, with women being employed in the household industries, and producing most of the colonies' manufactured goods. As labor shortages increased with the invasion of the frontier, the division of labor was modified to fit the needs of the society. Indeed, the transformation occurred during the journey itself. At the beginning of the westward journey, sex tasks were rigidly segregated; by mid-journey, due to the vicissitudes of the "Trail," most women worked at male tasks.[2] Increasing land shortages in the evolving frontier society found women in a variety of non-traditional occupations, including tavern keepers, traders, printers and publishers, as well as the more traditional domestic ones.[3] Despite the separation between the home and the workplace which industrialization fostered, women played a crucial role in the development of the factory system. With the introduction of the power loom in 1814 and the creation of the textile industry, women—working class women—comprised the bulk of this industrial work force. At various points during the 19th and 20th centuries, labor shortages, fluctuations in demand and technical innovations resulted in a shift toward greater numbers of female employees in such industries as shoe manufacturing, teaching, cigar making and clerical work. It appears that the question of whether or not women were in the home, of what they did or did not do, has been more related to class than to sex, determined by society rather than biology.

The discrepancy between the roles of women of different classes has perhaps been greater than that between men and women of the same class. While femininity was described in terms of non-participation in the labor force, and upper class women were allegedly fainting in parlors, immigrant working class women were laboring 12 hours a day in factories and Afro-American women were toiling for 16 hours or more in the fields. While womanliness was projected as intertwined with homemaking, and although single women comprised the majority of working women, the working wife seems to have been more prevalent than is generally assumed. An annual report of the Massachusetts Bureau of Statistics, cited in the April 1875 *Scientific American*, concluded on the basis of visits with 397 families that in the majority of cases working men did not support their families by their own earnings alone but depended on their wives and children for from one-fourth to one-third of the family earnings.

Perhaps the most dramatic, and heroic, example of the discrepancy between the ideology which holds that divisions of labor are biologically rooted, and the actual divisions that the socioeconomic system and the class position determine, is that of Afro-American women. Under conditions of chattel slavery where the goal was the greatest exploitation of labor, while the "flowers of southern womanhood" languished in plantation parlors, Afro-American women often did the same work as men—under conditions that no human being, male or female, should be subjected to.[10] The contradiction between the ideology of "women's place" as determined by their biology and what Afro-American women were actually doing is movingly described in Sojourner Truth's address to the Akron Convention for women's suffrage:

> That man over there says that women need to be helped into carriages, and lifted over ditches, and to have the best place everywhere. Nobody ever helps me into carriages, or over mud-puddles or gives me any best place, and am I not a woman? Look at me! Look at my arm. I have ploughed, and planted, and gathered into barns, and no man could head me! And am I not a woman? I could work as much and eat as much as a man—when I could get it—and bear the lash as well! And am I not a woman? I have borne thirteen children, and seen them most all sold off to slavery, and when I cried out with my mother's grief, none but Jesus heard me! And am I not a woman?[19] (2)

The effects of racism against Afro-American men and women in the areas of employment and wages, have compelled Afro-American women, since "emancipation," to work to help support themselves and their families, and their labor force participation has always exceeded that of Euro-American women.(3) Despite the desire of Afro-American married women to withdraw from the labor force after slavery, large numbers of rural women were forced to labor, alongside men, as field hands (relatively few worked as servants or washerwomen—occupations that were more common among urban Afro-Americans).[5]

While their long history of labor force participation may produce more egalitarian arrangements within the household, Afro-American women remain the most exploited in the public arena, receiving the lowest returns for the sale of their labor. The Census Department calculated that in 1973, the median annual income of minority women was 49.6% that of white men (as compared to 56.3% for Euro-American women(4)). This is primarily a result of the disproportionate confinement of Afro-American and other minority women to the lowest paying sectors of the labor force.(5) The examples of Afro-American and other working class women dramatically demonstrate the discrepancy between their roles as determined by the division of labor and the ideology that "the woman's place is in the home."

The relationship between the ideology of the division of labor—how differential roles of men and women are rationalized and explained—and the way in which these beliefs relate to the actual social relationships deserves much more elaborate treatment than I am able to undertake here. However, I would like to speculate a bit on how the ideology bears on the position of Afro-American and other working class women. We have noted that throughout the history of the United States, the normative notions of what a woman ought to be have tended to be a description of what upper class women were able to be. Rayna Rapp has portrayed the way in which upper class women, unlike all other women in society, have no need to work and therefore can present themselves as ideal wives, mothers and representatives of "high culture."[17] These women, who "become symbols of domesticity and of public service," influence our notions of what feminine behavior should be. The ideology of the division of labor, then, is often far removed from the reality of the experience of minority and other working women, yet it remains the cultural ideal, often buttressed by the canons of religion and rationalized as "natural" by the genetic explanations of science.

To bridge the gap between the ideology of sex roles and the real division of labor, between the biological gender of these women and their status as slaves and workers, requires a new ideological twist. In contemporary society, this takes the familiar form of blaming the victim: sex roles ideology is used by apologists for the social system to castigate women workers, and thus rationalize and deepen their oppression. The cynical theoretical circularity of the argument is most evident in the case of Afro-American women. African women, along with men, were captured, torn from their families, and forced into slave labor, without regard for the niceties of gender differentiation. (Of course, the ideological rationale at that time was to limit the definition of what was human—another pinnacle of genetic determinism.) After emancipation, Afro-American women were coerced, by necessity and otherwise, into the labor force. Gutman[5] reports numerous local situations where planters complained about the lack of cheap field labor because women did not want to work and wished to be supported by their husbands. One Louisiana planter instructed that rent be charged to any non-working wives of ex-slaves. Today, the effects of racism—wage and employment discrimination; the high rate of death and disability of Afro-American men as a result of poor health facilities, disproportionate death from war and more dangerous work conditions—as well as many other stressors of poverty, continue to force Afro-American women into the work force. In general, they do not have the option of choosing whether or not they wish to work. These women, who must work to ensure the survival of their families, are then attacked as "matriarchal."[13] Just as the ideology of racism bridges the gap between the folk belief of an open society with equal opportunity and the superexploitation of Afro-American labor, the ideology of the "castrating" Afro-American woman obscures the role of the socioeconomic system in oppressing them and, further, bridges the contradiction between sex role ideology and the actuality of what women in fact do. To the extent that the ideas of the ruling class become the ruling ideas of society, in the same way that the ideology of racism has confused and divided the working class, sex roles ideology penetrates the home and the workplace. In the home, where the wage paid by the employer will not support the subsistence of the family and the woman must work, tensions and strains arise from the inability of both spouses to "live up to" the role model as defined by the ruling class; in the workplace, it divides those who should be united.

It seems clear that the expression of the division of labor, while rationalized in terms of biological, genetic and personality differences, is ultimately determined by social conditions. There is much disagreement among social scientists about which configuration of social processes is most relevant to explicating the status of women, which I will not recount here. (See Amsden[1] for a discussion of the various economic explanations; these models also have their counterparts in the sociology literature.) While the point of production is not the only arena in which the inequality of women is expressed, the division of labor, its establishment and its perpetuation seem to be rooted in the productive processes, as well as in the relationship of the household to the resources of society. With this in mind, I will briefly indicate some of the functions served by the inequality of contemporary U.S. women in the workplace. (See Rapp,[17] for a discussion of the household.)

In a social system based on the accumulation of profit through the exploitation of labor, the sexual division of labor seems to function to strengthen that system and to increase profits. Clearly, sex-segregated occupations and less pay for the same work maximize profits. One well-documented example of this practice in process was the case of the American Telephone and Telegraph Company, whose discriminatory practices were investigated by the Equal Employment Opportunity Commission (EEOC). The EEOC report estimates that wage discrimination against women, through which AT&T was able to hold wages down and increase profits, amounted to $422 million a year in 30 metropolitan areas.[16] The widespread nature of such discriminatory practices is indicated in the male/female wage differential; women earn approximately 60% of what men earn.[1]

With the growth of an organized labor movement and labor militancy, where it is not always possible to put short-term profit-maximizing strategies into effect, the existence of components of the labor force that are subject to discriminatory practices may serve other functions. Because marginally and underemployed people have fewer options and a higher rate of unemployment, they constitute a "reserve army of unemployed" who can be utilized to inhibit wages and benefits demands of employed workers. Unemployment among women is 50% higher than among men, with the unemployment rate of minority women in the last quarter of the century averaging 80% above that of Euro-American women.[1] Again the AT&T

case illustrates the way in which this process operates. The EEOC report cites an AT&T Vice President Walter Straley's explanation of why, after years of discrimination, AT&T finally hired minority women: "What a telephone company needs to know about its labor market (is) who is available for work paying as little as $4,000 to $5,000 a year. It is therefore just a plain fact in today's world, telephone company wages are more in line with Black expectations—and the tighter the labor market the more this is true."[20] The report analyzes the results of this practice:

> The Operator job is, quite pointedly, a *horrendous* (italics theirs) job. No greater testimony to this fact exists than the unbelievably high rate at which employees bolt from the job. The Bell System's response is amazing: *rather than restructure the job, improve the wages and provide important new avenues for promotion and transfer*—changes which even common sense would suggest—*AT&T has decided to keep the wages depressed and simply hire more and more Black females* (italics mine).
>
> The inevitable effects of these policy decisions are all too obvious. Most of the Blacks in the Bell System will never have a real chance at a good job. The economic realities of the labor market will force large numbers of Blacks to apply for operator jobs. After all, *any* job is better than no job, any job except operator. The realities of the operator job will thus force Blacks to quit as fast as they are forced to apply.[20]

Since a large majority of the employees were white, we can surmise that the ability of AT&T to hire Afro-American workers, and particularly Afro-American women, at a lower wage and worse working conditions, because of their lack of options resulting from discrimination, contributed to AT&T's ability to hold down the salary and benefit level of white women workers to the level at which they could hire Afro-American women. Where males and females work at the same job, or where male workers can be replaced by female workers, this process can also be applied to male workers.

The threat of replacement, as well as the characterizations that are components of contemporary sex roles ideology, vaunting men as superior to women, insisting that the woman's place is in the home and that they are taking jobs from men, can be utilized to divide the working class and inhibit the formation of unified working class organizations that could, presumably, struggle more effectively for greater control of the workplace and better conditions for everyone. To make a case for the way in which the sexual inequality of women functions to increase profits does not require a "conspiracy theory." Although "conspiracy" among corporate interests undoubtedly occurs, overt collusion is not a precondition to perceiving their common interests and pursuing similar actions to advance those interests.

It is also possible for workers to perceive their common interests. The extent to which differences between men and women, among ethnic groups and populations, can be utilized to divide them and increase the profits of employers, depends on the extent to which people are organized to prevent it from occurring. Hopefully, the ability of corporations such as AT&T to perpetuate these circumstances will decrease as women are increasingly organized into trade unions and women's groups concerned with advancing the interests of women, in the context of the class struggle and the struggle against racism. It is interesting to note that Afro-American women have frequently assumed leadership roles in such organizing.[4, 10, 19] Of course, the success of such efforts will depend on the extent to which working people are able to unite in their own interests, across gender lines and race boundaries. It is interesting to note that the necessity for unity was proclaimed by the Colored National Labor Union, when it convened in 1869, in response to the exclusion of Afro-Americans from Euro-American unions. Upholding the rights of women in industry and unions, the Committee on Women's Labor recommended: "profiting by the mistakes heretofore made by our white fellow citizens in admitting women. . . . that women be cordially included in the invitation to further and organize cooperative societies."[4] While "the mistakes" have certainly not by any means been fully corrected, the necessity for unity is increasingly recognized. Most interesting are the scattered incidents where workers have been able to use protective legislation[(6)] measures designed for women in such a way as to extend them to increase benefits and protection for male workers as well.

In summary, then, it is undisputed that there are anatomical differences between men and women. However, what these differences come to mean, the significance they assume in a given society, appears to be determined not by the nature of the differences themselves, but by the way in which the society is organized. In a society where profit is the driving force, anatomical differences between males and females, like culture history differences between ethnic groups and phenotypic differences between populations, are utilized in such a way as to support that system and maximize profits. Where such differences converge, as in the case of Afro-American women, oppression will be particularly intense.[15]

Policy implications, then, must relate to changing the basic structure of the socioeconomic system. While all forms of gender asymmetry will not disappear once the social system ceases to be organized around profit, this seems to be the first step in creating the foundation for change. Explanations that do not account for the role of the social system in determining the division of labor, whether they attribute sexual inequality to the anatomy of women or to the congenital dispositions of men, ultimately function to assist in reproducing the socioeconomic system that so defines the division of labor, and divides the people who are oppressed by it. If gender inequality is socially, not naturally, determined the first step in eradicating inequality is addressing the system that profits from it—putting people before profits. Because the destinies of working people, men and women, are economically, politically and socially inextricably linked, this requires the unity of all working people and oppressed minorities, men and women, to create a better world for all our children.

Notes

(1) I would like to thank Eleanor Leacock for pointing out that the "exclusion" of women from hunting large game among gathering-hunting populations is a popular, but undocumented, stereotype. She notes that although men do most of the hunting, data on the Inuit and native Americans of the Canadian subarctic and for some Australian groups indicate that women hunt large game when they need or want to.

(2) This was originally recorded at the Akron Convention of the women's suffrage movement [in 1851] where Sojourner Truth said these words. I have taken the liberty of using "standard" English.

(3) In 1890 the labor force participation for white women was 16.3% compared to 39.7% for non-white women; however, the labor force participation rate for married white women was 2.5%, compared to 22.5% for married non-white women.[6] In 1948 31% of all Euro-American women and 45% of all non-white women were in the labor force;[3] by 1973, 3 out of 5 Afro-American women worked for wages or salary as compared to approximately half of Euro-American women.[16] While the differential between Afro-American and Euro-American women has been narrowing in recent years, the difference in the overall impact of the work experience can be understood more accurately if we examine in addition to marital status, the proportion of women working in specific age groups. In the 25–34 year range—the principal childbearing years—there is a sharp decline in the participation in the labor market of Euro-American women, but an increase in Afro-American women's participation; these are the years when the presence of children makes working more difficult, but for some, more necessary. It is in this age range that the excess of Afro-American women over Euro-American women reaches its peak, with 61.1% of Afro-American women working, as compared with 48.6% of Euro-American women.[16]

(4) There has been some confusion about the differential income of Afro-American women that has resulted from comparison of aggregate annual incomes of Euro-American and Afro-American women. Often these statistics, used to suggest that Afro-American women's wages are higher than those of Euro-American women, do not take into consideration the fact that a greater number of Euro-American women are able to afford to work part-time and to find suitable part-time work. In 1973, 35.5% of the number of full-time employed Euro-American women worked part-time by choice as compared to 24.5% of the number of Afro-American women employed full-time.[16]

(5) The U.S. Women's Bureau, in a survey of four states reported that prior to 1929 the Afro-American working woman averaged $300 annually or $6 per week. In 1955, 6 out of 10 Afro-American women worked in domestic and service jobs, with only 20% in industrial sales and office jobs, in which 59% of the Euro-

American women were employed.[4] In the last 15 years, the occupational distribution of Afro-American women workers has dramatically changed, with a move away from domestic work and a shift into clerical, professional and factory work.[16] However, although there have been gains related to social status, these have not necessarily registered as equivalent economic gains. In 1959, the median earnings of male clerical workers were $4,785; ten years later, the median annual earnings of female clerical workers were $4,232, and of Afro-American female clerical workers $4,152.[16]

(6) The issue of protective legislation is a very complex one. While it is true that protective legislation has been used in some cases to discriminate against women workers, it is also true that some of the measures ensure minimal protection against the hazards of the workplace, and thus offer some protection to women workers. Where women's movements have been dominated by intellectuals, professionals and housewives, the hazards faced by working class women, particularly those in industry, have not been understood nor considered. Where protective legislation is not clearly discriminatory, rather than seek to eliminate those few protective measures against the hazards of the workplace that are in existence, a more useful approach might be to fight to enact those protective measures and to extend them to all workers.

References

1. AMSDEN, A., *An Overview of the Economics of Women and Work.* New York: Center for the Social Sciences, Columbia University, 1978.

2. BERNARD, J., Historical and Structural Barriers to Occupational Desegregation. In *Women and the Workplace,* M. Blaxall and B. Reagan, eds. Chicago: University of Chicago Press, 1976.

3. BLAU, F., The Data on Women Workers, Past, Present and Future. In *Women Working,* A. Stromberg and S. Harkess, eds. California: Mayfield Publishing Company, 1978.

4. FONER, PHILIP, *Organized Labor and the Black Worker 1619–1973.* New York: International Publishers, 1974.

5. GUTMAN, HERBERT, *The Black Family in Slavery and Freedom.* New York: Pantheon Books, 1976.

6. GOLDIN, CLAUDIA, Female Labor Force Participation: *The Origin of Black and White Differences, 1870 and 1880: Journal of Economic His:* XXXVII: 87–1977.

7. HAMMOND, D. and A. JABLOW, *Women in Cultures of the World.* California: Cummings Publishing Company, 1976.

8. HARRIS, MARVIN, *Cannibals and Kings.* New York: Random House, 1977.

9. LEACOCK, E., Women's Studies in Egalitarian Society: Implications for Social Evolution. In *Current Anthropology* 19:247–255, 1978.

10. LERNER, GERDA, *Black Women in White America.* Pantheon Books, New York, 1972.

11. LEVI-STRAUSS, CLAUDE, The Family. In *Family in Transition,* A. and J. Skolnick, eds. Boston: Little, Brown, 1971.

12. LIEBOWITZ, L., *Females, Males, Families: A Biosocial Approach.* Massachusetts: Duxbury Press, 1978.

13. MOYNIHAN, P., Employment, Income & the Ordeal of the Negro Family. *Daedalus* 94:745-770, 1965.

14. MULLINGS, L., Women and Economic Change in Africa. In *Women in Africa,* N. Hafkin and E. Bay, eds. Stanford: Stanford University Press. California, 1976.

15. MULLINGS, L., Ethnicity and Stratification in the United States. In *Annals of the New York Academy of Sciences* 318:10-22, 1978.

16. PERLO, VICTOR, *Economics of Racism.* New York: International Publishers, 1975.

17. RAPP, R., Family and Class in Contemporary America. In *Science and Society* XLII:278-300, 1978.

18. REITER, RAYNA RAPP, The Search for Origins: Unraveling the Threads of Gender Hierarchy. In *Critique of Anthropology* 9 & 10: 5-24, 1977.

19. ROSSI, A., ed. *The Feminist Papers.* New York: Bantam Books, 1973.

20. U.S. Equal Employment Opportunity Commission, 'A Unique Competence': A Study of Employment Opportunity in the Bell System. In *Congressional Record,* February 17, 1972, pp. E 1260-E 1261.

21. WILSON, E., Human Decency is Animal. In *The New York Times Magazine,* October 12, 1975.

18

The "Maquila" Women

PATRICIA FERNANDEZ-KELLY

AFTER SHE WAS DESERTED by her husband of only two years, Rosario went to live with her mother, Mariana. Her young brother, Gerardo, and two aunts, Kica and Julia, also live there with their two children. Kica and Julia are production workers at clothing maquiladoras, as is Rosario. They work to support themselves and their children while Rosario works in the hope of moving to a better home and affording her brother a better education than the one she was able to get herself. They all live now in a drab, two-room adobe house in Juárez, Mexico, in sight of the shimmering skyline of downtown El Paso, Texas. Despite her youth, Rosario must always consider her family's situation:

> When I see my mother and aunts laugh and chat, I wish we were always happy. But the truth is that we have many problems. My mother wants to move to a different area because the barrio is full of idle bums. They have no jobs. There are a lot of unemployed men in this city. Mother does what she can to take care of the house and the children because neither Kica nor Julia can afford a place of their own.
>
> Both Kica and Julia were living here when I ran away with Carlos. He was my last hope! I wanted to get married because I thought my situation could only improve. Carlos was a student of architecture then. The first time we went out he took me to 'Cafe d'Europa' and ordered strawberries with cream. I had two servings, just like an elegant lady in a romantic novel. At sixteen I became pregnant and Carlos married me shortly afterwards. Then things changed. Even before the death

of my baby, Carlos had started to drink. He dropped out of school and could not support me. When he finally left me there was nothing to do but look for factory work. I was fortunate to land a job at RCA. They were expanding production and hiring people; all women.

Many could not be placed because they didn't have enough education. But I went to school for nine years and have some knowledge of typing and shorthand. For a time I thought management would find me a position as a receptionist or secretary, but you need to speak English to even be considered for that, so I guess I'll have to just keep on doing assembly work.

My shift runs from 6:30 in the morning to 3:30 in the afternoon from Monday to Friday. On Saturdays I work from 6:30 to 11:30 a.m.—forty-eight hours in total every week. On Fridays I get paid 1,001 pesos (slightly less than $43). I give my mother half of my weekly wage. Transportation, meals at the factory and personal expenses take care of the rest. I am buying a stereo system. At least I can purchase that for myself. As long as I work, I don't think I will get married again.

Rosario's story does not differ significantly from that of thousands of Mexican women employed by maquiladoras. She is young, single and childless, lacking support from either father or spouse. Like many women doing assembly work in Ciudad Juárez—especially those in the apparel sector—Rosario belongs to a female-headed household with children. (Even more frequent is the case of the young daughter who contributes to the support of both parents and siblings.) Although fathers, brothers, husbands and other male relatives may live under the same roof with these young women, evidence indicates that the majority are either unemployed or underemployed.

Seen in the context of Latin America, maquiladora workers represent a relatively recent and unusual occurrence. In Mexico as a whole, less than 1% of the women who work in the industrial sector get jobs as direct production operators.[1] In Ciudad Juárez, by contrast, almost half of the *total* work force is composed of women who work as maquila operators (85% of the maquiladora work force is female).

In the Mexican-American border area, racial, ethnic, national and religious differences are generally non-existent. Gender takes their place as a way to divide the labor force. Like Blacks or Latinos in the United States, women are preferentially hired to perform some of the worst paid and least rewarding jobs. This preference depends on stereotypes of and prejudice directed against the group in question.[2] Of course, from the point of view of the maquiladora managers, the prevailing ideological conception of women workers provides the necessary flexibility that adaptation in a fiercely competitive international market demands.[3] Their identification as submissive and supplementary income-earners tends to prevent women from acquiring legitimate status and being able to retain their jobs over extended periods of time.[4]

The two main industrial sectors making up the maquiladoras—electronics and apparel—offer very different conditions. The former, a relatively stable and capital-intensive sector, results in highly selective employment practices, i.e., women should be single, 17 to 25 years old, childless and with at least six years of formal education (compared to the average 3.8 years for Mexican workers in general).[5] In many cases workers must be available for morning and night shifts, and to get the job must pass one or several manual dexterity tests and a pregnancy exam. Such selective recruitment policies can be implemented due to the abundance of women searching for jobs in an environment where unemployment and underemployment reaches 30 %.[6]

In apparel, on the other hand, the precarious nature of the industry, due to intense competition, combined with a relatively low capital investment per plant, means that it tends to employ workers whose position in the local labor market is weaker than those hired in electronics. There are a larger number of older women (their average age is 26 as opposed to 20 for workers in the electric/electronic branch); many are single mothers who represent the only means of support for their children. Many have sought employment after being deserted by their husbands or after losing economic support from men belonging to their households. Indeed, one third of all women in apparel manufacturing in Ciudad Juárez are heads of households.[7] They also have lower average levels of schooling than workers in electronics.

A large number of assembly workers in the maquilas (some 70%) migrated to Ciudad Juárez, but only 3% came from a rural environment, and their average length of residence in Ciudad Juárez is 14 years, having typically arrived in the city as children in the company of their family. Only a small proportion left their hometowns as unaccompanied young women with the explicit purpose of finding a job in the city.

Many have taken courses in commercial academies or have studied to become professionals such as nurses or computer technicians. Yet particularly in electronics, the majority (60%) of the women had held no prior jobs, and in the apparel sector, approximately 30% were employed for the first time. Of the others, many had been maids, either in Ciudad Juárez or, usually without documents, in El Paso.

Among those interviewed, the consensus was that maquiladora work offered the best employment alternative in Ciudad Juárez, a striking revelation inasmuch as assembly operators earn an hourly wage of $1.00 and work 48 hours a week. Domestic work in the U.S. border towns is more rewarding and clerical work is more prestigious, but maquila work is less risky than the former and requires less training than the latter. Despite the rigorous work pace and inconvenient schedule, the subsistence wages and the access to medical care for themselves and their dependents—one of the "fringe benefits"—are vital to these women.[8]

This is particularly true given the size and age composition of their households. While the average number of household members in Ciudad Juárez is 5.3, the average for maquila workers is seven, three or four of whom are likely to be under 14 years of age.[9] Even more important is that the majority of men belonging to the same household are either unemployed or underemployed due to the scarcity of viable employment alternatives for men.

The result of this convergence of economic realities has been the swift transformation of women into the main providers of stable and regular income for their families. The pertinent question then becomes: how does the participation of women in wage labor affect family structure and organization? In a country in which, for better or worse, women aspire and are encouraged to become mothers and/or housewives, does factory work necessarily indicate an expansion of alternatives for women or their families? In short, will it bring about an improvement of women's political and economic position within and outside the household?

Maquila Mythologies

Impressionistic judgments and lack of empirical information have joined to generate a particular mystique, a nascent folklore, around maquiladora work and workers. What is noteworthy about these perceptions is their profound ambivalence toward female employment and its consequences. Women workers are trapped both by traditional suspicions about their participation in the world outside of home and family, and by corporate programs designed to reinforce the submissive "feminine" behavior that they have been taught all their lives. According to one common opinion, for example, the maquiladora program has effected a kind of "emancipation" by affording women the opportunity to earn their own income. Women, it is argued, can now spend money on clothes, jewelry and entertainment. This has led to the proliferation of clothing stores, discotheques and bars, an avalanche of consumer advertising in local newspapers, and a swarm of seductive opportunists waiting at the plant gates on payday.

On the other hand, critics of maquilas claim that a role reversal takes place which undermines traditional patterns of male authority and the overall cohesion of the family. Not only is this seen to have deleterious effects upon the "house husband's" sense of manhood, but it is also deplored for the alleged negative effect it has on the welfare of children. According to this view, as women gain economic power, daughters begin to challenge the authority of parents, wives refuse to comply with the demands of their husbands and, in general, disrespect for "traditional values" becomes rampant. This is extended to accusations of growing promiscuity and moral looseness among maquila workers. As a young woman working at an electronics components plant expressed with worry, "There are those who treat you differently as soon as they know you have a job at a maquiladora. Maybe they think that if you have to work, there is also a chance you're a whore."

Public relations managers for the maquiladoras have countered these accusations by pointing to specific policies implemented to reaffirm the value of femininity and a stable family life. Some companies offer courses on human sexuality, birth control and home economics to their workers. Annual beauty contests are held and, in many plants, operators receive red carnations on St. Valentine's Day. As is clear by these maneuvers, corporate-style "liberation" and more traditional expressions of women's oppression thus reinforce each other, defining the ideological framework within which real conflicts and fears are allowed to be articulated.

Myth and promotional hype aside, the employment of women in these transnational assembly plants has not inevitably led to gains in autonomy. Nor is there any indication of significant variations in family mores. In the vast majority of cases, single daughters live with their parents and siblings while these continue to hold traditional positions in the family hierarchy. Fathers are sources of authority. Mothers take care of daily domestic expenses and are responsible for housework. It is not uncommon for a young maquila worker to promptly transfer all her weekly wage to her mother, who in turn gives her a small allowance for essentials. Indeed, only in a very small number of cases are other housing arrangements found, e.g., young women living with other single friends with whom they share expenses.

Women's employment has not decreased their responsibility for domestic chores. Of more than 100 married workers interviewed, only one lived in a situation where her male companion had taken full charge of housework and child care while she acted as sole provider. In the majority of cases, women have a double work load.

Nina, for example, was employed at CENTRALAB, one of the largest electric manufacturers in Juárez. Although she had worked there almost three years, she was still on "temporary" status, enabling management to circumvent seniority and indemnification stipulations. For a time, Nina's husband, Manuel, was employed at the same plant. His earnings were being saved to buy a larger house, a goal to which both of them longingly aspired. When Manuel was fired from CENTRALAB, he did not take over any part of the domestic chores. He searched on and off for a job but was unable to find one. Finally he crossed the border without documentation. For three months he was employed as a maintenance worker in a factory in Phoenix, Arizona.

While Nina worked the morning shift, her two pre-school children remained in the care of an elderly acquaintance—even when Manuel was at home. She paid 100 pesos for babysitting out of her weekly wage of 875 pesos (roughly $4 out of $37). Nina would retrieve the children on her way home from work and stop at the barrio store to buy groceries. She would then cook dinner and tidy up the small adobe house which they leased for 500 pesos ($20 a month). On Saturdays, Nina washed and ironed clothes. She also put her background as a beautician to use by cutting and setting her neighbor's hair.

Although Manuel sometimes drank in excess and beat Nina occasionally, she earnestly prayed for his return from the United States. But when he finally returned with the intent of moving the family to Arizona, Nina was reluctant and afraid; she would have to leave her whole family behind. Nevertheless, she deferred, and on a Sunday afternoon, someone helped them cross the border at a relatively unsupervised spot.

Nina's not uncommon experience clearly does not suggest a shifting sense of shared responsibilities, nor an increase of women's participation in decision-making—either on the job or in the household—as a result of their factory employment.

More difficult to evaluate is the connection that some see between maquiladora work and a change in sexual mores. Extensive interviews with maquila workers indicate that their perceptions, attitudes and aspirations conform to traditional feminine definitions. Women often see their working status as temporary. They eagerly anticipate the prospect of marriage and motherhood, linked to their retirement from the work force. More importantly, they share a conventional differentiation between "decent" and "indecent" female behavior. To be confused for a prostitute is cause for grave preoccupation.

However, "decency" may be a difficult asset to preserve. The limited economic options of working class women is the reality in which they must come to terms with their sexual identity. Sexual harassment on the job is not uncommon; in many cases women complain that middle management and supervisory personnel ask for sexual favors in exchange for job security. Women are particularly vulnerable to advances made by men who have a superior status in the professional, economic and educational hierarchy. Some women, seeing their sexuality as the only viable means to gain access to employment, offer themselves to men in decision-making positions. Some evidence indicates that loyalties won through romantic entanglement can be fruitfully used by employers to insure efficiency and docility on the job. Thus it moves from a moral issue to one with vivid practical consequences.

In sum, the feeble economic and political position that women have in Ciudad Juárez has fettered any advances in consciousness these women have achieved as a result of their experiences. They have thus far been unable to erode female subordination, challenge established norms, or even achieve solidarity on the basis of class and gender. Mague, a maquila worker, summed up the predicament that she and her sisters confront on a daily basis: "No matter how you look at it, we are in a bind. Either as husbands, lovers or managers, men have power over us."

Notes

1. G. Gonzalez Salazar, "Participation of Women in the Mexican Labor Force," in June Nash and Helen I. Safa, eds., *Sex and Class in Latin America* (New York: Praeger, 1976), p. 188.

2. Helen I. Safa, "Multinationals and the Employment of Women in Developing

Areas: The Case of the Caribbean," Paper prepared for the Latin American Studies Association (Pittsburgh, 1979) and "Class Consciousness Among Working-Class Women in Latin America: Puerto Rico," in Nash and Safa, eds., *Sex and Class.*

3. Raúl Trajtenberg and J.P. Sajhau, "Las empresas transnacionales y el bajo costo de la fuerza de trabajo en los paises subdesarrollados," *Working Paper No. 15* (Geneva: International Labor Organization, World Employment Program Research, 1976); "U.S. Runaway Shops on the Mexican Border," *NACLA's Latin America & Empire Report,* Vol. IX, no. 5 (May–June 1975); "Capital's Flight: The Apparel Industry Moves South," *NACLA's LA & ER,* Vol IX, no. 3 (March 1977); and "Electronics: The Global Industry," *NACLA's LA & ER,* Vol. XI, no. 4 (April 1977).

4. Safa, "Multinationals and Employment;" and "Women, Production and Reproduction in Industrial Capitalism: A Comparison of Brazilian and U.S. Factory Workers," (mimeo, no date). See also June Nash, "Certain Aspects of the Integration of Women in the Development Process: A Point of View," Conference Background Paper—World Conference on the International Women's Year (New York: United Nations, 1975).

5. J. Bayer, "Unidad coordinadora para el empleo, capacitación y adiestramiento," Address before the Regional Convention of "Maquiladora" Associations (Ciudad Juárez, February 9, 1979).

6. J. R. Newton and F. Balli, "Mexican In-Bond Industry," Paper presented at the Seminar on "North-South Complementary Intra-Industry Trade" (Mexico City: UNCTAD, United Nations Conference, 1979), p. 11. See also, D. Nayar, "Transnational Corporations and Manufactured Exports from Poor Countries," *Economic Journal,* No. 88 (1977), pp. 59-84, and K. Martin and P. Tallock, *Trade and Developing Countries* (London: Croom Helm, 1977).

7. The empirical information about "maquiladora" workers in Ciudad Juárez included in the following pages is based on preliminary results of a sample survey conducted by Maria Patricia Fernandez-Kelly between September 1978 and February 1979. A random sample of 510 women working as direct production operators at 14 plants were extensively interviewed on questions of migration, income distribution and family composition.

8. By Mexican law all "maquiladora" direct production workers are affiliated to the Instituto Mexicano del Seguro Social (the Mexican Social Security System) and earn the minimum wage.

9. University of Texas, El Paso, *The Ciudad Juárez Plan for Comprehensive Socio-Economic Development: A Model for Northern Mexico Border Cities,* 1977.

Political Systems

There is no society without political processes, that is without some means by which individuals and groups obtain and use power. Even in the absence of formal political organizations, political organizing takes place in all societies. And in every society, even in the absence of formal leadership, we can identify people in the act of leading others.

In examining political systems cross-culturally, we must be particularly conscious of the pitfalls of an ethnocentric view. Our own political system is such a complex one that it is easy to forget that our local and national political offices, our written and highly technical laws, and our multifaceted international relations are only the particular forms by which we address the same basic political issues that all people confront. In other words, a two-party system, an electoral college, judges, courts, prisons, permanently armed forces, a state department, and a foreign diplomatic service are the *forms* that reflect the particular ways in which American society handles two universal problems: maintaining order within the society and regulating relations with other societies.

There is a considerable range in the ways the societies traditionally studied by anthropologists take care of their political affairs. At one end of the political continuum are those societies such as the Khoisan !Kung of the Kahalari desert (see Sahlins' article in the section on economic systems). Organized into bands of related kin, with no more than twenty to fifty people, and subsisting by hunting and gathering, there is no permanent centralized authority. And yet there are influential individuals who exercise their power in regulating internal !Kung affairs and relations with other bands. Skilled hunters and religious practitioners often fulfill this role. In short, how the !Kung carry out the universal political processes (maintaining internal order and sovereignty from outside forces) is in fact embedded in the nature of their social and economic systems.

Anthropologists have also described a number of societies as "tribes without rulers." Among peoples such as the Tiv and the Nuer of Africa (see Bohannan's article on the Tiv in the section on economic systems), political processes are associated with a particular form of patrilineal kinship organization known as the segmentary lineage.* When there is a conflict involving two closely related patrilineal villages, the local kinship units must resolve the issue. But when the conflict involves people who reside at a greater distance, residents of the nearby villages will band together against a similarly organized unit that stands on the opposite side of the dispute.

Whereas political organization among bands is based on the extended family, and among other groups it is based on the unilineal descent group, peoples of Melanesia and the New Guinea highlands entrust certain political responsibilities to "big men," entrepreneurial leaders who gain respect and support through the redistribution of wealth in feast-giving and exchange. When production is intensified and population density increases along with control over valuables, these leaders do more than command influence; the differences between them and other men widen to the point where they represent an incipient class.

In yet other societies the incipient class position of the "big men" is fully developed and power and authority are legitimized into chiefdomships. In these societies, such as the chiefdoms of Africa and the Hawaiian Islands, there is a clear association between the centralization of authority in a chief and his control over the process of economic redistribution. However, chieftainship tends to be hereditary, and thus political leadership is still tied to kinship.

These three political organizational levels—bands, tribes, and chiefdoms—are referred to as stateless forms of political organization. They stand in contrast to the state level of organization, where political institutions are centralized and reach an internal complexity and coherence, and where bureaucratic organization is highly developed. The state may not hold absolute power, but it alone has the right to exercise force and coercion of the population. The state has a territory within which it is sovereign. It can extract labor for civic and military purposes, and it can collect revenues. The state also has the responsibility to provide public services. The state's right to rule is legitimized by ideology.

---

*In a segmentary lineage system descent is defined by categories with reference to more and more remote ancestors—and thus the descent categories constitute a treelike structure.

Whether the state is that of the United States, the Ashanti of West Africa before British colonization, or the princely states of India under the invading Mughals, these complex levels of organization exhibit a number of distinctive patterns: densely populated urban units, intensive agriculture, advanced specialization, and an unequal distribution of surpluses.

The characteristics of a state are illustrated in John Beattie's description of the Bunyoro of the Republic of Uganda. With the British conquest in 1890 the Bunyoro kingdom lost its independence and underwent considerable changes. However, when Beattie conducted his anthropological research between 1952 and 1955, the traditional Bunyoro state had not totally disappeared as an independent political entity.

The Bunyoro state, like other African states, is referred to as feudal because of its resemblances to the political systems of medieval Europe. The Bunyoro state, as is characteristic of all states, monopolized the right to make crucial political decisions, and this right was enforced through its extensive administrative apparatus and the threat of sanctions that it alone could impose. Thus we see that political organizations range from that of hunting and gathering bands, such as the !Kung on the one end of the continuum, to that of modern industrial states, such as the United States on the other end.

We turn now to the political processes that constitute "law." In doing so, we do not escape the problem of definitions which indeed seems to haunt any consideration of behavior in cross-cultural perspective. For legal processes are more clearly defined and distinguishable from other processes in complex societies such as our own than in the tribal world. But struggling with what in fact is a minimal definition (of a legal process) is worth the battle, for it permits us to understand our own society, as well as those of other peoples, more pointedly.

In a society such as our own, where social relationships are of course a part of daily life but material goods are plentiful (although not equally distributed) and valued, a great deal of what constitutes a legal process has to do with breaches of norms about *things:* money and property. In the tribal world, where of course there are material goods associated with everyday affairs but kin and other social relationships are of paramount importance, many of the legal processes involve breaches of what is expected (required) within a given social relationship.

The size as well as the type of political organization in a society greatly affects the options available to individuals and groups seeking to redress a breach of norms. Take, for example, the continent of Africa. In certain chiefdoms and states in Africa the legal process can be as elaborate as that in our own society. Certain African societies have traditionally had hierarchial court systems. Anthropologists have described complex court litigations for the Lozi and the Tswana of south-central Africa. Among other peoples, such as the Kpelle of Liberia, the formal court system is supplemented by an informal process known as the moot—an ad hoc grouping of concerned kin and neighbors who function much like the New England town meeting.

As Gibbs explains in his article in this section, the Kpelle have a developed political structure of towns, districts, and regional chiefs which is paralleled by a hierarchy of formal courts. But a formal court system is not the Kpelle-preferred way to settle disputes among kin and neighbors, for too often a court settlement leaves the litigants polarized. Thus the Kpelle turn to a highly effective means of dispute settlement for individuals who must maintain good social relations: the "house palaver" or moot.

In those parts of Africa without formal political structures "above and beyond" kinship units, conflict resolution relies on individual and kin-group responses: what we might call "self-help justice," where the wronged individual or group has the right to take matters into their own hands; ordeals, where the dispute is settled by calling on supernatural forces to intervene; and contests, where, among the Tiv of Nigeria, a dispute is settled on the basis of who wins a song duel.

All of these responses to a breach of norm, custom, or law are considered legal processes, because the goal in each instance is to serve "justice" as defined by the society. This may involve the payment of a fine, excommunication from the group, imprisonment, or death—each of which is believed to restore order, whether by reconciliation, compensation, or punishment.

Some of the complexities of power and dispute settlement in our own society are discussed in the articles by Collins and Morgen. In each of the two U.S. settings described, there is an explicit analysis of racial, gender, and class dynamics and conflict and attempts to settle differences and disputes. In his analysis of a garbage strike in Memphis, Tennessee, in 1968, Collins documents how racial discrimination and class tensions were instrumental in the creation of urban conflict. Morgen shows how egalitarian principles, consensus decision making and assumed shared gender experiences were in contradiction with the increasing hierarchal structure, division of labor, as well as racial and class divisions within a feminist health clinic.

Anthropologists have devoted far less attention to the study of political relations between societies than within a given society, but from the literature that does exist we can make a few cross-cultural generalizations. Conflicts between societies are conducted in basically two ways: peacefully and violently. Efforts for peaceful resolutions of intergroup conflicts involve, cross-culturally, the use of mediation, intergroup laws, and diplomacy.

Although there are many anthropological—and other—theories about the cause or causes of war, there is considerable agreement among anthropologists and other social scientists that warfare is often, if not always, related to the control of scarce or strategic resources. One of the most explicit analyses of this relationship between war and resources is that of Andrew Vayda (1961), in which he suggests that warfare between horticultural societies is often brought on by population pressures on scarce land resources. As anthroplogists turn to the study of warfare in modern states, they have also postulated a relationship between armed conflict and economic resources, holding that wars are fought to protect raw materials and markets abroad.

From his review of the available literature (1970) Otterbein has also suggested that warfare is no more frequent in state-level political societies than in tribal societies. But the scale is of course drastically different, because a state has a far more specialized and complex military organization and far more sophisticated weapons than a tribal society. Small-scale tribal societies use spears, clubs, bows, and arrows in conflicts between various bands and tribes. Often, both sides will withdraw when there is serious injury to a combatant. Because of the relatively low population of tribal societies, the total casualty rate from warfare can be significantly higher in modern states, but the proportion of the population killed in battle may be higher in tribal societies. For example, it is calculated that among the Murgin of Australia, 28 percent of all male deaths occur in combat or as a result of it.

However, there is something distinctively different about modern warfare among the highly industrialized nations of today: at no other time in history has the possibility existed for the total destruction of humankind through the use of nuclear bombs. And therefore at no other time have we so deeply needed an understanding of the circumstances that create conflict and the possibilities for peaceful resolutions.

References

OTTERBEIN, KEITH. 1970. *The Evolution of War.* New Haven: Human Relations Area Files.

VAYDA, ANDREW. 1969. "The Study of the Causes of War, with Special Reference to Head Hunting Raids in Borneo." *Ethnohistory* 16:211–24.

19

The Bunyoro: An African Kingdom

J. BEATTIE

Rituals of Kingship

SOMETHING HAS ALREADY BEEN SAID of the kingship, and in the last chapter
we followed the fortunes of the most famous of Nyoro kings, the redoubtable
Kabarega. We now examine the Nyoro monarchy first as the symbol of
Nyoro nationhood, the focus of Nyoro ideas about political authority, and
second, as the center of the network of social relations which is what we mean
when we talk about the political system. Therefore in the first part of this
chapter I consider the ways in which the kingship is traditionally regarded;
this will entail a discussion of its ritual character. In the second part I discuss
the king's actual relationships with the different kinds of people who make up
Nyoro society; this will enable us to determine his position in the social
structure. Throughout, our main interest is in the present-day situation. But
we cannot understand this unless we understand the traditional elements
which still persist. What I describe is still in important respects a traditional
African monarchy, but it has been much modified by European influence,
and in the course of my account I shall take note of these modifications. This
will reflect the manner in which these modifications present themselves to the
field anthropologist, indeed to thoughtful Nyoro themselves; that is, as im-
pacting at various points and in various ways on a traditional political
organization.

We have seen how myth and traditional history validate the Mukama's claim to special distinction. He and his Bito kinsmen are thought of (and think of themselves) as quite different from ordinary people. Unlike some African rulers, Nyoro kings are not thought of as kin with the people they rule; they are not "fathers" of their people, but rulers of their people. Where the distinction between those born to rule and those born to be ruled is as sharply made as it is in Bunyoro, the intimacy of a blood tie (which in fact always exists through the female line since kings' mothers come from non-Bito clans) between these two quite different kinds of people is unlikely to be asserted, even in metaphor. The Mukama is the traditional ruler of all Nyoro, and in pre-European times all political authority in the state was seen as deriving from him. Nowadays, of course, outside political power is injected into the system at all levels by government officials, missionaries, and others, and nearly everybody knows this. But the Nyoro kingship is still essentially authoritarian. There are African kingdoms in which the king's importance is traditionally ritual rather than political; in Bunyoro this is not so. Though his power was not absolute, the Mukama was essentially a ruler. He is, indeed, surrounded by ritual, but this ritual makes sense only when it is seen as a symbolic expression of the king's political preeminence and power. A look at some of this ritual will make this point clear.

Broadly, Nyoro royal ritual falls into three categories. First, there are rites which express the ways in which Nyoro think about the kingship itself. Second, there is the ritual associated with the king's accession to and retention of authority, and his relinquishing of it at death. And third, there are those rites which are concerned with the ways in which the king may delegate his authority.

The rituals in the first category are mostly concerned with the Mukama in his aspect as "divine king," which means, for Nyoro, that he is mystically identified with the whole country of which he is the head. This means that the king must keep physically healthy; if he does not, the country and people as a whole will suffer. Formerly, a person, or even an ox, who was sick had to be removed at once from the royal enclosure, in case the king's health should be affected. The king had to avoid all contact with death; when I asked why the present Mukama did not attend his mother's funeral in 1953, I was told that it was because of this rule. In pre-European times, if the Mukama himself fell sick the matter was kept strictly secret. It is said that if his illness were serious, if he suffered any physical incapacity or mutilation, or if he grew too old and feeble to carry out his duties properly, he would either kill himself by taking poison or be killed by one of his wives. This was, of course, because any imperfection or weakness in the king was thought to involve a corresponding danger to the kingdom. We do not know for sure whether any kings ever were killed in this way, but the important thing is that it is thought that they were. This shows us how Nyoro traditionally thought about their country and their kingship.

As well as maintaining physical health, the Mukama had to keep himself in a good ritual or spiritual condition. This imposed on him certain ceremonial acts and avoidances. He was not allowed to eat certain kinds of food which were said to be of low status, such as sweet potatoes, cassava, and certain other vegetables. His numerous attendants also had to keep themselves ritually pure; for instance, his cooks had to abstain from sexual intercourse during and for some days before their periods of service in the palace, which were only for a few days at a time. On ceremonial occasions his special dairymaids, who had to be virgins, smeared themselves with white clay. This symbolized purity and goodness (for Nyoro, as for many other peoples, whiteness and purity are closely associated—indeed, one word is used for both). The king had to carry out certain rites associated with the royal herd of cattle "for the good of the country." These entailed his presence in the byre at milking time, and his ceremonial drinking of some of the new milk. Other usages also stress the Mukama's difference from and superiority to ordinary people. He has to be spoken to and greeted with special words (he is always addressed, and replies, in the third person singular), and he has a large number of distinctive names and titles. These refer to him as exceeding all men, ruling justly, relieving distress, and so on. Even today the most important officers of his own government kneel to hand him anything or to make a request of him in his own house. There is a special vocabulary referring to the king's person and activities, not used in regard to anyone else. He has extensive regalia, consisting of ancient crowns, drums, spears, stools, and other objects, and all of these have special names and their own custodians. In addition to these regalia keepers there are also a great many palace retainers and household officials of various kinds, most of whom have special names and titles.

The effect of these rituals and ceremonial usages, many of which are still observed, is to stress the Mukama's importance as the head of the state and the source of all political authority within it. By symbolically identifying him with the whole country, they justify his being treated as unique, and show why his physical and spiritual well-being must be sustained, while at the same time they enhance tribal unity by providing a set of symbols acceptable to everybody. But though ritual attaches to the kingship, it would be a mistake to think of the Mukama as a kind of priest, in the sense that he intercedes with a god or gods on behalf of his people. Such intercession is the work of the spirit mediums, initiates into the possession cult which is Bunyoro's traditional religion. The Mukama is not a priest, though he has his priests, just as he is not a rain maker, though he has his rain makers—magical experts who are subject to his discipline and control. In some African countries the real importance of chiefs lies in their magical or religious powers, and if they are secular rulers they are so only in a secondary capacity. In Bunyoro it is otherwise. The Mukama is first and foremost a ruler, and that is how everybody thinks of him.

The second of the broad categories of ritual which I distinguished was that concerned with the acquisition, retention, and relinquishing of kingly power. Nyoro accession ceremonies are lengthy and complex. This is what we should expect. In Bunyoro it is not known who is to be the new king until after the old king is dead. Traditionally the heir to the throne was supposed to be the prince who succeeded in killing whichever of his brothers (and he might have a good many) was his rival for the throne. Thus the successful prince undergoes a great change of status on his accession: formerly he was one of a considerable number of equally eligible princes; now he is king. Nyoro accession ritual marks this assumption of new status in the strongest and most emphatic terms. Both its ritual and political aspects are stressed. The accession ceremonies include washing, shaving, and nail-paring rites, anointment with a special oil and smearing with white chalk, ceremonial milk drinking and animal sacrifice. In pre-European times, it is said, they included the placing on the throne and the subsequent killing of a "mock king," who would, it was believed, attract to himself the magical dangers which attended the transition to kingship, so protecting the real king. The king's accession to political office is equally stressed. He is handed various objects symbolizing political and military power, such as spears, a bow and arrows, a dagger, and a stick, and he is formally admonished and instructed to rule wisely, to kill his enemies, and to protect his people. His territorial authority is also symbolized in a ceremony in which a man who represents neighboring regions formerly subject to Bunyoro presents him with ivory and some copper bracelets as "tribute." Another rite is the ceremonial acting-out of the settlement of a lawsuit in which one man sues another for debt. This is not really a judicial hearing; it is a symbolic way of impressing on both king and people the important part he is to play as lawgiver and judge. Finally, there is a ceremony in which the king shoots arrows with the bow he has been given toward the four points of the compass, saying as he does so: "Thus I shoot the countries to overcome them." Several of these rites are repeated at "refresher" ceremonies, which used to be held annually.

Accession and "refresher" rites stress the king's attainment to supreme political power equally with his accession to the high ritual status associated with this authority. These themes are also evident in the ritual connected with the Mukama's death. Here what is principally expressed is the continuity of the kingship, even though the king is dead. Traditionally there was an interregnum of several months during which two or more of the sons of the dead Mukama might fight for the succession, while civil disorder and confusion prevailed. For some days the king's death was concealed; then a man climbed to the top of one of the houses in the king's enclosure carrying a milk-pot, and hurled this to the ground, shouting "The milk is split; the king has been taken away!" As this man descended, he was killed, for such things may not be said. In pre-European times the royal corpse was preserved by disemboweling it and drying it over a slow fire. When a prince had succeeded in winning the kingdom he came and took the late king's jawbone, which had been separated from the corpse and carefully guarded, and had to bury this at a selected place, where a house was built and certain of the late king's regalia preserved under the supervision of a chosen member of the royal Bito clan. The rest of the corpse was buried separately and the grave forgotten; the tombs which are remembered and venerated today are those where the royal jawbones are buried.

The third kind of royal ritual which I distinguished related to the delegation of the Mukama's authority. A ruler—at least in the conditions of a tribal African kingdom—cannot keep all his power to himself, but must give some of it away; this is one of the major limitations on political authority. Thus, like other kings, the Mukama of Bunyoro traditionally had to confer quite a high degree of independent authority on his great chiefs; hence the loose, "feudal" type of organization (involving close interpersonal bonds between king and chiefs) characteristic of traditional Bunyoro.

To delegate political authority to his chiefs was at the same time to confer ritual status upon them. There is a Nyoro word, *Mahano*, denoting a special kind of spiritual power, which is applied to many objects and situations which are strange and awe inspiring. This mysterious potency may be dangerous, calling for the performance of special ritual to preserve or restore normality. It is especially associated with the Mukama; therefore, when he delegates political authority upon his chiefs, he also imparts to them something of his own ritual power. Thus the delegation of political authority is not just an administrative act, it is also a ritual act. The ritual involves, in particular, a ceremony known as "drinking milk" with the Mukama, and it is said that (in the case of important chiefs, at least) the milk formerly was taken from the cows of his special herd. Nowadays, it seems, milk is not used, but roasted coffee berries are handed by the Mukama to the person upon whom he is bestowing authority. The recipient of this favor is then supposed to kiss the Mukama's hand, a ceremony strikingly reminiscent of the kiss of fealty in medieval and later Europe. This expresses the chief's obligation and personal devotion to his sovereign, who has confirmed him in authority over a specific territory and its inhabitants. Theoretically, at least, all territorial authority in Bunyoro was held from the king and by his grace, and its grant implied enhancement of the recipient's ritual status as well as of his political status. Nyoro royal ritual is best understood as the symbolic expression of royal authority, and one of its effects is to sustain and validate this authority.

The King and His People

We now consider the king's relations, both in traditional times and at the present day, with the more important of the various categories of persons who make up Nyoro society. These are the members of the royal Bito line and their two heads, the Okwiri and the Kalyota, the king's mother, his regalia keepers, domestic officials, and advisers, his territorial chiefs of various grades and, finally, his people at large.

The word "Bito" denotes one of Bunyoro's hundred or more clans; it also denotes the present ruling dynasty. These are not quite the same thing. Though all Bito have the same avoidance object or "totem" (the bushbuck), only those who can establish a real genealogical link with the Mukama are accorded special prestige, and the closer the relationship the greater the prestige claimed and acknowledged. It is these close kinsmen of the king who are generally meant when the Bito are referred to; members of the Bito clan who can show no such explicit connection are not distinguished socially from members of commoner clans. Those who can demonstrate patrilineal descent from a Mukama of a few generations back (rarely more than four) regard themselves as a distinctive hereditary aristocracy, among whom the most distinguished are the "Bito of the drum," the actual sons of a Mukama. There are still a good many of these important Bito; former kings had many wives, and some were notably prolific: Kabarega had over a hundred children, some of whom are still living.

In the past, most important Bito received large estates from the Mukama, together with the political rights which such grants implied. They were thus important territorial chiefs. Nowadays, as we shall see in Chapter 4, European influence has broken down the traditional association between rights over land and political authority, and it has at the same time radically altered the basis on which land is held. A consequence of this is that Bito are no longer, as a class, the wealthy and powerful group which they formerly were. But they still claim special privileges and prestige; and they still preserve, under the nominal authority of their head, the Okwiri, the ability in certain contexts to act as a group.

The Okwiri, the Mukama's "official brother," is traditionally the eldest son of the late king, and he is formally appointed by the new Mukama after his accession. He is said to "rule" the Bito as the king rules the country as a whole. Structurally his office is interesting in that it provides a way of "detaching" the king from the exclusive Bito group to which he belongs by birth, so making possible his identification with the whole kingdom, non-Bito as well as Bito. For the King is not directly concerned with Bito interests, which often conflicted (and still do) with those of the people as a whole; these are the business of the Okwiri. This official nowadays represents the Bito on the central council of the native government, and resolutions (which are rarely if ever adopted) claiming for them special rights and privileges are still occasionally tabled through him. Even today, Bito claim special deference from commoners and are usually accorded it; many of them still hold large private estates which they administer autocratically; and they are sometimes said, not always without justification, to be arrogant and demanding, and heedless of others' rights. Like aristocracies elsewhere which have survived the political conditions in which they played an effective part, Bito still cling to the outward signs of an authority which they no longer have, and lord it over a peasant population which still shows little resentment. It might be thought that Bito, anxious for the reality of power, would have found places for themselves in the modern chiefly service. But very few have done so. This is consistent with traditional Bito values; service in the modern Nyoro government would involve official subordination to non-Bito, and to some of the more old-fashioned, this would be intolerable.

Corresponding to the Okwiri's position as the head of the Bito "princes" is that the king's "official sister," the Kalyota. She is a chosen half-sister of the king (she has a different mother), whom he appoints to be the head of the Bito women or "princesses." These royal ladies enjoy a prestige similar to their brothers'. They were, indeed, said to be "like men," for like the princes they ruled as chiefs over the areas allotted to them. Formerly they were not allowed to marry or bear children; this helped to preserve the unity and exclusiveness of the king's lineage, for it prevented the growth of lines of sisters' sons to the royal house. To old-fashioned Nyoro, it would have been unthinkable for persons of such high status to assume the markedly subordinate status of wives. Today, however, the king's daughters, like other Bito women, may marry and have children, but they usually marry men of high social standing who can afford to keep servants, for Bito princesses do not dig or carry water like ordinary women. Bridewealth is not paid in such marriages, for that would imply some degree of social equality. "How," an informant asked, "could a Bito and a commoner haggle about bridewealth? A Bito's word should be an order."

Like the Okwiri, then, the king's official sister was really a kind of chief; her appointment to office included the handing over to her of certain regalia, and like other persons succeeding to political authority she underwent the ceremony of "drinking milk" with the Mukama. She held and administered estates, from which she derived revenue and services, like other chiefs. She settled disputes, determined inheritance cases, and decided matters of precedence among the Bito women. She was not, as she is sometimes thought to have been, the queen, if by queen we mean the king's consort. It is said that in former times the Mukama could sleep with her if he wanted to, but he could do this with any of his royal sisters, so long as she was born of a different mother from his own. We may best regard her, then, as a kind of female counterpart of the king—the head of the Bito women, and so the chief lady in the land. We may see her office, like that of her brother the Okwiri, as one of the means whereby the royal authority was distributed. Though there is little place for her in the modern system, she still holds official rank, and her status is constitutionally recognized (as is the Okwiri's) by the payment to her of a small salary under the Bunyoro Agreement. Nowadays she is socially overshadowed by the king's true consort, the Omugo, whom he married in Christian marriage and who has borne him several children. It was she, not the Kalyota, who accompanied the Mukama on his visit to England for Queen Elizabeth's coronation in 1953, and she sits at his side at ceremonies and entertainments at which Europeans are present.

As in some other African monarchies, the king's mother also traditionally had considerable power, and kept her own court and ruled her own estates. She no longer has such authority today, but she is still much honored, and like the Okwiri and the Kalyota she receives a small official salary.

I referred above to the numerous regalia keepers and other palace officials who traditionally surrounded the king. Even today there are a great many such persons. Some are salaried officials; others, whose services are required only occasionally, receive gifts from the Mukama from time to time. These officials include the custodian of the royal graves, men responsible for the more important of the royal drums, caretakers, and "putters-on" of the royal crowns, custodians of spears, stools, and other regalia, cooks, bath attendants, herdsmen, potters, barkcloth makers, musicians, and many others. The more important of them have several assistants, and their duties are not onerous, for the care of a particular spear or attendance on the Mukama on ceremonial occasions occupies only a small part of a man's working life. This complex establishment is therefore not to be understood simply as an overcumbersome attempt to run a large household; neither in ancient times nor now can it be regarded as an economical or even as a particularly efficient way of doing this. Sociologically, the point of it is that it provided a means of involving a great many different groups and kinds of people in a common interest in the royal establishment and so in the maintenance of the kingship itself. It did this both through the clan system (for different offices were often hereditarily vested in particular clans, all of whose members shared in the honor of representation at the palace) and through occupational specialization (since it meant that all of Bunyoro's crafts were represented at the capital). In these ways the huge royal establishment served to integrate the Nyoro people around their center, and so to sustain the political system itself. Even in modern times prestige still attaches to these occupations, even where they are part time and unpaid, and I know of young men who have refused to take up profitable employment elsewhere in order to retain them. Moreover, a man who had served for some years in the palace might hope, if he gained the Mukama's personal favor, to be rewarded with a gift of an estate somewhere in the kingdom, thus becoming a kind of minor chief over its peasant inhabitants. Grants of this kind have been made even in recent times, though they have latterly rather taken the form of appointment to minor official chiefships. Such grants are not appropriate to a modern "civil service" type of administration; we shall return to this point.

In addition to this large body of palace and domestic officials, there was a loosely defined category of informal advisers and retainers. As well as certain officials in the last category, these included diviners and other persons who had attached themselves to the Mukama's household as dependants. These informal and private advisers had no official standing and they did not receive salaries. Some of them have, in the past, exerted considerable influence, and they have sometimes been said to be "nearer to the king" than the official chiefs. They acted at times as intermediaries between the chiefs and the king. They might expect to receive informal rewards from time to time, and they, too, might have received estates or minor chiefships for their services.

A much more important category of persons in traditional Bunyoro were the "crown wearers." To men whom the king wished specially to distinguish he gave elaborate beaded headdresses, with fringes or "beards" of colobus monkey skins. The award of a crown implied the grant of very high dignity and ritual status (recipients had to observe the same food restrictions as the king himself and were said to have a great deal of *mahano*). At the same time it involved accession to high political authority over considerable territories. Like other important chiefs the crown wearers had to take an oath of loyalty to the king, and to undergo the milk-drinking rite referred to above. In the past, crowns were awarded to persons who had performed some considerable service for the Mukama, such as winning a major victory in war; a crown was also traditionally awarded to the head of the king's mother's clan. Crowns, once awarded, were hereditary in the male line. The Bunyoro Agreement still provides for the grant of this award, which it describes as "an old-established order of distinction," but the institution is now falling into disuse, and no crown has been awarded for many years. The high ritual value that formerly attached to the Mukama's political authority no longer does so to the same extent, for such authority is seen nowadays to derive from other and more potent outside sources.

The system of territorial chiefship is discussed in the next chapter; here we need only note that traditionally all political authority was seen as deriving from the person of the king himself; as in feudal Europe, chiefs held their territories as gifts from the king, and this implied a close bond of personal dependence and attachment between him and them. Chiefship was essentially territorial; a chief was a person to whom the Mukama had granted rights over a particular territory and its inhabitants. These rights, even where they tended to become hereditary, were held only by the Mukama's favor: they could be withdrawn by him at any time, and sometimes they were. Though it does not seem that in pre-European times there was any such formal political hierarchy as there is now, there were different ranks of chiefs, from the great rulers of areas which roughly correspond with present-day counties, to minor chiefs with only a handful of peasant dependants.

This personal way of looking at the relationship between a ruler and his subordinates was quite appropriate to the relatively simple, "feudal" organization of pre-European times. Where political office is thought of as the sovereign's gift, it is important to seek and retain his personal favor, and it is natural that a return should be made for such a gift. If, even in modern times, chiefships should sometimes have been given, and promotion awarded, to persons who have rendered gifts or personal service to the king, and persons who have incurred his personal dislike should have been passed over, this would be wholly consistent with the values implicit in traditional Nyoro political structure, where personal attachment and loyalty were the supreme political values. It would be a serious mistake to regard such transactions, even now, as constituting breaches of tribal morality, although in terms of the impersonal standards of modern Western administration they are both wrong and politically harmful. It is natural, in such a system, that personal attachment should count for more than conformity to bureaucratic standards of efficiency and incorruptibility. And we must remember further that the exercise of political authority in pre-European times needed far less special training and knowledge than are demanded now. In Bunyoro, at all events, it is said that the expression of personal loyalty to the Mukama was until recent times hardly less necessary a qualification for political appointment than administrative experience or a high educational standard.

Appropriate though these attitudes were to the traditional system, they are plainly less so to modern times. Like other Western administrations, the British authorities are committed to encouraging the development of more modern and democratic political institutions, better adapted to the contemporary world of which Bunyoro is now a part. Traditional attitudes to chiefship are incompatible with these institutions. Many educated Nyoro realize this, and I have heard such people complain that faithful service in the Mukama's bathroom or kitchen is hardly an adequate qualification for even minor political office, and that the king's personal favor is not in itself an obvious qualification for the highest administrative posts. The situation, too, is greatly altered by the introduction of a cash economy, for when gifts formerly of kind are commuted to cash, they at once assume a different and more mercenary character. But it is an important part of the anthropologist's task to point out that such transactions are not properly understood when they are simply condemned as misdemeanors; rather, they have to be seen as usages surviving from a context in which they were proper and appropriate into one where they are no longer so. When values and patterns of behavior which are mutually incompatible come to coexist in the same rapidly changing political system, strains and conflict develop. We shall see in other contexts also that feudal values and bureaucratic ones do not always mesh smoothly.

Another example of uneasy coexistence of new and old values is found in the economic aspect of the relationship between the Mukama and his people at large. In the traditional system the king was seen both as the supreme receiver of goods and services, and as the supreme giver. Typically in systems of the Nyoro type, goods and services have to be rendered to the "lord," the person who stands next above one in the political hierarchy. Thus in Bunyoro the great chiefs, who themselves received tribute from their dependants, were required to hand over to the Mukama a part of the produce of their estates, in the form of crops, cattle, beer, or women. But everybody must give to the king, not only the chiefs. Even today the ordinary people make presents to him on certain ceremonial occasions. When he pays state visits to different parts of his country, as he often does, gifts of produce, for which there is a special Nyoro word, should be brought to him by peasants as well as chiefs. And larger gifts, in cash or kind, might be made to him from time to time by people who wish to obtain and retain his favor. All these various kinds of gifts express in traditional terms a kind of attachment between ruler and ruled which is important in a relatively small-scale feudal society. In addition, they formerly provided a sort of social insurance, for those who fell on hard times would naturally look for help to their chiefs and, ultimately, to the king.

The Mukama's role as giver was, accordingly, no less stressed. Many of his special names emphasize his magnanimity, and he was traditionally expected to give extensively in the form both of feasts and of gifts to individuals. But here, too, attitudes and values have survived the social conditions to which they were appropriate. People nowadays complain that the king no longer gives the great feasts which their grandfathers enjoyed. Their offerings of foodstuffs, they say, are taken away in a truck, and no feast, or at best a very inadequate one, is provided. They think that nowadays only the Mukama's circle of personal friends receives help from him. They do not see that the political changes of the past half-century, and in particular the advent of a cash economy, have made their attitudes and expectations anachronistic. For the truth is that the Mukama himself does not receive produce in the same quantities as his predecessors did, since the cultivators can now sell their surpluses for cash with which to satisfy their new needs. And to provide meat for huge feasts now, when cattle are virtually nonexistent and meat is prohibitively expensive, is economically impracticable. Also, as we have noted, many of the gifts which the Mukama now receives are in cash, not kind. And cash, unlike food and beer, does not have to be consumed quickly and communally in the form of gifts and feasts; it can be converted into many other desirable objects not formerly available. This state of affairs is not, of course, peculiar to Bunyoro; on the contrary, it is one of the most characteristic features of African kingdoms at the same stage of change. But in Bunyoro the economic aspect of political authority is particularly strongly institutionalized. It is thus inevitable that the incompatibility between the traditional idea of rulers as centers for the collection and redistribution of goods, and the new pattern of bureaucratic authority which is now developing, should lead to bewilderment and strain. Nor should we be surprised that the nature of these conflicts is not always fully understood by those most closely involved in them.

20

The Kpelle Moot: A Therapeutic Model for the Informal Settlement of Disputes[1]

JAMES L. GIBBS, JR.

AFRICA AS A MAJOR CULTURE AREA has been characterized by many writers as being marked by a high development of law and legal procedures. In the past few years research on African law has produced a series of highly competent monographs such as those on law among the Tiv, the Barotse, and the Nuer.[2] These and related shorter studies have focused primarily on formal processes for the settlement of disputes, such as those which take place in a courtroom, or those which are, in some other way, set apart from simpler measures of social control. However, many African societies have informal, quasi-legal, dispute-settlement procedures, supplemental to formal ones, which have not been as well studied, or—in most cases—adequately analysed.

In this paper I present a description and analysis of one such institution for the informal settlement of disputes, as it is found among the Kpelle of Liberia; it is the moot, the bɛrɛi mu meni saa or 'house palaver'. Hearings in the Kpelle moot contrast with those in a court in that they differ in tone and effectiveness. The genius of the moot lies in the fact that it is based on a covert application of the principles of psychoanalytic theory which underlie psychotherapy.

The Kpelle are a Mande-speaking, patrilineal group of some 175,000 rice cultivators who live in Central Liberia and the adjoining regions of Guinea.

This paper is based on data gathered in a field study which I carried out in 1957 and 1958 among the Liberian Kpelle of Panta Chiefdom in north-east Central Province.

Strong corporate patrilineages are absent among the Kpelle. The most important kinship group is the virilocal polygynous family which sometimes becomes an extended family, almost always of the patrilineal variety. Several of these families form the core of a residential group, known as a village quarter, more technically, a clan-barrio.[3] This is headed by a quarter elder who is related to most of the household heads by real or putative patrilineal ties.

Kpelle political organization is centralized although there is no single king or paramount chief, but a series of chiefs of the same level of authority, each of whom is superordinate over district chiefs and town chiefs. Some political functions are also vested in the tribal fraternity, the Poro, which still functions vigorously. The form of political organization found in the area can thus best be termed the polycephalous associational state.

The structure of the Kpelle court system parallels that of the political organization. In Liberia the highest court of a tribal authority and the highest tribal court chartered by the Government is that of a paramount chief. A district chief's court is also an official court. Disputes may be settled in these official courts or in unofficial courts, such as those of town chiefs or quarter elders. In addition to this, grievances are settled informally in moots, and sometimes by associational groupings such as church councils or cooperative work groups.

In my field research I studied both the formal and informal methods of dispute settlement. The method used was to collect case material in as complete a form as possible. Accordingly, immediately after a hearing, my interpreter and I would prepare verbatim transcripts of each case that we heard. These transcripts were supplemented with accounts—obtained from respondents—of past cases or cases which I did not hear litigated. Transcripts from each type of hearing were analysed phrase by phrase in terms of a frame of reference derived from jurisprudence and ethno-law. The results of the analysis indicate two things: first, that courtroom hearings and moots are quite different in their procedures and tone, and secondly, why they show this contrast.

Kpelle courtroom hearings are basically coercive and arbitrary in tone. In another paper[4] I have shown that this is partly the result of the intrusion of the authoritarian values of the Poro into the courtroom. As a result, the court is limited in the manner in which it can handle some types of disputes. The court is particularly effective in settling cases such as assault, possession of illegal charms, or theft where the litigants are not linked in a relationship which must continue after the trial. However, most of the cases brought before a Kpelle court are cases involving disputed rights over women, including matrimonial matters which are usually cast in the form of suits for divorce. The court is particularly inept at settling these numerous matrimonial disputes because its harsh tone tends to drive spouses farther apart rather than to reconcile them. The moot, in contrast, is more effective in handling such cases. The following analysis indicates the reasons for this.[5]

The Kpelle bɛrɛi mu meni saa, or 'house palaver', is an informal airing of a dispute which takes place before an assembled group which includes kinsmen of the litigants and neighbours from the quarter where the case is being heard. It is a completely *ad hoc* group, varying greatly in composition from case to case. The matter to be settled is usually a domestic problem: alleged mistreatment or neglect by a spouse, an attempt to collect money paid to a kinsman for a job which was not completed, or a quarrel among brothers over the inheritance of their father's wives.

In the procedural description which follows I shall use illustrative data from the Case of the Ousted Wife:

Wama Nya, the complainant, had one wife, Yua. His older brother died and he inherited the widow, Yokpo, who moved into his house. The two women were classificatory sisters. After Yokpo moved in, there was strife in the household. The husband accused her of staying out late at night, of harvesting rice without his knowledge, and of denying him food. He also accused Yokpo of having lovers and admitted having had a physical struggle with her, after which he took a basin of water and 'washed his hands of her'.

Yokpo countered by denying the allegations about having lovers, saying that she was accused falsely, although she had in the past confessed the name of one lover. She further complained that Wama Mya had assaulted her and, in the act, had committed the indignity of removing her headtie, and had expelled her from the house after the ritual hand-washing. Finally, she alleged that she had been thus cast out of the house at the instigation of the other wife who, she asserted, had great influence over their husband.

Kɔlɔ Waa, the Town Chief and quarter elder, and the brother of Yokpo, was the mediator of the moot, which decided that the husband was mainly at fault, although Yua and Yokpo's children were also in the wrong. Those at fault had to apologize to Yokpo and bring gifts of apology as well as local rum[6] for the disputants and participants in the moot.

The moot is most often held on a Sunday—a day of rest for Christians and non-Christians alike—at the home of the complainant, the person who calls the moot. The mediator will have been selected by the complainant. He is a kinsman who also holds an office such as town chief or quarter elder, and therefore has some skill in dispute settlement. It is said that he is chosen to preside by virtue of his kin tie, rather than because of his office.

The proceedings begin with the pronouncing of blessings by one of the oldest men of the group. In the Case of the Ousted Wife, Gbenai Zua, the elder who pronounced the blessings, took a rice-stirrer in his hand and, striding back and forth, said:

This man has called us to fix the matter between him and his wife. May vala [the supreme, creator deity] change his heart and let his household be in a good condition. May vala bless the family and make them fruitful. May He bless them so they can have food this year. May He bless the children and the rest of the family so they may always be healthy. May He bless them to have good luck. When Wama Nya takes a gun and goes to the bush, may he kill big animals. May vala bless us to enjoy the meat. May He bless us to enjoy life and always have luck. May vala bless all those who come to discuss this matter.

The man who pronounces the blessings always carries a stick or a whisk (kpung) which he waves for effect as he paces up and down chanting his injunctions. Participation of spectators is demanded, for the blessings are chanted by the elder (kpung namu or 'kpung owner') as a series of impera-tives, some of which he repeats. Each phrase is responded to by the spectators who answer in unison with a formal response, either e ka ti (so be it), or a low, drawn-out eeee. The kpung namu delivers his blessings faster and faster, building up a rhythmic interaction pattern with the other participants. The effect is to unite those attending in common action before the hearing begins. The blessing focuses attention on the concern with maintaining harmony and the well-being of the group as a whole.

Everyone attending the moot wears their next-to-best clothes or, if it is not Sunday, everyday clothes. Elders, litigants, and spectators sit in mixed fash-ion, pressed closely upon each other, often overflowing on to a veranda. This is in contrast to the vertical spatial separation between litigants and ad-judicators in the courtroom. The mediator, even though he is a chief, does not wear his robes. He and the oldest men will be given chairs as they would on any other occasion.

The complainant speaks first and may be interrupted by the mediator or anyone else present. After he has been thoroughly quizzed, the accused will answer and will also be questioned by those present. The two parties will question each other directly and question others in the room also. Both the testimony and the questioning are lively and uninhibited. Where there are witnesses to some of the actions described by the parties, they may also speak and be questioned. Although the proceedings are spirited, they remain or-derly. The mediator may fine anyone who speaks out of turn by requiring them to bring some rum for the group to drink.

The mediator and the others present will point out the various faults committed by both the parties. After everyone has been heard, the mediator expresses the consensus of the group. For example, in the Case of the Ousted Wife, he said to Yua: 'The words you used towards your sister were not good, so come and beg her pardon.'

The person held to be mainly at fault will then formally apologize to the other person. This apology takes the form of the giving of token gifts to the wronged person by the guilty party. These may be an item of clothing, a few coins, clean hulled rice, or a combination of all three. It is also customary for the winning party in accepting the gifts of apology to give, in return, a smaller token such as a twenty-five cent piece[7] to show his 'white heart' or good will. The losing party is also lightly 'fined'; he must present rum or beer to the mediator and the others who heard the case. This is consumed by all in attendance. The old man then pronounces blessings again and offers thanks for the restoration of harmony within the group, and asks that all continue to act with good grace and unity.

An initial analysis of the procedural steps of the moot isolates the descriptive attributes of the moot and shows that they contrast with those of the courtroom hearing. While the airing of grievances is incomplete in courtroom hearings, it is more complete in the moot. This fuller airing of the issues results, in many marital cases, in a more harmonious solution. Several specific features of the house palaver facilitate this wider airing of grievances. First, the hearing takes place soon after a breach has occurred, before the grievances have hardened. There is no delay until the complainant has time to go to the paramount chief's or district chief's headquarters to institute suit. Secondly, the hearing takes place in the familiar surroundings of a home. The robes, writs, messengers, and other symbols of power which subtly intimidate and inhibit the parties in the courtroom, by reminding them of the physical force which underlies the procedures, are absent. Thirdly, in the courtroom the conduct of the hearing is firmly in the hands of the judge, but in the moot the investigatory initiative rests much more with the parties themselves. Jurisprudence suggests that, in such a case, more of the grievances lodged between the parties are likely to be aired and adjusted. Finally, the range of relevance applied to matters which are brought out is extremely broad. Hardly anything mentioned is held to be irrelevant. This too leads to a more thorough ventilation of the issues.

There is a second surface difference between court and moot. In a courtroom hearing, the solution is, by and large, one which is imposed by the adjudicator. In the moot the solution is more consensual. It is, therefore, more likely to be accepted by both parties and hence more durable. Several features of the moot contribute to the consensual solution: first, there is no unilateral ascription of blame, but an attribution of fault to both parties. Secondly, the mediator, unlike the chief in the courtroom, is not backed by political authority and the physical force which underlies it. He cannot jail parties, nor can he levy a heavy fine. Thirdly, the sanctions which are imposed are not so burdensome as to cause hardship to the losing party or to give him or her grounds for a new grudge against the other party. The gifts for the winning party and the potables for the spectators are not as expensive as the fines and the court costs in a paramount chief's court. Lastly, the ritualized apology of the moot symbolizes very concretely the consensual nature of the solution.[8] The public offering and acceptance of the tokens of apology indicate that each party has no further grievances and that the settlement is satisfactory and mutually acceptable. The parties and spectators drink together to symbolize the restored solidarity of the group and the rehabilitation of the offending party.

This type of analysis describes the courtroom hearing and the moot, using a frame of reference derived from jurisprudence and ethno-law which is explicitly comparative and evaluative. Only by using this type of comparative approach can the researcher select features of the hearings which are not only unique to each of them, but theoretically significant in that their contribution to the social-control functions of the proceedings can be hypothesized. At the same time, it enables the researcher to pin-point in procedures the cause for what he feels intuitively: that the two hearings contrast in tone, even though they are similar in some ways.

However, one can approach the transcripts of the trouble cases with a second analytical framework and emerge with a deeper understanding of the implications of the contrasting descriptive attributes of the court and the house palaver. Remember that the coercive tone of the courtroom hearing limits the court's effectiveness in dealing with matrimonial disputes, especially in effecting reconciliations. The moot, on the other hand, is particularly effective in bringing about reconciliations between spouses. This is because the moot is not only conciliatory, but *therapeutic*. Moot procedures are therapeutic in that, like psychotherapy, they re-educate the parties through a type of social learning brought about in a specially structured interpersonal setting.

Talcott Parsons[9] has written that therapy involves four elements: support, permissiveness, denial of reciprocity, and manipulation of rewards. Writers such as Frank,[10] Klapman,[11] and Opler[12] have pointed out that the same elements characterize not only individual psychotherapy, but group psychotherapy as well. All four elements are writ large in the Kpelle moot.

The patient in therapy will not continue treatment very long if he does not feel support from the therapist or from the group. In the moot the parties are encouraged in the expression of their complaints and feelings because they sense group support. The very presence of one's kinsmen and neighbours demonstrates their concern. It indicates to the parties that they have a real problem and that the others are willing to help them to help themselves in solving it. In a parallel vein, Frank, speaking of group psychotherapy, notes that: 'Even anger may be supportive if it implies to a patient that others take him seriously enough to get angry at him, especially if the object of the anger feels it to be directed toward his neurotic behaviour rather than himself as a person.'[13] In the moot the feeling of support also grows out of the pronouncement of the blessings which stress the unity of the group and its harmonious goal, and it is also undoubtedly increased by the absence of the publicity and expressive symbols of political power which are found in the courtroom.

Permissiveness is the second element in therapy. It indicates to the patient that every-day restrictions on making anti-social statements or acting out anti-social impulses are lessened. Thus, in the Case of the Ousted Wife,

Yua felt free enough to turn to her ousted co-wife (who had been married leviratically) and say:

> You don't respect me. You don't rely on me any more. When your husband was living, and I was with my husband, we slept on the farm. Did I ever refuse to send you what you asked me for when you sent a message? Didn't I always send you some of the meat my husband killed? Did I refuse to send you anything you wanted? When your husband died and we became co-wives, did I disrespect you? Why do you always make me ashamed? The things you have done to me make me sad.

Permissiveness in the therapeutic setting (and in the moot) results in catharsis, in a high degree of stimulation of feelings in the participants and an equally high tendency to verbalize these feelings.[14] Frank notes that: 'Neurotic responses must be expressed in the therapeutic situation if they are to be changed by it.'[15] In the same way, if the solution to a dispute reached in a house palaver is to be stable, it is important that there should be nothing left to embitter and undermine the decision. In a familiar setting, with familiar people, the parties to the moot feel at ease and free to say *all* that is on their minds. Yokpo, judged to be the wronged party in the Case of the Ousted Wife, in accepting an apology, gave expression to this when she said:

> I agree to everything that my people said, and I accept the things they have given me—I don't have *anything else* about them on my mind. (*My italics.*)

As we shall note below, this thorough airing of complaints also facilitates the gaining of insight into and the unlearning of idiosyncratic behaviour which is socially disruptive. Permissiveness is rooted in the lack of publicity and the lack of symbols of power. But it stems, too, from the immediacy of the hearing, the locus of investigatory initiative with the parties, and the wide range of relevance.

Permissiveness in therapy is impossible without the denial of reciprocity. This refers to the fact that the therapist will not respond in kind when the patient acts in a hostile manner or with inappropriate affection. It is a type of privileged indulgence which comes with being a patient. In the moot, the parties are treated in the same way and are allowed to hurl recriminations that, in the courtroom, might bring a few hours in jail as punishment for the equivalent of contempt of court. Even though inappropriate views are not responded to in kind, neither are they simply ignored. There is denial of *congruent* response, not denial of *any* response whatsoever. In the *bɛrɛi mu meni saa*, as in group psychotherapy, 'private ideation and conceptualization are brought out into the open and all their facets or many of their facets exposed. The individual gets a "reading" from different bearings on the compass, so to speak,[16] and perceptual patterns . . . are joggled out of their fixed positions. . . .'[17]

Thus, Yua's outburst against Yokpo quoted above was not responded to with matching hostility, but its inappropriateness was clearly pointed out to her by the group. Some of them called her aside in a huddle and said to her:

> You are not right. If you don't like the woman, or she doesn't like you, don't be the first to say anything. Let her start and then say what you have to say. By speaking, if she heeds some of your words, the wives will scatter, and the blame will be on you. Then your husband will cry for your name that you have scattered his property.

In effect, Yua was being told that, in view of the previous testimony, her jealousy of her co-wife was not justified. In reality testing, she discovered that her view of the situation was not shared by the others and, hence, was inappropriate. Noting how the others responded, she could see why her treatment of her co-wife had caused so much dissension. Her interpretation of her new co-wife's actions and resulting premises were not shared by the co-wife, nor by the others hearing a description of what had happened. Like psychotherapy, the moot is gently corrective of behaviour rooted in such misunderstandings.

Similarly, Wama Nya, the husband, learned that others did not view as reasonable his accusing his wife of having a lover and urging her to go off and drink with the suspected paramour when he passed their house and wished them all a good evening. Reality testing for him taught him that the group did not view this type of mildly paranoid sarcasm as conducive to stable marital relationships.

The reaction of the moot to Yua's outburst indicates that permissiveness in this case was certainly not complete, but only relative, being much greater than that in the courtroom. But without this moderated immunity the airing of grievances would be limited, and the chance for social relearning lessened. Permissiveness in the moot is incomplete because, even there, prudence is not thrown to the winds. Note that Yua was not told not to express her feelings at all, but to express them only after the co-wife had spoken so that, if the moot failed, she would not be in an untenable position. In court there would be objection to her blunt speaking out. In the moot the objection was, in effect, to her speaking *out of turn*. In other cases the moot sometimes fails, foundering on this very point, because the parties are *too* prudent, all waiting for the others to make the first move in admitting fault.

The manipulation of rewards is the last dimension of therapy treated by Parsons. In this final phase of therapy[18] the patient is coaxed to conformity by the granting of rewards. In the moot one of the most important rewards is the group approval which goes to the wronged person who accepts an apology and to the person who is magnanimous enough to make one.

In the Case of the Ousted Wife, Kɔlɔ Waa, the mediator, and the others attending decided that the husband and the co-wife, Yua, had wronged Yokpo. Kɔlɔ Waa said to the husband:

From now on, we don't want to hear of your fighting. You should live in peace with these women. If your wife accepts the things which the people have brought you should pay four chickens and ten bottles of rum as your contribution.

The husband's brother and sister also brought gifts of apology, although the moot did not explicitly hold them at fault.

By giving these prestations, the wrong-doer is restored to good grace and is once again acting like an 'upright Kpelle' (although, if he wishes, he may refuse to accept the decision of the moot). He is eased into this position by being grouped with others to whom blame is also allocated, for, typically, he is not singled out and isolated in being labelled deviant. Thus, in the Case of the Ousted Wife the children of Yokpo were held to be at fault in 'being mean' to their step-father, so that blame was not only shared by one 'side', but ascribed to the other also.

Moreover, the prestations which the losing party is asked to hand over are not expensive. They are significant enough to touch the pocketbook a little; for the Kpelle say that if an apology does not cost something other than words, the wrong-doer is more likely to repeat the offending action. At the same time, as we noted above, the tokens are not so costly as to give the loser additional reason for anger directed at the other party which can undermine the decision.

All in all, the rewards for conformity to group expectations and for following out a new behaviour pattern are kept within the deviant's sight. These rewards are positive, in contrast to the negative sanctions of the courtroom. Besides the institutionalized apology, praise and acts of concern and affection replace fines and jail sentences. The mediator, speaking to Yokpo as the wronged party, said:

> You have found the best of the dispute. Your husband has wronged you. All the people have wronged you. You are the only one who can take care of them because you are the oldest. Accept the things they have given to you.

The moot in its procedural features and procedural sequences is, then, strongly analogous to psychotherapy. It is analogous to therapy in the structuring of the role of the mediator also. Parsons has indicated that, to do his job well, the therapist must be a member of two social systems: one containing himself and his patient; and the other, society at large.[19] He must not be seduced into thinking that he belongs only to the therapeutic dyad, but must gradually pull the deviant back into a relationship with the wider group. It is significant, then, that the mediator of a moot is a kinsman who is also a chief of some sort. He thus represents both the group involved in the dispute and the wider community. His task is to utilize his position as kinsman as a lever to manipulate the parties into living up to the normative requirements of the wider society, which, as chief, he upholds. His major orientation must be to the wider collectivity, not to the particular goals of his kinsmen.

When successful, the moot stops the process of alienation which drives two spouses so far apart that they are immune to ordinary social-control measures such as a smile, a frown, or a pointed aside.[20] A moot is not always successful, however. Both parties must have a genuine willingness to co-operate and a real concern about their discord. Each party must be willing to list his grievances, to admit his guilt, and make an open apology. The moot, like psychotherapy, is impotent without well-motivated clients.

The therapeutic elements found in the Kpelle moot are undoubtedly found in informal procedures for settling disputes in other African societies also; some of these are reported in the literature and others are not. One such procedure which seems strikingly parallel to the Kpelle *bɛrɛi mu meni saa* has been described by J.H.M. Beattie.[21] This is the court of neighbours or *ruku-rato rw'enzarwa* found in the Banyoro kingdom of Uganda. The group also meets as an *ad hoc* assembly of neighbours to hear disputes involving kins-men or neighbours.[22]

The intention of the Nyoro moot is to 'reintegrate the delinquent into the community and, if possible, to achieve reconciliation without causing bitter-ness and resentment; in the words of an informant, the institution exists "to finish off people's quarrels and to abolish bad feeling" '.[23] This therapeutic goal is manifested in the manner in which the dispute is resolved. After a decision is reached the penalty imposed is always the same. The party held to be in the wrong is asked to bring beer (four pots, modified downwards according to the circumstances) and meat, which is shared with the other party and all those attending the *rukurato*. The losing party is also expected to 'humble himself, not only to the man he has injured but to the whole assembly'.[24]

Beattie correctly points out that, because the council of neighbours has no power to enforce its decision, the shared feast is *not* to be viewed primarily as a penalty, for the wrong-doer acts as host and also shares in the food and drink. 'And it is a praiseworthy thing; from a dishonourable status he is promoted to an honourable one . . .'[25] and reintegrated into the community.[26]

Although Beattie does not use a psychoanalytic frame of reference in approaching his material, it is clear that the communal feast involves the manipulation of rewards as the last step in social-control measure which breaks the progressive alienation of the deviance cycle. The description of procedures in the *rukurato* indicates that it is highly informal in nature, convening in a room in a house with everyone 'sitting around'. However, Beattie does not provide enough detail to enable one to determine whether or not the beginning and intermediate steps in the Myoro moot show the permissiveness, support, and denial of reciprocity which characterize the Kpelle moot. Given the structure and outcome of most Nyoro councils, one would surmise that a close examination of their proceedings[27] would reveal the implicit operation of therapeutic principles.

The fact that the Kpelle court is basically coercive and the moot therapeutic does not imply that one is dysfunctional while the other is eufunctional. Like Beattie, I conclude that the court and informal dispute-settlement procedures have separate but complementary functions. In marital disputes the moot is oriented to a couple as a dyadic social system and serves to reconcile them wherever possible. This is eufunctional from the point of view of the couple, to whom divorce would be dysfunctional. Kpelle courts customarily treat matrimonial matters by granting a divorce. While this may be dysfunctional from the point of view of the couple, because it ends their marriage, it may be eufunctional from the point of view of society. Some marriages, if forced to continue, would result in adultery or physical violence at best, and improper socialization of children at worst. It is clear that the Kpelle moot is to the Kpelle court as the domestic and family relations courts (or commercial and labour arbitration boards) are to ordinary courts in our own society. The essential point is that both formal and informal dispute-settlement procedures serve significant functions in Kpelle society and neither can be fully understood if studied alone.[28]

Notes

1. The field work on which this paper is based was carried out in Liberia in 1957 and 1958 and was supported by a grant from the Ford Foundation, which is, of course, not responsible for any of the views presented here. The data were analysed while the writer was the holder of a pre-doctoral National Science Foundation Fellowship. The writer wishes to acknowledge, with gratitude, the support of both foundations. This paper was read at the Annual Meeting of the American Anthropological Association in Philadelphia, Pennsylvania, in November 1961.

   The dissertation, in which this material first appeared, was directed by Philip H. Gulliver, to whom I am indebted for much stimulating and provocative discussion of many of the ideas presented here. Helpful comments and suggestions have also been made by Robert T. Holt and Robert S. Merrill.

   Portions of the material included here were presented in a seminar on African Law conducted in the Department of Anthropology at the University of Minnesota by E. Adamson Hoebel and the writer. Members of the seminar were generous in their criticisms and comments.

2. Paul J. Bohannan, *Justice and Judgment among the Tiv*, Oxford University Press, London, 1957; Max Gluckman, *The Judicial Process among the Barotse of Northern Rhodesia*, Manchester University Press, 1954; P. P. Howell, *A Handbook of Nuer Law*, Oxford University Press, London, 1954.

3. Cf. George P. Murdock, *Social Structure*, Macmillan, New York, 1949, p. 74.

4. James L. Gibbs, Jr., 'Poro Values and Courtroom Procedures in a Kpelle Chiefdom', *Southwestern Journal of Anthropology* (in press). A detailed analysis of Kpelle courtroom procedures and of procedures in the moot together with transcripts appears in: James L. Gibbs, Jr., *Some Judicial Implications of Marital*

Instability among the Kpelle (unpublished Ph.D. Dissertation, Harvard University, Cambridge, Mass., 1960).

5. What follows is based on a detailed case study of moots in Panta Chiefdom and their contrast with courtroom hearings before the paramount chief of that chiefdom. Moots, being private, are less susceptible to the surveillance of the anthropologist than courtroom hearings, thus I have fewer transcripts of moots than of court cases. The analysis presented here is valid for Panta Chiefdom and also valid, I feel, for most of the Liberian Kpelle area, particularly the north-east where people are, by and large, traditional.

6. This simple distilled rum, bottled in Monrovia and retailing for twenty-five cents a bottle in 1958, is known in the Liberian Hinterland as 'cane juice' and should not be confused with the imported varieties.

7. American currency is the official currency of Liberia and is used throughout the country.

8. Cf. J. F. Holleman, 'An Anthropological Approach to Bantu Law (with special reference to Shona law)' in the *Journal of the Rhodes—Livingstone Institute*, vol. x, 1950, pp. 27–41. Holleman feels that the use of tokens for effecting apologies—or marriages—shows the proclivity for reducing events of importance to something tangible.

9. Talcott Parsons, *The Social System*, The Free Press, Glencoe, Ill., 1951, pp. 314–19.

10. Jerome D. Frank, 'Group Methods in Psychotherapy', in *Mental Health and Mental Disorder: A Sociological Approach*, edited by Arnold Rose, W. W. Norton Co., New York, pp. 524–35.

11. J. W. Klapman, *Group Psychotherapy: Theory and Practice*, Grune & Stratton, New York, 1959.

12. Marvin K. Opler, 'Values in Group Psychotherapy', *International Journal of Social Psychiatry*, vol. iv, 1959, pp. 296–8.

13. Frank, op. cit., p. 513.

14. Ibid.

15. Ibid.

16. Klapman, op. cit., p. 39.

17. Ibid., p. 15.

18. For expository purposes the four elements of therapy are described as if they always occur serially. They may, and do, occur simultaneously also. Thus, all four of the factors may be implicit in a single short behavioural sequence. Parsons (op. cit.) holds that these four elements are common not only to psychotherapy but to all measures of social control.

19. Parsons, op. cit., p. 314. Cf. loc. cit., chap. 10.

20. Cf. Parsons, op. cit., chap. 7. Parsons notes that in any social-control action the aim is to avoid the process of alienation, that 'vicious-cycle' phenomenon whereby each step taken to curb the non-conforming activity of the deviant has the effect of driving him further into his pattern of deviance. Rather, the need is to 'reach' the deviant and bring him back to the point where he is susceptible to the usual everyday informal sanctions.

21. J.H.M. Beattie, 'Informal Judicial Activity in Bunyoro', *Journal of African Administration*, vol. ix, 1957, pp. 188–95.

22. Disputes include matters such as a son seducing his father's wives, a grown son disobeying his father, or a husband or wife failing in his or her duties to a spouse. Disputes between unrelated persons involve matters like quarrelling, abuse, assault, false accusations, petty theft, adultery, and failure to settle debts. (Ibid., p. 190)

23. Ibid., p. 194.

24. Beattie, op. cit., p. 194.

25. Ibid., p. 193.

26. Ibid., p. 195. Moreover, Beattie also recognizes the functional significance of the Nyoro moots, for he notes that: 'It would be a serious error to represent them simply as clumsy, "amateur" expedients for punishing wrong-doers or settling civil disputes at an informal, sub-official level.' (Ibid.)

27. The type of examination of case materials that is required demands that field workers should not simply record cases that meet the 'trouble case' criterion (cf. K. N. Llewellyn and E. A. Hoebel, *The Cheyenne Way*, Norman, Okla., University of Oklahoma Press, 1941; and E. A. Hoebel, *The Law of Primitive Man*, Cambridge, Mass., Harvard University Press, 1954) but that cases should be recorded in some transcript-like form.

28. The present study has attempted to add to our understanding of informal dispute-settlement procedures in one African society by using an eclectic but organized collection of concepts from jurisprudence, ethno-law, and psychology. It is based on the detailed and systematic analysis of a few selected cases, rather than a mass of quantitative data. In further research a greater variety of cases handled by Kpelle moots should be subjected to the same analysis to test its merit more fully. It should prove useful in understanding dispute-settlement procedures in Africa and other parts of the world as well, for, since time immemorial, Freud's insights have undoubtedly been applied by man in many social-control mechanisms.

21

An Analysis of the Memphis Garbage Strike of 1968

THOMAS W. COLLINS

ON FEBRUARY 12, 1968, the city of Memphis Sanitation employees went on strike for higher wages and improved working conditions. Labor protests by public service employees had become quite common in the nation by the late 1960's but the Memphis strike was not just another labor dispute. In fact, it was highly unique, since it occurred in a metropolitan area with a long tradition of anti-union bias. Furthermore, the strikers were mostly black with poor education and little or no training. They were part of a regional sub-culture which had relegated them to the lowest rank in the political economy. The ramifications of their actions were enormous and extended well beyond their stated objectives in the walk-out. Indeed, it was a direct challenge to an entrenched life-style and value system. The purpose of this paper is to offer an analysis of the strike, the background factors leading to the initial confrontation, and the effects it had on the city. Special effort will be made to present this analysis from the point of view of the strikers, a view that has, thus far, been largely ignored.[1]

To understand the events leading to the strike, it is necessary to consider some important historical and environmental characteristics of Memphis. For example, its location on the Mississippi River and in the highly productive agricultural region of the Delta has molded the economy into a commercial and marketing center with only modest amounts of industrialization.

Demographically, Memphis has traditionally been a way-station for migrants moving from the Delta to northern urban centers (euphemistically known as the delta flow). The greater part of this migration consisted of economically impoverished families possessing only agricultural skills. Since the economy is non-industrial, the city has been able to absorb this labor, if only in menial service-type employment. Most of the migrants remained in Memphis only long enough to improve their resources and to gain essential techniques for survival in an urban environment. Therefore, the city has historically enjoyed a surplus of healthy labor, willing to work for low wages and yet, demanding very little in the way of public services. When the migrants reached a high level of dissatisfaction, they normally moved further north rather than attempting to change their local situation.

These demographic factors produced a rare sociopolitical structure, rare at least, in terms of 20th century United States. One sector is an affluent, service-consuming elite whose capital foundation rests in land and commercial activity. The second sector is larger and is primarily engaged in producing services for the elite sector. Vertical mobility between the two is minimal, nearly caste-like. Access to decision over the distribution of public resources has been retained by the elite. In fact, public power rested in the hands of one monolithic political machine for most of the first half of this century. Under the leadership of E. H. Crump, the machine effectively precluded any development of countervailing groups in city politics until well into the late 1950's.

Profile of Sanitation Workers

Predictably, the sanitation workers are migrants, thoroughly socialized in the economic hardships of depressed Delta counties. For example, Fayette County, Tennessee, where most of the informants in this study originated, is the third poorest county in the United States. Over 4 percent of the population survive on an income below that of the mean, $3,834. Unemployment among blacks, who make up 61% of the population, runs 68% and higher. Housing and education is especially poor; nearly 80% of the residences are substandard, i.e., without adequate plumbing facilities. The median educational attainment is 8.6 years. All the men interviewed from Fayette had either worked as share-croppers or in some phase of agro-business.

In nearly every case, the employees belong to informal mutual aid groups structured on the extended families. Developed as a means of survival in the rural environment, these networks continue to furnish vital support for migrants in the city. Resources, such as garden vegetables and fresh meat, produced in the county, sustain members in the city while limited amounts of cash and used consumer goods flow back to the county stem of the family. In some instances, these networks remain viable for years, providing workers with their major social outlet (i.e., visiting) and information on available employment. Over two-thirds (67%) of those surveyed indicated they had learned of their sanitation job opening through friends or relatives. On the other hand, none of the men had sought the aid of formal agencies such as the State Employment Office.

Shop foremen in the Sanitation Division have tended to encourage these informal communication links as a regular recruitment technique. Foremen frequently asked prospective employees if they were "a country boy" or, "who sent you?" The Division favored these men over those reared in Memphis because, as one foreman explained, "They work harder and are more stable." Given this hiring arrangement, it is quite common to find several men from the same family network together on a truck crew or other such assignment.

Work Conditions Prompting a Labor Dispute

When the migrant first arrives in Memphis, his major concern is to secure a job. Any job is important and relatively better than that which could be obtained in the country. The work attitude was expressed in a response to a question about types of employment. One worker tersely remarked, "there is no worst job. I would take anything." However, the economically deprived employee has his outer limits of tolerance to depressing work conditions. The sanitation men reached these limits by the beginning of the 1960's. The wage was $1.30 an hour with little or no job benefits. Only the truck drivers, who were mainly white, received vacations with pay. If an employee was injured on the job and could still work, he was offered a menial task around the office; otherwise he was let go. If one was killed, and a few were, his family received the equivalent of a month's salary plus burial expenses.

The job itself was little better than the wage and benefits. Each man was issued a tub for which he was responsible. Trash was collected from the back of the yard of each private residence and hauled to the truck waiting in the street. If the tub leaked, fluid from the trash would run down on the employee since he had to carry heavy loads on either his shoulder or his head. One retired worker described his situation, "In those days, I would sometimes get put off the bus 'cause I smelled so bad. I'd even have maggots in my pant cuffs at night. Some people called us the vultures 'cause we raided the garbage." A truck crew had responsibility for a neighborhood area. As a driver put it, "that meant if anything was thrown in the yard or in the street we had to pick it up. If a tree blew over in a private yard we had to go in with an ax and chop it up, then drag it out to the street and load it on the truck. If some guy was remodeling his house and threw bricks around the yard, we had to pick them up and carry them out on our heads. We had no guide lines as to what we had to do, we did everything." It should be noted here that Memphis was awarded the "Nations's Cleanest City" honor during many years of the 1950's.

Since the wages were so low, the employees had to "recycle" anything that was salvageable from their collections and apparently very little was missed including the coupons from discarded breakfast cereal boxes. "Ragging" was considered a reasonable income supplement by the management and the general public. In fact, during the strike a Memphis resident was reported to have questioned why the sanitation men were demanding a raise when they could keep anything found in the trash. People would sometimes leave used items on top of the trash container for the men, and if they kept the yard "picked up" they could expect a gift at the end of the year. Such paternalistic attitudes reflect the regional traditional values. John Dollard, in his study of a southern community in 1939, discussed a similar practice, "The Negroes seem to inherit the castoff clothes, automobiles, food, and social customs of the whites, and are marked by a general sort of second-handedness."[2]

Further injustices were inflicted on the workers by foremen. Several informants have reported that workers could be fired or suspended at the mere whim of a supervisor. For example, one reported, "My dad-in-law never took a drink in his life. But he was fired for being drunk on the job because some foreman said he saw him walking across the street with his head bobbing around. You never knew from one day to the next if you was going to get fired." Another worker said, "Once I picked up the trash from a house. After I left, the owner filled up the can again, and then called the bossman. He said the garbage had not been picked up. All I could say was that I'd picked up that house. I got three days off, no questions asked." A few of the informants related that some foremen and truck drivers demanded "kick-backs" from new employees during the six month probationary period. Perhaps the conditions were best assessed by a black minister shortly after the strike when he compared the city procedure to a slave system:

> ". . . The slave out on the field, he had no recourse to justice except if he went to the master and the master could give it to him if he wanted to, at his own dictates; his whim. Well no man wants to stand that any longer and when he is denied, a strike will come."[3]

Working conditions during the 1960's became increasingly more repressive as the city attempted to economize with tax dollars. Previously, men had been permitted to sit out a few hours of a rain storm on their route to draw a full day's pay. The city became more rigid in 1963 about such matters and began to send the men home with the short pay. The impact of this hardship must be considered in view of the fact that Memphis receives an average of 60 inches of rain a year. In the months from January through March it will often rain for days at a time. Employees often had to work under hazardous conditions. For example, men had to ride on the back of a truck, fireman style, which would sometimes reach a speed of 45 miles an hour between routes. For the sake of economy, men had to use equipment that was frequently obsolete and dangerous. When two workers were killed in a truck accident in 1964, the employees complained bitterly that the deaths could have been avoided by the installation of proper safety devices. In short, there were a number of grievances which led inexorably to a final confrontation between sanitation workers and the city. But even under such insufferable conditions, many employees still had to be convinced that striking was worth the risk of losing a salary. The activists had to labor hard to convince marginal men that something could be done to improve their condition.

City Attitude Toward Labor

Union activity is not unfamiliar to Memphis. The American Federation of Labor has represented the skilled workers in the city for most of this century. Indeed, preferential treatment was received by the AFL affiliated Memphis Trade and Labor Council in exchange for its political support of the Crump machine during the early 1930's. However, in 1936 this relationship was broken when the Council attempted to unionize city employees. In response to the union activity, the city fired fourteen employees of the fire department and blacklisted them.[4] The blacklist was so thorough it was impossible for them to gain other employment in the city for several months. During the same year, public school teachers and custodians formed a union which was also crushed. Crump's political lieutenants on the School Board forced the members to capitulate when served with an ultimatum: either give up the union or face dismissal.[5] City police were dealt a similar offer when they attempted to organize in 1943.[6] Thus, the city had established a policy of economic reprisals against employees in public service who attempted to carry on any union activity.

The Crump machine had other ways, too, to deal with organizers who were not directly employed by the city. When professionals were sent to the city by the CIO in the early 1940's to organize local plants, Crump's tactics shifted to the use of character assassination and the threat of terror. Organizers were labeled "communists" and "outside agitators engaging in un-American activity." When intimidation was not effective, union people were assaulted and often severely beaten by street toughs. Few assailants were ever apprehended in these affairs. Crump made his policy a matter of public record in 1943 when he announced: "I am opposed to the CIO. Their ruthless methods are destructive and retarding to the growth of communities wherein they are active ... if the CIO could entrench itself in Memphis, this city would go back ten years."[7] In spite of this opposition, the CIO did manage to unionize a few plants in Memphis during the 1940's. However, in the prevailing atmosphere, the city remained well out of the influence of national union organization.

The death of Crump and the subsequent disintegration of his political machine in 1954 did not soften the local attitude toward labor. Union ideology was and is the direct antithesis of values expressed by local political and business leaders, the media, and the general public. It is, therefore, understandable that it took twenty years for city employees to form another union. Surprisingly, it was the low-skilled workers of the Sanitation Division who were first to make the challenge. This fact in itself speaks of how deeply these workers felt oppression.

In 1964, the sanitation employees chartered Local 1733 and affiliated with the American Federation of State, County and Municipal Employees (AFSCME), an international union with a reputation for effectively organizing marginal occupational groups in the nation. Much of their national activity has centered on women and minorities who have been largely ignored by the major labor organizations. Needless to say, a radical organization of this type was not well received by the citizens and community leaders of Memphis. City administrators unquestionably had wide support in the effort to limit the effectiveness of Local 1733.

Direct Confrontation

Prior to the major confrontation of 1968, the sanitation workers attempted two strikes, the first in 1963 to protest general working conditions. Since there was little support for the strikers, either among the employees or in the black community, the action lasted only a few hours. Strike leader T.O. Jones recalls, "Even the black community was against us. Some ministers came down and literally got down on their knees and begged us to go back to work. We didn't have much chance." For their efforts, a few men were dismissed and others were reassigned to less desirable jobs. But these leaders were not to be denied. They continued their efforts until they finally secured a charter for Local 1733. It is noteworthy that the union leaders were similar in background and skill to other employees with the exception of their outside exposure. All of them had either served in the military or had worked in some northern city which in part explains their higher degree of militancy.

In 1965, another strike was attempted to secure recognition for the union local but again it was poorly organized and lacked support in the wider community. Word was leaked of their plans, and before the men had hit the street, the city was ready with a court injunction. The legal action was weak (based on a vague Tennessee Supreme Court ruling regarding government employees) but it was enough to intimidate the sanitation workers to return to work.

The black middle-class in Memphis was not willing at this time to make a commitment to any direct confrontation, out of consideration of what they felt to be good relations with city government. According to historian David

Tucker, the black middle class had been gaining a number of concessions in their efforts to desegregate the city.[8] Memphis public libraries, recreation facilities, and public accommodations had been opened to blacks. In 1965 they had helped elect a white mayor who was thought to favor further desegregation, particularly in industry and public schools. These expectations, however, proved to be false. Actually, little progress was made. Frustrations began to mount in the late 1960's. When a tough-minded mayor, Henry Loeb, was elected to office in 1967 without the support of any segment of the black electorate, the mood of the blacks changed to one of greater militancy with an emphasis on direct confrontation. The black middle-class organizations were waiting for an issue when the sanitation employees walked out on strike February 12, 1968. This time the employees were not ready to back down. They had organizational support, a militant union, and a city mayor who was capable of unifying the blacks.

The incident which sparked the walk-out actually occurred in another division of the Public Work Department. Thirty-five black employees had been sent home because of rain while several white employees, with identical work assignments, were permitted to remain and draw a full day's pay. The sanitation workers chose to strike in protest of the action. As predicted, the new strong-willed mayor took a firm stand in opposition to the employees. In the Crump tradition, he announced that Memphis was not New York and he would not yield to any union. A former City mayor reported that, "Loeb talked to the men like they might have expected to be talked to if they were still on a plantation working as sharecroppers." But the workers were just as adamant. As one put it, "Things were so bad back then that I made up my mind I wasn't coming back if we didn't win. The abuses were too much for us."

Once the administrators learned they could not force the men back on the job by intimidation, they set out to break the strike by hiring scab laborers, both white and black, to make collections on a limited basis. The fact that non-union black laborers would take jobs under the ominous threat of violence further relates how desperate rural men can be for employment. Employees who did not walk off their jobs at the beginning of the strike later joined the picket lines. A reluctant striker stated, "Henry Loeb's police couldn't protect me at home. I wanted to work, but I was afraid of the other men."

Actually, the greatest amount of violence in the strike came from the city, not the workers. Taking a cue from the late Mayor Crump's tactics, the city made a show of police force whenever possible. During the first protest march (one of many), the police reacted by macing (tear gasing) the strikers and black ministers indiscriminately. Additional gas was used in a black church where marchers had taken refuge from the attack. The police action stunned the black community and probably did more to unify it than any one incident in the history of Memphis. A minister in the march stated, "Police don't invade a black church. I mean, this is our sanctuary and they broke the law." This time people were not to be intimidated by their traditional adversary, the Memphis Police Department. Thus the dispute that began as a labor problem quickly turned into a major racial confrontation for the entire city.

Offered wide support, the strikers, with the influential black ministers, were able to escalate the pressure on city hall by calling for a boycott of white-owned downtown stores and selected companies. The city had managed to limit strike effectiveness by collecting trash but it could not cope with the economic pressures of a boycott. Also, a few white groups were formed to intercede in behalf of the strikers but such support was not widespread. On the contrary, there were cases where whites were voted out of their church membership for voicing an opinion of conciliation. Nor did the two daily newspapers print anything favorable to the black strikers (the papers were also boycotted). In the end, it was the boycott that finally brought the city around. The lost income of the downtown merchants during the two-month strike has not been made public, but it must have been staggering. This finally forced the mayor to make a settlement.

There was some question whether Dr. Martin Luther King should have been invited into the conflict in March. The boycott was working and opposition to the mayor was mounting. Also, it was understood that no protection could be expected for King since the police were clearly on the side of the city. Nevertheless, the ministers sent for the civil rights leader. His murder on April 4th brought nationwide focus on the city. Administrators had no choice but to make their peace with the strikers and the black community.

The city agreed to most of the union demands: recognition of the Local by establishing a dues check-off system; 10 cents an hour wage increase; merit promotion (a seniority system); and a realistic grievance procedure. For the first time in their lives, the men of the Public Works Department had job security. The occupation was the same and vertical mobility was still lacking, but the success in the strike was viewed as a beginning. They had challenged the system and won.

Attitudes Since the Strike

In the six years since the settlement, union members have demonstrated a surprising lack of willingness to push the city administration on hard bread and butter issues, i.e., wage increases and other benefits. Most members, thus far, appear content just to have a union. There is general consensus on the effectiveness of the union in terms of job security and grievance procedure. One worker summed up his feelings, "The Man can't run us out from down here anymore. If you stay straight, you have a job for life." Generally, the men react strongly to any attitude or action by foremen which can be interpreted as paternalism or vindictiveness. Men who submit to such treatment are sanctioned through the use of gossip or labeled an "Uncle Tom." Union stewards who are said to be soft on the city are quickly replaced. There are still a few employees who have been so thoroughly socialized in the traditions of rural southern life that it is difficult for them to lend their full support to the union. It is widely believed that these workers "will be shaped into line soon."

Job dissatisfaction is most often expressed by the younger men, particularly those who have been reared in the city or who have lived in Memphis long enough to change their network groups. Those with large families find it impossible to live on the base wage of $2.60 an hour. At least one-fourth of the men hold second jobs that extend their work week to 70 hours or more. A few are forced into "hustling" on weekends. Thus far, the union or the city has not been able to increase job mobility. A man cannot expect to be promoted to even the position of truck driver or crew chief until he has accumulated at least six years seniority. After 15 years, it is possible to be promoted to foreman, but the city has demonstrated a reluctance to offer this position to many black employees. Hence, the frustration tends to run high among those who are at the bottom of the seniority system.

In the past, men could quit their jobs and seek vertical mobility by moving north to industrial centers but this option is no longer open. A number of workers have expressed the belief that the cost of living is so high in the North that it is virtually impossible to improve their living situation. Therefore the ranks of sanitation employees are expanding with men who are willing to take a more militant stance to improve their current economic position. In future contract negotiations, the union leadership will be forced to assume a much harder line to keep these men satisfied.

Moreover, the strength of black blue-collar unionism has been steadily expanding since the 1968 strike. AFSCME has organized the Memphis City Hospital service staff and its membership now numbers over 5,000. Also, there are more blacks in formerly all-white unions in the city. In any future conflict it would appear impossible for these unions to ignore strike activity by AFSCME as they did in 1968. Thus the sanitation workers are in a position of power capable of making demands on the city political system quite independent of the black middle-class.

City administrators appear aware of this development. Therefore, they tend to take a more congenial approach in contract negotiations and grievance decisions. Although they have been slow to open up more available supervisory positions to blacks, administrators have attempted to introduce some training programs and upgrade existing positions. More employees are encouraged to apply for job openings outside the Sanitation Division in an attempt to increase their vertical mobility within the City structure. Foremen who have demonstrated a consistent unwillingness or inability to handle men in a biracial situation have been transferred. In some cases, however, the city is limited in the amount of change which can be made. If, for example, city administrators were to attempt to mechanize collections and hence pay higher salaries through increased productivity, it would reduce the number of jobs in the division. Moreover, the type of manpower training programs necessary to advance many of these employees to skilled-level jobs, is beyond the financial ability of any single municipal government. Therefore continuing innovation to upgrade the types of jobs available in the Sanitation Division will be somewhat restricted.

In summary, the sanitation strike was the single most important event in Memphis since the death of political boss Crump. Most notably, power relationships have changed. Not only have blacks improved their situation, but blue-collar blacks have become a factor in the decision-making process where before they existed only as a large minority to be ignored. For the employees who laid their jobs on the line, the actual increase in salary has been minimal, but their bargaining power is expanding with each contract negotiation. Furthermore, one cannot understate the value of the new status these men have achieved. As one worker succinctly put it, "That union makes me feel like a man."

Notes

1. Most of the data presented in this paper was collected over a twelve month period (December, 1972 through January, 1973), and utilized several traditional ethnographic methods, such as indepth interviewing and a structured survey. Additional data was obtained from the taped interviews stored in the Mississippi Valley Collection of the John Brister Library, Memphis State University. The latter interviews were collected by the Multi-Media Sanitation Strike Project.

2. John Dollard, *Caste and Class in a Southern Town* (New York: Doubleday, 1957, 3rd edition), p. 102.

3. Mississippi Valley Collections—Taped interview on File No. 41.

4. *Memphis Press-Scimitar*, February 14, 1936, p. 1.

5. *Ibid.*, May 20, 1936, p. 1.

6. *Ibid.*, October 15, 1943, pp. 1-2.

7. *Ibid.*, January 1, 1949, p. 1.

8. David Tucker, *Memphis Since Crump* (Ms, Memphis State University) ND.

22

The Dream of Diversity,
The Dilemma of Difference:
Race and Class Contradictions
in a Feminist Health Clinic

SANDRA MORGEN

WE OFTEN STUDY SOCIAL MOVEMENTS primarily to understand the changes they advance in the larger society. This article focuses instead on change within a social movement—the women's health movement of the 1970s in the United States. Like the larger feminist movement, women's health organizations during this period adopted the ideology of "sisterhood"—the belief that women share a common bond, a common oppression, and a common struggle for empowerment. Based on my research in a feminist health clinic, I explore the changing meaning of gender, that is, assumptions about the nature of sisterhood, for members of this organization as they faced the challenge of understanding how race and class differentiate women's experiences, needs, and political identities.

Between 1977 and 1979 I was a participant-observer in the Women's Health Center (WHC) (a pseudonym).[1] I was trained to provide a variety of health services and functioned as a member of the collective that ran the center. The center was founded in the early 1970s, and like hundreds of similar local feminist health groups, flourished in the wake of the women's health movement[2] in the United States. During the decade of the 1970s women organized a variety of health groups ranging from abortion and birth control referral services to comprehensive feminist health clinics. The movement is perhaps best known popularly through the publication *Our Bodies, Ourselves*[3] by the Boston Women's Health Book Collective. Like this book, the women's health movement aims to arm women with increased knowledge about their bodies and their reproductive, sexual, and physiological experiences and options.

The WHC was founded in 1972 by a consciousness-raising group of women who were "ready to stop talking and start doing something about our problems" (interview with founding member of WHC). They formed a small volunteer health information and referral center housed in the basement of a church that had as its goal the creation of

> a place where women can get involved . . . to talk, to share, to relax, or to get involved in collective action . . . to help ourselves and *all* women control our lives as much as possible. (Goals statement, Women's Health Center, 1973, emphasis mine)

In the next few years the center grew, and by the late 1970s it was an organization that employed six paid staff (almost all nonprofessional health workers), hosted twice-weekly family planning and routine gynecology clinics (staffed by physicians who provided those services that by law were restricted to doctors), and provided a wide array of peer counseling and crisis-intervention services (e.g., for rape, domestic violence, problem pregnancy, teen pregnancy, etc.) to women in the city.

The WHC, like other feminist health clinics of this period, embraced an egalitarian ideology emphasizing social relations based on equality, women's autonomy, self-help, and collective action. The vision of its members stressed equality in all phases of the organization's operation—decision making; the division of labor; and access to knowledge, wages and other rewards. WHC programs were formulated "by women, for women" (WHC document), manifesting the goal of self-determination by the collective and facilitating control by individual women over their lives. The feminist health service model, "the well woman model," explicitly challenged the unnecessary medicalization of women's lives imposed by largely male doctors, and embodied the premise that health care was a right, not a commodity designed to generate profits for those groups that control health services and products. The key issue of the movement is women's control of their own bodies and the WHC services and programs were designed to allow women themselves—as clients, lay health workers, and collective members—maximum control over their bodies and their lives.

The CETA Project

My focus here will be the analysis of changes that were associated with the center's receipt of a grant of over $100,000 from CETA (Comprehensive Employment and Training Act), the federal jobs training program for low-income persons.[4] This grant enabled the center to hire fifteen low-income women for a health education and training program. With the hiring of these women the composition of the staff changed substantially. In the years before receipt of these funds the staff of the center had been predominantly white, and middle-class women had served as the core of the health collective. This was probably due to the fact that most staff were volunteers (because there was no money to pay the health workers). The inability to pay staff had severely limited the participation of working-class women, who could rarely afford to work without being paid. Of the paid staff and volunteers who worked at the center just before the receipt of the CETA grant, only one was a woman of color, several were of Portuguese descent, and only a few were working class.[5] Of the fifteen women hired with CETA funds over one-third were women of color and almost all were AFDC (Aid to Families with Dependent Children) recipients or AFDC-eligible.

A major goal of the CETA project was this diversification of the staff. However, the CETA project initiated or accelerated a series of changes in the WHC over the next two years. During this period there was significant growth in the center's programs, staff, services, and budget. These changes had also involved a growing divergence between the center's feminist ideology and its everyday practice, particularly an erosion of egalitarian social relations, the demise of collectivity (participatory democracy), and an increasing distance from the political goals and the larger social movement that had spawned the center in the first place. Although the reality of collective decision making and egalitarian social relations had begun to erode before the CETA project, a series of decisions made regarding that project brought into bold relief the patterns of inequality that became pronounced in the months after the CETA project began.[6]

For example, the "regular" staff of the center (those on staff before the initiation of the CETA project) decided not to immediately incorporate the "CETA staff" (as they were called) into the collective decision-making structure, the weekly staff meeting. This decision was based on the feeling that because the newly hired women had no previous history of volunteering at the center and did not, in the interviews, evidence much knowledge of or specific commitment to feminism, they should undergo extensive training before they joined the collective. The plan was to wait several months, until the new staff had completed counselor-training and consciousness-raising sessions[7] and had become familiar with collective decision making through having a degree of control over their own project.

Admittedly, the incorporation of fifteen new staff members into an already existing staff of only ten women and the fact that only a few of the women hired for the CETA project had ever before been involved in any feminist organization were very real problems facing the center in implementing the new project. However, the staff had never before solved the problems of incorporating new members, almost always women with little to no previous feminist organizational or health experience, by denying them the opportunity to participate fully in the collective. In fact, the experience of participation in the collective was regarded as an important mechanism for fostering understanding of and commitment to feminism.

In addition, several of the CETA staff were assigned to full-time clerical duties, creating an explicit division of labor between health and clerical/administrative work for the first time in the center's history. Sine the center's inception clerical, administrative, health, and custodial duties had been done by all of the staff (sometimes in rotation, and sometimes to different degrees) in accordance with the ideal of egalitarianism. Both this division of labor and the failure to incorporate the CETA staff into the policy decision-making body created hierarchies within the staff and inequities of power, knowledge, and labor.

The counselor-training and consciousness-raising sessions organized for the new staff emphasized specific skills training, discussions of feminism, and discussions and exercises designed to develop an understanding of sexism. Discussions of differences in women's lives as shaped by race, ethnicity, and class did not occur, but there was an emphasis on the value of having a "diverse" staff so that more community women would feel comfortable coming to a health clinic where they could relate to "other women like themselves" (WHC document).

Interwoven throughout the training were messages concerning the importance of social relations of equality and the centrality of gender as a common bond between women. However, for the CETA staff this ideological message was belied by much of their actual experience—being referred to as "the CETA staff," which they later decried as a stigma, a mark of inferiority; being excluded from collective decision making; experiencing increasingly authoritarian treatment by the regular staff. Tensions simmered, but rarely did these issues come to the surface.

The distance between the dream of diversity and its reality was so great that change had to result. In this center, the nature and meaning of differences between women became thematic and were expressed in a series of events and conflicts that ultimately transformed the political meaning of gender for all. The process by which these contradictions were resolved was painful, enriching, and complex. The heart of it can be captured in three incidents that reflect the process of change and suggest the complexity of constructing a collective identity that encompasses gender commonality and race and class differences.

"Leftovers" and the Low-Income Women's Conference

One of the first and sharpest incidents in which race and class became explicit occurred in early 1978, almost six months after the CETA project began. The Department of Labor had planned a "Low-Income Women's Conference" for the city and had appointed as conference coordinator a white middle-class woman who had been associated with the WHC for years as a board member.[8] The conference coordinator scheduled several meetings with the CETA staff before the conference. Throughout these planning meetings, she often used the inclusive term "we" when discussing the goals and opportunities the conference offered low-income women; for example, "it's a great opportunity for us to tell them how we feel about their policies."

During one particular meeting she mentioned, rather proudly, a fight she was waging with the Department of Labor over the automatic deduction of five dollars from the fifteen-dollar stipend low-income women were to receive for attending the conference. The five dollars was to pay for lunch. She suggested to the CETA staff that they bring a sack lunch rather than pay the five dollars,

> You won't have to buy lunch. Bring a sack lunch, and the catering will be happening anyhow. Let's let the men pay their five dollars. You bring your sack lunches, and I'm sure there will be plenty of leftovers, and for sure we can go up after a while and have some coffee.

A number of the CETA staff rolled their eyes and were clearly angry with Cynthia. One Black woman said, "I'm going to pay for my lunch like everyone else." Another said, more pointedly, "I've been eating leftovers all my life, and I don't have to eat them at this conference." When the conference coordinator left the room the women exploded in anger and the theme of "not eating leftovers" was reiterated. One Black woman used this encounter as evidence that "women like her don't have a clue about the lives of low-income women," adding that "this kind of thing always happens when women like that get involved."

She elaborated on the meaning of "women like that," referring to a series of incidents from the history of the center that showed both the greater power of white middle-class women in the organization and their racist and class-biased actions, which alienated and excluded women of color and poor women. One example was the choice, the year before, of an almost all-white delegation from the community to an international women's conference in Mexico,

> They did nothing to involve anyone other than white middle-class women. Look at the delegates—one token Black and she is middle class. All those women had been in airplanes and to conferences. It would have been an excellent opportunity for poor or Black women to have gone to that conference and had it paid for, but no, those women had to go.

This incident exemplifies both the way women of color and working-class women experienced unequal social relations among women and their identification of race and class as shaping divisions among women. In contrast to the conference coordinator's use of the inclusive "we," presuming gender as the central social relationship, women of color and working-class women on the CETA staff perceived divisions among women that they expressed in the term "women like that" and in their refusal to set themselves apart by eating leftovers. The theme of exclusion based on race and class is linked to the privileges and power white middle-class women have wielded within the feminist community and parallels the experience of these women "eating leftovers" in the larger society. Although this incident did not lead to any further public discussion of racism or class bias in the WHC at that time, the incident did signal a shift from an assumption of gender bonds and commonalities in the consciousness and actions of the staff to a recognition, at least by the "CETA women," of the problem of differences among women.

"Minority" Women's Meeting

Several months later word reached the center that the Department of Labor was going to allocate several million dollars to grassroots organizations in the city as an experimental alternative to CETA. An ad hoc community coalition began to compile a series of proposals to submit as a package for projects involving minorities. The WHC staff decided that the minority women on the center staff should have a meeting to determine priorities and plans for a proposal from the center.

This was the first time in the center's history that a meeting had been held exclusively for women of color, although it should be noted that the decision to hold the meeting was made by the rest of the staff. Nevertheless, it suggests at least an initial awareness by the largely white middle-class "regular" staff that merely incorporating women of color into "their" organization was not enough. Rather, at least some of the staff realized that differences among women were significant enough to warrant both the relinquishment of control over the process of program development and autonomous action by minority women.

At that meeting Black and Hispanic women shared with each other their discomfort with and distrust of white women. For example, a Puerto Rican woman talked about being "uncomfortable" and "nervous" with white women. A Black woman made the suggestion that consciousness-raising groups be organized for minority women. She believed that minority women would not be comfortable in such an intimate group with white women and recalled an experience she once had with a white counselor,

> Now she wanted to get into my mind, pick my brain, find out how a woman like me feels, and I wasn't going to let her know, a white lady, sitting all dressed up and nice, no way.

The women also shared their perception that the WHC was regarded as a white middle-class woman's institution in the community. The Puerto Rican woman remarked

> Spanish women in this community have either not heard of the [WHC] or if they have they have heard really bad things. They think it a place to come for bullshit.

This was regarded as a real problem because, despite the distrust of white women expressed at the meeting, many members of this group admitted that they had grown enormously through their involvement with the WHC.

During most of the meeting the discussion centered on the kinds of programs minority women needed in order to better their own lives and those of their families. A consistently reiterated theme was the importance of minority women having the opportunity these women had experienced of a "changing sense of myself as a woman since being here at the WHC"(one of the CETA staff). There was no question that the experience of learning about their bodies, sharing and working with other women, and recognizing sexism had been very important for these women. They were very clear that their involvement with the WHC *had* been an invaluable experience. Their concern was to find a way to overcome the deeply rooted division and distrust between white middle-class women and poor and minority women in the community so that minority and poor women could participate in and benefit from an organization that was perceived to be controlled by and for women.

This meeting provides clear evidence that gender was an important part of the collective identity and concern of the women of color, but that gender consciousness was race-and-class-specific. Despite the lack of any explicit attention to race and class in the training of the new staff, they had filtered their growing awareness of gender through the lens of their own experiences, experiences shaped as much by race and class as by gender. Moreover, in the four months that elapsed between the first incident and this meeting, the staff as a whole had begun to recognize that women's lives were shaped by race, ethnicity, and class as certainly as by gender. Otherwise, they would not have planned a meeting exclusively for women of color at which they could consider their particular experiences, needs, and program ideas. This growing awareness can also be seen in the remarks of one of the "regular" staff members during a meeting about this time,

> Even though we always said we had respect for our clients as women and treated them as equals, it's different having your main contact with minority women being with them as clients and with them as fellow staff. Your relationship with clients is short-term and really defined through a helping relationship. Working together, though, Black, Hispanic, and white women—we really have to respect and understand the differences in our lives and values, not just say we do.

The Fair: A Turning Point in Collective Identity

A third incident took place one year later, when, as should become obvious, the texture of social relations within the staff had altered substantially.

This incident demonstrates that the group consciousness of the staff had changed and that the staff as a whole was more concerned to project an image of the WHC that reflected their new understandings about the intersection of gender, race, and class.

In late 1978, the board of the center decided to host a "fair" the following summer to celebrate the growth of the center and the anticipated move to its own building (donated by the city). Although the staff was invited to participate in planning the event, no one from the staff got involved until April, just two months before the fair was to be held. At that time a white middle-class woman, who had been involved with the center for most of its existence, went to a meeting of the committee planning the event and returned to the staff very concerned about the plans that had been made. In short—the plans for the fair were, to her mind, going to reinforce the image of the center as a place for white and middle-class women, going against what she called the "hard work of changing that image we have been about over the past couple of years." After a discussion in the staff (which now included about half of the ex-CETA workers hired through different grants), a decision was made to meet with the board committee to discuss their concerns.

The staff member who had attended the last meeting listed four concerns: the failure to organize child care for the fair, its location in the community arts center, the specific plans for preregistration for the conference, and the names and content of the proposed workshops. Each of the criticisms reflected the staff's concern that the fair not reflect an image of the WHC as an organization of and for white middle-class women.

The staff believed that working-class women would be discouraged from attending the fair if they had to preregister; if there were no arrangements made for child care; or if the fair was held in the arts center, a community organization clearly associated with the white middle class. Moreover, the staff felt that the proposed workshops, particularly the ones on "spirituality" and "career planning," did not reflect the needs and concerns of the majority of women in the city and would suggest an insensitivity to their priorities. As one of the staff put it,

> We feel that the content of the workshops draws barriers between women. A workshop on spirituality which focuses on the nonreligious kinds of spirituality denies the fact that for most working-class women in this community religion and spirituality are linked and turns off those women rather than reaching out to them to expand their ideas about spiritual matters. Worse, calling a workshop "career planning" in a community where most women have real limited job options makes it clear that you are really addressing professional white middle-class women.

Another staff member expressed her belief that the way the fair was planned would alienate many of the center's clients,

We are afraid it will set up a different relationship with our clients, one that is uncomfortable. We think they will come to the fair and see the membership as a group of people completely different from themselves. They could easily see the WHC serving low-income women by doling out services, without seeing it as a place they could work into, feel they belonged.

A heated and tense discussion followed, with several women from the board protesting that, in the words of one, the staff appeared to be "censoring" activities that were of concern to "a group of women who have been involved with the center for a long time but who are not interested in or in need of the services of the center." A staff member retorted, "We do see the fair as geared to a particular group of women, and we ourselves feel we cannot relate to it and don't want it labeled as representing the WHC." Another added, "It's one thing to schedule one speaker or event that is geared to the specific interests of a small group of women. It's another thing when the event is to symbolize who we are as an organization."

The staff succeeded in having the fair postponed until "we can work out some of these difficulties" (staff member); in fact, the fair was never held. But this event marked a turning point in the WHC, with the staff as a whole articulating a conception of gender that did not favor the experiences, priorities, needs, or values of the most powerful groups of women in the organization. Although there was still much struggle ahead for this group, with even more explicit and painful conflict over race and class issues, at this point the reality of differences and divisions among women was at least as influential in the group's political consciousness as was "sisterhood," that is, the common experiences of women.

Diversity, Difference, Changing Collective Identity

The WHC was able to move to a resolution of some of the tensions that the "dream of diversity" entailed for this organization. Within a few years of the events reported here even greater changes took place within the center. For example, a pamphlet developed by the WHC in celebration of International Women's Day[9] in 1980 explicitly addresses the breadth women's liberation takes on if truly diverse women's struggles are included and suggests that the process of changing group consciousness about "women's issues" has indeed been profound:

We have also realized that women's struggle for equality is closely connected with the struggles of other oppressed groups. . . . Some of these struggles [that the WHC has been involved in this year] do not concern narrowly defined "women's issues." . . . That's because women cannot achieve equality or decent lives unless all working people get a better deal, nor will women be liberated until racism is eliminated. . . . The struggle for women's liberation includes all women, including women struggling for equality and a better life as workers, as Black people, as Puerto Ricans, as lesbians, or other oppressed groups.

Within two years a woman of color involved with the CETA project became the center's director.

By focusing on the racism and class bias that existed among the staff of the WHC, I in no way mean to imply that these women should be singled out for their prejudices. Rather, the staff of the center are women who, from the beginning, recognized the necessity of including "other" women and who clearly believed that "sisterhood" was a sufficient foundation from which to practice egalitarian social relations. Within the context of their political commitment to women they faced the challenges of revising their assumptions about shared "sisterhood" and either dealing with their own racism and class privileges (the white and middle-class women) or their distrust and suspicions of white and middle-class women (the women of color and the working-class women).

Women who become involved in the women's movement and who adopt its values with respect to social, economic, and political equality do not automatically shed themselves of deeply ingrained assumptions and beliefs from the dominant culture. In the contemporary U.S. racism runs deep, and assumptions about class are pervasive. Racism and derogatory stereotypes about low-income people co-exist with ideological platitudes about equal opportunity and democratic pluralism.

What this case study suggests is that even progressive social movements—intentionally organized to foster egalitarian social relations and structures—must explicitly confront the underlying racism and class biases that are daily reinforced by the dominant society. It also shows that once this process begins, very significant changes can take place in the power relations between individuals and groups. The staff of the WHC shifted their emphasis from an assumption of shared sisterhood to a recognition that the bond women share is textured by the different experiences women have because of their position in the larger society. With that recognition, they moved from a desire to incorporate diverse groups of women into the center to the hard work of constructing a collective identity and organizational goals and actions that encompassed differences and entailed changing power relations between groups of women. In the process, sisterhood became less an assertion of commonality than a basis for alliances and for shared commitments to empower women.

Notes

1. For a much more in-depth description of the Women's Health Center, the community in which it is located, and some of the events discussed herein, see Sandra Morgen, "Ideology and Change in a Feminist Health Center: The Experience

and Dynamics of Routinization," Ph.D dissertation, Department of Anthropology, University of North Carolina, Chapel Hill, N.C., 1982.

2. For an excellent overview of the women's health movement, see Sheryl Ruzek, *The Women's Health Movement* (New York: Praeger, 1978).

3. Boston Women's Health Book Collective, *Our Bodies, Ourselves: A Book by and for Women* (New York: Simon and Schuster, 1976).

4. CETA was the federal jobs training program for most of the previous decade. Reagan abolished the program early in his administration. The program was administered by the Department of Labor, but local CETA agencies received and allocated funds. The program was designed to provide both training and short-term employment to eligible persons, with eligibility dependent largely on income.

5. My use of terms like "middle class" and "working class" is somewhat imprecise but essentially refers to a combination of income, occupation, and education and takes into consideration the self-designation of class position by the individuals involved in the center.

6. For a much-expanded discussion of the CETA project and the various changes in the WHC it spurred, see Sandra Morgen, "The Dynamics of Cooptation in a Feminist Health Clinic," *Social Science and Medicine* 23(2):201–210.

7. Consciousness-raising groups were a fundamental structure of the early women's movement in the U.S. Groups of five to ten women gathered on a regular basis to discuss problems they encountered in their everyday lives on account of their gender. The basic premise of the group is that if women share their everyday problems and insights, they can discover both the structural causes of their oppression and the potential to change society through collective action.

8. The WHC was essentially a staff (including volunteer)-run organization. A board was created in the center's early years to conform to regulations for nonprofit community organizations. The board usually met only once or twice a year. At different points in the center's history the board played different roles, but at no time did it preclude the centrality of staff collectivity.

9. International Women's Day, March 8, celebrates working women's struggles worldwide.

Ritual and Belief Systems

Men and women everywhere attempt to explain and control the world around them. Where do babies come from? What makes yams grow? What distinguishes women from men? What happens to an individual at death? Why does a rock thrown into the air always come down? Why do some men have more possessions than others? When did the world begin? These questions and countless others are posed in every human society. The very ability to pose such questions is a foundation of humanness—that which separates us from other forms of life. The explanations humans offer for themselves and the world around them are both secular and supernatural. They stem from, and are part of, magic, science, and religion. Our society is unlike the tribal world in its "mix" of explanations, rather than absolute dependence on one secular or religious belief system. As Malinowski argues in his classic article included here, all peoples have theories of the cosmos and methodologies for predicting, influencing, and, ideally, controlling it.

In the final analysis it is difficult to draw absolute lines of distinction between magic, science, and religion, but there are distinguishing aspects of each. Religion is a belief system involving *myths* that explain natural and supernatural phenomena and *rituals* by which beliefs and myths are acted out. It provides a rationale for human existence and makes intelligible and acceptable the world in which men and women live. Magic involves the manipulation of natural and supernatural forces to achieve desired results. Magic assumes human power over these forces; religion usually does not.

Science differs from both magic and religion in that it is grounded in observed relationships in the sphere of what is knowable, and its attempts to manipulate and control natural forces are based on experiments rather than supplications to and propitiations of supernatural powers.

In those societies traditionally studied by anthropologists, there is far less technological and scientific knowledge than in our own, and thus people more frequently resort to magic and religion. But it is possible to overemphasize the role of supernatural explanations in the tribal world, as it is to underestimate them in our own. Until we examine the ideology of our own and other societies, we may be unaware of how much technical and scientific explanations are a part of the ideology of the tribal world and how much our own is filled with magical and religious beliefs and rituals. Several of the articles in this section vividly point out the extent to which myth and ritual are a part of American society—one of the most scientifically and technologically complex and advanced in the world.

Today's studies of religion, science, and magic are of course different from those of the pioneers of the discipline like E. B. Tylor, Sir James Frazer, and Levy-Bruhl and such sociologists as Emile Durkheim and Max Weber. But it is a tribute to their scholarship to note how much of our current views on ideology continue to draw on their insights and theories, for example, Tylor's minimal definition of religion as a belief in spiritual beings and Durkheim's concept of the sacred and the profane. These early treatises on religion and magic were followed by studies that stand today among the monumental works of anthropology—for example, works by Malinowski on Trobriand magic, science, and religion; Evans-Pritchard on the religion of the Nuer and the Azande; and Herskovits on the kingdom of Dahomey.

Studies of religion reflect changes in the theories and methods of anthropology. For example, contemporary ecological anthropology, with an emphasis on cultures as adaptive responses to ecosystems, approaches the study of myth and ritual differently from earlier studies, though not necessarily contradicting them. Rappaport, in the article included here, does not reject sociological and psychological functions of ritual, but he offers material which indicates that the ritual cycles of the Tsembaga and of other local territorial groups of Maring speakers in the New Guinea interior are important in regulating the relationships of these groups with the human and nonhuman components of their immediate environments. Specifically, ritual helps maintain the biotic communities within their territories, redistributes land and people over land, helps mobilize allies for warfare, and redistributes local pig surpluses.

Human societies are constantly changing, and religion, science, and magic can be sources, as well as reflections, of such change. One brief example might make this point.

The anthropological literature focuses on the rituals and belief systems of peoples in the tribal world, with little attention to those within such societies whom we might describe as doubters or atheists. Especially after the impact of Western technology and ideology on the tribal world, do nonbelievers continue to represent only a minority group? In short, anthropologists who analyze religion, science, and magic must change the specifics of their questions in response to changes in the world view and material conditions of the peoples they study.

Religion from a Cross-cultural Perspective

From the earliest days of anthropology as a distinct discipline, studies of various cultures of the world have included descriptions and analyses of religion. But it is not easy to study these systems of beliefs and rituals. First of all, like magic, religion is deeply embedded in symbols, which can be easily misunderstood and misinterpreted. Imagine that an anthropologist from a tribal society arrives in the United States equipped with a passable command of the English language. This anthropologist attends and participates in a series of rituals in a Christian church and, after faithfully recording what is said in the rituals and the behavior of the churchgoers, writes in his fieldnotes that this particular people are polytheistic (they make constant references to the father, the son, and the holy ghost); they also engage in cannibalism in the religious rituals (the high priest offers them the body and the blood of one who has been sacrificed for their sins). To believers in Christian religions, these seem like foolish mistakes. Unfortunately, they are easily made when the symbolic character of religion is forgotten and the rituals and beliefs are interpreted literally.

The study of religions is also complicated by the tremendous variety among specific beliefs and rituals. The variety is reflected in terms of who and what is considered a supernatural force, how many there are, how the supernatural is to be worshipped and placated, how individuals become religious specialists, the kinds of rituals they perform, how supernatural forces are communicated with, and so on. The problem, in short, is that one is tempted to subsume a great deal of the specificity of a given religious system under broadly cast typologies, as when we say, for example, that all religions are either monotheistic or polytheistic or all religions do or do not practice "ancestor worship."

Anthropologists increasingly question the simplistic typologies that dominated the early studies of religion while recognizing the opposite pitfall of assuming that religions cannot be viewed in terms of a finite set of patterns and processes.

What Do Religions Do?

Anthropologists have not found a single explanation for the existence of religion in every human society. Rather, it appears that religions serve many purposes. We have noted above that religions help men and women to explain and control the universe that they see and participate in—and that which every people says is beyond its immediate experience. While there are often specialists who are particularly versed in the religious answers to essential questions, all those associated with a religion can be assured that there are answers! The specialists are also better equipped to influence what happens to human beings through prayers, sacrifices, and other rituals. But every believer takes comfort in knowing that there are means to communicate with and influence unseen beings and powers who are said to affect the daily events in a society.

Another way of phrasing this primary function of religions is to note the existence of fundamental problems in every society, problems that men and women must cope with as well as explain. Religions give people emotional support in times of tragedy—death, famine, failure. They provide a general order for what otherwise seems haphazard and unjust: Why did my crops fail and not his? Why am I poor when she is prosperous?

It is sometimes said that religions exist because crises exist. The truth in this statement is borne out by the fact that universally people engage in religious rituals at points of change and crisis in the life cycle. In a classic study, Van Gennep observed that many rituals are patterned after the stages of an initiation, that is, initiates are ritually separated from everyday life and are then ritually reincorporated into life in an altered state as they are "reborn." Such rites of passage occur at critical stages in the life cycle: birth, the transition into adulthood, marriage, and death. Rites of passage also occur in more secular forms. Nelson H. Graburn, in his chapter here, extends Van Gennep's notions to an examination of tourism. He finds that secular rituals involved in travel serve to mark the passage from the profane, daily world of work into the sacred world of vacation.

Rituals and religions also function to validate the moral and social order of a people. This is often accomplished by conceptualizing the supernatural as organized analogously to society. "Ancestor worship," for example, is most pronounced among societies where a unilineal descent group is of prime importance. In the pantheon of gods of West African and Caribbean religions, these supernatural forces marry, have offspring, and are often known to like certain foods and drinks—just as men and women on earth do.

Another example of how religion validates and gives meaning to human organization is the belief and ritual of *totemism,* a symbolic association between a social group and a natural phenomenon such as an animal or plant. The form of totemic religions varies, but their "classic" form involves special relationships between the social group and its totem such as food taboos and rules that forbid sexual relations with another member of the totemic group. The Australian aborigines have the most developed form of totemism. For them, totemism forms the basis for a moral code and is the organizational principle around which their society is ordered. In our own society there are many examples of the symbolic elements of totemism. Think of the number of sports teams associated with a plant, animal, or other natural object: the Ohio State Buckeyes, the Toronto Maple Leafs, the Detroit Lions, and the Baltimore Orioles are only a few of countless examples. In a classic article written in 1924, Ralph Linton described the development of totemic groups in the U.S. Army during World War I. For example, the 42d Division of the U.S. Army was assigned the name "Rainbow." The members of the division began to refer to themselves only by this term; to wear the insignia of a rainbow although officially forbidden to do so; and to assume that the appearance of a rainbow in the sky was a good omen for them. So strong was the belief that members of the division claimed to see rainbows in the sky before going into battle or after a victory, although weather conditions would have made this "scientifically impossible." The totemic idea spread and other divisions began to adopt "totems."

Finally, we note that a religious system can be viewed as a justification for the subordination of a given group, such as women, ethnic groups, or a class. It can also serve as a mechanism of resistance to inequality. For example, in prerevolutionary Cuba, although of much less importance today, there was an all-male secret cult called Abakua, based on a similar set of beliefs and rituals found among the Yoruba people of Nigeria. The notions of male supremacy of Abakua were based on the assumed ritual impurity of women. The Abukua, with its membership almost exclusively consisting of black males, also served as a means of fighting racial discrimination and guaranteeing employment for its members as port workers.

In other words, religious systems serve political, ecological, economic, and social functions, in addition to their "emotional" function in addressing the human need to explain what would otherwise remain both mysterious and uncontrollable. Anthropologists have handled this problem by studying the obviously religious and the "nonreligious" aspects of such systems; for example, Hinduism as a religion and as an ideological justification for the caste system.

In this section we include an article that specifically illustrates how religions function to validate and justify an existing social order. An anthropologist from India, Surajit Sinha, describes the relationship between religion and social structure in an American Midwestern town.

Finally, we note that in situations of rapid change, "new" religions and prophets often arise, addressing the chaos that is associated with such circumstances. Such religions and cults are variously called, by anthropologists, revitalization, nativistic, messianic, or millenarian movements. Some of these movements call for a return to the "old ways," while others predict conditions that have not been a part of their reality. One of the best known of these movements is the Ghost Dance religion of American Indians. In response to cultural changes stemming from contact with the numerically more powerful and technologically more advanced whites, the call was made for a retention of functionally obsolete patterns of behavior and involvement in cathartic dances and spirit possessions. The Cargo Cults of Melanesia, the Rastafarians of Jamaica, and the Black Muslims of the United States are other well-known cases of "new religions" that offer explanations for the causes of oppression and a ritual means for reducing frustration.

It is of interest to note how different denominations and religions in the United States are simultaneously espousing contradictory approaches to the period of upheaval in current American society. In recent years there has been a resurgence of religious fervor in the United States, sometimes called "born again" Christianity. This form of religion is basically conservative, calling for a return to an old morality rather than creating an adjustment to the new one. We note the integration of religions with other aspects of a culture as the "born again" express their conservative outlook in the politics of the so-called moral majority.

The opposite advice for bringing order to a chaotic world is offered by those individuals associated with what is known as "liberation theology." In its most developed form, it calls for the merging of religious principles like equality, charity, and justice with Marxist action to redress the problems of poverty, discrimination, and alienation.

Magic and Witchcraft

A particular logic is involved when Eskimos of the Bering Strait area create dolls in the image of a baby and give them to barren women to increase their ability to conceive; when a Louisiana sorcerer uses fingernail parings of an intended victim in performing certain rituals; when a Melanesian farmer places a peculiarly shaped stone, suspected to contain a supernatural force known as *mana*, in his garden in anticipation of a higher yield of yams. The "logic" of magic is based on assumptions that like produces like, which Sir James Frazer called the "law of similarity," and that things once in contact continue to exert an effect upon one another, which he called the "law of contact" or contagious magic. The system is insulated from attack by the belief that its success is proof that the magic is effective, whereas failure is not proof of the opposite. Failure only means that the ritual was not performed properly, that the practitioner was not in a proper ritual state, or that someone else has used a stronger magic to counteract the force.

One of the main contributions that Bronislaw Malinowski made to anthropology was his argument that the world cannot be simplistically and incorrectly divided into those who lean on science (us) and those whose world is filled with magic (them). In his study of the Trobriand Islanders (see page 404 in this volume), Malinowski pointed out that a farmer would never engage in magical practices to make his yams grow *without* first having followed all of the "scientific" procedures available and known to him. But, once all had been done according to Trobriand agricultural technology, there remained the possibility that forces beyond the control of that technology would interfere with the production of a bountiful harvest.

Similarly, in our own society, we turn to magic after we have exhausted the technological and scientific techniques available to us and in situations of uncertainty and chance. Thus we observe magical behavior among pitchers at a baseball game, students before an exam, and travelers before they board an airplane.

Magic can be used for socially approved or unapproved results; it can be practiced by an individual or a group and directed at either individuals or groups of people. Two particular forms of magic about which anthropologists have written a great deal are witchcraft and sorcery. Where a distinction exists between the two, witchcraft involves an inherent trait while sorcery is a learned skill.

The pervasiveness of witchcraft, even in our own society, as the article by Leininger indicates, is no doubt traceable to the functions it can serve. It can provide an outlet for aggression and hostility; it can serve as a means for resolving conflicts and settling tensions; and it can serve as a mechanism for social control as individuals follow the rules of society because they are afraid either of being victims of a witch or of being accused of being witches themselves.

Nadel (1952) argues that witchcraft beliefs are related to specific anxieties and stresses in social life. Nadel also suggests that witchcraft accusations function to perpetuate the status quo in a society by identifying the witch as one who transgresses the existing values and behavior patterns. For example, in the 1950s in our own society, under the leadership of Senator Joseph McCarthy, the evils of American society were to be cleansed through the identification and punishment of communists, whom McCarthy assumed were lurking in every corner of American society.

A Final Word on Rituals and Beliefs

We might conclude this discussion of ideology by returning to the notion that religion is a set of rituals that "act out" a belief system. Anthropologists pose fundamental questions about these beliefs: What creates and sustains them in a society? The answer, quite simply, is *myths*. As the modes through which a society expresses beliefs about things it holds sacred, myths are stories that explain how things came to be the way they are and, importantly, how they should be maintained.

Levi-Strauss and other anthropologists suggest that symbolic expressions in myths are arranged in a common pattern: (1) There is an action or value; (2) there is the antithesis of that action or value; and (3) there is a mediating set of values that resolve the conflict between (1) and (2). Levi-Strauss also argues that myths are highly abstract models that have an internal logic unrelated to the real world. Thus they are open to many interpretations and thereby allow individuals a great deal of room to define their position in the real world (Levi-Strauss: 1955).

The "primitives" studied by Rappaport and Malinowski, as well as the "modern" peoples studied by Leininger, Sinha, and Graburn, participate in magic and religion along with practical or scientific activities. Universally, daily practical life is inextricably linked with spiritual beliefs and mythical frameworks.

References

FRAZER, SIR JAMES. 1922. *The Golden Bough*. Abridged ed. New York: Macmillan.

LINTON, RALPH. 1924. "Totemism and the A.E.F." *American Anthropologist* 26: 296–300.

LEVI-STRAUSS, CLAUDE. 1955. "The Structural Study of Myth." *Journal of American Folklore* 67: 428–444.

NADEL, S. F. 1952. "Witchcraft in Four African Societies: An Essay in Comparison." *American Anthropologist* 54: 18–29.

VAN GENNEP, A. 1960. Originally published in 1908. *Rites of Passage*. Chicago: University of Chicago Press.

23

Ritual Regulation of Environmental Relations Among a New Guinea People[1]

ROY A. RAPPAPORT

MOST FUNCTIONAL STUDIES of religious behavior in anthropology have as an analytic goal the elucidation of events, processes, or relationships occurring within a social unit of some sort. The social unit is not always well defined, but in some cases it appears to be a church, that is, a group of people who entertain similar beliefs about the universe, or a congregation, a group of people who participate together in the performance of religious rituals. There have been exceptions. Thus Vayda, Leeds, and Smith (1961) and J. K. Moore (1957) have clearly perceived that the functions of religious ritual are not necessarily confined within the boundaries of a congregation or even a church. By and large, however, I believe that the following statement by Homans (1941: 172) represents fairly the dominant line of anthropological thought concerning the functions of religious ritual:

> Ritual actions do not produce a practical result on the external world—that is one of the reasons why we call them ritual. But to make this statement is not to say that ritual has no function. Its function is not related to the world external to the society but to the internal constitution of the society. It gives the members of the society confidence, it dispels their anxieties, it disciplines their social organization.

No argument will be raised here against the sociological and psychological functions imputed by Homans, and many others before him, to

389

ritual. They seem to me to be plausible. Nevertheless, in some cases at least, ritual does produce, in Homans' terms, "a practical result on the world" external not only to the social unit composed of those who participate together in ritual performances but also to the larger unit composed of those who entertain similar beliefs concerning the universe. The material presented here will show that the ritual cycles of the Tsembaga, and of other local territorial groups of Maring speakers living in the New Guinea interior, play an important part in regulating the relationships of these groups with both the nonhuman components of their immediate environments and the human components of their less immediate environments, that is, with other similar territorial groups. To be more specific, this regulation helps to maintain the biotic communities existing within their territories, redistributes land among people and people over land, and limits the frequency of fighting. In the absence of authoritative political statuses or offices, the ritual cycle likewise provides a means for mobilizing allies when warfare may be undertaken. It also provides a mechanism for redistributing local pig surpluses in the form of pork throughout a large regional population while helping to assure the local population of a supply of pork when its members are most in need of high quality protein.

Religious ritual may be defined, for the purposes of this paper, as the prescribed performance of conventionalized acts manifestly directed toward the involvement of nonempirical or supernatural agencies in the affairs of the actors. While this definition relies upon the formal characteristics of the performances and upon the motives for undertaking them, attention will be focused upon the empirical effects of ritual performances and sequences of ritual performances. The religious rituals to be discussed are regarded as neither more nor less than part of the behavioral repertoire employed by an aggregate of organisms in adjusting to its environment. The data upon which this paper is based were collected during fourteen months of field work among the Tsembaga, one of about twenty local groups of Maring speakers living in the Simbai and Jimi Valleys of the Bismarck Range in the Territory of New Guinea. The size of Maring local groups varies from a little over 100 to 900. The Tsembaga, who in 1963 numbered 204 persons, are located on the south wall of the Simbai Valley. The country in which they live differs from the true highlands in being lower, generally more rugged, and more heavily forested. Tsembaga territory rises, within a total surface area of 3.2 square miles, from an elevation of 2,200 feet at the Simbai river to 7,200 feet at the ridge crest. Gardens are cut in the secondary forests up to between 5,000 and 5,400 feet, above which the area remains in primary forest. Rainfall reaches 150 inches per year.

The Tsembaga have come into contact with the outside world only recently; the first government patrol to penetrate their territory arrived in 1954. They were considered uncontrolled by the Australian government until 1962, and they remain unmissionized to this day.

The 204 Tsembaga are distributed among five putatively patrilineal clans, which are, in turn, organized into more inclusive groupings on two hierarchical levels below that of the total local group.[2] Internal political structure is highly egalitarian. There are no hereditary or elected chiefs, nor are there even "big men" who can regularly coerce or command the support of their clansmen or co-residents in economic or forceful enterprises.

It is convenient to regard the Tsembaga as a population in the ecological sense, that is, as one of the components of a system of trophic exchanges taking place within a bounded area. Tsembaga territory and the biotic community existing upon it may be conveniently viewed as an ecosystem. While it would be permissible arbitrarily to designate the Tsembaga as a population and their territory with its biota as an ecosystem, there are also nonarbitrary reasons for doing so. An ecosystem is a system of material exchanges, and the Tsembaga maintain against other human groups exclusive access to the resources within their territorial borders. Conversely, it is from this territory alone that the Tsembaga ordinarily derive all of their foodstuffs and most of the other materials they require for survival. Less anthropocentrically, it may be justified to regard Tsembaga territory with its biota as an ecosystem in view of the rather localized nature of cyclical material exchanges in tropical rainforests.

As they are involved with the nonhuman biotic community within their territory in a set of trophic exchanges, so do they participate in other material relationships with other human groups external to their territory. Genetic materials are exchanged with other groups, and certain crucial items, such as stone axes, were in past obtained from the outside. Furthermore, in the area occupied by the Maring speakers, more than one local group is usually involved in any process, either peaceful or warlike, through which people are redistributed over land and land redistributed among people.

The concept of the ecosystem, though it provides a convenient frame for the analysis of interspecific trophic exchanges taking place within limited geographical areas, does not comfortably accommodate intraspecific exchanges taking place over wider geographic areas. Some sort of geographic population model would be more useful for the analysis of the relationship of the local ecological population to the larger regional population of which it is a part, but we lack even a set of appropriate terms for such a model. Suffice it here to note that the relations of the Tsembaga to the total of other local human populations in their vicinity are similar to the relations of local aggregates of other animals to the totality of their species occupying broader and more or less continuous regions. This larger, more inclusive aggregate may resemble what geneticists mean by the term population, that is, an aggregate of interbreeding organisms persisting through an indefinite number of generations and either living or capable of living in isolation from similar aggregates of the same species. This is the unit which survives through long periods of time while its local ecological (*sensu stricto*) subunits, the units more or less independently involved in interspecific trophic exchanges such as the Tsembaga, are ephemeral.

Since it has been asserted that the ritual cycles of the Tsembaga regulate relationships within what may be regarded as a complex system, it is necessary, before proceeding to the ritual cycle itself, to describe briefly, and where possible in quantitative terms, some aspects of the place of the Tsembaga in this system.

The Tsembaga are bush-fallowing horticulturalists. Staples include a range of root crops, taro (*Colocasia*) and sweet potatoes being most important, yams and manioc less so. In addition, a great variety of greens are raised, some of which are rich in protein. Sugar cane and some tree crops, particularly *Pandanus conoideus*, are also important.

All gardens are mixed, many of them containing all of the major root crops and many greens. Two named garden types are, however, distinguished by the crops which predominate in them. "Taro-yam gardens" were found to produce, on the basis of daily harvest records kept on entire gardens for close to one year, about 5,300,000 calories[3] per acre during their harvesting lives of 18 to 24 months; 85 per cent of their yield is harvested between 24 and 76 weeks after planting. "Sugar-sweet potato gardens" produce about 4,600,000 calories per acre during their harvesting lives, 91 per cent being taken between 24 and 76 weeks after planting. I estimated that approximately 310,000 calories per acre is expended on cutting, fencing, planting, maintaining, harvesting, and walking to and from taro-yam gardens. Sugar-sweet potato gardens required an expenditure of approximately 290,000 calories per acre.[4] These energy ratios, approximately 17:1 on taro-yam gardens and 16:1 on sugar-sweet potato gardens, compare favorably with figures reported for swidden cultivation in other regions.[5]

Intake is high in comparison with the reported dietaries of other New Guinea populations. On the basis of daily consumption records kept for ten months on four households numbering in total sixteen persons, I estimated the average daily intake of adult males to be approximately 2,600 calories, and that of adult females to be around 2,200 calories. It may be mentioned here that the Tsembaga are small and short statured. Adult males average 101 pounds in weight and approximately 58.5 inches in height; the corresponding averages for adult females are 85 pounds and 54.5 inches.[6]

Although 99 per cent by weight of the food consumed is vegetable, the protein intake is high by New Guinea standards. The daily protein consumption of adult males from vegetable sources was estimated to be between 43 and 55 grams, of adult females 36 to 48 grams. Even with an adjustment for vegetable sources, these values are slightly in excess of the recently published WHO/FAO daily requirements (Food and Agriculture Organization of the United Nations 1964). The same is true of the younger age categories, although soft and discolored hair, a symptom of protein deficiency, was noted in a few children. The WHO/FAO protein requirements do not include a large "margin for safety" or allowance for stress; and, although no clinical assessments were undertaken, it may be suggested that the Tsembaga achieve nitrogen balance at a low level. In other words, their protein intake is probably marginal.

Measurements of all gardens made during 1962 and of some gardens made during 1963 indicate that, to support the human population, between .15 and .19 acres are put into cultivation per capita per year. Fallows range from 8 to 45 years. The area in secondary forest comprises approximately 1,000 acres, only 30 to 50 of which are in cultivation at any time. Assuming calories to be the limiting factor, and assuming an unchanging population structure, the territory could support—with no reduction in lengths of fallow and without cutting into the virgin forest from which the Tsembaga extract many important items—between 290 and 397 people if the pig population remained minimal. The size of the pig herd, however, fluctuates widely. Taking Maring pig husbandry procedures into consideration, I have estimated the human carrying capacity of the Tsembaga territory at between 270 and 320 people.

Because the timing of the ritual cycle is bound up with the demography of the pig herd, the place of the pig in Tsembaga adaptation must be examined.

First, being omnivorous, pigs keep residential areas free of garbage and human feces. Second, limited numbers of pigs rooting in secondary growth may help to hasten the development of that growth. The Tsembaga usually permit pigs to enter their gardens one and a half to two years after planting, by which time second-growth trees are well established there. The Tsembaga practice selective weeding; from the time the garden is planted, herbaceous species are removed, but tree species are allowed to remain. By the time cropping is discontinued and the pigs are let in, some of the trees in the garden are already ten to fifteen feet tall. These well-established trees are relatively impervious to damage by the pigs, which, in rooting for seeds and remaining tubers, eliminate many seeds and seedlings that, if allowed to develop, would provide some competition for the established trees. Moreover, in some Maring-speaking areas swiddens are planted twice, although this is not the case with the Tsembaga. After the first crop is almost exhausted, pigs are penned in the garden, where their rooting eliminates weeds and softens the ground, making the task of planting for a second time easier. The pigs, in other words, are used as cultivating machines.

Small numbers of pigs are easy to keep. They run free during the day and return home at night to receive their ration of garbage and substandard tubers, particularly sweet potatoes. Supplying the latter requires little extra work, for the substandard tubers are taken from the ground in the course of harvesting the daily ration for humans. Daily consumption records kept over a period of some months show that the ration of tubers received by the pigs approximates in weight that consumed by adult humans, i.e., a little less than three pounds per day per pig.

If the pig herd grows large, however, the substandard tubers incidentally obtained in the course of harvesting for human needs become insufficient and it becomes necessary to harvest especially for pigs. In other words, people must work for the pigs and perhaps even supply them with food fit for human consumption. Thus, as Vayda, Leeds, and Smith (1961:71) have pointed out, there can be too many pigs for a given community.

This also holds true of the sanitary and cultivating services rendered by pigs. A small number of pigs is sufficient to keep residential areas clean, to suppress superfluous seedlings in abandoned gardens, and to soften the soil in gardens scheduled for second plantings. A larger herd, on the other hand, may be troublesome; the larger the number of pigs, the greater the possibility of their invasion of producing gardens, with concomitant damage not only to crops and young secondary growth but also to the relations between the pig owners and garden owners.

All male pigs are castrated at approximately three months of age, for boars, people say, are dangerous and do not grow as large as barrows. Pregnancies, therefore, are always the result of unions of domestic sows with feral males. Fecundity is thus only a fraction of its potential. During one twelve-month period only fourteen litters resulted out of a potential 99 or more pregnancies. Farrowing generally takes place in the forest, and mortality of the young is high. Only 32 of the offspring of the above-mentioned fourteen pregnancies were alive six months after birth. This number is barely sufficient to replace the number of adult animals which would have died or been killed during most years without pig festivals.

The Tsembaga almost never kill domestic pigs outside of ritual contexts. In ordinary times, when there is no pig festival in progress, these rituals are almost always associated with misfortunes or emergencies, notably warfare, illness, injury, or death. Rules state not only the contexts in which pigs are to be ritually slaughtered, but also who may partake of the flesh of the sacrificial animals. During warfare it is only the men participating in the fighting who eat the pork. In cases of illness or injury, it is only the victim and certain near relatives, particularly his co-resident agnates and spouses, who do so.

It is reasonable to assume that misfortune and emergency are likely to induce in the organisms experiencing them a complex of physiological changes known collectively as "stress." Physiological stress reactions occur not only in organisms which are infected with disease or traumatized, but also in those experiencing rage or fear (Houssay et al. 1955: 1096), or even prolonged anxiety (National Research Council 1963: 53). One important aspect of stress is the increased catabolization of protein (Houssay et al. 1955: 451; National Research Council 1963: 49), with a net loss of nitrogen from the tissues (Houssay et al. 1955: 450). This is a serious matter for organisms with a marginal protein intake. Antibody production is low (Berg 1948: 311), healing is slow (Large and Johnston 1948: 352), and a variety of symptoms of a serious nature are likely to develop (Lund and Levenson 1948: 349; Zintel 1964: 1043). The status of a protein-depleted animal, however, may be significantly improved in a relatively short period of time by the intake of high quality protein, and high protein diets are therefore routinely prescribed for surgical patients and those suffering from infectious diseases (Burton 1959: 231; Lund and Levenson 1948: 350; Elman 1951: 85ff; Zintel 1964: 1043ff).

It is precisely when they are undergoing physiological stress that the Tsembaga kill and consume their pigs, and it should be noted that they limit the consumption to those likely to be experiencing stress most profoundly. The Tsembaga, of course, know nothing of physiological stress. Native theories of the etiology and treatment of disease and injury implicate various categories of spirits to whom sacrifices must be made. Nevertheless, the behavior which is appropriate in terms of native understandings is also appropriate to the actual situation confronting the actors.

We may now outline in the barest of terms the Tsembaga ritual cycle. Space does not permit a description of its ideological correlates. It must suffice to note that Tsembaga do not necessarily perceive all of the empirical effects which the anthropologist sees to flow from their ritual behavior. Such empirical consequences as they may perceive, moreover, are not central to their rationalizations of the performances. The Tsembaga say that they perform the rituals in order to rearrange their relationships with the super-natural world. We may only reiterate here that behavior undertaken in reference to their "cognized environment"—an environment which includes as very import elements the spirits of ancestors—seems appropriate in their "operational environment," the material environment specified by the anthropologist through operations of observation, including measurement.

Since the rituals are arranged in a cycle, description may commence at any point. The operation of the cycle becomes clearest if we begin with the rituals performed during warfare. Opponents in all cases occupy adjacent territories, in almost all cases on the same valley wall. After hostilities have broken out, each side performs certain rituals which place the opposing side in the formal category of "enemy." A number of taboos prevail while hostilities continue. These include prohibitions on sexual intercourse and on the ingestion of certain things—food prepared by women, food grown on the lower portion of the territory, marsupials, eels, and, while actually on the fighting ground, any liquid whatsoever.

One ritual practice associated with fighting which may have some physiological consequences deserves mention. Immediately before proceeding to the fighting ground, the warriors eat heavily salted pig fat. The ingestion of salt, coupled with the taboo on drinking, has the effect of shortening the fighting day, particularly since the Maring prefer to fight only on bright sunny days. When everyone gets unbearably thirsty, according to informants, fighting is broken off.

There may formerly have been other effects if the native salt contained sodium (the production of salt was discontinued some years previous to the field work, and no samples were obtained). The Maring diet seems to be deficient in sodium. The ingestion of large amounts of sodium just prior to fighting would have permitted the warriors to sweat normally without a lowering of blood volume and consequent weakness during the course of the fighting. The pork belly ingested with the salt would have provided them with a new burst of energy two hours or so after the commencement of the engagement. After fighting was finished for the day, lean pork was consumed, offsetting, at least to some extent, the nitrogen loss associated with the stressful fighting (personal communications from F. Dunn, W. MacFarlane, and J. Sabine, 1965).

Fighting could continue sporadically for weeks. Occasionally it terminated in the rout of one of the antagonistic groups, whose survivors would take refuge with kinsmen elsewhere. In such instances, the victors would lay waste their opponents' groves and gardens, slaughter their pigs, and burn their houses. They would not, however, immediately annex the territory of the vanquished. The Maring say that they never take over the territory of an enemy for, even if it has been abandoned, the spirits of their ancestors remain to guard it against interlopers. Most fights, however, terminated in truces between the antagonists.

With the termination of hostilities a group which has not been driven off its territory performs a ritual called "planting the *rumbim*." Every man puts his hand on the ritual plant, *rumbim* (*Cordyline fruticosa* (L.), A. Chev; *C. terminalis*, Kunth), as it is planted in the ground. The ancestors are addressed, in effect, as follows:

> We thank you for helping us in the fight and permitting us to remain on our territory. We place our souls in this *rumbim* as we plant it on our ground. We ask you to care for this *rumbim*. We will kill pigs for you now, but they are few. In the future, when we have many pigs, we shall again give you pork and uproot the *rumbim* and stage a *kaiko* (pig festival). But until there are sufficient pigs to repay you the *rumbim* will remain in the ground.

This ritual is accompanied by the wholesale slaughter of pigs. Only juveniles remain alive. All adult and adolescent animals are killed, cooked, and dedicated to the ancestors. Some are consumed by the local group, but most are distributed to allies who assisted in the fight.

Some of the taboos which the group suffered during the time of fighting are abrogated by this ritual. Sexual intercourse is now permitted, liquids may be taken at any time, and food from any part of the territory may be eaten. But the group is still in debt to its allies and ancestors. People say it is still the time of the *bamp ku*, or "fighting stones," which are actual objects used in the rituals associated with warfare. Although the fighting ceases when *rumbim* is planted, the concomitant obligations, debts to allies and ancestors, remain outstanding; and the fighting stones may not be put away until these obligations are fulfilled. The time of the fighting stones is a time of debt and danger which lasts until the *rumbim* is uprooted and a pig festival (*kaiko*) is staged.

Certain taboos persist during the time of the fighting stones. Marsupials, regarded as the pigs of the ancestors of the high ground, may not be trapped until the debt to their masters has been repaid. Eels, the "pigs of the ancestors of the low ground," may neither be caught nor consumed. Prohibitions on all intercourse with the enemy come into force. One may not touch, talk to, or even look at a member of the enemy group, nor set foot on enemy ground. Even more important, a group may not attack another group while its ritual plant remains in the ground, for it has not yet fully rewarded its ancestors and allies for their assistance in the last fight. Until the debts to them have been paid, further assistance from them will not be forthcoming. A kind of "truce of god" thus prevails until the *rumbim* is uprooted and a *kaiko* completed.

To uproot the *rumbim* requires sufficient pigs. How many pigs are sufficient, and how long does it take to acquire them? The Tsembaga say that, if a place is "good," this can take as little as five years; but if a place is "bad," it may require ten years or longer. A bad place is one in which misfortunes are frequent and where, therefore, ritual demands for the killing of pigs arise frequently. A good place is one where such demands are infrequent. In a good place, the increase of the pig herd exceeds the ongoing ritual demands, and the herd grows rapidly. Sooner or later the substandard tubers incidentally obtained while harvesting become insufficient to feed the herd, and additional acreage must be put into production specifically for the pigs.

The work involved in caring for a large pig herd can be extremely burdensome. The Tsembaga herd just prior to the pig festival of 1962-63, when it numbered 169 animals, was receiving 54 per cent of all of the sweet potatoes and 82 per cent of all of the manioc harvested. These comprised 35.9 per cent by weight of all root crops harvested. This figure is consistent with the difference between the amount of land under cultivation just previous to the pig festival, when the herd was at maximum size, and that immediately afterwards, when the pig herd was at minimum size. The former was 36.1 per cent in excess of the latter.

I have estimated on the basis of acreage yield and energy expenditure figures, that about 45,000 calories per year are expended in caring for one pig 120-150 pounds in size. It is upon women that most of the burden of pig keeping falls. If, from a woman's-daily intake of about 2,200 calories, 950 calories are allowed for basal metabolism, a woman has only 1,250 calories a day available for all her activities, which include gardening for her family, child care, and cooking, as well as tending pigs. It is clear that no woman can feed many pigs; only a few had as many as four in their care at the commencement of the festival; and it is not surprising that agitation to uproot the *rumbim* and stage the *kaiko* starts with the wives of the owners of large numbers of pigs.

A large herd is not only burdensome as far as energy expenditure is concerned; it becomes increasingly a nuisance as it expands. The more numerous pigs become, the more frequently are gardens invaded by them. Such events result in serious disturbances of local tranquillity. The garden owner often shoots, or attempts to shoot, the offending pig; and the pig owner commonly retorts by shooting, or attempting to shoot, either the garden owner, his wife, or one of his pigs. As more and more such events occur, the settlement, nucleated when the herd was small, disperses as people try to put as much distance as possible between their pigs and other people's gardens and between their gardens and other people's pigs. Occasionally this reaches its logical conclusion, and people begin to leave the territory, taking up residence with kinsmen in other local populations.

The number of pigs sufficient to become intolerable to the Tsembaga was below the capacity of the territory to carry pigs. I have estimated that, if the size and structure of the human population remained constant at the 1962–1963 level, a pig population of 140 to 240 animals averaging 100 to 150 pounds in size could be maintained perpetually by the Tsembaga without necessarily inducing environmental degradation. Since the size of the herd fluctuates, even higher cyclical maxima could be achieved. The level of toleration, however, is likely always to be below the carrying capacity, since the destructive capacity of the pigs is dependent upon the population density of both people and pigs, rather than upon population size. The denser the human population, the fewer pigs will be required to disrupt social life. If the carrying capacity is exceeded, it is likely to be exceeded by people and not by pigs.

The *kaiko* or pig festival, which commences with the planting of stakes at the boundary and the uprooting of the *rumbim*, is thus triggered by either the additional work attendant upon feeding pigs or the destructive capacity of the pigs themselves. It may be said, then, that there are sufficient pigs to stage the *kaiko* when the relationship of pigs to people changes from one of mutualism to one of parasitism or competition.

A short time prior to the uprooting of the *rumbim*, stakes are planted at the boundary. If the enemy has continued to occupy its territory, the stakes are planted at the boundary which existed before the fight. If, on the other hand, the enemy has abandoned its territory, the victors may plant their stakes at a new boundary which encompasses areas previously occupied by the enemy. The Maring say, to be sure, that they never take land belonging to an enemy, but this land is regarded as vacant, since no *rumbim* was planted on it after the last fight. We may state here a rule of land redistribution in terms of the ritual cycle: *If one of a pair of antagonistic groups is able to uproot its rumbim before its opponents can plant their rumbim, it may occupy the latter's territory.*

Not only have the vanquished abandoned their territory; it is assumed that it has also been abandoned by their ancestors as well. The surviving members of the erstwhile enemy group have by this time resided with other groups for a number of years, and most if not all of them have already had occasion to sacrifice pigs to their ancestors at their new residences. In so doing they have invited these spirits to settle at the new locations of the living, where they will in the future receive sacrifices. Ancestors of vanquished groups thus relinquish their guardianship over the territory, making it available to victorious groups. Meanwhile, the *de facto* membership of the living in the groups with which they have taken refuge is converted eventually into *de jure* membership. Sooner or later the groups with which they have taken up residence will have occasion to plant *rumbim*, and the refugees, as co-residents, will participate, thus ritually validating their connection to the new territory and the new group. A rule of population redistribution may thus be stated in terms of ritual cycles: *A man becomes a member of a territorial group by participating with it in the planting of rumbim.*

The uprooting of the *rumbim* follows shortly after the planting of stakes at the boundary. On this particular occasion the Tsembaga killed 32 pigs out of their herd of 169. Much of the pork was distributed to allies and affines outside of the local group.

The taboo on trapping marsupials was also terminated at this time. Information is lacking concerning the population dynamics of the local marsupials, but it may well be that the taboo which had prevailed since the last fight—that against taking them in traps—had conserved a fauna which might otherwise have become extinct.

The *kaiko* continues for about a year, during which period friendly groups are entertained from time to time. The guests receive presents of vegetable foods, and the hosts and male guests dance together throughout the night.

These events may be regarded as analogous to aspects of the social behavior of many nonhuman animals. First of all, they include massed epigamic, or courtship, displays (Wynne-Edwards 1962: 17). Young women are presented with samples of the eligible males of local groups with which they may not otherwise have had the opportunity to become familiar. The context, moreover, permits the young women to discriminate amongst this sample in terms of both endurance (signaled by how vigorously and how long a man dances) and wealth (signaled by the richness of a man's shell and feather finery).

More importantly, the massed dancing at these events may be regarded as epideictic display, communicating to the participants information concerning the size or density of the group (Wynne-Edwards 1962:16). In many species such displays take place as a prelude to actions which adjust group size or density, and such is the case among the Maring. The massed dancing of the visitors at a *kaiko* entertainment communicates to the hosts, while the *rumbim* truce is still in force, information concerning the amount of support they may expect from the visitors in the bellicose enterprises that they are likely to embark upon soon after the termination of the pig festival.

Among the Maring there are no chiefs or other political authorities capable of commanding the support of a body of followers, and the decision to assist another group in warfare rests with each individual male. Allies are not recruited by appealing for help to other local groups as such. Rather, each member of the groups primarily involved in the hostilities appeals to his cognatic and affinal kinsmen in other local groups. These men, in turn, urge other of their co-residents and kinsmen to "help them fight." The channels through which invitations to dance are extended are precisely those through which appeals for military support are issued. The invitations go not from group to group, but from kinsman to kinsman, the recipients of invitations urging their co-residents to "help them dance."

Invitations to dance do more than exercise the channels through which allies are recruited; they provide a means for judging their effectiveness. Dancing and fighting are regarded as in some sense equivalent. This equivalence is expressed in the similarity of some pre-fight and pre-dance rituals, and the Maring say that those who come to dance come to fight. The size of a visiting dancing contingent is consequently taken as a measure of the size of the contingent of warriors whose assistance may be expected in the next round of warfare.

In the morning the dancing ground turns into a trading ground. The items most frequently exchanged include axes, bird plumes, shell ornaments, an occasional baby pig, and, in former times, native salt. The *kaiko* thus facilitates trade by providing a market-like setting in which large numbers of traders can assemble. It likewise facilitates the movement of two critical items, salt and axes, by creating a demand for the bird plumes which may be exchanged for them.

The *kaiko* concludes with major pig sacrifices. On this particular occasion the Tsembaga butchered 105 adult and adolescent pigs, leaving only 60 juveniles and neonates alive. The survival of an additional fifteen adolescents and adults was only temporary, for they were scheduled as imminent victims. The pork yielded by the Tsembaga slaughter was estimated to weigh between 7,000 and 8,500 pounds, of which between 4,500 and 6,000 pounds were distributed to members of other local groups in 163 separate presentations. An estimated 2,000 to 3,000 people in seventeen local groups were the beneficiaries of the redistribution. The presentations, it should be mentioned, were not confined to pork. Sixteen Tsembaga men presented bridewealth or child-wealth, consisting largely of axes and shells, to their affines at this time.

The *kaiko* terminates on the day of the pig slaughter with the public presentation of salted pig belly to allies of the last fight. Presentations are made through the window in a high ceremonial fence built specially for the occasion at one end of the dance ground. The name of each honored man is announced to the assembled multitude as he charges to the window to receive his hero's portion. The fence is then ritually torn down, and the fighting stones are put away. The pig festival and the ritual cycle have been completed, demonstrating, it may be suggested, the ecological and economic competence of the local population. The local population would now be free, if it were not for the presence of the government, to attack its enemy again, secure in the knowledge that the assistance of allies and ancestors would be forthcoming because they have received pork and the obligations to them have been fulfilled.

Usually fighting did break out again very soon after the completion of the ritual cycle. If peace still prevailed when the ceremonial fence had rotted completely—a process said to take about three years, a little longer than the length of time required to raise a pig to maximum size—*rumbim* was planted as if there had been a fight, and all adult and adolescent pigs were killed. When the pig herd was large enough so that the *rumbim* could be uprooted, peace could be made with former enemies if they were also able to dig out their *rumbim*. To put this in formal terms: *If a pair of antagonistic groups proceeds through two ritual cycles without resumption of hostilities their enmity may be terminated.*

The relations of the Tsembaga with their environment have been analyzed as a complex system composed of two subsystems. What may be called the "local subsystem" has been derived from the relations of the Tsembaga with the nonhuman components of their immediate or territorial environment. It corresponds to the ecosystem in which the Tsembaga participate. A second subsystem, one which corresponds to the larger regional population of which the Tsembaga are one of the constituent units and which may be designated as the "regional subsystem," has been derived from the relations of the Tsembaga with neighboring local populations similar to themselves.

It has been argued that rituals, arranged in repetitive sequences, regulate relations both within each of the subsystems and within the larger complex system as a whole. The timing of the ritual cycle is largely dependent upon changes in the states of the components of the local subsystem. But the *kaiko*, which is the culmination of the ritual cycle, does more than reverse changes which have taken place within the local subsystem. Its occurrence also affects relations among the components of the regional subsystem. During its performance, obligations to other local populations are fulfilled, support for future military enterprises is rallied, and land from which enemies have earlier been driven is occupied. Its completion, furthermore, permits the local population to initiate warfare again. Conversely, warfare is terminated by rituals which preclude the reinitiation of warfare until the state of the local subsystem is again such that a *kaiko* may be staged and completed. Ritual among the Tsembaga and other Maring, in short, operates as both transducer, "translating" changes in the state of one subsystem into information which can effect changes in a second subsystem, and homeostat, maintaining a number of variables which in sum comprise the total system within ranges of viability. To repeat an earlier assertion, the operation of ritual among the Tsembaga and other Maring helps to maintain an undegraded environment, limits fighting to frequencies which do not endanger the existence of the regional population, adjusts man-land ratios, facilitates trade, distributes local surpluses of pig throughout the regional population in the form of pork, and assures people of high quality protein when they are most in need of it.

Religious rituals and the supernatural orders toward which they are directed cannot be assumed *a priori* to be mere epiphenomena. Ritual may, and doubtless frequently does, do nothing more than validate and intensify the relationships which integrate the social unit, or symbolize the relationships which bind the social unit to its environment. But the interpretation of such presumably *sapiens*-specific phenomena as religious ritual within a framework which will also accommodate the behavior of other species shows, I think, that religious ritual may do much more than symbolize, validate, and intensify relationships. Indeed, it would not be improper to refer to the Tsembaga and the other entities with which they share their territory as a "ritually regulated ecosystem," and to the Tsembaga and their human neighbors as a "ritually regulated population."

Notes

1. The field work upon which this paper is based was supported by a grant from the National Science Foundation, under which Professor A. P. Vayda was principal investigator. Personal support was received by the author from the National Institutes of Health. Earlier versions of this paper were presented at the 1964 annual meeting of the American Anthropological Association in Detroit, and before a Columbia University seminar on Ecological Systems and Cultural Evolution. I have received valuable suggestions from Alexander Alland, Jacques Barrau, William Clarke, Paul Collins, C. Glen King, Marvin Harris, Margaret Mead, M. J. Meggitt, Ann Rappaport, John Street, Marjorie Whiting, Cherry Vayda, A. P. Vayda and many others, but I take full responsibility for the analysis presented herewith.

2. The social organization of the Tsembaga will be described in detail elsewhere.

3. Because the length of time in the field precluded the possibility of maintaining honest records on single gardens from planting through abandonment, figures were based in the case of both "taro-yam" and "sugar-sweet potato" gardens, on three separate gardens planted in successive years. Conversions from the gross weight to the caloric value of yields were made by reference to the literature. The sources used are listed in Rappaport (1966: Appendix VIII)

4. Rough time and motion studies of each of the tasks involved in making, maintaining, harvesting, and walking to and from gardens were undertaken. Conversion to energy expenditure values was accomplished by reference to energy expenditure tables prepared by Hipsley and Kirk (1965: 43) on the basis of gas exchange measurements made during the performance of garden tasks by the Chimbu people of the New Guinea highlands.

5. Marvin Harris, in an unpublished paper, estimates the ratio of energy return to energy input ratio on Dyak (Borneo) rice swiddens at 10:1. His estimates of energy ratios on Tepotzlan (Meso-America) swiddens range from 13:1 on poor land to 29:1 for the best land.

6. Heights may be inaccurate. Many men wear their hair in large coiffures hardened with pandanus grease, and it was necessary in some instances to estimate the location of the top of the skull.

Bibliography

BERG, C. 1948. Protein Deficiency and Its Relation to Nutritional Anemia, Hypoproteinemia, Nutritional Edema, and Resistance to Infection. Protein and Amino Acids in Nutrition, ed. M. Sahyun, pp. 290-317. New York.

BURTON, B. T., ed. 1959. The Heinz Handbook of Nutrition. New York.

ELMAN, R. 1951. Surgical Care. New York.

FOOD AND AGRICULTURE ORGANIZATION OF THE UNITED NATIONS. 1964. Protein: At the Heart of the World Food Problem. World Food Problems 5. Rome.

HIPSLEY, E., and N. KIRK. 1965. Studies of the Dietary Intake and Energy Expenditure of New Guineans. South Pacific Commission, Technical Paper 147. Noumea.

HOMANS, G. C. 1941. Anxiety and Ritual: The Theories of Malinowski and Radcliffe-Brown. American Anthropologist 43: 164-172.

HOUSSAY, B. A., et al. 1955. Human Physiology, 2nd edit. New York.

LARGE, A., and C. G. JOHNSTON. 1948. Proteins as Related to Burns. Proteins and Amino Acids in Nutrition, ed. M. Sahyun, pp. 386-396. New York.

LUND, C. G., and S. M. LEVENSON. 1948. Protein Nutrition in Surgical Patients. Proteins and Amino Acids in Nutrition, ed. M. Sahyun, pp. 349-363. New York.

MOORE, O. K. 1957. Divination—a New Perspective. American Anthropologist 59: 69-74.

NATIONAL RESEARCH COUNCIL. 1963. Evaluation of Protein Quality. National Academy of Sciences—National Research Council Publication 1100. Washington.

RAPPAPORT, R. A. 1966. Ritual in the Ecology of a New Guinea People. Unpublished doctoral dissertation, Columbia University.

VAYDA, A. P., A. LEEDS, and D. B. SMITH. 1961. The Place of Pigs in Melanesian Subsistence. Proceedings of the 1961 Annual Spring Meeting of the American Ethnological Society, ed. V. E. Garfield, pp. 69-77. Seattle.

WAYNE-EDWARDS, V. C. 1962. Animal Dispersion in Relation to Social Behaviour. Edinburgh and London.

ZINTEL, HAROLD A. 1964. Nutrition in the Care of the Surgical Patient. Modern Nutrition in Health and Disease, ed. M. G. Wohl and R. S. Goodhart, pp. 1043-1064. Third edit. Philadelphia.

24

Rational Mastery by Man of His Surroundings

BRONISLAW MALINOWSKI

... FIRST, has the savage any rational outlook, any rational mastery of his surroundings, or is he, as M. Lévy-Bruhl and his school maintain, entirely "mystical"? The answer will be that every primitive community is in possession of a considerable store of knowledge, based on experience and fashioned by reason.

The second question then opens: Can this primitive knowledge be regarded as a rudimentary form of science or is it, on the contrary, radically different, a crude empiry, a body of practical and technical abilities, rules of thumb and rules of art having no theoretical value? This second question, epistemological rather than belonging to the study of man, will be barely touched upon at the end of this section and a tentative answer only will be given.

In dealing with the first question, we shall have to examine the "profane" side of life, the arts, crafts and economic pursuits, and we shall attempt to disentangle in it a type of behavior, clearly marked off from magic and religion, based on empirical knowledge and on the confidence in logic. We shall try to find whether the lines of such behavior are defined by traditional rules, known, perhaps even discussed sometimes, and tested. We shall have to inquire whether the sociological setting of the rational and empirical behavior differs from that of ritual and cult. Above all we shall ask, do the natives distinguish the two domains and keep them apart, or is the field of knowledge constantly swamped by superstition, ritualism, magic or religion?

Since in the matter under discussion there is an appalling lack of relevant and reliable observations, I shall have largely to draw upon my own material, mostly unpublished, collected during a few years' field work among the Melanesian and Papuo-Melanesian tribes of Eastern New Guinea and the surrounding archipelagoes. As the Melanesians are reputed, however, to be specially magic-ridden, they will furnish an acid test of the existence of empirical and rational knowledge among savages living in the age of polished stone.

These natives, and I am speaking mainly of the Melanesians who inhabit the coral atolls to the N.E. of the main island, the Trobriand Archipelago and the adjoining groups, are expert fishermen, industrious manufacturers and traders, but they rely mainly on gardening for their subsistence. With the most rudimentary implements, a pointed digging-stick and a small axe, they are able to raise crops sufficient to maintain a dense population and even yielding a surplus, which in olden days was allowed to rot unconsumed, and which at present is exported to feed plantation hands. The success in their agriculture depends—besides the excellent natural conditions with which they are favored—upon their extensive knowledge of the classes of the soil, of the various cultivated plants, of the mutual adaptation of these two factors, and, last not least, upon their knowledge of the importance of accurate and hard work. They have to select the soil and the seedlings, they have appropriately to fix the times for clearing and burning the scrub, for planting and weeding, for training the vines of the yam plants. In all this they are guided by a clear knowledge of weather and seasons, plants and pests, soil and tubers, and by a conviction that this knowledge is true and reliable, that it can be counted upon and must be scrupulously obeyed.

Yet mixed with all their activities there is to be found magic, a series of rites performed every year over the gardens in rigorous sequence and order. Since the leadership in garden work is in the hands of the magician, and since ritual and practical work are intimately associated, a superficial observer might be led to assume that the mystic and the rational behavior are mixed up, that their effects are not distinguished by the natives and not distinguishable in scientific analysis. Is this so really?

Magic is undoubtedly regarded by the natives as absolutely indispensable to the welfare of the gardens. What would happen without it no one can exactly tell, for no native garden has ever been made without its ritual, in spite of some thirty years of European rule and missionary influence and well over a century's contact with white traders. But certainly various kinds of disaster, blight, unseasonable droughts rains, bush-pigs and locusts, would destroy the unhallowed garden made without magic.

Does this mean, however, that the natives attribute all the good results to magic? Certainly not. If you were to suggest to a native that he should make his garden mainly by magic and scamp his work, he would simply smile on your simplicity. He knows as well as you do that there are natural conditions and causes, and by his observations he knows also that he is able to control these natural forces by mental and physical effort. His knowledge is limited, no doubt, but as far as it goes it is sound and proof against mysticism. If the fences are broken down, if the seed is destroyed or has been dried or washed away, he will have recourse not to magic, but to work, guided by knowledge and reason. His experience has taught him also, on the other hand, that in spite of all his forethought and beyond all his efforts there are agencies and forces which one year bestow unwonted and unearned benefits of fertility, making everything run smooth and well, rain and sun appear at the right moment, noxious insects remain in abeyance, the harvest yields a superabundant crop; and another year again the same agencies bring ill luck and bad chance, pursue him from beginning till end and thwart all his most strenuous efforts and his best-founded knowledge. To control these influences and these only he employs magic.

Thus there is a clear-cut division: there is first the well-known set of conditions, the natural course of growth, as well as the ordinary pests and dangers to be warded off by fencing and weeding. On the other hand there is the domain of the unaccountable and adverse influences, as well as the great unearned increment of fortunate coincidence. The first conditions are coped with by knowledge and work, the second by magic. . . .

An interesting and crucial test is provided by fishing in the Trobriand Islands and its magic. While in the villages on the inner lagoon fishing is done in an easy and absolutely reliable manner by the method of poisoning, yielding abundant results without danger and uncertainty, there are on the shores of the open sea dangerous modes of fishing and also certain types in which the yield greatly varies according to whether shoals of fish appear beforehand or not. It is most significant that in the lagoon fishing, where man can rely completely upon his knowledge and skill, magic does not exist, while in the open-sea fishing, full of danger and uncertainty, there is extensive magical ritual to secure safety and good results.

Again, in warfare the natives know that strength, courage, and agility play a decisive part. Yet here also they practice magic to master the elements of chance and luck.

Nowhere is the duality of natural and supernatural causes divided by a line so thin and intricate, yet, if carefully followed up, so well marked, decisive, and instructive, as in the two most fateful forces of human destiny: health and death. Health to the Melanesians is a natural state of affairs and, unless tampered with, the human body will remain in perfect order. But the natives know perfectly well that there are natural means which can affect health and even destroy the body. Poisons, wounds, burns, falls, are known to cause disablement or death in a natural way. And this is not a matter of private opinion of this or that individual, but it is laid down in traditional lore and even in belief, for there are considered to be different ways to the nether world for those who died by sorcery and those who met "natural" death. Again, it is recognized that cold, heat, overstrain, too much sun, overeating, can all cause minor ailments, which are treated by natural remedies such as massage, steaming, warming at a fire and certain potions. Old age is known to lead to bodily decay and the explanation is given by the natives that very old people grow weak, their oesophagus closes up, and therefore they must die.

But besides these natural causes there is the enormous domain of sorcery and by far the most cases of illness and death are ascribed to this. The line of distinction between sorcery and the other causes is clear in theory and in most cases of practice, but it must be realized that it is subject to what could be called the personal perspective. That is, the more closely a case has to do with the person who considers it, the less will it be "natural," the more "magical." Thus a very old man, whose pending death will be considered natural by the other members of the community, will be afraid only of sorcery and never think of his natural fate. A fairly sick person will diagnose sorcery in his own case, while all the others might speak of too much betel nut or overeating or some other indulgence.

But who of us really believes that his own bodily infirmities and the approaching death is a purely natural occurrence, just an insignificant event in the infinite chain of causes? To the most rational of civilized men health, disease, the threat of death, float in a hazy emotional mist, which seems to become denser and more impenetrable as the fateful forms approach. It is indeed astonishing that "savages" can achieve such a sober, dispassionate outlook in these matters as they actually do.

Thus in his relation to nature and destiny, whether he tries to exploit the first or to dodge the second, primitive man recognizes both the natural and the supernatural forces and agencies, and he tries to use them both for his benefit. Whenever he has been taught by experience that effort guided by knowledge is of some avail, he never spares the one or ignores the other. He knows that a plant cannot grow by magic alone, or a canoe sail or float without being properly constructed and managed, or a fight be won without skill and daring. He never relies on magic alone, while, on the contrary, he sometimes dispenses with it completely, as in fire-making and in a number of crafts and pursuits. But he clings to it, whenever he has to recognize the impotence of his knowledge and of his rational technique. . . .

The use of leaves, notched sticks, and similar aids to memory is well known and seems to be almost universal. All such "diagrams" are means of reducing a complex and unwieldy bit of reality to a simple and handy form. They give man a relatively easy mental control over it. As such are they not—in a very rudimentary form no doubt—fundamentally akin to developed scientific formulas and "models," which are also simple and handy paraphrases of a complex or abstract reality, giving the civilized physicist mental control over it?

This brings us to the second question: Can we regard primitive knowledge, which, as we found, is both empirical and rational, as a rudimentary stage of science, or is it not at all related to it? If by science be understood a body of rules and conceptions, based on experience and derived from it by logical inference, embodied in material achievements and in a fixed form of tradition and carried on by some sort of social organization—then there is no doubt that even the lowest savage communities have the beginnings of science, however rudimentary.

Most epistemologists would not, however, be satisfied with such a "minimum definition" of science, for it might apply to the rules of an art or craft as well. They would maintain that the rules of science must be laid down explicitly, open to control by experiment and critique by reason. They must not only be rules of practical behavior, but theoretical laws of knowledge. Even accepting this stricture, however, there is hardly any doubt that many of the principles of savage knowledge are scientific in this sense. The native shipwright knows not only practically of buoyancy, leverage, equilibrium, he has to obey these laws not only on water, but while making the canoe he must have the principles in his mind. He instructs his helpers in them. He gives them the traditional rules, and in a crude and simple manner, using his hands, pieces of wood, and a limited technical vocabulary, he explains some general laws of hydrodynamics and equilibrium. Science is not detached from the craft, that is certainly true, it is only a means to an end, it is crude, rudimentary, and inchoate, but with all that it is the matrix from which the higher developments must have sprung.

If we applied another criterion yet, that of the really scientific attitude, the disinterested search for knowledge and for the understanding of causes and reasons, the answer would certainly not be in a direct negative. There is, of course, no widespread thirst for knowledge in a savage community, new things such as European topics bore them frankly and their whole interest is largely encompassed by the traditional world of their culture. But within this there is both the antiquarian mind passionately interested in myths, stories, details of customs, pedigrees, and ancient happenings, and there is also to be found the naturalist, patient and painstaking in his observations, capable of generalization and of connecting long chains of events in the life of animals, and in the marine world or in the jungle. It is enough to realize how much European naturalists have often learned from their savage colleagues to appreciate this interest found in the native for nature. There is finally among the primitives, as every fieldworker well knows, the sociologist, the ideal informant, capable with marvelous accuracy and insight to give the *raison d'être*, the function, and the organization of many a simpler institution in his tribe.

Science, of course, does not exist in any uncivilized community as a driving power, criticizing, renewing, constructing. Science is never consciously made. But on this criterion, neither is there law, nor religion, nor government among savages.

The question, however, whether we should call it *science* or only *empirical and rational knowledge* is not of primary importance in this context. We have tried to gain a clear idea as to whether the savage has only one domain of reality or two, and we found that he has his profane world of practical activities and rational outlook besides the sacred region of cult and belief. . . .

The study of the texts and formulas of primitive magic reveals that there are three typical elements associated with the belief in magical efficiency. There are, first, the phonetic effects, imitations of natural sounds, such as the whistling of the wind, the growling of thunder, the roar of the sea, the voices of various animals. These sounds symbolize certain phenomena and thus are believed to produce them magically. Or else they express certain emotional states associated with the desire which is to be realized by means of the magic.

The second element, very conspicuous in primitive spells, is the use of words which invoke, state, or command the desired aim. Thus the sorcerer will mention all the symptoms of the disease which he is inflicting, or in the lethal formula he will describe the end of his victim. In healing magic the wizard will give word pictures of perfect health and bodily strength. In economic magic the growing of plants, the approach of animals, the arrival of fish in shoals are depicted. Or again the magician uses words and sentences which express the emotion under the stress of which he works his magic, and the action which gives expression to this emotion. The sorcerer in tones of fury will have to repeat such verbs as "I break—I twist—I burn—I destroy," enumerating with each of them the various parts of the body and internal organs of his victim. In all this we see that the spells are built very much on the same pattern as the rites and the words selected for the same reasons as the substances of magic.

Thirdly there is an element in almost every spell to which there is no counterpart in ritual. I mean the mythological allusions, the references to ancestors and culture heroes from whom this magic has been received. And that brings us to perhaps the most important point in the subject, to the traditional setting of magic.

The Tradition of Magic

Tradition, which, as we have several times insisted, reigns supreme in primitive civilization, gathers in great abundance round magical ritual and cult. In the case of any important magic we invariably find the story accounting for its existence. Such a story tells when and where it entered the possession of man, how it became the property of a local group or of a family or clan. But such a story is not the story of its origins. Magic never "originated," it never has been made or invented. All magic simply "was" from the beginning an essential adjunct of all such things and processes as vitally interest man and yet elude his normal rational efforts. The spell, the rite, and the thing which they govern are coeval.

Thus, in Central Australia, all magic existed and has been inherited from the *alcheringa* times, when it came about like everything else. In Melanesia all magic comes from a time when humanity lived underground and when magic was a natural knowledge of ancestral man. In higher societies magic is often derived from spirits and demons, but even these, as a rule, originally received and did not invent it. Thus the belief in the primeval natural existence of magic is universal. As its counterpart we find the conviction that only by an absolutely unmodified immaculate transmission does magic retain its efficiency. The slightest alteration from the original pattern would be fatal. There is, then, the idea that between the object and its magic there exists an essential nexus. Magic is the quality of the thing, or rather, of the relation between man and the thing, for though never man-made it is always made for man. In all tradition, in all mythology, magic is always found in the possession of man and through the knowledge of man or man-like being. It implies the performing magician quite as much as the thing to be charmed and the means of charming. It is part of the original endowment of primeval humanity, of the *mura-mura* or *alcheringa* of Australia, of the subterrestrial humanity of Melanesia, of the people of the magical Golden Age all the world over.

Magic is not only human in its embodiment, but also in its subject matter: it refers principally to human activities and states, hunting, gardening, fishing, trading, love-making, disease, and death. It is not directed so much to nature as to man's relation to nature and to the human activities which affect it. Moreover, the effects of magic are usually conceived not as a product of nature influenced by the charm, but as something specially magical, something which nature cannot produce, but only the power of magic. The graver forms of disease, love in its passionate phases, the desire for a ceremonial exchange and other similar manifestations in the human organism and mind, are the direct product of the spell and rite. Magic is thus not derived from an observation of nature or knowledge of its laws, it is a primeval possession of man to be known only through tradition and affirming man's autonomous power of creating desired ends.

Thus, the force of magic is not a universal force residing everywhere, flowing where it will or it is willed to. Magic is the one and only specific power, a force unique of its kind, residing exclusively in man, let loose only by his magical art, gushing out with his voice, conveyed by the casting forth of the rite.

It may be here mentioned that the human body, being the receptacle of magic and the channel of its flow, must be submitted to various conditions. Thus the magician has to keep all sorts of taboos, or else the spell might be injured, especially as in certain parts of the world, in Melanesia for instance, the spell resides in the magician's belly, which is the seat of memory as well as of food. When necessary it is summoned up to the larynx, which is the seat of intelligence, and thence sent forth by the voice, the main organ of the human mind. Thus, not only is magic an essentially human possession, but it is literally and actually enshrined in man and can be handed on only from man to man, according to very strict rules of magical filiation, initiation, and instruction. It is thus never conceived as a force of nature, residing in things, acting independently of man, to be found out and learned by him, by any of those proceedings by which he gains his ordinary knowledge of nature.

25

Witchcraft Practices and Psychocultural Therapy with Urban U.S. Families

MADELEINE LEININGER

WITCHCRAFT, A PSYCHOCULTURAL and social interactional phenomenon, continues to hold the interest of cultural anthropologists, humanists, and many lay persons. Until recently in this country, witchcraft has been a fairly taboo topic and has not been discussed in an open manner in public educational and service institutions. For many health professionals, witchcraft is a new and intriguing subject and they have a limited understanding of its nature and dynamic process. Many persons in our society characterize witchcraft as demon possession, superstition, antireligious, nonscientific, and as a mystical power over human and supernatural phenomena. Some persons find the idea of witchcraft very frightening, others find it amusing, and still others remain sufficiently intrigued to explore the phenomenon with an open-minded attitude.

In recent years, adolescents, religious groups, and individuals interested in mysticism, astrology, and transcendental media have shown increased interest in witchcraft. As a consequence, magazine and newspaper articles, television and radio programs, and film productions have provided information about witchcraft. In addition, educational institutions have offered special courses, group discussions, and public sessions on witchcraft. Thus witchcraft has become a more common and open topic of public discourse than it was a decade ago. Furthermore, witchcraft has generated sufficient interest in several settings to become a topic for systematic investigation.

In this paper, witchcraft refers to the psychocultural and sociological process by which an individual and group(s) subtly and skillfully influence the behavior of others primarily in a harmful way, but there is also evidence of *positive* secondary consequences which may alleviate life stresses for the persons involved in witchcraft. In general, witchcraft is viewed as a malevolent phenomenon and as a situational misfortune to cope with psychocultural problems and social stresses. Witchcraft practices have been generally characterized as involving mysterious actions, the use of impersonal powers, reliance upon supernatural beliefs, and the use of symbolic modes of communication to affect the behavior of others in a harmful way. From a structural-functional analysis, however, social scientists have also identified some *positive* functions or consequences related to witchcraft practices.

For several decades, Kluckhohn (1944), Nadel (1952), Evans-Pritchard (1937), and other anthropologists have studied witchcraft behavior in Western and non-Western societies and have presented theoretical interpretations and descriptive accounts of witchcraft from cultural, psychological, and social viewpoints. Anthropological findings and explanations of witchcraft have been the primary source for understanding witchcraft, especially in non-Western societies. There is, however, an urgent need to study and understand the prevalence of witchcraft in modern American society, giving fresh thought to the psychocultural forces and changing social structure features which influence the development of witchcraft. Accordingly, efforts should be made to use these insights to help anxiety-ridden witchcraft victims and their families and to make known the means by which therapists can help them. The purpose of this paper is, therefore, to make a modest contribution toward these latter efforts.

Contrary to popular belief, witchcraft is *not* a unique behavior phenomenon restricted to primitive, nontechnological, or non-Western societies. Forms and processes of witchcraft continue to be found in highly developed and technological cultures such as that of the United States. Moreover, witchcraft practices and victims have been reported recently in almost every part of the United States in mental health clinics, general hospitals, community health agencies, educational situations, and in social gatherings.[1] Unfortunately, statistical data on precise witchcraft occurrences are not available; however, the author received reports of nearly 200 witchcraft cases in a three-year period through her work with and interest in witchcraft victims. Since witchcraft is generally a highly secretive ingroup experience, and because victims fear that witchcraft may not be accepted by professional health workers, it often goes undetected and unreported.

The author contends that there may be several significant reasons for the increased interest in and prevalence of witchcraft. First, the very rapid movement in this country over a short period of time to reduce inequities and to provide equal rights and opportunities for all ethnic, cultural, and social groups has produced tensions and a fertile climate for witchcraft accusations. Signs of unrest and distrust and challenges between and among different groups who may have never interacted with one another until recently are evident.

Second, there has been a heightened interest and involvement in extra-sensory perceptual experiences, transcendental media, and other forms of special psychic experiences, particularly by adolescents. These youths have also been actively involved in the use of a wide variety of drugs and other stimuli in an attempt to obtain special psychophysiological "release experiences" to assuage current societal problems and stresses.

Third, there is evidence of an increased use of secretive and highly symbolic forms of communication in order to relate differently and intimately with humans, superhumans, animals, and nature. The use of special modes, mediums, and seemingly strange forms of communication provides the climate for witchcraft practices which are secretive, mystical, and symbolic in form and function.

Fourth, in recent years there has been a marked increase in a belief in astrology as a guide for one's actions and thought patterns. Many people today will not leave their homes or begin a day's work without checking their horoscope reading. This reading often provides a perceptual set and a psychosocial guide for one's thinking and actions. Witchcraft behavior is frequently linked with horoscope readings and astrological predictions, especially with predictions of what forces may cause a witchcraft victim harm.

Fifth, there is also an increase in the use of magical explanations by people who are nonscientifically disposed to explain unusual and unknown scientific findings. Undoubtedly, these magical explanations have arisen because of the tremendous gap in understanding highly scientific and technological data and they are used to cognitively bridge two different perceptual worlds, namely, the highly scientific and nonscientific. Supernatural and mystical explanations are important means to reduce conceptual incongruencies and to understand complex phenomena and the many unknowns in our society.

Sixth, many youths today are actively seeking and testing what is "real" and "not real," and in so doing, they may test witchcraft spells and incantations with their peers. The youth are faced with trying to understand divergent cultural norms and conflicts in value systems, and witchcraft practices are used to test such value orientations and to make life more congruent with one's interests and identity.

Finally, witchcraft practices may be increasing in our society in order to cope with problems related to acculturational stresses which may be exceedingly troublesome for some individuals and groups. The necessity for rapid and sudden adjustments to groups with different life styles is producing obvious psychocultural stresses on various groups. Witchcraft behavior, as discussed in this paper, reveals the psychocultural struggle of certain groups to adjust to rural-urban acculturational situations.

Theoretical Framework and Empirical Phases

Using a theoretical framework which was inductively developed through direct participant-observation experiences with witchcraft victims, the author focused primarily upon Spanish-speaking (Spanish and Mexican-Americans) families and a few Anglo-American students attending college in a large university setting in the United States. In the process of providing therapy to four of the Spanish-speaking families and two Anglo-American families as well as observing and studying 40 additional Spanish-speaking families (the latter without being involved in therapy), the author developed the following theoretical formulation which was used as a guide for helping the bewitched victim and his family.

Witchcraft behavior reflects the process by which some individuals and groups experience psychocultural and social stresses which arise within a designated primary group (to be referred to as the ingroup). Later, these stresses are perceptually and cognitively displaced to a secondary group (to be referred to as the outgroup) which the primary group has known for some time. Figure 1 depicts this conceptual framework with the three phases which will be discussed shortly. Throughout this paper, the terms "ingroup" and "outgroup" are used in a general sense to represent all the cases studied. Furthermore, the term, ingroup or primary, refers to the initial locus of the family stresses and the term, outgroup or secondary, to the group receiving the displaced stresses of the ingroup.

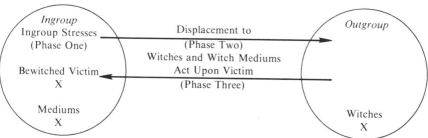

This conceptual framework reflects a processual scheme covering three major phases and ranging from the prewitchcraft stress period to the resolution or the coping phase which deals with the witchcraft victim, witches, and mediums.

FIGURE 1. Ingroup-Outgroup Witchcraft and Phases

Phase One: The Prewitchcraft Stress Period

Phase one of the prewitchcraft period was characterized by the intended victim and his family (primary ingroup) experiencing intense interpersonal conflicts which arose from identifiable social, economic, and acculturational problems. One of the early signs of prewitchcraft stress was a decrease in the traditionally shared verbal communication among family members and a general distrust of each other's behavior. As the communication problems increased and the interpersonal stresses became more evident, the family members began to distort and misinterpret one another's behavior.

Since the majority of families had shifted from a rural to an urban way of life, economic stresses related to maintaining an adequate income to live in the city were often a basis of quarrels and subtle antagonisms among the family members.

But most importantly, the families were in conflict with and/or ambivalent about "new" cultural values encroaching upon their traditional values. Generally, some of the younger family members, in an annoying and semi-hostile manner, would "try on" the new values to which they had been recently exposed. Sometimes the "new" ways of acting were openly challenged or verbally suppressed when the behavior appeared completely out of harmony with past behavior modes.

Scapegoating behavior was clearly evident in the ingroup with one family member serving as the victim. This victim was frequently blamed for matters which were generally unresolved problems or conflicts which the total family needed to face. Many unresolved family problems could be identified, and most of them were related to discrepancies in "new" and "old" cultural values and family practices. Because of the intense and largely covert interpersonal tensions and communication problems along with the economic concerns and conflicting values, no family member was able to assume a group leadership role to discuss these problems openly. Instead, the intrafamily tensions increased with the scapegoat victim being harrassed more and more by all family members. The family accusations became formalized, the tension mounted, and later (phase three) the scapegoat victim became legitimately the witchcraft victim. By the time phase three occurred, the victim had been emotionally and socially conditioned to take the bewitched victim role.

Phase Two: Displacement to the Outgroup

Phase two was characterized by the family ingroup members becoming increasingly angry with and distrustful of one another and finally displacing their feelings and problems to a known outgroup. The ingroup members continued to openly accuse each other of not helping and of not being concerned about one another's most urgent needs, e.g., food, sleep, clothing, and money. Although all ingroup members intended to blame each other for their problems, the scapegoat member continued to receive the greatest share of blame. There was evidence that family members denied their feelings about one another, especially when directly confronted about them. As the ingroup members became increasingly angry with one another, they withdrew to their bedrooms or left the house. Their silent periods reflected passive hostility to one another. In general, the ingroup members were afraid to express their pent-up feelings openly to one another, except for some periodic blasts of anger at the scapegoat family member.

Soon the primary ingroup began to cognitively displace its problems and feelings to a secondary outgroup. In all cases studied, the ingroup knew the outgroup, whose members were distant kinsmen—for example, "second or third cousins." In some cases, the outgroup was a social group whom the ingroup had known for at least six months, and in most cases, the ingroups and outgroups had been socially and economically dependent upon one another prior to the displacement phenomenon.

After the displacement of feelings and problems to the outgroup markedly decreased their contact with each other. Gradually, they showed increased fear and open anger toward one another and accusatory statements were secretively passed between the two groups. The intense fear and anger between each group led to avoidance behavior, and soon the groups began to talk cautiously and secretively about one another. The "terrible" ways and "horrible" witches in the outgroup were commonly discussed by the ingroup for a number of months and during the third phase.

Phase Three: Identification of the Bewitched Victim, the Witches, and the Witch Mediums

The third phase was characterized by intense ingroup-outgroup antagonisms and by identification of the bewitched victim, the witches, and the witch mediums. At this time, the scapegoat victim in the ingroup was clearly victimized and identified as the bewitched person. In all cases studied, the bewitched member was a female who was conditioned to assume the role because she had been the scapegoat family member, as described in phase one. The bewitched person became increasingly ill (emotionally and physically) as the witches in the outgroup were perceived to be affecting her in a covertly destructive manner. As the witchcraft accusations increased, the victim felt more and more frightened, helpless, and controlled by the outgroup witches. She would remain silent and angry and would often stay in bed for hours with the door closed or locked. The witchcraft accusations and the perceived malevolent acts were talked about by both groups in a cautious, angry manner, but without direct verbal exchanges. As the malevolent acts were perceived to increase, the ingroup noted that the bewitched victim became more acutely ill; as the acts decreased, the victim got better. The bewitched victim was sometimes brought to a hospital or to a mental health clinic for relief of her symptoms during the intense period of witchcraft accusations between the two groups.

During the third phase, *witchcraft mediums* who had the power to transmit covert messages from the outgroup witches into the body or mind of the bewitched victim were also identified. As these frightening auditory and visual messages were relayed to the bewitched victim, she became extremely tense or openly aggressive to those near her. The witch mediums (usually one or two) were found in the ingroup and were thought to have been "chosen" by the outgroup witch to transmit her malevolent directives to the bewitched victim. That the witch medium was in the ingroup and near the bewitched person was terrifying to the medium himself as well as to the victim. It was almost an untenable situation since neither the medium nor the victim thought they could change their roles—they, too, were helpless in influencing the witches to be less destructive and horrible. In all cases studied, the witch medium was usually a female who was terribly distraught that she had been "picked" as the medium because it pinpointed her as the immediate person causing harm to the victim. Often the witch medium was the mother or an older sister of the victim. Thus one can envision the tense daughter-mother relationships that existed, accompanied with feelings of intense fear, helplessness, and hostility. Occasionally, the witch medium would use her indirect power upon other ingroup family members to threaten and control their behavior when family relationships seemed out of control. All family members greatly feared the power of the witch mediums as well as the witches and thought that they themselves might become bewitched at any moment.

Psychocultural Approach and Therapy

The author attempted psychocultural therapy with six families (four Spanish-speaking and two Anglo-American families) in their homes. She saw each family about three hours each week (two sessions) and for a period of four to eight months of therapy. The therapy with the four Spanish-speaking families will be described in this first section, followed by a brief account of one of the two Anglo-American families.

In working with all cases, the author was identified as a professional nurse who had come into the home to help and study the sick member of the family. The Spanish-speaking families identified her as a *medicas*—a person who combined indigenous practitioner skills with professional practices; whereas the Anglo-American families saw her as someone providing help in a "crisis situation." In working with the families I used a similar psychocultural nursing therapy approach, employing psychotherapy methods and cultural data such as kinship ties, ethnohealth beliefs, economic aspects, social concerns, and religious beliefs. The families seemed responsive to this comprehensive and multidimensional approach.

The Spanish-speaking Families

As the author began working with the six Spanish-speaking families, she learned that two of the young females (20 and 25 years of age) had been in psychiatric hospitals for varying periods of time, one for seven months and another for one year. In each case, the victims' conditions had been diagnosed as "paranoid schizophrenia" and they had been dismissed with a "guarded prognosis."[2] Their families felt that the hospital's professional staff had not helped their daughters and commented: "She is worse than before she went to the hospital. They did not seem to understand our situation. It was hard to tell them about it." One of the Spanish-speaking patients had made a serious suicidal attempt three months before the author began working with her. A number of the psychiatric staff were baffled about the patient's "secretive behavior" and the meaning of her communication referents.

The Spanish-speaking families seemed desperate for help since the bewitched victim in each family had not improved and the indigenous curers had "given up on the victim." Thus the climate for helping them seemed favorable. Fortunately, the author had known two of these families through her study of an urban Spanish-speaking community and its health care system (Leininger 1969)—and it was important to these families that they knew the author.

At the start of therapy with the four Spanish-speaking families, the author focused upon their family ties and past relationships and took their genealogies. The latter seemed to be extremely important to the families, enabling them to tell about each family member and what had happened to them in recent months as well as to their family and friends. Furthermore, the genealogies were the key means for discovering the male and female witches as well as the witch mediums. When the families spoke about the witches, they whispered their names and always spoke of them with intense fear because of their great power and malevolent ways.

After the initial warm-up sessions using the genealogies and other relevant sociocultural data, the family members gradually became more at ease in talking about their family concerns and the sick members in the family. In a short time, they discussed the anger, fear, and distrust which existed among them. The author listened attentively to each family member's concerns, fears, and conflicts with no attempt to modify their behavior. It was felt that this approach was important in this initial phase of the therapy so that the members could openly express their feelings to an outsider who was actively interested in them, but who was not trying to suppress their feelings. Family members made direct and hostile accusations to one another, but especially to the bewitched victim. Initially, the victim was completely overwhelmed at these accusations and occasionally cried or left the room. Gradually, the author interceded in behalf of the victim and offered her emotional and social support by protecting and defending her feelings. When this occurred, the victim's ego became stronger and more confident. She would talk in a more coherent manner and would try to handle the accusations that she felt were unfair. For example, one victim stated: "You (family) 'caused' me to become ill. You have picked on me too long in this family. I did not do everything you said I did. Whenever I tried something different, I was pounced upon. I don't know why you always pick upon me."

During the course of the family "talk-out" sessions, the members discussed their past and current problems in adjusting to different "kinds of people and new ways in the city." There was evidence of conflict between their traditional cultural norms and the different sets of norms they were being exposed to in the urban community. Several common themes became evident in the family therapy sessions and will be highlighted and summarized below.

First, there had been unresolved family problems related to value changes and their ambivalence about changing traditional family relationships. For example, in one Mexican-American family the daughter was very angry with her mother for not permitting her to be more independent and "to be like other teenagers in the city." From a cultural viewpoint, this mother believed in maintaining close surveillance on her daughter, but after the family moved to the city, the daughter wanted to try some of the urban norms and to "live a different life." The mother, however, was extremely reluctant to let her daughter be so free and felt she needed even greater surveillance and protection than when they had lived in the rural area.

Second, the ingroup families were feeling the impact of the diverse ideologies of the different people encountered in their work and school settings and they were experiencing ambivalence about changing their own values. The families talked about how much they valued the warm, friendly, and generous attitudes which they had maintained traditionally with their extended family kinsmen. Lately, they felt these values were changing and that even their distant kinsmen (the outgroup) were becoming "cold, impersonal, and ungenerous people like the rest of these city people." The ingroup family members gave several examples of how their outgroup kinsmen or friends (toward whom they now felt hostile and frightened) had become extremely selfish and inconsiderate. In fact, the ingroup members were highly critical of the outgroup's behavior and were unwilling to forgive or forget such inconsiderate behavior. They said the outgroup had been stingy in giving gifts, loaning money, and helping them with occasional family celebrations. It was, therefore, no wonder that the outgroup became the ingroup's target for the displacement of its angry, distrustful, and suspicious feelings.

Third, a series of traditional cultural norms had been broken in each of the family ingroups, and the witchcraft victim was blamed for breaking them. And since the victim was perceived in each family to have violated the norm most flagrantly, she was vulnerable to most of the witchcraft accusations. In addition, the ingroup had become emotionally tense with one another because of a "cultural awkwardness" in changing their life style from one set of norms to another. They did not seem to know how to act as they "tried out" new or different behaviors in the family context and they were uncomfortable with the new ways.

Fourth, as the ingroup families spoke about their angry and antagonistic feelings toward the outgroup, they were oblivious to the dynamics of their own internal family relationships and their displacement of family problems and hostilities to the outgroup. None of the families studied were aware of this important aspect of their behavior until the author helped them to see such relationships. In time, some of their anger, which had been displaced to the outgroup, subsided as the author forcused therapy upon ingroup behavior and explored ways to resolve family conflicts.

In the process of working with the families, the specific incidents, problems, and feelings of the ingroup that seemed to have precipitated the cycle of events were dealt with. As a consequence, it was observed that as feelings of anger and hostility shifted from the ingroup to the outgroup, the ingroup members became more comfortable with one another and gradually began to work on their own problems. It was also apparent that as the ingroup dealt with their problems as a group, family unity and solidarity increased. It was, however, a difficult task for the therapist to help the ingroup see the relationship between their own behavior and the displacement of problems to the outgroup. This goal was not achieved until after the ingroup learned to trust each other and work as a family unit again.

During the therapy, the victim challenged the family members who called her "sick" for she felt *all* the family members were involved in similar stresses and were also "sick." As she made these counter-challenges, the author encouraged her to express other feelings and reassured her that other family members would not be allowed to harm her.

The families also talked about the economic pressures they had experienced and how they had to work long hours to meet the monthly costs of urban living. They had expected their outgroup friends to help them economically, however, the outgroup was also feeling economic pressures and was unable to provide the gifts, food, or help that they had earlier. Hence, the ingroup began to realize that their expectations of the outgroup were probably unrealistic and that they would have to deal with their own problems as best they could.

The author talked with some outgroup members who were accused of acting malevolently toward the group. Interestingly, the outgroup members were aware of their culturally defined role in witchcraft and that there were witches among them who were causing harm to the ingroup victim and his family. They were, however, very cautious in talking with the author as they were uncertain about her role since they had never experienced an "outside professional" person who wanted to help them with "their witchcraft." Two outgroup "witches" said that they were acting protectively in order to control the behavior of the ingroup whom they greatly feared—and so, they did not mind being accused of being witches since they felt they were protecting their families.

Occasionally, members of the ingroup would meet or see a member of the outgroup at the store, church, or school. There was always great fear of each other and efforts were made to avoid direct contacts—even if it meant walking or driving several blocks away from the person. In one instance, a male "witch" from the outgroup boarded a bus driven by a member of the victim's ingroup. The "witch" started to enter the front of the bus, quickly recognized the ingroup member driving the bus, and then entered the bus at the rear. He sent another person to the front to pay his fare. Later, the driver said he had been extremely frightened to have the "witch" riding "his bus" and wanted to leave his job. The author was able to help this ingroup member retain his job, and in time, he gradually changed his feelings, but only after his sister (the bewitched victim) showed signs of health improvement. In general, the ingroup and outgroup members were not able to confront one another about their actions and feelings. The author chose not to work with the outgroup members but rather to help the ingroup members modify their behavior so that they themselves could deal with the outgroup in time—which did occur in the majority of families.

With two of the Spanish-speaking families, a large black cat was the symbol which indicated that the family and home were bewitched. For example, in one of these families the ingroup believed that the black cat had been sent by the outgroup witches who desired to cause them evil. They contended that the outgroup had broken the window and dropped the cat in their basement. Initially, they were terrified of removing the cat because they feared it would cause the victim's death or provoke outright family revenge toward them. Instead, they kept the cat well cared for and fed each day. Finally, as their group unity increased, they decided to release the cat from the basement, after which the victim's husband repaired the window. The decision to remove the cat was a major one and caused great fear; however, once they felt "strong enough" to remove the cat, the ingroup became greatly relieved and more relaxed in their home. Symbolically, it meant that the outgroup was no longer living in their basement since the cat was the symbol of oppressive witchcraft practices from the outgroup which brought harm to the bewitched victim and the family. Removal of the cat was a significant factor in achieving a positive direction in the family therapy. The ingroup used the author to support them in their decision because in the past they had had to wait until the outgroup "released" the cat from their house. Having the cat in the house clearly sustained the illness associated with witchcraft behavior.

Since the goals of the therapy for both the Spanish-speaking and the Anglo-American families were similar, with only slight modification according to symbolic referents, they are presented now. The therapy or treatment goals were based upon empirical cultural, psychological, economic, and social data which were conceptualized into a theoretical framework as described earlier. The author attempted to: (1) provide expressive therapy for the ingroup members by focusing upon their social tensions and daily living problems, (2) provide an emotional supportive relationship using cultural referents for an extremely harrassed bewitched victim, (3) assist the group to cope with acculturation changes and the concomitant shift in value orientations, and (4) help the family to function again as a viable and cohesive social group under the duress of cultural changes.

Anglo-American Families

Turning briefly to the two Anglo-American families I worked with for approximately six months, I found similar dynamics in operation as noted above with the Spanish-speaking families. Although there was some variation in the linguistic expression and symbolic cultural forms, the same ingroup-outgroup theoretical model was used and similar therapy goals were applied. While both Anglo-American cases were similar, only one of the families will be discussed.

Reo, a fictitious name, was a 21-year-old college student who had lived in a small midwestern rural community. According to Reo and her family, she had been "hexed" by two college students (referred to as the "hex-witches") at the end of her first year of college in a large urban community. The family had taken Reo to a psychiatric clinic because "she was acting strangely toward us and her classmates." During the interview with the clinic staff she said she had been "hexed" by some classmates who were distant friends, but with whom she had quarreled prior to being bewitched. Since then, Reo felt that these two "witches" were acting unfriendly toward her and influencing her behavior "from a distance." With her closest classmates and family she felt she was being accused of things she did not do. (Scapegoat behavior toward Reo was evident within her family and close ingroup classmates and was based upon social tensions and interpersonal antagonisms.)

Reo said that previously her "close classmates" and family had been good, dependable persons, but lately they seemed to be suspicious, unfriendly, cold, and even fearful of her. She told the clinic staff that one friend, who was now a terrible "hex-witch," was forcing her roommate and also her sister to influence her (Reo's) thoughts and actions by using "McLuhan's medium techniques" and by making her feel strange and sick. The clinic staff were baffled by "the hexing" phenomenon, but diagnosed her case as "paranoid schizophrenia with a guarded prognosis." She was sent home after two weeks of hospitalization (largely on a medication regime) with some mild tranquilizers and was told to return "if things got worse for her and the family." Things did seem to get worse and they returned to the outpatient clinic where the author agreed to provide therapy in the home.

There was no difficulty in working with this Anglo-American family because they viewed the author as another "Anglo" and as a professional nurse who had worked with other families with similar difficulties. The family members desperately wanted help because they were very frightened of what Reo might do to herself or to them and commented that "we believe she is being influenced by that college group (outgroup), but we don't know what to do about it and what she might do."

After Reo was "hexed," she attended some of her classes, but gradually withdrew from them as she became more emotionally disturbed and experienced periodic episodes of nausea and vomiting. Reo also feared she would encounter the hex-witches on the campus and she was most fearful of them and what they might do to her—ranging from being haunted mentally to being killed by the witches.

As I worked with Reo and her family in their home, using indirect interview therapy techniques similar to those used with the Spanish-speaking families, Reo explained how she had been initially victimized by a large black spider. She said her distant college "hex-witches" had put the spider on her dormitory door, after which "she knew they were going to cause her harm." She also told how this college outgroup had once been kind to her, but had become harsh and unkind. She said that they used to have snacks with her, but suddenly became angry and hostile toward her after they "hexed" her. Reo felt her older sister was also involved in making her ill since her sister also knew this college outgroup. Reo thought the latter were sending messages through her sister.

The changes taking place in Reo's family life were similar to those taking place in the Spanish-speaking families. Reo's family also had moved from a rural to an urban community about three years before, and they were encountering acculturational stresses and conflicts in rural-urban value systems. They were able to identify some of the differences they were experiencing between rural and city life, but were unable to cope with their ambivalence about "which ways would be better for them." They found rural life with its many warm and friendly neighbors a real asset in contrast with their cold and busy city neighbors whom they really did not know. Nor could they depend upon their city neighbors in times of crisis like they did with their rural counterparts. They had had many ambivalent feelings about sending Reo to college and they "just knew something would happen to her there and that is why the oldest daughter did not go to college." They had two other daughters who would soon be ready for college (the reason they had moved to an urban community), and they did not know how to handle this problem.

Also, all adult family members were employed in semiskilled and unskilled jobs in the city. They often left the house at 7 a.m. and returned at 6 p.m., and had little time to discuss their family problems and be together as a group as they had been previously in the rural community. Economic problems were evident and they were deeply concerned about how to make a living in the city. There was no question that many of the initial problems which were related to witchcraft had begun with ingroup family problems and interpersonal tensions. Even before Reo was "hexed" at college, the family relationships had become tense with the family members growing increasingly irritable, impatient, and suspicious of one another. They were not fully aware of what was happening to their family relationships, except that "it was not going well." Reo was the family scapegoat member who received their accusations. Moreover, Reo revealed in the family therapy sessions that she had decided to go to college to "get away from all this family bickering and the unfair accusations placed upon me—I just could not take it any longer." The displacement phenomenon to the college outgroup occurred after the family social tensions had become unbearable and the family members were unable to talk with one another without quarreling or physically fighting.

Fortunately, the author was able to talk with Reo's college outgroup who also spoke about the noticeable change in Reo's behavior. They said they had become frightened of her and decided to "leave her at a distance" since they "could no longer understand her." They did feel that they sent "wave lengths" to her and were influencing her behavior unfavorably by the use of "transcendental power communication modes." Later they asked about Reo's health and wondered if they could "use their power to help her get well." They had been very angry with her because "she did not treat us fairly and was unkind, scary and uncharitable to us." They also admitted that they had placed the black spider on her door because "we wanted to scare her."

In working with Reo and her family, the same approach and goals described above were used over a period of four months. Most of the time was spent talking about: changes in rural-urban values and what to do about them; perceptions and anxieties about college life; and how to cope with social, economic, interpersonal family problems in the future in a city way of life with different cultural norms. The family also was extremely sensitive and, hence, secretive about sharing their "family problems with the whole hospital staff or psychiatric group" as they were sure the staff "would not believe" their daughter was hexed, and did not know "how to help her." Because Reo's behavior became worse, they had decided to try the clinic but were disappointed that she did not improve while in the hospital.

Perhaps because they desperately wanted help, this family responded quite readily to family therapy. They liked that therapy was given in their home. The author also worked with Reo on other hostilities and offered her emotional support as she talked about her role as a scapegoat member of the family. Family antagonisms gradually subsided and the family was still functioning as a group one year after the author left them. Reo subsequently completed a college degree and another daughter has enrolled in college.

General Observations and Functional Analysis of Witchcraft Dynamics

The author observed that as the initial tensions and conflicts mounted in the family ingroup, there seemed to be *no* traditional institutionalized norms and practices which the family could rely on to cope with its problems. Moreover, the family contacts to obtain help from outside groups were limited because of the differing cultural norms involved. In general, the family members felt socially and culturally alienated and alone with their problems with no way to deal with them or resolve them.

Although most of the ingroup families had been living in an urban community for at least two years, it was apparent that their traditional values had been challenged only recently by their own family members and by outsiders. The exposure to a number of individuals and groups through work, school, and church seemed to increase their insecurity about themselves as a social group and about the values that they held. Interestingly, each family member was trying to resolve his value conflicts by himself and was afraid to talk openly about them with other family members. In time, the unresolved cultural value differences and social tensions increased so that the family members were unable to converse with one another in an acceptable manner.

The displacement of anger and the maintenance of stresses between the ingroup and the outgroup were dynamic features of the witchcraft practices and had several important social, cultural, and psychological functions which can be summarized here.

First, the displacement of angry feelings from the ingroup to the outgroup helped the ingroup become socially and psychologically more comfortable with one another and kept them united during the heightened ingroup conflict period.

Second, the identified witches in the outgroup (who were perceived to be highly destructive and powerful) were important in explaining the sick victim's behavior to the ingroup. While this temporarily served to relieve the ingroup family members by focusing their group problems on one family member, it also disguised the family's critical problems which ultimately had to be dealt with in the family therapy sessions. Concomitantly, the witches functioned as a powerful external threat to the ingroup and brought them together from fear in order to prevent the witches from generating more "deadly power" upon the sick victim.

Third, the scapegoating behavior exerted upon an ingroup member not only localized the emotional and social conflicts of the family in one member, but it also prepared and conditioned the victim and the others for the roles they would play in the witchcraft practices. Most importantly, the bewitched victim knew the role she would be expected to play, and she served as a barometer for determining the strength and nature of the ingroup-outgroup relationships by the degree of her illness.

Fourth, witchcraft practices were clues to cultural, social, economic, and psychological stresses which were extremely difficult for the ingroup to handle and required a nonfamily member to be helpful and objective. Reports of other victims who had not been helped in this way revealed either a prolonged illness in the hospital or increased social pathology in the family.

Fifth, symbolic referents such as cats and lizards served the important function of legitimizing the witchcraft phenomenon and of alerting the victim and the family to difficulties with an outgroup.

Summary

In this paper, the author has presented a theoretical framework, based upon empirical data, regarding witchcraft behavior and its functions in selected urban families in the United States. Through an intensive study and the provision of psychocultural therapy to four Spanish-speaking and two Anglo-American families, the author was able to help the bewitched victims and their families.

An analysis of the six families, plus other families who did not receive therapy, disclosed that ingroup tensions and problems (which were largely a consequence of acculturation and the ensuing economic, social, and psychocultural stresses) were displaced in time to a known outgroup whose witches acted upon the scapegoat or bewitched victim in the ingroup. Witchcraft practices in these families were important psychocultural and social mechanisms to cope with ingroup problems generated by external societal concerns.

The theoretical model with three major phases served as an important guide in providing psychocultural nursing therapy to the six families. The therapy was largely supportive and expressive in form involving the use of cultural value orientations adapted to the current life and environmental situation of the families. Although witchcraft behavior has been described in the anthropological literature since the early part of this century, there have been no known reports of professional groups attempting to relieve bewitched victims and their families through psychocultural therapy. However, with the reported increase of interest in witchcraft in this country and the increase of bewitched victims seeking help, it seems important that professional staff (and especially mental health personnel) become more knowledgeable of the witchcraft phenomenon and explore ways to relieve victims and their families of such stress.

Notes

1. The majority of the witchcraft cases were reported to the author by anthropologists who were doing field work in local communities, and by a few who were employed at a medical center or hospital.
2. This diagnosis and prognosis statement was commonly found with many witchcraft victims studied, and generally with no indication on the patient's record of his suffering from bewitchment phenomena.

References

EVANS-PRITCHARD, E. E. 1937. Witchcraft, Oracles and Magic Among the Azande. Oxford: Clarenton Press.

KLUCKHOHN, C. 1944. Navajo Witchcraft. Boston: Beacon Press.

NADEL, S. F. 1952. Witchcraft in four African societies: an essay in comparison. American Anthropologist 54:18.

LEININGER, M. 1969. Study of the Health-Illness System of Spanish-Americans in an Urban Community. Unpublished report.

26

Religion in an Affluent Society

SURAJIT SINHA

THIS STUDY WAS TAKEN UP primarily out of curiosity about a pattern of living that operates today as a powerful model for modernity and as a generator of induced change throughout the economically underdeveloped world.[1] The study deals with these problems: (1) why and how formal religion persists in the most technologically advanced country in the world, contrary to the expectations of Comte, Spencer, and Tylor; and (2) the relation between religion and secular life.

Data Collection

I sought an American village with a fairly stable core population (i.e., with a sense of local history), clear evidence of economic affluence, and a fair balance between Protestants and Roman Catholics. A population under 5,000 was desirable in order that much of the village life could be directly visible or, at least, easily approached. I found such a community, which I shall call "Mapletown," in the Midwest.

With my family I moved into a big modern house in the predominantly lower-middle class section. I became a member of the local chapter of the

Kiwanis Club. We stayed for about 3 months—from June 5 until September 5, 1963. I revisited the village alone for about 2 weeks in May, 1964.[2]

I observed as much of the religious and related secular behavior as possible, although I collected the bulk of my data through informally guided conversation and open-ended questionnaires. Responses were often tape recorded. In framing the questionnaires, I took advantage of being a foreigner and of not knowing much about Christianity or about American society. I also did a census survey of about 10% of the families of Mapletown.

My American field experience was quite different from my earlier encounter with tribes of Central India.[3] There I studied the groups with a considerable sense of sociocultural distance, detachment, and, I must confess, condescension. In my commitment to record fully the customs of the tribe as a "natural system," I did not always pay adequate attention to the reaction of the respondents to my encroachment on the privacy of their customs and social relations. In Mapletown I was much more cautious about the sensitivities of my respondents. In tribal Central India, while I utilized the insights of exceptionally perceptive informants, the analysis of behavior was primarily done by me. In Mapletown, there were many local intellectuals who thought reflectively about the structures or processes of their community life. I could approach these specialized respondents—the priests, doctors, lawyers, educated farmers, school teachers, journalists, etc.—as fellow "intellectuals," or "learned informants." I occasionally asked selected informants for a guided tour of the village and tried to follow their mental charts of the community.

The shifting cluster of playmates around my 5½-year-old daughter often brought into relief the class structure of the community. The neighborhood children provided us with ready subjects for enquiring into the imprint of religion on 6- to 9-year-old children.

Our coming as foreigners gave us easy access to some of the marginal people who were somewhat critical of the community, such as a local newspaper reporter, the Negro leaders of the local chapter of the NAACP, and the few agnostics. In theological discussion with the local ministers, my sometimes posing contrasting alternatives from Hindu theological background stimulated discussion.

Mapletown

Mapletown became an incorporated village in 1859. The pioneering families were all Protestants from the eastern states. They worked hard, cleared large farmlands, built decent, commodious houses, and prospered.

Later immigrants to the community included members of other ethnic groups, nearly all Catholic. Of these, the Irish are no longer distinguishable from the Protestants. The other groups are: Poles, Italians, Slovaks, and

Croatians. There are also 3 Jewish families, all shop-owners, and about a dozen Negro families, living mostly in the rural area.

Mapletown township today has a population of 4,939 of whom 1,967 live in rural areas and 2,972 in the village. About ¼ of the 1,245 families in the township depends mainly or subsidiarily on farming. (Grape-growing, introduced by Southern European immigrants about 1910, is an important specialty.) The rest depend on labour, business, service, professions, and industries. Since the major industries in this township are connected with the processing of farm products, the nonfarming section of the population keeps close track of what is happening to the farmers. About 100 family heads commute daily to an industrial city about 18 miles away.

To a person coming from India, Mapletown has no characteristics of a "village" other than population size. It has all the modern amenities: electricity, telephones, television, radio, supermarkets, automatic laundry, hotels, and restaurants. Within the last 30 years, the village has developed industries; it has 3 wineries, 2 juice-processing companies, 2 canning companies, 2 fish bait companies, 1 electronics factory, 1 plating company, 1 fruit-packaging company, 1 cement products company, 1 notebook and looseleaf binder company, and 1 dairy processing plant. About 1,700 people are employed by these concerns.

Two men tried to impress upon me that class structure is not very visible in the residential pattern and that there is really "no rich man towering above others in the village." Mr. D., the leading drugstore owner gave a breakdown of the class structure in terms of annual income as follows:

Level 1)   Industry leaders and owners: about $100,000 or more.
Level 2)   Doctors, dentists and lawyers: $15–70,000.
            Automobile dealers: $15–40,000.
            Outstanding farmers: $10–30,000.
Level 3)   Salesmen, insurance agents, etc.: $10–30,000.
Level 4)   Teachers: $4–10,000; medium farmers: $4–10,000.
Level 5)   Skilled industrial workers: $4–8,000.
Level 6)   Small farmers, unskilled industrial labourers, store clerks, retired people: $2–4,000.
Level 7)   Transient laborers: $2,000

Mr. D. estimated that about three-fourths of the population of the township would belong to levels 4–6.

Nearly all the families from levels 1–5 have electricity, central heating, car, refrigerator, telephone, television, and at least 1 radio. Most of these items are also available in level 6, only a few not having a telephone. In level 7, telephones become rare and even television is missing in a number of families, and the car is usually dilapidated.

Within the upper 5 levels, variations occur in the size of the house and its lawn; lake frontage; number and quality of possessions; and ownership of special items such as record player, piano or organ, tape recorder, expensive camera, and power mower. A trip to Florida for the retired has recently become a symbol of prestige widely shared by people from levels 1-4. A pleasure trip to Europe is becoming common for the younger people from levels 1-3. A private swimming pool and horses for the children are also marks of economic distinction.

With the rising income level, increased consumption, and growth of industries, the society is aware that it is affluent, compared to its past and especially compared to other countries. However, the lower classes, from level 5 down, are aware that they are not influential in the community. They are outside the prestige churches and the prestige clubs. Although organizations like the volunteer fire department, American Legion, Masonic Lodge, and Knights of Columbus tend to blur class lines, the lower classes are involved to a lesser extent in such social activities as bridge clubs, boating, hunting, and golfing. The marginal position of these people has, of course, important bearing upon their religious behavior (Harrington 1963). They either do not go to church at all or go to the "emotional" ones that promise the coming of the Lord and the inheritance of the earth by the meek.

The Churches

Every Friday, the local newspaper publishes a Durkheimian statement: "Strong Church makes strong communities." The theme is further elaborated as follows:

> The Church is the greatest faith on earth for the building of character and good citizenship. It is a storehouse of spiritual values. Without a strong Church, neither democracy nor civilization can survive.

The full page announcement includes church-service notices for 11 churches in the township: St. Mary's Catholic, St. Mark's Episcopal, First Presbyterian, First Methodist, Trinity Lutheran, First Baptist, Christian (Disciples of Christ), Assembly of God, Full Gospel Pentecostal, Seventh Day Adventist, and Jehovah's Witnesses.

These messages are sponsored every week by 23 industries and business establishments in Mapletown. They include a pictorial feature and a lengthy moral message obtained through a national advertising service. These announcements say much about the place of formal religion in the community: (a) It is generally felt that church going generates the requisite individual and social ethics that support "democracy" and "civilization," which are identical; (b) the business world is behind the church; (c) there is considerable tolerance, on a formal level, of the various churches, denominations, and sects; and (d) religious life in small communities is guided by a nationwide network of mass communication.

Yet the village president and the village clerk are not church members. Both of them are highly regarded by the community, not only for their official position and efficiency, but also for their general uprightness. In other words, churchgoing is not an essential indicator of normal conduct. About ¼ of the adult population of the village does not belong to any church, and another ¼ does not attend church regularly. The bulk of the unchurched comes from the low-income groups. These unchurched people, however, believe in God and want a minister to preside over their funeral ceremonies.

Six of the most important churches of Mapletown—Methodist, Presbyterian, First Baptist, Christian, Episcopal, and Catholic—were established between 1835 and 1872. The other 5 churches have been built since World War II. With 1 exception, all of these latecomers are fundamentalist churches.

The class structure of the churches is fairly explicit in broad terms, except for the Roman Catholic, which includes a wide spectrum, from industrialists to unskilled factory workers and farm laborers, but very few professionals. In terms of economic status the Protestant churches may be arranged in the following descending order: Presbyterian, Methodist, Episcopal, Christian, Lutheran, Baptist Seventh Day Adventist, Assembly of God, and Pentecostal. The members of the first 5 churches are predominantly middle-class; while the last 4 churches (all fundamentalist) recruit members mainly from the lower classes. The Jehovah's Witnesses seem to stand apart; although predominantly of the lower-middle class, they also include stray members from the upper-middle class.

The leaders of all the above churches claim to welcome Negroes, but the latter are found only in the Baptist, Episcopal, Roman Catholic, and Jehovah's Witnesses churches.

The membership of the various churches of Mapletown is given in Table 1. St. Mary's Catholic Church is the largest single church group in the township, but the 9 Protestant churches together have more members. Among the Protestant churches, the standard churches have the bulk of the membership. (It may be mentioned here that only about 12 families of the village proper belong to the fundamentalist churches.) The unchurched include about 25% of the total number of families.

How the Ministers View Their Churches

The ministers of the various churches in Mapletown have a number of conventional categories for describing the basic characteristics of churches: "high" (ritualistic and formal) and "low" (informal), "conservative" (accepting literal interpretation of the Bible) and "liberal" (willing to rein-

TABLE 1.   Church Membership in Mapletown Township

CHURCH	NO. OF FAMILIES	% OF TOTAL
Standard Protestant		
1. Presbyterian	160	13.0
2. Methodist	150	12.0
3. Lutheran	90	7.1
4. Episcopal	25	2.0
5. Christian	25	2.0
Total	450	36.1
Fundamentalist Protestant		
1. Baptist	15	1.2
2. Assembly of God	10	0.8
3. Seventh Day Adventist	29	2.3
4. Pentecostal	2	0.2
Total	56	4.5
Roman Catholic	400	32.1
Jehovah's Witnesses	2	0.1
Miscellaneous churches outside Mapletown	25	2.0
Jews	3	0.2
Unchurched	309	25.0
TOTAL	1,245	100.0

terpret the letter of the scripture in terms of the spirit of modern times), "emotional" and "rational," and so on. There is also the usual distinction between the fundamentalists and the standard denominations. The fundamentalists are noted for their disregard of ritual symbolism, emotional exuberance in songs and sermons, literal interpretation of the Bible, belief in miraculous experiences like speaking in tongues and divine healing, strict rules of abstention, and excessive aversion to Catholicism.

By collating the views of the ministers with my observations on their religious services, the churches of Mapletown may be arranged in a variety of continua:

    a. Formalistic-Informal: (1) Catholic; (2) Episcopal; (3) Lutheran; (4) Presbyterian, Methodist, and Christian; (5) Baptist; (6) Assembly of God, Seventh Day Adventist, and Pentecostal.

    b. Ritualistic-Rational: (1) Catholic; (2) Episcopal; (3) Lutheran; (4) Christian; and (5) Presbyterian and Methodist. (The fundamentalist churches such as Assembly of God, Seventh Day Adventist, etc. fall outside the continuum since they are neither rgitualistic nor rational.)

    c. Cold-Hot: (1) Presbyterian and Methodist; (2) Christian; (3) Baptist and Lutheran; (4) Seventh Day Adventist; (5) Assembly of God; (6)

Pentecostal. (The Catholic Church, although lacking the emotional exuberance of the shouting and rolling fundamentalist churches, does not share the cold intellectual persuasiveness of the rational Protestant churches.)

d. Puritanical-Permissive: (1) Assembly of God, Pentecostal, and Seventh Day Adventist; (2) Christian and Baptist; (3) Methodist; (4) Presbyterian; (5) Episcopal; and (6) Catholic. (Here "Puritanism" is judged mainly by abstention from drinking, smoking, gambling, cardplaying, etc.)

e. Authoritarian-Democratic: (1) Roman Catholic; (2) Episcopal; (3) Methodist; (4) Presbyterian and the rest. (Jehovah's Witnesses, again, do not clearly fall into any of the above continua. Like the fundamentalists they are concerned with literal interpretation of the Bible and have "fanatical" dedication to their cause. But although their services have an informal atmosphere like that of the fundamentalist churches, there is not the same emphasis on emotional singing and shouting.)

The atmosphere of church services seemed to me distinctly non-secular in the ritualistic (i.e., Roman Catholic and Episcopalian) and in the fundamentalist churches. In the Catholic and the Episcopalian churches, the numerous esoteric symbolic elements, such as the figure of Jesus on the cross, candles, robe of the minister, and his symbolic gestures and Latin chants, create an atmosphere of sanctity quite distinct from ordinary life. The fundamentalist churches effect the separation from day-to-day life by their emotionalism: "singing of the heart," shouting of "hallelujah," and "speaking in tongues." In contrast, the "rationalist" Protestant churches give the impression of being social clubs with special emphasis on sober moralizing.

We attended a marriage ceremony in the Catholic Church and one in the Presbyterian Church. Here also the contrasts in atmosphere were quite evident—the elaborate Catholic marriage ritual ending with the couple kneeling submissively before the statue of Mary created a sacred atmosphere which was lacking in the relatively brief and contractual mode of the Presbyterian ceremony.

Below are a few statements on the position of their respective churches made by some ministers of Mapletown which will bring into relief the range of ideological positions.

The Presbyterian minister, Rev. K., whose educational background included psychology and philosophy, stated:

Ours is very definitely a middle class church. They place heavy emphasis on education in this denomination. It is not an emotional appeal. They want a reasoned approach.

Rev. K. is proud of the fact that many of his parishioners are well-educated and that they control the power structural of the community. At the same time, he views the community as "politically and economically very conservative" and considers himself the spokesman for the young intellectuals.

In his "liberal" sermons, the themes of "youth," "modernity," and "intelligence" appear repeatedly, and also an uncomfortable admission that the Christian churches tend to avoid vital issues and that "all of the good forces may be working outside the Church at the present moment." In this venture into radical ideas among an upper-middle-class congregation in a politically and socially conservative community, there is the tacit understanding between the minister and his congregation that there will be no call for action. When the previous minister of the Presbyterian church impressed upon his Board of Elders the moral necessity of letting a Negro buy a plot of land in the fashionable quarter where some of his younger influential parishioners lived, he was fired.

Brother M. of the newly established Pentecostal Church stated that the core doctrine of his church was based on the 2nd chapter of *Acts*, which prescribes communion with the Holy Ghost and speaking in tongues:

> That is the basic doctrine of our church plus holiness and righteous living. . . . our women don't put on makeup, . . . cut their hair nor adorn themselves. The Bible teaches modest dress . . . The Bible says that the Zealous of God will have to be a *peculiar* people to cut yourself [off] from the whole world. We consider ourselves as the First Church that was established in the world of God. Therefore we are not Protestants.[4] We are all labourers. The Gospel came to the Poor. And I suppose you might say we are amongst the poorest.

The Pentecostal church is also noted for its belief in ritual healing.

Father R. of St. Mary's Catholic Church stated that among the Protestant churches, he felt more at home with the standard churches than with the fundamentalists. But he complained that the former "have watered down or weakened the basic teachings":

> Historically ours is old and has "completeness" of the teachings of Christ. Their [the "liberal" Protestants'] emphasis is more on the "external," "to lead a good life," than to "a body of beliefs." . . . Whereas the Protestant churches have the idea of "serving" the people, we emphasize the idea of "receiving" the grace of God.
>
> I don't think the terms "liberal-conservative" are too applicable in describing the Catholic and the Protestant churches. Our bulk members are of lower or middle class. As lower- and middle-class people tend to vote Democratic party nationally, the majority of Roman Catholics in America are Democratic. In [Mapletown] and the surrounding areas, however, many of the Roman Catholics tend to be Republican. I don't see how a Catholic could hold to "rugged individualism" too rigorously.

The Catholic Church runs an elementary school which has about 400 students. The textbooks of this school come from the diocese. Every morning the students have 40 minutes of religious teaching. It appears that the Catholic school maintains stricter discipline than the local public schools. Sister D., the principal, said:

> We teach the students not to argue a point. Our children learn good discipline. You will find that our students will say 'Yes, sir,' instead of 'Yeah.'

Brother P., minister of the Jehovah's Witnesses congregation, brings out the idiosyncratic position of his church as follows:

> We are neither Protestant nor Catholic . . . . We consider ourselves as Bible students—advocates of the Truth from the Bible. The Bible puts a great emphasis on the name of God so we call him Jehovah. The cross is of pagan origin. We do not use any pagan symbol . . . . We do not salute the American flag . . . . We regard salute as an act of worship. We do not worship a flag, although we respect it. We feel that our life belongs to God who gave it to us. And for that reason we cannot give our life to any nation. So Jehovah's Witnesses refuse military service . . . . Armageddon . . . is the Great Day of Judgment of God the Almighty. Only true believers of Jehovah's Witnesses will survive the Armageddon and live happily in the new kingdom of God.

Members of all the other churches in Mapletown refer to Jehovah's Witnesses as "fanatics," "screwballs," "nuts," "pests," and so on. Only the Presbyterian minister added that the existence of such an extremist sect provided a test for religious tolerance.

Mr. B., of a neighboring village, belongs to the Spiritualist church about 50 miles away and knows 3 persons in Mapletown who occasionally attend seances and who usually attend the spiritual centers in Florida during the winter. Mr. B. explained his position as a spiritualist as follows:

> All things are controlled by one Divine Power and the object of our seances is to contact spirits who advance on different planes of life. . . . Christ was one of the greatest examples of spiritual phenomena. I have no superstition whatsoever. There are good spirits and bad spirits. I send the bad spirits back by prayer. . . . I get messages and give messages.

Mr. B. invited me to participate in a seance at his house and showed me his collection of pictures of spirits that appear before him and Mrs. B. during seances. In the state of possession, he prescribed cures for his ailing wife.

Although statistically the cult of the spiritualists does not carry any weight, its existence in a small community like Mapletown has some significance. Like the various fundamentalist groups, the spiritualists are a reminder to the rest of the community that the respectable churches have been secularized and have lost any meaningful contact with the supernatural sphere.

What People Say They Believe In

Apart from interviewing 9 pastors and listening to informal conversation, I interviewed 27 adults and 5 children (ages 7 to 9) regarding their religious beliefs with the help of an open-end questionnaire. The adult respondents covered all the denominations, sects, and economic classes in the community.

Only 1 person declared himself to be an atheist. He does not believe in God, but sings in the Presbyterian choir and sends his children to Sunday School.

One person declared:

I am not an atheist, but an agnostic. I believe there is an order behind the running of the Universe. I don't know the nature of this order. We should be concerned more with social progress than with religion.

Some who claim to be believers complain against the churches. P. L., an unchurched factory worker, said, "They look upon you in church in a way that you don't belong there." P. M., a retired mail-carrier, raised as a German Lutheran but not now a member of any church, strongly believes in God and is now active in the American Legion and the Masonic Lodge. He stated:

I know men, so-called pillars of the church, who are dishonest. . . . I think religion today is pretty much commercialized. I have heard ministers talk about "living like Christ." There isn't a minister in the world living like Christ.

Mrs. M., an elderly widow of Catholic descent, is bitter about the role of the churches:

I see a lot of these people that go to church every Sunday and they are terrible people. They steal and think nothing of robbing the poor.

The theme of hypocrisy in religious behavior and divergence between what is preached and practiced is widespread in the community. The role of the aggressive village atheist, however, is dead, so that the Presbyterian minister could say: "The old struggle between science and religion is a dead issue and has been thoroughly reconciled."

In a community where there is so little overt dependence on God and where there is widespread skepticism about the depth of religious commitment, one naturally wonders how seriously the people rely on the supernatural.

From the answers of educated respondents belonging to the "liberal" Protestant churches, I got the impression that there has been a general decline of "supernaturalism," "superstition," and "asceticism." Respondents repeatedly said: "I have no superstition." "Heaven" and "Hell" are considered states of mind rather than places. Devil and angels are ruled out as mythical and allegorical symbols. God is invisible and is an abstract ethical principle symbolizing what is best in men. Evolution is generally accepted. The Bible is not infallible and is not to be taken literally; the Biblical accounts are colored by the world view of the writers of those times.

The members of the Roman Catholic church in general took a less secular stand than those of the liberal Protestant churches. All Catholic respondents stated that they believed in "virgin birth," saints, and taboos on birth control and on divorce, but some of them expressed their doubts about the reality of Heaven, Hell, and the Devil and felt that at least half of the Catholic families in the town used contraceptives.

Whereas the majority of the church-goers in the liberal churches appear as striving to preserve their belief in God along with their commitment to modernization and science, members of fundamentalist churches have more clear commitment to God-centered beliefs. Mrs. G. of the Pentecostal church gave the following statement:

> In 1934 I believed in the Lord. It was raining hard in Missouri and the people were running away to the hills. . . . I . . . called God for help. I did not know Him but He knew me. While I was talking to the Lord, the Lord talked to my son and the storm ceased.

Such intense reliance upon the Lord is not limited to the poorly educated. B. C., who is a schoolteacher with an M.A. degree and belongs to the Church of God in a neighboring village, said:

> I believe very strongly in miracles. . . . When I was in Japan, I prayed and asked God to lead me to the right girl for my wife and He said "Don't worry about this . . . this will be taken care of." As soon as I went home to America, I met the girl who is my present wife and I knew she was the girl right from the first time I met her.

The children I interviewed all came from Protestant families, 4 of them lower-class and 1 upper-middle-class.

The 4 children of the lower-income parents, belonging to the Baptist and Lutheran churches, conceived of God as "white-skinned, old, putting on a robe." Jesus and Mary are the father and the mother of God, and "Jesus is the best American." They vaguely believe in angels and "devils with horns." The latter sometimes "makes you shiver with cold." The sins are "to swear, drink, disobeying father and mother, and to lie." "The Sunday School teaches you to love others, to be kind and to good to others." "Half of the world are Christians and the other half are sinners. They would go down to the Devil."

C. S. (8 years old), daughter of a lawyer who attends the Presbyterian Sunday School, strikes a more critical and rational tone. She stated:

> Nobody really knows what God looked like. Everybody says the soul goes up to the angels. Hell is not a good word to use. Some people say there is a Devil, but I don't think so. The President and Governors are good Americans, they help to build the country, doctors also.

Religion and the Secular Sphere

In a farming community with so many churches, one might expect religion to offer some support to farming activities. But the farmer, whether Roman Catholic or Protestant, does not seek divine help to solve any agricultural problems. Although in the Roman Catholic church there are formal provisions for "blessing of the grape vineyards" and for petition to God on the Rogesian days for bountiful crops, these customs have become completely obsolete in Mapletown in recent years.

According to N. H., a well-known farmer, there are still some "folk beliefs" half-heartedly adhered to by some of the old farmers in the area:

> I think there are still some people who believe that you should plant certain things in the light of the moon and others in the dark phase of the moon. My hired hand did not want to start plowing a field on Friday. It is just the fact of the old saying that if you start something on a Friday, you'll never finish.

The prevailing notions are that "God is not to be manipulated for the purpose of farming" and that "rain falls on the fields of the virtuous and the sinners alike." God is prayed to in order to build "character" with which to face one's problems. In both the Catholic school and the Protestant Sunday schools, children learn that kindliness, honesty, and obedience to parents are good and that swearing, drinking, smoking, lying, stealing, and hurting others are sins. The children begin life with a notion that God is watching their conduct. None of the churches *directly* emphasizes worldly virtues such as hard work, thrift, and cleanliness.

It is difficult to assess the role of the teaching of the churches in the maintenance of a high level of civic activity. Mapletown has had a volunteer fire department since 1868, with an excellent record of performance of which everyone is proud. The Conservation Club, whose members have built a club building and planted thousands of trees, is another example of civic cooperation. Similar effort and zeal have gone into the improvement of the local school system, the running of the village council, and the organization of the American Legion, the Farm Bureau, 4H clubs, and the Sixty Plus Club. It is customary to open these meetings by a formal prayer.

Although the Baptist minister pointed out that it is the Protestant, and not the Catholic, countries which have successfully developed industries, my respondents, whether Catholic or Protestant, did not see any direct connection between initiative in industry and Christian upbringing. A few suggested that Christian ethics provided the basis for trustworthy business transactions. People do not see their civic performance in the various voluntary associations and the level of initiative in livelihood activities as *necessarily* derived from Christian ethics. The villagers seem to imbibe their civic sense by participating in the orderly life of both secular and religious associations. Although all the churches warn against pursuit of material pleasures, it is only the fundamentalist churches that may be regarded as distinctly "otherworldly."

To a Hindu visitor, it is striking that in all the churches of Mapletown, with the exception of the Jehovah's Witnesses, the American flag is displayed as prominently as the church flag. Also, at the end of the service there is a formal prayer in which the minister invokes the blessing of God on the President and on others in power. In spite of the Protestant insistence on the separation of the church and the state, there is the underlying theme: "The church and God are the protectors of the nation." One also gains the impression that not only does the church bless the American flag, but the autonomous sacredness of the flag also lends sanctity to the church.

The ritualized repetition of the oath of allegiance to the flag in the schools, in 4H clubs, and in such voluntary associations as the Kiwanis Club, Lions Club, and American Legion is indeed impressive. A brief prize essay on "What Civil Defense means to me," written by a high school student is an example of the loyalty generated by nationalistic rituals:

> First of all . . . Civil Defense means the protecting of your country, your home and yourself from destruction by the enemy. By protecting this country you're preserving a light that is leading the free world to peace, prosperity and happiness. . . I'm fighting for the Bill of Rights, the Constitution, the individual and the home. And all the people that make up the greatest country in the world.

Yet the leaders of the community are worried that patriotism is softening. At a Kiwanis meeting, the vice president read aloud extracts from a pamphlet, *What Happened to Patriotism*, by Max Rafferty (1953).

It appears that various nationalistic voluntary associations join forces with the churches to impress upon the people that they are indeed citizens of the most prosperous and civilized nation in the world. With prosperity, democracy, freedom, and Christian ethics, they are convinced that they have the best of everything. Protestants, Catholics, and Jews, whites and negroes, share this with equal conviction. Mapletown seems to bear out Will Herberg's observation (1960:263-64) that:

> . . . the new religiosity pervading America seems to be very largely the religious validation of the social pattern and cultural values associated with the American Way of Life.

In a recent study of the impact of religion on politics, economics, and family life in Detroit, Gerhard Lenski (1963:320-21) found a confirmation of the Weberian thesis:

> White Protestants and Jews have a positive attitude toward work more often than the Negro Protestants or Catholics, especially in the upper-middle class jobs. They are likelier to believe that ability is more important than family connections; to be self-employed; to believe in intellectual autonomy and to have small families.

I did not follow up Lenski's observations by detailed study, but it is obvious that compared with the "liberal" Protestants, the Catholics are brought up in a more authoritarian elementary school system and live in more stable family units. However, an outsider is impressed with how both segments of the population are predominantly committed to rational technological orientation in agriculture and industry, in medical care, cleanliness, punctuality, and thrift.

It is true that the Catholics, most of whom are relatively recent European immigrants or their 1st-generation descendants, have not yet contributed any "professionals" to the community (with the exception of a dentist), but some of the top industrialists and businessmen belong to the Catholic church and so also do many technologically progressive farmers. Until further research is carried on, I am inclined to stick to my general impression that through their common exposure to the high school system, and to the various civic organizations, Catholics and Protestants of Mapletown share fundamentally similar secular values of economic initiative, saving, civic responsibility, and national pride. Religious upbringing does not *directly* cause any major deflection from the common American course.

Conclusions

General Impressions

This was my first field encounter with a cultural system effectively committed to technological development. The spread of economic well-being in a village like Mapletown is indeed very impressive in the contrastive perspective of an underdeveloped village in India. Also impressive is the general absence of overt violence and loud quarrels and the low level of mutual suspicion among villagers in Mapletown. The people of this village are accustomed to leave the doors of their houses unlocked even when they are away from home. The many village organizations indicate a high level of "civic culture."

Although the full roster of customs is long, one cannot escape noticing that compared to an Indian peasant community, the load of custom on the minds of the people of Mapletown is relatively light in the face of rational dedication to economic mobility. Farming is practically free of religious or esoteric customs, although some farmers still cling to the sentiment that "farming is a way of life." Many also state: "It is a matter of the almighty dollar," and "The younger generation is trying to get out of farming." The elder generation of farmers does not expect the younger generation to stay in Mapletown out of sentiment for locality and kin instead of pursuing better opportunities elsewhere.

One would expect to find the pace of life in a small community like Mapletown quite relaxed, with people meeting in many different contexts and being well acquainted. But in comparison with the Bhumij tribe of West Bengal-Bihar (India), the spontaneity of interpersonal relations in Mapletown appears considerably restrained by the discipline of a high standard of living. People are hesitant to visit one another without a formal engagement over the telephone, and everyone is aware that one should be careful not to encroach upon the time of another person. When people get together for a potluck meeting of the Sixty Plus Club or a family reunion, the affair is preceded by a planned effort and lacks the spontaneity and spirit of abandon in human interaction observed in an informal gathering of the Bhumij. One misses the spirit of *adda* found in a Bengali home (even in a city like Calcutta), where people may spend hours talking on random topics without concern about the expenditure of time. It appears that a happy village like Mapletown has had to sacrifice a good portion of the "spirit of abandon" in favor of the discipline of industrialization. As a result, compared to the Indian base-line, whether tribal or peasant or urban, Mapletown gives the impression of dehydration of interpersonal sentiments.[6]

As one reads the local newspapers, attends the village council meetings, or meets people in more informal gatherings, one feels that a sense of optimism and achievement thrives in the community in spite of occasional complaints that "the younger generation is getting soft," "religion is getting hypocritical," "there is too much cut-throat competition among social climbers," and so on. The people are thoroughly convinced that they live in [one] of the best small communities of the best nation in the world. Good life has a vivid visual image: a clean house and a clean yard indicate that the individual has pride in himself and in his family. Although the leaders of the village continue to plan improvements in living conditions, an outsider gets the feeling that in Mapletown one has come close to the end of a fairy tale: "And they lived happily ever after."

How and Why Religion Still Holds Ground

Although I stand by my general impression that reliance on God is irreversibly on the decline, it is also true that formal religion tenaciously holds a residual ground. Some of the factors sustaining religion in Mapletown today are as follows:

1. Along with the numerous secular associations, the churches play an important role in the condensation of human interaction in the town and make community life vivid.
2. The churches, instead of disturbing the social structure, closely follow its contours.

3. Religion continues to provide a *certain* and coherent world view in a changing world, so that a person can conveniently think that he goes by a set of absolutes, namely, "Christian ethics."
4. Religion sanctifies the important social event of marriage and by its ritual and ideas helps people to face the crisis of death.
5. Religion is a source of aesthetic activity in the choirs and the architecture of the churches.
6. By sponsoring a series of festivals like Christmas and Easter, religion provides a vivid frame of cultural continuity between the generations.
7. Religion bolsters the common image of America as the best nation having the best ethical standards.
8. Internal competition between the various denominations and the major competition between the Roman Catholics and the Protestants maintains the vigor of social and moral commitment to the church. The Protestants cannot afford to give up while the Catholics are thriving.

Some Dysfunctional Aspects of Religion

So far I have written mainly about the extraordinarily good fit, in a value-neutral way, between religion and social structure in Mapletown. Taking a more value-laden position, one can point to some dysfunctional aspects of religion in Mapletown:

1. Although it provides the poor with the consolation of salvation and a certain emotional boost, it also pushes them to irrationality or to a symbolic acceptance of social marginality and inferiority. The upper class is perpetually charged with cynicism and hypocrisy.
2. It bolsters the national image too strongly to be desirable in the modern age.
3. By becoming too thin, it fails to provide adequate security in times of stress. The activities of the churches tend to camouflage the growing spiritual vacuum on account of lack of faith.

In facing the dilemma of how to preserve and promote secular values and yet not be spread too thinly in the spiritual realm, I feel that the Roman Catholic and the Episcopal churches have been relatively successful so far. They tend to preserve an aesthetically vivid and serene religious platform while allowing their members to imbibe the requisite secular values by directly participating in secular associations. The vows of chastity and poverty of Catholic nuns and priests help to emphasize the sacred nature of their institutions. The liberal Protestant churches, with their pride in being "rational" and "modern," are troubled with the problem of where to draw the line between secular idealism and belief in God.[7] Perhaps by letting secular idealism vigorously engulf almost the entire domain of the church, as is the case with Unitarianism, the liberal Protestant churches of Mapletown could find a special solution to their dilemma. But such a radical denomination is not likely to have a comfortable stay in Mapletown.

Contrasts With Hinduism

The religion of the people of Mapletown, especially of the liberal Protestant churches, contrasts with Hinduism of rural as well as urban Bengal, in the following ways:[8]

1. The role of divine intervention in natural phenomena as well as in human problems such as economics, health, and litigation is very much attenuated in Mapletown.
2. There is less of a *dependent* relation to God in the American village. Instead of praying to God to get something done, people seek divine help to build morality or character with which to face their problems.
3. The rituals in the churches of Mapletown are relatively simple.
4. Through Sunday school teachings and the general influence of the simple code of the Ten Commandments, Christian teachings tend to be more directly ethical, whereas in Hinduism the ethical elements are often immersed in pragmatic rituals.
5. Ascetic rigor and denial of "pleasures" is less emphasized in local Christianity.
6. The religious practices of the standard Christian churches, whether of the ministry or of the laity, are very close to the secular mode of life. There is little seeking of "mystical" or "transcendental" experience.
7. Religion is organized in rigid associations like the local churches, connected to national or international networks of organization, rather than such loose organizational units as family, temple, pilgrim centers, and so on, as in Hinduism.
8. The prescribed patterns of religious behavior of the people of Mapletown come mainly from outside, from the centers of the various church organizations, although the local pastor and the lay leaders of the congregation may give particular color to the local congregation. In the case of a Hindu village, the Great Traditions reach the small community in a much less organized way and are refracted to a much greater degree in the context of the little community, and there are also unique local cults of particular villages or of very narrow regions.[9]
9. The churches of Mapletown are strongly committed to reinforcing nationalism, in contrast to the general indifference of peasant Hinduism to nationalism.

10. There is no clear counterpart to the Hindu search for "spiritual freedom" by renunciation of worldly ties or by becoming a wandering ascetic in the distinctly more "this-worldly" religion of the Christians of Mapletown.

The Catholic Church, with its greater content of esoteric rituals, its images of Christ, and its pantheon of the saints and the Virgin Mary, comes nearer to the Hindu mode. The singers of the fundamentalist congregations remind one of the congregation of Vaishnavites singing highly emotional *Kirtana* songs, except that the contents of the latter songs are not heavy with the concept of sin.

Notes

1. There have been surprisingly few field studies of American culture by anthropologists from Afro-Asian countries. In this regard, I can think only of the publications of Francis Hsu (1953, 1961, 1963), all on the level of national character. Kluckhohn once commented: "We badly need people from India, Japan, and China to come and study our American values and *vice versa*. This is an indispensable step. We have to see a value system from this point, that point, and the other point." (Tax *et al.* 1953:340).

2. This field study was made possible by the generous support of The Wenner-Gren Foundation for Anthropological Research and the Center for Advanced Study in the Behavioral Sciences. I am particularly grateful to Sol Tax for encouraging me in many ways to take up this study. This preliminary report will be followed by a detailed monographic account of religion in Mapletown.

3. See my article "State Formation and Rajpur Myth in Tribal Central India" (1962).

4. Interviews with a few members of this church made it clear that the respondents felt themselves to be part of the Protestant order and were definitely against the Catholic church.

5. The Bengali word *adda* has many shades of meaning. Essentially it involves an informal get-together to spend time in leisurely and spontaneous conversation.

6. Jules Henry (1963:25) speaks of "personality impoverishment" in contemporary America.

7. Here I am in agreement with the observation of the Lynds: "The Catholics, Jews, and Episcopalians, who stress ritual somewhat more and rely less upon 'sermon,' i.e., verbalized message, maintain a liaison between the permanent and the immediate with more dignity and less apparent sense of uneasiness than do most of the Protestant churches" (Lynd and Lynd 1937:311).

8. These points could be considerably elaborated, but I am pointing out only the more important aspects. Needless to say, considerable simplification is involved in the process of homogenizing my complex exposure to various strata and regional versions of Bengali Hinduism. The same is true in my considering the complex range of religious behavior in Mapletown as a single entity. For a general account of peasant Hinduism see O'Malley (1935).

9. McKim Marriott (1955:211) speaks about the process of "parochialization" of religious culture in Indian village communities.

References

HARRINGTON, MICHAEL. 1963. *The other America*. Baltimore: Penguin Books.

HENRY, JULES. 1963. *Culture against man.* New York: Random House.

HERBERG, WILL. 1960. *Protestant, Catholic, Jew.* New York: Doubleday Anchor Books.

HSU, FRANCIS L. K. 1953. Americans and Chinese: *Two ways of life.* New York: Abelard-Schuman.

—1961. "American core values and national character," in *Psychological anthropology: Aspects of culture and personality.* Edited by F. L. K. Hsu, Homewood, Illinois: Dorsey Press.

—1963, *Clan, caste and club.* Princeton: Van Nostrand.

LENSKI, GERHARD. 1963. *The religious factor: A sociological enquiry.* New York: Doubleday Anchor Books.

LYND, ROBERT S. and HELEN M. LYND. 1937. *Middletown in transition: A study in cultural conflicts.* New York: Harcourt, Brace.

MARRIOTT, McKIM. 1955. "Little communities in an indigenous civilization," in *Village India.* Edited by McKim Marriott, pp. 171–222. American Anthropological Association Memoir 83.

O'MALLEY, L. S. S. 1935. *Popular Hinduism.* Cambridge: Cambridge University Press.

RAFFERTY, MAX. 1953. *What happened to patriotism?* West Orange, New Jersey: Economic Press.

SINHA, SURAJIT. 1962. State formation and Rajput myth in tribal central India, *Man in India* 42(1):35–80.

TAX, SOL, LOREN C. EISELEY, IRVING ROUSE and C. F. VOEGELIN. 1953. *An appraisal of anthropology today.* Chicago: University of Chicago Press.

27

Tourism: The Sacred Journey

NELSON H. H. GRABURN

> The human organism . . . is . . . motivated to keep the influx of novelty, complexity, and information within an optimal range and thus escape the extremes of confusion [This is Tuesday, so it must be Belgium] and boredom [We never go anywhere!].
>
> D. Berlyne (1968, p. 166)

THE ANTHROPOLOGY OF TOURISM, though novel in itself, rests upon sound anthropological foundations and has predecessors in previous research on rituals and ceremonials, human play, and cross-cultural aesthetics. Modern tourism exemplifies that part of the range of human behavior Berlyne calls "human exploratory behavior," which includes much expressive culture such as ceremonials, the arts, sports, and folklore; as diversions from the

This chapter is derived from a series of revisions made of the remarks that I delivered as a discussant to the Symposium on Tourism, organized by Valene Smith at the American Anthropological Association meetings in Mexico City, November 1974. A draft of this chapter was presented as "The Anthropology of Tourism" in June 1975 and discussed at a meeting of the faculty of the Department of Anthropology at the University of California, Berkeley, to whom I direct my gratitude for many suggestions and criticisms. In addition I owe particular thanks to Sheldon Rothblatt and Ian Dengler of the Department of History at Berkeley, for suggestions concerning the development of tourism in European history, and to Valene Smith I owe special gratitude for her stimulating pursuit of this new branch of anthropology and for particular insightful comments on the nature of travel itself, which are incorporated in this chapter.

ordinary, they make life worth living. Tourism does not universally exist but is functionally and symbolically equivalent to other institutions that humans use to embellish and add meaning to their lives. In its special aspect—travel—it has antecedents and equivalents in other seemingly more purposeful institutions such as medieval student travel, the Crusades, and European and Asian pilgrimage circuits.

All Work and No Play Makes Jack a Dull Boy

A major characteristic of our conception of tourism is that it is *not* work, but is part of the recent invention, *re*-creation, which is supposed to renew us for the workaday world. Tourism is a special form of play involving travel, or getting away from "it all" (work and home), affording relaxation from tensions, and for some, the opportunity to temporarily become a nonentity, removed from a ringing telephone. Stemming from our peasant European (or East Asian) traditions, there is a symbolic link between staying:working and traveling:playing, which may be expressed as a model (Figure 1).

Norbeck (1971) points out that in Western society and Japan, and particularly in Northern European-derived cultures, the work ethic is so important that very strong moral feelings are attached to the concepts of work and play, including an association of what is "proper" in time and place. From the model, compulsory or serious activities such as making a living properly take place in the workaday world and preferably "at home." Conversely, "proper" travel is voluntary, does not involve routine work, and therefore is "good for you." A majority of Americans and Europeans see life as properly consisting of alternations of these two modes of existence: living at home and working for longish periods followed by taking vacations away from home for shorter periods. However, some sanctioned recreation is often another kind of "hard work," especially in the rites-of-passage or self-testing types of tourism such as those of youthful travelers (Teas 1976; Vogt 1975). Many tourists admittedly return home to "rest up" from their vacations.

The model also indicates that staying at home and *not* working is consid-

	STAY	TRAVEL
VOLUNTARY	"Doing nothing" at home	Tourism and/or Recreation
COMPULSORY/ SERIOUS	Work (including school-work and housework)	Occupations requiring travel

FIGURE 1

ered improper for normal people. Many would complain that to not go away during vacations is "doing nothing" as if the contrasting "something" must take place away from home or it is "no vacation at all." The very word vacation comes from the Latin *vacare*, "to leave (one's house) empty," and emphasizes the fact that we cannot properly vacation at home.* People who stay home for vacation are often looked down upon or pitied, or made to feel left behind and possibly provincial, except for the aged and infirm, small children, and the poor. Within the framework of tourism, normal adults travel and those who do not are disadvantaged.

By contrast, able-bodied adults who do not work when living at home are also in a taboo category among contemporary Western peoples. If they are younger or poorer they are labelled "hippies," "bums," or even "welfare chiselers"; otherwise they may be labelled the "idle rich." In both cases, most people consider them some kind of immoral parasites.

The other combination—work that involves compulsory travel—is equally problematic. Somehow, it is improper to travel when we work, as it is improper to work when we travel. The first category includes traveling salesmen, gypsies, anthropologists, convention goers, stewards, and sailors, and our folklore is full of obscene jokes about such people—for their very occupation is questionable, whatever their behavior! Alternately, people on vacation don't want to work, and justifiably complain about their "busman's holiday." Among them are housewives whose families, to save money, rent a villa rather than stay in a hotel; doctors who are constantly consulted by their co-travelers; and even anthropologists who are just trying to vacation in a foreign country.

To Tour or Not to Tour: That Is the Problem

Tourism in the modal sense emphasized here is but one of a range of choices, or styles, of vacation or recreation—those structurally necessary, ritualized breaks in routine that define and relieve the ordinary. For the present discussion our focus is consciously on the more extreme examples of tourism such as long distance tours to well-known places or visiting exotic peoples, in the most enchanting environments. However, the most minimal kinds of tourism, such as a picnic in the garden, contain elements of the magic of tourism. The food and drink might be identical to that normally eaten indoors, but the magic comes from the movement and the nonordi-

---

*Though the sense of "leaving one's house" now implies a holiday or tourism, it was originally intended to describe the itinerant work of people such as craftsmen, apprentices, and circuit judges. Such changes in meaning from: holiday = to celebrate a holy day in the home community, and vacation = to go off to work, to the present usage reflects the post-Renaissance changes in ideology that account for the rise of modern tourism.

nary setting. Furthermore, it is not merely a matter of money that separates the stay-at-homes from the extensive travelers. Many very wealthy people never become tourists, and most "youthful" travelers are, by Western standards, quite poor.

The stay-at-home who participates in some creative activity such as remodeling the house, redoing the garden, or seriously undertaking painting, writing, or sports activities, shares some of the values of tourism in that recreation is involved that is nonordinary and represents a *voluntary* self-indulgent choice on the part of the practitioner. Still others who, through financial stringency or choice, do not go away during vacations but celebrate the released time period by making many short trips, take the non-workaday aspects of the vacation and construct events for the satisfaction of their personal recreational urges. Even sending the children away to camp may count as a vacation for some parents. Though not tourism in the modal sense, camping, backpacking, renting a lake cottage, or visiting relatives who live far away function as kinds of tourism, although their level of complexity and novelty may not be as high.

The Sacred and the Profane, or a Change Is as Good as a Rest

Taking our cue from Berlyne, who suggests that all human life tries to maintain a preferred level of arousal and seeks "artificial sources of stimulation . . . to make up for shortcomings of their environment" (Berlyne 1968, p. 170), tourism can be examined against its complement: ordinary, workaday life. There is a long tradition in anthropology of the structural examination of events and institutions as markers of the passage of natural and social time and as definers of the nature of life itself. This stems partly from Durkheim's (1912) notions of the sacred—the nonordinary experience—and the profane. The alternation of these states and the importance of the transition between them was first used to advantage by Mauss (1898) in his analysis of the almost universal rituals of sacrifice, which emphasized the process of leaving the ordinary, i.e., sacralization that elevates participants to the nonordinary state wherein marvellous things happen, and the converse process of desacralization or return to ordinary life.

Leach (1961, pp. 132–36), in his essay on "Time and False Noses," suggests that the regular occurrence of sacred-profane alternations marks important periods of social life or even provides the measure of the passage of time itself. The passing of each year is usually marked by the annual vacation (or Christmas), and something would be wrong with a year if it didn't occur, as if one had been cheated of time. "The notion that time is a 'discontinuity of repeated contrasts' is probably the most elementary and primitive of all ways of regarding time. . . . The year's progress is marked by a succession of festivals. Each festival represents a temporary shift from the Normal-Profane order of existence into the Abnormal-Sacred order and back again.'' The total flow of time has a pattern, which may be represented as in Figure 2.

Vacations involving travel, i.e., tourism, since all ''proper'' vacations involve travel, are the modern equivalent for secular societies to the annual and lifelong sequences of festivals for more traditional, God-fearing societies. Fundamental is the contrast between the ordinary/compulsory work state spent ''at home'' and the nonordinary/voluntary ''away from home'' sacred state. The stream of alternating contrasts provides the meaningful events that measure the passage of time. Leach applies the diagram to ''people who do not possess calendars of the Nautical Almanac type,'' implying that those who have ''scientific'' calendars and other tacit reminders such as newspapers, radio, and TV rely on the numerical calendar. I believe the ''scientific, secular'' Westerner gains greater meaning from the personal rather than the numerical in life. We are happier and better recall the loaded symbolic time markers: ''That was the year we went to Rome!'' rather than ''that was 1957,'' for the former identifies the nonordinary, the festive, or ritual.

Each meaningful event marks the passage of time and thus life itself. Each secular or sacred period is a micro-life, with a bright beginning, a middle, and an end, and the beginnings and endings of these little ''lives'' are marked by rituals that thrust us irreversibly down life's path. Periods A and C in Figure 2 are both segments of our lives but of a different moral quality. The profane period, A, is the everyday life of the ''That's life!'' descriptive of the ordinary and inevitable. The period of marginality, C, is another life, which, though extraordinary, is perhaps more ''real'' than

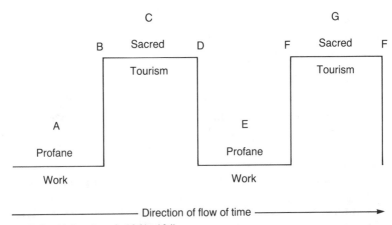

FIGURE 2   (After Leach 1961: 134)

"real life." Vacation times and tourism are described as "I was really living, living it up . . . I've never felt so alive," in contrast to the daily humdrum often termed a "dog's life," since dogs are not thought to "vacation." Thus, holidays (holy, sacred days now celebrated by traveling away from home) are what makes "life worth living" as though ordinary life is not life or at least not the kind of life worth living.

Our two lives, the sacred/nonordinary/touristic and the profane/ workaday/stay-at-home, customarily alternate for ordinary people and are marked by rituals or ceremonies, as should the beginning and end of lives. By definition, the beginning of one life marks the end of the other. Thus, at time B, we celebrate with TGIF (Thank God it's Friday) and going-away parties, to anticipate the future state and to give thanks for the end of the ordinary. Why else would people remain awake and drink all night on an outbound plane enroute to Europe when they are going to arrive at 6:40 A.M. with a long day ahead of them? The re-entry ritual, time D, is often split between the ending-party—the last night in Europe or the last night at sea—and the welcome home or welcome back to work greetings and formalities, both of which are usually sadder than the going away.

In both cases the transition formalities are ambivalent and fraught with danger or at least tension. In spite of the supposedly happy nature of the occasion, personal observation and medical reports show that people are more accident prone when going away; are excited and nervous, even to the point of feeling sick; and Van Gennep (1914) suggests that the sacralization phase of symbolic death lies within our consciousness. It is implied in phrases such as, "Parting is such sweet sorrow," : or even, "To part is to die a little." Given media accounts of plane, train, and automobile accidents, literally as tourists we are not sure that we will return. Few have failed to think at least momentarily of plane crashes and car accidents or, for older people, dying while on vacation. Because we are departing ordinary life and may never return, we take out additional insurance, put our affairs in order, often make a new will, and leave "final" instructions concerning the watering, the pets, and the finances. We say goodbye as we depart and some even cry a little, as at a funeral, for we are dying symbolically. The most difficult role of a travel agent is to hand someone their tickets to travel to a funeral, for the happy aspect of the journey is entirely absent, leaving only a double sorrow.

The re-entry is also ambivalent. We hate to end a vacation, and to leave new-found if temporary excitement; on the other hand, many are relieved to return home safely and even anticipate the end of the tense, emotion-charged period of being away. We step back into our former roles (time E), often with a sense of culture shock. We inherit our past selves like an heir to the estate of a deceased person who has to pick up the threads, for we are *not* ourselves. We are a new person who has gone through recreation and, if we do not feel renewed, the whole point of tourism has been missed.

For most people the financial aspects of tourism parallel the symbolic. One accumulates enough money with which to vacation, much as one progressively acquires the worries and tedium of the workaday world. Going away lightens this mental load and also one's money. Running out of money at the end of the holiday is hopefully accompanied by running out of cares and worries—with the converse accumulation of new perspectives and general well-being. The latter counteract the workaday worries with memories of the more carefree times. In turn, they stimulate the anticipation and planning for the next vacation, and F and G will be different from B and C because we have experienced times A through E.

While traveling, each day is a micro-model of the same motif. After the stable state of sleep, the tourist ventures forth to the heightened excitement of each new day. Nightfall is often a little sad for the weary tourist; the precious vacation day is spent. Perhaps the often frantic efforts at nightlife on the part of tourists who may never indulge at home are attempts to prolong the "high"—to remain in the sacred, altered state—and delay the "come down" as long as possible.

The Profane Spirit Quest: The Journey Motif in Tourism

Life is a succession of events marked by changes in state. It is both cyclical, in that the same time-marking events occur day after day, year after year, and it is progressive or linear in that we pass through life by a series of changes in status, each of which is marked by a different (though similarly structured) rite of passage. An almost universal motif for the explanation and description of life is the journey, for journeys are marked by beginnings and ends, and by a succession of events along the way.

The travel involved in tourism is more than geographical motion or a symbolically altered state. For Westerners who value individualism, self-reliance, and the work ethic, tourism is the *best* kind of life for it is sacred in the sense of being exciting, renewing, and inherently self-fulfilling. The tourist journey is a segment of our lives over which we have maximum control, and it is no wonder that tourists are disappointed when their chosen, self-indulgent fantasies don't turn out as planned.

A journey is seldom without purpose, but culturally specific values determine the goal of travel. In many American Indian societies, a young man left the camp alone to travel and suffer, and to meet the right spirit in order to advance to the next higher status on the journey through life. In India, in medieval Europe, and in the Islamic world, people made difficult pilgrimages to find spiritual enlightenment. Visitors to Las Vegas are also enlightened and often return home with a flat wallet, having sacrificed dearly for their pleasures.

Even if one regards tourism as voluntary, self-interested travel, the tourist journey must be morally justified by the home community. Because the touristic journey lies in the nonordinary sphere of existence, the goal is symbolically sacred and morally on a higher plane than the regards of the ordinary workaday world. Tourists spend substantial sums to achieve the altered state—money that could be invested for material gain or alternately used to buy a new car or redecorate their home.

"Human exploratory behavior," says Berlyne (1968, p. 152), "is behavior whose principle function is to change the stimulus field and introduce stimulus elements that were not previously accessible." Thus, as art uplifts and makes meaningful the visual environment, so tourism provides an aesthetically appropriate counterpoint to ordinary life. Tourism has a stated, or unstated but culturally determined, goal that has changed through the ages. For traditional societies the rewards of pilgrimages were accumulated grace and moral leadership in the home community. The rewards of modern tourism are phrased in terms of values we now hold up for worship: mental and physical health, social status, and diverse, exotic experiences.

In medieval Europe, travel was usually for avowedly religious purposes, as were pilgrimages and crusades; for ordinary people travel was difficult and dangerous, and even for the ruling classes, who also traveled for reasons of state, travel required large protective entourages. Those who could afford it often retired to retreats or endowed religious institutions in their spiritual quest for the ultimate "truth." It was the Renaissance that changed the world view by bringing forth the kind of consciousness that provides the cosmological foundation for modern tourism: the idea that truth lay outside the mind and spirit. In all fields this outward, materialist turning, this urge to explore and understand, showed up in such new forms as the new astronomy, the explorations, the new historical and scientific investigations of the fifteenth and sixteenth centuries. Means of land and sea transportation improved, and curiosities and exciting tales of discovery were brought back from all over the world.

By the seventeenth century the aristocracy and the wealthy were traveling to and in Europe to see the evidence of old historical truths and to converse with the discoverers of the new geographical and scientific ones. For eighteenth-century England the Grand Tour became a fully developed institution; the tourist motive for going abroad was not only cultural but highly educational and political. The post-medieval decline of the universities and the great public and grammar schools as institutions of liberal learning meant the rise of alternative means of instruction: the tutor and the tour were the two principal ones. Milord went abroad not only to see the classical sights, but to learn languages, manners and accomplishments, riding, dancing, and other social graces. The tour was deemed a very necessary part of the training of future political and administrative leaders, as well as patrons of the arts.

The Industrial Revolution took hold at the end of the eighteenth century and set in motion further changes affecting travel and tourism. It enhanced the need for scientific exchange and learning, for trade and raw materials, and for imperial expansion. (See Nash, chapter 2.) In addition it gave rise to the romanticism that glorified nature and the countryside, ideas stemming partly from the formerly neoclassical pastoral games of British and French aristocracy. As the Grand Tour in its elitist form declined in significance, new modes of transportation and new political arrangements made travel safer and cheaper for the bourgeoisie.

Thomas Cook, a Baptist minister and social reformer, taking advantage of the new railway system, in 1842 organized an all-inclusive tour to a temperance meeting. Other successful and morally uplifting tours followed; Cook combined his visions of democratic travel and the promotion of sobriety with the chance to profit financially from the opportunities for taking townspeople to the countryside or abroad. His tours expanded from the Lake District, Wales, the Isle of Man, and Scotland, to reach France, Italy, and the glories of the Middle East by the 1870s. Promoting railway expansion everywhere, and the standardization of hotels and restaurants, Cook's coupons and later traveler's checks made travel easy for the masses, opening approved parts of the world to the inspection and edification of the educated middle classes. Imitators arose in Europe and America and travel-made-easy followed closely on the heels of imperial and commercial expansion.

Displaced from their command of the historical and cultural centers of Europe and the Far East, the aristocracy pioneered another form of tourism, which was later to become a form of mass escape: the ruling families and the very wealthy began to leave their palaces and their homes for recreational and health reasons on a regular, yearly basis. Not since Roman times had this been done on such a massive scale. Prior to the eighteenth century the royal families regularly moved between their several castles, for the hunting and falconry seasons; and after the Renaissance a larger part of the ruling stratum began to take "cures" at spas within their own countries, such as at Bath or Baden-Baden. These were the forerunners of the strongly re-creational theme in tourism. Starting in the eighteenth century and becoming the mode in the nineteenth century, luxurious rivieras were built along the Mediterranean and Adriatic shores to house the royalty and idle rich from the nations of Northern and Eastern Europe. Like the national health spas they displaced, these resorts were often only thinly disguised excuses for gambling and more lascivious pleasures. As the winter abodes for the Northerners were opened in the warmer South, this pleasure-seeking trend led to the establishment of Monte Carlo and other casino resorts. By the beginning of the twentieth century even rich Americans came to partake of the idle winter life-style, and great liners and trains made long distance travel safe all over the world for those who could afford to pay.

The final cultural revolution that set the stage for the mass tourism of today was prompted by the First World War. Not only did this catastrophe pauperize the elite rivieras, but it did away with many of the ruling families and other European aristocrats whose fortunes had fueled the life-style. By the 1920s the newly wealthy Americans came to be the dominant tastemakers, not only in Paris but along the Cote d'Azur. The winter vacation retreats of the elitist "international set" became summer pleasure resorts. No longer was nature shunned and white skin universally admired. American experience in Florida and the Caribbean, along with an increasing realization of the healthy aspects of exposure to sunlight (pioneered by the discovery of Vitamin D and German experiments in World War I) made the suntan fashionable. An air of freedom from the old mores and the overthrow of the (superficially) stuffy old aristocracies brought out the excesses of the 1920s in every sphere of life. Features of the life-style of common people were studiedly imitated, folk music and jazz were heard, and a snobbish kind of "slumming" that equated dark skins and sexuality provided a spark for these changing attitudes, which are now well nigh universal. During this period aspects of "ethnic" tourism and anthropology itself became popular. Though the Depression put a lid on some of the excesses, the themes of nature, recreation, and ethnic interest were securely added to the previous cultural, historical, and educational motivations that underlie tourism today.

Nature Tourism and Cultural Tourism

Symbolically, Nature tourism has two different manifestations, both of which are strongly with us. The purest form is represented by Environmental tourism where varied aspects of the land, sea, and sky perform their magical works of renewal—it's the "pure" air, the soothing waters, or the vast vistas that are curative. In its most extreme form the absence of humans is a factor: "There I was, the only person for miles . . . alone in the woods." If Nature is curative, performs magical recreations and other miracles otherwise assigned to Lourdes, God, or *gurus*, the medicine is weakened by the presence of other humans. To share is to lose power. Recently, Environmental tourism has bifurcated into Ecological tourism (see Figure 3), wherein the tourist tries to leave as little effect from his visit as possible—concentrating perhaps on photographs and tape recordings— rather than the variant, Hunting and Gathering tourism. The latter includes environmental tourism and nature appreciation, including hunting, wherein little thought is given to impact, and at least some souvenirs are brought home.

To others, however, Nature in the "raw" is nice but somewhat boring because there is no dialogue; Nature is unresponsive even when threatened

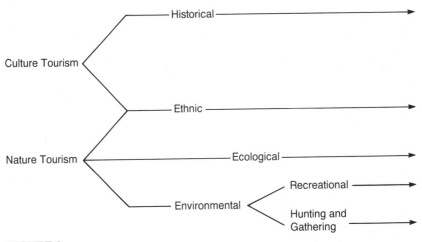

FIGURE 3

by capture on film or violation by campfire. Another way to get close to Nature's bosom is through her children, the people of Nature, once labelled Peasant and Primitive peoples and considered creatures of instinct. Interaction with them is possible and their naturalness and simplicity exemplifies all that is good in Nature. What more exciting and uplifting experience could one imagine than to share a few words or, even better, a meal and a bed with such delightful people? Again, the magic is spoiled by the presence of too many other tourists. The approach to Nature through Her People is Ethnic tourism, whereas the use of Nature for her specified attributes of sun (tanning), wind (sailing), snow (skiing), surf (fishing), and sky (gliding) is Recreational tourism.

The relation between the various forms of tourism is diagrammed in Figure 3.

Each touristic type has its own special scale of values and its hierarchy of prestigious places, i.e., those having more "magic." However, two or more kinds are frequently combined in one trip. For instance, one might visit the museums and cathedrals in Europe (Historical) and then go to Northern Scandinavia to see the Midnight Sun (Environmental) and the Lapps (Ethnic), or one might combine the Historical, Cultural, and Ethnic by touring India. Certain types of tourism are closer in fact and function than others; for instance, Ethnic tourism is a combination of Culture and Nature tourism. Others are conceptually further removed, such as Cultural tourism, with its emphases on the great traditions, in contrast to Hunting and Gathering tourism represented by African hunting safaris. Within these categories of tourism, there are an almost infinite variety of substyles including class, and ethnic and national variations. The rush of urban Germans to the southern and western coasts of Europe is different from the Scandinavians' junket to the Adriatic; the French take to their countryside quite differently than do the British to theirs. The levels of preferred arousal and the nature of the touristic goals vary almost as much by age group and personality as by national origin and sex, and cannot all be described here.

The Holy Grail: Symbols and Souvenirs

Few tourists come home from a vacation without something to show for it, whether it is matchcovers, folk art, or rolls of exposed film. The type of vacation chosen and the proof that we really did it reflect what we consider "sacred." The Holy Grail is the myth sought on the journey, and the success of a holiday is proportionate to the degree that the myth is realized.

Souvenirs are tangible evidences of travel that are often shared with family and friends, but what one really brings back are memories of experiences. As Carpenter (1973, p. 17) puts it so well:

> The connection between symbol and things comes from the fact that the symbol—the word or picture (or artifact)—helps give the 'thing' its identity, clarity, definition. It helps convert given reality into experienced reality, and is therefore an indispensable part of all experience.

The chosen style of tourism has its counterpart in types of souvenirs. The Environmental tourist is usually content with pictures and postcards but the Hunter and Gatherer wants rocks and sea shells, or even pieces of an archaeologic ruin. Bolder members bring back heads or even whole animals to stuff, to testify to their vacation glory. The Ethnic tourist rarely has the opportunity to bring home the "whole Primitive" but is content with arts or crafts, particularly if they were made by the ethnic for his/her own (preferably sacred) use. Items made specifically for the tourist market have much less symbolic appeal, and this authenticity is often overstated (Graburn 1976).

The limitations of tourist travel, especially for jet-setters who cover so much ground so fast, diminishes experienced reality and the momentos and souvenirs serve as cues by which to relive the experience at a slower pace. In photography, to get oneself in the picture is common to tourists of both Occidental and Oriental origins as evidence of identity and placement. If they are not afraid of soul-loss, native peoples often project themselves into tourist's pictures as a momentary escape from their environment and as a means of "getting into" the imagined happiness and affluence of the tourist's home situation. As one impoverished African in a remote ex-colonial country said to the anthropologist who was taking last-minute photos of all his informants, "And when you develop the photo, please make me come out white."

"Wish You Were Here"

Tourists almost ritualistically send postcards from faraway places to those whom they wish to impress as well as to those they love. Partly, it is to let the latter know they are well and enjoying themselves, and partly to be remembered and awaited. Conversely, the sacred charisma rubs off; those left at home feel partly uplifted, though perhaps jealous, when they receive such cards and may even display them near their work desks or on bulletin boards. The next best thing to traveling is to know someone who did.

Yet if they did go along, had already been there, or were about to visit the same area, there would be heightened excitement in sharing, which parallels Huizinga's (1950, p. 12) observations about play:

> The [co-traveling] community tends to become permanent even after it is over . . . the feeling of 'being apart' together in an exceptional situation, of sharing something important, or mutually withdrawing from the rest of the world and rejecting the usual norms, retains its magic beyond the duration . . . surrounds itself with an air of secrecy . . . dressing up . . . disguised together as other beings.

Even aboard jets, we all know the "stranger on the train" phenomenon, or the "shipboard romance" that didn't last. The magic of sharing a touristic activity lasts only when (1) the event is really nonordinary; (2) participants initially share similar value systems; and most importantly, when (3) they already know each other or are in the same profession or institution. The popularity of conferences (held in vacation settings such as Hawaii or Disneyland), or touring groups of farmers or attorneys as well as "in-house" travel planned for factory workers, attest to the fact that the magic of tourism is enhanced by group identity and, later, reliving the experience with associates. Analogous to the truism that "Distance is to love as wind to fire; it enflames the great and puts out the feeble," experiences shared at a distance strengthen relationships between the like-minded but may push others further apart.

Tourism is rife with snobbery, and within each of its basic forms hierarchies of rank and prestige exist that illustrate the continuum and the contrast between the ordinary/nonordinary. Obviously, what is extraordinary for some—for a rural Britisher, a trip up to London to the theater—may be an almost daily affair for others (a London suburbanite). Thus one man's excitement may be another man's boredom and threshold from which the more urbane measures his sacred.

To measure the hierarchies of prestige, the journey motif suggests that the further removed from the ordinary, the better; the sacred/profane motif suggests that the more extra-ordinary, the better; while the time measuring aspect suggests that the longer the period or more frequent the trips, the better. Each theme can be translated into the one-upmanship of the genre of tourists. For the young, rebellious Ethnic and Environmental tourist (or nontourist as they proudly claim), distant and exotic places such as Kathmandu or Goa are "in," and prestige is enhanced by the length of uninterrupted travel.

Others of a more rugged bent, the elite tourists, emphasize the struggle against Nature, and gain their prestige through solitude, and a high degree of self-reliance in the communion. Driving alone from Cairo to Capetown, or daring raft trips down wild rivers are pale imitations of what were once rugged individual efforts worthy of Explorer's Club membership.

A common theme in these contrasting examples of Ethnic and Environmental tourism is the emphasis on the "spirit quest" or the self-testing, often maturing, pioneer endurance that they both effect in their different ways. This spirit quest may be imagined, for Cohen (1973) suggests that modern drifter-tourism is as safe and commonplace as riding a New York subway. Nevertheless, these apparently dangerous and effortful styles of tourism seem to attract the young, as a kind of self-imposed rite of passage to prove to themselves and to their peers that they can make their own way in life—probably never to repeat it later on. Or, this high adventure attracts the affluent, often highly educated middle-aged for whom social constraints and a Depression denied their youthful wanderlust. Money is not the criterion of prestige. For the youthful traveler, Cohen (1973) notes that voluntary poverty is the sacred/non-ordinary quality of tourism for the middle-class "Nomads from Affluence."

In sharp contrast is the tourism of the timid—often parents of the youthful travelers—who have money and don't mind spending it, as long as they can carry the home-grown "bubble" of their life style around with them. They rely on the advice and blandishments of tourist brokers in order to live as comfortably as at home or even more luxuriously, for the holiday is nonordinary, and one should eat, drink, and spend beyond the rules of the ordinary. Though undoubtedly enchanted by the view of God's handiwork through the pane of the air-conditioned bus or the porthole, they worship "plumbing that works" and "safe" water and food. The connection with the unfamiliar is likely to be purely visual, and filtered through sunglasses and a camera viewfinder. These tourists are likely to have the greatest impact on the culture and environment of the host peoples both by virtue of their greater numbers and by their demands for extensions of their home environments for which they are willing to pay handsomely. Cohen (1973) points out that mass drifter-tourism stimulates the hosts to maintain specially designed receptive institutions, even if the travelers are unaware of the degree to which they are being catered.

Although the outward rationale for tourism has as many variations as there are tourists, the basic motivation seems to be the human need for recreation. Tourism is one manifestation of the fulfillment of this need—

one, that because of the more affluent economic status of the developed world, is enabling many people to see "how the other half lives."

Reference List and Bibliography

BERLYNE, D. E. 1962. New directions in motivation theory. In *Anthropology and human behavior*, T. Gladwin and W. C. Sturtevant, eds., pp. 150-73. Washington, D.C.: Anthropological Society of Washington.

CARPENTER, E. 1972, 1973. *Oh, what a blow that phantom gave me!* New York: Holt, Rinehart and Winston.

COHEN, E. 1973. Nomads from affluence: notes on the phenomenon of drifter-tourism. *International Journal of Comparative Sociology* 14 (1-2): 89-103.

DURKHEIM, E. 1912. *Elementary forms of religious life.* London: Allen and Unwin.

GRABURN, N. H. H., ed. 1976. *Ethnic and tourist arts: cultural expressions from the fourth world.* Berkeley and Los Angeles: University of California Press.

HUIZINGA, J. 1950. *Homo Ludens: a study of the play element in culture.* Boston: Beacon.

LEACH, E. R. 1961. Time and false noses. In *Rethinking anthropology*, E. R. Leach, ed., pp. 132-36. London School of Economics, Monographs in Social Anthropology No. 22. London: Athlone Press.

MAUSS, M. and MAUSS, H. H. 1898. Essaie sur la nature et la fonction au sacrifice. *L'Année Sociologique* 2: 29-138.

NASH, D. 1970. *A community in limbo: an anthropological study of an American community abroad.* Bloomington: Indiana University Press.

NORBECK, E. 1971. Man at play. *Natural History.* Special supplement: Play, pp. 48-53.

TEAS, J. 1976. I'm studying monkeys: What do you do? Youth and travelers in Nepal. Unpublished manuscript.

VAN GENNEP, A. 1914. *The rites of passage.* London: Routledge and Kegan Paul.

VOGT, J. W. 1975. Wandering: youth and recreation travel behavior. Paper read at the symposium on Tourism and Culture Change, American Anthropological Association, 6 December 1975, San Francisco, California.

PART III

Toward a New Anthropology: On Systems of Inequality

Anthropology continues to grow and change in response to new and different phenomena within world societies, to discoveries and insights within the discipline itself, and to the mandate for ever-increasing relevancy that comes from the very people whom anthropologists study, from students such as yourselves. The dynamic quality of the discipline is such that at any point in time one can speak of movement toward a new anthropology. The articles in the preceding sections of this volume illustrate this dynamic quality of the discipline. Some are now classics in the field, but when first published a number of years ago they represented new and in some cases radically different approaches to long-standing questions in anthropology. Other articles address current issues and themes in the discipline and employ more recent theoretical and methodological approaches. In this final section we concentrate on the latter type of articles as we survey three trends in cultural anthropology. Our survey is necessarily selective, a reflection of the considerable range and diversity in the current state of anthropology. The three themes deal with questions about who should study whom, and what in fact should be studied in anthropology. Their focuses:

On studying the full range of human societies
Native anthropology
On studying systems of inequality

On Studying the Full Range of Human Societies

A number of articles in this volume present findings of anthropologists who have studied "Western" societies, that is the United States, Canada, and Western Europe. While studies of complex industrialized societies date back to the works of pioneering anthropologists such as Tylor, Boas, Linton, and Kroeber, the proportion of such studies, compared to those of small tribal societies, has grown substantially in the last two decades. In addition to this emphasis on studying *all* societies, from the largest and most technologically complex to the relatively small-scale in terms of technology and population, a number of anthropologists have called for two additional kinds of studies that would bring the discipline even closer to the objective of studying the full range of humankind: the need to study up as well as down and the need to study societies with a socialist form of organization.

In an article first published in 1972 and reprinted here, Laura Nader challenged anthropologists to study centers of power such as multinational corporations, state institutions, and Western elites. It is important to note that Nader does not call for the abandonment of the typical kinds of anthropological studies of poor and Third World societies; rather, she argues for the sharpened insights that will accrue from anthropologists studying up, down, and, we might add, on the same levels of power as themselves.

There are, of course, particular problems associated with studying in each of these directions. Nader points to the problem of gaining access to the life-ways of the powerful. There are also a number of difficulties in studying on the same level of power and influence as that of most anthropologists, that is, the "middle class." And in the literature of anthropology there are references to the theoretical, methodological, and ethical pitfalls that should be avoided in studying communities of poor and powerless peoples. But with the difficulties in studying on each of these levels, there are also the rewards, and when the results from studying these three levels are compiled, anthropology advances.

In an article titled "In a Pig's Eye: Daily Life and Political Economy in Southeastern Europe," John Cole (1980) calls for anthropologists to engage in research on the conditions of everyday life in Southeastern Europe. He makes a point that stands in interesting contrast with the thrust of Laura Nader's argument. Criticizing the bulk of studies of Southeastern European societies for the overemphasis on studying the formal institutions and structures of decision making and their overdependence on statistical trends, Cole calls for research "with a pig's eye," that is, research that looks at the various social groupings in these socialist societies—not simply at the leaders of the political party and state organizations. Like Nader, Cole does not call for mechanical substitution of one approach for another. Rather, he makes the point that

. . . scholars are generally agreed that studying a particular problem from a variety of perspectives and comparing results is a better way to advance knowledge than to have numbers of like-minded individuals working on the same problem. [1980, p. 27]

Native Anthropology

Writing over a period of several years, and drawing on different but complementary points, a number of anthropologists have made the plea for more native anthropology. (See, for example John L. Gwaltney's recent book *Drylongso*, 1980.) In his article discussing some of the problems facing black anthropologists (see page 30 in this volume), Delmos Jones made one of the earliest calls for correcting the biases of the outsider by having those inside a culture study and analyze their own way of life. In one of the most recent statements in defense of anthropologists studying themselves, Gwaltney (1980) describes the technique of folk seminars where the anthropologist serves as a facilitator while members of his community discuss and analyze their lives.

Anthropology has suffered from a lack of studies of a people by the people themselves. But it would also suffer were the field to become exclusively "native anthropology." In the same sense in which anthropologists have called for studying up and down, and on the same level, our understanding of the human condition will surely increase to the extent that all combinations of the studier and the studied are developed: anthropologists of tribal societies studying their own cultures and those of the West; Western anthropologists continuing their traditional studies of tribal societies but also engaging in analyses of their own ways of life; members of racial and ethnic minorities studying their own communities and those of the politically dominant group.

Those who call for and engage in native anthropology are quick to point out that this is not a problem-free method for analyzing and understanding a culture. It is not an easy matter to decide who is a native anthropologist. Whitehead describes the problem:

In recent years, . . . Third world anthropologists have called for the development of a "native anthropology," in which members from traditional anthropological study populations would begin to study themselves as a means of correcting the ethnographic record. But in today's small, pluralistic and cosmopolitan world, a relevant question is: who truly represents such membership? It is possible for an ethnographer to only belong to the same cultural areas, as his study population, or must he be a member of the same nation? Must he or she belong to the same region, or to the same community? Will ethnic congruency across regional or national boundaries suffice, or is membership in the same local voluntary association necessary? [1980:40]

An important issue surrounding native anthropology is that of involvement and detachment. The opinion of most anthropologists who have written on this issue is that an anthropologist's identification with the people of the community strengthens the field experience and is a source of innumerable insights, but "overidentification" inevitably presents problems.

These are problems that will continue to occupy anthropologists as American and European scholars increasingly study their own communities, and as the number of anthropologists from Third World countries interested in studying their own societies grows.

On Studying Systems of Inequality

Prominent aspects of world economic, political, and social relations revolve around issues of inequality: those based on class, caste, race, and gender. Anthropological attention to two of these forms of discrimination, racism, and sexism represents a major trend in the discipline. It is helpful to review briefly the history of anthropological interest in these issues in order to understand the current analyses in the discipline. Race as a biological concept has always been of concern to physical anthropologists. However, major shifts have occurred in the way that physical differences among human populations are conceptualized and studied. The early physical anthropologists concentrated on the outward physical differences among human groups, and the categorizing of these phenotypic traits ended in unresolved debates about the exact number of races that exist in the world. Today physical anthropologists, more often called biological anthropologists, are moving toward agreement that if "race" is to be used as a meaningful term, it must be thought of in the Mendelian sense as a group of breeding populations. Thus it is to genetics that these anthropologists have turned for an understanding of physical differences.

Racism is a social concept and as such is within the province of social anthropologists. For regardless of the fuzziness of the concept of "races," there are, in the folk taxonomies of many peoples, categories of individuals who are held to be not simply different but "superior" to other categories of individuals. A concern with racism was a highly emphasized part of the academic and "popular" writings of early American anthropologists under the leadership of Franz Boas. Deeply troubled by the Nazi notions of "Aryan racial superiority," Boas spoke out in newspapers and articles about the danger of this myth. He was also outspoken about the myth of black inferiority and was among the first anthropologists to caution us about differences among the concepts of race, culture, and language. Many of Boas's students—Ruth Benedict, Melville Herskovits, Hortense Powdermaker, and Margaret Mead—turned their attention to questions of race relations. (See for example, Ruth Benedict's *Race: Science and Politics* [1940], Powdermaker's *After Freedom* [1939].)

Following an era of Boasian anthropology, racism did not receive a great deal of attention in anthropological writings. Sometimes referred to as an element in colonialism, racism has not been a major focus in the ethnologies of African, Asian, and Latin American peoples. Today, however, the call comes from within and outside of the discipline for systematic analyses of the impact of racism on the lives of many of the world's peoples.

Today, with the resurgence of biological determinist theories concerning "race," the writings of Shockley and Jensen being the most noted, social and biological anthropologists have a special responsibility to present their findings, which unquestionably contradict the notion of "superior races."

Gerald Berreman, in the article reprinted here, compares the relationship among "touchable" and "untouchable" castes in India with the relationship between Afro-Americans and white Americans in the South of the United States. Not all anthropologists or social scientists agree with Berreman's conclusion that "race relations" in the Southern United States constitute a caste system. Regardless of one's theories about racism and caste stratification, this is an important work because it illustrates the value and the necessity of cross-cultural comparisons of "invidious distinctions." In her chapter Angela Gilliam linguistically analyzes how cultural evaluations of color and race appear in Latin American phrases. She finds that many expressions reveal a concern with reproduction and interethnic relationships between men and women.

It is not an exaggeration to say that the 1970s ushered in an explosion of anthropological interest in "the woman question." Since the very first writings of anthropologists there have been references to women's roles and statuses in various societies, but the literature was largely written by and about the world of men, into which women periodically intruded as the bearers and socializers of children. This is true despite the contribution of such very prominent female anthropologists as Margaret Mead, Ruth Benedict, Hortense Powdermaker, Elizabeth Colson, Mary Douglas, Lucy Mair, and many others.

It is not that we lack information on women cross-culturally. As Rayna Reiter (1975) indicates, the problem is that most of that information has been gathered by asking questions of men about their wives, daughters, and sisters—while the women of a society remain untapped sources on their own lives. In other words, the reality of a group is portrayed as identical to the perceptions and behaviors of the males of that group. This gender-biased anthropology is concretely expressed in ways such as the following.

A study by Rohrlich-Leavitt *et al.* (1975) offers striking evidence of the schisms that can exist between male and female perspectives on the culture of the same people. The authors examined the writings of male and female anthropologists on the Tiwi of Australia in terms of differences in their theoretical, methodological, and ideological orientations, and they conclude that male-gender-biased studies distort the status and role of women *and* men in a society.

The women's movement raised American and European consciousness about gender inequality and turned to anthropology for enlightenment about the sources and cross-cultural expressions of sexism. Anthropological responses to these inquiries are voluminous, as evidenced by "an entirely new literature on the status of women cross-culturally" (Quinn 1977). However, the literature contains what Quinn calls a bewildering number of disconnected hypotheses. In time these various and often contradictory theories on women's status and power will be sorted out.

The issues being addressed in the anthropology of women cover a broad spectrum: the origins of gender inequality; the evolution of sex roles and the division of labor; the impact of child care on women's status and roles; women's roles in the "public and private" spheres of societal life; the influence of family relations on gender inequalities; women's economic roles in precapitalist and capitalist societies; the intersections of race, gender, and class; and the status of women in socialist societies. The article by J. B. Cole, reprinted here, addresses some of these issues through a specific exploration of gender inequality in Cuba before and after the 1959 revolution.

A direction in which anthropologists might profitably move is that of systematic comparisons of racism and sexism in those societies where racism is present as well as sexism—and we know of no societies that have eliminated sexism at this point in history—such comparative analyses may well advance our understanding of the most fundamental nature of systems of inequality and, in fact, we may learn more about what is required to eliminate these forms of discrimination.

References

BENEDICT, RUTH. 1940. *Race: Science and Politics.* New York: Modern Age.

BOAS, FRANZ. 1948. *Race: Language and Culture.* Originally published in 1888. New York: Macmillan.

COLE, JOHN W. 1980. "In a Pig's Eye: Daily Life and Political Economy in Southeastern Europe." *IREX Occasional Papers* vol. 1, no. 4. International Research and Exchanges Board.

GWALTNEY, JOHN L. 1980. *Drylongso.* New York: Random House.

POWDERMAKER, HORTENSE. 1939. *After Freedom: A Cultural Study in the Deep South.* New York: Viking Press.

REITER, RAYNA R. 1975. *Toward an Anthropology of Women.* New York: Monthly Review Press.

ROHRLICH-LEAVITT, RUBY, BARBARA SYKES, and ELIZABETH WEATHERFORD, 1975. "Aboriginal Woman: Male and Female Anthropological Perspectives." In Rayna R. Reiter, ed. *Toward an Anthropology of Women*. New York: Monthly Review Press.

QUINN, NAOMI. 1977. "Anthropological Studies of Women's Status." *Annual Review of Anthropology* 6:181–225.

WHITEHEAD, TONY L. 1980. "Identity, Subjectivity and Cultural Bias in Fieldwork." *The Black Scholar* 11, 7:40–44; 83–87.

28

Up the Anthropologist—Perspectives Gained from Studying Up

LAURA NADER

IN THIS ESSAY I shall describe some opportunities that anthropologists have for "studying up" in their own society, hoping to generate further discussion of why we study what we do (Nader, 1964). Anthropologists have a great deal to contribute to our understanding of the processes whereby power and responsibility are exercised in the United States. Moreover, there is a certain urgency to the kind of anthropology that is concerned with power (cf. Wolf, 1969), for the quality of life and our lives themselves may depend upon the extent to which citizens understand those who shape attitudes and actually control institutional structures. The study of man is confronted with an unprecedented situation: never before have a few, by their actions and inactions, had the power of life and death over so many members of the species. . . .

Scientific Adequacy

If we look at the literature based on field work in the United States, we find a relatively abundant literature on the poor, the ethnic groups, the disadvantaged; there is comparatively little field research on the middle class and very little first hand work on the upper classes. Anthropologists might indeed ask themselves whether the entirety of field work does not depend upon a certain power relationship in favor of the anthropologist, and whether indeed such dominant-subordinate relationships may not be affecting the kinds of theories we are weaving. What if, in reinventing anthropology, anthropologists were to study the colonizers rather than the colonized, the culture of power rather than the culture of the powerless, the culture of affluence rather than the culture of poverty?

Studying "up" as well as "down" would lead us to ask many "common sense" questions in reverse. Instead of asking why some people are poor, we would ask why other people are so affluent? How on earth would a social scientist explain the hoarding patterns of the American rich and middle class? How can we explain the fantastic resistance to change among those whose options "appear to be many"? How has it come to be, we might ask, that anthropologists are more interested in why peasants don't change than why the auto industry doesn't innovate, or why the Pentagon or universities cannot be more organizationally creative? The conservatism of such major institutions and bureaucratic organizations probably has wider implications for the species and for theories of change than does the conservatism of peasantry.

If, in reinventing anthropology, we were principally studying the most powerful strata of urban society, our view of the ghetto might be largely in terms of those relationships larger than the ghetto. We would study the banks and the insurance industry that mark out areas of the city to which they will not sell insurance or extend credit. We would study the landlord class that "pays off" or influences" enforcement or municipal officials so that building codes are not enforced. Slums are technically illegal; if building codes and other municipal laws were enforced, our slums would not be slums (if enforcement were successful), or they might be called by another name which would indicate that they were results of white-collar crime. One might say that if business crime is successful, it will produce street crime. With this perspective on white-collar crime, our analysis of gang delinquency might be correspondingly affected, and in developing theories of slum-gang behavior we might ask: Is it sufficient to understand gangs as products of the value systems of that subculture alone? We might study the marketing systems or the transportation system which, as in Watts, makes virtual islands of some ghetto areas. We might study the degree to which legal practices, or the kind of legal services, mold the perceptions of law that are present in the ghettos.

The consequences of not studying up as well as down are serious in terms of developing adequate theory and description. If one's pivot point is around those who have responsibility by virtue of being delegated power, then the questions change. From such a perspective, one notices different facets of culture—the ghetto may be viewed as being without law, lawless. The courts are not geared to the complaints of the poor (which would fall in the $20 to $80 range): furthermore, they are not geared for cheap and quick resolution of conflict—crucial features for the poor. From this perspective, ghetto communities may be said to be shut out of the legal system except as defendants, and indeed they are often shut off from other municipal services ranging from garbage-collecting to police protection. From this orientation, then, the question may be raised again: In our studies of delinquency, is it sufficient to understand gangs as products of the value systems of that subculture alone?

Let's ask another question: What have been the consequences of social science research on crime? By virtue of our concentration on lower-class crimes, we have aided in the public definition of the "law and order problem" in terms of lower-class or street crimes. Let's assume that the taxpaying public in a democracy, after listening to a presidential speech calling for more tax money for enforcement and protection from street crimes, decides to see for itself. No matter what library they went to, the most they could get is some information on crimes committed by the lower class. They would have no way of evaluating, given present descriptive materials, whether, in a situation of limited money, they would do better to put their money on street crime or on white-collar crime, both of which, after all, imperil the lives of all taxpayers every day in many ways.

As Clyde Mitchell has noted, it was with such problems in mind that anthropologists first introduced the concept of "social field."

> The classical anthropological study takes a unit—a "tribe" or "society" or "community"—and presents the behavior of its members in terms of a series of interlocking institutions, structures, norms, and values. It is not only anthropologists working in urban areas who have found this sort of assumption difficult to maintain, but also those who have been conducting "tribal" studies in modern Africa (and presumably also elsewhere). They have found that the effect of groups and institutions not physically present in the tribal area influences the behavior of people in it. The unit of interacting relationships, in other words, is larger than the tribe. (Mitchell, 1966, p. 56)

Lowie may have studied the Crow, Llewellyn and Hoebel the Cheyenne, as if they were "islands" unrelated to the wider society and even unrelated to the policies and actions of the Bureau of Indian Affairs, but there has raged a whole literature since the fifties challenging the limited ethnographic community view of the world, and a recognition of methodological need has been, as Mitchell noted, what has perhaps stimulated the development of network theory and the development of nation state studies (Adams, 1970).

If anthropology were reinvented to study up, we would sooner or later need to study down as well. We are not dealing with an either/or proposition; we need simply to realize when it is useful or crucial in terms of the problem to extend the domain of study up, down, or sideways. If we become interested in the determinants of family patterns (rather than the poor or the rich as such), then studying this problem across class, or at least on a vertical slice, would be a way to test hypotheses regarding whether certain aspects of lower-class or upper-class plight are somehow due to a particular kind of family pattern (serially monogamous, matrifocal, father-absent), whether poverty, for example, is generated by certain types of employment patterns or external factors. At least posing the problems in a comparative frame would help improve our chances for understanding the forces that generate excessive poverty or affluence and the origins of those forces, whether intrusive from the larger society or "determined by cultural transmission within the group." Depending on one's view of the processes that generate behavior, one would seek solutions to social problems either by a policy directed to reforming the society as a whole or by one directed to modifying the behavior of the subculture, or both (Valentine, 1969; Gladwin, 1969).

On the basis of such work in our own society,[1] we could rewrite the books on American Society, whose indexes make no mention of the advertising, insurance, banking, realty, or automobile industries, which most people on the street know have played a major role in forming modern American society. Ethnographic reports would describe the communications industries, the agencies which regulate them, the institutions that undergird the industrial sector, such as the legislative bodies, the universities and professional organizations, and such descriptions would be from the point of view of the *users* as well as the managers. It is appropriate that a reinvented anthropology should study powerful institutions and bureaucratic organizations in the United States, for such institutions and their network systems affect our lives and also affect the lives of people that anthropologists have traditionally studied all around the world.

It is particularly appropriate that anthropologists should lead the way in this work by virtue of a number of characteristics of our discipline. The study of man has had to be eclectic in its methods, broad in its vision of what it takes to understand man—his past, his present, his culture, his biology. We have specialized in understanding *whole* cultures in a cross-cultural context. We should, for example, be at home in studying the law firm as a secret society, in finding and analyzing the networks of power—which on paper may not be there—in describing those unwritten customary behaviors that are completely indispensable for understanding, for example, what makes Congress tick. The anthropologist should, above all, by virtue of his understanding of the principle of reciprocity, be able to analyze why it is that decisions of Federal Communications Commissioners may not be "rational," or the cultural dimensions involved in the failure of national programs ostensibly geared to reintegrate society. It is the anthropologist who, by virtue of his populist values, may be able to define the role of citizen-scholar—a science of man for man.

Democratic Relevance

"Studying up" seems to be one track for integrating paramount social concerns with the goals and aims of the science of man. The service function we have performed in the past could be amplified to include another service, social as well as scientific, that is, writing ethnographies for the "natives." A monograph that should be taken into account by managers for the benefit of people concerned is Colson's recent (1971) book on *The Impact of the Kariba Resettlement upon the Gwembe Tonga.*

> Massive technological development hurts. This is a fact largely ignored by economic planners, technicians, and political leaders. In planning drastic alterations in environment that uproot populations or make old adjustments impossible, they count the engineering costs but not the social costs. After all, they do not think of themselves as paying the latter. . . . This book is a study in the impact of forced change upon some of its victims.

Another example is Spradley's *You Owe Yourself a Drunk*, an ethnographic description of the interaction and the consequences of the interaction that drunks have with the legal and enforcement systems. This monograph is already serving to educate managers of that system about the consequences of specific legal decisions and procedures. This is not a novel role for social scientists to play, and unfortunately our findings have often served to help manipulate rather than aid those we study. Another role, however, is related to the concept of citizenship in a country that is to be run on a democratic framework and the control that citizens must have to harness managerial manipulation. We cannot, as responsible scientists, educate "managers" without at the same time educating those "being managed." A democratic framework implies that citizens should have access to decision-makers, institutions of government, and so on. This implies that citizens need to know something about the major institutions, government or otherwise, that affect their lives. Most members of complex societies and certainly most Americans do not know enough about, nor do they know how to cope with, the people, institutions, and organizations which most affect their lives. I believe that anthropologists would be surprisingly good at applying their descriptive and analytical tools to a major problem: How can a citizenry function in a democracy when that citizenry is woefully ignorant of how the society works and doesn't work, of how a citizen can "plug in" as a citizen, of what would happen should citizens begin to exercise rights other than voting as a way to make the "system" work for them? But first, as we know, we have to describe the bureaucracy and its culture.

Love and Eaton (1970) began their study of the Bay Area Air Pollution Control Agency with questions about the functions of the agency: How does the agency perceive itself? Who uses it? How do the users perceive the agency? Public access was a key question.

> Our approach was, at first, guarded due to our doubts. We pretended innocence, and in fact found out that we really were innocent. We then began to realize that we were "outsiders." We were the public who did not understand the professional language being spoken. The avenues we approached were those the public gen-

erally approached. Gradually, a picture of the agency and its position in the legal system emerged.

Its structure, the personalities of the decision-makers, the limitations reality places on any ideal system, and finally the kinds of uses made of it became clearer. . . . (Pp. 2-3)

When the citizen goes to the agency, he is translated into statistical data which separate him from the actual procedure or use of the agency. . . . Assumed in this is the notion that since the agency is supposed to protect the public interest, the public will seek access to it. The reality of the situation is very different. The agency acts as autonomously as possible to combat air pollution and in so doing, comes into close contact with the industry officials who speak the same technical and legal language. It is industry which has the greatest access to the agency, especially at the legislative level. It is industry which makes the greatest *use* of the agency to protect *its* interests. (Pp. 32-33)

This same study notes that, in the legal division of the agency, violation notices are treated like parking tickets—after so many are collected the violator is prosecuted. But what does prosecution consist of, given the intimate patterns of social interaction described above? These were not ordinary criminals.

In the legal division, the agency lawyer emphasized that the principles of criminal law were not a solution, hence the civil fines. The type of "crime" committed does not merit the "responsible" official being put in jail with "prostitutes and muggers." . . . An interesting footnote to this procedure is that Regulation I, which does *not* apply to most large industries but to private citizens and land developers, is treated as a misdemeanor where the violator can be put in jail with the "prostitutes and muggers." (P. 33)

Apart from being a useful report on bureaucratic culture, this thirty-seven-page report is the kind of ethnographic information that citizens need prior to an attempt to gain *access* to, or attempt to *use*, a public agency. Such reports would introduce them to the structure and culture of the subgroup in such a way as to allow them to gauge whether the cards are stacked and in what direction they are stacked in terms of real access to, and use of, a public agency.

The study of the California Department of Insurance, and in particular the processing of complaints by the Policy Services Bureau of that same agency, is another attempt to describe the workings of an organization whose acts of omission or commission affect the lives of many (Serber, 1971). Serber concludes (p. 62) that the Department of Complaints does not meet the needs of the people of the State of California because "the vast majority of the people are not aware of its existence." He adds, by means of a quote, a further insight which has been noted by other student studies of governmental agencies (and it is not much different for private agencies that purport to serve the public) and which suggests that such public institutions are not structured for public access:

It is much worse to deal with someone in the public because you know that you are very limited in what kinds of answers you can give them and the results you can get for them. They expect more and often get impatient. With the industry, it's different: they are usually friendly and polite, at least to our faces; we always know where we stand and how far we can go. It's less stressful because I feel less responsible for the outcome of the conversations. (Insurance Officer III).

The report goes on to note that "there is a qualitative difference in the nature of the interaction between the complainants and the Insurance Officer and the representative of the industry and the Insurance Officer."

It's not very pleasant to arrive here at a quarter of eight in the morning after battling to cross the Bay Bridge for forty-five minutes and before I can finish a cup of coffee some *hysterical* fat bitch who can hardly talk, she's so stupid and excited, will come in, and they will call me. When I catch sight of her my stomach tightens and my mouth gets dry; sometimes the burning in my pipe starts before I can even get up to the desk, and I'll have to take a sip of water. (Insurance Officer IV)

This same report makes a set of predictions as to what might happen to this Department of Complaints were access by the public easily available; the structure and function of the department would move more closely in line with a major goal of the Department of Insurance "to enforce insurance laws so as to achieve the highest possible degree of protection for the public in general and all policy holders and beneficiaries in particular" (Serber, 1971, p. 64). . . .

Some years ago, the criminologist Edwin H. Sutherland wrote a book entitled *White-Collar Crime*. A landmark finding documented in that work was the simple fact that white-collar personnel commit crimes, a fact which should have helped combat the belief, at least among social scientists, that the poor had a monopoly on crime. If, as scientists, we are interested in understanding the determinants of crime, then the "discovery" that the rich as well as the poor commit "crimes" (something that is well known to the average citizen and most certainly known by the poor) is very important. The fact that crimes are differentially stigmatized and prosecuted according to class should lead us to disregard oversimplistic theories explaining criminal behavior. Very few sociological works of this type followed Sutherland's study, and indeed there was a long dry period between the muckraking of the turn of the century and Sutherland.

Instead, sociologists such as Lewis Coser (1968) prefer to tell us why some poor do and why some poor do not commit crimes in terms of the theory of related criminal behavior. If we look at the question in relation to a vertical slice, it is a well-known fact that the criminal law has been oriented toward individual crimes, preferably street crime, and collective criminal behavior by an agency or corporation is often dealt with in administrative agencies or in ways which leave very little stigma on those involved (Pound, 1906; Sutherland, 1949). Yet our analyzed data base is slim. Henry Ruth, Director of the National Institute of Law Enforcement and Criminal Justice, noted as late as 1970 that

> the National Institute of Law Enforcement and Criminal Justice has developed an intensive concern that so-called "white-collar crime" receives scant attention from the law enforcement and research communities. . . . The entire field of white-collar crime represents a national priority for action and research—to define the problem, to examine its many faces, to measure its impact, to look for ways in which its victims can be helped, and to determine how such crime can be prevented, deterred, and effectively prosecuted. (Edelhertz, 1970, p. iii)

With regard to benefit to citizens, it is astounding that in as legalistic a country as the United States, nowhere in the educational system does one get a *working* knowledge of the law as part of a general education. In fact, after years of studying the Zapotec legal system of Oaxaca, Mexico, I would conclude that the single most important difference between the Zapotec legal system of southern Mexico and the American legal system (from the point of view of a middle-class consumer) is that Zapotecs have access to, know how to *use* access to, the legal system. In the United States, most citizens do not have access to the legal system, either because they are ignorant of the workings of the system or because they cannot afford the professional (lawyer) who would have adequate knowledge of the workings of the system. In California, for example—and I imagine this is much more wide-spread—there are few books for citizens describing the legal system, what it is, and how it works.

This situation is representative of the larger problem of citizen education. Most of what we learn about the law we absorb vicariously from TV westerns and Perry Mason—style shows. Ethnographic works on the subject of law would be filling a scientific and descriptive need, as well as informing the native about a system which at times heavily weights the direction his life takes. For example, one student began a study of the Immigration and Naturalization Service in an effort to find out how immigration and the INS have molded and influenced the communities of third-world immigrants. The basic hypothesis was that the INS is the historical product of negative American attitudes toward non-Northern European immigrants—fear of foreigners, dislike of strange cultures, isolationism, and the like; that while there has been a major liberalization of the laws, the administration of immigration, and indeed recruitment to the agency, continue to be affected by these historical attitudes. Other anthropological studies that might involve the use of personal documents—the memoirs of judges, lawyers, and corporate executives are more noticeable for their absence from the bookshelves. The Washington law firms whose lobbying functions have earned them the label of fourth branch of government would be a fascinating place to test some of Elizabeth Bott's hypotheses about networks. What shapes and functions do the networks of such firms have in an organization where, at mid-career, the majority of firm members fan out into positions about Washington, yet still maintain relations with the law firm even after they are no longer on the payroll? What kind of reciprocity is involved here?

Obstacles and Objections

But there are those who would not want to entertain any such reorientation of anthropology, and it is important to appreciate the reasons why present-day anthropologists would say "impossible," "improbable," "irrelevant," "off the mark," even "impertinent." The obstacles that are posed are many, but for our purposes here they may be discussed in terms of *access, attitudes, ethics,* and *methodology.*

Departments of anthropology have generally believed that students should do their dissertation field work in a non-Western culture. At some points in time that was a useful policy to implement, if in training anthropologists one valued the importance of culture shock and the detachment which accompanies it. For many students today, the experience of working in a Washington law firm, in a company town, or in an international industrial complex would be more bizarre than anything a student anthropologist could find in a Mexican village, or in New Guinea for the matter. We anthropologists have studied the cultures of the world only to find in the end that ours is one of the most bizarre of all cultures and one, by virtue of its world influence for "bad" or "good," in urgent need of study.

The most usual obstacle is phrased in terms of access. The powerful are out of reach on a number of different planes: they don't want to be studied; it is dangerous to study the powerful; they are busy people; they are not all in one place, and so on. As some of our students found out in their studies of corporate use of the courts:

> The belief that corporations work secretly and surreptitiously in their own interests has been somewhat verified. Their desire for secrecy, their paranoid fear of all but self-fashioned publicity, their refusal to discuss questions on their operation, and the overconscious regard of their lawyers for the confidential nature of the lawyer-client relationship (even when the public's interests are at stake), all serve to eliminate any free flow of information which should be available to the public forum, and are reminiscent of secret societies. The stealth of the corporation is epitomized in those wily chess masters they employ to handle their cases, the corporate lawyers. (Zeff and Bush, 1970)

These difficulties are true of the people that anthropologists have studied in many different places. That problems of access are any different, or at least any more problematic, in studying up in the United States is a proposition which has not been adequately tested. Anthropologists have had problems of access everywhere they have gone; solving such problems of access is part of what constitutes "making rapport." In view of our successes among peoples of the world who have been incredibly hostile, it is rather surprising that anthropologists could be so timid at home (see Riesman, 1954, pp. 440-66). Furthermore, it could be argued that access to bureaucratic organizations (such as governmental agencies) frequented by the wealthy and powerful should be open to social scientists by virtue of laws which protect public access to information affecting the public interest. In addition, there are wealthy anthropologists who would presumably have access "up." Cleveland Amory (1947) and E. Digby Baltzell (1964) have made substantial contributions to understanding the power status of the upper class, although neither one is an anthropologist. No, there must be more plausible reasons why the less powerful are more attractive for study in the United States.

It has been said that anthropologists value studying what they like and liking what they study and, in general, we prefer the underdog. Braroe and Hicks (1967), discussing the mystique of anthropology, make reference again to the traditional alienation from their own culture that characterizes anthropologists, and they explore how such alienation relates to their lack of intense commitment to social reform. This could be phrased more positively: Anthropologists have favored studying non-Western cultures as a way of fulfilling their mission to study the diverse ways of mankind; they have not had an intense commitment to social reform because of their relativistic stance and a belief that such a stance was necessary to a truly "objective, detached, scientific perspective," or because they thought that others, such as sociologists, were involved in social reform. While scientific findings may be ideally viewed as "value-free," certainly the choice of subject for scientific inquiry is most certainly not. Anthropologists of the future will have a greater responsibility for what they choose to study as well as how they study.

The ethical problems that are raised in studying up almost always appear to be confused, particularly in discussing ethics of working in one's own society. One student made the following comment:

> To say that kula-ring participants don't perform in practice what they say they do has very different consequences from saying that a government agency is not living up to its standards. This isn't to say that the government agency shouldn't be studied, or that the fact it isn't living up to its standards shouldn't be pointed out. The question is: Can the anthropologist do a structural study and then in his role as citizen point out that the agency is screwing the American public?

The same student asked:

> How can we gain access to the same kinds of information as when we "study down" without being dishonest (i.e., a fake secretary or other role)? If we did get information without letting informants know we were social scientists, how could we publish it? It seems that the only "open" way of doing a study would end up being fairly superficial—questionnaires and formal interviews as versus what we learn by participant observation.

The problems raised by this student are ethical problems anthropologists have had to face no matter what culture they are studying. In discussing such ethical questions involved in studying up in our society, I have the impression that confusion results depending on whether or not one recognizes the implicit double standard—is there one ethic for studying up and another for studying down? Or is it, as this student suggests, that the consequences of describing what may be systemic inadequacies may be greater for government agencies than peasant economic systems or for conflict resolution (or just plain conflict) in a small fishing village, and that therefore our subjects of study should be treated accordingly?

There is an important distinction to be recognized as to "public" and "private," even though informant anonymity may be important to both sectors. For the most part, anthropologists working in the United States can be said to have worked in the "private" sphere: we study families, small groups, those aspects of communities which are more private than public. We should not necessarily apply the same ethics developed for studying the private, and even ethics developed for studying in foreign cultures (where we are guests), to the study of institutions, organizations, bureaucracies that have a broad public impact. In reinventing anthropology, any discussion of ethics should consider the public-private dimensions as well as the home-abroad component. Furthermore, in the present anthropology, work that is considered in the objective social science mode, when carried out abroad might well be dubbed "journalistic" by the subjects. Telling it like it is may be perceived as muckraking by the subjects of study (Oscar Lewis' work on Mexico was so viewed), *or* by fellow professionals who feel more comfortable if data is presented in social science jargon which would protect the work from common consumption.

The concept of participant observation plays a determining role in *what* anthropologists choose to study. The power of participant observation as such was only discovered in the twentieth century. Malinowski and Radcliffe-Brown, among the first to do field work by the techniques of participant observation, set a new standard for ethnographic descriptions. When an anthropologist goes to study the culture of a people, he lives with them; the resultant description is rich in contextual information and is the result of the many points of view that one is opened to by virtue of "living with the natives." Hortense Powdermaker has described the components of participant observation as follows:

> The conditions for successful mutual communication include 1) physical proximity of the field worker to the people he studies, 2) knowledge of their language, and 3) psychological involvement. (1966, p. 287)

She goes on to say:

> The ability to be psychologically mobile is important in hierarchical situations where it is necessary to move easily between different levels in the power struc-

ture. Some field workers identify so completely with the underdog that they are unable to make effective contacts with those on the top level of the social (or political) hierarchy. (P. 291)

At the same time that Hortense Powdermaker has described the value of participant observations, she has also alluded to the limitations of such complete acceptance of participant observation as a distinctive feature of all social anthropological field work. When the anthropologist participant observes, he or she resides and generally partakes with the "natives." Such a method has weighed heavily in the decisions as to where anthropologists study: we prefer residential situations, whether the residence is in a primitive village or a modern hospital.

The degree to which our field choices might be determined by whether or not we can observe as participant was made clear to me when two of my students went to Washington to study a law firm that did not want to be studied (even though individual members were willing to cooperate in a limited way). How could they participant-observe if the firm wouldn't let them in the door, and *if they couldn't participant-observe, how could they do anthropology?* These questions have, of course, been raised before in anthropology, and when anthropologists thought it important enough they surmounted the problems raised. Witness the culture-at-a-distance studies that cropped up during World War II, or witness the work of Elizabeth Bott (1957) in her network study of kinship in London, which was based principally on face-to-face interviewing.

The point here is that there is a mystique about participant observation that carries points with it, yet it remains that the anthropologist's image of himself is shattered (Fischer, 1969) if he cannot participant-observe, and for the most part our students are not generally trained in the kinds of techniques that they would need to work on problems in nonresidential settings such as banks, insurance companies, government agencies, electronics industries, and the like. How many anthropologists know how to find out who owns a city? If Sol Tax is right in pointing out that anthropologists are not working on the most relevant problems of the world today—such as population, pollution, and war—because they cannot participant-observe such problems in a community, then, in reinventing anthropology, we might have to shuffle around the value placed on participant observation that leads us to forget that there are other methods (see Gussow and Tracy, 1971) more useful for some of the problems and situations we might like to investigate. The use of personal documents, memoirs, may substitute for anthropological participation in some areas of culture that take long years of participation to really understand. . . .

Interviews of various sorts (formal/informal, face-to-face/telephone) were used by my students. Documents were used (see the *NACLA Guide*, 1970)—public relations documents for understanding the preferred self-image of the organization, internal documents on the structure and statistics of work planned and accomplished by the organization, all useful in discovering trends and what is thought of as problematic by the actors. Also important is what Marian Eaton has labeled "self-analysis"—an awareness on the part of the student of how he as a social scientist is perceived, run around, enculturated, and described in the veiled and not-so-veiled encounters with informants and the members of organizations and the like whose job it is to deal with outsiders. We may have to give higher priority to traditional anthropological values such as using our knowledge of others as a mirror for ourselves and allowing questions to lead us to mthodology (rather than vice versa).

We may have to reorder our conception of urgent anthropology. Surely it should be the needs of mankind for the study of man that lead the way.

Notes

I am very grateful to Elizabeth Colson, Marian Eaton, Dell Hymes, and Julio Ruffini for taking the time to read and criticize earlier versions of this paper. Marian Eaton deserves special recognition for helping research and edit these pages. The undergraduate students who have been pioneering in "studying up" deserve recognition for their vision, their persevering attitudes, their delight in doing ethnography of everyday life situations at home, and for trying to do so in better than the usual way. Physicist Arthur Rosenfeld deserves special thanks for funding two anthropology students in an early effort to study up in Washington, D.C., an effort which led to the formulation of ideas for this paper.

1. See M. N. Srinivas' book *Social Change in Modern India*, Chapter 5, "Some Thoughts on the Study of One's Own Society," for a discussion of the problems involved in such an endeavor.

References

ADAMS, RICHARD NEWBOLD. 1970. *Crucifixion by Power*. Austin: University of Texas Press.

AMORY, CLEVELAND. 1947. *The Proper Bostonians*. New York: E. P. Dutton & Co.

BALTZELL, E. DIGBY. 1964. *The Protestant Establishment: Aristocracy and Caste in America*. New York: Vintage Books.

BENEDICT, RUTH. 1946. *The Chrysanthemum and the Sword*. Boston: Houghton Mifflin Co.

BOTT, ELIZABETH. 1957. *Family and Social Network: Roles, Norms and External Relationships in Ordinary Urban Families*. London: Tavistock Publications.

BRAROE, NIELS WINTHER, and GEORGE L. HICKS. 1967. "Observations on the Mystique of Anthropology." *Sociological Quarterly* 7, No. 2:173–86.

COLSON, ELIZABETH. 1971. *The Impact of the Kariba Resettlement upon the Gwembe Tonga*. Manchester: University of Manchester Press.

COSER, LEWIS A. 1968. "Violence and the Social Structure." In *Violence in the Streets,* ed. Shalom Endleman. Chicago: Quadrangle Books. Pp. 71–84.

EATON, MARION. 1971. "An Ethnography of BBB Oakland: One Consumer's View." Unpublished undergraduate thesis, Department of Anthropology, University of California, Berkeley.

EDELHERTZ, HERBERT. 1970. *The Nature, Impact, and Prosecution of White-Collar Crime.* Washington, D.C.: Government Printing Office.

FELLMETH, ROBERT, ed. 1971. *Power and Land in California, Preliminary Draft.* Center for the Study of Responsive Law, Washington, D.C.

FISCHER, ANN. 1969. "The Personality and Subculture of Anthropologists and Their Study of U.S. Negroes." In *Concepts and Assumptions in Contemporary Anthropology,* ed. Stephen A. Tyler. Proceedings of the Southern Anthropological Society No. 3. Athens: University of Georgia Press. Pp. 12-17.

GELLHORN, WALTER. 1966. *When Americans Complain.* Cambridge, Mass.: Harvard University Press.

GLADWIN, THOMAS. 1969. Review of *Culture and Poverty: Critique and Counter-Proposals,* by Charles Valentine. *Current Anthropology,* 10, Nos. 2–3:185.

GUSSOW, ZACHARY, and GEORGE S. TRACY. 1971. "The Use of Archival Materials in the Analysis and Interpretation of Field Data: A Case Study in the Institutionalization of the Myth of Leprosy as 'Leper.' " *American Anthropologist* 73, No. 3:695–709.

HANNERZ, ULF. 1969. *Soulside: Inquiries Into Ghetto Culture and Community.* New York: Columbia University Press.

HENRY, JULES. 1963. *Culture Against Man.* New York: Random House.

KLUCKHOHN, CLYDE. 1960. *Mirror for Man.* Greenwich, Conn.: Fawcett Publications.

LEACOCK, ELEANOR BURKE, ed. 1971. *The Culture of Poverty: A Critique.* New York: Simon & Schuster.

LOVE, NORMA, and MARIAN EATON. 1970. "The Bay Area Air Pollution Control District: An Anthropological Perspective." Unpublished undergraduate paper, Department of Anthropology, University of California, Berkeley.

MALINOWSKI, BRONISLAW. 1922. *Argonauts of the Western Pacific.* London: Routledge & Kegan Paul.

MITCHELL, J. CLYDE. 1966. "Theoretical Orientations in African Urban Studies." In *The Social Anthropology of Complex Societies,* ed. Michael Banton. Association of Social Anthropologists Monograph No. 4. London: Tavistock Publications. Pp. 37–68.

NADER, LAURA. 1964. "Perspectives Gained from Field Work." In *Horizons of Anthropology,* ed. Sol Tax. Chicago: Aldine Press. Pp. 148–59.

NORTH AMERICAN CONGRESS ON LATIN AMERICA. 1970. *NACLA Research Methodology Guide.* New York.

POUND, ROSCOE. 1906. "The Causes of Popular Dissatisfaction with the Administration of Justice." *Reports of the American Bar Association* 29, Part I: 395-417.

POWDERMAKER, HORTENSE. 1966. *Stranger and Friend: the Way of an Anthropologist.* New York: W. W. Norton & Co.

RESEK, CARL. 1960. *Lewis Henry Morgan, American Scholar.* Chicago: University of Chicago Press.

REISMAN, DAVID. 1954. *Individualism Reconsidered and Other Essays.* Glencoe, Ill.: Free Press.

SERBER, DAVID. 1971. "A Discussion of the Policy Services Bureau of the California Department of Insurance, with Specific Reference to the Interaction with the Insured Public and the Insurance Industry." Unpublished undergraduate thesis, Department of Anthropology, University of California, Berkeley.

SPRADLEY, J. P. 1970. *You Owe Yourself a Drunk: An Ethnography of Urban Nomads.* Boston: Little, Brown & Co.

SRINIVAS, M. N. 1966. *Social Change in Modern India.* Berkeley: University of California Press.

SUTHERLAND, EDWIN H. 1949. *White-Collar Crime.* New York: Dryden Press.

VALENTINE, CHARLES. 1969. Book review of his *Culture and Poverty: Critique and Counter-Proposals. Current Anthropology* 10, Nos. 2–3: 181–200.

WEAKLAND, J. H. 1960. " 'The Double Bind' Hypothesis of Schizophrenia and Three-Party Interaction." In *The Etiology of Schizophrenia,* ed. Don D. Jackson. New York: Basic Books.

WOLF, E. 1969. "American Anthropologists and American Society." In *Concepts and Assumptions in Contemporary Anthropology,* ed. Stephen A. Tyler. Proceedings of the Southern Anthropological Society No. 3. Athens: University of Georgia Press. Pp. 3–11.

ZEFF, DAVID, and PEGGY BUSH. 1970. "Corporate Use of the Courts." Unpublished undergraduate paper, Department of Anthropology, University of California, Berkeley.

29

Race, Caste, and Other Invidious Distinctions in Social Stratification

GERALD D. BERREMAN

A SOCIETY is socially stratified when its members are divided into categories which are differentially powerful, esteemed, and rewarded. Such systems of collective social ranking vary widely in the ideologies which support them, in the distinctiveness, number, and size of the ranked categories, in the criteria by which inclusion in the categories is conferred and changed, in the symbols by which such inclusion is displayed and recognized, in the degree to which there is consensus upon or even awareness of the ranking system, its rationale, and the particular ranks assigned, in the rigidity of rank, in the disparity in rewards of rank, and in the mechanisms employed to maintain or change the system.

For purposes of study, such systems have been analysed variously depending upon the interests and motives of the analyst. One of the most frequently used bases for categorizing and comparing them has been whether people are accorded their statuses and privileges as a result of characteristics which are regarded as individually acquired, or as a result of characteristics which are regarded as innate and therefore shared by those of common birth. This dichotomy is often further simplified by application of the terms 'achieved' versus 'ascribed' status. Actually, what is meant is *non*-birth-ascribed status versus birth-ascribed status. The former is usually described as class stratification, referring to shared statuses identified by such features as income, education, and occupation, while the latter is frequently termed caste or racial stratification or, more recently, ethnic stratification, referring to statuses defined by shared ancestry or attributes of birth.

Regardless of its characteristics in a particular society, stratification has been described as being based upon three primary dimensions: class, status, and power, which are expressed respectively as wealth, prestige, and the ability to control the lives of people (oneself and others).[1] These dimensions can be brought readily to mind by thinking of the relative advantages and disadvantages which accrue in Western class systems to persons who occupy such occupational statuses as judge, garbage man, stenographer, airline pilot, factory worker, priest, farmer, agricultural labourer, physician, nurse, big businessman, beggar, etc. The distinction between class and birth-ascribed stratification can be made clear if one imagines that he encounters two Americans, for example, in each of the above-mentioned occupations, one of whom is white and one of whom is black. This quite literally changes the complexion of the matter. A similar contrast could be drawn if, in India, one were Brahmin and one untouchable; if in Japan one were Burakumin and one were not; if in Europe one were Jew and one were Gentile; or if, in almost any society, one were a man and one a woman. Obviously something significant has been added to the picture of stratification in these examples which is entirely missing in the first instance—something over which the individual generally has no control, which is determined at birth, which cannot be changed, which is shared by all those of like birth, which is crucial to social identity, and which vitally affects one's opportunities, rewards, and social roles. The new element is race (colour), caste, ethnicity (religion, language, national origin), or sex. The differences in opportunities and behaviour accorded people as a result of these criteria are described by such pejorative terms as racism, casteism, communalism (including especially ethnic and religious discrimination), and sexism. To be sure, the distinctions are manifest in class, status, and power, but they are of a different order than those considered in the first examples: they are distinctions independent of occupation, income, or other individually acquired characteristics. While the list includes a variety of criteria for birth-ascription and rank with somewhat different implications for those to whom they are applied, they share the crucial facts that: 1. the identity is regarded as being a consequence of birth or ancestry and hence immutable; 2. the identity confers upon its possessor a degree of societally defined and affirmed worth which is regarded as intrinsic to the individual; 3. this inherent worth is evaluated relative to that of all others in the society—those of different birth are inherently unequal and are accordingly adjudged superior or inferior, while those regarded as being of similar birth are innately equal. The crucial fact about birth-ascription for the individual and for society lies not so much in the source of status (birth), as in the fact that it cannot be repudiated, relinquished, or altered. Everyone is sentenced for life to a social cell shared by others of like birth, separated from and ranked relative to all other social cells. Despite cultural differences, therefore, birth-ascribed stratification has common characteristics of structure, function, and meaning, and has common consequences in the lives of those who experience it and in the social histories of the societies which harbour it.

The specific question motivating the present discussion is this: is social ranking by race absolutely distinctive, not significantly distinctive at all, or is race one criterion among others upon which significantly similar systems of social ranking may be based? While identifying the last of these as 'correct' from my perspective, I shall insist that the answer depends entirely upon what one means by 'race', and by 'distinctive', and what one wishes to accomplish by the inquiry. No satisfactory answer can be expected without comparative, cross-cultural analysis encompassing a number of systems of social differentiation, social separation, and social ranking, based on a variety of criteria, embedded in a variety of cultural *milieux*, analysed by reference to various models of social organization, and tested against accounts of actual social experience. The attempt to do this leads to a number of issues central and tangential to the study of stratification and race, some of which have been overlooked or given short shrift in the scholarly literature, while others are well-discussed in particular disciplinary, regional, or historical specialities without necessarily being familiar to students of other academic domains to whose work and thought they are nevertheless relevant.

There is not space here to present ethnographic and historical documentation for particular instances of birth-ascribed stratification. I have done so briefly in another paper, citing five societies on which there is fortunately excellent published material vividly exemplifying the kinds of social systems I refer to in this paper, and their implications for those who comprise them: Ruanda, India, Swat, Japan, and the United States. I recommend those accounts to the reader.[2]

Models For Analysis

In the course of scholarly debate concerning the nature and comparability of systems of collective social ranking, a number of models and concepts have been suggested, implied, or utilized. A framework can be provided for the present discussion by identifying some of these and analysing whether and to what extent each is relevant and applicable to all or some systems of birth-ascribed social separation and inequality, with special attention to the five societies cited above.

Stratification

By definition, stratification is a common feature of systems of shared social inequality—of ranked social categories—whether birth-ascribed or not.

Where membership in those categories is birth-ascribed, the ranking is based on traditional definitions of innate social equivalence and difference linked to a concept of differential intrinsic worth, rationalized by a myth of the origin, effect, and legitimacy of the system, perpetuated by differential power wielded by the high and the low, expressed in differential behaviour required and differential rewards accorded them, and experienced by them as differential access to goods, services, livelihood, respect, self-determination, peace of mind, pleasure, and other valued things including nourishment, shelter, health, independence, justice, security, and long life.

Louis Dumont, in *Homo Hierarchicus*, maintains that the entire sociological notion of stratification is misleading when applied to South Asia, for it is of European origin, alien and inapplicable to India. He holds that the term implies an equalitarian ideology wherein hierarchy is resented or denied, and that it therefore obscures the true nature of India's hierarchical society, based as it is on religious and ideological premises peculiar to Hinduism which justify it and result in its endorsement by all segments of Indian society. Stratification, he maintains, is thus a 'sociocentric' concept which cannot cope with the unique phenomenon of Indian caste.[3] My response to this is twofold: first, the caste hierarchy based on the purity-pollution opposition as Dumont insists, is well within any reasonable definition of stratification, for the latter refers to social structure and social relations rather than to their ideological bases; and second, Dumont's description of the functioning of, and ideological basis for, the caste hierarchy is idealized and similar to the one commonly purveyed by high caste beneficiaries of the system. Few low caste people would recognize it or endorse it. Yet their beliefs and understandings are as relevant as those of their social superiors to an understanding of the system. The low caste people with whom I have worked would find Dumont's characterization of 'stratification' closer to their experience than his characterization of 'hierarchy'.[4]

Use of the stratification model focuses attention upon the ranking of two or more categories of people within a society, and upon the criteria and consequences of that ranking. Often, but not inevitably, those who use this concept place primary emphasis upon shared values and consensus, rather than power and conflict, as the bases for social ranking and its persistence. This emphasis is misleading, at best, when applied to systems of birth-ascribed ranking, as I shall show. It is obvious, however, that while many systems of stratification are not birth-ascribed, all systems of birth-ascribed ranking are systems of social stratification, and any theory of social stratification must encompass them.

Ethnic Stratification

Probably the most recent, neutral, and non-specific term for ascriptive ranking is 'ethnic stratification'. 'An ethnic group consists of people who conceive of themselves as being alike by virtue of common ancestry, real or fictitious, and are so regarded by others', [5] or it comprises 'a distinct category of the population in a larger society whose culture is usually different from its own [and whose] members . . . are, or feel themselves, or are thought to be, bound together by common ties of race or nationality or culture.' [6] Undoubtedly the systems under discussion fit these criteria. Use of the adjective 'ethnic' to modify 'stratification' places emphasis upon the mode of recruitment, encompassing a wide variety of bases for ascription, all of which are determined at birth and derive from putative common genetic makeup, common ancestry, or common early socialization and are therefore regarded as immutable. This commonality is held responsible for such characteristics as shared appearance, intelligence, personality, morality, capability, purity, honour, custom, speech, religion, and so forth. Usually it is held responsible for several of these. The ranked evaluation of these characteristics, together with the belief that they occur differentially from group to group and more or less uniformly within each group serves as the basis for ranking ethnic groups relative to one another.

Van den Berghe has held that 'ethnic' should be distinguished from 'race' or 'caste' in that the former implies real, important, and often valued social and cultural differences (language, values, social organization), while the latter are artificial and invidious distinctions reflecting irrelevant (and sometimes non-existent) differences in physiognomy, or artificial differences in social role. [7] This is a useful point. In the recent sociological literature, however, 'ethnic' has increasingly been used to refer to *all* social distinctions based on birth or ancestry, be they associated with race, language, or anything else. This is the usage adopted here. Moreover, as I shall elaborate in discussing pluralism below, race and caste entail the kinds of cultural distinctions cited by van den Berghe as diagnostic of ethnic diversity, for the social separation implied by those systems ensures social and cultural diversity. For example, van den Berghe's assertion that 'notwithstanding all the African mystique, Afro-Americans are in fact culturally Anglo-American,' [8] has been countered by ample evidence that the African origin, social separation, and collective oppression of blacks in America *has* resulted in an identifiable Afro-American culture. [9]

All systems of ethnic stratification are thus based on ancestry, approximating a theory of birth-ascription, and if the definitions set forth by advocates of this term are accepted, most systems of birth-ascribed stratification can properly be designated ethnic stratification. Perhaps the only recurrent exception is sexual stratification, wherein inherent, birth-ascribed, and biologically determined characteristics which are *independent* of ancestry are the basis for institutionalized inequality. This instance, exceptional in several respects, will be discussed separately below, and hence will not be alluded to repeatedly in intervening discussions although most of what is said applies to it also.

Caste

A widely applied and frequently contested model for systems of birth-ascribed rank is that of 'caste', deriving from the example of Hindu India where the *jati* (almost literally 'common ancestry') is the type-case. *Jati* in India refers to interdependent, hierarchically ranked, birth-ascribed groups. The ranking is manifest in public esteem accorded the members of the various groups, in the rewards available to them, in the power they wield, and in the nature and mode of their interaction with others. *Jatis* are regionally specific and culturally distinct, each is usually associated with a traditional occupation and they are usually (but not always) endogamous. They are grouped into more inclusive, pan-Indian ranked categories called *varna* which are frequently confused with the constituent *jatis* by those using the term 'caste'. The rationale which justifies the system is both religious and philosophical, relying upon the idea of ritual purity and pollution to explain group rank, and upon the notions of right conduct (*dharma*), just deserts (*karma*), and rebirth to explain the individual's fate within the system. As an explanation of caste inequalities this rationale is advocated by those whom the system benefits, but is widely doubted, differently interpreted, or regarded as inappropriately applied by those whom the system oppressed.

Many students of stratification believe that the term 'caste' conveys an impression of consensus and tranquillity that does not obtain in systems of rigid social stratification outside of India. That notion, however, is no more applicable to, or derivable from, Indian caste than any other instance of birth-ascribed stratification.[10]

If one concedes that caste can be defined cross-culturally (i.e., beyond Hindu India), then the systems under discussion here are describable as caste systems. That is, if one agrees that a caste system is one in which a society is made up of birth-ascribed groups which are hierarchically ordered, interdependent, and culturally distinct, and wherein the hierarchy entails differential evaluation, rewards, and association, then whether one uses the term 'caste', or prefers 'ethnic stratification', or some other term is simply a matter of lexical preference. If one requires of a caste system that it be based on consensus as to its rationale, its legitimacy, and the legitimacy of the relative rank of its constituent groups, then none of the examples mentioned here is a caste system. If one requires social tranquillity as a characteristic, then too, none of these is a caste system. If one allows that a caste system is held together by power and the ability of people within it to predict fairly accurately one another's behaviour while disagreeing on almost anything or everything else, then all of these systems will qualify. If one requires a specifically Hindu rationale of purity and pollution and/or endogamy and/or strict and universal occupational specialization, then one restricts caste to India and to only certain regions and groups within India at that. If one requires for castes, as some do, a tightly organized corporate structure, then too one would exclude even in India some *jatis* and other groups commonly called 'castes'. (This, however, does seem to me to be the structural criterion which comes closest to differentiating Indian *jati* from other systems of birth-ascribed stratification such as that of the United States. Corporateness evidently emerges as a response to oppression and as a mechanism for emancipation even where it has been previously minimal, e.g., in Japan, Ruanda, and the United States. Thus, the corporateness of Indian *jatis* may represent a late state of development in caste systems rather than a fundamental difference in the Indian system.)

Jati in Hindu India and the equivalent but non-Hindu *quom* organization in Swat and Muslim India, are each unique, yet both share the criteria by which I have defined caste, as do the tri-partite system of Ruanda and the essentially dual systems of Japan and the United States, and all share in addition (and in consequence, I believe) a wide variety of social and personal concomitants. Caste is a useful and widely used term because it is concise, well-known, and in fact (as contrasted to phantasy), the structural, functional, and existential analogy to Indian caste is valid for many other systems.

Race

Systems of 'racial' stratification are those in which birth-ascribed status is associated with alleged physical differences among social categories which are culturally defined as present and important. Often these differences are more imagined than real, sometimes they are entirely fictional and always a few physical traits are singled out for attention while most, including some which might differently divide the society if they were attended to, are ignored. Yet systems so described share the principle that ranking is based on putatively inborn, ancestrally derived, and significant physical characteristics.

Those who use this model for analysis generally base it upon the negative importance attached by Europeans to the darker skin colour of those they have colonized, exterminated, or enslaved. A good many have argued that racially stratified societies are *sui generis*; that they are unique and hence not comparable to societies stratified on any other basis.[11] There is often a mystical quality to these arguments, as though race were an exalted, uniquely 'real', valid, and important criterion for birth ascription, rendering it incomparable to other criteria. An element of inadvertent racism has in such instances infected the very study of race and stratification. In fact, as is by now widely recognized, there is no society in the world which ranks people on the basis of biological race, i.e., on the basis of anything a competent geneticist would call 'race', which means on the basis of distinctive shared genetic makeup derived from a common gene pool. 'Race', as a basis for social rank is always a *socially* defined phenomenon which at most only very imperfectly corresponds to genetically transmitted traits and then, of course, only to phenotypes rather than genotypes. Racists regard and treat people as alike or different because of their group membership defined in terms of socially significant ancestry, not because of their genetic makeup. It could not be otherwise, for people are rarely geneticists, yet they are frequently racists.

To state this point would seem to be superfluous if it were not for the fact that it is continually ignored or contested by some influential scholars and politicians as well as the lay racists who abound in many societies. To cite but one well-known recent example, Arthur Jensen, in his article on intelligence and scholastic achievement, maintains that there is a genetic difference in learning ability between blacks and whites in the United States.[12] Nowhere, however, does he offer evidence of how or to what extent his 'Negro' and 'White' populations are genetically distinct. All of those, and only those, defined in the conventional wisdom of American folk culture to be 'Negro' are included by Jensen, regardless of their genetic makeup, in the category whose members he claims are biologically handicapped in learning ability. Thus, large numbers of people are tabulated as 'Negroes', a majority of whose ancestors were 'white', and virtually all of Jensen's 'Negroes' have significant but highly variable percentages of 'white' ancestry. Although, also as a result of social definition, the 'whites' do not have known 'Negro' ancestry, the presumed genetic homogeneity of the 'whites' is as undemonstrated and unexplored as that of the 'Negroes'. In short, there was no attempt to identify the genetic makeup or homogeneity of either group, the genetic distinctiveness of the two groups, or whether or how genetic makeup is associated with learning ability, or how learning ability is transmitted. This kind of reasoning is familiar and expectable in American racism, but not in a supposedly scientific treatise—a treatise whose author berates those who deplore his pseudo-science as themselves unscientific for failing to seriously consider his 'evidence'. The fallacy in Jensen's case is that he has selected for investigation two socially defined groupings in American society which are commonly regarded as innately different in social worth and which as a result are accorded widely and crucially divergent opportunities and life experiences. Upon finding that they perform differentially in the context of school and test performance, he attributes that fact to assumed but undemonstrated and uninvestigated biological differences. Thus, socially defined populations perform differently on socially defined tasks with socially acquired skills, and this is attributed by Jensen to biology. There are other defects in Jensen's research, but none more fundamental than this.[13] One is reminded of E. A. Ross's succinct assessment of over fifty years ago, that ' "race" is the cheap explanation tyros offer for any collective trait that they are too stupid or too lazy to trace to its origin in the physical environment, the social environment, or historical conditions'.[14]

The point to be made here is that systems of 'racial' stratification are social phenomena based on social rather than biological facts. To be sure, certain conspicuous characteristics which are genetically determined or influenced (skin colour, hair form, facial conformation, stature, etc.) are widely used as convenient indicators by which ancestry and hence 'racial' identity is recognized. This is the 'colour bar' which exists in many societies. But such indicators are never sufficient in themselves to indicate group membership and in some instances are wholly unreliable, for it is parentage rather than appearance or genetics which is the basis for these distinctions. One who does not display the overt characteristics of his 'racial' group is still accorded its status if his relationship to the group is known or can be discovered. The specific rules for ascertaining racial identity differ from society to society. In America, if a person is known to have had a sociologically black ancestor, he is black regardless of how many of his ancestors were sociologically white (and even though he looks and acts white). In South Africa, most American blacks would be regarded as 'coloured' rather than 'black'. Traditionally, in a mixed marriage, one is a Jew only if one's mother is a Jew. In contemporary India, an Anglo-Indian has a male European ancestor in the paternal line; female and maternal European ancestry are irrelevant. In racially stratified societies, phenotypical traits are thus never more than clues to a person's social identity.

As Shibutani and Kwan have noted, 'a color line is something existing in the presuppositions of men,'[15] . . . what is decisive about "race relations" is not that people are genetically different but that they approach one another with dissimilar perspectives.'[16] Van den Berghe makes a similar point: 'Race, of course, has no intrinsic significance, except to a racist. To a social scientist, race acquires meaning only through its social definition in a given society.'[17]

This is illustrated by the title of DeVos and Wagatsuma's book, *Japan's Invisible Race*, dealing with the hereditarily stigmatized and oppressed Burakumin. The Japanese believe that these people are physically and morally distinct, and their segregation and oppression are explained on that basis when in fact they are not so at all. Instead they are recognizable only by family (ancestry), name, occupation, place of residence, life style, etc. The Burakumin thus comprise a 'race' in the sociological sense of Western racism, but an 'invisible' (i.e., not genetic or phenotypic) one. The authors subtitled the book, *Caste in Culture and Personality*, shifting the analogy from that of race (in the West) to that of caste (in India). The book could as well have been entitled: *Caste in Japan: Racial Stratification in Culture and Personality*.

The Japanese example brings up a point which needs to be made about the alleged uniqueness of 'racial' stratification. *All* systems of birth-ascribed stratification seem to include a belief that the social distinctions are reflected in biological (i.e., 'racial') differences. That is, caste and other ethnic differences are said to be revealed in physical makeup or appearance. Associated with these supposed natural and unalterable inherited physical characteristics are equally immutable traits of character, morality, intelligence, personality, and purity. This is the case in Japan, where no actual physical differences can be detected; it is true in India and Swat where physical stereotypes about castes abound but actual differences are minimal; it is true in Ruanda where the ranked groups all are black but are said to differ in stature and physiognomy as well as in culture; it is true in the United States where the physical differences are commonly and erroneously thought to be absolute. Cultural factors have to be relied upon in addition to whatever biological ones may be present, in order to make the important discriminations upon which ranked social interaction depends, and even then mistakes are frequently made. Throughout the world, people who look distinctive are likely to be regarded as socially different; people who are regarded as socially different are likely to be thought to look distinctive. They are also likely to be required to dress and act distinctively.

I suggest that, just as societies frequently dramatize the social differences among kin groups (e.g., sibs, clans, phratries) by giving to them totemic names and attributing to them characteristics of animals or plants, thereby identifying the social differences with biological species differences,[18] so also, societies with birth-ascribed status hierarchies dramatize and legitimize *these* crucial social differences by attributing to them innate biological, hence 'racial', differences. As a result, the concept of miscegenation arises, based on an ideology of innate difference contradicted by a persistent and recurrent perception of similarity by people of opposite sex across social boundaries.[19]

Thus, caste organization and ethnic stratification include racism; racial stratification is congruent with caste and ethnic stratification. Their ultimate coalescence is in the imputation of biological differences to explain and justify birth-ascribed social inequality. In this regard, sexual stratification can be seen to be a phenomenon of the same order.

This universality of racism in birth-ascribed stratification can be understood in the fact that physical traits not only dramatize social differentiation, but can also explain and justify it. The effect of such explanation is to make social inequality appear to be a natural necessity rather than a human choice and hence an artificial imposition. Social distinctions are man-made and learned; what man makes and learns he can unmake and unlearn. What God or biology has ordained is beyond man's control. The former may be defined as artificial, unjust, untenable, and remediable; the latter as inevitable or divinely sanctioned. This is important because birth-ascribed stratification is widely or universally resented by those whom it oppresses (at least as it affects them), and advocated by those it rewards. Both categories share the human capability of empathy, and it inspires envy and resentment in the one and fear or guilt in the other. Racism—the self-righteous rationalization in terms of biology—is a desperate and perhaps ultimately futile attempt to counteract those subversive emotions.

In sum, 'race', as commonly used by social scientists, emphasizes common physical characteristics (as does 'sex'); 'caste' emphasizes common rank, occupational specialization, endogamy, and corporate organization; 'ethnic stratification' emphasizes cultural distinctiveness. These are real differences in meaning, but the degree of empirical overlap in systems so described, and the commonalities in the existential worlds of those who live within them are so great as to render the distinctions among them largely arbitrary, and irrelevant, for many purposes. Individual cases differ, but as types of social stratification, they are similar. With equal facility and comparable effect, they utilize as evidence of social identity anything which is passed on within the group: skin colour, hair form, stature, physiognomy, language, dress, occupation, place of residence, geneology, behaviour patterns, religion. None is wholly reliable, all are difficult to dissimulate. In any case, strong sanctions can be brought to bear to minimize the temptation to 'pass' among those who might be capable and tempted. As the case of India suggests and Japan confirms, social criteria can be as rigid as physical ones.

'Race' Versus 'Caste'

Considerable controversy has surrounded the terms 'race' and 'caste' when applied outside of the contexts in which they originated and to which they have been most widely applied: Western colonialism and Hindu India, respectively. This is understandable because there are important peculiarities in each of these situations, and to extend the terms beyond them requires that those peculiarities be subordinated to significant similarities. Systems of birth-ascribed inequality are sufficiently similar, however, to invite comparative study, and some general term is needed to refer to them. 'Caste' has seemed to me more useful than 'race', because it refers to social rather than allegedly biological distinctions, and it is the social distinctions which are universal in such systems. If it were a catchier term, 'ethnic stratification' might replace both in the social scientific literature. Unfortunately it is not, so we must probably await a better term or tolerate continuing terminological dispute and confusion. In any case, it is the nature of birth-ascribed stratification—the ideas, behaviours, and experiences which comprise it, the effects it has on persons and societies and, quite frankly, the means by which it may be eliminated—in which I am interested. The words applied to it are of little importance. When I try to explain American race relations to Indians, I describe and analyse America as a caste stratified society, with attention to the similarities and differences in comparison with India. If I am trying to explain Indian caste stratification to Americans, I describe and analyse India as a racist society, with attention to the similarities and differences in comparison to the United States. I do this as a matter of translation from the social idiom of one society to the other. It is the most economic, vivid, and accurate way I know to convey these phenomena to people whose experience is limited to one system or the other. I do not think Indian caste *is* American race, or vice versa, but neither do I think that race stratification in America *is* race stratification in South Africa, or that caste in India *is* caste in Swat, or that caste in the Punjab *is* caste in Kerala. Neither do I think racial stratification and racism are the same for blacks, Chicanos, and whites in America, or that caste stratification and casteism are the same for sweepers, blacksmiths, and Rajputs in Hindu India. There are features in all of these which are the same in important ways, and by focusing on these I think we can understand and explain and predict the experience of people in these diverse situations better than if we regard each of them as unique in every way.

Objections to the cross-cultural comparison of race and caste depend either on an insistence that the two would have to be wholly identical to justify such comparison, or more commonly, on misconceptions about one or both of the systems being compared. It is worthwhile to identify and comment upon some of these objections.

1. The most prevalent objection among experts on Western social stratification is that caste status is accepted and endorsed by those in the system whereas racial stratification is objected to and striven against by those it oppresses. Thus Cox asserts that 'while the caste system may be thought of as a social order in stable equilibrium, the domination of one race by another is always an unstable situation. . . . The instability of the situation produces what are known as race problems, phenomena unknown to the caste system.' I have contended with this claim in some detail elsewhere.[20] Suffice it to say here that anyone who has known low caste people in India can affirm that this particular contrast is imaginary, as can anyone who knows the history of religious conversion, social reform, and social mobility striving in India, who has followed the reports of the Commissioner of Scheduled Castes and Tribes, or who simply reads the news releases from India today.

2. It is often argued that caste in India is unique and noncomparable because of the elaborate religio-philosophical rationale which underlies it, and that racial stratification is unique because it is based on colour.[21] As I have pointed out, these contentions are questionable on empirical grounds. Few would deny, for example, that caste exists in Swat as well as India, and that it exists in Mysore, India, among both the Lingayats and the Hindus, yet the rationale is very different in each of these cases. On the other hand, few would deny that colour consciousness is an important part of the ideology and metaphor of caste in India.

But on another level, these arguments are not necessarily relevant to the issue of comparison. That phenomena are in some respects different does not make them incomparable. They may still be similar in crucial respects. Everything is, after all, unique, but there can be no science of the unique. The claim for comparability can be refuted by showing that the facts are in error, or that the interpretations of their significance are fallacious, not by citing differences extraneous to the argument being made. Moreover, comparability (or incomparability) for one purpose or in one context does not imply comparability (or incomparability) for another purpose or in another context. The test must be whether or not and how well explanation can be derived from a particular comparison.

If one knows that a society is characterized by birth-ascribed stratification, he can predict a great deal about the experiences and attitudes of people at different levels within it, about the social, political, and economic behaviour they are likely to engage in under various circumstances, and about the nature and consequences of social conflict.[22] This, to my mind, justifies the comparison.

3. A number of specific characteristics of caste in India or race in the West have been cited as bases for non-comparability with other systems of birth-ascribed stratification. (a) *Endogamy* has been cited as essential to caste. However, what is crucial and universal in a caste system is not endogamy, but birth-ascribed membership in a ranked category or group. Endogamy is the most common method for achieving this in India and elsewhere, but a firm patrilineal or matrilineal rule of status assignment will do as well, and so will a rule which assigns to an individual the caste of his higher status parent or of his lower status parent, or one which designates that an individual whose parents are of castes A and B will be of caste C. All of these rules of birth-ascription occur in South Asian castes.[23]

(b) *Occupational distinctiveness* has been cited as essential to caste. This is indeed an almost inevitable concomitant of social separation, stratification, and interdependence, be it birth-ascribed or not. But again, it is not universal among castes even in India, nor is it lacking in racial and sexual stratification. Some have maintained that caste, without a conspicuous racial basis, cannot exist in a complex society simply because the anonymity of such a society would make dissimulation and passing too easy to sustain a caste system where no physical indicators of identity existed.[24] It is probably true that in the anonymity and mobility of contemporary urban life, rigid ethnic stratification is increasingly difficult to maintain when the indicators of identity are learned, for learned characteristics can be unlearned, suppressed, or learned by those to whom they are inappropriate. To manipulate these indicators is often difficult, as the persistence of the Burakumin of Japan makes clear, because the identifying characteristics may be learned very early (language, gesture), and may be enforced from without as well as from within (dress, deference, occupation), but it is possible, as instances of passing make clear.[25] The more personal relationships of traditional, small-scale societies, together with their formal and informal barriers and sanctions against casual or promiscuous interaction militate against the learning or expression of inappropriate status characteristics and conspicuous indicators of status are largely unnecessary. Reliable, immutable, and conspicuous indicators of identity are thus more important to systems of birth-ascribed stratification in the anonymity and mobility of the city than in the village, but the internal pressures of ethnic pride combined with the external pressures of ethnic discrimination and the vested interests which sustain it make such systems possible in even the most unlikely-seeming circumstances.

(c) Some have argued that the corporate structure of many Indian castes renders them incomparable to most instances of ethnic stratification, a point which I have discussed above (pp. 505–506) and will therefore not repeat.

(d) The comparison between black-white stratification in America and Indian caste is occasionally contested on grounds that the former is a *dichotomy* while the latter is a *complex hierarchy*. This is a real difference between the two, but it does not make them incomparable. It is a difference in numbers of groups, not in race versus caste. For one thing, there are other racial or caste-like groups in American society: Native Americans, Chicanos, Puerto Ricans, Asians, etc. In India, on the other hand, most interaction is not caste specific so much as it is specific to categories of castes (categories such as 'untouchables', 'twice-born', the *varnas*, etc.), thereby simplifying the interactional situation greatly. For example, the *Khas-Dom* (twice-born versus untouchable) dichotomy in the mountain area of my research[26] and the Brahmin-non-Brahmin dichotomy in South India are quite comparable to the situation described as the colour-bar elsewhere. One probable difference between dichotomous and multiple hierarchies may be that in the former the oppressed characteristically oppose the system as such. To rise within it would be to displace the privileged—to reverse the hierarchy—and that is impracticable. To overthrow the system is to erase their oppression and vice versa. They have nothing to lose but their inferiority. In multiple hierarchies, objection may more characteristically be made not to the system, but to the place of one's own group within it, the reason being that to overthrow the system is not feasible for any one of the many groups within it, each of which is relatively small, weak, and in competition with others. Moreover, successful overthrow would result not only in equality with elites, but equality with erstwhile inferiors. Therefore, it is regarded as more practicable and more rewarding to attempt to rise within the system than to eliminate the system itself. These remarks apply to systems of birth-ascribed stratification regardless of the criteria used.

(e) Finally, it is sometimes held that racial stratification is an outgrowth of Western colonialism, and hence India can be regarded as an example thereof only in the relationship of Indians to the British, not in the relationship among indigenous castes. I would maintain that caste in India is in fact a product of colonialism and that its present manifestations are closely analogous to the 'internal colonialism' which Blauner, among others has described for the United States (see below).[27] In India this is an instance of what has recently been termed 'fourth-world' colonialism, i.e., exploitation inflicted by 'third-world' (non-Western) people on their internal minorities, analogous to that they have often experienced themselves at the hands of 'first-' and 'second-world' colonialists (Western non-communist and communist nations, respectively).

In short, the further one probes into the nature and dynamics of race and caste, and into the experience of those who live them, the more it becomes apparent that they are similar, comparable, phenomena.

Colonialism

The concept of colonialism has gained popularity in recent years for the analysis of racism and racial stratification in the West.[28] It therefore merits further discussion. This model focuses on the history of Western expansion and the exploitation of alien peoples, emphasizing notions of the superiority of the dominant, Western, white society whose members arrogated privilege to themselves through the exercise of power (usually technological, often military) to dominate, control, exploit, and oppress others. Racism has been an integral aspect of this process, for there usually have been differences in colour between the colonizer and the colonized which were used to account for the alleged inferiority in ability, character, and mentality which in turn were used to justify colonial domination. Colonialism has been most often described as the result of overseas conquest, in which case the colonizing group has usually comprised a numerical minority. Less often colonialism has included conquest or expansion across national boundaries overland, but the results are the same, if the romance is less. These phenomena have recently come to be termed 'external colonialism', in contrast to 'internal colonialism' which refers to similar domination and exploitation, within a nation, of an indigenous, over-run, or imported minority. This distinction directs attention to the *locus* of colonial domination whereas the distinction between third-world and fourth-world colonies cited above, directs attention to the *sources* of that domination.

While it has not been much easier to gain acceptance of the colonial model for analysis of American race relations than it has been to gain acceptance of the caste model, it is clear that here again, the problem is semantic rather than substantive. Some of those who argue persuasively the cross-cultural and multi-situational applicability of the colonial model, deny such applicability for the caste model and in so doing use precisely the logic and data they deplore and regard as faulty when their intellectual adversaries deny applicability of 'colonialism' outside of the classical overseas context.[29]

Colonialism, external and internal, is a process which has occurred repeatedly, in many contexts, with many specific manifestations and many common results. It long antedates the recent period of European and American expansion. Caste stratification, racial stratification, ethnic stratification, and 'pluralism' have been its recurrent products.[30] The point can be made with specific reference to caste in India. Rather than regarding colonialism as an antecedent condition which excludes traditional India from the category of racially or ethnically stratified societies, it can well be used as a basis for assigning India historical priority among such societies, in the contemporary world. That is, traditional India may represent the most fully evolved and complex post-colonial society in the world. It is easy to obtain explanations of caste from informants or books in India which refer directly to the presumed early domination of primitive indigenes by advanced invaders. There is little doubt that the present caste system had its origins some 3,000 to 3,500 years ago in a socio-cultural confrontation that was essentially colonial. Low status was imposed on technologically disadvantaged indigenes by more sophisticated, militarily and administratively superior peoples who encroached or invaded from the north and west, arrogating to themselves high rank, privileges, and land. The large number of local and ethnically distinct groups on the sub-continent were fitted into a scheme of social hierarchy which was brought in or superimposed by the high status outsiders, culminating in the caste system we know today.[31] Social separation and social hierarchy based on ancestry became the essence of the system; colonial relations were its genesis. Even today, most tribal people—those who are geographically and economically marginal and culturally distinct—are incorporated into Hindu society, if at all, at the bottom of the hierarchy (except in those rare instances where they have maintained control over land or other important sources of income and power).

If one were to speculate on the course of evolution which ethnic stratification might take in the United States in the context of internal colonialism, of rigid separation, hierarchy, and discrimination which are part of it, and the demands for ethnic autonomy which arise in response to it, one possibility would be a caste system similar to, though less complex than that of India. The historical circumstances may be rather similar despite the separation of many hundreds of years, many thousands of miles and a chasm of cultural difference. Actually, development of the degree of social separation common in India seems at this point unlikely given the mass communications and mass education in the United States, its relative prosperity, and the rather widespread (but far from universal) commitment to at least the trappings of social equality. But surely if anything is to be learned from history and from comparison, the case of the Indian sub-continent should be of major interest to students of American race and ethnic relations, social stratification, and internal colonialism.

In sum, colonialism is as inextricable from caste and race as caste and race are from one another. There may be instances of colonialism where birth-ascription is or becomes irrelevant, but every instance of caste, race, and ethnic stratification includes, and relies for its perpetuation upon, the kind of ethnic domination and exploitation that defines colonialism.

Class

Closely associated with each of the models discussed here is that of social class. Class is a matter of acquired status rather than of birth-ascription, and is in this respect distinct from race, caste, and ethnic stratification, with different social consequences. In a class system, one is ranked in accord with his behaviour and attributes (income, occupation, education, life style, etc.).

In a birth-ascribed system, by contrast, one behaves and exhibits attributes in accord with his rank. In a class system, individual mobility is legitimate, albeit often difficult, while in ascribed stratification it is explicitly forbidden. Systems of acquired rank—class systems—prescribe the means to social mobility; systems of ascribed rank proscribe them. As a consequence, a class system is a continuum; there are individuals who are intergrades, there are individuals in the process of movement, there are individuals who have experienced more than one rank. Miscegenation is not an issue because there are no ancestrally distinct groups to be inappropriately mixed. A birth-ascribed system is comprised of discrete ranks on the pattern of echelon organization, without legitimate mobility, without intergrades; the strata are named, publicly recognized, clearly bounded. Miscegenation is therefore a social issue. In a system of acquired ranks, the strata may be indistinct, imperfectly known, or even unknown to those within the system. In fact, there is considerable debate among students of stratification as to whether or not awareness of class is essential to a definition of class. Some hold that social classes are properly defined by social analysts who use such criteria as income to designate categories which may be entirely unrecognized by those in the society.

In a class system individuals regard themselves as potentially able to change status legitimately within the system through fortune, misfortune, or individual and family efforts. In a birth-ascribed system, individuals know that legitimate status change is impossible—that only dissimulation, revolution, or an improbable change in publicly accorded social identity can alter one's rank and hence life-chances.

Despite these differences, class is in no way incompatible with birth-ascribed systems. In fact, in so far as it is a term for categories of people ranked by income, occupation, education, and life style, it co-occurs with them. Low castes, despised races, ethnic minorities, and colonized people comprise economically and occupationally depressed, exploited classes who are politically and socially oppressed; high castes, exalted races, privileged ethnic groups, and colonizers comprise economically and occupationally privileged, power-wielding, elite classes who live off the labour of others. In this respect, class differences pervade and reinforce systems of birth-ascribed stratification. Furthermore, it is not unusual to find significant class differentials within a caste, racial, or ethnic group or within a colonized or colonial group.[32] That is, class, in the conventional sense often occurs conspicuously within such groups, and may also bridge their boundaries without obscuring them. But it is not possible to analyse birth-ascribed stratification solely in terms of class, for no amount of class mobility will exempt a person from the crucial implications of his birth in such systems.

Those who have sought to identify the positions of European immigrants to America such as the Poles, Italians, and Irish, with the position of blacks, Native Americans, Chicanos, and Asians have failed to discern the essential fact that racism is the basis of American caste, and that it bestows upon those who experience it a unique social, political, and economic stigma which is not bestowed by class or national origin. Second generation white Europeans can meet all of the criteria for acceptance into the American white race-caste for they are regarded as being only culturally different. A fifteenth generation American black, or a fifteen-hundredth generation American Indian cannot, for their differences are regarded as innate, immutable, and crucial. Equalitarianism has produced no 'American dilemma' among racists, as Myrdal believed, simply because it is an equality for whites only, and its extension to other groups has moved slowly, painfully, and with vehement opposition, even where it has moved at all.

Systems of collective social rank, whether ascribed or acquired, are systems for retaining privilege among the powerful and power among the privileged, reserving and maintaining vulnerability, oppression, and want for those upon whom it can be imposed with minimal risk while retaining their services and their deference. In this way they are similar. In the principles of recruitment and organization by which that similarity is effected and in the individuals' prospects for mobility they differ, and those differences have important consequences for individual life experience and social processes in the societies which harbour them.

Pluralism

Pluralism is a model which has been applied to socially and culturally diverse societies since the writings of Furnivall on South-East Asia.[33] Cultural pluralism obtains when 'two or more different cultural traditions characterize the population of a given society'; it is 'a special form of differentiation based on institutional divergences'.[34] Systems of birth-ascribed stratification are inevitably systems of social and cultural pluralism because they are accompanied by social separation. In a caste system, 'Because intensive and status-equal interaction is limited to the caste, a common and distinctive caste culture is assured. This is a function of the quality and density of communication within the group, for culture is learned, shared and transmitted.'[35] The same is true for any system of racial or ethnic stratification. M. G. Smith has noted, 'it is perfectly clear that in any social system based on intense cleavages and discontinuity between differentiated segments the community of values or social relations between these sections will be correspondingly low. This is precisely the structural condition of the plural society.'[36] And I have noted elsewhere that,

> . . . castes are discrete social and cultural entities. . . . They are maintained by defining and maintaining boundaries between castes; they are threatened when boundaries are compromised. Even when interaction between castes is maximal and cultural differences are minimal, the ideal of mutual isolation and distinc-

tiveness is maintained and advertised among those who value the system. Similarly, even when mobility within, or subversion of the system is rampant, a myth of stability is stolidly maintained among those who benefit from the system.[37]

Mutual isolation of social groups inevitably leads to group-specific institutions (an important criterion for pluralism according to Furnivall), because members are excluded from participation in the institutions of other groups.

Caste, race, and ethnic stratification, like all plural systems therefore, are systems of social separation and cultural heterogeneity, maintained by common or over-riding economic and political institutions rather than by agreement or consensus regarding the stratification system and its rationale.[38] This does not deny consensus, it only defines its nature:

> In caste systems, as in all plural systems, highly differentiated groups get along together despite widely differing subjective definitions of the situation because they agree on the objective facts of what is happening and what is likely to happen—on who has the power, and how, under what circumstances, and for what purposes it is likely to be exercised. They cease to get along when *this* crucial agreement changes or is challenged.[39]

The constituent social elements of plural societies need not be birth-ascribed, and they need not be (and sometimes are not) ranked relative to one another, although by Furnivall's definition, one element must be dominant. In fact, unranked pluralism is the goal many ethnic minorities choose over either stratification or assimilation. But a system of birth-ascribed stratification is always culturally, socially and hence institutionally heterogeneous, and thus pluralistic.

Hierarchy as Symbolic Interaction

I have elsewhere described the universality among social hierarchies of patterns of interaction which symbolize superiority and inferiority.[40] Social hierarchy, after all, exists only in the experiences, behaviours, and beliefs of those who comprise it. Interpersonal interaction becomes the vehicle for expression of hierarchy: for asserting, testing, validating, or rejecting claims to status. Almost every interaction between members of ranked groups expresses rank claimed, perceived, or accorded. When the hierarchy is birth-ascribed, the membership of its component groups is ideally stable, well-known, and easily recognizable. In such systems people are perceived by those outside of their groups almost wholly in terms of their group identity rather than as individuals. They are regarded as sharing the characteristics which are conventionally attributed to the group and they share the obligations, responsibilities, privileges, and disabilities of their group. In intergroup relations, therefore, one individual is substitutable for another in his group, for all are alike, and interchangeable. This is the setting for prejudice, discrimination, bigotry, chauvinism, and is an ideal situation for scapegoating. These attitudes and their behavioural consequences are designated and deplored by such terms as racism, casteism, communalism (referring to ethnic chauvinism of various sorts), and recently, sexism. They are characterized by domination, deprivation, oppression, exploitation, and denigration directed downward; obedience, acquiescence, service, deference, and honour demanded from above. They result in envy, resentment, dissimulation, and resistance arising from below, balanced from above by fear, guilt, and that combination of arrogant self-righteousness and rationalization which is found in all such systems. Maya Angelou has aptly characterized the result in American race relations as 'the humorless puzzle of inequality and hate'; the question of worth and values, of aggressive inferiority and aggressive arrogance'[41] which confronts and exacts its toll not only from black Americans, but from the denizens of all those jungles of inherited inequality I call caste systems. It is this quality of interpersonal relations rather than any particular event or structural feature which struck me most vividly, forcefully, and surprisingly as similar in Alabama and India when I first experienced them for over a year each within a period of five years.[42] For me, this is the hallmark of oppressive, birth-ascribed stratification.

A specifically interactional definition of caste systems applies equally to all systems of birth-ascribed stratification: '*a system of birth-ascribed groups each of which comprises for its members the maximum limit of status-equal interaction, and between all of which interaction is consistently hierarchical.*'[43] The cultural symbols of hierarchical interaction vary; the presence and importance of such symbols is universal and essential to racism, casteism, and their homologues.

Hierarchy as Ideology

Dumont has emphasized the point that Indian caste is unique in that it is based on an ideology of hierarchy defined in terms of ritual purity and pollution.[44] He regards other systems of hierarchical social separation as non-comparable because of the inevitable differences in the ideologies supporting them. In the comparative framework which I advocate, I maintain simply that the Hindu rationale is one of several ideologies (cf. those of Islamic Swat, of the South Indian Lingayats to whom purity is irrelevant, of Ruanda, of Japan, and the United States) which can and do underlie and justify systems of birth-ascribed social hierarchy. Each is unique to the culture in which it occurs; each is associated with remarkably similar social structures, social processes, and individual experiences. I believe that anyone who has experienced daily life in rural India and the rural American South, for example, will confirm the fact that there is something remarkably similar in the systems of social relations and attitudes. I believe that anyone who has experienced daily life in an urban slum, a public market, or a factory in India and the United States would come to the same conclusion. That similarity is generated by birth-ascribed stratification and it is not concealed by differential ideologies.[45]

Contrary to another of Dumont's assumptions (shared with Cox), there is nothing incompatible between an ideology which underwrites a hierarchy of groups and a notion of equality within each group. This combination, in fact, is found not only in the United States where it accounts for the above-mentioned absence of a real 'American dilemma' in race relations, but also in each of the other systems described here. Members of each ranked group are *inherently unequal* to those of each other group and are by birth *potentially equal* to those of their own group. More importantly, the existence of an ideology of hierarchy does not mean that this ideology is conceived and interpreted identically by all within the system it is presumed to justify or even that it is shared by them. Acquiescence must not be mistaken for concurrence. Dumont's assumption to the contrary is the most glaring weakness in his analysis of Indian caste.[46]

Sexual Stratification

Finally, in my discussion of models for analysis, I turn to the controversial and sociologically puzzling matter of sex as a basis for social separation and inequality. The special problems which the sexual criterion poses for the student of stratification are both academic and substantive. The academic problems derive from the history of the study of stratification. Although the role of women in various non-Western societies has been discussed by anthropologists (including prominently Margaret Mead), and the position of women in European societies has been discussed by some social historians, the sexual dichotomy rarely appears in sociological works on stratification. That this criterion has been largely ignored or dismissed by stratification theorists is attributable to several factors not the least of which is no doubt that members of the privileged sex have authored most of the work and to them such ranking has not been a problem and hence has not been apparent. Also, their culturally derived biases have been such that this kind of ranking was taken for granted as a manifestation of biological differences. 'Many people who are very hip to the implications of the racial caste system . . . don't seem to be able to see the sexual caste system and if the question is raised they respond with: "that's the way it's supposed to be. There are biological differences." Or with other statements which recall a white segregationist confronted with integration.'[47] The biological rationale—what Millett refers to as the 'view of sex as a caste structure ratified by nature'[48]—recalls also the justification offered for *all* birth-ascribed dominance-exploitation relationships be they caste in India, Burakumin status in Japan, sexual roles, or any other. In each instance the plea is that these are uniquely *real*, significant, unavoidable, and natural differences, and therefore they must be acted upon. Thus, in an interview about their new book, *The Imperial Animal*, which is said to claim that males have dominated human history because 'the business of politics . . . is a business that requires skills and attitudes that are peculiarly male,' anthropologists Robin Fox and Lionel Tiger were reported to have vehemently denied that their theory about the reasons for women's roles might be a sexist theory. ' "These are the facts, don't accuse us of making up the species," Tiger said.' And again, ' "Because this is a racist country, people relate sexism to racism." But these two reactions are actually different because while there are no important biological differences between races, there are very important differences between the sexes.'[49] Whether the differences are real or not (and who would deny that males and females differ in important ways?), the sociological and humanistic question is whether the differences require or justify differential opportunities, privileges, responsibilities, and rewards or, put negatively, domination and exploitation.

Birth-ascribed stratification, be it sexual, racial, or otherwise, is always accompanied by explanations, occasionally ingenious but usually mundane and often ludicrous, as to why putative natural differences *do* require and justify social differences. Those explanations are widely doubted by those whose domination they are supposed to explain, and this includes increasing numbers of women.

The substantive issues which becloud the topic of sexual stratification have to do with the mode of recruitment, the socialization, membership, and structural arrangements of sexually ranked categories. First, there is the fact that while sex is determined at birth, it is not contingent upon ancestry, endogamy, or any other arrangement of marriage or family, and is not predictable. It is the only recurrent basis for birth-ascribed stratification that can be defensibly attributed solely to undeniably physical characteristics. Even here there are individual or categorical exceptions made for transvestites, hermaphrodites, homosexuals, etc., in some societies as in the case of *hijaras* in India.[50] The significance (as contrasted to the fact) of the diagnostic physical traits—of sexual differences—is, however, largely socially defined, so that their cultural expressions vary widely over time and space. Second, as a concomitant to the mode of recruitment, males and females have no distinct ethnic or regional histories. It must not be overlooked, however, that they do have distinct social histories in every society. Third, the universal co-residence of males and females within the household precludes the existence of lifelong separate male and female societies as such, and usually assures a degree of mutual early socialization. But note that it does not preclude distinct male and female social institutions, distinct patterns of social interaction within and between these categories, or distinguishable male and female subcultures (in fact the latter are universal) including, for example, distinct male and female dialects.

Partly as a consequence of these factors, the nature and quality of segregation of the sexes has not been defined by sociologists as comparable to that of the other ascriptive social categories discussed here. Nevertheless, most of the characteristics of birth-ascribed separation and stratification (racial, caste, ethnic, colonial, class, and pluralistic characteristics), and virtually all of the psychological and social consequences of inborn, lifelong superiority-inferiority relations are to be found in the relationship of males and females in most societies. These stem from similar factors in early socialization and from stereotypes and prejudices enacted and enforced in differential roles and opportunity structures, rationalized by ideologies of differential intrinsic capabilities and worth, sustained and defended through the combination of power and vested interest that is common to all birth-ascribed inequality. I have elsewhere contrasted some of the consequences of these assumptions and behaviours in the United States and India as reflected in the political participation of women in the two nations although this is dwarfed by Millet's more recent work on male domination, its sources, and manifestations in the West.[51]

If we agree with van den Berghe that 'race can be treated as a special case of invidious status differentiation or a special criterion of stratification,'[52] I think we are bound to agree that sex is another.

Consequences of Inherited Inequality

Assuming that there are significant structural and interactional similarities among systems of birth-ascribed stratification, the question can still be legitimately asked, 'so what?' Is this merely a more or less interesting observation—even a truism—or does it have some theoretical or practical significance? My answer would be that it has both, for such systems have common and predictable consequences in the individual lives of those who live them and in the cumulative events which comprise the ongoing histories of the societies which harbour them.

> Caste systems are living environments to those who comprise them. Yet there is a tendency among those who study and analyse them to intellectualize caste, and in the process to squeeze the life out of it. Caste is people, and especially people interacting in characteristic ways and thinking in characteristic ways. Thus, in addition to being a structure, a caste system is a set of human relationships and it is a state of mind.[53]

Their 'human implications' are justification enough for studying and comparing systems of birth-ascribed stratification. There are neither the data nor the space to discuss these implications fully here, but I will suggest the nature of the evidence briefly, identifying psychological and social consequences. I am well aware that many features of such systems are found in all sharply stratified societies. Some are characteristic of all relationships of superordination and subordination, of poverty and affluence, of differential power. Others are found in all societies made up of distinct sub-groups whether stratified or not. It is the unique combination of characteristics in the context of the ideal of utter rigidity and unmitigable inequality which makes systems of stratification by race, caste, ethnicity, and sex distinctive in their impact on people, individually and collectively.

Psychological Consequences

Beliefs and attitudes associated with rigid stratification can be suggested by such terms as paternalism and dependence, *noblesse oblige*, arrogance, envy, resentment, hatred, prejudice, rationalization, emulation, self-doubt, and self-hatred. Those who are oppressed often respond to such stratification by attempting to escape either the circumstances or the consequences of the system. The realities of power and dependence make more usual an accommodation to oppression which, however, is likely to be less passive than is often supposed, and is likely to be unequivocally revealed when the slightest change in the perceived distribution of power occurs. Those who are privileged in the system seek to sustain and justify it, devoting much of their physical effort to the former and much of their psychic and verbal effort to the latter. When these systems are birth-ascribed, all of these features are exacerbated.

Kardiner and Ovesey conclude their classic, and by now outdated, study of American Negro personality, *Mark of Oppression*, with the statement: 'The psycho-social expressions of the Negro personality that we have described are the *integrated* end products of the process of oppression.'[54] Although it is appropriate to question their characterization of that personality in the light of subsequent events and research, there is no doubt that such oppression has recurrent psychological consequences for both the oppressor and the oppressed, as Robert Coles has demonstrated in *Children of Crisis* and subsequent works.[55]

Oppression does not befall everyone in a system of birth-ascribed inequality. Most notably, it does not befall those with power. What does befall all is the imposition by birth of unalterable membership in ranked, socially isolated, but interacting groups with rigidly defined and conspicuously different experiences, opportunities, public esteem and, inevitably, self-esteem. The black in America and in South Africa, the Burakumin of Japan, the Jarijan of India, the barber or washerman of Swat, the Jutu or Twa of Ruanda, have all faced similar conditions as individuals and they have responded to them in similar ways. The same can be said for the privileged and dominant groups in each of these societies, for while painful consequences of subordination are readily apparent, the consequences of superordination are equally real and important. Thus, ethnic stratification leaves its characteristic and indelible imprint on all who experience it.

The consequences of such stratification include many of the attitudes and responses vividly described in literature on black-white relations in the United States. Immediately to mind come accounts of the black experience, such as James Baldwin's *Notes of a Native Son, Nobody Knows My Name*, and *Go Tell it On the Mountain*; Claude Brown's *Manchild in the Promised Land*; Eldridge Cleaver's *Soul on Ice*; Ralph Ellison's *Invisible Man*; Richard Wright's *Native Son* and *Black Boy*; and Malcolm X's *The Autobiography of Malcolm X*. Outstanding among those dealing with the white experience in relation to blacks are W. J. Cash's *The Mind of the South*; Lillian Smith's *Killers of the Dream* and *Strange Fruit*. The psychiatrist Robert Coles has provided insights into both sides of the American caste barrier in his works cited above.

Corresponding literature on other caste-like systems include, for India, Mulk Raj Anand's *Untouchable*; Hazari's *An Indian Outcaste: The Autobiography of an Untouchable*; Harold Isaac's *India's Ex-Untouchables*; and, from the British side, E. M. Forster's *Passage to India*; and in Burma, George Orwell's *Burmese Days*. On Japan, we can refer to the contributors to DeVos and Wagatsuma's *Japan's Invisible Race*, and, cited therein, Ninomiya's 'An Inquiry Concerning the Origin, Development and Present Situation of the *Eta* . . .', and Shimazaki Tōson's *Hakai (Breach of Commandment)*. Works on South Africa include Alan Paton's *Cry the Beloved Country* and *Too Late the Phalarope*; Albert Luthuli's *Let My People Go*; and van den Berghe's *Caneville* and *South Africa: A Study in Conflict*. Telling analyses of colonial situations include Franz Fanon's *Wretched of the Earth*, and Albert Memmi's *The Colonizer and the Colonized*, both deriving from Algeria; O. Mannoni's *Prospero and Caliban*, from Madagascar; J. C. Heinrich, *The Psychology of a Suppressed People*, on India. This listing does not do justice to the relevant literature, but is suggestive of it.

Research on the psychological consequences of racism in the United States is well-known and voluminous, though restricted almost exclusively to black-white relations. Although this literature has followed many blind leads and has been distorted by many subtle (and some not-so-subtle) biases, stereotypes, and prejudices, it nevertheless suggests that the public and self-disparagement or aggrandizement and the differential opportunities which go with birth-ascribed status, low and high, result in characteristic psychological problems and resort to characteristic psychological mechanisms.[56] Comparable literature on non-Western societies is scanty but increasing.[57]

The consequences of birth-ascribed stratification are self-fulfilling and self-perpetuating, for although low status groups do not adopt views of themselves or their statuses which are consistent with the views held by their superiors, they are continually acting them out and cannot avoid internalizing some of them and the self-doubts they engender, just as high status groups internalize their superiority and self-righteousness. The oppression of others by the latter serves to justify and bolster their superiority complex and to rationalize for them the deprivation and exploitation of those they denigrate. 'Once you denigrate someone in that way,' say Kardiner and Ovesey, 'the sense of guilt makes it imperative to degrade the subject further to justify the whole procedure.'[58] Gallagher notes that in the southern United States,

> By the attitudes of mingled fear, hostility, deprecation, discrimination, amused patronage, friendly domination, and rigid authoritarianism, the white caste generates opposite and complementary attitudes in the Negro caste. It is a touch of consummate irony that the dominant group should then argue that the characteristics which exhibit themselves in the submerged group are 'natural' or 'racial'.[59]

The products of oppression are thus used to justify oppression.

Change and Emancipation

The self-reinforcing degradation described above combines with greed and fear of status-loss or revolt to comprise a dynamic of oppression which, in birth-ascribed stratification, probably accounts for the widespread occurrence of pariah status or untouchability. Elites characteristically justify oppression by compounding it; they enhance their own rewards by denying them ever more stringently to social inferiors, and they strive to protect themselves from challenges to status and privilege from below by rigidifying the status boundaries, reinforcing the sanctions which enforce them, and increasing the monopoly on power which makes the sanctions effective. This assures increasing social separation and hierarchical distance between groups until such time as it generates rebellion, reform, or disintegration.

The fact that social order prevails most of the time in any given instance of inherited inequality does not mean that all of those in the system accept it or their places within it willingly, nor does it mean that the system is either stable or static. It most often means that power is held and exercised effectively by those in superordinate statuses, for the time being. Such systems are based on conformity more than consensus, and are maintained by sanctions more than agreement. Nevertheless, change is inherent, resistance and mobility-striving are universal, and effective challenges to such systems are probably ultimately inevitable because the response they elicit from those they oppress is subversive. The possibility of acting out the subversion depends largely upon the balance of power among the stratified groups and the definitions of the situation their members hold. The processes of change and patterns of conflict which lead to them are major areas of commonality in such systems.[60]

The history of every caste system, of every racially stratified system, of every instance of birth-ascribed oppression is a history of striving, conflict, and occasional revolt. That this is not generally acknowledged is largely a result of the fact that most of these actions occur in the context of overwhelming power and uncompromising enforcement by the hereditary elites and are therefore expressed in the form of day-to-day resentment and resistance handled so subtly and occurring so routinely that it goes unremarked.[61] Even conspicuous manifestations are likely to be quickly and brutally put down, confined to a particular locality or group, and knowledge of their occurrence suppressed by those against whom they have been directed. These phenomena often can only be discovered by consulting and winning the confidence of members of oppressed groups, and this is rarely done.

Only the most spectacular instances of resistance, and the few successful ones are likely to be well-known. Immediately to mind come such martyrs to the cause of emancipation of oppressed peoples as the Thracian slave Spartacus, who led a rebellion against Rome; the American slave rebellion leaders Gabriel and Nat Turner, the white abolitionist John Brown, and the contemporary leaders of black emancipation in America, Martin Luther King, Medgar Evers, and others (too many of them martyred) among their fellow leaders and supporters, black and white. No doubt there are many more, most of them unknown and unsung, in the history of all groups whose members society condemns by birth to oppression. In the folk history of every such group, and in the memory of every member, are instances of courageous or foolhardy people who have challenged or outwitted their oppressors, often at the cost of their own foreseeable and inevitable destruction.

Better-known and better-documented than the individuals who led and sometimes died for them, are the emancipation movements which have occurred in most such societies—movements such as those for black power and black separatism in the United States, anti-casteism and anti-untouchability in India, Hutu emancipation in Rwanda and Burundi, Burakumin emancipation in Japan, and anti-apartheid in South Africa. All have depended primarily upon concerted efforts to apply political, economic, or military power to achieve their ends. They have comprised direct challenges to the systems. Most have followed after the failure of attempts less militant, less likely to succeed, and hence less threatening to social elites—attempts towards assimilation or mobility within the systems such as those of status emulation.

The movements among black Americans (and more recently among other ethnically stratified groups in America such as Chicanos and Native Americans, and among women), are too well-known and well-documented to require enumeration here.[62] Anyone who reads the American press and especially the black and left press, cannot avoid being aware of the main currents in this area.

Emancipation movements outside of the West are less known to European and American readers, but they are more numerous than can be indicated here albeit quite poorly documented. Any list would have to include the following obvious examples:

India: Escape from the consequences of caste stratification has been a primary appeal of every religion and social reform movement to gain adherents in India from the beginnings of Jainism and Buddhism in the sixth century B.C., through Islam which became a significant religion in India from the eleventh century A.D.; Sikhism from the early sixteenth century; Christianity, dating from the 'Syrian Christians' of the first or sixth century A.D. in Kerala, followed in the sixteenth century by converts of Portuguese and French Catholic missionaries and in the nineteenth century by Anglican and Protestant converts; various Hindu reform movements including the Brahmo Samaj and Arya Samaj of the early and late nineteenth century, respectively; the post-Independence resurgence of 'neo-' Buddhism among low castes as an explicitly anti-caste phenomenon under Dr. B. R. Ambedkar, the revered leader of Indian untouchables for many decades and founder of the Scheduled Castes Federation and its successor in the later 1950s, the All-India Republican Party.

Regional movements have been many, among the best-known of which are the Maharashtrian anti-Brahmin movement under the leadership of Jotirao Phule in the 1870s, a largely middle-caste Maratha movement, and in the same area an emancipation movement among untouchable Mahars which matured into the above-mentioned Scheduled Caste Federation under Ambedkar.[63]

Innumerable local and regional movements, primarily in urban centers, have arisen whose aim has been to emancipate the members of a caste or cluster of castes, to force public recognition of higher status for a caste, or to ameliorate their caste-based disabilities through solidarity and political action.[64] There can be little doubt that contemporary revolutionary parties and movements in India depend to a significant extent on their appeal to oppressed castes whose members see them as vehicles to emancipation.

In addition to these sophisticated efforts at emancipation, upward mobility movements among low castes are endemic to all regions of India, and have evidently been so throughout its history. These movements entail a claim to high status that has not been recognized. They co-ordinate and enforce among the members of a caste emulation of the behaviours and attributes of high castes in the hope that this will result in public recognition of the claim. This process has been termed 'Sanskritization', in recognition of the fact that the behaviours adopted are often those prescribed for high castes in the sacred Sanskrit literature.[65] Emulation alone, however, no matter how successfully done, is not enough to confer status, for status in a caste system is not based on behaviour but on birth. To change the societal definition of a caste's status requires a concerted, sustained, and powerful group effort, and it is most often unsuccessful.

In addition, as Harold Isaacs has documented in *India's Ex-Untoucha-bles*, individuals occasionally escape the consequences of their caste status into rewarding caste-free occupations in cities, often as a result of education and sometimes by the successful concealment of their caste identities (passing). In rural areas, some people emigrate to cities to escape the disabilities of their caste status; some cluster together in low-caste communities to avoid daily contact with, and humiliation by, their caste superiors; a few are able to acquire a degree of exemption at the cost of conventional family life through adoption of non-priestly religious roles or resort to various socially deviant identities.[66]

Japan: Publicly recognized emancipation movements among the Burakumin of Japan have been many, militant, and frequently violent following the official Edict of Emancipation of 1871. They have been so well documented and conveniently summarized by Totten and Wagatsuma that to repeat the information would be superfluous. Wagatsuma has carried the chronology of political militance through the post-World War II period, and has also documented non-political, religious, and educational approaches to amelioration of Burakumin oppression.[67] The similarities to emancipation efforts in India and the United States are little short of uncanny. The occurrence and problems of 'passing' among Burakumin, and the limited rewards to be acquired through educational, occupational, and residential mobility are closely parallel to those reported for India and the United States.[68]

Ruanda: In Ruanda and nearby Urundi, the dominant Tutsi seemed until fifteen years ago to be in firm control, with the subordinate Hutu and Twa relegated to dependent economic and political roles.[69] But this proves to have been a false calm. In 1957, while Ruanda was still part of the Belgian trust territory of Ruanda-Urundi, the Jutu issued the Bahutu Manifesto which initiated an emancipation movement. Opposing political parties then arose, advocating Hutu revolution on the one hand and Tutsi supremacy on the other. The brutality of the latter unleashed a successful Hutu revolution in 1959, in which most of the Tutsi were driven from the country. The resultant Hutu government was confirmed when the emancipation party won overwhelmingly in a plebiscite in 1961. That party was in power when Ruanda became independent Rwanda in 1962, and has remained so despite frequent incursions by Tutsi from across the Rwanda borders. In the adjacent kingdom of Burundi (formerly Urundi and part of the same trust territory), the Hutu emancipation movement was suppressed by the Tutsi-dominated government after independence in 1962, and inter-caste tension thereafter increased. When the Hutu won a majority of governmental seats in the election of 1965, the king refused to name the majority government. This lead to an unsuccessful Hutu coup, put down by the army, after which most of the Hutu leadership was shot. These Hutu emancipation efforts were perhaps a surprise to the Tutsi overlords, but they came as no surprise to any serious student of birth-ascribed oppression, for such systems are always fraught with tension and resentment which await only a belief in the possibility of success for drastic change to be attempted from below.

Henry Adams characterized the slave society of Virginia in 1800, as 'ill at ease'.[70] This seems to be the chronic state of societies so organized—the privileged cannot relax their vigilance against the rebellious resentment of the deprived. That such rigid, oppressive systems do function and persist is a credit not to the consensus they engender any more than to the justice or rationality of the systems. Rather, it is a tribute to the effectiveness of the monopoly on power which the privileged are able to maintain. When in such systems deprived people get the vote, get jobs, get money, get legal redress, get guns, get powerful allies, get public support for their aspirations, they perceive a change in the power situation and an enhancement of the likelihood of successful change in their situation, and they are likely to attempt to break out of their oppressed status. These conditions do not generate the desire for change, for that is intrinsic; they merely make it seem worthwhile to attempt the change. Sometimes the triggering factor is not that the deprived believe conditions have changed so that success is more likely, but rather that conditions have led them to define the risk and consequences of failure (even its virtual certainty) as acceptable. Resultant changes are often drastic and traumatic of achievement, but they are sought by the oppressed and by enlightened people of all statuses precisely because of the heavy individual and societal costs of maintaining inherited inequality and because of its inherent inhumanity.

An important difference between the dynamics of inherited stratification and acquired stratification results from the fact that in the latter, power and privilege accompany achievable status, emulation is at least potentially effective, and mobility and assimilation are realistic goals. Therefore energies of status resentment may rationally be channelled toward mobility. Most immigrant groups in the United States, for example, have found this out as they have merged with the larger society after one or two generations of socialization. But in a system where inherited, unalterable group identity is the basis for rewards, emulation alone cannot achieve upward mobility, and assimilation is impossible so long as the system exists (in fact, prevention of assimilation is one of its main functions). Only efforts to destroy, alter, or circumvent the system make sense. In the United States, blacks, Chicanos, and Native Americans have found this out. Only in response to changes in the distribution of power is such inherited status likely to be re-evaluated and the distribution of rewards altered.

Conclusion

'Race' as the term is used in America, Europe, and South Africa, is not qualitatively different in its implications for human social life from caste, *varna*, or *jati* as applied in India, *quom* in Swat and Muslim India, the 'invisible race' of Japan, the ethnic stratification of Rwanda and Burundi. Racism and casteism are indistinguishable in the annals of man's inhumanity to man, and sexism is closely allied to them as man's inhumanity to woman. All are invidious distinctions imposed unalterably at birth upon whole categories of people to justify the unequal social distribution of power, livelihood, security, privilege, esteem, freedom—in short, life chances. Where distinctions of this type are employed, they affect people and the events which people generate in surprisingly similar ways despite the different historical and cultural conditions in which they occur.

If I were asked, 'What practical inference, if any, is to be drawn from the comparative study of inherited inequality—of ascriptive social ranking?' I would say it is this: There is no way to reform such institutions; the only solution is their dissolution. As Kardiner and Ovesey said long ago *'there is only one way that the products of oppression can be dissolved, and that is to stop the oppression'*.[71] To stop the oppression, one must eliminate the structure of inherited stratification upon which it rests. Generations of Burakumin, Hutu, blacks, untouchables, and their sympathizers have tried reform without notable success. Effective change has come only when the systems have been challenged directly.

The boiling discontent of birth-ascribed deprivation cannot be contained by pressing down the lid of oppression or by introducing token flexibility, or by preaching brotherly love. The only hope lies in restructuring society and redistributing its rewards so as to end the inequality. Such behavioural change must come first. From it may follow attitudinal changes as meaningful, status-equal interaction undermines racist, casteist, communalist, and sexist beliefs and attitudes, but oppressed people everywhere have made it clear that it is the end of oppression, not brotherly love, which they seek most urgently. To await the latter before achieving the former is futility; to achieve the former first does not guarantee achievement of the latter, but it increases the chances and makes life liveable. In any case, the unranked pluralism which many minorities seek requires only equality, not love.

To those who fear this course on the grounds that it will be traumatic and dangerous, I would say that it is less so than the futile attempt to prevent change. Philip Mason spoke for all systems of inborn inequality when he called the Spartan oppression of the Helots in ancient Greece a trap from which there was no escape.

It was the Helots who released the Spartans from such ignoble occupations as trade and agriculture.... But it was the Helots who made it necessary to live in an armed camp, constantly on the alert against revolt.... They had a wolf by the ears; they dared not let go. And it was of their own making they had decided—at some stage and by what process one can only guess—that the Helots would remain separate and without rights forever.[72]

That way, I believe, lies ultimate disaster for any society. A thread of hope lies in the possibility that people can learn from comparison of the realities of inherited inequality across space, time, and culture, and can act to preclude the disaster that has befallen others by eliminating the system which guarantees it. It is a very thin thread.

References

1. Max Weber, *From Max Weber: Essays in Sociology*, H. H. Gerth and C. W. Mills trans. and ed. (New York, Oxford University Press, 1946); W. G. Runciman, 'Class, Status and Power?', in *Social Stratification*, J. A. Jackson, ed. (London, Cambridge University Press, 1968), pp. 25-61.

2. See for Ruanda: Jacques J. Maquet, *The Premise of Inequality in Ruanda* (London, Oxford University Press, 1961); for India: F. G. Bailey, 'Closed Social Stratification in India', *European Journal of Sociology* (Vol. IV, 1963); Gerald D. Berreman, 'Caste: The Concept', in *International Encyclopedia of the Social Sciences*, D. Sills, ed. (New York, Macmillan and The Free Press, 1968), Vol. II, pp. 333-9; André Béteille, *Castes Old and New* (Bombay, Asia Publishing House, 1969); Louis Dumont, *Homo Hierarchicus* (London, Weidenfeld and Nicolson, 1970); J. H. Hutton, *Caste in India, Its Nature, Functions and Origins* (London, Cambridge University Press, 1946); Adrian C. Mayer, 'Caste: The Indian Caste System', in D. Sills, ed., op. cit., pp. 339-44; M. N. Srinivas, *Caste in Modern India and Other Essays* (Bombay, Asia Publishing House, 1962), and *Social Change in Modern India* (Berkeley, University of California Press, 1966); for Swat: Fredrik Barth, 'The System of Social Stratification in Swat, North Pakistan', in *Aspects of Caste in South India, Ceylon and North-West Pakistan*, E. Leach, ed. (London, Cambridge University Press, 1960), pp. 113-48; for Japan: George DeVos and Hiroshi Wagatsuma, eds., *Japan's Invisible Race: Caste in Culture and Personality* (Berkeley, University of California Press, 1966); Shigeaki Ninomiya, 'An Inquiry Concerning the Origin, Development and Present Situation of the *Eta* in Relation to the History of Social Classes in Japan', *The Transactions of the Asiatic Society of Japan* (Second series, Vol. 10, 1933); cf. Herbert Passin, 'Untouchability in the Far East', *Monumenta Nipponica* (Vol. 2, No. 3, 1955); for the United States: Allison Davis, B. B. Gardner, and M. R. Gardner, *Deep South: A Social Anthropological Study of Caste and Class* (Chicago, The University of Chicago Press, 1941); John Dollard, *Caste and Class in a Southern Town* (Garden City, New York, Doubleday, 1957); Gunnar Myrdal, *An American Dilemma: The Negro Problem in Modern Democracy* (New York, Harper, 1944); Alphonso Pinkney, *Black Americans* (Englewood Cliffs, New Jersey, Prentice-Hall, 1969); Peter I. Rose, ed., *Americans from Africa*, Vol. 1: *Slavery and its Aftermath* and Vol. II: *Old Memories, New Moods* (New York, Atherton Press, 1970). See also contrasts with South Africa: Pierre van den Berghe, *South Africa, a Study in Conflict* (Berkeley, University of California Press, 1967); Latin America: Marvin Harris, *Patterns of Race in the Americas* (New York, Walker, 1964); Julian Pitt-Rivers, 'Race, Color and Class in Central America and the Andes', *Daedalus*

(Spring, 1967); the Caribbean: M. G. Smith, *The Plural Society in the British West Indies* (Berkeley, University of California Press, 1965). G. D. Berreman, *Caste in the Modern World* (New York, General Learning Press, forthcoming).

3. Dumont, op. cit.

4. Gerald D. Berreman, 'A Brahmanical View of Caste: Louis Dumont's *Homo Hierarchicus*', *Contributions to Indian Sociology* (New Series, No. V, 1972).

5. Tamotsu Shibutani and Kian M. Kwan, *Ethnic Stratification: A Comparative Approach* (New York, Macmillan, 1965), p. 572.

6. H. S. Morris, 'Ethnic Groups', in D. Sills, ed., op. cit., Vol. 5, p. 167.

7. Pierre van den Berghe, 'The Benign Quota: Panacea or Pandora's Box', *The American Sociologist* (Vol. 6, Supplementary Issue, June 1971).

8. Ibid., p. 43.

9. Cf. Robert Blauner, 'Black Culture: Myth or Reality?', in Rose, *Old Memories, New Moods*, pp. 417–43.

10. Gerald D. Berreman, 'Caste in India and the United States', *The American Journal of Sociology* (Vol. LXVI, September, 1960); cf. Berreman, 'A Brahmanical View of Caste . . .'; op. cit.

11. Oliver C. Cox, 'Race and Caste: A Distinction', *The American Journal of Sociology* (Vol. L, March, 1945); cf. Oliver C. Cox, *Caste, Class and Race* (Garden City, New York, Doubleday, 1948).

12. Arthur R. Jensen, 'How Much Can We Boost I.Q. and Scholastic Achievement?', *Harvard Educational Review* (Vol. 39, No. 1, Winter, 1969).

13. See the various articles comprising the 'Discussion', of Jensen's article in *Harvard Educational Review* (Vol. 39, No. 2, Spring, 1969).

14. E. A. Ross, *Social Psychology* (New York, Macmillan, 1914), p. 3.

15. Shibutani and Kwan, op. cit., p. 37.

16. Ibid., p. 110.

17. Pierre van den Berghe, *Race and Racism* (New York, Wiley, 1967), p. 21.

18. Claude Lévi-Strauss, 'The Bear and the Barber', *Journal of the Royal Anthropological Institute* (Vol. 93, Part 1, 1963).

19. Winthrop D. Jordan, *White Over Black* (Baltimore, Penguin Books, 1969), p. 137–8.

20. Cox, *Caste, Class and Race*, p. 433, cf. Berreman, 'Caste in India and the United States', op. cit.; Berreman, 'A Brahmanical View of Caste . . .'; op. cit.; Gerald D. Berreman, 'Caste, Racism and "Stratification" ', *Contributions to Indian Sociology* (No. VI, December 1962); Martin Orans, 'Caste and Race Conflict in Cross-Cultural Perspective', in *Race, Change and Urban Society*, P. Orleans and W. R. Ellis, eds., comprising *Urban Affairs Annual Reviews* (Vol. 5, 1971).

21. Dumont, op. cit., Cox, *Caste, Class and Race*.

22. Berreman, 'Caste in India and the United States', op. cit., Gerald D. Berreman, 'Caste in Cross-Cultural Perspective: Organizational Components' comprising Chapter 14, 'Structure and Function of Caste Systems', and Chapter 15, 'Concomitants of Caste Organization', in *Japan's Invisible Race*, DeVos and Wagatsuma, eds., op. cit.; Gerald D. Berreman, 'Stratification, Pluralism and

Interaction: A Comparative Analysis of Caste', in *Caste and Race: Comparative Approaches*, A. de Reuck and J. Knight, eds., (London, J. and A. Churchill, 1967); Orans, op. cit.

23. Cf., Berreman, 'Caste in Cross-Cultural Perspective . . .' op. cit., pp. 279–81.

24. F. G. Bailey, 'Closed Social Stratification in India', op. cit., p. 113.

25. Cf., George DeVos and Hiroshi Wagatsuma, 'Group Solidarity and Individual Mobility' in *Japan's Invisible Race*, pp. 245–8; Harold R. Isaacs, *India's Ex-Untouchables* (New York, John Day Company, 1965), pp. 143–9 et passim.

26. Gerald D. Berreman, *Hindus of the Himalayas: Ethnography and Change* (Berkeley, University of California Press, 1972), pp. 200 ff.

27. Robert Blauner, 'Internal Colonialism and Ghetto Revolt', *Social Problems* (Vol. 16, No. 4, Spring, 1969); Robert Blauner, *Racial Oppression in America* (New York, Harper and Row, 1972).

28. Cf., Blauner, 'Internal Colonialism . . .', op. cit.; Stokely Carmichael and Charles Hamilton, *Black Power* (New York, Random House, 1967); Frantz Fanon, *The Wretched of the Earth* (New York, Grove Press, 1966); O. Mannoni, *Prospero and Caliban: The Psychology of Colonization* (New York, Praeger, 1956); Albert Memmi, *The Colonizer and the Colonized* (Boston, Beacon Press, 1967).

29. Cf. Blauner, 'Internal Colonialism . . .'p. 395-6.

30. Gerald D. Berreman, 'Caste as Social Process', *Southwestern Journal of Anthropology* (Vol. 23, No. 4, Winter, 1967); Blauner, *Racial Oppression in America*; S. F. Nadei, 'Caste and Government in Primitive Society', *Journal of the Anthropological Society of Bombay* (Vol. 8, 1954); J. S. Furnivall, *Colonial Policy and Practice: A Comparative Study of Burma and Netherlands India* (London, Cambridge University Press, 1948); M. G. Smith, *The Plural Society in the British West Indies* (Berkeley, University of California Press, 1965); James B. Watson, 'Caste as a Form of Acculturation', *Southwestern Journal of Anthropology* (Vol. 19, No. 4, Winter 1963).

31. Cf. Irawati Karve, *Hindu Society: An Interpretation* (Poona, Deccan College Postgraduate and Research Institute, 1961).

32. Davis, Gardner, and Gardner, op. cit.; St. Clair Drake and Horace R. Cayton, *Black Metropolis* (New York, Harcourt, Brace, 1945); Dollard, op. cit.; Marina Wikramanayake, 'Caste and Class Among Free Afro-Americans in Ante-bellum South Carolina', paper delivered before the 70th Annual Meeting of the American Anthropological Association (New York, November 1971).

33. Furnivall, op. cit.; cf. Malcolm Cross, ed., *Special Issue on Race and Pluralism, Race* (Vol. XII, No. 4, April 1971).

34. M. G. Smith, op. cit., pp. 14, 83.

35. Berreman 'Stratification, Pluralism and Interaction . . .', op. cit., p. 51.

36. M. G. Smith. op. cit., p. xi.

37. Berreman, 'Stratification, Pluralism and Interaction . . .', op. cit., p. 55.

38. Cf. Furnivall, op. cit.

39. Berreman, 'Stratification, Pluralism and Interaction . . .', op. cit., p. 55.

40. Ibid., cf. McKim Marriott, 'Interactional and Attributional Theories of Caste Ranking', *Man in India* (Vol. 39, 1959).

41. Maya Angelou, *I Know Why the Caged Birds Sings* (New York, Bantam Books, 1971), p. 168.

42. Cf. Berreman, 'Caste in India and the United States', op. cit.

43. Berreman, 'Stratification, Pluralism and Interaction . . .', op. cit., p. 51.

44. Dumont, op. cit.

45. Cf. Berreman, 'Caste in India and the United States', op. cit.; Berreman, 'Caste in Cross-Cultural Perspective . . .', op. cit.; Gerald D. Berreman, 'Social Categories and Social Interaction in Urban India', *American Anthropologist* (Vol. 74, No. 3).

46. Cf. Berreman, 'A Brahmanical View of Caste . . .', op. cit.

47. Kate Millett, *Sexual Politics* (New York, Avon Books, 1971), p. 19.

48. Casey Hayden and Mary King, 'Sex and Caste', *Liberation* (April, 1966), p. 35; cf. Millett, op. cit.

49. Fran Hawthorne, 'Female Roles Examined by Rutgers Professors', *Daily Californian* (Berkeley, 6 October, 1971), p. 5. See also Millett, op. cit., p. 57, for a summary of the common psychological traits and adaptational mechanisms attributed to blacks and women in American society as reported in three recent sociological accounts.

50. Cf. G. Morris Carstairs, *The Twice-Born* (Bloomington, Indiana University Press, 1958), pp. 59–62 *et passim*; Morris E. Opler, 'The Hijarä (Hermaphrodites) of India and Indian National Character: A Rejoinder', *American Anthropologist* (Vol. 62, No. 3, June, 1960).

51. Gerald D. Berreman, 'Women's Roles and Politics: India and the United States', in *Readings in General Sociology*, R. W. O'Brien, C. C. Schrag, and W. T. Martin, eds., (4th Edition, Boston, Houghton Mifflin Co., 1969). First published, 1966. Cf. Millett, op. cit.

52. van den Berghe, *Race and Racism*, op. cit., p. 22.

53. Berreman, 'Stratification, Pluralism and Interaction . . .', op. cit., p. 58.

54. Abram Kardiner and Lionel Ovesey, *Mark of Oppression* (Cleveland, The World Publishing Co., 1962), p. 387.

55. Robert Coles, *Children of Crisis* (Boston, Atlantic-Little, Brown, 1964); with Jon Erikson, *The Middle Americans* (Boston, Little, Brown, 1971).

56. Berreman, 'Stratification, Pluralism and Interaction . . .', op. cit., Cf. Thomas F. Pettigrew, *A Profile of the Negro American* (Princeton, D. Van Nostrand, 1964); Stanley M. Elkins, *Slavery* (Chicago, University of Chicago Press, 1959); Mina Davis Caulfield, 'Slavery and the Origins of Black Culture: Elkins Revisited', in *Americans From Africa: Slavery and Its Aftermath*, P. I. Rose, ed., J. H. Rohrer and M. S. Edmonson, *The Eighth Generation Grows Up* (New York, Harper and Row, 1960).

57. Santokh S. Anant, 'Child Training and Caste Personality: The Need for Further Research', *Race* (Vol. VIII, No. 4, 1967); Santokh S. Anant, *Inter-Caste Attitudes* (provisional title), (Delhi, Vikas Publications, 1972); K. K. Singh, *Patterns of Caste Tension* (Bombay, Asia Publishing House, 1967); DeVos and Wagatsuma, op. cit.

58. Kardiner and Ovesey, op. cit., p. 379.

59. B. G. Gallagher, *American Caste and the Negro College* (New York, Columbia University Press, 1938), p. 109.

60. Berreman, 'Caste as Social Process', op. cit.

61. Raymond Bauer and Alice Bauer, 'Day to Day Resistance to Slavery', *Journal of Negro History* (Vol. 27, October 1942); Douglas Scott, 'The Negro and the Enlisted Man: An Analogy', *Harpers* (October 1962), pp. 20–1; cf. Berreman, 'Caste in India and the United States', op. cit.

62. Cf. Carmichael and Hamilton, *op. cit.*; Eldridge Cleaver, *Soul on Ice* (New York, Dell Publishing Co., 1968); E. U. Essien-Udom, *Black Nationalism* (New York, Dell Publishing Co., 1962); Lewis M. Killian, *The Impossible Revolution? Black Power and The American Dream* (New York, Random House, 1968); Martin Luther King, *Stride Toward Freedom* (New York, Harper Brothers, 1958); C. Eric Lincoln, *The Black Muslims in America* (Boston, Beacon Press, 1962); Louis E. Lomax, *The Negro Revolt* (New York, New American Library, 1962); Raymond J. Murphy and Howard Elinson, *Problems and Prospects of the Negro Movement* (Belmont, California, Wadsworth, 1966); Pinkney, op. cit.; Rose, op. cit.; Charles E. Silberman, *Crisis in Black and White* (New York, Random House, 1964); Stan Steiner, *The New Indians* (New York, Harper and Row, 1968); Stan Steiner, *La Raza: The Mexican Americans* (New York, Harper and Row, 1970); Howard Zinn, *S.N.C.C., The New Abolitionists* (Boston, Beacon Press, 1964).

63. Charles H. Heimsath, *Indian Nationalism and Hindu Social Reform* (Princeton, Princeton University Press, 1964); Owen M. Lynch, *The Politics of Untouchability* (New York, Columbia University Press, 1969); Gail Omvedt, 'Jotirao Phule and the Ideology of Social Revolution in India' (Dept. of Sociology, University of California, Berkeley, 1971), mimeographed paper; cf. B. R. Ambedkar, *The Untouchables: Who were They and why They became Untouchables* (New Delhi, Amrit Book Co., 1948); B. R. Ambedkar, *What Congress and Gandhi have done to the Untouchables* (Bombay, Thacker and Co., 1946); B. R. Ambedkar, *Annihilation of Caste* (Bombay, Bharat Bhusan Press, 1945).

64. Orans, op. cit.; Martin Orans, *The Santal: A Tribe in Search of a Great Tradition* (Detroit, Wayne State University Press, 1965); Lloyd I. Rudolph and Susan H. Rudolph, 'The Political Role of India's Caste Associations', *Pacific Affairs* (Vol. 33, 1960); James Silverberg, ed., *Social Mobility in the Caste System in India, Supplement III: Comparative Studies in Society and History* (The Hague, Mouton, 1968).

65. M. N. Srinivas, *Caste in Modern India and Other Essays* (Bombay, Asia Publishing House, 1962), pp. 42-62; M. N. Srinivas, *Social Change in Modern India* (Berkeley, University of California Press, 1966), pp. 1–45.

66. Cf. Berreman, *Hindus of the Himalayas*, Epilogue, 'Sirkanda Ten Years Later'.

67. George O. Totten and Hiroshi Wagatsuma, 'Emancipation: Growth and Transformation of a Political Movement', in DeVos and Wagatsuma, op. cit., pp. 33–67; Hiroshi Wagatsuma, 'Postwar Political Militance', and 'Non-Political Approaches: The Influences of Religion and Education', in DeVos and Wagatsuma, op. cit., pp. 68–109.

68. George DeVos and Hiroshi Wagatsuma, 'Group Solidarity and Individual Mobility', in DeVos and Wagatsuma, op. cit., pp. 245-56.

69. Maquet, op. cit.

70. Henry Adams, *The United States in 1800* (Ithaca, New York, Cornell University Press, 1961), p. 98.

71. Kardiner and Ovesey, op. cit., p. 387.

72. Philip Mason, *Patterns of Dominance* (London, Oxford University Press for the Institute of Race Relations, 1970), p. 75.

30

Telltale Language: Race, Class, and Inequality in Two Latin American Towns

ANGELA GILLIAM

Language as Mirror of Society

WHAT DO POPULAR PHRASES reveal about society? For one thing, they can give clues to the student of anthropology about how a society is organized, what values and beliefs are held to be important, and how rewards and punishments are distributed in that culture. That is, common phrases expose the powerful and the powerless as well. The reason for this is that language is an integral part of culture, and culture represents behavior and values that are both learned from and shared with other people. A phrase is popular or common by virtue of its wide circulation in a society.

Language can also inform the careful listener about personal attitudes and how the beliefs of individuals reflect the collective thinking of the society as a whole. Hence, phrases that define values about beauty and ugliness, poverty and wealth, social legitimacy and marginality have significant social meaning. When these values merge with attitudes about race, ethnicity, class, and gender, the structure of the society is revealed. Thus, the social relations among various sectors of that culture are manifest within the language.

Sometimes, power and status—or lack of same—is carried in the pronunciation of the language, choice of vocabulary, or the structure of language itself. For example, in the Western hemisphere, use of Indian-influenced pronunciation or words of Indian origin may signal to the listener that the speaker has low social status. That person will experience social treatment different from that received by a person whose speech is identified with the ruling elite. Moreover, these types of linguistic factors are often accompanied by paralinguistic elements that also mark class or ethnic identity. The way hands, head, and the rest of the body are used while talking can disclose cultural meaning as well.

This chapter compares some of the terms and phrases that are the telltale signs of social inequality in both Pinotepa Nacional on the southwestern coast of Mexico and Salvador, Bahia, in the Brazilian Northeast. These phrases divulge historical, racial, and socioeconomic stratification and are rooted in the colonial plantation past.

Reinterpreting the Double Heritage of Slavery and Colonialism

Increasingly, Mexicans, Brazilians, and other Latin American peoples are reassessing the double heritage of colonialism and slavery. Conventionally, many scholars of Brazilian or Mexican colonial plantation systems overlook the signs of hierarchy and stratification still remaining in those societies. The strength of official concepts like "Brazilian racial democracy" or "Mexican assimilation" then become difficult to modify with new interpretation of the data. One cause of this is that some social scientists assert that slavery in Luso-Iberian (Portuguese and Spanish) America was less brutal than that of Anglo-Saxon America and therefore led to more social and ethnic integration. The extensive miscegenation in Latin America is frequently used as evidence of this theory. And, plantation social science in Brazil, led by the Gilberto Freyre school of thought, holds that the Portuguese man built a society in the tropics through "his" creation of the *mulata*, the mixed-race woman. Such an analysis ignores the role of the indigenous or slave woman in the development of the nation and national culture. In any colonial plantation system, the slave woman was a participant in the cultural transformation and linguistic transmission to succeeding generations. As shall be seen in another part of this chapter, popular expressions and phrases in both Brazil and Mexico demonstrate that colonial plantation patterns of sexual union can be interpreted as oppression of women rather than as positive examples of ethnic integration.

In Mexico, demographic evidence of the colonial plantation system is principally in the southern coastal regions. The Mexican anthropologist Gonzalo Aguirre Beltrán (1958), renowned for his study of African influences in Mexican society, suggests that the pattern of ethnic interaction in Mexico is characterized by the disappearance of blacks as a differentiated group. In spite of the value of his famous study of the southern Pacific town of Cuijla, it nonetheless reflects the upper-class bias of his informants in the region.

A by-product of the belief that slavery in Latin America was more benign than that in the English-speaking part of the hemisphere is that racism is associated primarily with former British colonies—such as the United States—and is not considered a problem for scholars concerned with Latin America. While patterns of inequality in the United States are acknowledged by many citizens to be a target for national action, many Latin American elites have identified African or Indian physical or cultural characteristics as merely biological or social infirmities for which the remedies are miscegenation or cultural absorption. However, the phrases, terms, and folk expressions that developed in the colonial plantation systems of Brazil and Mexico reveal that the social position of an individual is determined not only by his or her wealth but also by the degree to which European ancestry and a familiarity with European culture are present.

Remnants of Two Different Colonial Plantation Systems

Most of the Western hemisphere was characterized by simultaneous colonialism and slavery from the sixteenth until the nineteenth centuries, with Brazil eliminating slavery as recently as 1888. The system of forced labor, initially of Indian peoples but later predominantly African, was seen as the principal factor that enabled the enrichment and subsequent industrialization of European monarchies.

There are certain similarities between Mexico and Brazil, which were Spanish and Portuguese colonies, respectively. They had both achieved national independence by 1830. As was true of other Latin American countries, state power within the new nations was held by elites who were mostly European in their identity but born in the Western hemisphere. This group frequently had some Indian or African heritage as well, but defined themselves and the new national culture as European-derived, even though the image and the heritage of the Indian *past* was romanticized in the formation of the new state.

In analyzing Latin American societies, some scholars have referred to a triumvirate of power in Latin America composed of church, military, and landowners. Elite Latin American families were expected to commit sons to each of those sectors in order to assure continuity of their social and economic power.

In both Mexico and Brazil, the Indian peoples and descendants of African slaves were relegated to the levels of least prestige and privilege, with their physical *and* cultural traditions used as markers of lower-class status. The double heritage of colonialism and slavery meant the adoption of European languages and cultures as the official culture. Yet, both countries exhibit cultural elements that reveal a blending of many peoples, especially European, Indian, and African. Nonetheless, there are significant differences between the two countries as well as between the towns of this study.

The Brazilian town of Salvador, Bahia, in northeastern Brazil, was the site of one of the earliest and richest colonial plantation systems, as well as one of the first places where sugar was grown in the Americas. The port city of Salvador was also the capital of the Portuguese crown for two centuries, and its past is evident in both the colonial architecture of the city and in its African cultural influences. Modern Salvador has a population of more than a million inhabitants, the majority of whom appear to be of West African origin. As such, popular food, patterns of worship, the Yoruba-based language of the *candomblé* religion, styles of dress, music and dance, and even the self-defense, martial arts dances of *capoeira* and *maculelê* all attest to the African origins of much of contemporary Bahian culture.

Vestiges of indigenous populations are to be found in the interior of the state of Bahia. Indian communities of Brazil were never part of large, populous city-states such as those in Mexico or Peru. When the Portuguese crown established itself in Bahia, the response of many indigenous people was to strategically retreat into the interior where inaccessibility afforded them some protection.

The Indian populations of Mexico however, were renowned for their stratified social organization, densely populated urban centers, and material and technological achievements. During the sixteenth and seventeenth centuries, colonial invasion caused considerable depopulation in a great part of Mexico, including the southern Pacific region of *La Mixteca*, land of the Mixtecan Indians. Although the Indian peoples were the principal laborers and workers of the land throughout the Spanish colony of New Spain, the trade in African people was known in virtually every Spanish possession. Yet, Aguirre Beltrán (1958, 1972) maintains that no more than 250,000 persons entered Mexico as African slaves during the course of the three centuries of the Atlantic slave trade. The southern Pacific region—also known as *La Costa Chica*—where Pinotepa Nacional is located became home to the most hunted of runaway slaves.

Today, there are three distinct types of towns in the region. First, there are the Mixtecan Indian communities; then, there are towns of *morenos* ("dark people"), which is a polite way of referring to blacks. In addition to these two categories, there are larger towns in which it is understood that most of the inhabitants are *mestizos*, or persons of mixed ancestry. However, *mestizos* consider themselves—and are considered by others—to be essentially white. Pinotepa Nacional is just such a *mestizo* center. It functions like a provincial center of trade and exchange as regards the other smaller towns or communities in this region, and individuals in authority in the town maintain positions of regional power. There are no towns of

Mixtecan Indians or *morenos* that function as centers of regional trade. Many of the *moreno* towns are presumed to have had their origin as runaway slave settlements. In addition, even the *morenos* who live in *mestizo* towns say that only *la brosa* ("lowlife") live in *moreno* villages. "Don't go there; *la brosa* will kidnap you" is the warning given to strangers who are traveling to these villages. Some peasant farmers maintain that originally *la brosa* helped poor people to take land from the big landowners, but "now that assistance is not needed because everybody has a plot of land." The fact that even freed slaves were forbidden by decree to own land lends historical context to beliefs about *la brosa*.

The Language of "Whitening" and Becoming "Of Reason"

The study of the phrases of ethnicity applied to women and men illuminates the problem of class and color in Salvador as well as Pinotepa Nacional. There is a popular saying in Brazilian Portuguese that summarizes the basic aspects of ethnicity, class, and gender relations in Bahia: *Preta p'ra trabalhar, branca p'ra casar, e mulata p'ra fornicar* (English translation: [A Brazilian man's idea of heaven on earth is] a black woman to work, a white woman to marry, and a brown-skinned woman as a mistress.) Viewing this saying as a sociological paradigm, the social scientist can clearly imagine the social pressure that exists to *melhorar a raça* ("improve the breed") or *limpar o sangue* ("cleanse the blood") by producing lighter children.

Thus, social mobility is commonly perceived to be based on a process of *embranquecimento* ("whitening"). This can mean straightening very wavy or fluffy hair or selecting a mate who will subsequently help to "improve" the children. Whitening oneself is converted into a type of cultural conditioning through the acquisition of formal education and through constant vigilance in order to avoid Africanisms, real or imagined, linguistic or paralinguistic. Thus, someone concerned with bettering himself or herself would watch carefully phonology (accent) in speech, as well as grammar and the very words chosen for conversation.[1] In addition, one's conduct and behavior would be guarded. These values and perceptions are shared by all social classes and racial groups in Bahian society, even though there is much resistance on the part of blacks and mulattoes to total absorption and internalization of those values.

In Salvador, one hears terms such as *branco da terra* ("home-grown white person") or *branco bahiano* ("Bahian white"). These terms mean "not really white." This also applies to the Bahian words *saruaba* and *sarará*, except that these words specifically describe someone with light-colored eyes, skin, and blonde-to-light-brown hair that is fluffy and with African facial features.

On the other hand, one also hears the Bahian term *nego* ("black one"), a derivative of *negro*, as a term of endearment towards any close friend or relative, irrespective of ethnicity and in its feminine form of *nega* as well. Likewise, the diminutive form, *neguinho*, can be either affectionate or paternalistic, depending on the social context. Yet, the simple descriptive—*negro*—is offensive, as is the augmentative, *negrão*. The latter word translates into English as "big black," is always used to describe a male, and denotes a person who is menacing.

As in Salvador, the word for "black"—*negro*—has an aggressive connotation in *La Costa Chica*. The word *moreno* is euphemistically used instead and has many linguistic derivatives with similar meanings. The augmentative form, *morenote*, means "big, dark one"; the diminutive is *morenito* and can either mean "little, dark one" or be affectionate, in which case the term can soften the cultural significance of the word itself. The repetitive—*moreno moreno*—is emphatic, relates primarily to pigmentation, and means "really dark." All of the above words are either nouns or adjectives, and are sometimes used in the feminine form of *morena* or *morenita* (the augmentative is almost always masculine).

It is commonly accepted that the European-identified *mestizos* who maintain positions of regional power in Pinotepa Nacional are designated by definition as being *gente de razón* ("people of reason"). This is a term that has been used since colonial times to mean "white." Those who consider themselves to be *gente de razón* affirm that neither *morenos* nor Mixtecans can be. *Morenos* in turn consider themselves to be *gente de razón*, but they do not consider the Mixtecans to be. As for the Mixtecans, as long as they speak their language and wear traditional Mixtecan dress, they tolerate other ethnic groups saying that they are not. To be "of reason" is determined by a combination of factors: ethnicity, language, dress, level of education, and financial resources at one's disposal. When a Mixtecan man decides to *abandonar el calzón de manta* ("take off the white pants") and his sandals, he is making a decision to leave an Indian community. He can become *gente de razón* as long as he leaves his village and adopts the social and cultural characteristics of national culture. Nevertheless, he runs the risk of being called an *indio revestido* ("dressed over Indian") or *igualado* ("uppity"—an Indian or dark-skinned man who presumes to be *gente de razón*). On the other hand, the Mixtecan man who no longer uses the white cotton pants, but who still lives in a Mixtecan town, maintains his ethnic identity as a Mixtecan person.[2]

The desire for upward mobility is considered a negative characteristic when found among poor men of Indian or African ancestry in both Salvador and Pinotepa Nacional. The very word *mulato* in Brazilian history has been associated with aggressive goals of self-improvement. The same identification is related to expressions in the Spanish language in Pinotepa Nacional. *Chango vestido* (literally meaning "dressed ape") refers to a *moreno* in expensive clothing; *acotejado* signifies a *moreno* who only associates with women whose skin is lighter than his own.

In the feminine form, the term *mulata* in Brazil has sexual connotations; the brown-skinned woman is the traditional sexual object with the similar projection that the concept of "dumb blonde" receives in the United States.

Terms that define degrees of whiteness also exist in *La Costa Chica* and are embodied in the Mexican Spanish terms *güera sucia* ("dirty blonde"), and *morena limpia* ("clean brunette") which refers to a "dark-skinned" woman with European facial features and straight hair. The concern with blondness is also related to the great number of albinos, who are known in Pinotepa Nacional as *hi jos del sol* ("children of the sun"). Some of the *morena* women interviewed for this study affirmed that they would have preferred to be albinos, partly because albinos generally had Indian features and hair. In addition, some *morena* women also admitted that they would prefer to have illegitimate children by a man who was *gente de razón* than be married to a man who was very *moreno*. This value has cultural meaning since television, magazines, and advertisements promote the notion of the blonde woman as the physical ideal. Indeed, one famous Mexican beer commercial refers to *rubias de cateqoría* ("blondes of quality"). One of the consequences of colonialist values is that the models of humanity and beauty are different from the actual appearance of the majority of the people who actually reside in a given locale.

Hair is one of the most important indices of ethnicity in all parts of the hemisphere. The terms "good hair" in English, *cabelo bom* in Portuguese, and *pelo bueno* in Spanish, mean hair that resembles European hair. In Latin America, it does not mean very straight hair; Indian women are also pressured to feel that very straight hair like theirs cannot be "good." However, "bad hair," *cabelo ruim* or *pelo malo*, means hair that indicates African ancestry. A pejorative term for very wavy or fluffy hair in Pinotepa Nacional is *chanda*, and like other parts of the hemisphere, represents more social pressure on the woman than on the man. Recently, young people from Salvador have been resisting this concept and use terms like *cabelo afro* or *blequepau* (a word derived from the English "black power") to be positive phrases for fluffy hair.

The underlying cultural significance of many of these terms relates to marriage choice and patterns of choosing the parents of one's children.

Interracial Unions and Conflicts

There are two primary patterns of interethnic sexual union between men and women in Salvador and Pinotepa Nacional. The most common pattern of union across ethnic boundaries historically is the one in which a man from the dominant sector exercises control over a woman from a subordinate group. Women from poor families in Latin America rarely have the option of refusing advances by elite men or from their employers. This is especially true when official culture assumes that such overtures are proper, socially sanctioned behavior. That this process has been a manifestation of inequality in the structure of Latin American societies is reflected in the common phrases and expressions used by many in both Salvador and Pinotepa Nacional. Even marriage choice in stratified societies becomes a way of mediating the requirements for social approval set by those in power.

Another example of interethnic sexual union occurs in Pinotepa Nacional when the Mixtecan woman marries or lives with a *moreno* man. Many believe that marrying a *moreno* man is the only way for a Mixtecan woman to become *gente de razón*. Even then, it is primarily her children who will have different status. This process has deep roots in the culture. Davidson (1973), in his work on slave rebellions in Mexico, cites a letter sent to Felipe I and written by the viceroy in 1574, in which the former specifies that "indigenous women prefer to marry with black men and not with indigenous men, and neither more nor less, black men prefer to marry indigenous women rather than black women, since in this way their children will be free." And Aguirre Beltrán (1958, 1972) has demonstrated that marriage or cohabitation among the blacks in Mexico was usually prohibited by the slave owners who, following the Church, fixed days and hours for conjugal union with the view to controlling sin and adultery. Thus, the bases, not only of the historical relations among Indians and *morenos* but also of the very structure of marriage and conjugal unions, are related to questions of power and control.

The Mixtecan woman who marries a non-Mixtecan man has a difficult decision; she not only relinquishes a culture but family and kinship networks. (Mixtecan men rarely marry exogamously.) This pattern of union has also been one of the reasons for the delicate coexistence between Indian and *moreno* villages. The children of such unions only have contact with the father's family, creating a situation of one-sided lineage and kinship affiliation.[3] In addition, the history of tense relations between Mixtecan and *moreno* villages stems from the fact that descendants of slaves worked as overseers of Indian laborers for big landowners in the region.

Although *morenos* and Indians often denigrate the other, all manner of social relations exist between members of both groups. In addition, the two groups have been in a similar relationship to power and property in spite of the historically generated antagonisms.

Conclusion

There is an interdependence in Latin America between the social structure of society and the nature of interethnic bonding and sexual unions, as

Martinez-Alier (1974) has noted. This relationship is visible in the common expressions, phrases, and terms that are part of the attitudes, beliefs, and values expressed in both Spanish and Portuguese. The language thus reveals that often black and indigenous women and men feel social pressure to marry exogamously in order to further their future children's access to the resources in the places where they live and work. Furthermore, when carried out across class and power boundaries, some interethnic bonding reflects exploitation, not voluntary ethnic integration, as the phrases and folk language demonstrate. It exemplifies the extent and nature of the existing inequality.

Notes

1. One of the cultural aspects of society in *La Costa Chica* is described as *hablar payo* ("speak country"). The adjective *payo* refers to Africanized impact on phonology, or accent. As on the Mexican Atlantic Coast and in the Spanish-speaking Caribbean, the \s\ sound is suppressed or muted before consonants. Moreover, there is a lexicon, or vocabulary, that is peculiar to the region which is also identified as *hablar payo*. For example, the term *mba*, most likely of Bantu origin in South Central Africa, is given the conjunction of \m\ and \b\ as initial consonant cluster. In *La Costa Chica*, this word means "umhmm" and is used to accompany conversation as an indication of listening. Such linguistic influences are often seen as negative, however, and one member of a powerful family in Pinotepa Nacional explained that *morenos* deform the "civilized languages" that they try to speak. Thus, the *morenos*, especially the peasant ones, manifest a certain linguistic insecurity on speaking with a person who is considered to be wealthy and *gente de razón*.

2. This was the situation of two of the teachers of the *Centro Coordinador Indigenista* ("Coordinating Indian Center") who refused to relinquish their Mixtecan identity, even though their employment as teachers facilitated the process of wearing urban attire. For these two men, their very responsibilities on the job—teaching Mixtecan children to speak Spanish—produced psychosocial problems. They both felt that they were functioning as deculturizing agents for Mixtecan youth. The teachers saw themselves trapped in the dilemma that is so familiar to many dominated peoples: They must learn the language of the ruling elite in order to get employment, but with each additional year of formal education, they feel progressively more isolated from the community of their childhood.

3. The family that adopted the author during the field experience was just such an interethnic, kinship situation. The mother—a Mixtecan Indian—said that she wanted to give her children the best of the Mixtecan and *moreno* worlds. Upon marriage, she went to live in a *moreno* village, her children knew only one group of relatives, and she did not like to talk about her family or the village that she left. She always affirmed that she had made a happy marriage.

Bibliography

AQUIRRE BELTRÁN, GONZALO. 1972. "La Población Negra de México." Mexico: Fondo de Cultura Económica: 248–259.

———. 1958. *Cuijla*. Mexico: Fondo de Cultura Económica.

BECKFORD, GEORGE. 1972. *Persistent Poverty: Underdevelopment in Plantation Economies of the Third World*. New York: Oxford University Press.

DAVIDSON, DAVID. 1973. "Negro Slave Control and Resistance in Colonial Mexico 1519–1650," in *Maroon Societies*, R. Price, ed. Garden City, N.Y.: Anchor Books.

FONTAINE, PIERRE MICHEL (ed.). 1986. *Race, Class, and Power in Brazil*. Los Angeles: University of California, Los Angeles, Center for Afro-American Studies.

GONZALEZ-CASANOVA, PABLO. 1960. *Democracy in Mexico*. New York: Oxford University Press: 67–120.

GONZALEZ-OBREGÓN, LUIS. 1951. *Rebeliones Indígenas y Precursores de la Independencia Mexicana*. México: Ediciones Fuente Cultural.

MARTINEZ-ALIER, VERENA. 1974. *Marriage, Class and Colour in Nineteenth Century Cuba*. Cambridge, Mass.: Cambridge University Press.

WARMAN, ARTURO. 1970. "Todos Santos y Todos Difuntos," in *De Eso Que Llaman la Antropología Mexicana*, A. Warman, M. Nolasco, *et al.*, eds. México: Editorial Nuestro Tiempo: 9–38.

31

Women in Cuba: The Revolution Within the Revolution

JOHNNETTA B. COLE

> And if they were to ask what the most revolutionary aspect of this Revolution is, we'd tell them that the most revolutionary aspect is the revolution that is taking place among the women in our country.
>
> Fidel Castro, December 10, 1966
> Congress of the Federation of Cuban Women

FOR THOSE OF US who live in the Americas, and perhaps on a global scale, the situation among Cuban women today presents, in sharp relief, the complexities, the problems, and the possibilities for the genuine liberation of women. The cultures, histories, and current realities of Third World women involve a range of differences, and yet there are common bases of oppression, whether the physical setting and time period are Alabama in 1860, Cuba in 1958, Mozambique in 1970, or India in 1978. Without denying the influence, and indeed the importance, of tradition and culture, and without minimizing the pain that women can feel from bigoted attitudes and behavior, we can say with overwhelming evidence that the condition of women in a society is fundamentally a reflection of economic structures and relationships. The 1959 Revolution, by radically changing the economic organization of Cuban society, destroyed the overall material basis of inequalities, including the inequalities suffered by women. That revolution did not instantly provide the material means for full incorporation of women into the productive, political, and cultural life of the nation. And that revolution did not (and no revolution can) immediately wipe away centuries old myths and attitudes concerning the "proper places" for men and women. In short, the 1959 Cuban Revolution presented, for the first time, the *possibility* for all women in Cuba to fully share the rewards and responsibilities of their society.

In this brief chapter, we will contrast the conditions of Cuban women in the 1950s before the revolution with the years after, indicating the accomplishments as well as problem areas that still exist.

Before the Revolution

Before the Revolution of 1959 life for the majority of Cuba's people conformed to the patterns that are repeated in poor, underdeveloped Third World countries all over the world: chronic unemployment, meager health facilities, high rates of illiteracy, and grossly inadequate and unsanitary housing conditions. But while this was the condition for the majority of Cuba's people, the plight of women was particularly harsh.

In the year preceding the revolution, Havana may have been a playland paradise for the North American rich, but it was an inferno for the majority of Cuban women. Approximately 464,000 Cuban women knocked on doors of houses and offices looking for work—but no work existed for them. Over 70,000 eked out a living as servants in the homes of wealthy Cubans and North Americans, receiving between $8 and $25 a month. Of the thousands of beggars on the streets of Havana, at least 25,000 of them were women. In Havana alone, it is estimated that there were 11,500 prostitutes. The Havana of the 1950s had 270 brothels, 700 bars with hostesses (one step away from prostitution), and dozens of rent-by-the-hour hotels.[1]

In 1958 there were only 100,000 working women in Cuba—including all of the servants and the underemployed.[2] Put in slightly different terms, in 1958, 85 percent of Cuban women were housewives.

In the years immediately preceding the revolution, the educational level of Cuban women was dismally low. For example, in 1958, one out of every five women in urban areas could not read or write; two out of every five in rural areas. Of all women over 25 years of age, only 1 out of every 100 had any university education. This generally low educational level prepared the overwhelming majority of Cuban women for their jobs primarily as housewives or maids for rich folks; when all else failed, as prostitutes. Those few Cuban women who did manage to work outside their homes (or someone else's home or "a house"—in 1953 only one out of seven women worked outside) were mainly in tobacco (women formed 37 percent of the tobacco workers in 1953) and textiles (women formed 46 percent of the textile workers).[3]

Housing was particularly poor in Cuba before the revolution: 80 percent of the Cuban people lived in *bohios*—huts with thatched roofs, dirt floors, and no running water or indoor plumbing. The Cuban and North American bourgeoisie lived in quite different conditions. Their mansions, which before the revolution were private dwellings, are today the national headquarters of organizations like the Federation of Cuban Women. The DuPonts had a home on Varadero Beach, which they occupied for a few months each year, where 122 servants attended the family. Today that mansion is the Las Americas restaurant.

The housing situation as dismal as this was doubly oppressive for Cuban women, since 85 percent of them spent the greatest amount of their time in and around them, performing the drudgery of housework. In 1953 in his speech "History Will Absolve Me," Fidel Castro described the housing situation of the 5.8 million Cuban population:

> There are two hundred thousand huts and hovels in Cuba; 400,000 families in the country and in the cities live cramped into barracks and tenements without even the minimum sanitary requirements; 2,200,000 of our urban population pay rents which absorb between one-fifth and one-third of their income; and 2,800,000 of our rural and suburban population lack electricity.

The situation with respect to health was consistent with that in other areas of services. In 1959 over 60 percent of the population of Cuba (6.5 million) had virtually no access to health care.[4] The people of rural Cuba and the majority of the urban poor lived under "the constant threat of the most serious diseases and epidemics."[5] Before the 1959 Revolution in Cuba, there were high rates of infant mortality, malnutrition, and infectious and contagious diseases such as polio, malaria, tuberculosis, intestinal parasitism, diphtheria, and tetanus.[6]

Again, the nature of an exploitative society is such that women will often suffer additional jeopardies because they are women. For example, health care provided for pregnant women, women in childbirth, and newborns is critical in the prevention of chronic illnesses and death among mothers and infants. Indeed, infant mortality is a particularly good indicator of a nation's health and a very sharp indicator of the condition of women's health. In Cuba before the revolution, 5 out of every 50 children died before their first birthday.

Sports and culture, while not on the same level as health, education, and housing, nevertheless serve as excellent barometers of equality and inequality in a society. In terms of sports before the revolution, Jane McManus notes, "It would be hard to overestimate the importance of basic gymnasium for women in a country like Cuba. At the triumph of the Revolution in 1959, the 'ideal' Cuban woman was pampered and passive. Mild exercise, followed by massages and steam baths, were available only to the wealthy clients of the most expensive and exclusive beauty salons. The lower classes got their 'exercise' working. Organized, mass physical fitness programs were unknown."[7] And, even in the highly exploitative professional sports world of the 1950s, women were not given "a place." In the arts, while a few women managed to lead respectable lives based on their talents, too often Cuban women were associated with entertainment for wealthy Cubans and North Americans.

The conditions of Cuban women in the areas described above—work, education, health, housing, sports, and culture—were fundamentally outgrowths of the type of economic system in operation in Cuba. Edward Boorstein has captured the dominant characteristics of that 1950s economy in these words:

> The central fact about the Cuban economy before the Revolution was neither its one-crop concentration on sugar nor the monopoly of most of the agricultural land by huge latifundia nor the weakness of the national industry, nor any other such specific characteristic. Until the Revolution, the central fact about the Cuban economy was its domination by American monopolies—by American imperialism. It was from imperialist domination that the specific characteristics flowed.[8]

In concrete terms this meant that U.S. business interests owned Cuba; and specifically, these business interests were not concerned with the plight of Cuban women. There were enough Cuban men to work the jobs associated with U.S. business interests—indeed, more than enough since in 1958, 28 percent of the labor force were unemployed or underemployed.

But in addition to this primary cause of the oppression of women in Cuba (an inequalitarian economic system designed for the financial interests of a small national bourgeoisie and a sizable group of foreign investors), there were certainly a number of traditions, attitudes, and values in Cuban society that buttressed the notion of women as the rightful occupiers of the bottom rung of society's ladder. In short, machismo was a bolster to class oppression. And for some Cuban women there was racism, too, as yet another instrument for securing the stratification of Cuban society.

Machismo, as it developed in Cuba, is more complex in derivation and current expression than what is implied in the everyday notion of attitudes of male supremacy among Latin American men, a legacy from Spanish culture. Cultural sources of male supremacy attitudes include Africa and the United States as well as Spain.

The Spanish base of machismo was strongly cast in a sexual division of expected and possible behavior within the typical prerevolutionary Cuban family. The husband and father worked, though poor men spent considerable amounts of time as victims of unemployment. The wife and mother seldom worked outside the home—the exceptions being the poor. For women, the control and dominance of their homes and children were often the only outlets they had to express themselves. They cooked heavy Spanish meals and kept spotless homes. Many Cuban men supported a legal family and one or more mistresses. The standard moral code was: "Anything goes for men"; the treasured signs of masculinity were demonstrated in a man's control of his wife and children and his conquering other women. As Margaret Randall notes, "Children grew up with these images of 'man' and 'woman'; proper young girls didn't wear pants and didn't go out unchaperoned."[9]

The African influence in Cuban machismo has received little attention. In part, this is a reflection of the general Western scholarly disregard for African cultural elements in Cuba, elements that, however, do play a part in Cubans' daily lives (art, language, food habits, and the like). Indeed, some scholars and activists in the United States have tended to ascribe egalitarian roles to men and women in West Africa, often mistakenly citing matrilineal societies (usually misnamed *matriarchal*) as proof. There is an important line of research here, especially since there is an African base to the cultures of the Americas varying in degree and specific cultural origin. Margaret Randall has commented on one African source of machismo in Cuba:

> In Cuba the African religions produced another side to the particular Cuban *machismo* which has strongly influenced the lives of Cuban women: the *abakua*. *Abakua* is a secret society of men who came from religious sects in the Congo and Nigeria that held the age-old beliefs about women being unclean and inferior. The Cuban derivative is often called *nanigo*. Not only did membership in the *abakua* (which degenerated from "good husbands, fathers and sons" to include professional killers and other delinquent elements) involve masculine pride; it also became a prerequisite for working in construction, the docks, and port work. At the beginning of this century, approximately 90% of all workers in these sectors were *abakua*.
>
> The women were proud of the fact that their men were members of this all-male society with its job security and status, and so *this false pride based on their own inferiority was deepened in themselves as well as in men*. . . . The *nanigos* were not only Black men, there was a large percentage of whites as well.[10]

The third source of machismo in Cuba—the United States—has received little attention in published sources on Cuba; yet, it takes very little reflection to realize that the very aspects of U.S. society that "went" to Cuba are the most brutally sexist. The same point could be made with respect to racism in Cuba; that is, during the period of U.S. domination, U.S.-styled Jim Crow practices of segregation were brought to Cuba.[11]

Havana, the capital city of Cuba having approximately 1 million inhabitants, was a major site for prostitution and gambling for U.S. vice men. It was also a playground for U.S. sailors and others who had money to spend. And, Cuba developed an international reputation for pornography and dirty movies. As Randall vividly states, in the eyes of the world, Cuban women "were caged in the tourist-poster image of the big-assed, rumba-dancing, bandanna-topped mulatto carrying a basket of tropical goodies belonging to United Fruit and swaying under a palm tree belonging to Eisenhower-via-Batista."[12]

This is not to suggest that the island of Cuba was free of such practices and accompanying attitudes before U.S. penetration. It is to say that the domination of Cuba by the United States increased what were already Spanish- and African-based attitudes of male supremacy. In terms of the practices of vice and prostitution, the patterns can be directly tied to the period of U.S. imperialism.

> As is always the case with this kind of cultural as well as economic exploitation, the worst of American contemporary tradition was exaggerated and made even more grotesque in the colony. . . . *Superman* and *Tarzan* became values which filtered from the colonizers through the local ruling class to the population in general, adding a U.S.-edge to Cuban *machismo*.[13]

After the Revolution

The triumph of the revolution on January 1, 1959, marks the beginning of fundamental changes in the organization of Cuban society that have deeply affected the lives of the Cuban people. In the same sense that the ills of prerevolutionary Cuba disproportionately affected Cuban women, the benefits of the new political and economic order are dramatically experienced by Cuban women. Those who suffered the most before the revolution—Black people, women, and, in general, the poor—have gained the most. In the specific case of women, this is not to suggest that the total battle has been won; in fact, all evidence suggests that it is the area of Cuban society where old attitudes are particularly rigid. Cuba has managed to eliminate much institutionalized racism and substantially affect racist attitudes in only 20 years. A comparable statement cannot be made about sexism in Cuba—a reflection, no doubt, of the greater degree of sexism than racism in prerevolutionary Cuba.

Cuba has not eliminated sexist attitudes nor fully incorporated women into the work force and daily life of the revolution. But what has taken place over the past 20 years is a highly impressive series of changes—changes that can be accurately described as a revolution within a revolution. There are two sources of these changes in "women's place" in Cuban society: the revolution itself and specific laws, actions, and organizations within the revolution. We turn now to a discussion of these two sources of change.

Impact of the Cuban Revolution on Women

Of all aspects of the society—health, education, housing, work, culture, and the like—work is clearly the area that has most significantly changed the face of Cuba. In the process of changing its society from one where 25 percent unemployment per year was a constant to one where there is no unemployment, there is a labor shortage. Cuba has become a different place. In concrete terms this means that every adult who wishes to work can do so. Because so much of the society's productive labor is at work (under the priorities of a socialist economy), there are free and modestly priced social services for the entire population.[14]

One of the first massive efforts following the triumph of the revolution was an extensive literacy campaign. In 1961 young boys *and* girls traveled throughout Cuba, teaching their elders to read and write (in one year 707,000 adults learned to read and write). Of those who learned to read and write, 56 percent were women. The formation of these brigades was a serious challenge to the old ideas of what was proper for young girls to do, and the success of the campaign is measured in the fact that Cuba has virtually eliminated illiteracy.

By 1975 one of every three Cubans was studying something in an educational system that provided free training from the elementary through the university level. In 1975, of the 80,000 university students enrolled, women accounted for 49 percent in science, 47 percent in pedagogy, and 33 percent each in the medical sciences and economics. The aim of "*every* Cuban with a sixth grade education" is now a realizable goal in a country where women were once the least educated in a sparsely educated population. Women are, of course, the recipients of tremendous improvements in a Cuba where 11 times more resources are put into education than before the revolution; 70 percent of the present school facilities have been built, adapted, or begun since 1959. Finally, with respect to education, we must note the importance in Cuba of the study-work principle. The entire educational system of Cuba has been remolded on this principle—that those who study can simultaneously contribute to the country's economic development through work in the countryside or urban areas. There are important long-range consequences for Cuba when young girls (as is the case with young boys) reach adulthood with the firmly rooted notion of their responsibility to *work*.

The transformation of health care since the revolution has earned the respect and admiration of even the most severe of Cuba's critics. The transformation is reflected in such measures as the eradication of diseases (for example, polio, diphtheria, and malaria), life expectancy (under 55 years before the revolution but has now gone up to 70 years), expenditure for public health (20 million pesos before the revolution; today over 400 million pesos—a 20-fold increase), and the widespread distribution of free clinics (for example, in 1958 there was not a single free dental clinic in Cuba; in 1976 there were 115 scattered throughout the island). Specifically related to questions of maternity, today pregnant women in Cuba receive an average of 8.5 medical visits each, and 97 percent of all births now take place in a maternity hospital.

Infant mortality is a particularly sensitive indicator of a people's health, Margaret Gilpin and Helen Rodriquez-Trias point out: "Whether children will live or die before they are a year old is determined by a complex interplay of biological and environmental factors such as nutrition, employment income, housing, educational level, the age of the mother, the parents' health, etc. Health care provided for pregnant women, for women in childbirth and for newborn infants is critical in the prevention of illness and death among mothers and infants."[15] Since the revolution, infant mortality has been reduced from 5 out of 50 children before the first birthday to 1 out of 50, the lowest rate of Latin America.

Of the three fundamental services, health, education, and housing, it is the latter that has been the most difficult challenge for Cubans to meet, a reflection, in part, of the severe labor and capital-intensive requirements to eradicate a situation where 80 percent of the Cuban people lived in huts before the revolution. In 1961 the revolution began to reverse its emphasis on home ownership and began to provide for the renting of new housing built by the state for a rent of not more than 10 percent of the family's income. This was a decisive move toward the ultimate goal of free housing for all Cubans. However, the attainment of this goal requires mass mobilization of Cuban men and women. Beginning in 1971 the Cuban people formed micro-brigades, a system whereby a percentage of the workers of a work center (factory or a port) spend one and a half to two years constructing houses, while the other workers in the center keep up production by extra effort. The homes built belong to the work collective, and it makes the decision on distribution. It is, of course, particularly striking that Cuban women have incorporated themselves into this process, for the idea of women doing such work is a sharp challenge to prerevolutionary notions of womanhood.

Because of the persistent association of women with housework, these new housing units with running water, electricity, and many modern conveniences bring the greatest relief to those who still do most of the housework.

The priority given to the construction of adequate housing for the Cuban population is captured in the allocations of the national budget:

> Housing and social service construction has a national budget twice that for defense purposes, and the annual investment in housing alone is some 184 million pesos. By comparison, housing and community development allocations in the United States represent less than 2% of the national budget, compared with over 30% for defense. Housing expenditures per capita in the U.S. are less than half of Cuba.[16]

The explosion in participation in cultural activities and sports includes monumental increases in the involvement of women. In the "amateur arts movement" of Cuba, women are actively involved in musical, community-based theater and art groups. And on a national level, women have taken major responsibilities in ballet, theater, literature, and the graphic and plastic arts.

In the area of sports, Fidel Castro was able to report to the First Party Congress of Cuba in 1975: "People have been encouraged in every possible way to do physical exercises and to go in for sports. The diversification of sports has been promoted to include sports in which the country had no tradition or experience. Sports have been encouraged at work centers and in units of the Armed Forces and the Ministry of the Interior. Women's participation has grown considerably."[17] Sports and culture have been defined by the revolution as rights, not privileges, of every Cuban. The material means for participating in these rights have been provided. What is left is the destruction of the age-old attitudes and prejudices against women's participation.

Before the revolution in a typical year, 25 percent of the work force would have been unemployed. Today, Cuba has totally eliminated unemployment (indeed, Cuba suffers from a labor shortage). The effects of such a dramatic change are to be found throughout Cuban society. Men and women can walk with dignity, knowing that they will never again have to beg for work and "be good" in order to keep work when they have found it. The elimination of unemployment has also meant that with the intensive use of Cuban productive labor, the social services described above are available to all for free or at modest costs to individuals. The incorporation of women into the Cuban work force has steadily improved since the triumph of the revolution; however, there are still far too many Cuban women who choose not to work. In 1953 women occupied 9.8 percent of the total labor force (which included the 70,000 domestics); today close to 30 percent of the work force are women.

For some percentage of Cuban women (it is difficult to be more precise), the opportunity to work was all that was needed to bring them into the work force. However, for the majority of Cuban women it has taken more than mere opportunity. First, the provision of basic social services at free-to-minimal cost has meant that many Cuban women chose not to work because they could remain in their homes and still enjoy the fruits of the revolution (for example, free health care and education). For many Cuban women who chose to work, the material conditions to support that choice did not (and still do not) exist. As Vilma Espin, president of the Federation of Cuban Women (FMC), has said, "Obtaining the participation of women in work requires overcoming numerous obstacles of a material nature such as day nurseries, workers' dining rooms, student dining rooms, semi-boarding schools, laundries and other social services which would make it possible for the housewife to work."[18] And, finally, for many women attitudes and prejudices about women working keep them out of the work force.

The Cuban Revolution Moves on the Question of Women

The incorporation of Cuban women into the work force, and indeed into the full productive life of Cuban society, has required more than the availability of jobs and statements by the leadership. We turn now to a brief review of the major steps taken by the revolution.

When the revolution triumphed in 1959, it immediately took measures to incorporate women into the work force. Approximately 20,000 women began to study in special "Schools for the Advancement of Domestic Servants." Many of these women became the staff workers of day-care centers. In those early days of the revolution, much of the door-to-door work of talking with women and urging them to join the work force was done by the FMC. In 1969/70 members of the FMA reached 400,000 women in their door-to-door conversations. That was a crucial year for Cuba with the thrust to harvest 1 million tons of sugarcane. Through the work of the FMC, as well as the work by the Committee for the Defense of the Revolution, thousands of women volunteered to cut cane. But as women moved into the work force, they also moved out again. For example, in the last three months of 1969, 140,000 women entered the labor force; but 80,000 left; so there was a net gain of only 27,000. Major reasons for this enormous turnover were, as Fidel Castro noted, "all the residual male chauvinism and supermanism and all those things that are still a part of us." Many men were encouraging their wives not to work; and many women grew tired of the double burden of working outside the home and then coming home to dishes, laundry, and cooking.

This period, 1959 to 1970, has been described as the period when the revolution moved on long-standing notions of the home (*casa*) as the place for women and the streets (*calles*) as the place for men. Carollee Bengelsdorf and Alice Hagerman characterize this period:

> Although it had now been made clear that women had the "social duty" to work, and although they were entering the labor force in increasing numbers, no nationally organized attempt was made during this period to challenge the assumption that children, laundry, and cooking were women's work. The expectation remained firm that women would be relieved of this work to the extent that the society could take on those responsibilities. In conditions of underdevelopment this has meant a *de facto* "second shift" for most women who work. For, given the scarcity of resources, the full services to relieve women of household tasks simply could not be immediately provided.[19]

In the years since 1970, the Cuban revolution has more seriously attacked the problem of "the second shift." The government of Cuba has placed a great emphasis on the construction of day-care centers, for it is clear that the absence of sound day care for their children is a major deterrent to many women working. By 1974 the revolution had constructed 610 day-care centers caring for over 50,000 children—but these still were not enough.

Since 1972 the shopping bag plan (*plan jaba*) has been in effect in order to give working women priority service at their local grocery stores. They may either drop off their lists in the morning and pick up their groceries in the evening, or they may immediately go to the front of each counter. In a country where the realities of underdevelopment and the U.S.-imposed blockade create long lines, this is a means of saving time for working women. Working women have also received preferential access to a variety of goods and services. For example, working women have preferential access to medical appointments, dry cleaners, shoe stores, hairdressers, and tailors.

The revolution has also worked to extend laundry services for workers at their work places and hot meals in workers' cafeterias. Although all workers benefit by these services, it is working women who benefit most, for it means that these "household" tasks are done outside of their homes. The basic problem with all of these efforts is that the needs of the Cuban people exceed their capabilities at the present time.

The problem of the second shift has also put women at a disadvantage within their workplaces. "Women who must pick up children at day care centers and take care of their household often cannot stay at their work place to attend assemblies or do voluntary work. Therefore, they have less chance to develop and display attitudes which might lead to their selection by workers' assemblies to leadership positions or for special material rewards."[20]

A structure was created to attempt to ease and, where possible, eliminate some of these jeopardies. In 1969 the Feminine Front was incorporated into the Cuban trade union structure—a secretariat within the Central Trade Union Federation to focus on problems of women in their work centers. The Feminine Front is now known as the Department of Feminine Concerns.

There are also problems in the area of women's participation in political leadership. Today, as throughout the history of Cuba, there are many examples of the heroism and strong leadership qualities of individual women. However, in a more general way, there is much work to be done in this area. Women comprise only 13 percent of the membership of the Communist party of Cuba; 2.9 percent of the leadership at a base level and 0 percent at the top level of the politburo.

This problem is also expressed in the involvement of women in leadership roles in popular power, the municipal, provincial, and national assemblies in charge of all the service and production units operating at those various levels (schools, courts, hospitals, and the like); on the national level, it is the body with the authority to pass all laws and discuss and approve the general outlines of foreign and domestic policy. Before this new system of popular power went into effect, an experiment was carried out in the province of Matanzas. In the Matanzas experiment, women comprised only 7.6 percent of the individuals nominated as candidates and only 3 percent of those elected to municipal assemblies in the province. In a speech in which he discussed the results of the elections, Fidel Castro emphasized that these figures demonstrate how "we still have residues of cultural backwardness and how we still retain old thinking patterns in the back of our minds." And, he continued, "There are certain theories alleging that women don't like to be led by women. . . . If there is a speck of truth to it, it will serve to show that a hard struggle must be waged among women themselves." As a result of the efforts of many organizations in Cuba, but most especially the efforts of the FMC, the percentage of women candidates for municipal assemblies in 1976 rose to 13.6 percent, a doubling of the Matanzas figure for 1974.[21] This increase in female participation in the most important organs of mass political power in Cuba represents important changes in the attitudes of certain women and men who make the nominations as well as some of those women who agree to accept nomination.

In the past few years, Cuba has passed substantial legislation that deeply affects women. In 1975 the Maternity Law was passed, and in that same year the Family Code went into effect. These laws have the potential to cut away the very fiber of discrimination against women.

The Maternity Law of Cuba is based on certain assumptions: that every adult Cuban is a worker, that children will be borne by working women, and that children represent the future of the revolution. These assumptions, within the context of the Cuban revolution, have led to one of the most far-reaching maternity laws in the world:

> The Maternity Law requires that pregnant women take an eighteen week paid leave of absence—six weeks prior to the birth and three months after. Pregnant women are granted six full days, or twelve half days, off for prenatal care. Mothers are entitled to one day per month during the first year after the birth for the child's medical care; in practice, the father can also take responsibility for this assignment. At the end of the paid maternity leave, if the mother feels she needs or wants to continue to care for her child full time, she can take up to one year's leave without pay; at the end of the year she can return to her former position.[22]

With respect to the Family Code, it is important to note that for one year preceding its adoption there was constant dialogue on the code—on buses and in work centers, homes, and shops. Then, following discussion by the people and approval by more than 98 percent of the participants in meetings and assemblies, the Family Code went into effect on International Women's Day in 1975.

The Family Code is a comprehensive piece of legislature that goes a long way toward bringing equality into social relationships that were hitherto considered "too private" for the law. Today, as a result of the Family Code, divorce is far easier than in the past; illegitimacy is no longer a viable concept. But certainly the most significant aspect of the law, and that which will take the longest to put into full effect, is the stipulation that men are required to shoulder 50 percent of the housework and child care when women work. The difficulty with such a law is, of course, in the necessity of women bringing legal action against their husbands. However, the immediate positive result is that the case for equal responsibilities and rights is given public sanction.

Margaret Randall describes the code in this way: "The sense of the new Code rests entirely on mutual respect between women and men, and respect on the part of parents for their children. The family nucleus as we know it is in fact strengthened, but its private property or bourgeois capitalist-sexist aspects are largely removed."[23] Today, because of the availability of free education, jobs for all, and legal provisions (such as the ease with which divorces can be obtained), no woman in Cuba need put up with an exploitative personal situation in a relationship with a man. But this does not mean no woman does.

Since its founding in August 1960, the Federation of Cuban Women has played instrumental roles in the range of efforts to incorporate women more fully into the productive and active life of their society. In order to carry out this work, the FMC continues to be a center for analyzing the problems women face and creating and suggesting solutions. Each of the specific activities or laws described here have been closely associated with the FMC: from the literacy campaign in 1961 to the passing of the Family Code in 1975; from incorporating women into the work force to suggesting the shopping bag plan. At present the FMC has a membership of over 2,264,000 or 81.5 percent of all Cuban women above the age of 14.

Conclusion

Without question, the Cuban revolution has brought enormous changes in the position of women, and it has done so in a short period of 22 years. Serious problems remain, however—problems that grow out of Cuba's legacy of underdevelopment and that are the result of the tenacity of prejudices about women. As Cuba develops its economy, those problems that stem from the lack of a material base to support the integration of women into the work force and life of Cuba will tend to disappear. For example, by the end of the Five-Year Plan (1976-80), Cuba will have 400 new day-care centers, raising the national capacity from 50,000 to 150,000 children cared for and educated in these centers. Similarly impressive growth in other areas suggests that the objective conditions that tie women to hours of housework and child care are being steadily removed.

The subjective problems—machismo and sexism—that keep women out of the workplace, leadership, and full participation in the life of their country are more difficult to root out. There is one particularly protective cushion for attitudes of male supremacy in Cuba, which appears all the more powerful when we realize that it never existed in the same way for racial prejudices. The perpetuation of sexist attitudes is aided by the fact that the setting for so many of the interpersonal relations between men and women is the home. Women may experience tremendous gains in their workplaces but return to situations within the privateness of the household that are filled with old myths and prejudices. Children are taught and practice equality of the sexes in schools but may come home in the evenings, or on weekends, to see their mothers, sisters, and other female relatives in statuses "reserved for women."

The Family Code is a dramatic challenge to the attitude that housework and child care are tasks for women and not for men. The code states that working men and women in a household must share these tasks equally. But these tasks take place, by and large, in the privateness of one's home. It must take an extremely confident woman to bring her husband to public sanction for failure to honor the code. (In contrast, the most frequent settings for racial discrimination were public ones: beaches, clubs, schools, hospitals, and work centers. Because the offenses were committed in public, they were rather quickly dealt with and eliminated by the revolutionary government.)

There is a great deal that is inspiring and instructive about the Cuban Revolution's efforts to eliminate gender inequality. In the short span of 22 years, the changes in the status of Cuban women genuinely warrant the description of a Revolution within a Revolution. We should remember that the material conditions for attacking sexism are far greater in Cuba than in most of the Third World, but certain material conditions are necessary but not sufficient conditions for gender equality. Thus the Cuban case underlines the necessity of on-going attacks on the level of the superstructure *even after* socialist transformation is in process.

Finally, the Cuban case reminds us that revolutionary changes are processes, not discrete events. It will no doubt take generations before gender equality is a reality in Cuba; but the humor and openness with which the issue is discussed and criticisms raised in Cuba is a most encouraging sign.

We conclude this paper with a taste of the on-going process of change which grows out of open criticism as expressed in selected lines from a poem by Milagros Gonzalez:

FIRST DIALOGUE
(With our comrades, who daily . . .)

> In that way, put an end to the
> old non-communist psychology.
>   V.I. LENIN

Where are you: manspirit of my time,
every afternoon home from work

become exactly that fountain of rude stares
reproaching me the quick lunch,
pile of unwashed clothes,
the handkerchiefs not perfectly ironed,
This daily existence

. . . . .

And you make Revolution from the Five Year Plan
but as you can, straddling Rocinante
while Dulcinea admires your prowess, the spear, the windmills,
and you, in the neighborhood, defending the social advantages
of our new Constitution!
    You make Revolution:
    starched shirt
    clean refrigerator,
    beds made,
    shining pots
floors so clean you can eat on them or spit on them.

. . .

Because Revolution is more than I want
    more than Party member
    more than Congress, Assembly
your eyelid closing over the book, the seed,
gun raised, fraternal death.

    REVOLUTION
is also we who make and do
who plough with you,
who pencil, who trench . . .

. . .

Revolution, my love, will also be
when day breaks one of these centuries
and pride strokes the militant home,
and honey in your hands turned sweet again.

Comrade, when the day breaks,
you'll have risen finally
TO THE HIGHEST HUMAN PLANE.

Notes

1. "Women in Cuba," *Granma*, March 5, 1978, p. 6.
2. Ibid.
3. Carollee Bengelsdorf and Alice Hagerman, "Emerging from Underdevelopment: Women and Work," *Cuba Review* 9, no. 2 (1974): 4.

4. Margaret Gilpin and Helen Rodriquez-Trias, "Looking at Health in a Healthy Way," *Cuba Review* 7, no. 1 (1978): 4.

5. Ibid.

6. Ibid.

7. Jane McManus, "Stretching Out," *Cuba Review* 7, no. 2 (1977): 29-30.

8. Edward Boorstein, *The Economic Transformation of Cuba* (New York: International, 1968), p. 1.

9. Margaret Randall, *Cuban Women Now* (Toronto: Canadian Women's Educational Press, 1974), p. 27.

10. Ibid., p. 28.

11. Ibid., p. 7.

12. Ibid.

13. Ibid.

14. Since this article was written in 1979, there have been a number of changes in Cuba, including the exodus of one hundred twenty thousand people, representing a little over 1 percent of the Cuban population. With respect to the employment situation, *Latin America Weekly Report* indicates the following: "The government has been campaigning vigorously for the past 18 months to increase efficiency and eliminate unproductive employment. This has created a labour glut which has been exacerbated by the increase in women and young people arriving on the employment market.

    Government economists are confident that the economy will be able gradually to absorb the extra capacity." (*Latin America Weekly Report*, 31 July, 1981:3-4)

15. Gilpin and Rodriquez-Trias, "Looking at Health," p. 4.

16. Tony Schuman, "Housing, Progress and Prognosis," *Cuba Review* 5, no. 1 (1975): 17.

17. Fidel Castro, *First Congress of the Communist Party of Cuba* (Moscow: Progress, 1976), p. 165.

18. Sheila Rowbotham, "Colony within a Colony," in *Women, Resistance and Revolution: A History of Women and Revolution in the Modern World* (New York: Vintage, 1974), p. 227.

19. Bengelsdorf and Hagerman, "Emerging from Underdevelopment: Women and Work," p. 8.

20. Ibid., p. 11.

21. "Women in Cuba."

22. Bengelsdorf and Hagerman, "Emerging from Underdevelopment: Women and Work," p. 11.

23. Margaret Randall, "Introducing the Family Code," *Cuba Review* 4, no. 2 (1974): 31.

References

BENGELSDORF, CAROLLEE, and ALICE HAGERMAN. "Emerging from Underdevelopment: Women and Work." *Cuba Review* 4, no. 2 (1974): 3-18.

"Emerging from Underdevelopment: Women and Work in Cuba." In *Capitalist Patriarchy and the Case for Socialist Feminism*, edited by Zillah R. Eisenstein, pp. 271-96. New York: Monthly Review Press, 1979.

BOORSTEIN, EDWARD. *The Economic Transformation of Cuba*. New York: International, 1969.

CASTRO, FIDEL. *First Congress of the Communist Party of Cuba*. Moscow: Progress, 1976.

"History Will Absolve Me." In *Revolutionary Struggle*, edited by Rolando Bonachea and Nelson Valdes. Cambridge: Massachusetts Institute of Technology Press, 1972.

FOX, GEOFFREY E. "Honor, Shame, and Women's Liberation in Cuba: Views of Working Class Emigre Men." In *Female and Male in Latin America*, edited by Ann Pescatello, pp. 273-90. Pittsburg: University of Pittsburg Press, 1973.

GILPIN, MARGARET, and HELEN RODRIQUEZ-TRIAS. "Looking at Health in a Healthy Way." *Cuba Review* 7, no. 1 (1978): 3-15.

KING, MARJORIE. "Cuba's Attack on Women's Second Shift 1974-1976." *Latin American Perspectives* 4, nos. 1 and 2 (Winter and Spring 1977): 106-19.

MCMANUS, JANE. "Stretching Out." *Cuba Review* 7, no. 2 (1977): 29-30.

NELSON, LOWRY. "The Cuban Family." In *Rural Cuba*. Minneapolis: University of Minnesota Press, 1950.

PURCELL, SUSAN K. "Modernizing Women for a Modern Society: The Cuban Case." In *Female and Male in Latin America*, edited by Ann Pescatello, pp. 257-71. Pittsburg: University of Pittsburgh Press, 1973.

RANDALL, MARGARET. *Cuban Women Now*. Toronto: Canadian Women's Educational Press, 1974.

"Introducing the Family Code." *Cuba Review* 4, no. 2 (1974): 31.

" 'We Need a Government of Men and Women. . . .' Notes on the Second National Congress of the Federación de Mujeres Cubanos, November 25-29, 1974." *Latin American Perspectives* 4, nos. 1 and 2 (Winter and Spring 1975): 111-17.

ROWBOTHAM, SHEILA. "Colony within a Colony." In *Women, Resistance and Revolution: A History of Women and Revolution in the Modern World*. New York: Vintage, 1974.

SCHUMAN, TONY. "Housing, Progress and Prognosis." *Cuba Review* 5, no. 1 (1975): 17-19.

SUTHERLAND, ELIZABETH. "The Longest Revolution." In *The Youngest Revolution: A Personal Report on Cuba*. New York: Dial, 1969.

"WOMEN IN CUBA." *Granma*, March 5, 1978, p. 6.

Index